AUTOMOTIVE DRIVE TRAINS
Automatic and Manual

Second Edition

Frank J. Thiessen
Davis N. Dales

Prentice Hall
Englewood Cliffs, New Jersey   Columbus, Ohio

Data

Automotive drive trains : automatic and manual / Frank J.
Thiessen, Davis N. Dales.—2nd ed.
    p.   cm.
    Includes index.
    ISBN 0-13-339979-6 (alk. paper)
    1. Automobiles—Power trains.   2. Automobiles—Power trains—
Maintenance and repair.   I. Dales, D. N.   II. Title.
TL260.T5   1996
629.24—dc20   95-24807
                                                              CIP

Cover photo:© J. Whitmer/H. Armstrong Roberts
Editor: Ed Francis
Production Editor: Alexandrina Benedicto Wolf
Design Coordinator: Jill E. Bonar
Production Manager: Deidra M. Schwartz
Marketing Manager: Debbie Yarnell

This book was set in Century Book by The Clarinda Company and was printed and bound by Quebecor
Printing/Semline. The cover was printed by Phoenix Color Corp.

 © 1996 by Prentice-Hall, Inc.
A Simon & Schuster Company
Englewood Cliffs, New Jersey 07632

Earlier edition © 1984 by Reston Publishing, Inc.

Printed in the United States of America

10 9 8 7 6 5 4 3 2 1

ISBN: 0-13-339979-6

Prentice-Hall International (UK) Limited, *London*
Prentice-Hall of Australia Pty. Limited, *Sydney*
Prentice-Hall of Canada, Inc., *Toronto*
Prentice-Hall Hispanoamericana, S. A., *Mexico*
Prentice-Hall of India Private Limited, *New Delhi*
Prentice-Hall of Japan, Inc., *Tokyo*
Simon & Schuster Asia Pte. Ltd., *Singapore*
Editora Prentice-Hall do Brasil, Ltda., *Rio de Janeiro*

PREFACE

This edition of *Automotive Drive Trains* details the design, operation, diagnosis, service, and repair of the various drive train types. This includes front-wheel-drive, rear-wheel-drive, and four-wheel-drive systems, manual transmissions and transaxles, and automatic transmissions and transaxles. The easy-to-read style and increased emphasis on "how-to, hands-on" information make this a valuable source of information for those already in the automotive field and for those desiring to enter it. The information in this book may be used to prepare for ASE certification tests in the following areas.

Test A2. Automatic Transmission/Transaxle

Content Area. General Transmission/Transaxle Diagnosis, Maintenance and Adjustment, In-Vehicle Repair, Off-Vehicle Repair, Removal, Disassembly and Assembly, Oil Pump and Converter, Gear Train, Shafts, Bushings, Case, Friction, and Reaction Units.

Test A3. Manual Transmissions and Drive Axles

Content Area. Clutch Diagnosis and Repair, Transmission Diagnosis and Repair, Transaxle Diagnosis and Repair, Drive (Half) Shaft and Universal Joint Diagnosis and Repair, Rear-Axle Diagnosis and Repair, Ring and Pinion Gears, Differential Case Assembly, Limited Slip Differential, Axle Shafts, and Four-Wheel-Drive Component Diagnosis and Repair.

The information in this book is divided into chapters as follows:

I. Introduction
1. Front-Wheel-Drive Axle Principles and Service
2. Drive Shaft Principles and Service
3. Differential and Drive Axle Principles and Service
4. Clutch Principles and Service
5. Manual Transmission and Transaxle Principles
6. Manual Transmission and Transaxle Service
7. Automatic Transmission and Transaxle Principles
8. Automatic Transmission and Transaxle Service
9. Four-Wheel-Drive System Principles and Service

Each chapter includes the following features:

- INTRODUCTION Introduces the subject matter covered in the chapter.
- LEARNING OBJECTIVES A list of the major areas of *skill* and *knowledge* that the student is expected to acquire during completion of the chapter.
- TERMS YOU SHOULD KNOW A list of the *automotive* terms used in the chapter. Tells the student what to expect in the chapter and the terms the student must learn in order to discuss the operation and service of the automobile.
- SAFETY CAUTIONS AND PRO TIPS These appear throughout the text to emphasize potential *problems*, *safe procedures*, and the avoidance of *accidents and injury*.
- REVIEW QUESTIONS Short-answer, fill-in-the-blank, and true-false questions. May be used by the student and the instructor to review comprehension and progress.
- TEST QUESTIONS Test questions of the type used in certification tests. Provides practice for writing technician certification tests.

These features are designed to make it easier for the student to understand the technical language commonly used in the automotive service industry without which effective communication in the shop is not possible. Emphasis is on the terminology that must be understood, the potential hazards that may be encountered, and the safe work habits that are essential to productivity and profit.

IMPORTANT SAFETY NOTICE

Proper service and repair are important for the safe and reliable operation of motor vehicles. The service procedures described in this book are effective general methods of performing service operations. Some of these operations require the use of tools especially designed for the purpose. These special tools should be used as recommended in the appropriate service manuals.

This book contains various general precautions that should be read carefully to minimize the risk of personal injury or damage to the vehicle being serviced. It must be noted that these precautions are not exhaustive. The authors could not possibly know, evaluate, and advise the service trade of all the conceivable ways in which service may be carried out or of the possible hazardous consequences of such methods. Accordingly, anyone using any given service procedure, tool, or equipment must first confirm that neither personal safety nor the safety of the vehicle or equipment will be jeopardized by the service method selected. This book is not a service manual and should not be used as such. Always refer to the appropriate manufacturer's service manual for specific procedures and specifications.

ACKNOWLEDGMENTS

Special appreciation is hereby extended to Ed Francis, Alex Wolf, Colleen Brosnan, and the many vehicle and equipment manufacturers, colleagues, and educational and training institutions across the United States and Canada for their most valuable assistance. Their help is what makes this book possible.

BRIEF CONTENTS

CONTENTS

Chapter 3   Differential and Drive Axle Principles and Service, 61

Chapter 4   Clutch Principles and Service, 91

Chapter 5 Manual Transmission and Transaxle Principles 119

Chapter 6 Manual Transmission and Transaxle Service, 147

Chapter 7 Automatic Transmission and Transaxle Principles, 197

Chapter 8   Automatic Transmission and Transaxle Service, 257

Chapter 9 Four-Wheel-Drive System Principles and Service, 367

Index, 405

◆ 1 ◆

INTRODUCTION

This chapter describes the function and types of automotive drive trains. It describes engine location and position in the vehicle. The location and position of the engine are factors in drive train design. The various types of drive train are discussed as well as how the drive train applies power to the engine to make the vehicle move.

Practicing safety in the shop is vital to the well-being of the technicians and the productivity of the shop. It includes avoiding injury to yourself and to others near you and avoiding damage to vehicles and equipment. Practicing safety involves recognizing hazardous situations and taking the necessary precautions to ensure safety. It means developing safe work habits that eventually become routine. Practicing safety does not waste time—it saves time. This chapter deals with the basic considerations required to develop safe working habits and conditions.

Many kinds of fasteners are used in the automotive service industry. Each fastener is designed for a specific purpose and for specific conditions that are encountered during vehicle operation. Using an incorrect type or size of fastener, a damaged fastener, or one of inferior quality can result in early failure, accident, and injury to the driver and passengers of the repaired vehicle. It is important, therefore, to be able to distinguish among the various fastener sizes, types, and usage, as you will learn from this chapter.

LEARNING OBJECTIVES

After successfully completing this chapter, you should be able to:

- Describe the function of the drive train.
- Describe the different ways engines are positioned and located in the vehicle.
- Distinguish between rear-wheel drive, front-wheel drive, four-wheel drive, and all-wheel drive.
- Distinguish between manual and automatic transmission and transaxle drive trains.
- Describe how engine power is applied to the drive train to make the vehicle move.
- Recognize the importance of safe work habits and conditions.
- Adopt safe dress habits appropriate to an automotive shop.
- Use proper protective clothing and devices for specific procedures.
- Use proper exhaust venting equipment when required.
- Use proper procedures and protection when handling dangerous chemicals.
- Drive a customer's car safely.
- Avoid any practice that may cause a potential fire hazard.
- Practice basic first aid.
- Recognize common causes of accidents.
- Distinguish between different types and sizes of threaded fasteners.
- Select and use the correct size and type of fastener required for each application.

- Use a torque wrench and torque chart and tighten fasteners to torque specifications.
- Repair damaged threads with a thread repair insert.
- Select and use the correct snap rings, washers, and keys for proper application.

TERMS YOU SHOULD KNOW

Watch for these terms as you study this chapter and learn what they mean.

Drive train	air bag module
engine location	spontaneous combustion
front engine	carbon monoxide
mid-engine	exhaust ventilation
rear engine	fire extinguisher
engine position	eyewash station
drive shaft	chemical burns
longitudinal	first-aid kit
transverse	bolts
two-wheel drive	studs
rear-wheel drive	nuts
(RWD)	tensile strength
front-wheel drive	grade
(FWD)	pitch
four-wheel drive	class
(4WD)	UNC
part-time four-wheel drive	UNF
	UNEF
full-time four-wheel drive	SAE
	pipe thread
all-wheel drive	machine thread
(AWD)	metric thread
transfer case	coarse
manual transmission	fine
manual transaxle	torque
automatic transmission	torque turn
automatic transaxle	thread insert
face mask	heli-coil
protective gloves	flat washer
safety goggles	

lock washer	straight key
snap ring	woodruff key
spline	

DRIVE TRAIN FUNCTION

The automotive drive train has several jobs to perform. It provides the means to propel as well as help stop vehicle movement while the engine is running. It provides the driver with several speed and power options to adapt to changing driving conditions. Since it takes more power to drive up a hill than it does to go downhill, proper speed and power combinations are needed for both situations. The drive train provides the means to increase or decrease driving torque from the engine to the drive wheels as required.

The drive train provides the following functions:

1. It provides the means to connect or disconnect the engine to or from the drive wheels while the engine is running.
2. It provides the means whereby engine power is transmitted from the engine to the drive wheels.
3. It provides several different speed and power combinations to accommodate changes in road and load conditions.
4. It provides both forward and reverse speeds.

DRIVE TRAIN TYPES

Drive train design depends on:

1. Engine location (front, rear, or middle of vehicle)
2. Engine position (longitudinal or transverse)
3. Drive type (rear-wheel drive, RWD; front-wheel drive, FWD; four-wheel drive, 4WD; all-wheel drive, AWD)

ENGINE LOCATION AND POSITION

The engine may be located in the front, rear, or middle of the vehicle depending on vehicle design as follows (**Figure I–1**):

1. *Front engine vehicle.* The engine is located just in front of the passenger compartment.

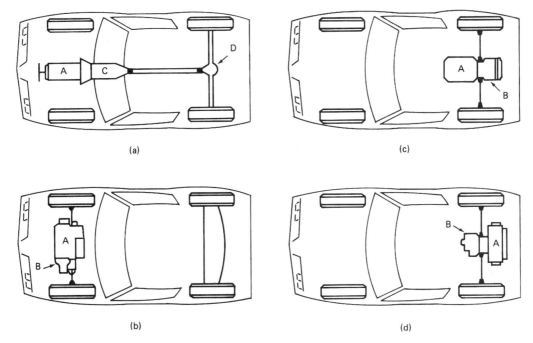

(a)

(c)

(b)

(d)

FIGURE I–1 Possible engine locations (a) front engine with rear-wheel drive: (b) front engine with front-wheel drive; (c) mid-engine with rear-wheel drive; (d) rear engine with rear-wheel drive. A, engine; B, transaxle; C, transmission; D, differential.

2. *Rear engine vehicle.* The engine is located in the rear just behind the rear axle.

3. *Mid-engine vehicle.* The engine is located behind the passenger compartment just in front of the rear axle.

The engine may be placed in a longitudinal or transverse position regardless of engine location as follows (see **Figure I–1**):

1. *Longitudinal engine.* The engine is placed in a lengthwise position parallel to the frame in the vehicle.

2. *Transverse engine.* The engine is placed in a crosswise position perpendicular to the frame in the vehicle.

REAR-WHEEL DRIVE

The conventional rear-wheel-drive power train has the engine mounted in the front of the vehicle. It is positioned longitudinally between the front wheels. A clutch and manual transmission, or torque converter and automatic transmission, transmit engine power to a drive shaft.

The drive shaft transmits power to the rear axle final drive gear and the differential **(Figure I–2)**. The

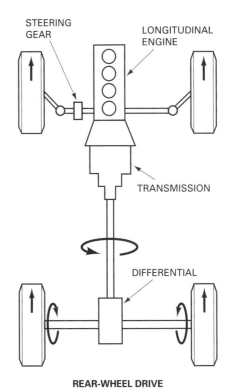

REAR-WHEEL DRIVE

FIGURE I–2 Conventional rear-wheel drive with the engine positioned longitudinally in the front.

differential transmits power through the rear axles to the rear wheels. The final drive gears change the direction of powerflow 90 degrees from that of the drive shaft. The differential splits the power equally to each rear wheel under normal straight-ahead driving **(Figure I–3)**. Rear-wheel-drive systems use the rear wheels to push the vehicle during forward travel. Rear-wheel drive is used on some compact, mid-size, and full-size cars, compact and full-size pickup trucks, minivans, full-size vans, and on medium and heavy trucks.

The mid-engine rear-wheel-drive system has the engine positioned just in front of the rear axle **(Figure I–4)**. This eliminates the need for a long drive shaft as required in the front engine rear-wheel-drive design. The engine may be in a longitudinal or transverse position. The transverse engine position eliminates the need to change the direction of powerflow 90 degrees since the engine's crankshaft is parallel to the drive axles. This arrangement is currently limited to use in some sports car designs.

The rear engine design has the engine positioned just behind the rear axle in either a transverse or longitudinal position **(Figure I–5)**.

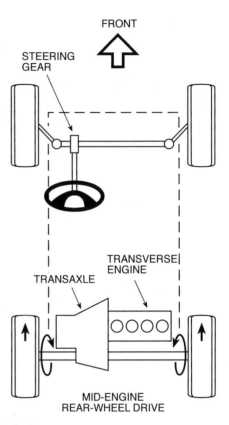

FIGURE I–4 Mid-engine rear-wheel drive with transverse engine position. Engine may be longitudinal on some models.

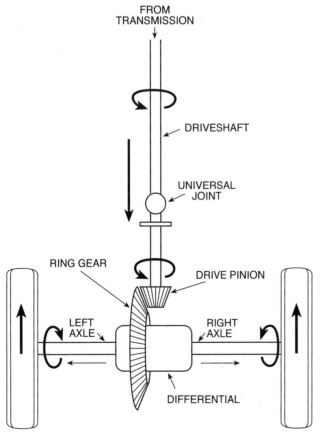

FIGURE I–3 In the conventional rear-wheel drive power train, the final drive gears (drive pinion and ring gear) change the direction of power flow 90 degrees.

FRONT-WHEEL DRIVE

The front-wheel-drive power train has the engine mounted in the front of the vehicle. It may be mounted in a transverse or longitudinal position. In the longitudinal engine design, a clutch and manual transaxle, or torque converter and automatic transaxle, transmit engine power to the front-wheel-drive half-shafts **(Figure I–6)**. The half-shafts drive the front wheels. With the longitudinal engine position, the transaxle final drive must change the direction of powerflow 90 degrees from that of the engine crankshaft **(Figure I–7)**.

With the transverse engine design, the clutch and manual transaxle, or torque converter and automatic transaxle, transmit engine power to the half-shafts and front-drive wheels. Since the engine crankshaft is parallel, the direction of powerflow is not changed 90 degrees as in the longitudinal engine design.

The front-wheel-drive design is currently the most commonly used drive train and is used on compact, mid-size, and full-size cars, and on minivans.

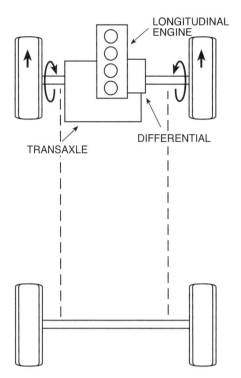

FIGURE I–7 Front-wheel drive with longitudinal engine.

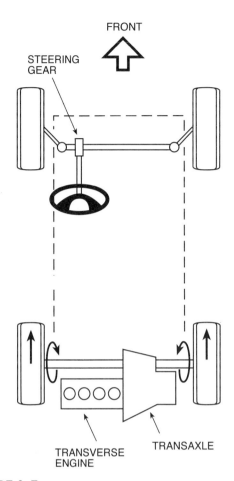

FIGURE I–5 Rear engine rear wheel drive with transverse engine. Engine may be longitudinal on some models.

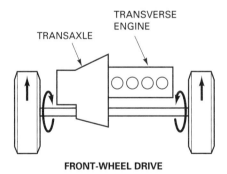

FRONT-WHEEL DRIVE

FIGURE I–6 Front-wheel drive (FWD) with transverse engine. (Rear wheels not shown.)

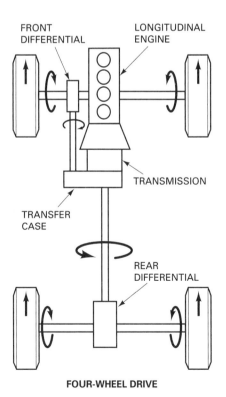

FOUR-WHEEL DRIVE

FIGURE I–8 Four-wheel drive (4WD) with longitudinal engine.

PART-TIME FOUR-WHEEL DRIVE

The part-time four-wheel-drive system is a modification of the conventional rear-wheel-drive design with the engine in the front. Part-time four-wheel drive has a transfer case mounted on the rear of the transmission. A set of gears and shafts in the transfer case provide the means to select two-wheel drive or four-wheel drive. Power from the transfer case is transmitted to the rear drive axle through the rear drive shaft. Power can also be transmitted to the front drive axle if the driver selects the four-wheel-drive mode. A front drive shaft connects the transfer case to the front drive axle **(Figures I–8 and I–9).**

The transfer case usually has four possible gearshift lever positions: Neutral, Two-Wheel Drive (rear wheels only doing the driving), four-wheel drive Low, and Four-Wheel Drive High **(Figure I–10).** This system is designed to be operated in the two-wheel-drive mode only on the highway or other hard surfaces and in the two-wheel-drive or four-wheel-drive modes off the highway. Mud, snow, and rough terrain may also require using the four-wheel-drive mode. Since there is no differential in the transfer case, interaxle conflict occurs between the front and rear axles when used in the four-wheel-drive mode on hard surfaced roads. Speed fluctuations between the front and rear drive axles cause severe strain on the drive train when all four wheels are driving on good traction surfaces. This also results in rapid tire wear. During off-road four-wheel-drive operation on poor traction surfaces, there is enough wheel slippage to keep interaxle conflict at a minimum. See Chapter 9 for a detailed description of part-time four-wheel-drive systems.

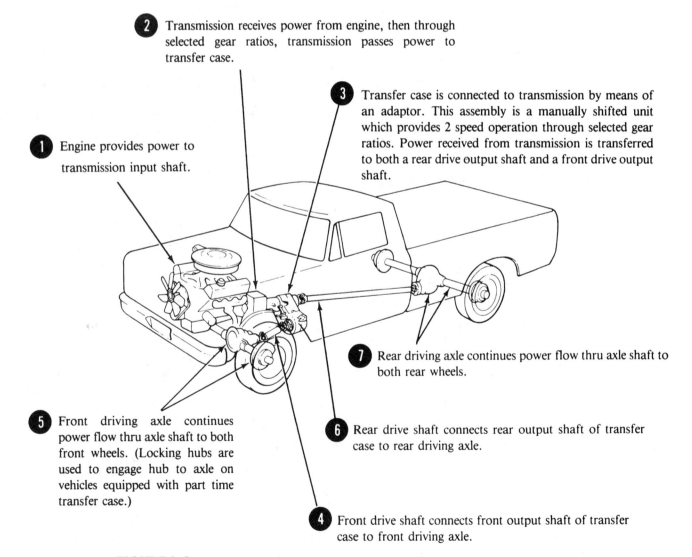

2 Transmission receives power from engine, then through selected gear ratios, transmission passes power to transfer case.

3 Transfer case is connected to transmission by means of an adaptor. This assembly is a manually shifted unit which provides 2 speed operation through selected gear ratios. Power received from transmission is transferred to both a rear drive output shaft and a front drive output shaft.

1 Engine provides power to transmission input shaft.

7 Rear driving axle continues power flow thru axle shaft to both rear wheels.

5 Front driving axle continues power flow thru axle shaft to both front wheels. (Locking hubs are used to engage hub to axle on vehicles equipped with part time transfer case.)

6 Rear drive shaft connects rear output shaft of transfer case to rear driving axle.

4 Front drive shaft connects front output shaft of transfer case to front driving axle.

FIGURE I–9 (Courtesy of Ford Motor Co. of Canada Ltd.)

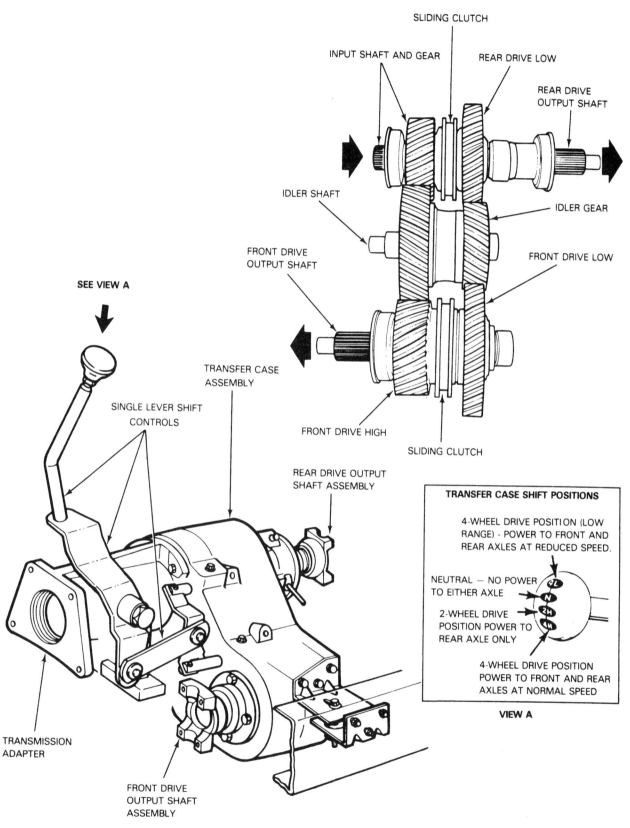

SLIDING CLUTCH

INPUT SHAFT AND GEAR

REAR DRIVE LOW

REAR DRIVE
OUTPUT SHAFT

IDLER SHAFT

IDLER GEAR

FRONT DRIVE
OUTPUT SHAFT

FRONT DRIVE LOW

SEE VIEW A

TRANSFER CASE
ASSEMBLY

FRONT DRIVE HIGH

SLIDING CLUTCH

SINGLE LEVER SHIFT
CONTROLS

REAR DRIVE OUTPUT
SHAFT ASSEMBLY

TRANSFER CASE SHIFT POSITIONS

4-WHEEL DRIVE POSITION (LOW
RANGE) - POWER TO FRONT AND
REAR AXLES AT REDUCED SPEED.

NEUTRAL — NO POWER
TO EITHER AXLE

2-WHEEL DRIVE
POSITION POWER TO
REAR AXLE ONLY

4-WHEEL DRIVE POSITION
POWER TO FRONT AND REAR
AXLES AT NORMAL SPEED

VIEW A

TRANSMISSION
ADAPTER

FRONT DRIVE
OUTPUT SHAFT
ASSEMBLY

FIGURE I–10 (Courtesy of Ford Motor Co. of Canada Ltd.)

7

FULL-TIME FOUR-WHEEL DRIVE

Full-time four-wheel drive is similar to part-time four-wheel drive. The major difference is that the transfer case has a differential or viscous coupling that is active when in the four-wheel-drive mode. This prevents interaxle conflict by allowing the front and rear drive axles to turn at different speeds. This allows the vehicle to be operated full time in four-wheel drive both on and off the highway. Transfer case range selections include Neutral, Two-Wheel Drive, Four-Wheel Drive Low, and Four-Wheel Drive High. The two-wheel-drive mode is used whenever four-wheel drive is not required to reduce fuel consumption. This transfer case can be shifted from two-wheel drive to four-wheel drive while the vehicle is driving in forward speeds. Full-time four-wheel drive is used on compact and full-size pickup trucks and on sport utility vehicles. Another version provides a lockup of the transfer case differential for positive drive to both axles for off-road operation.

ALL-WHEEL DRIVE

The all-wheel-drive system was developed from the front-wheel-drive design. It uses the same transaxle as the front-wheel drive. A specially designed single-speed transfer case is attached to the transaxle. A viscous coupling or differential in the transfer case prevents interaxle conflict. Power is transmitted to both axles at all times. An all-wheel-drive cutout switch is provided on some models. The switch controls an electromagnetic clutch in the transfer case that allows the rear axle to be connected or disconnected from the transfer case. Power from the transfer case is transmitted to the rear drive axle through a drive shaft. During turns, the transfer case differential or viscous coupling allow the front and rear axles to turn at different speeds **(Figure I–11).**

ALL-THE-TIME FOUR-WHEEL DRIVE

The all-the-time four-wheel-drive system is designed for both off-road and highway driving. It eliminates the need for shifting between two-wheel drive and four-wheel drive. The transfer case has three shift lever positions: 4WD All-Time High, Neutral, and 4WD Part-Time Low. A differential in the transfer case prevents drive line windup and interaxle conflict. A viscous cou-

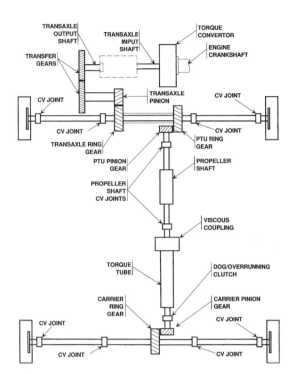

FIGURE I–11 All-wheel-drive schematic. (Courtesy of Chrysler Corporation.)

pling automatically distributes driving torque to the front and rear axles as required.

MANUAL AND AUTOMATIC TRANSMISSIONS AND TRANSAXLES

Manual transmissions and transaxles are shifted into and out of the different drive ranges by hand or manually **(Figures I–12** and **I–13).** This is accomplished by depressing the clutch pedal (disengaging the clutch) and moving the shift selector lever to the desired drive range. The shift lever may be mounted on the steering column, in a floor-mounted console, or directly on the floor. The clutch is controlled by a foot-operated pedal. Shifting is achieved by depressing the clutch pedal (disengaging the clutch), moving the shift lever into the desired gear range, and releasing the clutch pedal to engage the clutch. Both upshifts and downshifts are made this way.

Automatic transmissions and transaxles shift up and down automatically. A shift lever provides the means to select the desired drive range. When the vehicle reaches the required road speed, the transmission or transaxle automatically shifts to the next higher gear ratio. Three or four forward gear ratios are usually provided as well as reverse. The top gear ratio may be

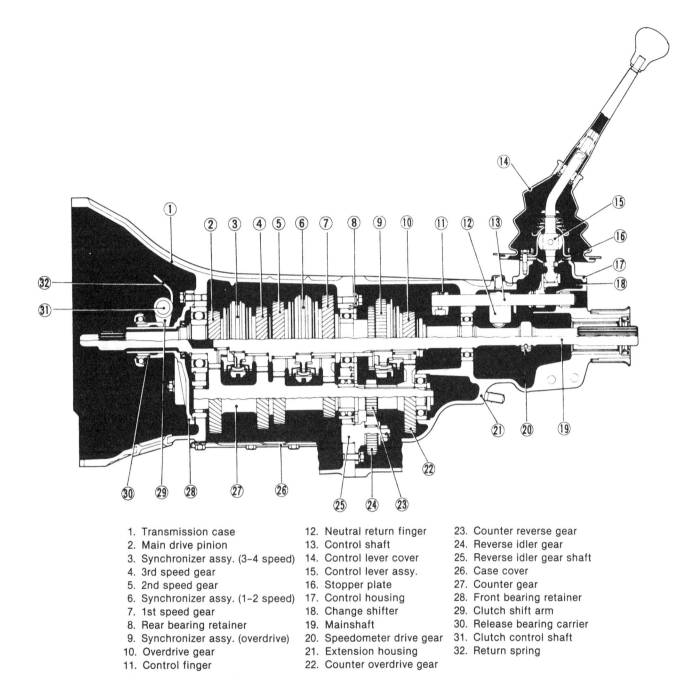

1. Transmission case
2. Main drive pinion
3. Synchronizer assy. (3–4 speed)
4. 3rd speed gear
5. 2nd speed gear
6. Synchronizer assy. (1–2 speed)
7. 1st speed gear
8. Rear bearing retainer
9. Synchronizer assy. (overdrive)
10. Overdrive gear
11. Control finger
12. Neutral return finger
13. Control shaft
14. Control lever cover
15. Control lever assy.
16. Stopper plate
17. Control housing
18. Change shifter
19. Mainshaft
20. Speedometer drive gear
21. Extension housing
22. Counter overdrive gear
23. Counter reverse gear
24. Reverse idler gear
25. Reverse idler gear shaft
26. Case cover
27. Counter gear
28. Front bearing retainer
29. Clutch shift arm
30. Release bearing carrier
31. Clutch control shaft
32. Return spring

FIGURE I–12 Typical five-speed overdrive manual transmission for rear-wheel-drive vehicle. (Courtesy of Chrysler Corporation.)

1:1 (direct drive) or overdrive (about 0.7:1). Vehicles with manual or automatic transmissions transmit power from the transmission through a drive shaft to the final drive gears and the differential. These are located in the rear drive axle housing. On vehicles with manual or automatic transaxles, the final drive gears and differential are built into the transaxle assembly. A drive shaft is therefore not required (**Figures I–14** and **I–15**).

HOW ENGINE POWER IS APPLIED TO MOVE THE VEHICLE

Engine power must be applied to some point on the vehicle to cause vehicle movement. On rear-wheel-drive vehicles, engine power is transmitted through the drive train to turn the rear wheels. Since the tires are in contact with the road surface, a rolling action takes place.

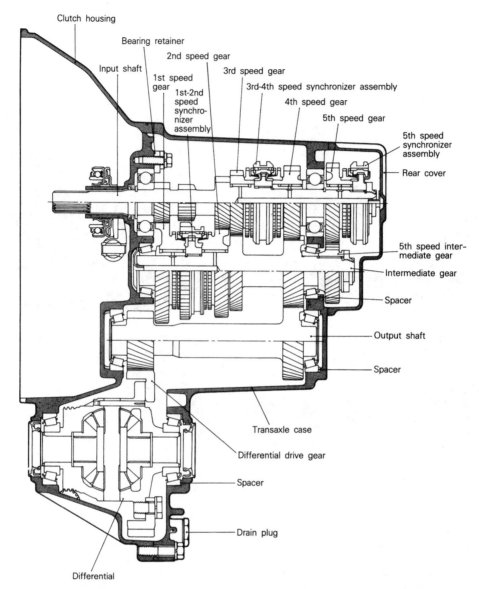

FIGURE I–13 Cutaway view of five-speed manual transaxle gears, shafts, and synchronizers. (Courtesy of Chrysler Corporation.)

The weight of the vehicle tends to resist this action. However, when enough engine power is applied and there is enough gripping action of the tires (traction), the wheels are forced to turn. As the wheels roll forward, the drive axles push forward against the axle bearings and the axle housing. This force is transmitted to the vehicle frame and body through control arms or struts (on coil spring suspension) or through leaf springs, thereby pushing the vehicle forward **(Figures I–16** and **I–17).**

On front-wheel-drive systems, the action is similar except that the force is applied through the front wheels and front suspension linkage to the front of the vehicle frame and body **(Figure I–18).**

PERSONAL SAFETY IN THE SHOP

1. Wear proper clothing. Loose clothing, ties, uncontrolled long hair, rings, and so on, can get caught in rotating parts or equipment and cause injury. Wear shoes that provide protection for your feet; steel-capped work boots with nonskid soles are best. Keep clothing clean.

2. Use protective clothing and equipment where needed. Use rubber gloves and an apron as well as a face mask for handling batteries. Protective goggles or safety glasses are recommended at all times.

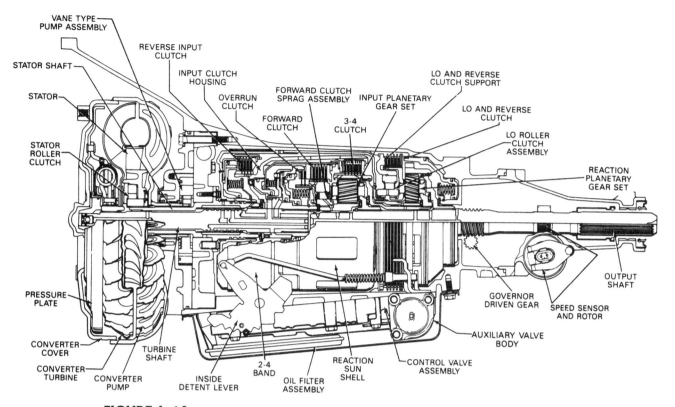

FIGURE I–14 Four-speed automatic transmission used on rear-wheel-drive cars has two simple planetary gears. (Courtesy of General Motors Corporation.)

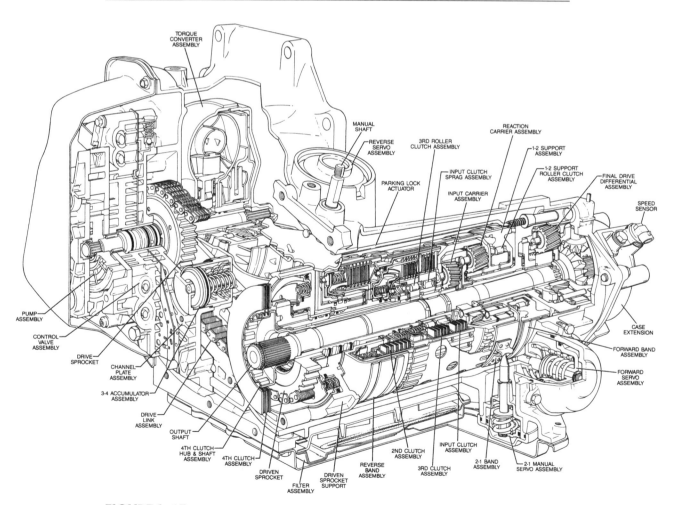

FIGURE I–15 Four-speed electronic automatic transaxle with planetary gear final drive. (Courtesy of General Motors Corporation.)

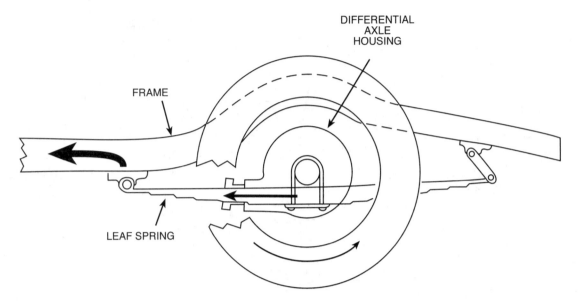

FIGURE I–16 On rear-wheel-drive vehicles with longitudinal rear leaf springs, the driving force is transferred from the axle housing through the leaf springs to the frame.

3. Keep hands and tools clean to avoid injury to hands and to avoid falling due to slipping when pulling on a wrench. Wash hands with soap and water after contact with oil, brake fluid, and other fluids.

4. Do not use compressed air to clean your clothes. This can cause dirt particles to be embedded in your skin and cause infection. Do not point the compressed air hose at anyone. Use eye protection.

5. Be careful when using compressed air to blow away dirt from parts. You should not use compressed air to blow dirt from brake parts since cancer-causing asbestos dust may be inhaled as a result.

6. Do not carry screwdrivers, punches, or other sharp objects in your pockets. You could injure yourself or damage the car you are working on.

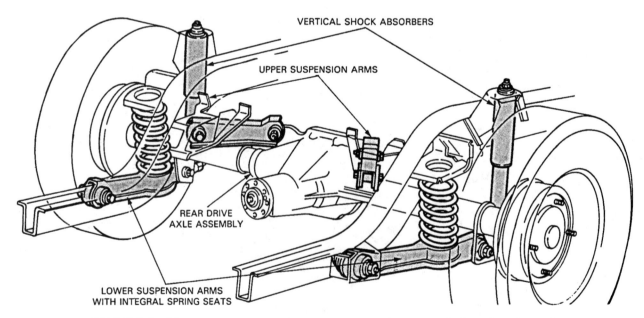

FIGURE I–17 Driving force is transmitted from the rear axle housing through four control arms to the frame on this rear-wheel-drive design. (Courtesy of Ford Motor Company.)

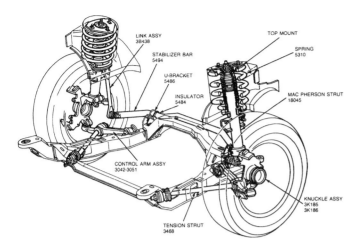

FIGURE I–18 Driving force is transmitted through tension struts and lower control arms on this front-wheel-drive design. (Courtesy of Ford Motor Company.)

7. Never get involved in dares, horseplay, or other practical jokes. They can lead to injury.

8. Make sure that you use the proper tool for the job and use it the right way. The wrong tool or its incorrect use can damage the part you are working on, cause injury, or both.

9. Never work under a car or under anything else that is not properly supported. Use safety stands properly placed to work under a car. Also, use a creeper.

10. Do not jack a car while someone is under it.

11. Never run a car engine without proper ventilation and adequate means of getting rid of exhaust gases. Exhaust gas contains deadly carbon monoxide. It can and does kill.

12. Keep your work area clean at all times. Your safety and the quality of work you do depend on it.

13. Lifting and carrying should be done properly to avoid injury. Heavy objects should be lifted and moved with the right equipment for the job.

14. Do not stand in the plane of rotating parts such as fans.

15. Never smoke while working on any vehicle.

SHOP SAFETY

1. Familiarize yourself with the way the shop is laid out. Find out where things are in the shop. You will need to know where the shop manuals are kept in or-der to obtain specifications and service procedures. Make sure that you know the route to the exit in case of fire.

2. Find out whether there are certain stalls that are reserved for special jobs. Abide by these rules.

3. Take note of all the warning signs around the shop. No-smoking signs, special instructions for some shop tools and equipment, danger zones, and so on, are all there to help the shop run smoothly and safely.

4. Note the location of fire extinguishers. Take time to read their operating instructions and the type of fire on which they are meant to be used.

5. Follow local regulations with regard to storing gasoline and other flammable liquids. Gasoline should be stored only in approved containers and locations.

6. Never use gasoline to clean parts. Never pour gasoline into a carburetor air horn to start the car.

7. Always immediately wipe up any gasoline that has been spilled. Never pour gasoline down a floor drain.

8. Fuel vapors are highly explosive. If vapors are present in the shop, have the doors open and the ventilating system turned on to get rid of these dangerous vapors.

9. Repair any fuel leak immediately. The potential fire hazard is very high. The smallest spark can set off an uncontrollable or fatal fire or explosion.

10. Dirty and oily rags should be stored in closed metal containers to avoid catching fire by spontaneous combustion.

11. Keep the shop floor and work benches clean and tidy. Oil on the floor can cause serious personal injury.

12. Do not operate shop tools or equipment that are in unsafe condition. Electrical cords and connectors must be in good condition. Bench grinding wheels and wire brushes should be replaced if defective. Floor jacks and hoist must be in safe operating condition and should not be used above their rated capacity. The same applies to mechanical and hydraulic presses, drills, and drill presses. Draw the attention of your instructor or shop supervisor to unsafe equipment or conditions. Do not operate equipment without prior instruction.

13. Never string extension cords across walkways as these would pose a hazard.

14. Do not leave jack handles in the down position across the floor. Someone could trip over them.

15. Do not drive cars over electrical cords. This could cause short circuits.

Chemical Safety

Automotive shops use a variety of chemicals in liquid, powder, or crystalline form. They can cause skin irritation, rashes, and burns. Always read the instructions on the package label to find out how to use the chemical and how to treat a chemical burn. Always wear hand and face protection when handling dangerous chemicals. Some of the more common chemicals used can cause skin rash and/or severe burns. These include:

- *Cleaning solvents:* petroleum-based products used for parts cleaning
- *Sulfuric acid:* used in batteries
- *Muriatic acid:* used to clean metal parts to be soldered. Extremely corrosive
- *Alkaline chemicals:* used for hot-tank cleaning of parts; like ordinary lye, extremely corrosive
- *Emulsion chemicals:* used in cold-soak cleaning of parts

Fire Safety

Several classes of fires can occur in the shop. Classifications of fires are determined by the type of combustible material involved. Fire extinguishers are classified in a similar manner, depending on their effectiveness on a particular class of fire. In some cases the use of an improper fire extinguisher may, in fact, increase the intensity of the flames. The use of water on a gasoline fire is one example of this hazard.

Following is a list of fire classifications.

1. *Class A fires.* These fires occur in normal combustible materials such as paper, wood, rags, and rubbish.

2. *Class B fires.* These fires result from flammable liquids such as diesel fuel, gasoline, oil, grease, paint, paint thinners, and similar substances being ignited.

3. *Class C fires.* These fires occur in electrical equipment and usually involve insulating materials and overheated electrical wiring due to electrical overload in switch panels, electric motors, and the like.

4. *Class D fires.* Although not common in auto shops, these fires can occur where combustible metals such as lithium, sodium, potassium, magnesium, titanium, and zirconium are present.

Following is a list of the appropriate fire extinguishers for use on each classification of fire:

1. *Pressurized water:* usually, a hose with a hand-squeezed, trigger-operated valve. Use on class A fires.

2. *Dry chemical:* usually, a portable hand-held tank with a valve operated by squeezing a handle or lever and aiming the chemical at the base of the fire. Use on class B and C fires. Dry chemical fire extinguishers that are suitable for three classes of fires—classes A, B, and C—are also available.

3. *Carbon dioxide (CO_2):* usually, a portable hand-held tank with a valve operated by squeezing a trigger or handle and aiming the CO_2 at the fire. Use on class B and C fires.

Driving a Customer's Car Safely

Be sure to follow these rules whenever you must drive a customer's car:

1. Make sure that your hands are clean before getting into a customer's car.

2. Use a shop seat cover and a floor mat to protect the upholstery and carpet in the car.

3. Make sure that there are no flat tires before getting in the car.

4. Test the brakes to make sure that you can stop when necessary.

5. Watch for other cars and for people on the move as you drive the car into and in the shop.

6. Position the car where you want it, place the transmission in Park, and apply the parking brake.

7. Use the same precautions when moving a customer's car out of the shop.

USED AND WASTE MATERIALS DISPOSAL SAFETY

The automotive service industry is concerned about energy conservation and the consequences of the indiscriminate disposal of used materials resulting from normal automotive service operations. Waste materials generated by the auto service industry must be recovered and recycled or disposed of in an environmentally friendly manner. The quality of the air we breathe, the purity of the water we use, and the condition of the land we live on are critical to the survival of all living creatures and plant life on earth.

Among the materials commonly handled in the automotive service industry, many can be recovered and recycled, while others must be disposed of in accordance with federal and local regulations. These include engine oil, gasoline, diesel fuel, solvents, transmission/transaxle and differential fluids, engine coolant (ethylene glycol), A/C refrigerants, batteries, sulphuric acid, tires, belts, cleaning fluids and chemicals, paints, brake fluid, and the like. Federal and local regulations governing the recovery, recycling, and safe disposal of these materials must be followed. As more is learned about the harmful effects of improper handling and disposal of materials, these regulations will become more and more stringent.

COMMON CAUSES OF ACCIDENTS

Many accidents can be prevented if the causes are recognized and anticipated before the accident happens. The technician and shop supervisor must always be alert for any conditions that develop which could lead to accidents. Here are some common causes of accidents which, if given due attention, can be corrected:

1. *Inexperience or lack of training.* If a technician does not know or follow the correct procedure, he or she should not proceed until this is remedied.

2. *Fatigue.* Working excessively long hours over a period of time can cause fatigue. Fatigue impairs judgment and alertness.

3. *Bad work habits.* Unsafe work habits can be developed or acquired from fellow workers. New or inexperienced workers must not pick up poor work habits from others.

4. *Shortcuts.* Shortcuts can result in accidents and should be avoided unless proven to be safe.

5. *Dirty shop.* A dirty, poorly organized shop or stall is prone to cause accident and injury. Tools and equipment left lying around can cause a fall; so can slippery floors.

6. *Bravado.* Under no circumstances should one employee goad another into an unsafe act by a dare.

Nor should anyone accept and follow through on such a dare. Dares and bravado are foolish and unsafe; they indicate immaturity.

7. *Skipping essential steps or procedures.* Trying to get a job done faster by skipping essential steps or procedures often results in dangerous situations. All necessary steps and procedures should be followed.

8. *Inability to recognize hazards.* This is usually the result of insufficient or poor training and experience. Proper training includes developing an awareness of the consequences of hazardous situations and recognizing them in time to avoid accidents.

FIRST AID

1. Make sure that you know the location and contents of the first-aid kit in your shop.

2. Find out if there is a resident nurse in your shop or school, and find out where the nurse's office is.

3. If there are specific first-aid rules in your school or shop, make sure you are aware of them and follow them. You should be able to locate emergency telephone numbers quickly, such as ambulance, doctor, and police.

4. There should be an eyewash station in the shop so that you can rinse your eye thoroughly should you get acid or some other irritant into it.

5. Burns should be cooled immediately by rinsing with water and then treating as recommended.

6. If someone is overcome by carbon monoxide, get him or her to fresh air immediately.

7. In case of severe bleeding, try to stop blood loss by applying pressure with clean gauze on or around the wound, and summon medical aid.

8. Do not move someone who may have broken bones unless the person's life is otherwise endangered. Moving a person may cause additional injury. Call for medical assistance.

Safety is the responsibility of everyone. The following is a good procedure to use:

- Study safety regulations.
- Set up a safe working area.
- Report any unsafe working conditions.
- Be safety conscious.
- Practice safety on every job.

"RIGHT TO KNOW" LAWS

The U.S. "Right to Know" law originated with the Occupational Safety and Health Administration specifically for companies where hazardous materials were stored and handled. Most states extended these regulations to include the automotive service industry. Canadian workplace safety and health regulations are similar.

These laws require the employer to provide a safe working environment for their employees in three areas of responsibility.

1. Employers must provide training to their employees about their rights under the legislation, the nature of hazardous materials present in the workplace, the proper labeling of the hazardous materials, the posting of safety data sheets that provide precautionary information about the handling of these materials, protective equipment required, and procedures to follow in case of accidental spills and other safe handling procedures.

2. All hazardous materials must be labeled indicating their health, fire, and reactivity hazards. These labels must be clearly understood by users before product application or usage. A list of all hazardous materials used in the work area must be posted where the employees can read it.

3. Employers and shops must maintain documentation in the workplace on proof of training provided, records of accidents or spills involving hazardous materials.

Hazardous waste includes both solids and liquids and is categorized in four ways. Waste is hazardous if it is listed on the government's list of hazardous materials or falls into any of the following categories:

1. *Ignitability.* If the liquid flash point (temperature at which liquid will ignite) is below 140°F (45.8°C) or if the solid will spontaneously ignite (self-ignite due to heat generated by reaction of the materials).

2. *Corrosivity.* If it burns the skin or dissolves metals.

3. *Reactivity.* If it reacts violently with water or other substances, or releases dangerous gases when exposed to low pH acid solutions, or generates toxic vapors, fumes, mists or flammable gases.

4. *EP toxicity.* If it leaches any of eight listed heavy metals in concentrations greater than 100 times the concentration found in standard drinking water.

Every automotive shop should obtain all the current applicable information regarding workplace safety and health, and the handling and disposal of hazardous materials and waste. Failure to comply with regulations may result in heavy fines or imprisonment.

AUTOMOTIVE FASTENERS

Bolt Identification

Standard bolts are identified by size and thread type as given in the following examples (see **Figure I–19**). A bolt identified as 1/2–13 UNC 2A 1 is one that is 1/2 in. in diameter, has 13 threads per inch, has Unified National Coarse threads, has a class 2A thread fit, and is 1 in. long. The three lines on the bolt head indicate an SAE grade 5 bolt strength. Metric bolts are identified similarly but in metric dimensions, as follows. A bolt identified as M12 × 1.75–6g × 25–9.8 is one that has metric thread, is 12 mm in diameter, has a 1.75-mm thread pitch, has a 6g thread fit, is 25 mm long, and has a tensile strength rating of 9.8. These terms are explained in this chapter. A variety of fasteners is shown in **Figure I–20** (see also **Figures I–21 to I–23**).

Bolt Size

The size of the bolt or stud is expressed in terms of its length and its diameter. Nut size is expressed in terms of its inside diameter. A 1/2-in. nut, for example, fits a 1/2-in.-diameter bolt. Fastener size is not to be confused with the wrench size required to fit the bolt head or the nut. Fasteners used in automotive applications may be dimensioned in the customary inch system or in the metric system.

Tensile Strength

The tensile strength of a bolt is the amount of load required to break the bolt when the load is applied longitudinally.

Fastener Grade

Bolts, cap screws, and studs are classified according to standards established by the Society of Automotive Engineers (SAE) and the American Society for Testing and Materials (ASTM). The grade or quality of a fastener is determined by the type of material and the process

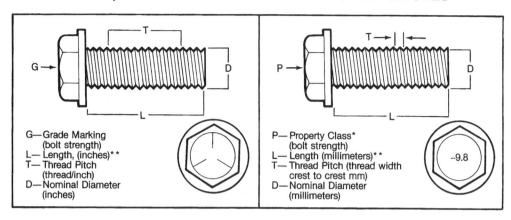

(ENGLISH) INCH SYSTEM
Bolt, 1/2-13x1

METRIC SYSTEM
Bolt M12-1.75x25

G—Grade Marking
(bolt strength)
L—Length, (inches)**
T—Thread Pitch
(thread/inch)
D—Nominal Diameter
(inches)

P—Property Class*
(bolt strength)
L—Length (millimeters)**
T—Thread Pitch (thread width
crest to crest mm)
D—Nominal Diameter
(millimeters)

*The property class is an Arabic numeral distinguishable from the slash SAE English grade system.
**The length of all bolts is measured from the underside of the head to the end.

FIGURE I–19 Examples of English and metric bolt dimensions and terminology. (Courtesy of Ford Motor Company.)

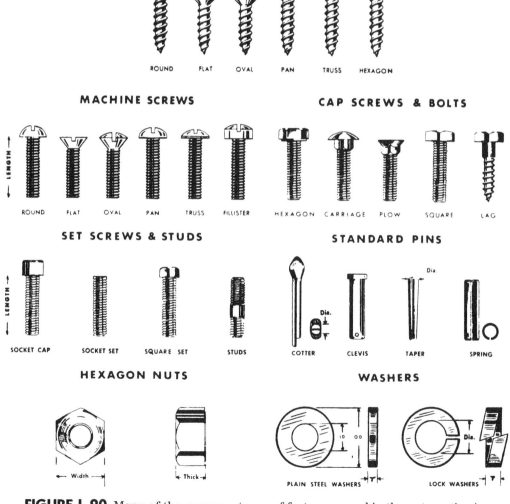

TAPPING SCREWS

SHEET METAL SCREWS

ROUND   FLAT   OVAL   PAN   TRUSS   HEXAGON

MACHINE SCREWS

ROUND   FLAT   OVAL   PAN   TRUSS   FILLISTER

CAP SCREWS & BOLTS

HEXAGON   CARRIAGE   PLOW   SQUARE   LAG

SET SCREWS & STUDS

SOCKET CAP   SOCKET SET   SQUARE SET   STUDS

STANDARD PINS

COTTER   CLEVIS   TAPER   SPRING

HEXAGON NUTS

Width   Thick

WASHERS

PLAIN STEEL WASHERS   LOCK WASHERS

FIGURE I–20 Many of the common types of fasteners used in the automotive industry. (Courtesy of H. Paulin & Co. Limited.)

used in its manufacture and is indicated by special head markings (**Figures I–21** and **I–22**). Nuts are marked with numbers or dots in the SAE system. Increasing number or dots indicate increased strength (**Figure I–23**).

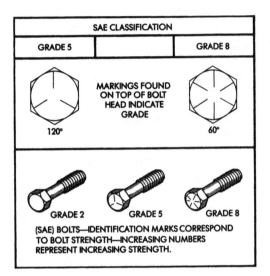

FIGURE I–21 Bolt head markings indicate fastener grade (tensile strength) on SAE bolts. (Courtesy of Chrysler Corporation.)

METRIC BOLTS—IDENTIFICATION CLASS NUMBERS CORRESPOND TO BOLT STRENGTH— INCREASING NUMBERS REPRESENT INCREASING STRENGTH.

FIGURE I–22 Metric bolt strength is indicated by numbers on bolt head. (Courtesy of Chrysler Corporation.)

Yield Point

The yield point of a bolt or cap screw is the point at which it continues to stretch without increasing the load on the assembly. This point is reached at or near the tensile strength rating.

Shear Strength

The shear strength of a bolt is the point at which a force applied at 90 degrees to the bolt axis results in the bolt shearing in two. The shear strength of a bolt is just over half of its tensile strength.

Thread Pitch and Type

The thread pitch is defined as the distance from the apex of one thread to the apex of the next thread. It is expressed as the number of threads per inch in the U.S. customary system and the distance in millimeters from crest to crest of adjoining threads in the metric system. Thread types with regard to pitch are classified as follows:

- Unified National Coarse (UNC or NC)
- Unified National Fine (UNF or NF) (formerly SAE)
- Unified National Extra Fine (UNEF or NEF)
- Unified National Pipe Thread (UNPT or PT)
- Machine Screw (MS)
- Metric Coarse and Fine (SI)

A thread pitch gauge with both metric and U.S. gauge blades is used to check fastener thread pitch and type (**Figure I–24**).

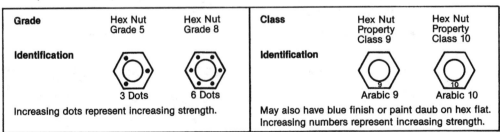

FIGURE I–23 Nut strength markings. (Courtesy of Ford Motor Company.)

FIGURE I–24 Thread pitch gauge with SAE and metric gauges. (Courtesy of KD Tools, Inc.)

Thread Class Fit

The thread class symbol identifies the fit between the internal and external threads of an assembled bolt and nut. In the Unified series, symbols such as 1A, 2A, and so on, are used. Metric fasteners also use alphanumeric symbols for thread fit, such as 6g, with lowercase letters instead of capitals.

Bolt Torque

Factors that affect the tightening specifications for fasteners include the following:

1. Bolt size, length, and diameter
2. Tensile strength (property class)
3. Thread type and fit
4. Whether threads are dry or lubricated
5. Whether or not bolts are plated
6. Whether threads are self-locking or self-tapping
7. The type of material being bolted together: iron, aluminum, plastic, and so on.

The wide variety of fasteners, thread types, and materials used in the modern automobile no longer allows any standard torque values to be followed. The only safe method is to follow the vehicle manufacturer's torque specifications in each specific instance.

Torque is defined as a twisting force. To turn a bolt or cap screw into a threaded part requires torque. Although the proper way to express torque in the English system is in pound inches or pound feet, the automotive trade commonly uses the terms *inch pounds* and *foot pounds*. Fifteen foot pounds applied to a bolt is the equivalent of a 15-lb force be-

ing applied at the end of a 1-ft wrench measured from the exact center of the bolt to the point where the force is applied. One foot pound is equal to 12 in.-lb. In the metric system, torque is measured in newton meters or kilogram meters (**Figures I–25** and **I–26**). (See the Appendix for conversion factors.) Always use a torque wrench to tighten fasteners properly. Where applicable, the torque-turn method may be used.

Torque-Turn Tightening. This is done as follows:

1. Tighten the nut or cap screw to the torque specified in the appropriate service manual.
2. Tighten the nut or cap screw an additional amount as specified in the service manual (e.g., 1/3 turn, 1/2 turn, 60°, etc.; **Figure I–27**).

Fastening Integrity

Thread-Locking Compound. To prevent bolts, nuts, and screws from loosening due to vibration, a liquid thread-locking compound is applied to the fastener threads during installation. The compound is applied to the entire length of the threaded portion of the fastener. It is then installed and tightened to specifications. To remove a fastener installed with liquid thread-locking compound after any time period, use an ordinary socket and handle. Some extra turning effort may be required, but removal should not be difficult.

Antiseize Compound. Over a period of time, extreme temperature changes and other environmental factors, certain bolts, nuts, screws, and other threaded parts may become seized and extremely difficult or impossible to remove without component damage. The exhaust oxygen sensor is a good example of this. If the oxygen sensor is installed without antiseize compound on its threads, it may not be possible to remove it without damaging the exhaust pipe to which it is threaded. An antiseize compound used on threaded fasteners and components such as the oxygen sensor, exhaust manifold bolts, and pipe connections makes removal easy even after an extended time period.

Causes of Fastener Failure. The following are some of the common causes of fastener failure:

1. Using a grade of fastener below that called for in the specifications

Size	GRADE 5		GRADE 8	
	In. Lbs. Ft. Lbs.	Newton meters	In. Lbs. Ft. Lbs.	Newton meters
1/4–20	95 In. Lbs.	11	124 In. Lbs.	14
1/4–28	95 In. Lbs.	11	150 In. Lbs.	17
5/16–18	200 In. Lbs.	23	270 In. Lbs.	31
5/16–24	20 Ft. Lbs.	27	25 Ft. Lbs.	34
3/8–16	30 Ft. Lbs.	41	40 Ft. Lbs.	54
3/8–24	35 Ft. Lbs.	48	45 Ft. Lbs.	61
7/16–14	50 Ft. Lbs.	68	65 Ft. Lbs.	88
7/16–20	55 Ft. Lbs.	75	70 Ft. Lbs.	95
1/2–13	75 Ft. Lbs.	102	100 Ft. Lbs.	136
1/2–20	85 Ft. Lbs.	115	110 Ft. Lbs.	149
9/16–12	105 Ft. Lbs.	142	135 Ft. Lbs.	183
9/16–18	150 Ft. Lbs.	156	150 Ft. Lbs.	203
5/8–11	115 Ft. Lbs.	203	195 Ft. Lbs.	264
5/8–18	160 Ft. Lbs.	217	210 Ft. Lbs.	285
3/4–16	175 Ft. Lbs.	237	225 Ft. Lbs.	305

FIGURE I–25 Typical bolt-tightening specifications. Always refer to the service manual for bolt torque specifications. (Courtesy of Chrysler Corporation.)

GRADE OF BOLT		5D	8G	10K	12K	
MIN. TENSILE STRENGTH		71,160 P.S.I.	113,800 P.S.I.	142,200 P.S.I.	170,679 P.S.I.	
GRADE MARKINGS ON HEAD		5D	8G	10K	12K	SIZE OF SOCKET OR WRENCH OPENING
METRIC						METRIC
BOLT DIA.	U.S. DEC EQUIV.	FOOT POUNDS				BOLT HEAD
6mm	0.2362	5	6	8	10	10mm
8mm	0.3150	10	16	22	27	14mm
10mm	0.3937	19	31	40	49	17mm
12mm	0.4720	34	54	70	86	19mm
14mm	0.5512	55	89	117	137	22mm
16mm	0.6299	83	132	175	208	24mm
18mm	0.709	111	182	236	283	27mm
22mm	0.8661	182	284	394	464	32mm

FIGURE I–26 Metric bolt torque values. (Courtesy of Mac Tools Inc.)

2. Overtightening (above specified torque)

3. Undertightening (below specified torque)

4. Cross-threading

5. Mixing thread types (metric and SAE, for example)

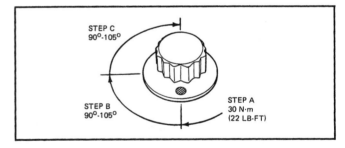

FIGURE I–27 Typical torque-turn bolt-tightening steps. (Courtesy of Ford Motor Company.)

6. Mixing bolt and nut grades

7. A washer that is incorrectly installed under a bolt or cap screw head

8. Using the same fastener too many times

Studs

Studs are threaded at both ends and do not have a head **(Figure I–28)**. Studs are screwed into the main part to specified torque. A mating part is positioned on the studs and held in place by stud nuts tightened to speci-

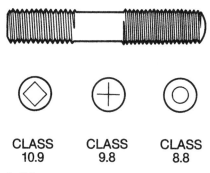

CLASS
10.9

CLASS
9.8

CLASS
8.8

FIGURE I-28 Some studs carry the property class number. Smaller studs use a geometric code on the end. (Courtesy of Ford Motor Company.)

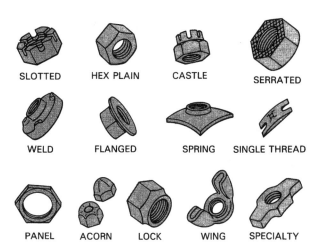

SLOTTED   HEX PLAIN   CASTLE   SERRATED

WELD   FLANGED   SPRING   SINGLE THREAD

PANEL   ACORN   LOCK   WING   SPECIALTY

FIGURE I-29 Different nut designs. (Courtesy of Deere and Company.)

fications. Thread types, sizes, and tensile strengths are the same as those for bolts.

Nut Types

Many different nut styles are used in automotive service. Hexagonal nuts are the most common **(Figure I-29)**. Castellated or slotted nuts are locked in place with a cotter pin **(Figure I-30)**. Acorn or cap nuts are used where better appearance is desired. Self-locking nuts are used to prevent loosening due to vibration. Wing nuts are used where low tightening torque is sufficient and where removal and tightening by hand is desired. Thread types for nuts are the same as for bolts.

Washer Types

Flat washers are used under bolt heads and nuts to increase the area being clamped and to prevent the bolt head or nut from damaging the part during tightening. Lock washers are used to prevent bolts or nuts from loosening from vibration. Split-ring and toothed lock washers are used **(Figure I-31)**.

Machine Screws

Machine screws are similar to bolts but are smaller. They usually have slotted, square, Phillips, Torx, Pozi, 6-point, or 12-point drive heads. They are used where heavy clamping is not needed.

Self-Tapping Screws

Self-tapping screws are used to hold sheet metal and plastic parts in place (trim panels, body sheet metal,

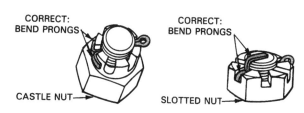

CORRECT:
BEND PRONGS

CORRECT:
BEND PRONGS

CASTLE NUT

SLOTTED NUT

FIGURE I-30 Castle nut and slotted nut locked with a cotter pin. (Courtesy of Deere and Company.)

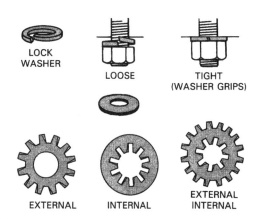

LOCK
WASHER

LOOSE

TIGHT
(WASHER GRIPS)

EXTERNAL   INTERNAL   EXTERNAL
INTERNAL

FIGURE I-31 Split-ring lock washer use (top), flat washer (middle), and toothed lock washers (bottom). (Courtesy of Deere and Company.)

and plastic parts). Self-tapping screws have a tapered, coarse thread that usually comes to a point for ease in starting the screw. They screw into thin metal nuts or into the sheet metal itself. Different head designs and drive types are used.

Self-Locking (Prevailing Torque) Fasteners

Self-locking or prevailing torque fasteners are used where low clamping force is adequate. They have a built-in self-locking feature to prevent loosening due to vibration. Deformed threads, nylon inserts, adhesive coatings, and out-of-round threads are methods used to provide the self-locking feature (**Figure I–32**).

Setscrews

Setscrews are used to lock a part to a shaft. Automotive setscrews are usually headless with a recessed hex drive. Setscrews may be used with or without a key and keyway.

Keys and Keyways

A metal key may be used to lock a part to a shaft. The key fits into a groove in the shaft and a mating groove in the part (collar, gear, or pulley). The key prevents the shaft and part from turning independently. Straight keys and woodruff (half-moon) keys are used (**Figure I–33**).

Splines

Splines are a series of parallel grooves cut into a shaft and mating part. They prevent the part and shaft from rotating independently. Splines allow the part

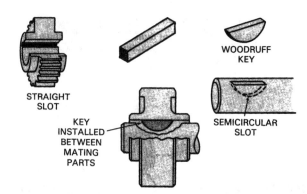

FIGURE I–33 Straight key and woodruff key use. (Courtesy of Deere and Company.)

to slide back and forth on the shaft without affecting rotation. Splines are used in transaxles, transmissions, clutches, drive shafts, differentials, and drive axles.

Snap Rings

Snap rings may be used to keep bearings, gears, collars, pins, shafts, and other parts in place. The snap ring fits into a groove in a shaft or housing. There are internal and external snap rings. Snap rings are made from spring steel so that their tension keeps them firmly in place. Snap ring ends may have holes or square or angled ends that require special snap ring pliers to remove or install (**Figure I–34**).

Roll Pins (Spring Pins)

Roll pins are split, tubular steel pins used to lock two parts together. The pin fits tightly in a hole slightly smaller than the pin diameter in its relaxed state. The tension of the pin in the hole keeps it in place. Roll pins come in different sizes and lengths. Other pin types are also used (**Figure I–35**).

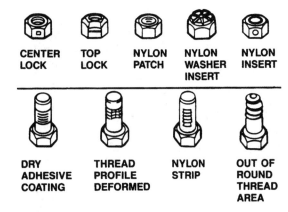

FIGURE I–32 Various kinds of self-locking or prevailing torque type fasteners. (Courtesy of General Motors Corporation.)

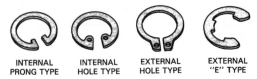

FIGURE I–34 Snap ring designs. (Courtesy of Deere and Company.)

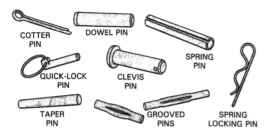

FIGURE I–35 Various types of pins. (Courtesy of Deere and Company.)

Cotter Pins

Cotter pins are split steel pins with a rounded head section on one end. They are used to lock slotted nuts and other parts in place. The cotter pin is inserted into the hole and the protruding end is split apart and bent over to lock it in place.

Rivets

Rivets are metal pins with a head at one end. They may be solid metal or tubular. They are used to lock two parts together. The solid rivet is inserted into the holes in the parts to be joined and the protruding end is mushroomed with a ball-peen hammer to lock it in place. Tubular rivets are used in a similar manner. Pop rivets are designed to be used in blind holes where access is limited to one side only. Pop rivets are installed with a special pop riveting tool that deforms the rivet on the end opposite the rivet head after insertion.

REMOVING DAMAGED OR BROKEN FASTENERS

Removing damaged or broken fasteners that may also be seized or whose heads are rounded off is a skill required of all technicians. Different tools and methods are used depending on the particular problem encountered. Here are some common methods:

1. *Locking pliers.* These can be used to remove bolts whose heads are rounded off, nuts that are rounded off or broken bolts or studs that are broken off far enough above the part surface to allow gripping with locking pliers. A sharp blow with a hammer on the end of the fastener and some penetrating oil can help the process.

2. *Stud remover.* This tool can be used to remove or install studs and to remove fasteners that are broken off far enough above the surface to allow tool usage.

3. *Screw driver.* If enough of the fastener extends above the surface, saw a slot in the fastener with a hacksaw and remove the fastener with a screw driver.

4. *Welding.* Weld a nut onto the broken fastener and use a wrench to remove the stud or bolt.

5. *Screw extractor.* Sometimes called an "easy out." To use, drill an appropriate size hole in the exact center of the fastener. Tap the extractor snugly into the hole and use a wrench to remove the fastener.

SAFETY CAUTION: Be careful not to break the extractor in the drilled hole. It is case hardened and cannot be removed by drilling. Do not use excessive turning force on the wrench.

---

6. *Hammer and punch.* These may be used on some broken fasteners where seized threads are not a problem. Place the point of the punch near the outer edge of the fastener at an angle that will unscrew the bolt when you strike the punch with a hammer.

After broken fastener removal, always inspect internal threads for possible damage. Clean threads by running the appropriate size tap through the threads.

THREAD REPAIR

Threads in good condition can be cleaned up with a tap or die to remove any foreign material or minor burrs. Damaged threads must be repaired by drilling out the damaged threads, tapping new threads in the hole thus prepared, and installing a suitable-size thread repair insert (**Figures I–36** and **I–37**). First establish the size, pitch, and length of thread required. Refer to the kit manufacturer's instructions for the proper-size drill to

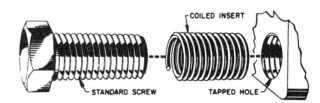

FIGURE I–36 Thread repair insert may be used to repair damaged threads.

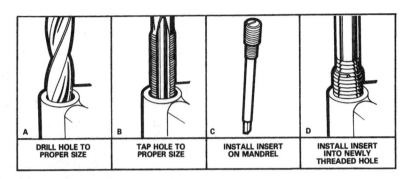

A	B	C	D
DRILL HOLE TO PROPER SIZE	TAP HOLE TO PROPER SIZE	INSTALL INSERT ON MANDREL	INSTALL INSERT INTO NEWLY THREADED HOLE

FIGURE I–37 How to use a thread repair kit to repair damaged internal threads. (Courtesy of General Motors Corporation.)

use for the thread size to be repaired. Drill out the damaged threads with the specified drill. Clean out all metal chips from the hole. Tap new threads in the hole using the specified tap. Lubricate the tap while threading the hole. Back out the tap every turn or two. When the hole is threaded to the proper depth, remove the tap and all metal chips from the hole. Select the proper-size thread insert and thread it onto the installing mandrel. Lubricate the thread insert with motor oil if in cast iron (do not lubricate if installing in aluminum). Install the thread insert into the hole until flush with, or to one turn below, the surface. Remove the installer. If the tang of the insert does not break off during mandrel removal, break the tang off with a drift punch and remove it. This completes the repair and allows normal fastener use and torque.

REVIEW QUESTIONS

1. Drive train design depends on:

   a. _____ _____   b. _____ _____

   c. _____ _____

2. When the engine is located behind the passenger compartment and just in front of the rear axle, it is called a _____ vehicle.

3. On a rear-wheel-drive vehicle, the engine is positioned _____ between the front wheels.

4. On a front-wheel-drive vehicle, the engine may be mounted in a _____ or a _____ position.

5. On the front-wheel-drive vehicle, the _____ drive the front wheels.

6. Part-time four-wheel drive has a _____ _____ mounted to the rear of the transmission.

7. What kind of shoes are best for automotive shop use?

8. Why should compressed air not be used to blow dirt from your clothing?

9. Never use _____ _____ to blow dirt away from brake parts.

10. Exhaust gases contain deadly _____ _____.

11. Never use _____ to clean parts.

12. Gasoline vapors are highly _____.

13. Name four automotive shop chemicals that can cause skin rash and chemical burns.

14. List five common causes of accidents.

15. What is an eyewash station?

16. Why should water not be used on a gasoline fire?

17. Standard bolts are identified by _____ and _____ type.

18. The size of a bolt is determined by its _____ and _____.

19. The thread pitch of a bolt in the English system is determined by the number of _____ per _____.

20. An increasing number of "slashes" on a bolt head represents increased _____ _____.

21. Name the six thread types used in automobiles. (Use abbreviations.)

22. Name six factors that affect the tightening specifications for fasteners.

23. Torque is defined as a _____ force.

24. List eight causes of fastener failure.

25. A damaged internal thread can be repaired by drilling, tapping, and installing a _____ _____ _____.

26. Name five kinds of washers used in automobiles.

TEST QUESTIONS

1. Technician A says the drive train provides the means to increase or decrease the driving torque. Technician B says the drive train is used to increase or decrease speed. Who is correct?
   a. Technician A
   b. Technician B
   c. Both are correct
   d. Both are wrong

2. Engines are located in the vehicle:
   a. front and rear only
   b. front, rear, and transverse
   c. rear, front, and middle
   d. front only

3. Front-wheel-drive vehicles may have engines located in a longitudinal or transverse position.   True or False.

4. A transfer case usually has four possible gearshift positions:
   a. low, second, third, and overdrive
   b. neutral, low, second, and third
   c. neutral, two-wheel drive, four-wheel drive high, and four-wheel drive low.
   d. none of the above

5. A full-time four-wheel-drive transfer case has a
   a. differential
   b. viscous coupling
   c. direct drive
   d. differential and a viscous coupling

6. Manual transmissions are shifted into different drive ranges automatically.   True or False.

7. Automotive shop safety includes
   a. avoiding injury to yourself
   b. avoiding injury to others in the shop
   c. avoiding damage to vehicles and equipment
   d. all of the above

8. The type of clothing that should be worn in the automotive shop includes
   a. shoes with nonslip soles
   b. shoes with steel-capped toes
   c. clothing that is not loose, baggy, or torn
   d. all of the above

9. Compressed air can be used to
   a. blow dirt from clothing
   b. dry hands after washing
   c. clean the floor
   d. none of the above

10. Automobile exhaust gases contain deadly
   a. carbon dioxide
   b. nitric oxides
   c. carbon monoxide
   d. hydrocarbon

11. Face shields should be used when working with
   a. grinders
   b. cold chisels
   c. batteries
   d. all of the above
   e. none of the above

12. Class B fires can be extinguished by using
   a. water
   b. CO_2 fire extinguisher
   c. dry chemical fire extinguisher
   d. any of the above

13. Class A fires occur with such materials as
   a. gasoline and diesel fuel
   b. electrical wiring
   c. paper and rags
   d. sodium and lithium

14. Automotive chemicals that may cause skin rash or severe burns include
   a. sulfuric acid, cold-soak cleaners, and muriatic acid

b. muriatic acid, soapstone, and sulfuric acid

c. cold-soak cleaners, alkaline chemicals, and seltzer water

d. alkaline chemicals, soapstone, and seltzer water

15. Which of the following is not a common cause of accidents?
    a. bravado
    b. fatigue
    c. good work habits
    d. inexperience

16. The thread pitch on a U.S.-dimensioned bolt is determined by
    a. a number on the bolt head
    b. radial lines on the bolt head
    c. the required wrench size
    d. the number of threads per inch

17. The property class or strength of a metric bolt is determined by
    a. a number on the bolt head
    b. radial lines on the bolt head
    c. the required wrench size
    d. the number of threads per inch

18. Prevailing torque bolts use
    a. an adhesive coating
    b. an out-of-round thread
    c. a deformed thread
    d. a nylon strip or patch
    e. all of the above
    f. none of the above

19. Bolt size is determined by
    a. wrench size
    b. nut size
    c. length and diameter
    d. thread pitch and tensile strength

20. Fastener head drive designs include
    a. Phillips, Pozi, Torx, clutch, and hex
    b. clutch, ISO, Torx, Pozi, and Phillips
    c. Pozi, Phillips, SAE, and Torx
    d. Torx, clutch, Phillips, and Negy

21. The torque capacity of a bolt is determined by bolt
    a. length, diameter, thread pitch, and head size
    b. diameter, thread pitch, length, and tensile strength
    c. tensile strength, head size, length, and diameter
    d. diameter, wrench size, length, and thread pitch

22. Which of the following is not a cause of fastener failure?
    a. undertightening
    b. cross threading
    c. overtightening
    d. torque-turn tightening

23. A stud is
    a. a male fastener
    b. threaded at both ends
    c. a bolt with no nut
    d. less reliable than a bolt

24. Setscrews are used to
    a. set thread depth
    b. set torque values
    c. lock a part to a shaft
    d. lock at set torque values

25. Splines may be
    a. internal or external
    b. self-locking or internal
    c. sliding or external
    d. self-locking or sliding

◆ CHAPTER 1 ◆

FRONT-WHEEL-DRIVE AXLE PRINCIPLES AND SERVICE

INTRODUCTION

Many front-wheel-drive vehicles use two open drive axles with a constant velocity (CV) universal joint at each end of each axle. Some designs have three shafts with two constant-velocity (CV) universal joints on each outer shaft, and another U-joint on the inner shaft. This chapter discusses the function, design, operation, and service of front-wheel-drive axles and CV joints.

LEARNING OBJECTIVES

After completing this chapter, you should be able to:

- Describe the function of front-wheel-drive axles and CV joints.
- Describe the construction of front-wheel-drive axles and CV joints.
- Diagnose front-wheel-drive axle and CV joint problems.
- Remove and replace front-wheel-drive axles and CV joints.

TERMS YOU SHOULD KNOW

Look for these terms as you study this chapter and learn what they mean.

transaxle	outboard joint
front drive axle	tripod joint
inner stub shaft and housing	spider
outer stub shaft and housing	Rzeppa joint
interconnecting shaft	cage
intermediate shaft	boot
CV joint	boot straps
inboard joint	

FRONT-WHEEL-DRIVE AXLE FUNCTIONS AND COMPONENTS

Front-wheel-drive axles perform the following functions:

1. Transfer driving torque from the transaxle differential to the drive hubs and the front wheels.
2. Transfer driving torque at various angles as the front wheels turn right or left and as the suspension moves up or down.

A front-wheel-drive axle consists of the following major parts (**Figures 1–1** to **1–4;** some front-wheel-drive systems do not use an intermediate shaft).

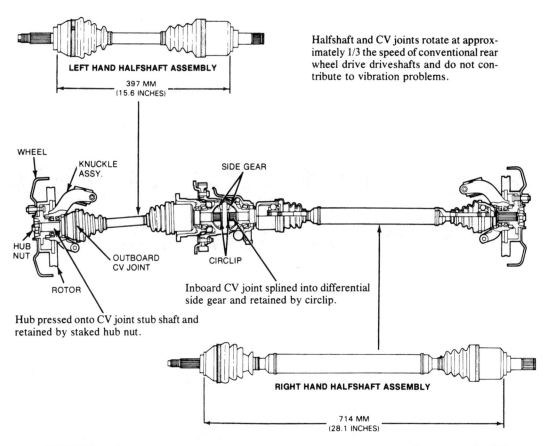

LEFT HAND HALFSHAFT ASSEMBLY

397 MM
(15.6 INCHES)

Halfshaft and CV joints rotate at approximately 1/3 the speed of conventional rear wheel drive driveshafts and do not contribute to vibration problems.

WHEEL

KNUCKLE ASSY.

SIDE GEAR

HUB NUT

OUTBOARD CV JOINT

CIRCLIP

ROTOR

Inboard CV joint splined into differential side gear and retained by circlip.

Hub pressed onto CV joint stub shaft and retained by staked hub nut.

RIGHT HAND HALFSHAFT ASSEMBLY

714 MM
(28.1 INCHES)

FIGURE 1–1 Front-wheel-drive axles and how they connect to the transaxle differential and front wheel hubs. (Courtesy of Ford Motor Company.)

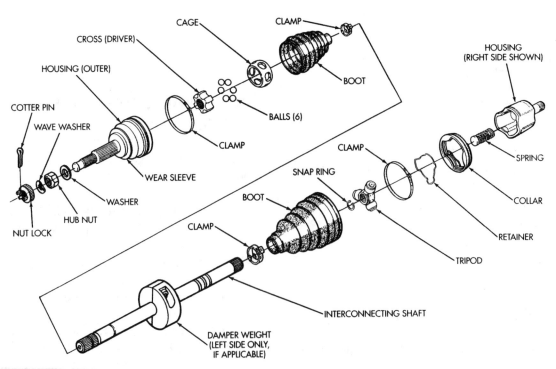

CAGE

CLAMP

CROSS (DRIVER)

HOUSING (RIGHT SIDE SHOWN)

HOUSING (OUTER)

BOOT

COTTER PIN

BALLS (6)

SPRING

WAVE WASHER

CLAMP

CLAMP

SNAP RING

COLLAR

CLAMP

WEAR SLEEVE

WASHER

BOOT

RETAINER

HUB NUT

TRIPOD

NUT LOCK

CLAMP

INTERCONNECTING SHAFT

DAMPER WEIGHT
(LEFT SIDE ONLY,
IF APPLICABLE)

FIGURE 1–2 Front-wheel-drive axle parts. (Courtesy of Chrysler Corporation.)

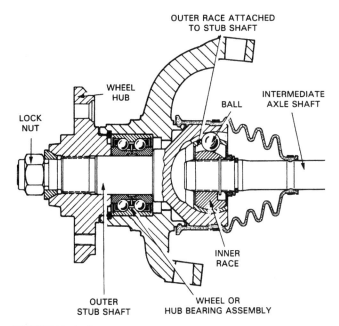

FIGURE 1–3 Cross section of outer CV joint, wheel hub, and bearing assembly. (Courtesy of Ford Motor Company.).

1. *Inner stub shaft and housing:* splined to axle side gears in transaxle differential and connected to inboard universal joint.
2. *Interconnecting shaft:* connects inboard universal joint to outboard universal joint. Shaft ends are splined.

3. *Outer stub shaft and housing:* splined to wheel hub and connected to outboard universal joint.
4. *Intermediate shaft:* connects inner stub shaft to drive axle shaft through a universal joint.
5. *Intermediate shaft support bearing:* used to support the outer end of the intermediate shaft.
6. *Universal joints:* connect the shafts together and allow shafts to operate at various angles.

Axle shafts are machined with splines for drive connections and grooves for snap rings and boots. Axle shafts turn at about one-third the speed of a drive shaft on a rear-wheel-drive car. Constant-velocity universal joints (CV joints) are used to transmit driving torque at various angles. A cross and roller U-joint may be used on vehicles with an intermediate shaft. Each shaft has one fixed and one sliding or telescoping CV joint.

FRONT-WHEEL-DRIVE AXLE OPERATION

Tripod CV Joint

A tripod CV joint is usually used at the inboard end of the drive axle. It may or may not provide for sliding or telescoping action depending on design. Most tripod joints are the sliding type. It consists of a spider with three trunnions and balls with needle bearings, splined

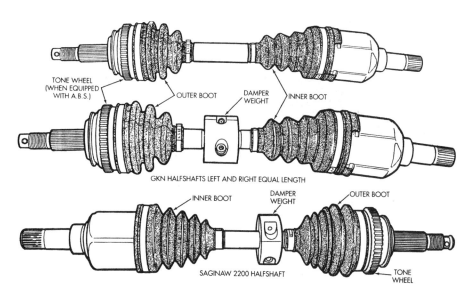

FIGURE 1–4 Various drive axle designs. Note tone wheel (wheel speed sensor ring) used on cars with antilock brakes. (Courtesy of Chrysler Corporation.)

to the drive axle, a housing, or a yoke connected to the stub shaft. A bellows type of rubber boot keeps dirt and moisture out and the special CV joint lubricant in Retaining straps keep the boot in place (see **Figures 1–2 and 1–3**).

Rzeppa CV Joint

A Rzeppa CV joint is usually used at the outboard end of the drive axle. It may or may not (depending on design) provide sliding or telescoping action to accommodate the changes in the effective length of the axle caused by up-and-down movement of the suspension. Most Rzeppa joints do not slide. A Rzeppa joint consists of an inner race splined to the outer end of the axle shaft, a set of drive balls and a ball cage, and an outer race connected to the stub shaft. A bellows type of rubber boot keeps dirt and moisture out and the special CV joint lubricant in. Retaining straps keep the boot in place **(Figure 1–5)**.

Equal- and Unequal-Length Drive Axles

Some vehicles use half-shafts of unequal length, while others use shafts of equal length. The equal-length system is used to reduce torque steer. Torque steer occurs on acceleration. It is the tendency of the vehicle to self-steer under heavy acceleration to the side with the long drive axle. This results from the fact that there is less torque loss between the transaxle and drive wheel with the short shaft. This causes the drive wheel with the short shaft to lead (be slightly ahead of) the other wheel during acceleration. A damper weight is used on the short shaft in some applications to reduce shaft vibration **(Figure 1–6)**. Some systems use an intermediate shaft assembly to accommodate the off-center position of the transaxle on a transverse engine front-drive system. The intermediate shaft assembly consists of a single cardan universal joint, a short intermediate shaft, and a support bearing and bracket **(Figure 1–7)**.

FRONT-WHEEL-DRIVE AXLE PROBLEMS

Rubber boots may become ruptured or torn since they are exposed to the weather and any gravel or debris on the road. Dirt and water can enter and cause CV joint failure. CV joint noise (clicks, clunks, or a grinding noise) indicate excessive wear or lack of lubricant. Clicking during turns usually indicates an outer joint problem. Clunking during acceleration or deceleration usually indicates an inner joint problem. The noise is especially evident when engaging the transaxle or clutch in drive or reverse. A grinding noise may be more pronounced during turns. CV joint boots that are cracked or ruptured must be replaced. Worn CV joints must be replaced.

FRONT-DRIVE AXLE REMOVAL

Front-drive axle procedures vary depending on design. The following procedures are typical:

1. In some cases it may be necessary to remove the right-side shaft first before the left shaft can be removed, or the other way around, depending on design. On some models, either shaft may be removed without being affected by the other. Follow the service manual sequence.

2. Remove the drive wheel hub nut (staked, cotter pinned, or prevailing torque nut). **Figures 1–8 and 1–9)**. Raise the vehicle and remove the wheel.

3. Separate the steering knuckle from the suspension arm. Support the drive axle and wire tie it to some part of the vehicle. Slide the wheel hub and steering knuckle assembly from the outer stub shaft. Be sure not to put excessive strain on the flexible brake line during this procedure **(Figures 1–10 to 1–12)**.

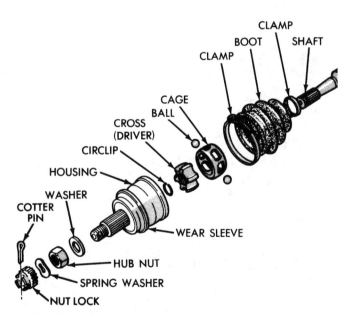

FIGURE 1–5 A Rzeppa CV joint provides swiveling action and telescoping action. (Courtesy of Chrysler Corporation.)

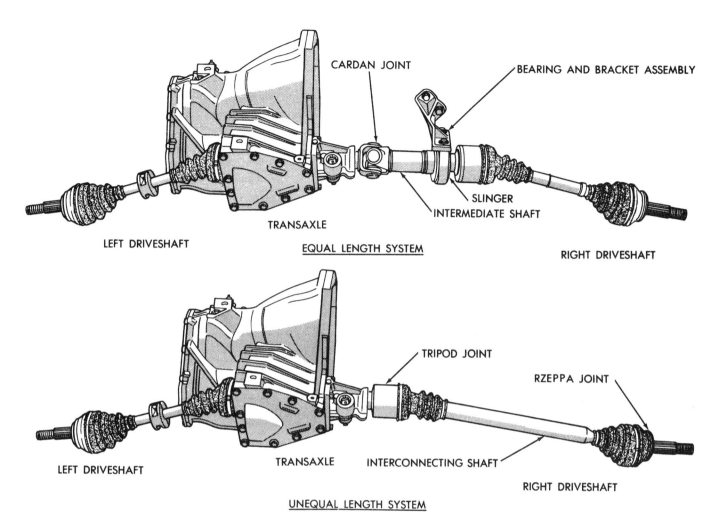

FIGURE 1–6 Typical transaxle and front-drive axle system. Shown here are equal-length (top) and unequal-length (bottom) drive axle systems. Equal-length systems are designed to reduce torque steer. (Courtesy of Chrysler Corporation.)

4. In some cases the control arm ball joint may have to be disconnected to provide clearance for axle shaft removal.

> **CAUTION:** Never remove both inner CV joints at the same time. Doing so may allow the differential to drop out of position requiring complete disassembly to correct.

5. Disconnect the inner end of the drive axle from the transaxle in one of the following ways, depending on design:

    a. Simply slide the stub shaft out of the transaxle.

    b. Remove the retaining flange bolts and slide the stub shaft from the transaxle.

    c. Remove the access cover from the transaxle; push the stub shaft into the transaxle to gain access to the retaining circlip, and remove the circlip; then slide the shaft out of the transaxle.

    d. Use a slide hammer puller to release the circlip and allow the stub shaft to be removed **(Figure 1–13).**

In each case, loss of lubricant either through the shaft hole or through the inspection cover may be expected. Use a clean pan to catch any escaping lubricant.

RZEPPA CV JOINT REPLACEMENT

The general procedure for the disassembly of a Rzeppa (ball and cage) CV joint is as follows. (Refer to the ser-

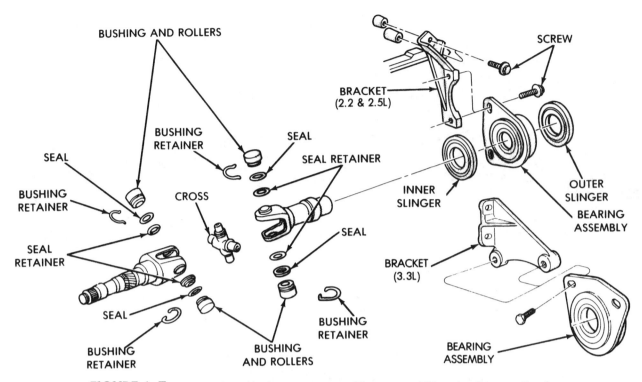

FIGURE 1–7 Intermediate shaft components. (Courtesy of Chrysler Corporation.)

CAUTION: Discard the hub retainer nut. It is a torque prevailing design and cannot be reused.

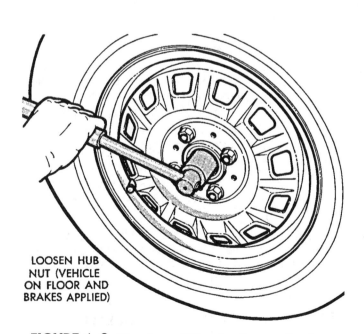

LOOSEN HUB NUT (VEHICLE ON FLOOR AND BRAKES APPLIED)

FIGURE 1–8 (Courtesy of Chrysler Corporation.)

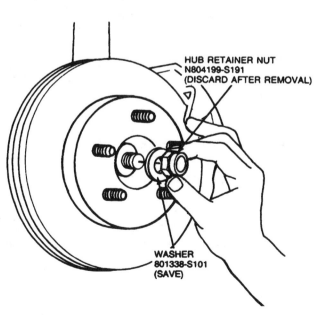

HUB RETAINER NUT N804199-S191 (DISCARD AFTER REMOVAL)

WASHER 801338-S101 (SAVE)

FIGURE 1–9 (Courtesy of Ford Motor Company.)

CAUTION: Never use a hammer to separate the outboard CV joint stub shaft from the hub. Damage to the CV joint threads and internal components may result.

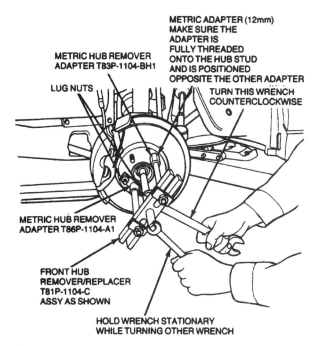

FIGURE 1–10 Using a puller to remove a front wheel hub assembly from the outer shaft. (Courtesy of Ford Motor Company.)

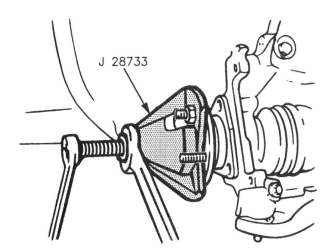

FIGURE 1–11 Pushing the drive axle out of the wheel hub. (Courtesy of General Motors Corporation.)

vice manual for specific procedures.) *Note:* The usual practice is to replace the entire joint if any parts are worn or damaged.

1. Clamp the half-shaft securely in a vise with soft jaws.

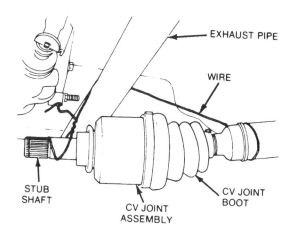

FIGURE 1–12 Using a piece of wire to support the outer end of the drive axle. (Courtesy of Ford Motor Company.)

2. Remove the boot retaining clamps or straps **(Figure 1–14)**.

3. Slide the rubber boot back to expose the cage retaining ring.

4. Mark the shaft and housing to ensure that alignment is maintained during reassembly **(Figure 1–15)**. Remove the retaining ring with suitable snap ring pliers.

5. Slide the joint off the shaft. Use a soft hammer and tap it off if necessary.

6. Tilt the cage and inner race in the housing, using your thumbs.

7. Remove the exposed balls. Use a blunt screwdriver if needed. Tilt the cage in different directions to remove the remaining balls in the same manner **(Figure 1–16)**.

8. Remove the dust seal if so equipped.

9. Remove the ABS sensor ring (if equipped) using special tools for the purpose **(Figure 1–17)**.

10. Remove the dust seal if so equipped.

11. Inspect all parts for wear or damage. Replace faulty parts with a CV joint repair kit.

To assemble the Rzeppa joint, the usual procedure is as follows using a CV joint repair kit which contains all the necessary parts and lubricant.

1. Wash in recommended cleaning solvent and blow dry all parts to be reused.

2. Install the ABS sensor ring (if equipped) using the special tools required **(Figure 1–18)**.

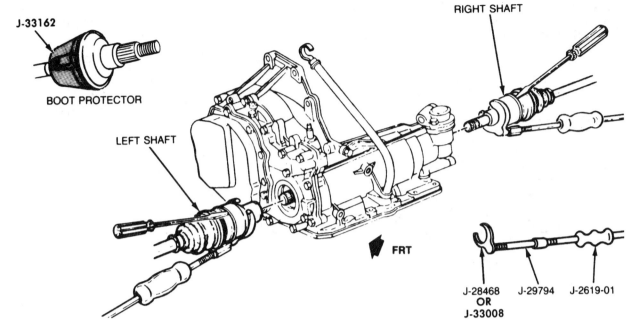

FIGURE 1–13 Using a slide hammer puller to remove the drive axles from the transaxle. (Courtesy of General Motors Corporation.)

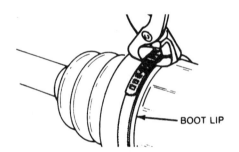

FIGURE 1–14 Using a pair of cutters to remove the boot retaining strap. (Courtesy of Chrysler Corporation.)

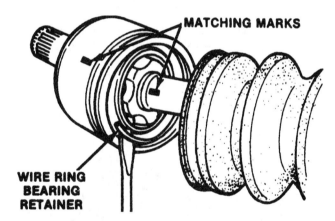

FIGURE 1–15 Marks on shaft and CV joint housing ensure proper alignment during assembly. (Courtesy of Ford Motor Company.)

3. Using the special grease supplied with the new kit, grease the inner race and cage.

4. Install the race and cage into the housing.

5. Tilt the cage in various positions to install all the drive balls **(Figure 1–19)**.

6. Slide the joint onto the splined shaft with the marks aligned.

7. Install the cage retaining ring. Make sure that it is fully seated.

8. Pack the joint with the remaining special grease in the boot and slide the boot over the joint. Make sure the boot fits snugly in the grooves at each end **(Figure 1–20)**. Position the small end of the boot and tighten the clamp. Before clamping the larger end, slide a thin screwdriver under the boot to allow any trapped air to escape.

9. Install the boot retaining straps or clamps using the special tools that may be required. Do not overtighten **(Figures 1–21 and 1–22)**.

10. Install a new dust seal if so equipped **(Figure 1–23)**.

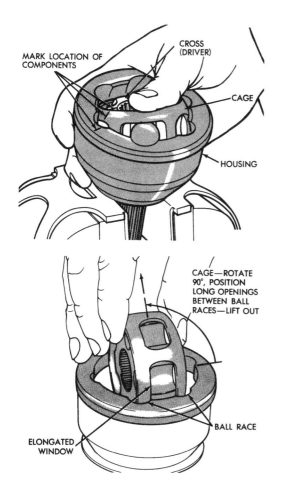

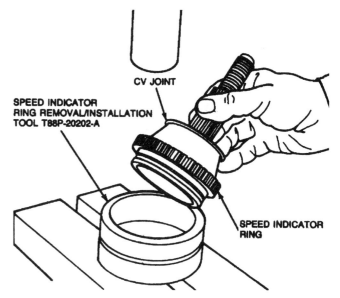

FIGURE 1–17 Speed indicator ring removal tool and press. (Courtesy of Ford Motor Company.)

FIGURE 1–16 Removing the ball cage from the CV joint housing (typical). (Courtesy of Chrysler Corporation.)

Tripod CV Joint Replacement

The general procedure for the disassembly of a tripod CV joint is as follows. **(Figure 1–24):**

1. Clamp the shaft in a soft-jaw-equipped vise. Be careful not to dent or deform the tubular shafts. They should not be clamped too tightly since any dent can cause imbalance and vibration.

2. Remove the boot retaining rings. Cut the strap type or pry off the spring type. (See **Figure 1–14**.)

3. Mark the housing, spider, and axle shaft if parts are to be used again. (See **Figure 1–15**.)

4. Separate the housing from the tripod, being careful to keep the bearings in place if they are to be reused. *Note:* The usual procedure is to replace the entire joint if any parts are worn or damaged.

5. Remove the spider retaining ring.

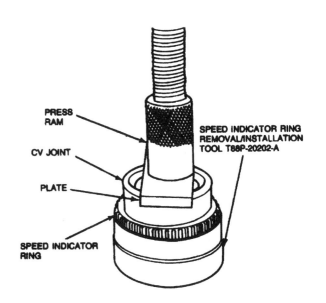

CAUTION: Extra care should be taken not to damage the speed indicator ring during installation. If teeth are damaged, brake performance will be affected.

FIGURE 1–18 Installing the speed indicator ring on the CV joint housing. (Courtesy of Ford Motor Company.)

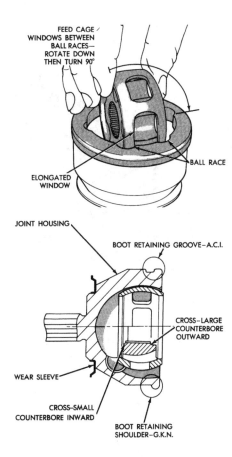

FEED CAGE WINDOWS BETWEEN BALL RACES—ROTATE DOWN THEN TURN 90°

BALL RACE

ELONGATED WINDOW

JOINT HOUSING

BOOT RETAINING GROOVE–A.C.I.

CROSS–LARGE COUNTERBORE OUTWARD

WEAR SLEEVE

CROSS–SMALL COUNTERBORE INWARD

BOOT RETAINING SHOULDER–G.K.N.

CROSS LANDS FEED THROUGH ELONGATED WINDOWS–CITROEN

JOINT HOUSING

CAGE CHAMFERED SIDE OUT

WEAR SLEEVE

CROSS CHAMFER OUTWARD

CROSS–SMALL COUNTERBORE INWARD

BOOT RETAINING GROOVE

FIGURE 1–19 Assembling a Rzeppa CV joint (typical). (Courtesy of Chrysler Corporation.)

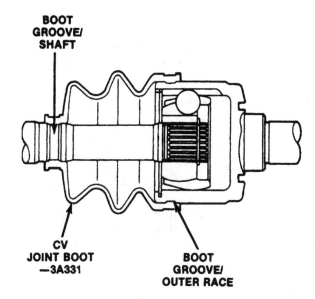

BOOT GROOVE/ SHAFT

CV JOINT BOOT —3A331

BOOT GROOVE/ OUTER RACE

FIGURE 1–20 Make sure the dust boot is positioned properly in the grooves in the shaft and housing during assembly. (Courtesy of Ford Motor Company.)

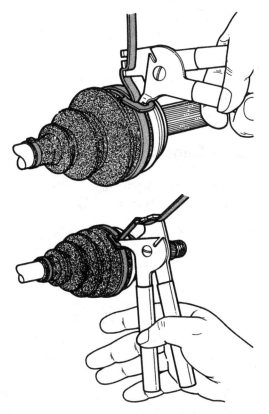

FIGURE 1–21 A special tool is needed to install CV joint boot straps. (Courtesy of Chrysler Corporation.)

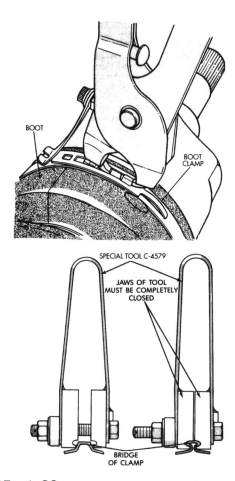

FIGURE 1–22 Two kinds of axle boot clamps and clamping procedures. (Courtesy of Chrysler Corporation.)

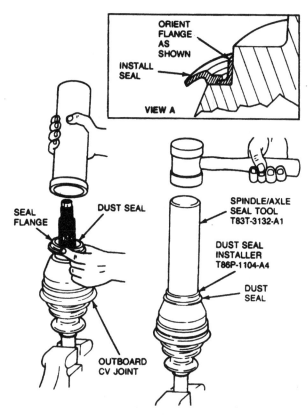

FIGURE 1–23 Installing a new CV joint dust seal. (Courtesy of Ford Company.)

6. Using a brass punch and hammer, drive the spider from the axle shaft.

7. Remove the rubber boot.

To assemble the joint, proceed as follows, using a new CV joint kit **(Figure 1–25):**

1. Wash in solvent and blow dry all the parts to be reused.

2. Slide the rubber boot onto the axle shaft.

3. Slide the spider and bearing assembly onto the axle shaft. If one side is chamfered, be sure that it faces the correct direction.

4. Install the spider retaining ring. Be sure that it is fully seated.

5. Install the spring and seat into the housing (if so equipped).

6. Grease the tripod assembly with the special grease from the kit. Pack the joint fully using all the grease.

7. Slide the tripod into the housing.

8. Using the special grease supplied with the new kit, place the grease in the rubber boot. Grease the spider with the same grease.

9. Position the boot over the housing and install the boot clamps or straps. Do not overtighten. (See **Figures 1–20** to **1–22.**)

INSTALLING THE DRIVE AXLES

To install the drive axle, follow the removal directions in reverse order. Be sure the snap rings and circlips are fully seated **(Figure 1–26).** Lubricate the seal at the transaxle before installing the drive axle. If the transaxle cover was removed, clean the sealing surfaces thoroughly, apply the required gasket or sealer, and install the cover, starting all the bolts by hand. Tighten the bolts to specifications in a crisscross pattern. Fill the transaxle with the correct type of lubri-

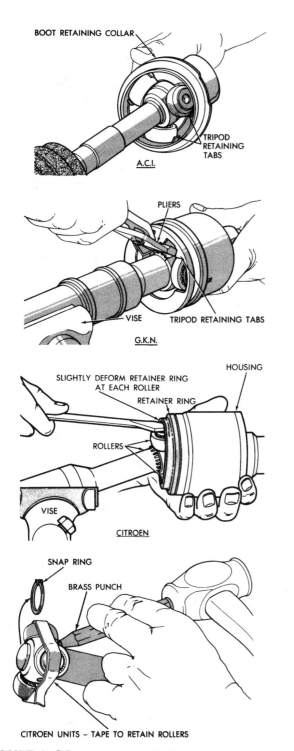

FIGURE 1–24 Typical tripod joint disassembly procedures. (Courtesy of Chrysler Corporation.)

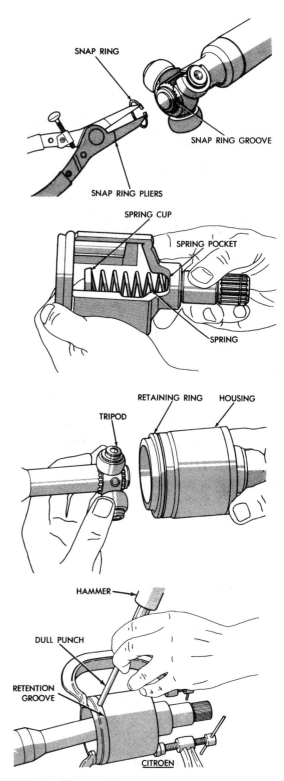

FIGURE 1–25 Typical tripod CV joint assembly. Make sure that proper side of tripod faces end of shaft. Pack housing with specified CV joint lubrication. (Courtesy of Chrysler Corporation.)

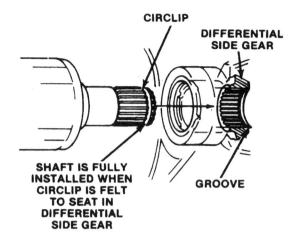

CIRCLIP

DIFFERENTIAL
SIDE GEAR

SHAFT IS FULLY
INSTALLED WHEN
CIRCLIP IS FELT
TO SEAT IN
DIFFERENTIAL
SIDE GEAR

GROOVE

FIGURE 1–26 (Courtesy of Ford Motor Company.)

cant to the specified level. Install the spindle (if disconnected) and the front wheels. Tighten the wheel bearing nut to specifications and lock the nut as required.

On some models a prevailing torque nut is used. A new nut must be used any time the nut is removed. (See **Figure 1–9**.)

REVIEW QUESTIONS

1. What functions do front-wheel-drive axles perform?

2. What are the six major components of a front-wheel-drive axle?

3. True or false? The tripod-type CV joint is usually used at the inboard end of the drive axle.

4. True or false? A Rzeppa CV joint uses three balls supported by needle bearings on the spider trunnions.

5. A bellows-type _____ _____ keeps dirt and moisture out of the CV joints.

6. A car with unequal-length drive axles will _____ _____ to the side with the _____ axle shaft under heavy _____.

7. Some front-drive-axle inner stub shafts are retained in the transaxle by _____ _____, while others may be held in place by _____.

8. Before disassembling the tripod CV joint, _____ _____ the housing, spider, and axle shaft.

9. To remove the balls from a Rzeppa CV joint, _____ the _____ in different directions and remove the exposed balls.

10. True or false? Use all-purpose pressure gun grease to lubricate CV joints.

TEST QUESTIONS

1. Front-drive-axle CV joints must accommodate
   a. changes in effective length of drive axle
   b. changes in steering wheels left to right
   c. changes in suspension height
   d. all of the above

2. The front-drive axle is connected to the drive wheel hub by means of
   a. splines
   b. a woodruff key
   c. a cotter pin
   d. all of the above

3. CV joint boots
   a. are designed to contain lubricant
   b. prevent entry of dirt

   c. must be replaced when punctured

   d. all of the above

4. "A tripod CV joint is usually used at the inner end of the drive axle." "The tripod CV joint does not provide any telescoping action." Which of these statements is correct?

   a. the first

   b. the second

   c. both are correct

   d. both are incorrect

5. Technician A says that front-wheel-drive axles are always the same length on both sides. Technician B says that some cars have half-shafts of unequal length. Who is right?

   a. technician A

   b. technician B

   c. both are right

   d. both are wrong

6. A clicking sound during turns usually indicates

   a. an outer CV joint problem

   b. an inner CV joint problem

   c. a ball joint problem

   d. a strut problem

7. To remove the drive balls from a Rzeppa CV joint

   a. remove the cage first

   b. tilt the cage as required

   c. both (a) and (b)

   d. none of the above

8. When installing a CV joint boot, make sure that

   a. the boot fits snugly in the grooves at each end

   b. you use the special lubricant supplied with the kit

   c. the boot retaining straps or clamps are properly secured

   d. all of the above

◆ CHAPTER 2 ◆

DRIVE SHAFT PRINCIPLES AND SERVICE

INTRODUCTION

Drive shafts are used on rear-wheel-drive, four-wheel-drive, and all-wheel-drive vehicles. The drive shaft transmits power from the transmission, transaxle, or transfer case to the differential drive pinion. Universal joints provide the connections that allow the shaft to operate at changing angles due to suspension movement. Drive shaft speeds may exceed 2500 rpm in direct drive. This chapter discusses drive shaft and universal joint construction, operation, and service.

LEARNING OBJECTIVES

After completing this chapter, you should be able to:

- Describe drive shaft and universal joint construction.
- Describe drive shaft and universal joint operation.
- Diagnose universal joint and drive shaft problems.
- Service and repair drive shafts and universal joints.

TERMS YOU SHOULD KNOW

Look for these terms as you study this chapter and learn what they mean.

drive shaft	pinion flange
universal joint	torsional damper
slip yoke	drive shaft vibration
cross and roller	drive shaft noise
trunnion	universal joint noise
needle bearings	drive shaft runout
constant velocity	drive shaft balance
ball and trunnion	drive shaft angle
drive shaft yoke	pinion yoke

DRIVE SHAFT FUNCTION

The drive shaft transmits driving torque from the transmission or transfer case to the drive axle differential; it must be able to accommodate changes in the angle of the drive shaft **(Figure 2–1)**. It must be able to change the effective length of the drive shaft as the drive axle moves up or down. It must be able to transmit power smoothly without torsional vibration.

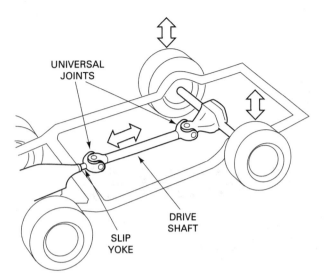

FIGURE 2–1 Drive shaft connects transmission output shaft to differential drive pinion. The effective length of the drive shaft changes with up-and-down suspension movement. Universal joints allow power to be transmitted at an angle.

DRIVE SHAFT CONSTRUCTION AND OPERATION

The basic drive shaft consists of a tubular shaft with a universal joint at each end. A splined, sliding slip yoke at the transmission end allows the effective length of the drive shaft to change. The universal joints, one at each end of the shaft, accommodate the change in drive shaft angle as the drive axle moves up and down **(Figure 2–2)**. The tubular shaft may be made from steel, aluminum or carbon compound. The large-diameter tube construction provides the stiffness needed to prevent the shaft from flexing. A two-piece tube with a rubber insulator between is sometimes used to reduce torsional and frequency vibration **(Figure 2–3)**. A torsional damper consisting of a heavy metal ring and rubber insulator is used on some vehicles to reduce torsional vibration. A cardboard liner is used in some drive shafts to reduce the effects of vibration and noise. Rubber inserts between the liner and drive shaft increases the effectiveness of this feature **(Figure 2–4)**. A two-piece shaft with a center support and three universal joints is used on many trucks because of the greater distance between the transmission and drive axle **(Figure 2–5)**. A one-piece shaft that is too long will flex and "whip" as it turns. If the transmission output shaft and differential pinion shaft positions were fixed in a straight line, universal joints would not be needed.

UNIVERSAL JOINTS AND SLIP YOKES

Cross and Roller Universal Joint (Single Cardan)

The cross and roller universal joint consists of two Y-shaped yokes connected to each other by a "spider" shaped like a "+" **(Figures 2–6 to 2–10)**. The ends of the spider are called trunnions. Each trunnion is fitted with a needle roller bearing, bearing cup, and grease seal. The bearing cups are a press fit in the eyes of the yoke and are held in place by snap rings. Some universal joints have a grease fitting for lubrication. Most U-joints are prelubricated during assembly.

When torque is transmitted at an angle through a single universal joint, the drive yoke transmits torque

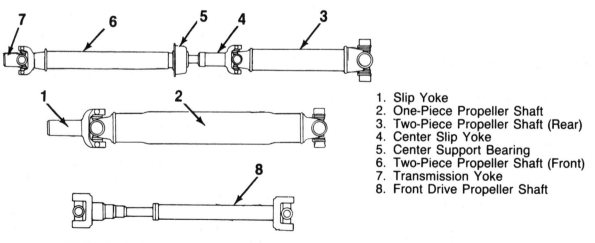

1. Slip Yoke
2. One-Piece Propeller Shaft
3. Two-Piece Propeller Shaft (Rear)
4. Center Slip Yoke
5. Center Support Bearing
6. Two-Piece Propeller Shaft (Front)
7. Transmission Yoke
8. Front Drive Propeller Shaft

FIGURE 2–2 Different drive shaft designs. (Courtesy of General Motors Corporation.)

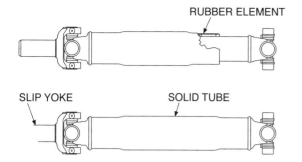

RUBBER ELEMENT

SLIP YOKE   SOLID TUBE

FIGURE 2–3 Drive shaft with rubber element between two connecting tubes (top) and one piece tubular shaft (bottom). (Courtesy of General Motors Corporation.)

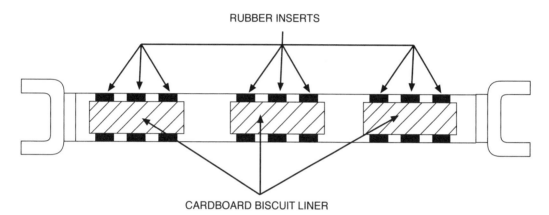

RUBBER INSERTS

CARDBOARD BISCUIT LINER

FIGURE 2–4 A cardboard liner with rubber inserts reduces the effects of noise and vibration.

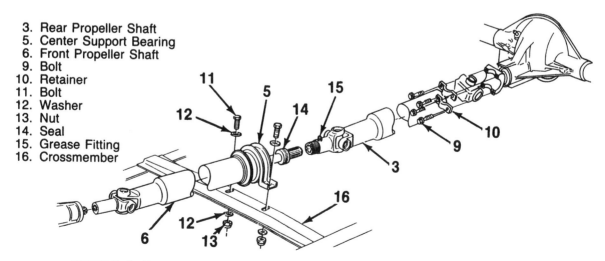

3. Rear Propeller Shaft
5. Center Support Bearing
6. Front Propeller Shaft
9. Bolt
10. Retainer
11. Bolt
12. Washer
13. Nut
14. Seal
15. Grease Fitting
16. Crossmember

FIGURE 2–5 Two-piece shaft with center support bearing often used on trucks. (Courtesy of General Motors Corporation.)

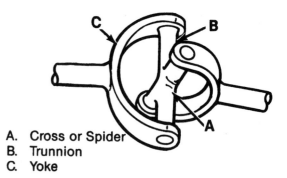

FIGURE 2–6 Basic universal joint swivels in both directions. (Courtesy of General Motors Corporation.)

A. Cross or Spider
B. Trunnion
C. Yoke

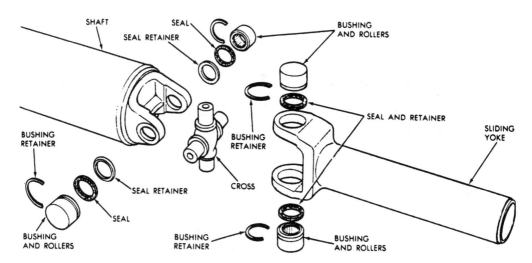

FIGURE 2–7 Single cardan cross and roller universal joint and sliding yoke as used at the transmission end of the driveshaft. (Courtesy of Chrysler Corporation.)

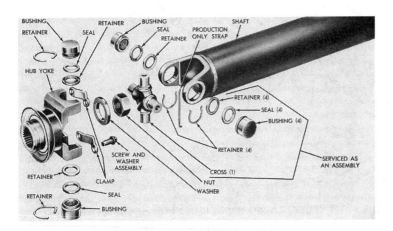

FIGURE 2–8 Exploded view of typical universal joint at the differential end of the drive shaft. (Courtesy of Chrysler Corporation.)

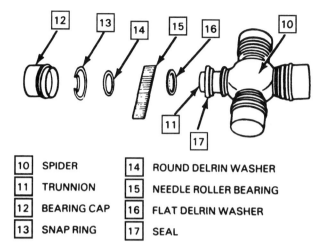

10 SPIDER	**14** ROUND DELRIN WASHER
11 TRUNNION	**15** NEEDLE ROLLER BEARING
12 BEARING CAP	**16** FLAT DELRIN WASHER
13 SNAP RING	**17** SEAL

FIGURE 2–9 Cross and roller universal joint. Needle bearings are grease packed. Snap rings keep bearing caps in position in yokes. (Courtesy of General Motors Corporation.)

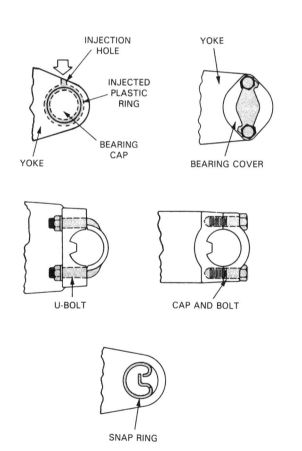

FIGURE 2–10 Different methods are used to hold the universal joint bearing cup in place in the yoke.

at a constant speed while the drive yoke speeds up and slows down twice during each revolution. This change in velocity increases as the angle of the universal joint is increased. On a one-piece drive shaft, this change in velocity can be eliminated by arranging the two drive yokes at 90 degrees to each other. However, when the two universal joints operate at different angles, this no longer applies. The installation angles of the transmission output shaft and the differential pinion shaft are designed to keep the universal joint operating angles and drive line fluctuation at a minimum (**Figure 2–11**).

Constant-Velocity Universal Joint (Double Cardan)

A constant-velocity universal joint consists of two cross and roller U-joints connected to each other by a ball and socket in the center and by a double center yoke. A constant-velocity U-joint is used on drive shafts where the difference in the operating angle at the two ends is too great for a single cardan U-joint to be used at each end. The CV joint is used at the end with the larger operating angle to reduce fluctuations in velocity (**Figures 2–12** and **2–13**).

Ball-and-Trunnion U-Joint

The ball-and-trunnion design is a constant-velocity U-joint that also accommodates changes in drive shaft length. It is not commonly used on today's cars.

Slip Yoke

The slip yoke (**Figures 2–14** and **2–15**) slides forward and back on the splined output shaft. The yoke has internal splines that match the external splines on the output shaft. The outer surface of the slip yoke is machined smooth to slide back and forth in the housing bushing and seal. The seal prevents transmission or transfer case fluid from leaking past the slip yoke. A vent prevents hydrostatic lock. The extension housing bushing supports the slip yoke. The outer surface of the slip yoke is lubricated by transmission or transfer case lubricant. The splines may be lubricated from the lubricant in the transmission or by a special lubricant applied during assembly.

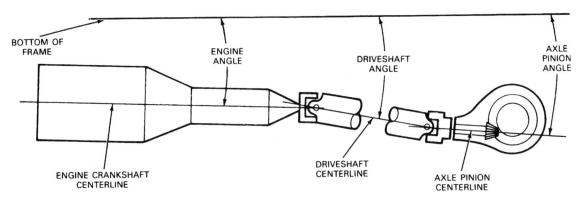

FIGURE 2–11 Drive shaft installation angle is designed to keep drive shaft speed fluctuation at a minimum. (Courtesy of Ford Motor Company.)

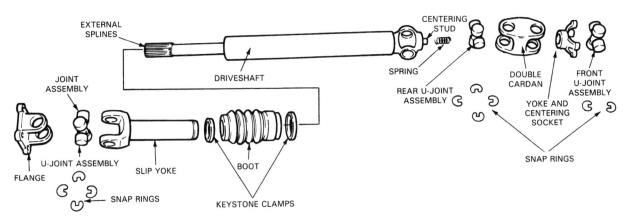

FIGURE 2–12 Drive shaft with double cardan constant-velocity universal joint. (Courtesy of Ford Motor Company.)

FIGURE 2–13 Constant-velocity universal joint consists of two cross and roller joints, center yoke, and ball socket. Ball socket ensures that universal joints operate at the same angle. (Courtesy of General Motors Corporation.)

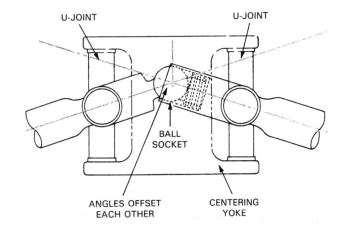

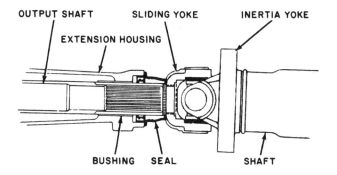

FIGURE 2-14 Internal splines on slip yoke slide on external splines of transmission output shaft. Outer surface of slip yoke is machined smooth and is supported in the extension housing by a bushing. The output shaft and slip yoke rotate as a unit. Seal prevents lubricant leakage. (Courtesy of Chrysler Corporation.)

Differential Pinion Yoke or Flange

The differential pinion yoke or flange is splined to the differential drive pinion and held in place by a washer and nut. The outer surface of the yoke hub is machined smooth to provide a smooth surface for the lip of the pinion shaft oil seal **(Figures 2–16** and **2–17).**

DRIVE SHAFT BALANCE

The drive shaft turns at engine crankshaft speeds when the transmission is in direct drive. Drive shaft weight must be even around the center of shaft rotation to prevent vibration. During the balancing process, the drive shaft is turned at high speed on a balancing machine. Small metal weights are welded to the light side of the shaft to counterbalance heavy sections **(Figure 2–18).** When a drive shaft becomes unbalanced in use, screw-type metal hose clamps are clamped to the drive shaft to restore balance.

Torsional Dampeners

A heavy metal inertia ring rubber mounted on the drive shaft is sometimes used to reduce torsional vibration resulting from acceleration, deceleration, and drive axle torque fluctuation. Another method is to use a rubber insert between two tubular sections of the drive shaft. (See **Figures 2–3, 2–14,** and **2–15.**)

DRIVE SHAFT SERVICE PRECAUTIONS

1. Place the vehicle safely on stands or hoist for under-vehicle work.

2. Make sure that the problem is in the drive line before proceeding with drive line removal.

3. Do all in-shop drive line diagnosing (vehicle running) with the vehicle at normal curb weight and height. (The vehicle should be supported under

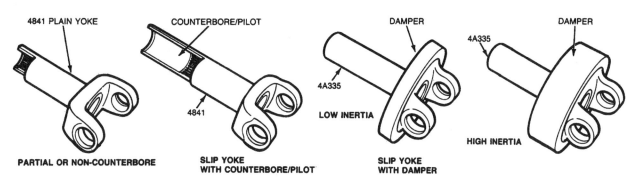

FIGURE 2–15 Different styles of slip yokes. Dampers reduce torsional vibrations. (Courtesy of Ford Motor Company.)

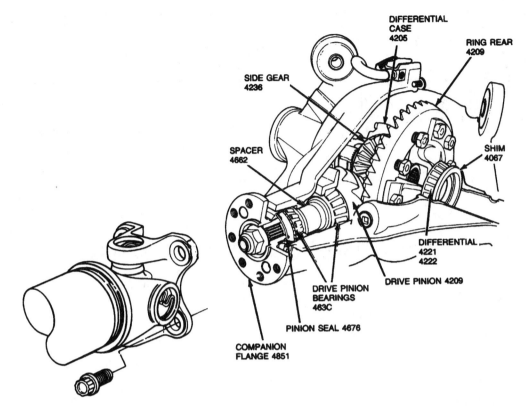

FIGURE 2–16 Drive shaft yoke is bolted to companion flange of differential in this design. (Courtesy of Ford Motor Company.)

the axle housing.) Consult the vehicle manufacturer's manual for proper lift points and diagnostic procedures.

4. Be careful of oil running out of the transmission when the slip yoke is removed, or gear oil when the differential drive flange is removed. Correct fluid levels after repairs have been made.

5. Never distort the drive shaft by clamping in a vise and overtightening. Be especially careful with aluminum or graphite drive shafts.

6. Never collapse or distort universal joint yokes while removing or installing U-joint bearing cups. Use proper support for the yoke during this operation.

FIGURE 2–17 Differential pinion yoke (hub yoke) provides seats for U joint bearing cups in this design. (Courtesy of Chrysler Corporation.)

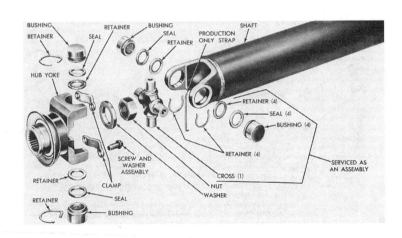

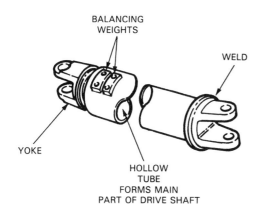

BALANCING
WEIGHTS

WELD

YOKE

HOLLOW
TUBE
FORMS MAIN
PART OF DRIVE SHAFT

FIGURE 2–18 Metal weights welded to light side of drive shaft provide balance. (Courtesy of Ford Motor Company.)

7. Beware of needle bearings dropping out of place during assembly and preventing bearing cups from being properly installed.

8. Be sure that bearing cups are inside alignment lugs on the differential drive flange yoke before tightening the clamp bolts.

9. Always lubricate the yoke externally and internally on splines with the recommended lubricant before assembly.

10. Tighten all bolts to specifications.

DRIVE SHAFT PROBLEMS

There are two major categories of drive shaft problems: vibration and abnormal noise. Both can be checked during a road test. (See **Figures 2–19** to **2–21**.)

1. *Vibration:* may be caused by a bent shaft (runout), a severe U-joint operating angle, a lost balance weight, a dented shaft, or buildup of undercoating or mud.

2. *Abnormal noise:* includes a click or clunk when engine torque is applied, squeaking or grinding noises during operation, and a whining, almost ringing sound or rattles. Clicks, clunks, squeaks, and squeals are usually caused by worn or dry universal joints. A whining sound can be caused by a dry or worn center bearing on a two-piece drive shaft. A tinny kind of rattle can be caused by a loose deflector shield on the differential drive pinion yoke.

DRIVE SHAFT INSPECTION

Inspect the rear transmission seal for any oil leaks. If there is an oil leak, check for any slip yoke looseness in the extension housing bushing by moving the yoke up and down. If it is loose, both the bushing and seal must be replaced after the drive shaft is removed.

Inspect the differential pinion seal for oil leakage. If there is an oil leak, check for any looseness of the pinion bearings by forcing the drive shaft and pinion back and forth. If there is any end play, the pinion bearings must be serviced and the seal replaced. (See Chapter 3 for procedure.) If the pinion bearings are not loose, the pinion seal must be replaced after drive shaft removal. Check the seal journal on the pinion yoke hub for grooved wear and replace it if present. Follow service manual procedures for replacement.

Inspect the entire drive shaft for dents, undercoating, missing balance weights, and other damage. Inspect the universal joints for any sign of lube leakage or rust escaping past the bearing cup seals. Check for any looseness by grasping the drive shaft and forcing it up and down while observing any looseness. Turn the U-joint a quarter turn to check the other two bearing cups. If there is any lube, leakage, seal damage, rust escaping, or bearing looseness, the U-joint must be replaced.

DRIVE SHAFT RUNOUT

If a noise or vibration is present at high speed, which might be caused by a bent shaft, or if a shaft has been damaged through rough handling or a collision, it may be checked for straightness as follows:

1 Raise the vehicle on a twin-post hoist so that the rear is supported on the rear-axle housing with wheels free to rotate.

2. Mount a dial indicator on a movable support that is high enough to permit contact of the indicator button with the propeller shaft, or mount a dial indicator to a magnetic base and attach to a suitable smooth place on the underbody of the vehicle. Readings are to be taken at points indicated in **Figure 2–22.**

3. With the transmission in Neutral (engine off), check for runout by turning a rear drive wheel so that the propeller shaft will rotate.

ROAD TEST FORM

1. Did condition exist when vehicle was new? ☐ Yes ☐ No

   How did condition begin?

   ☐ Gradually occurred   Mileage_____

   ☐ Suddenly occurred   Mileage_____

2. Vehicle NVH between_____MPH and_____MPH

3. Neutral engine run-up NVH?   ☐ Yes ☐ No

4. What driving conditions affect the NVH?

   ☐ Light to medium acceleration

   ☐ Hard acceleration

   ☐ Deceleration (foot off accelerator pedal)

   ☐ Constant speed

5. If a vibration, where is the vibration noticed?

   ☐ Seat

   ☐ Steering wheel

   ☐ Instrument panel pad

   ☐ Floor

   ☐ Hood and fenders

6. If a noise, define as:

   ☐ Buzz

   ☐ Moan

   ☐ Drone

   ☐ Rumble

   ☐ Hum

   ☐ Other   Describe:_____

FIGURE 2–19 This form may be used to describe road test results. (Courtesy of Ford Motor Company.)

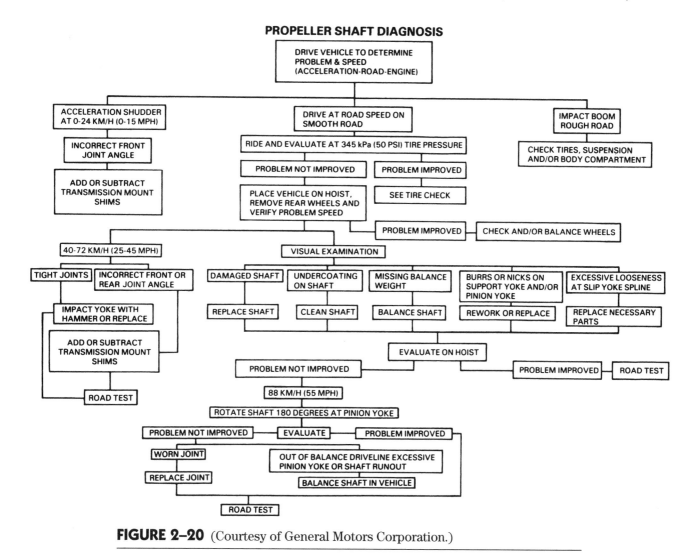

FIGURE 2–20 (Courtesy of General Motors Corporation.)

PRO TIP

Different cars may have different drive shafts. Specifications for runout are different on different shafts. See the service manual for specifications. Care must be taken not to include indicator variation caused by ridges, flat spots, or other surface variations in the tube.

4. If runout exceeds specifications, rotate the shaft 180 degrees at companion flange and reinstall. Check runout again. Rotating the shaft 90 degrees may also work.

5. If runout is still over specifications at one or more locations, replace the drive shaft, but only after checking vibration or noise. The replacement shaft must be rechecked for runout also.

6. If the new drive shaft runout is still over specifications, check for a bent companion flange or slip yoke. Refer to the balancing procedure if noise or vibration persists.

Runout specifications vary depending on vehicle make and model from approximately 0.020 in. (0.50 mm) to 0.045 in. (1.27 mm).

DRIVE SHAFT BALANCING (ON VEHICLE METHOD)

Use the hose clamp method as follows:

1. Place the car on a twin-post hoist so that the rear of the car is supported on the rear axle housing and the rear wheels are free to rotate. Remove both

PROPELLER SHAFT DIAGNOSIS

CONDITION	POSSIBLE CAUSE	CORRECTION
Roughness, Vibration or Body Boom at any Speed.	a. Bent or dented propeller shaft.	a. Replace propeller shaft.
	b. Undercoating on propeller shaft.	b. Clean propeller shaft.
	c. Tire unbalance (48-105 km/h, 30-65 mph, not throttle conscious).	c. Balance or replace as required.
	d. Worn universal joints.	d. Replace universal joints.
	e. Burrs or gouges on pinion yoke. Check snap ring locating surfaces on pinion yoke.	e. Rework or replace pinion yoke.
	f. Excessive propeller shaft or pinion yoke unbalance, or runout.	f. Check for missing balance weights on propeller shaft. Remove and reassemble propeller shaft to pinion yoke, 180 degrees from original position.
	g. Excessive looseness at slip yoke spline.	g. Replace damaged parts.
Roughness - above 56 km/h (35 mph) felt and/or heard.	a. Tires unbalanced or worn.	a. Balance or replace as required.
Leak at front slip yoke. An occasional drop of lubricant leaking from splined yoke is normal.	a. Rough outside surface on splined yoke.	a. Replace seal if cut by burrs on yoke. Minor burrs can be smoothed by careful use of crocus cloth or honing with a fine stone. Replace yoke if outside surface is rough or burred badly.
	b. Damaged transmission rear oil seal.	b. Inspect bushing for damage or wear and replace transmission rear oil seal if required. Bring transmission oil up to proper level after correction.
Knock in driveline, clinking noise when vehicle is operated under floating condition at 16 km/h (10 mph) in gear or neutral.	a. Worn or damaged universal joints.	a. Replace universal joints.
	b. Side gear counterbore in differential worn oversize.	b. Replace differential case and/or side gears as required.
Ping, Snap or Click in driveline. Usually occurs on initial load application after transmission has been put into gear, either forward or reverse.	a. Loose differential carrier assembly upper or lower arm bushing bolts.	a. Tighten bolts to specified torque.
	b. Loose pinion yoke.	b. Remove propeller shaft from pinion yoke. Turn 180 degrees from its original position and reinstall.

FIGURE 2–21 (Courtesy of General Motors Corporation.)

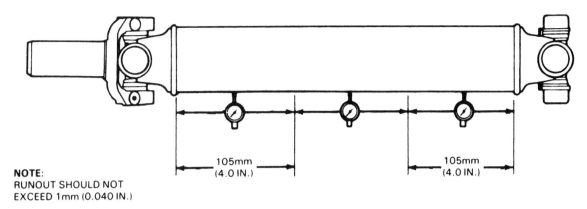

NOTE:
RUNOUT SHOULD NOT
EXCEED 1mm (0.040 IN.)

105mm
(4.0 IN.)

105mm
(4.0 IN.)

FIGURE 2–22 Drive shaft runout should be checked at three positions with a dial indicator. (Courtesy of General Motors Corporation.)

rear tire and wheel assemblies and reinstall wheel lug nuts with flat side next to drum.

2. Mark and number the propeller shaft at four points 90 degrees apart at the rear of the shaft just forward of the balance weight.

3. Install two hose clamps on the rear of the propeller shaft, and slide them rearward until the clamps stop at the nearest balance weight welded to the tube. Align both clamps to any one of the four marks made on shaft in step 2. Tighten the clamps (see **Figure 2–23**). Be sure that sufficient clearance is maintained so that the clamp heads do not contact the floor pan of car when the axle is in contact with the rebound bumper in frame. To gain sufficient clearance, it may be necessary to position the clamps over the balance weights.

4. Run the car through the speed range 50 to 55 mph (80 to 90 km/h). Note the amount of imbalance.

PRO TIP

Never run a car higher than 55 mph (90 km/h). Also, all personnel should stay clear of the drive line.

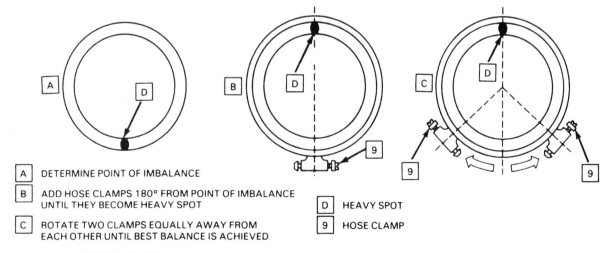

A	DETERMINE POINT OF IMBALANCE
B	ADD HOSE CLAMPS 180° FROM POINT OF IMBALANCE UNTIL THEY BECOME HEAVY SPOT
C	ROTATE TWO CLAMPS EQUALLY AWAY FROM EACH OTHER UNTIL BEST BALANCE IS ACHIEVED

| D | HEAVY SPOT |
| 9 | HOSE CLAMP |

FIGURE 2–23 Using hose clamps to balance a drive shaft. (Courtesy of General Motors Corporation.)

5. Loosen the clamps and rotate clamp heads 90 degrees to the next mark on the shaft. Tighten the clamps and repeat step 4.

6. Repeat step 5 until the car has been run with clamp heads located at all four marks on the shaft.

7. Position the clamps at point of minimum imbalance. Rotate the clamp heads away from each other 45 degrees (one each way from the point of minimum imbalance). Do not position clamps more than 120 degrees apart. Run the car and note if imbalance has improved. In some cases it may be necessary to use one clamp or possibly three clamps to obtain good balance. Replace the shaft if three hose clamps do not improve the imbalance.

8. Continue to rotate the clamps apart in smaller angular increments until the feel for imbalance is best. Do not run the car on the hoist for extended periods due to the danger of overheating the transmission or engine.

9. Reinstall the tire and wheel assemblies and road test the car for final check of balance. Vibration felt in the car on the hoist may not show up in a road test, which is the final determining factor.

DRIVE SHAFT REMOVAL

PRO TIP

Do not pound on the original propeller shaft yoke ears, as injection joints may fracture.

Several different methods are used to attach the rear of the drive shaft to the differential pinion flange or end yoke as described earlier.

1. Raise the vehicle on a hoist. Mark the relationship of the shaft to the pinion flange **(Figure 2–24)** and disconnect the rear universal joint by removing the bolts, straps, or U-bolts. If the bearing cups are loose, tape them together to prevent dropping and loss of bearing rollers.

2. Withdraw the propeller shaft slip yoke from the transmission by moving the shaft rearward, passing it under the axle housing. Do not allow the drive shaft to drop or allow the universal joints to bend to an extreme angle, as this might fracture the joint internally. Support the propeller shaft during removal.

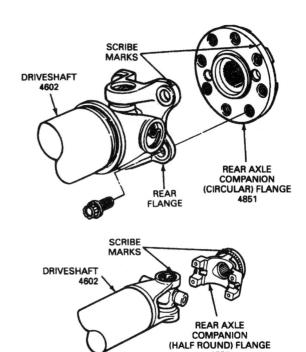

FIGURE 2–24 Scribe mark shaft and differential pinion flange (or yoke) position for assembly in same position later. (Courtesy of Ford Motor Company.)

After drive shaft removal, move the U-joints in each direction to check for any binding or gritty feeling. Replace U-joints if these conditions are present.

UNIVERSAL JOINT SERVICE

First remove all the bearing retaining snap rings **(Figure 2–25)**. Clamp the U-joint tool securely in a bench vise. Using the appropriate-size adapters, press the bearing cup in on one side. This will push the opposite bearing cup out. If it is not pushed out completely, remove it with a pair of pliers using a twisting motion. Reposition the shaft 180 degrees in the U-joint tool and push the other cup out by pushing against the U-joint spider. Do the same with the other two bearing cups **(Figure 2–26)**. Be careful not to bend the ears of the yoke during this procedure.

Assembling the Universal Joints

When reassembling a propeller shaft, install complete new universal joint repair kits, which include a spider, four bearing assemblies, spacers, seals, and shields.

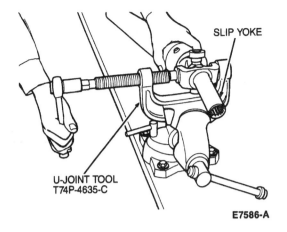

E7586-A

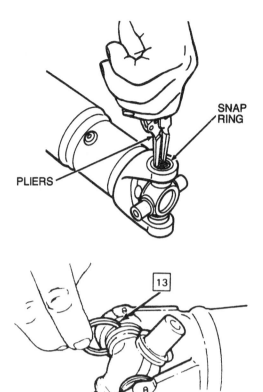

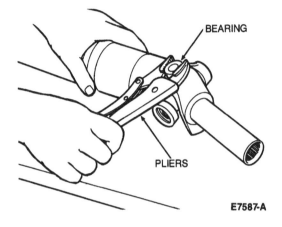

E7587-A

FIGURE 2–25 To replace a universal joint, first remove all bearing retaining snap rings. [Courtesy of Ford Motor Company (top) and General Motors Corporation (bottom).]

The four bearings come equipped with snap rings (**Figure 2–27**) to retain the bearings.

The following procedure is typical:

1. Make certain that the shields and seals are in position and install the spider in the yoke. The spider may face in either direction if there is no grease fitting. If there is a grease fitting, make sure to position the spider to provide access to the fitting with a grease gun when assembled.

2. Push the opposite journal to extend slightly above the yoke bore. Spider journals and bearings must be free of dirt and foreign material.

3. Place the propeller shaft and yoke assembly in position in the U-joint tool. Position the bearing straight over the yoke bore and onto the spider journal. Failure to pilot the spider journal into the bearing could cause the bearing needles to become dislodged during installation of the bearing cup.

Force the bearing into the yoke. The bearing cup is properly positioned in the yoke when the snap ring groove is exposed enough to install the snap ring. When

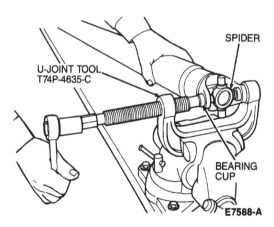

E7588-A

FIGURE 2–26 Universal joint removal (top and center) and installation (bottom). (Courtesy of Ford Motor Company.)

the bearing is correctly positioned in the yoke, turn the assembly over, and again place bearing over the bore in the yoke (**Figure 2–26**).

Carefully slide the spider partially out of the previously seated bearing and start it carefully into the bear-

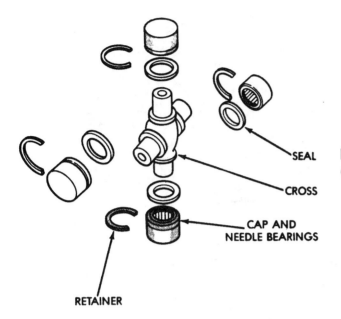

FIGURE 2–27 Replacement universal joint kit contents. (Courtesy of Chrysler Corporation.)

ing being installed. This prevents the bearing needles from burning the edge of the spider journal if they are forced over journal other than in straight. Even slight burring of the journal can cause premature failure.

While pressing the bearings into position, move the spider back and forth to make certain that the spider journals engage the bearings squarely. This avoids damage and binding. If binding exists, remove the bearings and spider and examine for dislodged rollers or damaged journals.

If excessive resistance is encountered, the bearings should be removed as this is an indication that one or more of the needles is out of place.

4.   While observing the previous precautions, install the balance of the bearings necessary to complete the assembly and install snap rings.

5.   Strike the yoke firmly with a plastic hammer to fully seat the snap rings against the yoke. Turn the spider to make certain that it is free **(Figure 2–28).**

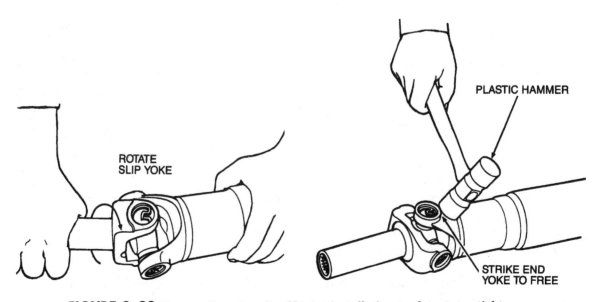

FIGURE 2–28 Rotate slip yoke after U-joint installation to detect any tightness. Strike the yoke with a plastic hammer if necessary to free the joint. (Courtesy of Ford Motor Company.)

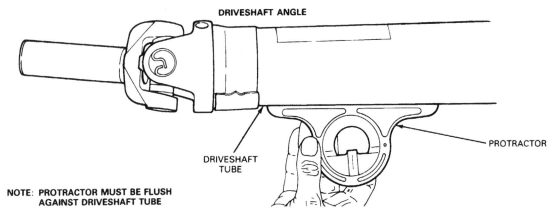

NOTE: PROTRACTOR MUST BE FLUSH
AGAINST DRIVESHAFT TUBE

FIGURE 2–29 Checking drive shaft angle with protractor. (Courtesy of Ford Motor Company.)

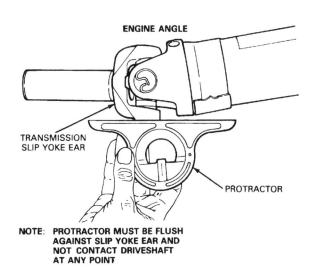

NOTE: PROTRACTOR MUST BE FLUSH
AGAINST SLIP YOKE EAR AND
NOT CONTACT DRIVESHAFT
AT ANY POINT

FIGURE 2–30 Checking universal joint angle with protractor. (Courtesy of Ford Motor Company.)

DRIVE SHAFT INSTALLATION

The propeller shaft must be supported carefully during handling to avoid jamming or bending any of the parts.

1. Inspect the outer diameter of the splined yoke to ensure that it is not burred, as this will damage the transmission seal. Inspect the seal for damage and replace as needed. Inspect the splines of the slip yoke for damage.

2. Lubricate all splined propeller shaft yokes; then slide the yoke and drive shaft assembly onto the transmission output shaft.

PRO TIP

Do not drive the propeller shaft into place with a hammer. Check for burrs on transmission output shaft spline, twisted slip yoke splines, or possibly the wrong U-joint yoke. Make sure that the splines agree in number and fit. To prevent trunnion seal damage, do not place any tool between the yoke and the splines. When making rear shaft connections, be sure to align the mark on pinion flange or end yoke with the mark on the drive shaft.

3. Position the rear universal joint to the rear axle pinion flange; make sure that the bearings are properly seated in the pinion flange yoke.

4. Install the rear joint fasteners and tighten evenly to the torque specified.

PRO TIP

The propeller shaft to pinion flange or end yoke fasteners are important attaching parts in that they may affect the performance of vital components and systems, which may result in major repair expense. They must be replaced with one of the same part number or with an equivalent part, if replacement becomes necessary. Do not use a replacement part of lesser quality or substitute design. Torque values must be used as specified during reassembly to assure proper retention of these parts.

DRIVE SHAFT OPERATING ANGLE

To measure the drive shaft operating angle, the vehicle must be in a level position and its weight supported by the springs. Different types of measuring devices are used. Generally, a protractor gauge is placed on the drive shaft and the reading in degrees is shown **(Figures 2–29 and 2–30).** Other types take measurements from the universal joint. In this way the offending U-joint can be identified (front or rear) and the correction made at the appropriate end of the drive shaft. Shims may be placed under the rear transmission mount to correct the front U-joint operating angle. On leaf-spring vehicles, tapered shims can be used between the leaf spring and axle housing to correct the rear U-joint angle. Coil spring solid rear axles have adjustable eccentrics on the control arms for adjustment.

REVIEW QUESTIONS

1. The drive shaft transmits torque from the _____ to the _____ _____ _____.

2. The drive shaft must be able to accommodate changes in the _____ and effective _____ of the shaft.

3. The tubular drive shaft is made from _____, _____, or _____.

4. The cross and roller universal joint has two _____ and a _____ with _____ bearings.

5. Torque transmitted at an angle through a single universal joint _____ _____ and _____ twice each revolution.

6. A constant-velocity universal joint consists of two _____ and _____ U-joints connected to each other at the center by a _____ and _____ and by a double _____.

7. The slip yoke slides forward and back on the _____ _____ shaft.

8. A heavy metal ring rubber mounted on the drive shaft is sometimes used to dampen _____ _____.

9. Drive shaft vibration may be caused by a _____ _____, a severe U-joint _____ _____, a lost _____ _____, a _____ shaft, or a buildup of _____ or _____.

10. Drive shaft runout is measured with a _____ _____.

11. A drive shaft can be balanced on the car using the _____ _____ method.

12. To disassemble a universal joint, first remove the _____ _____.

13. If excessive resistance is encountered while pressing a U-joint bearing into position, it is possible that one or more of the _____ are out of place.

TEST QUESTIONS

1. "The drive shaft must be able to transmit power smoothly without torsional vibrations." "The effective length of the drive shaft must not change during operation." Which of these statements is correct?
   a. the first
   b. the second
   c. both are correct
   d. both are incorrect

2. The yokes on the ends of a one-piece drive shaft must be
   a. at 90 degrees to each other
   b. in phase
   c. in opposite phase
   d. at 45 degrees to each other

3. Torsional vibrations of a drive shaft can be reduced by using
   a. aluminum instead of steel
   b. solid shafts instead of the tubular design
   c. torsional shafts
   d. a torsional damper

4. A single cardan universal joint has how many bearings?
   a. one
   b. two
   c. three
   d. four

5. The slip yoke of a drive shaft
   a. slides back and forth on the transmission output shaft
   b. has internal splines
   c. forms one yoke of the front universal joint
   d. all of the above

6. Drive shaft imbalance may be caused by
   a. undercoating material stuck to the shaft
   b. a lost balance weight
   c. a dented shaft
   d. all of the above

7. Drive shaft runout may be measured with
   a. outside calipers
   b. a dial indicator
   c. an outside micrometer
   d. all of the above

8. An out-of-balance drive shaft can be balanced with the use of
   a. radiator hose clamps
   b. a dial indicator
   c. an outside micrometer
   d. scales

9. To measure the operating angle of a drive shaft, use a
   a. micrometer
   b. dial indicator
   c. retractor
   d. protractor

10. If a U-joint bearing cup cannot be fully seated during assembly, the probable cause is
   a. too much grease in the cup
   b. the seat is too shallow
   c. a dislodged roller
   d. all of the above

CHAPTER 3

DIFFERENTIAL AND DRIVE AXLE PRINCIPLES AND SERVICE

INTRODUCTION

Rear-wheel-drive cars and trucks use a differential to transmit power from the drive shaft and change the direction of power to the drive axles. Front-wheel-drive cars use a differential to transmit power from the final drive shaft to the differential. Four-wheel-drive vehicles use two differentials, one in the rear axle and one in the front axle. All-wheel-drive vehicles with a transaxle use a differential to transmit torque from the transaxle output shaft to the rear drive axles. Differential action is similar in most applications. This chapter deals with how differentials work and how to diagnose and service them. See Chapters 5 through 8 for transaxle differentials and Chapter 9 for transfer case differentials.

LEARNING OBJECTIVES

After completing this chapter, you should be able to:

- Describe rear wheel drive differential construction and operation.
- Describe rear wheel drive axle construction and operation.
- List the different types of differential designs.
- Diagnose differential and drive axle problems.
- Service the differential and drive axles.

TERMS YOU SHOULD KNOW

Look for these terms as you study this chapter and learn what they mean.

differential

drive pinion

ring gear

differential case

side bearings

pinion shaft

pinion gears

axle gears

drive axles

integral axle housing

removable carrier housing

differential carrier

spiral bevel gears

hypoid gear

straddle mounted pinion

overhung mounted pinion

drive

coast

float

concave

convex

hunting and nonhunting gears

limited slip

swing axle

drive axle noise

differential noise

breakaway torque

slide hammer puller

bearing retainer ring

bearing retainer plate

axle shaft oil seal

C-clip

ring gear backlash

ring gear runout

pinion depth

pinion bearing preload

side bearing preload

tooth contact pattern

DIFFERENTIAL AND DRIVE AXLE FUNCTIONS

The differential and drive axle assembly performs the following functions:

1. Transmits torque from drive shaft to drive axles and rear wheels
2. Transmits torque at a 90 degree angle
3. Provides a gear reduction between the drive pinion and drive axles
4. Splits driving torque between the two wheels
5. Allows drive wheels to turn at different speeds when turning corners
6. Supports the chassis, drive axles, and differential
7. Provides the means to attach the suspension system, brake assemblies, and drive wheels

DIFFERENTIAL AND DRIVE AXLE COMPONENTS

The major components of a differential and drive axle assembly include (**Figures 3–1** and **3–2**):

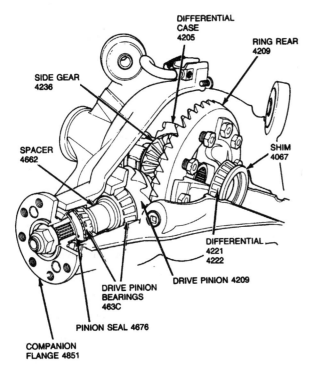

FIGURE 3–1 Cutaway view of differential. (Courtesy of Ford Motor Company.)

1. *Differential drive pinion yoke (flange):* connects drive shaft to differential drive pinion
2. *Drive pinion:* transmits torque from drive shaft to differential ring gear
3. *Ring gear:* transmits torque from drive pinion to differential case
4. *Differential case:* transmits torque from ring gear to differential pinion shaft; contains differential pinion shaft, differential pinion gears, and axle side gears
5. *Differential case side bearings:* support differential case in axle housing.
6. *Differential pinion shaft:* transmits torque from differential case to differential pinion gears
7. *Differential pinion gears:* transmit torque from differential pinion gears to axle side gears; allow axle gears to turn at different speeds when cornering
8. *Axle side gears:* transmit torque from differential pinion gears to drive axles
9. *Drive axles:* transmit torque from axle side gears to drive wheels
10. *Axle housing:* supports and contains the differential assembly and drive axles and supports the chassis

DIFFERENTIAL AND DRIVE AXLE OPERATION

In operation, engine torque is delivered by the drive shaft to the differential drive pinion. The drive pinion is in mesh with the ring gear and causes it to turn. There is a gear reduction between the pinion and ring gear, causing the ring gear to turn at about one-third to one-fourth the speed of the drive pinion. The ring gear is bolted to the differential case, and the two turn as a unit. The small differential gears are mounted on a pinion shaft that passes through the gears and the case. The pinion gears are in mesh with the axle side gears, which are splined to the axle shafts.

During normal straight-ahead driving, the rotating differential case causes the small pinion shaft and pinion gears to rotate end over end with the case. Since the pinion gears are in mesh with the side gears, the side gears and axle shafts are also forced to rotate. This is what happens during straight-ahead vehicle motion when both wheels have adequate traction (**Figure 3–3**).

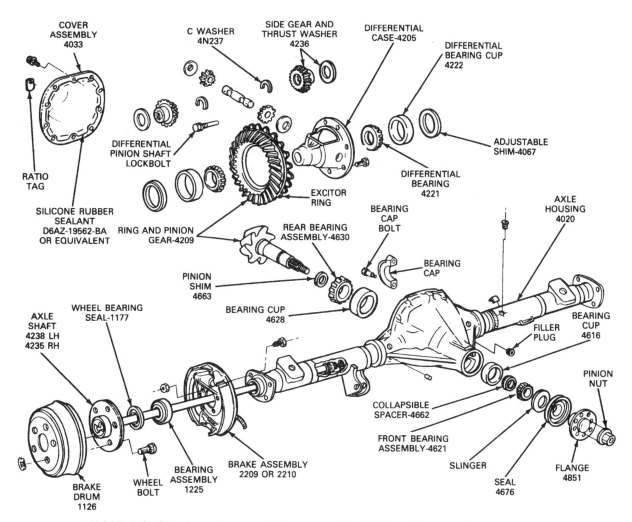

FIGURE 3–2 Drive axle parts. (Courtesy of Ford Motor Company.)

When the vehicle turns a corner, the inner wheel travels a shorter distance (smaller circle) than the outer wheel. This causes the inner wheel axle gear to slow down, causing the small differential pinion gears to "walk" around the slower turning axle gear. This results in these pinion gears rotating on the pinion shaft. This rotational torque is transmitted to the outer wheel-side gear, causing it to turn faster, but still providing equal torque to both wheels **(Figure 3–4).**

When one of the driving wheels has little or no traction, the torque required to turn the wheel without traction is very low. The wheel with good traction is in effect "holding" the axle gear on that side stationary. This causes the pinions to walk around the stationary side gear and drive the other wheel at twice the normal speed but without any vehicle movement.

With one wheel stationary, the other wheel turns at twice the speed shown on the speedometer. Excessive spinning of one wheel can cause severe damage to the differential. The small pinion gears can actually become welded to the pinion shaft or differential case.

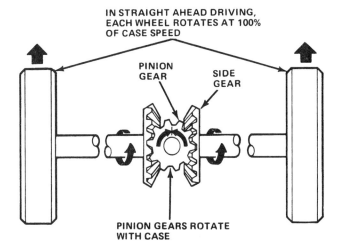

FIGURE 3–3 Differential action in straight-ahead driving. (Courtesy of General Motors Corporation.)

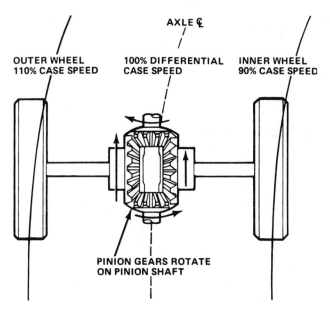

FIGURE 3–4 Differential action when turning a corner. (Courtesy of General Motors Corporation.)

DRIVE PINION AND RING GEAR TYPES AND OPERATION

The differential drive pinion and ring gear are a matched set and should not be interchanged with gears from another set. There are two types of differential gears: spiral bevel gears and hypoid gears **(Figure 3–5)**.

The spiral bevel gear has the drive pinion center line intersect with the centerline through the ring gear. The hypoid gearset has the pinion mounted well below the centerline of the ring gear. The hypoid gearset is the most common type of differential gearing used in passenger cars.

Hypoid gears are quiet running, allow several teeth to absorb the driving force, and allow a lower hump in the floor of the vehicle body. The teeth are curved, causing a wiping action during meshing. The inner end of the teeth on the ring gear is known as the toe and the outer end of the teeth as the heel of the teeth. The drive side of the teeth is curved in a convex shape, while the coast side of the teeth is concave **(Figure 3–6)**.

While engine torque is being applied to the drive pinion, the pinion teeth exert pressure on the drive or convex side of the ring gear teeth. During coast or engine braking, the concave side of the ring gear teeth exerts pressure on the drive pinion. When there is no torque being applied either in drive or in coast, the condition is known as float.

Upon heavy acceleration, the drive pinion attempts to climb up the ring gear and raises the front of

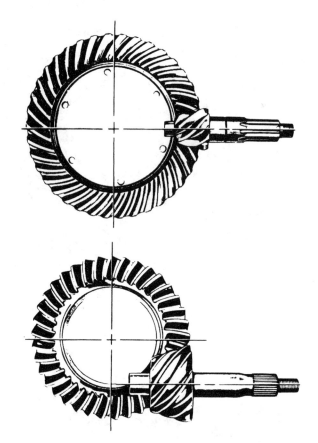

FIGURE 3–5 Spiral bevel differential gears (top) and hypoid gears (bottom). (Courtesy of Ford Motor Co. of Canada Ltd.)

the differential. A rubber bumper between the car body and differential prevents metal-to-metal contact on heavy acceleration or when the vehicle is heavily loaded and accelerated. Normally, the leaf springs or the torque arms on coil spring suspension absorb the torque.

Pinion Mounting Methods

The drive pinion is commonly mounted in either of two ways: (1) straddle mounted or (2) overhung mounted. The straddle-mounted pinion has two opposed tapered roller bearings close together with a spacer between the inner races ahead of the pinion gear and a third bearing, usually a straight roller bearing, supporting the rear of the pinion gear **(Figure 3–7)**.

The overhung-mounted pinion has two opposed tapered roller bearings somewhat farther apart than the bearings on the straddle-mounted type but no third bearing. The two roller bearings must be farther apart to provide adequate pinion support since there is no third bearing behind the pinion gear **(Figure 3–7)**.

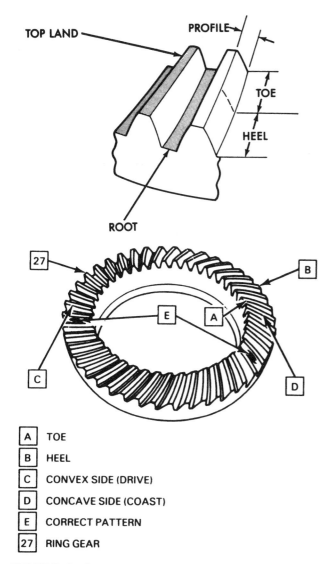

A | TOE
B | HEEL
C | CONVEX SIDE (DRIVE)
D | CONCAVE SIDE (COAST)
E | CORRECT PATTERN
27 | RING GEAR

FIGURE 3–6 Ring gear teeth terminology. [Courtesy of Chrysler Corporation (top) and General Motors Corporation (bottom).]

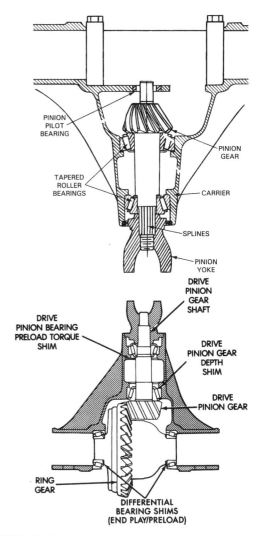

FIGURE 3–7 Straddle-mounted pinion (top) is supported by three bearings. (Courtesy of Ford Motor Company.) Over-hung mounted pinion (bottom) is supported by two bearings. (Courtesy of Chrysler Corporation.)

Drive Pinion Bearing Preload

A collapsible spacer is used between the two large tapered roller bearings to provide for proper pinion bearing preload. Some differentials use a solid noncollapsible spacer with selective thickness shims to adjust pinion bearing preload. When the pinion shaft nut is tightened, pressure is exerted by the pinion drive flange against the inner race of the front pinion bearing. This applies pressure against the spacer and the rear bearing, which cannot move because it is located against the drive pinion. When the nut is tightened to specifications, a slight load is placed on the two pinion bearings. This assures that there will be no pinion shaft end play.

During drive, the angle on the gear teeth attempts to move the pinion forward, and during coast it tries to move to the rear. If there is any pinion shaft end play, the result is a "walking" pinion (fore and aft moving pinion) and rapid gear and bearing wear.

Hunting and Nonhunting Gears

Differential gears are also classified as nonhunting, partial nonhunting, and hunting gears. During assembly, the nonhunting and partial nonhunting gears must be assembled with the timing marks properly aligned. The reason for this is that during manufacture they have

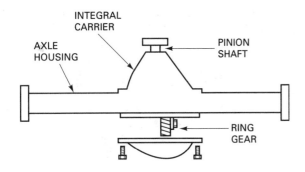

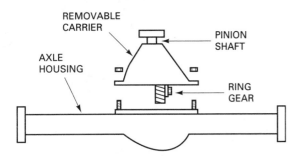

FIGURE 3-8 Integral carrier axle housing (top) and removable carrier axle housing (bottom).

been lapped, and since specified teeth on the pinion will always meet specific teeth on the ring gear (owing to the gear ratios), a noisy gear will result if not properly timed.

All ratios ending in .00 (3.00:1, 4.00:1) are non-hunting gears and must be timed. All ratios with a .50 ending (3.50:1, 4.50:1) are partial nonhunting gears and must also be timed. All gear ratios that do not fall into the categories above are called hunting gears and need not be timed.

DIFFERENTIAL CASE AND AXLE HOUSING

In most cases, the differential case is supported in the carrier by two tapered roller side bearings. This assembly can be adjusted from side to side to provide (1) the proper backlash between the ring gear and pinion, and (2) the required side bearing preload. This adjustment is achieved by threaded bearing adjusters on some units and selective shims and spacers on others.

There are two types of solid drive axle housings: the removable carrier type and the integral carrier type (**Figure 3-8**). The removable carrier type has a differential carrier assembly that is removable from the front of the housing. The integral type of drive axle assembly

consists of a housing and differential carrier assembly that are integral (carrier not removable). On this unit, the differential is removed from the rear of the housing. In the transaxle assembly, the differential and final drive are enclosed in the same housing as the transmission or in a separate housing bolted to the transaxle housing.

LIMITED SLIP DIFFERENTIALS

The limited slip differential performs an additional function over standard differentials; that is, it provides more driving force to the wheel with traction when one wheel begins to spin. Therefore, it modifies load-equalizing action with certain amounts of speed-equalizing action to enhance vehicle capability and operation. With a standard differential, if one wheel is on a slippery surface such as ice, snow, or mud, and the other wheel is on dry ground, the wheel on the slippery surface would spin, and the other would not drive the car. A limited slip unit would drive the wheel with traction and reduce the possibility of becoming immobile.

Limited slip differentials fall into three categories: those with clutch plates, those with clutch cones, and those with a viscous coupling. All three units perform the same task. The differential cases are similar to standard cases except for a large internal recess in the area of each side gear. This recess accepts either a clutch pack or a clutch cone depending on design (**Figures 3-9** to **3-16**). The clutch pack consists of clutch discs and plates. The clutch discs are splined to the side gear, and the clutch plates are tanged and fit into the case. The discs rotate with the side gear and the plates with the differential case. In the other unit, the cone is splined to the axle shaft, and it rotates with the side gear only.

A preload spring or springs provides the necessary clutch apply pressure to provide drive to both axles and wheels during unequal traction on the drive wheels. The spring tension is low enough to allow clutch slippage on the inner drive axle when turning corners. A viscous limited slip differential has a viscous coupling with alternate plates connected to the two output connections. The plates are evenly spaced and operate in a thick silicone fluid. The shear strength of the fluid between the plates provides the drive connection and the limited slip required for cornering.

ELECTROMAGNETIC CLUTCH LOCKUP

The rear-drive-axle differential on some models is equipped with an electromagnetic clutch lockup fea-

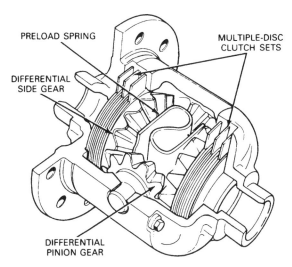

FIGURE 3–9 Cutaway view of limited slip differential with two clutch packs and wave-shaped preload spring. (Courtesy of Ford Motor Company.)

ture. The magnetic clutch operates in the same manner as the clutch on an air conditioning compressor. The clutch may be controlled manually by a switch on the dash or by a traction control computer based on signals from wheel speed sensors. When one wheel loses traction and speeds up, the computer activates the magnetic clutch to lock up the differential and provide equal power to both wheels.

DRIVE AXLE SHAFTS AND BEARINGS

On solid drive axles, the inner end of the axle shaft is splined to the axle side gears of the differential, and the outer end of the shaft has a flange to mount the wheel. The inner end of the shaft is supported through the side gear in the differential case, and the outer end is supported by a bearing between the axle and axle

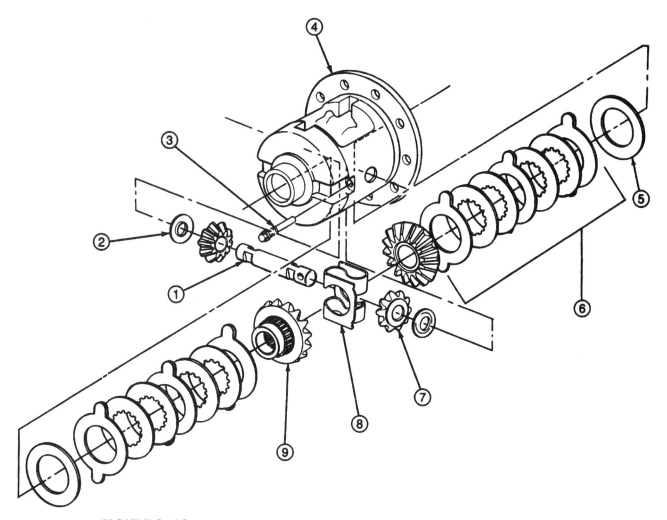

FIGURE 3–10 Parts detail for differential shown in Figure 3–9. (Courtesy of Ford Company.)

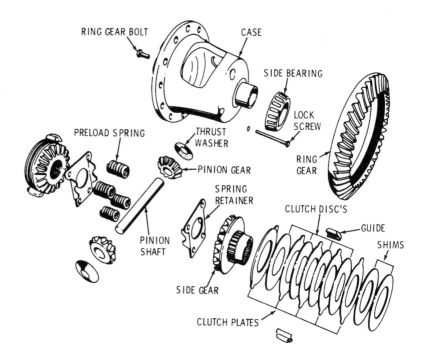

FIGURE 3–11 Limited slip differential with one multiple-disc clutch pack and coil-type preload springs. Earlier model of this unit used a Belleville type of preload spring (dished plate). (Courtesy of General Motors Corporation.)

housing. A seal and retaining plate prevent lubricant leakage.

The axle endwise movement is controlled by a C-type retainer on the inner end of the axle shaft or by a bearing retainer and retaining plate at the outer end of the axle shaft. Axle bearing types include ball bearings, tapered roller bearings, and a straight roller bearing that uses the axle shaft as the inner race **(Figure 3–17).**

SWING AXLES

The swing axle rear-wheel-drive system has the differential bolted to the frame cross member. The axle shafts are not enclosed. Each axle shaft has an inner and outer universal joint to allow each wheel to move up and down independently. The universal joints may be the cross and roller type or the tripod ball-and-trunnion type.

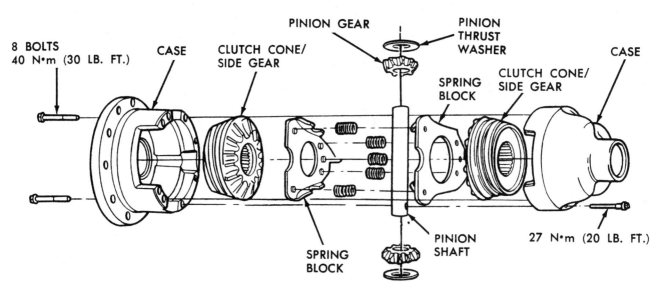

FIGURE 3–12 Cone clutch limited slip differential. (Courtesy of General Motors Corporation.)

DIFFERENTIAL AND DRIVE AXLE SERVICE PRECAUTIONS

1. Avoid getting lubricant or other contamination on brake linings, drums, discs, or pads.

2. Be sure that all axle mounting components are in good condition and are properly attached.

3. Observe all precautions specified by manufacturer on limited slip differentials as well as standard differentials.

4. Always use new seals and gaskets when overhauling.

5. Be sure that all metal filings are removed from entire axle housing.

6. Tighten all bolts to specifications.

7. Never allow FWD axles or swing type RWD axles to rotate with the suspension hanging free while the vehicle is up on a hoist.

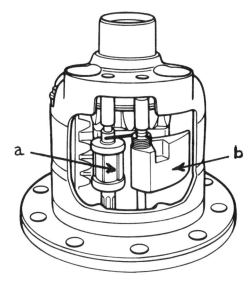

FIGURE 3–13 Limited slip differential with governor (a) and latching device (b) to control limited slip action. (Courtesy of General Motors Corporation.)

PRELIMINARY CHECKS

Lubricant Leaks

Lubricant may leak from the differential pinion seal, carrier gasket, cover gasket, the two axle seals or the axle housing tube connections to the differential housing. Inspect the leak carefully to determine whether it is differential lubricant or brake fluid. They can be distinguished by their feel and smell.

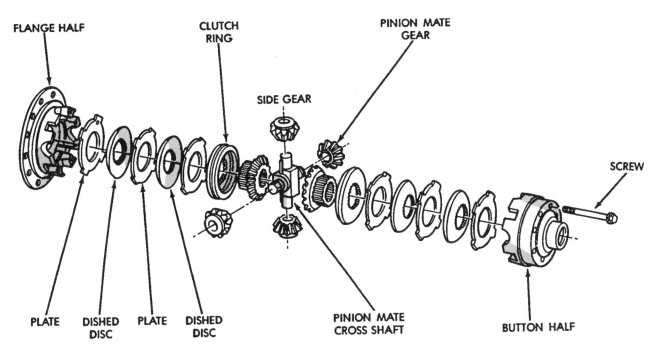

FIGURE 3–14 Power-Lok differential has two clutch packs, one for each axle. (Courtesy of Chrysler Corporation.)

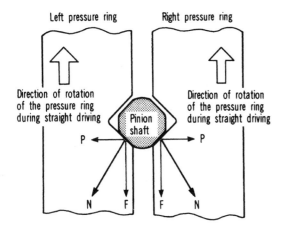

Reaction force symbol code
P = Pressing force of the pressure rings
on the clutch plates
F = Pressing force of the pressure rings
on the pinion shaft
N = Resultant force of P + F

Opposing force symbol code
P, P' = Pressing force of the pressure rings
on the clutch plates
F, F' = Pressing force of the pressure rings
on the pinion shaft
N, N' = Resultant force of P + F and P' + F'

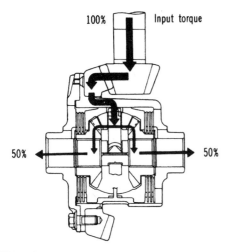

FIGURE 3–15 Power-Lok differential operation during straight-ahead driving. (Courtesy of Chrysler Corporation.)

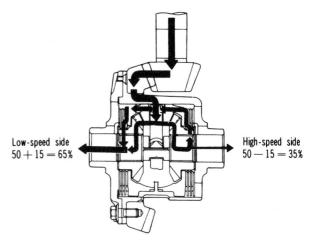

FIGURE 3–16 Power-Lok differential operation when one wheel is on a slippery surface. (Courtesy of Chrysler Corporation.)

Limited Slip Differential Check

The limited slip differential is subject to the same kinds of problems as the conventional differential but may also encounter clutch problems. The clutch discs or cones may wear, causing too much slip. This results in the differential acting like a conventional differential.

To check the clutch action of a limited slip differential, raise one drive wheel off the floor. Bolt a special adapter to the wheel. With the engine off, place the transmission in Neutral. Turn the wheel with a torque wrench. Observe the reading on the torque wrench when the wheel begins to turn **(Figure 3–18).** This is the clutch breakaway torque. Compare the reading to specifications. If the breakaway torque is too low, the clutches are worn, or the springs are too weak, and the benefits of limited slip action are lost. If the breakaway torque is too high, there may be excessive chatter and vibration when turning corners. The clutch must be repaired.

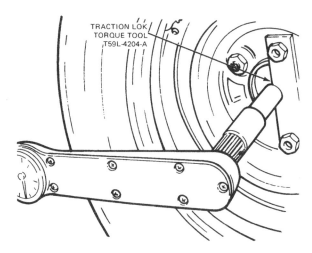

FIGURE 3–18 Checking limited slip clutch action with a torque wrench. (Courtesy of Ford Motor Company.)

3. Jack up the rear wheels and place a rigid jack at the specified part of the side sill.

4. Disconnect the coupling of the differential and propeller shaft.

5. When one wheel is being rotated slowly, check whether or not the wheel on the other side turns in the same direction.

6. If the second wheel turns in the opposite direction, replace the viscous unit.

ROAD TEST

A road test is a must for any complaint of noise and/or vibration that is not eliminated by the on-hoist check of chassis components. The diagnosis check has four operating conditions or modes in which some axle noises come and go: drive, cruise, coast, and float.

It is important to a good diagnosis check to operate in all four modes and check off those in which the noise occurs. It is important that rear axle noise complaints be evaluated with the transmission in direct drive and not in overdrive. Transmission noise can be mistaken for rear axle noise when in overdrive. Follow the diagnosis charts to isolate rear axle noise **(Figure 3–19)**.

AXLE AND DIFFERENTIAL NOISE

1. Gear noise is the typical howling or whining of the ring gear and pinion due to an improper gear pat-

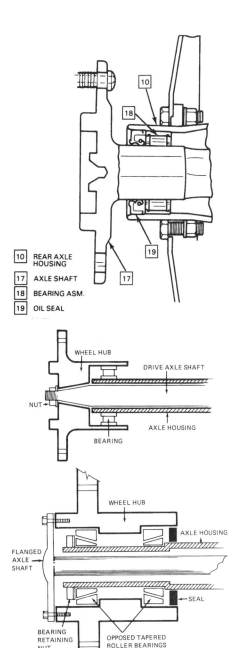

10	REAR AXLE HOUSING
17	AXLE SHAFT
18	BEARING ASM.
19	OIL SEAL

FIGURE 3–17 Drive axle types: semifloating (top), three-quarter floating (middle), and full floating (bottom). (Courtesy of General Motors Corporation and F T Enterprises.)

Viscous Coupling Limited Slip Differential Check

1. Block the front wheels and move the shift lever to Neutral.

2. Release the parking brake completely.

SERVICE DIAGNOSIS

Condition	Possible Cause	Correction
WHEEL NOISE	(a) Wheel loose.	(a) Tighten loose nuts.
	(b) Faulty, brinelled wheel bearing.	(b) Faulty or brinelled bearings must be replaced.
AXLE SHAFT NOISE	(a) Misaligned axle shaft tube.	(a) Inspect axle shaft tube alignment. Correct as necessary.
	(b) Bent or sprung axle shaft.	(b) Replace bent or sprung axle shaft.
	(c) End play in drive pinion bearings.	(c) Refer to Drive Pinion Bearing Pre-Load Adjustment.
	(d) Excessive gear backlash between ring gear and pinion gear.	(d) Check adjustment of ring gear backlash and pinion gear. Correct as necessary.
	(e) Improper adjustment of drive pinion gear shaft bearings.	(e) Adjust drive pinion shaft bearings.
	(f) Loose drive pinion gearshaft yoke nut.	(f) Tighten drive pinion gearshaft yoke nut with specified torque.
	(g) Improper wheel bearing adjustment.	(g) Readjust as necessary.
	(h) Scuffed gear tooth contact surfaces.	(h) If necessary, replace scuffed gears.
AXLE SHAFT BROKE	(a) Misaligned axle shaft tube.	(a) Replace broken axle shaft after correcting axle shaft tube alignment.
	(b) Vehicle overloaded.	(b) Replace broken axle shaft. Avoid excessive weight on vehicle.
	(c) Erratic clutch operation	(c) Replace broken axle shaft after inspecting for other possible causes. Avoid erratic use of clutch.
	(d) Grabbing clutch.	(d) Replace broken axle shaft. Inspect clutch and make necessary repairs or adjustments.
DIFFERENTIAL CASE CRACKED	(a) Improper adjustment of differential bearings.	(a) Replace cracked case; examine gears and bearings for possible damage. At reassembly, adjust differential bearings properly.
	(b) Excessive ring gear backlash.	(b) Replace cracked case; examine gears and bearings for possible damage. At reassembly, adjust ring gear backlash properly.
	(c) Vehicle overloaded.	(c) Replace cracked case; examine gears and bearings for possible damage. Avoid excessive weight on vehicle.
	(d) Erratic clutch operation.	(d) Replace cracked case. After inspecting for other possible causes, examine gears and bearings for possible damage. Avoid erratic use of clutch.
DIFFERENTIAL GEARS SCORED	(a) Insufficient lubrication.	(a) Replace scored gears. Scoring marks on the drive face of gear teeth or in the bore are caused by instantaneous fusing of the mating surfaces. Scored gears should be replaced. Fill rear differential housing to required capacity with proper lubricant. Refer to Specifications.
	(b) Improper grade of lubricant.	(b) Replace scored gears. Inspect all gears and bearings for possible damage. Clean and refill differential housing to required capacity with proper lubricant.
	(c) Excessive spinning of one wheel/tire.	(c) Replace scored gears. Inspect all gears, pinion bores and shaft for damage. Service as necessary.
LOSS OF LUBRICANT	(a) Lubricant level too high.	(a) Drain excess lubricant by removing fill plug and allow lubricant to level at lower edge of fill plug hole.

FIGURE 3–19 (Courtesy of Chrysler Corporation.)

SERVICE DIAGNOSIS (CONT'D)

Condition	Possible Cause	Correction
	(b) Worn axle shaft seals.	(b) Replace worn seals.
	(c) Cracked differential housing.	(c) Repair or replace housing as necessary.
	(d) Worn drive pinion gear shaft seal.	(d) Replace worn drive pinion gear shaft seal.
	(e) Scored and worn yoke.	(e) Replace worn or scored yoke and seal.
	(f) Axle cover not properly sealed.	(f) Remove cover and clean flange and reseal.
AXLE OVERHEATING	(a) Lubricant level too low.	(a) Refill differential housing.
	(b) Incorrect grade of lubricant.	(b) Drain, flush and refill with correct amount of the correct lubricant.
	(c) Bearings adjusted too tight.	(c) Readjust bearings.
	(d) Excessive gear wear.	(d) Inspect gears for excessive wear or scoring. Replace as necessary.
	(e) Insufficient ring gear backlash.	(e) Readjust ring gear backlash and inspect gears for possible scoring.
GEAR TEETH BROKE (RING GEAR AND PINION)	(a) Overloading.	(a) Replace gears. Examine other gears and bearings for possible damage. Replace parts as needed. Avoid overloading of vehicle.
	(b) Erratic clutch operation.	(b) Replace gears and examine the remaining parts for possible damage. Avoid erratic clutch operation.
	(c) Ice-spotted pavements.	(c) Replace gears. Examine the remaining parts for possible damage. Replace parts as required.
	(d) Improper adjustments.	(d) Replace gears. Examine other parts for possible damage. Ensure ring gear backlash is correct.
AXLE NOISE	(a) Insufficient lubricant.	(a) Refill axle with correct amount of the proper lubricant. Also inspect for leaks and correct as necessary.
	(b) Improper ring gear and drive pinion gear adjustment.	(b) Check ring gear and pinion gear teeth contact pattern.
	(c) Unmatched ring gear and drive pinion gear.	(c) Remove unmatched ring gear and drive pinion gear. Replace with matched gear and drive pinion gear set.
	(d) Worn teeth on ring gear or drive pinion gear.	(d) Check teeth on ring gear and drive pinion gear for correct contact. If necessary, replace with new matched set.
	(e) Loose drive pinion gear shaft bearings.	(e) Adjust drive pinion gearshaft bearing preload torque.
	(f) Loose differential bearings.	(f) Adjust differential bearing preload torque.
	(g) Misaligned or sprung ring gear.	(g) Measure ring gear runout.
	(h) Loose differential bearing cap bolts.	(h) Tighten with specified torque.

FIGURE 3–19 *(Continued)*

tern, gear damage, or improper bearing preload. It can occur at various speeds and driving conditions, or it can be continuous.

2. Chuckle is a particular rattling noise that sounds like a stick against the spokes of a spinning bicycle wheel. It occurs while decelerating from 40 mph (65 km/h) and usually can be heard all the way to a stop. The frequency varies with the speed of the car.

3. Knock is very similar to chuckle, although it may be louder and occurs on acceleration or deceleration. The teardown will disclose what has to be corrected.

4. Clunk may be a metallic noise heard when the automatic transmission is engaged in Reverse or Drive, or it may occur when throttle is applied or released. It is caused by a broken tooth on a pinion gear or backlash somewhere in the drive line; it is felt or heard in the axle.

5. Bearing whine is a speed sensitive high-pitched sound similar to a whistle. It is usually caused by malfunctioning pinion bearings that are operating at drive shaft speed. Roller wheel bearings may whine the same way if they run completely dry. Bearing noise occurs at all driving speeds, distinguishing it from gear whine, which usually comes and goes as speed changes and is caused by excessive gear backlash.

6. Bearing rumble sounds like marbles being rumbled. This condition is usually caused by a malfunctioning wheel bearing. The lower pitch is because the wheel bearing turns at only about one-third of drive shaft speed.

7. Chatter on corners is a condition where the whole rear end vibrates only when the car is moving. The vibration is as plainly felt as it is heard. In conventional axles, extra differential thrust washers cause a condition of partial lockup that creates this chatter. Chatter noise on traction-lock axles can usually be traced to erratic movement between adjacent clutch plates and can be corrected with a lubricant change and the addition of a friction modifier available for the purpose.

8. Click at engagement is a condition on axles of a slight noise, distinct from a clunk, which happens in Reverse or Drive engagement.

Nonaxle Noise

There are a few other conditions that can sound just like axle noise and have to be considered in prediagnosis. The four most common are exhaust, tires, roof racks, and trim moldings.

1. In certain conditions, the pitch of the exhaust may sound very much like gear whines. At other times, it can be mistaken for a wheel bearing rumble.

2. Tires (especially snow tires) can have a high-pitched tread whine or roar similar to gear noise. Radial tires, to some degree, have this characteristic. Also, any nonstandard tire with an unusual tread construction may emit a roar or whine-type noise.

3. Roof racks on station wagons may, because of an airfoil effect, make roaring or rumbling sounds which seem to come from the "rear end."

4. Trim and moldings also can cause a whistling or whining noise.

Therefore, be sure that none of these is the cause of the noise before proceeding with an axle teardown and diagnosis.

The chart on page 75 may be used to identify the source of noise problems.

DRIVE AXLE, SEAL, AND BEARING SERVICE

On cars with solid axle rear-wheel-drive, axle shafts are retained in the axle housing either by a C-clip at the inner end of the axle or by a press-fit axle bearing and retainer plate at the outer end. A removable cover provides access to the C-clip retainers. Axle shaft removal is required for seal, bearing, or shaft replacement and for differential removal.

C-Clip Axle Shaft Service

To remove an axle retained by a C-clip:

1. Raise the car and support it safely to allow access to the drive axle. Support the car under the frame to allow the drive wheels to turn.

2. Remove the wheel assembly and the brake drum.

3. Place a drain pan under the differential to catch the lubricant. Remove the rear cover from the housing. Note the location of any clips or tags as the retaining bolts are removed.

4. Remove the differential pinion shaft retaining pin or bolt.

5. Rotate the differential one-half turn and tap the pinion shaft inward about one inch.

6. Rotate the differential back one-half turn. Insert a suitable punch into the retaining pin hole and pull the shaft out of the differential case. A twisting, pulling action may be needed to remove the shaft. *Note:* The differential pinions and thrust washers may fall out of place during this procedure.

7. Push the axle shaft inward toward the differential to expose the C-clip and remove the C-clip **(Figure 3–20)**.

Condition	Cause
1. Noise is the same in drive or coast.	a. Road noise. b. Tire noise. c. Front wheel bearing noise. d. Incorrect driveline angles.
2. Noise changes on a different type of road.	a. Road noise. b. Tire noise.
3. Noise tone lower as vehicle speed is lowered.	a. Tire noise.
4. Noise is produced with vehicle standing and driving.	a. Engine noise. b. Transmission noise.
5. Vibration.	a. Rough rear wheel bearing. b. Unbalanced or damaged propeller shaft. c. Tire unbalance. d. Worn universal joint in propeller shaft. e. Incorrect driveline angles. f. Mis-indexed propeller shaft at pinion yoke. g. Pinion yoke runout too great.
6. A knock or click approximately every two revolutions of the rear wheel.	a. Rear wheel bearing noise.
7. Noise most pronounced on turns.	a. Rear axle side gear and pinion noise.
8. A continuous low pitch whirring or scraping noise starting at relatively low speed.	a. Pinion bearing noise.
9. Drive noise, coast noise or float noise.	a. Ring and pinion gear noise.
10. Clunk on acceleration or deceleration.	a. Worn rear axle pinion shaft in case or side gear hub counterbore in case worn oversize. b. Worn universal joint on propeller shaft. c. Slip yoke lubrication insufficient.
11. Groan in forward or reverse.	a. Wrong lubricant in rear axle. b. Worn bushings.
12. Chatter on turns.	a. Wrong lubricant in rear axle. b. Clutch cone worn and/or spring worn.
13. Clunk or knock on rough road operation.	a. Excessive end play of axle shafts. b. Worn bushings.

8. Carefully pull the axle shaft out of the housing while supporting it to avoid damaging the seal if it is not to be replaced.

9. Inspect the axle shaft for wear or damage. Look for wear or roughness in the bearing and seal contact areas of the shaft. Look for excessive wear or cracking in the splined area (**Figure 3–21**).

Seal and Bearing Removal and Replacement

1. Use a slide hammer puller with the appropriate adapter to remove the seal and bearing.

2. Inspect the housing bore in the area where the seal and bearing contact the housing for any

scoring that may allow lubricant to leak past the seal.

3. Inspect the bearing rollers and cage for wear or damage. Replace the bearing if damaged or worn.

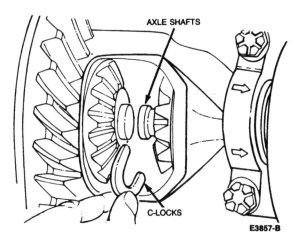

FIGURE 3–20 With axle shaft pushed in, C-lock can be removed. (Courtesy of Ford Motor Company.)

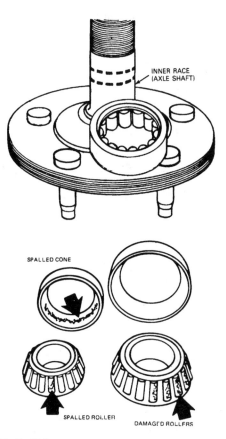

FIGURE 3–21 Examine axle bearing race, rollers, and cones carefully for wear and damage. (Courtesy of Ford Motor Company.)

4. Use a special driver with an adapter slightly smaller in diameter than the housing bore to install the bearing. Drive the bearing in until it bottoms in its bore.

5. Coat the outer shell of the new seal with a good sealer. Install the seal with the lip facing inward using the same tool as for bearing installation **(Figure 3–22).**

C-Clip Axle Shaft Installation

1. Lubricate the axle bearing and seal as well as the bearing and seal contact area on the axle.

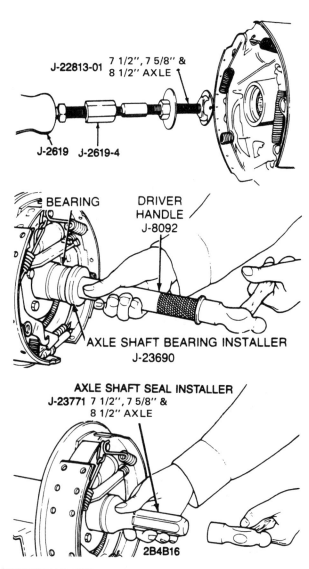

FIGURE 3–22 Using axle bearing puller (top). Installing axle bearing (middle). Installing axle seal (bottom). (Courtesy of General Motors.)

2. Carefully insert the axle into the housing while supporting it to avoid seal damage.

3. When the inner end of the shaft contacts the carrier bearing area, grip the axle flange and tilt the inner end of the shaft upward to engage the differential side gear. Turn the shaft slightly if necessary to align the splines and push the axle into place.

4. Install the C-clip into its groove in the axle and then pull outward on the axle so the C-clip fits into its recess.

5. Install the differential pinions, thrust washers, and pinion shaft making sure the retaining pin hole is properly aligned.

6. Install the interference fit retaining pin or threaded retaining pin (as equipped). Tighten the threaded pin to specified torque.

7. Check the axle shaft end play by pushing the axle in and out. End play should be as specified in the service manual (usually 0.005 to 0.030 in. (0.12 to 0.76 mm). Selective thickness C-clips or shims may be used to correct end play.

8. Clean the rear cover thoroughly and wipe it dry. Use a new gasket or form-in-place gasket material (as specified) and install the cover. Tighten the bolts to specified torque.

9. Fill the axle to the correct level with the specified lubricant.

10. Install the brake drum and wheel assembly and lower the vehicle to the floor.

Drive Axle with Press-Fit Bearing Service

The rear wheel bearing and bearing retainer ring both have a heavy press fit on the axle shaft. Because of this fit, they should be removed or installed separately. Both the retainer ring and the bearing must be removed to replace the seal.

> **DANGER:** Always wear safety glasses for protection.

1. Position and tighten the axle shaft in a vise at an angle so that the retainer ring rests on the vise jaws. Use a heavy chisel and hammer to crack the retainer ring **(Figures 3–23 and 3–24).**

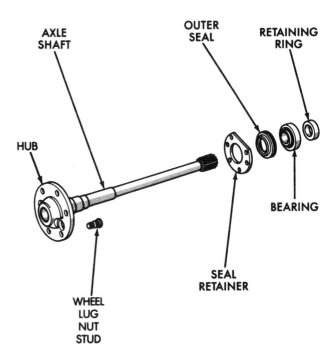

FIGURE 3–23 Axle assembly with press-fit bearing and retainer ring. (Courtesy of Chrysler Corporation.)

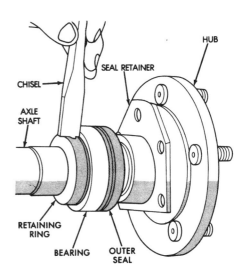

FIGURE 3–24 Use a hammer and chisel to cut into retaining ring. This spreads the ring for easy removal. (Courtesy of Chrysler Corporation.)

PRO TIP

Do not use heat to remove the retainer ring, as this may temper the axle shaft and result in axle shaft failure.

2. Press the axle bearing off, using the recommended tools and equipment. Follow the equipment manufacturer's directions for setting up the axle and press to avoid damage to parts and equipment and to avoid injury to yourself and others (**Figure 3–25**).

3. Remove the axle shaft seal and retainer plate.

4. Install a new retainer plate and seal on the axle shaft, then install the bearing.

5. Press the bearing into place, using the recommended tools and equipment and following the manufacturer's instructions for setting up and operating the equipment. Make sure that the bearing is pressed fully against the shoulder or on the axle shaft.

6. Press the new bearing retainer on the axle shaft with the proper tool and make sure that the retainer is seated against the bearing.

7. If the axle housing has an inner seal, remove and replace it with a new seal. On this type, the axle bearing is either a sealed bearing or must be packed with wheel bearing grease.

8. Install the axle shaft in the housing and install and tighten the retaining plate bolts and nuts to specified torque.

9. Clean the differential inspection cover and mounting surface on the axle housing. Do not allow any foreign matter to enter the differential housing. Apply new gasket or RTV sealer to cover as recommended and install cover and bolts. Tighten bolts to specified torque and fill the differential to the proper level with the lubricant type specified by the vehicle manufacturer.

10. Install the drum or disc and wheel assembly and tighten all bolts to specified torque.

DIFFERENTIAL REMOVAL

Removal: Carrier Type

1. Remove the drive shaft.

2. Remove the drive axle shafts as described earlier.

3. Place a drain pan under the differential.

4. Remove the carrier retaining nuts.

5. Separate the carrier from the axle housing to allow the lubricant to drain (**Figure 3–26**).

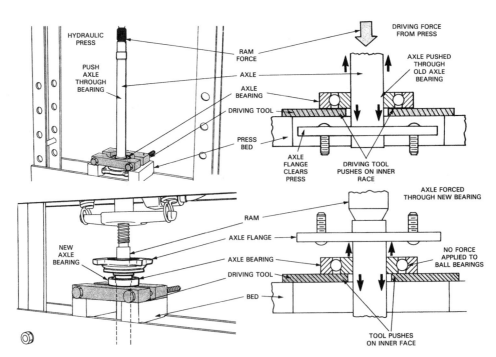

FIGURE 3–25 Press-fit bearing removal (top) and installation (bottom). (Courtesy of Chrysler Corporation.)

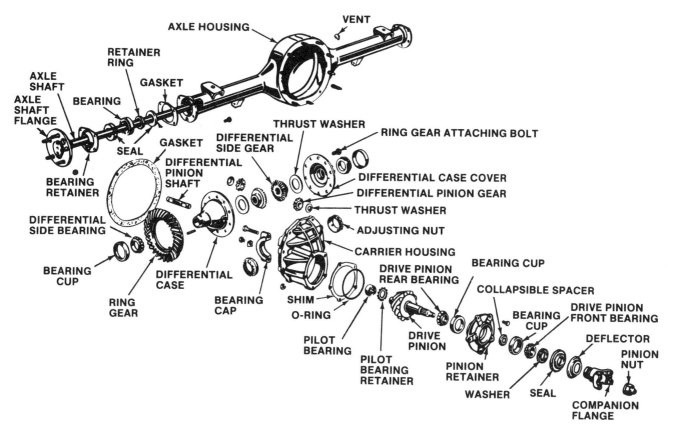

FIGURE 3–26 Rear axle with removable differential carrier. (Courtesy of Ford Motor Company.)

PRO TIP

The differential carrier assembly is very heavy. Maintain a firm grasp on it during removal, and if necessary, support it on a jack.

Inspection Before Disassembly: Carrier Type

1. Mount the carrier in a holding fixture.
2. Rotate the gears and note any bearing roughness.
3. Inspect the ring gear teeth for excessive wear or damage.
4. Set up a dial indicator and measure ring gear backlash and ring gear backface runout **(Figure 3–27).** If runout is excessive, the case flange may be bent.

Removal: Integral Type

1. Remove the drive shaft.
2. Place a drain pan under the differential.
3. Remove the rear cover.
4. Remove the drive axles as described earlier.
5. Rotate the gears and note any bearing roughness.
6. Inspect the teeth for excessive wear or damage.
7. Set up a dial indicator and measure ring gear backlash and ring gear backface runout (see **Figure 3–27**). If runout is excessive, the case flange may be bent.
8. Mark or label all the parts as they are removed to ensure that they are installed in the same location during assembly. This includes bearing caps, shims, bearing cups, bearings, and gears.
9. Remove the bearing retaining caps.

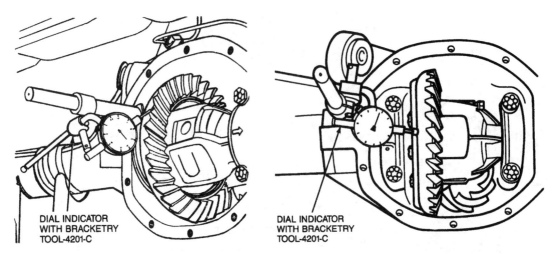

FIGURE 3–27 Using a dial indicator to measure ring gear backlash (left) and backface runout (right.) (Courtesy of Ford Motor Company.)

10. Use a bearing spreader if required or pry the differential out of the housing **(Figure 3–28)**. Mark or label caps, bearing cups, and shims.

11. Remove the drive pinion nut, yoke, and pinion shaft **(Figure 3–29).**

DIFFERENTIAL DISASSEMBLY AND INSPECTION

Disassemble the differential by following the directions in the appropriate service manual. Procedures vary depending on differential design **(Figures 3–30 and 3–31).** After disassembly, thoroughly clean and inspect all parts. Always use clean solvent when cleaning bearings. Oil the bearings immediately after cleaning to prevent rusting. Inspect the parts for defects. Clean the inside of the carrier before rebuilding it. When a scored gear set is replaced, the axle housing should be washed thoroughly and steam cleaned. This can be done effectively only if the axle shafts and shaft seals are removed from the housing. Inspect individual parts as outlined below.

Gears

Examine the pinion and ring gear teeth for scoring or excessive wear **(Figure 3–32)**. Extreme care must be taken not to damage the pilot bearing surface of the pinion. Worn gears cannot be rebuilt to correct a noisy condition. Gear scoring is the result of excessive shock loading or the use of an incorrect lubricant.

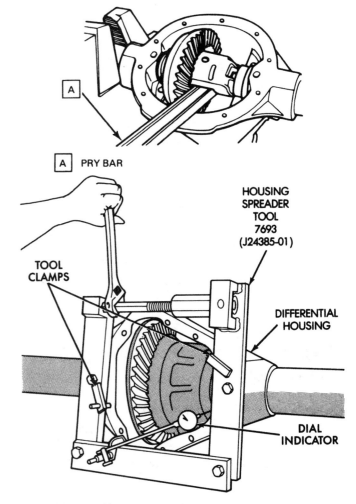

FIGURE 3–28 Differential removal methods. Some can be pried out while others are in so tight that a housing spreader must be used. [Courtesy of General Motors Corporation (top) and Chrysler Corporation (bottom).]

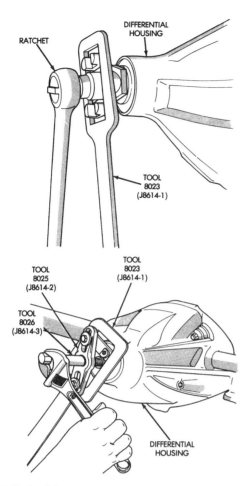

FIGURE 3–29 Removing the drive pinion nut (top) and yoke (bottom) (Courtesy of Chrysler Corporation)

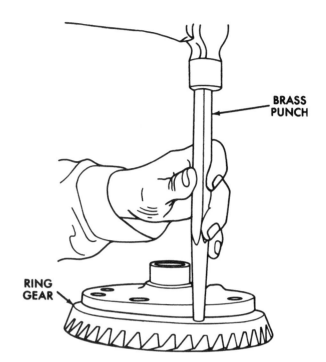

FIGURE 3–30 Ring gear removal. (Courtesy of Chrysler Corporation.)

Scored gears cannot be reused. Examine the teeth and thrust surfaces of the differential gears. Wear on the hub of the differential gear can cause a checking noise known as chuckle when the vehicle is driven at low speeds. Wear of splines, thrust surfaces, or thrust washers can contribute to excessive drive line backlash.

Bearing Cups and Cone and Roller Assemblies

Check bearing cups for rings, scores, galling, or excessive wear patterns. Pinion cups must be solidly seated. Check for seating by attempting to insert a 0.0015-in. (0.0381-mm) feeler gauge between these cups and the bottoms of their bores.

When operated in the bearing cups, cone and roller assemblies must turn without roughness. Examine the large roller ends for wear. If the original blend radius has worn to a sharp edge, the cone and

roller assembly should be replaced. If inspection reveals either a worn bearing cup or a worn cone and roller assembly, both parts should be replaced to avoid damage.

Universal Joint Flange

Be sure that the surfaces of the flange have not been damaged in removing the drive shaft or in removing the flange from the axle. The end of the flange that contacts the front pinion bearing inner race, as well as the flat surface of the pinion nut counterbore, must be smooth. Polish these surfaces if necessary. Roughness aggravates backlash noises and causes wear of the flange and pinion nut, with a resultant loss in pinion bearing preload. Flange seal surface must be smooth and not grooved due to wear from seal contact.

Carrier Housing

Make sure that the differential bearing bores are smooth and the threads are not damaged. Remove any nicks or burrs from the mounting surfaces of the carrier housing.

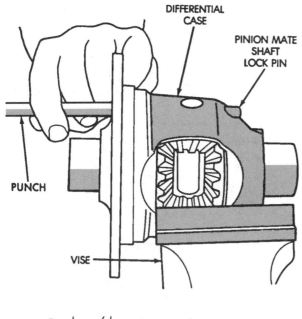

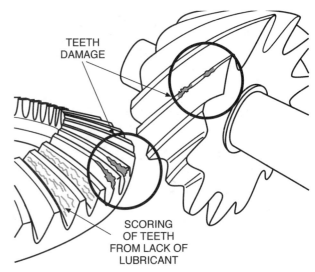

FIGURE 3–32 Typical pinion and ring gear tooth damage. (Courtesy of Ford Motor Company.)

surfaces of the two parts of the case are smooth and free from nicks or burrs.

Limited Slip Differential Parts

Inspect the clutch plates or cones for uneven or extreme wear. The dog-eared clutch plates must be free from burrs, nicks, or scratches, which could cause excessive or erratic wear to the internally splined clutch plates. The internally splined clutch plates should be inspected for condition of the material and wear. Replace the plates if their thickness is less than specified or if the material is scored or badly worn. Inspect the plate

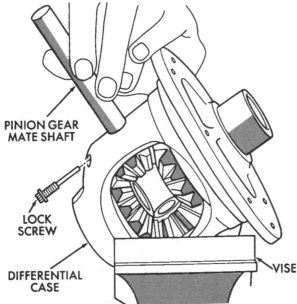

FIGURE 3–31 Lock pin (top) or lock screw (bottom) must be removed before pinion gear shaft can be removed. (Courtesy of Chrysler Corporation.)

Differential Case

Make sure that the hubs where the bearings mount are smooth. Carefully examine the differential case bearing shoulders, which may have been damaged when the bearings were removed. The bearing assemblies will fail if they do not seat firmly against the shoulders. Check the fit (free rotation) of the differential side gears in their counterbores. Be sure that the mating

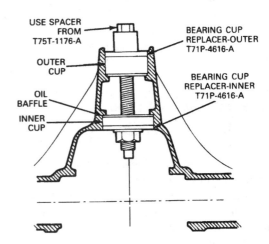

FIGURE 3–33 Installing drive pinion bearing cups. (Courtesy of Ford Motor Company.)

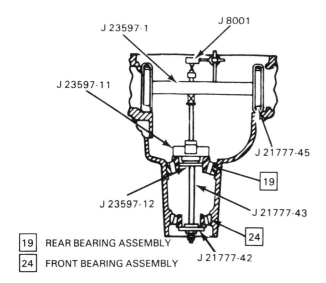

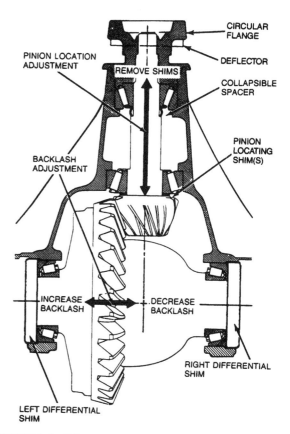

[19] REAR BEARING ASSEMBLY

[24] FRONT BEARING ASSEMBLY

FIGURE 3–34 Pinion depth setting gauge in place in differential carrier. (Courtesy of General Motors Corporation.)

FIGURE 3–36 Pinion depth adjustment is made by changing shim thickness between pinion gear and bearing. (Courtesy of Ford Motor Company.)

internal teeth for wear. Replace them if excessive wear is evident. Plates should be replaced as a set only. Examine all thrust surfaces and hubs for wear. Abnormal wear on these surfaces can contribute to a noisy axle.

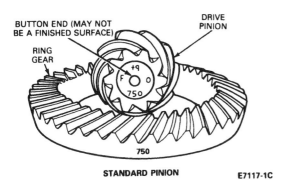

On the end of each drive pinion is marked a plus figure (+), a minus figure (-) or a (0). These figures indicate the position for each gear set. The position is determined by the thickness of the baffle between the inner pinion bearing cup and carrier bearing bore and the thickness of the selective oil slinger between the pinion head and inner pinion bearing. Any pinion depth change is made by changing the thickness of the selective oil slinger. Refer to the charts.

FIGURE 3–35 Pinion markings determine the thickness of pinion depth shim required. Matched gear sets have the same number stamp, 750 in this case. Paint marks on nonhunting ring gear and pinion teeth must be aligned during assembly to ensure proper gear timing. (Courtesy of Ford Motor Company.)

DIFFERENTIAL ASSEMBLY AND INSTALLATION

Refer to **Figures 3–33** to **3–45** for examples of procedures.

1. Assemble the differential case, clutches (if applicable), ring gear, and bearings using the procedures in the service manual.

2. Install the pinion cups.

3. Install the drive pinion spacer and bearings as outlined in the service manual using a pinion depth setting gauge to ensure proper pinion depth adjustment.

PINION GEAR DEPTH VARIANCE

Original Pinion Gear Depth Variance	Replacement Pinion Gear Depth Variance								
	−4	**−3**	**−2**	**−1**	**0**	**+1**	**+2**	**+3**	**+4**
+4	+0.008	+0.007	+0.006	+0.005	+0.004	+0.003	+0.002	+0.001	0
+3	+0.007	+0.006	+0.005	+0.004	+0.003	+0.002	+0.001	0	−0.001
+2	+0.006	+0.005	+0.004	+0.003	+0.002	+0.001	0	−0.001	−0.002
+1	+0.005	+0.004	+0.003	+0.002	+0.001	0	−0.001	−0.002	−0.003
0	+0.004	+0.003	+0.002	+0.001	0	−0.001	−0.002	−0.003	−0.004
−1	+0.003	+0.002	+0.001	0	−0.001	−0.002	−0.003	−0.004	−0.005
−2	+0.002	+0.001	0	−0.001	−0.002	−0.003	−0.004	−0.005	−0.006
−3	+0.001	0	−0.001	−0.002	−0.003	−0.004	−0.005	−0.006	−0.007
−4	0	−0.001	−0.002	−0.003	−0.004	−0.005	−0.006	−0.007	−0.008

FIGURE 3–37 Typical pinion gear depth setting chart. (Courtesy of Chrysler Corporation.)

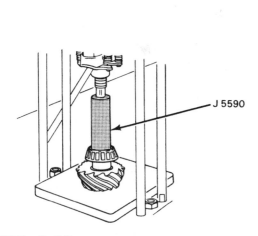

FIGURE 3–38 Installing the rear pinion bearing. (Courtesy of General Motors Corporation.)

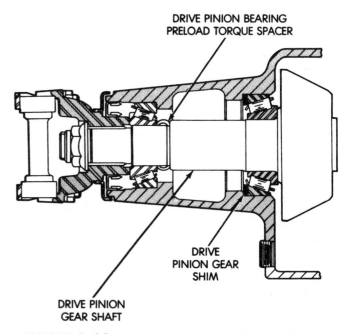

DRIVE PINION BEARING PRELOAD TORQUE SPACER

DRIVE PINION GEAR SHIM

DRIVE PINION GEAR SHAFT

FIGURE 3–39 On differential with a collapsible pre-load spacer, tighten pinion shaft nut to specified torque to obtain proper bearing preload. (Courtesy of Chrysler Corporation.)

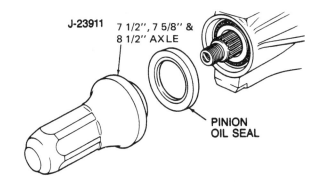

FIGURE 3–40 Installing pinion seal (typical). (Courtesy of General Motors Corporation.)

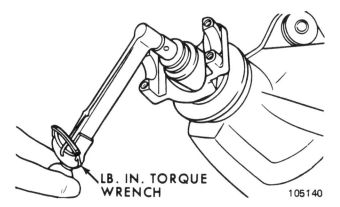

FIGURE 3–41 Checking pinion bearing preload. (Courtesy of General Motors Corporation.)

4. Install the pinion seal and drive flange.

5. Install the drive pinion nut to the specified torque to ensure correct pinion bearing preload.

6. Install the differential case assembly by following the specifications regarding shim packs at each side to provide the correct side bearing preload and gear backlash on integral units.

7. Install the bearing retaining caps and bolts to the specified torque.

8. Recheck the ring gear backlash and runout to make sure that they remain within specifications.

9. If desired, a tooth pattern check may be made at this point **(Figure 3–46)**. Follow the manufacturer's service manual for procedure.

10. Install the axle shafts, differential pinions, shaft, and shaft retainer as required. Check and adjust axle shaft end play. Install the wheels.

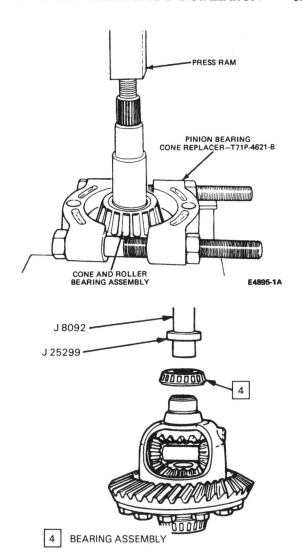

FIGURE 3–42 Differential case side bearing removal (top) and installation. [Courtesy of Ford Motor Company (top) and General Motors Corporation (bottom).]

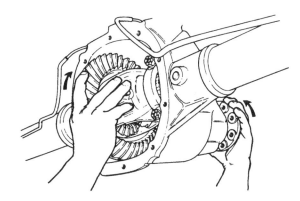

FIGURE 3–43 Rotate the differential assembly to ensure proper positioning during installation. (Courtesy of Ford Motor Company.)

11. Install the differential cover using gasket or recommended sealer. Tighten the bolts to specifications. On carrier-type differentials, adjust the side bearing preload using the threaded adjuster rings. Follow the service manual procedures to obtain proper ring gear backlash and bearing preload. Perform a tooth contact pattern check. Install the carrier into the hous-

ing using a new gasket and gasket sealer. Tighten retaining nuts to specifications.

12. Fill the unit to the specified level with lubricant specified by the manufacturer.

13. Install the drive shaft.

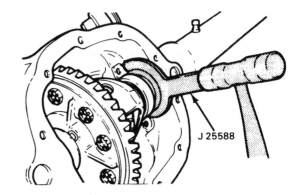

FIGURE 3–44 Installing side bearing preload shims. (Courtesy of General Motors Corporation.)

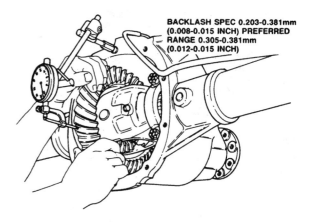

FIGURE 3–45 Measure and correct backlash according to service manual specifications. This shows a typical example. (Courtesy of Ford Motor Company.)

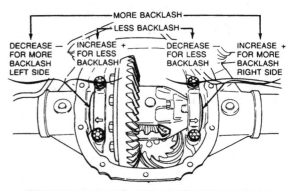

BACKLASH CHANGE REQUIRED	THICKNESS CHANGE REQUIRED	BACKLASH CHANGE REQUIRED	THICKNESS CHANGE REQUIRED
.001 inch	.002 inch	.009 inch	.012 inch
.002 inch	.002 inch	.010 inch	.014 inch
.003 inch	.004 inch	.011 inch	.014 inch
.004 inch	.006 inch	.012 inch	.016 inch
.005 inch	.006 inch	.013 inch	.018 inch
.006 inch	.008 inch	.014 inch	.018 inch
.007 inch	.010 inch	.015 inch	.020 inch
.008 inch	.010 inch		

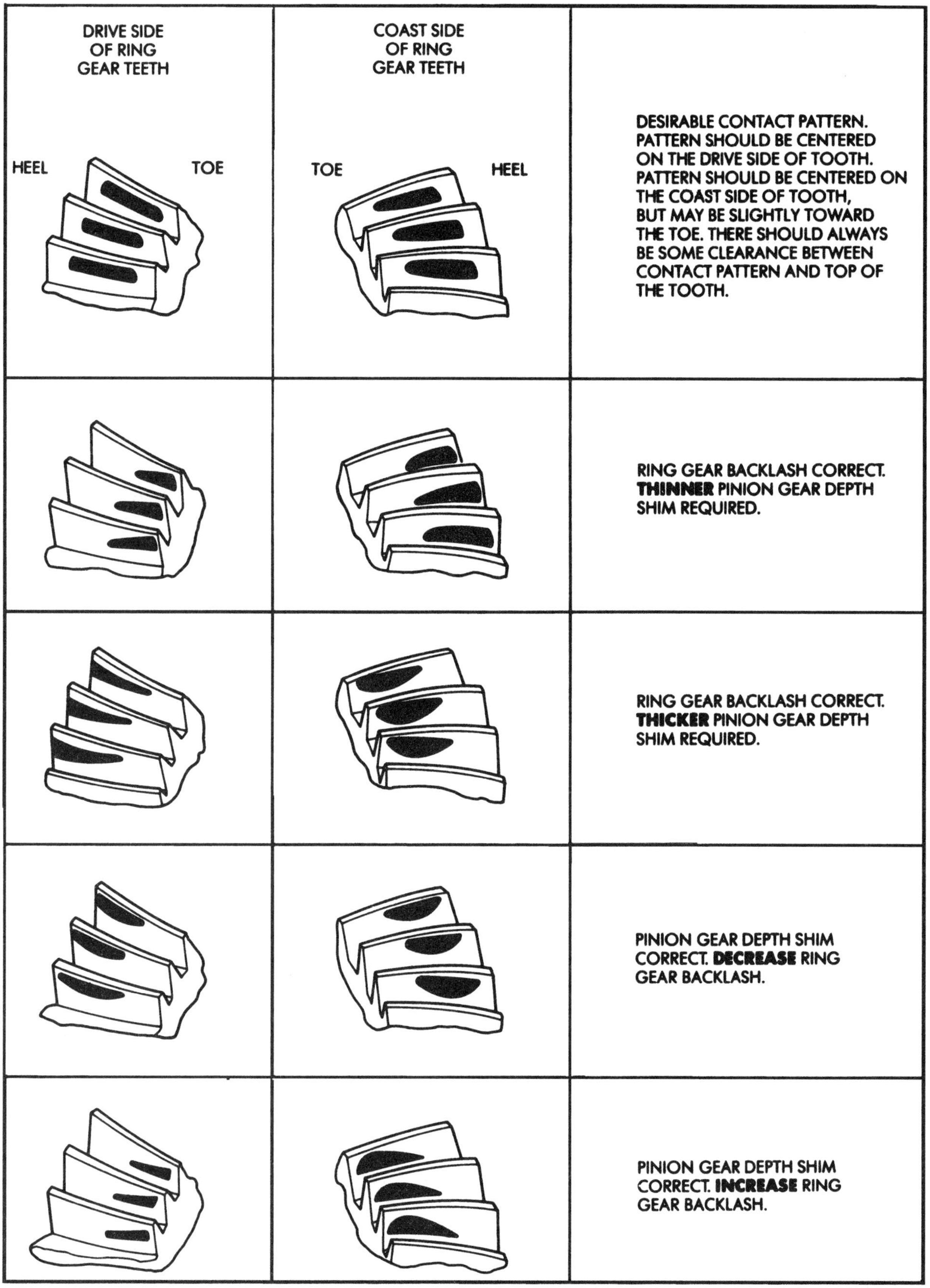

DRIVE SIDE OF RING GEAR TEETH	COAST SIDE OF RING GEAR TEETH	
HEEL ... TOE	TOE ... HEEL	DESIRABLE CONTACT PATTERN. PATTERN SHOULD BE CENTERED ON THE DRIVE SIDE OF TOOTH. PATTERN SHOULD BE CENTERED ON THE COAST SIDE OF TOOTH, BUT MAY BE SLIGHTLY TOWARD THE TOE. THERE SHOULD ALWAYS BE SOME CLEARANCE BETWEEN CONTACT PATTERN AND TOP OF THE TOOTH.
		RING GEAR BACKLASH CORRECT. **THINNER** PINION GEAR DEPTH SHIM REQUIRED.
		RING GEAR BACKLASH CORRECT. **THICKER** PINION GEAR DEPTH SHIM REQUIRED.
		PINION GEAR DEPTH SHIM CORRECT. **DECREASE** RING GEAR BACKLASH.
		PINION GEAR DEPTH SHIM CORRECT. **INCREASE** RING GEAR BACKLASH.

FIGURE 3–46 Gear tooth contact pattern correction chart. (Courtesy of Chrysler Corporation.

REVIEW QUESTIONS

1. True or false? The differential drive pinion drives the differential pinions.

2. The differential ring gear transmits torque to the differential pinion _____.

3. The differential case is supported in the axle housing by _____ _____.

4. When a vehicle turns a corner, the inner wheel travels a _____ distance than the outer wheel.

5. When turning a corner the small differential pinions walk around the slower turning _____ _____.

6. The most common type of differential ring gear and pinion is the _____ type.

7. The differential drive pinion may be _____ mounted or _____ mounted.

8. The limited slip differential provides more drive force to the wheel with more _____.

9. With the swing axle rear-wheel-drive system, the drive axles are not _____.

10. Each swing axle has two _____ _____.

11. The axle housing may have a _____ differential carrier, or it may be _____ with the housing.

12. To check limited slip differential _____ torque, use a torque wrench.

13. Use a _____ and _____ to remove a drive axle bearing retainer ring.

14. To remove a drive axle held in place by a C-clip, remove the _____ _____ retaining pin and push the axle inward to expose the C-clip.

15. True or false? The carrier type of differential is removed from the rear of the axle housing.

16. Before disassembling the differential, check the ring gear _____.

17. Pinion depth is set with the use of a pinion _____ _____ gauge.

18. Differential side bearing preload and backlash are adjusted with _____ on the integral carrier drive axle.

TEST QUESTIONS

1. "The drive axle differential transmits torque from the drive shaft to the drive axles." "The drive axle differential transmits torque at a 90 degree angle." Which of these statements is correct?
   a. the first
   b. the second
   c. both are correct
   d. both are incorrect

2. The differential drive pinion is in mesh with the
   a. axle gears
   b. pinion gears
   c. ring gear
   d. sun gear

3. The differential case encloses the
   a. axle shafts and axle gears
   b. pinion shaft, pinion gears, and axle gears
   c. ring gear, pinion gear, and axle gears
   d. pinion gears, sun gear, and axle gears

4. The hypoid rear axle is designed to
   a. lower the body profile
   b. provide more tooth contact
   c. provide quieter operation
   d. all of the above

5. The overhung-mounted pinion has how many bearings?
   a. one
   b. two
   c. three
   d. four

6. Technician A says that the differential pinions turn on the pinion shaft during straight-ahead driving. Technician B says that the differential pinions are in mesh with the drive pinion. Who is right?
   a. technician A
   b. technician B

c. both are right

d. both are wrong

7. The collapsible sleeve between the pinion bearings in the differential controls
   a. pinion depth
   b. backlash
   c. tooth contact pattern
   d. pinion bearing preload

8. The type of differential gear that must be timed during assembly is the
   a. hypoid
   b. spur and bevel
   c. hunting
   d. nonhunting

9. "A limited slip differential may have a viscous coupling or clutches." "A limited slip differential allows more wheel slip than a standard differential." Which of these statements is correct?
   a. the first
   b. the second
   c. both are correct
   d. both are incorrect

10. Side bearing preload and gear backlash is determined by
    a. ring gear-to-pinion position
    b. side bearing shim thickness

c. side bearing threaded adjusters

d. all of the above

11. Technician A says that the swing axle rear-wheel-drive system has a differential that is part of the unsprung weight. Technician B says that the swing axle differential is bolted to the frame. Who is right?
    a. technician A
    b. technician B
    c. both are right
    d. both are wrong

12. On many solid axle drive axles, the axle shafts cannot be removed before removing the
    a. C-clips from the inner end of the axle shafts
    b. setscrews from the inner end of the axle shafts
    c. locknuts from the inner end of the axle shafts
    d. none of the above

13. "On a removable carrier rear axle, the differential is removed from the front of the axle housing." "On an integral carrier rear axle, the differential is removed from the rear of the axle housing." Which of these statements is correct?
    a. the first
    b. the second
    c. both are correct
    d. both are incorrect

◆ CHAPTER 4 ◆

CLUTCH PRINCIPLES AND SERVICE

INTRODUCTION

The clutch is a driver-controlled mechanical connection between the engine and the transmission or transaxle. This chapter discusses the function, design, operation, and service of the automotive clutch.

LEARNING OBJECTIVES

After completing this chapter, you should be able to:

- Describe the function of the clutch.
- List the major components of a clutch.
- Describe the operation of the clutch.
- Describe the different clutch designs.
- Describe the different types of clutch controls.
- Describe typical clutch problems.
- Diagnose clutch problems.
- Service and replace a clutch assembly.

TERMS YOU SHOULD KNOW

Look for these terms as you study this chapter and learn what they mean.

clutch	clutch disc
clutch housing	pressure plate
diaphragm spring	clutch noise
coil spring	chatter
clutch finger	drag
release bearing	grab
clutch fork	slippage
clutch linkage	vibration
hydraulic clutch	overheating
clutch master cylinder	clutch adjustment
clutch slave cylinder	clutch alignment
pedal free play	bleeding

CLUTCH FUNCTION AND COMPONENTS

The clutch provides the means for the driver to connect and disconnect the engine from the manually shifted transmission or transaxle. The clutch (when engaged) provides a direct 1:1 drive connection from the engine to the transmission/transaxle. It is disengaged during gear shifting and engaged whenever engine power is applied to the transmission. The clutch is disengaged (released) when the clutch pedal is depressed, and engaged (applied) when the clutch pedal is released. With the engine running and the transmission in neutral, engine power is not transmitted through the transmission.

Clutch components are shown in **Figure 4–1.**

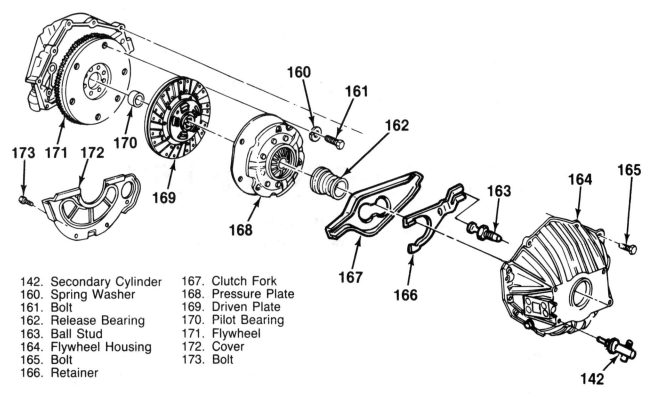

142. Secondary Cylinder
160. Spring Washer
161. Bolt
162. Release Bearing
163. Ball Stud
164. Flywheel Housing
165. Bolt
166. Retainer

167. Clutch Fork
168. Pressure Plate
169. Driven Plate
170. Pilot Bearing
171. Flywheel
172. Cover
173. Bolt

FIGURE 4–1 Clutch components for rear-wheel-drive car. (Clutch shaft is not shown here.) (Courtesy of General Motors Corporation.)

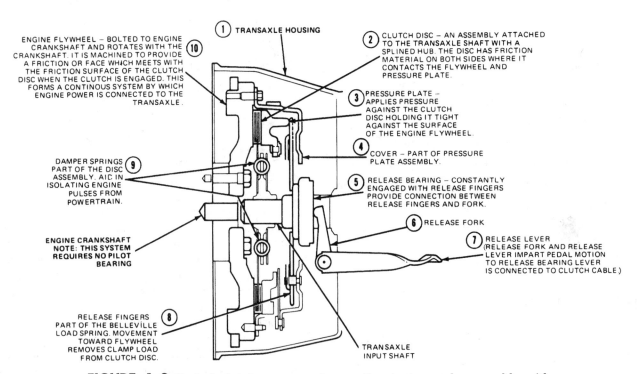

① TRANSAXLE HOUSING

② CLUTCH DISC – AN ASSEMBLY ATTACHED TO THE TRANSAXLE SHAFT WITH A SPLINED HUB. THE DISC HAS FRICTION MATERIAL ON BOTH SIDES WHERE IT CONTACTS THE FLYWHEEL AND PRESSURE PLATE.

③ PRESSURE PLATE – APPLIES PRESSURE AGAINST THE CLUTCH DISC HOLDING IT TIGHT AGAINST THE SURFACE OF THE ENGINE FLYWHEEL.

④ COVER – PART OF PRESSURE PLATE ASSEMBLY.

⑤ RELEASE BEARING – CONSTANTLY ENGAGED WITH RELEASE FINGERS PROVIDE CONNECTION BETWEEN RELEASE FINGERS AND FORK.

⑥ RELEASE FORK

⑦ RELEASE LEVER (RELEASE FORK AND RELEASE LEVER IMPART PEDAL MOTION TO RELEASE BEARING LEVER IS CONNECTED TO CLUTCH CABLE.)

⑩ ENGINE FLYWHEEL – BOLTED TO ENGINE CRANKSHAFT AND ROTATES WITH THE CRANKSHAFT. IT IS MACHINED TO PROVIDE A FRICTION OR FACE WHICH MEETS WITH THE FRICTION SURFACE OF THE CLUTCH DISC WHEN THE CLUTCH IS ENGAGED. THIS FORMS A CONTINOUS SYSTEM BY WHICH ENGINE POWER IS CONNECTED TO THE TRANSAXLE.

⑨ DAMPER SPRINGS PART OF THE DISC ASSEMBLY. AID IN ISOLATING ENGINE PULSES FROM POWERTRAIN.

ENGINE CRANKSHAFT NOTE: THIS SYSTEM REQUIRES NO PILOT BEARING

⑧ RELEASE FINGERS PART OF THE BELLEVILLE LOAD SPRING. MOVEMENT TOWARD FLYWHEEL REMOVES CLAMP LOAD FROM CLUTCH DISC.

TRANSAXLE INPUT SHAFT

FIGURE 4–2 Typical clutch component operation in transaxle assembly with constant-running release bearing. (Courtesy of Ford Motor Co. of Canada Ltd.)

1. *Clutch housing:* cast aluminum housing that is bolted to the engine block and encloses the clutch assembly.
2. *Flywheel:* bolted to the engine crankshaft, it provides a friction surface for the clutch and the mounting surface for the pressure plate.
3. *Pressure plate:* spring-loaded plate and cover bolted to the flywheel clamps and the clutch disc to the flywheel when the clutch is applied.
4. *Clutch disc:* disc with friction facing on each side is splined to the transmission input shaft. Disc is clamped tightly between the flywheel and pressure plate when the clutch is applied to drive the transmission input shaft.
5. *Clutch control:* clutch pedal, cable, linkage, or hydraulic system used by driver to release and apply the clutch.
6. *Clutch fork:* lever that pushes the release bearing against the clutch fingers in the pressure plate to disengage the clutch.
7. *Release bearing:* positioned between the clutch fork and release fingers to reduce friction.
8. *Clutch switch:* prevents starting until the clutch pedal is fully depressed.

CLUTCH OPERATION AND TORQUE CAPACITY

See **Figure 4–2.**

The flow of power through the clutch is accomplished by bringing the rotating drive members (flywheel and pressure plate) secured to the crankshaft into gradual contact with the driven member (clutch disc) which is splined to the input shaft of the transmission or transaxle. These members are either stationary or rotating at different speeds. Contact is established and maintained by strong spring pressure controlled by the driver through the clutch pedal and suitable linkage. When full spring pressure is applied, the speed of the driving and driven members is the same. All slipping has stopped, and there is, in effect, a direct connection between the driving and driven parts. Some slight slippage or clutch creep may occur.

The application of engine power to the load must be gradual to provide smooth engagement and to lessen the shock on the driving parts. After engagement, the clutch must transmit all the engine power to the transmission without slipping. Further, to avoid gear damage, it is desirable to disconnect the engine from the power train during the time the gears in the transmission are being shifted from one gear ratio to another.

Torque Capacity. The ability of a clutch to transmit torque depends on several factors:

1. Applied pressure (springs and centrifugal devices)
2. Coefficient of friction of clutch frictional surfaces
3. Surface area of frictional surfaces (square inches or square centimeters)
4. Internal and external diameter of driven disc

The clutch is designed with sufficient overcapacity to allow for deterioration due to normal wear. The clutch is also designed to prevent flying apart or bursting. High-performance vehicles are usually equipped with a scatter shield or blanket designed to contain flying parts should the clutch assembly fly apart at high speeds.

CLUTCH DISC DESIGN

The clutch disc is made of spring steel in the shape of a single flat disc consisting of a number of flat segments. Suitable frictional facings provide the wear surface and are attached to each side of the disc by means of rivets. These facings are heat resistant since friction produces heat. The most commonly used facings are made of cotton and other fibers woven or molded together and impregnated with resins or similar binding agents. Very often, copper wires are woven or pressed into material to give it additional strength. To make clutch engagement as smooth as possible and eliminate chatter, the steel segments attached to the splined hub are slightly twisted (cushion springs), which causes the facings to make gradual contact as the disc flattens out (**Figure 4–3**).

The clutch disc is provided with a flexible center to absorb the torsional vibration of the crankshaft, which would be transmitted to the power train unless it were eliminated. The flexible center has steel compression springs placed between the hub and the steel disc. The springs permit the disc to rotate slightly with relation to its hub. The slight backward and forward rota-

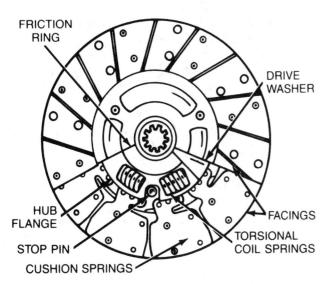

FIGURE 4–3 Clutch disc components. (Courtesy of General Motors Corporation.)

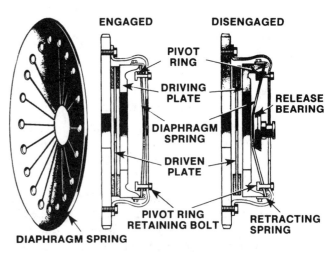

FIGURE 4–4 Diaphragm spring pressure plate operation. (Courtesy of General Motors Corporation.)

tion permitted by the springs allows the clutch shaft to rotate at a more uniform rate than the crankshaft, thereby eliminating some of the torsional vibration from the crankshaft.

CLUTCH SHAFT AND PILOT BEARING

The splined transmission input shaft is sometimes called the clutch shaft because the clutch disc is located on this shaft. The clutch shaft is supported at the front by a pilot bearing or bushing and at the other end

by the front bearing in the transmission. The clutch disc is free to slide on the clutch shaft. The shaft keeps the disc centered between the flywheel and pressure plate. The pilot bushing is located in the end of the crankshaft.

CLUTCH PRESSURE PLATE

The driving and driven members are held in contact by spring pressure. This pressure may be exerted by a one-piece diaphragm spring or by a number of small coil springs located around the outer portion of the pressure plate **(Figures 4–4 to 4–8).** In the

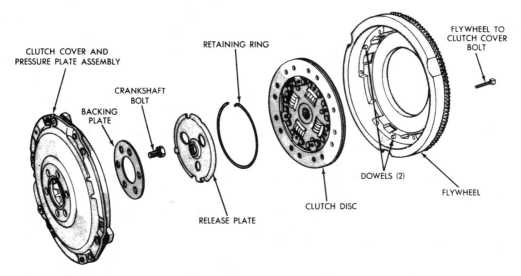

FIGURE 4–5 Diaphragm spring pressure plate clutch with recessed flywheel. (Courtesy of Chrysler Corporation.)

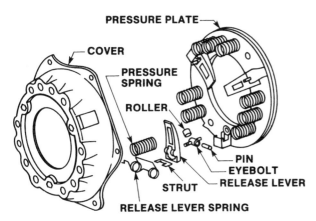

FIGURE 4–6 Coil spring pressure plate parts. (Courtesy of General Motors Corporation.)

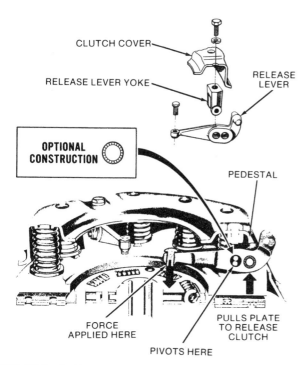

FIGURE 4–7 Semi-centrifugal pressure plate operation. As the clutch assembly spins, the weighted release levers provide added clutch apply pressure due to centrifugal force acting on the levers. (Courtesy of Ford Motor Company.)

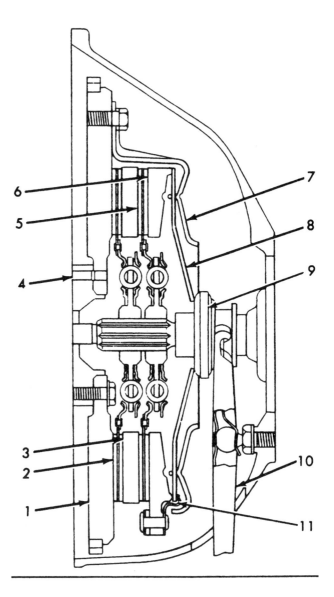

1. Flywheel
2. Front Driven Disc
3. Front Pressure Plate
4. Dowel Hole
5. Rear Driven Disc
6. Rear Pressure Plate
7. Cover
8. Diaphragm Spring
9. Throwout Bearing
10. Fork
11. Retracting Spring

FIGURE 4–8 Dual plate clutch has increased torque capacity due to increased frictional surface area. (Courtesy of General Motors Corporation.)

diaphragm design clutch, the throw-out bearing moves forward against the spring fingers, forcing the diaphragm spring to pivot around the inner pivot ring, dishing the fingers toward the flywheel. The outer circumference of the spring now lifts the pressure plate away from the driven disc through a series of retracting springs placed around the outer cir-

cumference of the pressure plate. In the helical-spring clutch, a system of levers pivoted on the cover forces the pressure plate away from the driven disc and against the pressure of the springs, thus performing the same function as the dish-shaped diaphragm spring.

CLUTCH HOUSING

The clutch housing (also called a flywheel or bell housing, due to its shape) is bolted to the engine block. It encloses the clutch assembly. The transmission is bolted to the back of the clutch housing. The clutch release fork is mounted through a hole in the housing and pivots on a ball stud or bracket. The housing may be cast aluminum, magnesium, or cast iron. The bottom of the housing may have a thin steel plated covering an opening through which the starter ring gear can be inspected (see **Figure 4–1**).

CLUTCH LINKAGE

Mechanical Clutch Control

Two basic types of clutch linkages are used: mechanical and hydraulic control. The mechanical linkage consists of a series of rods and levers or a flexible cable connecting the clutch pedal to the clutch release fork **(Figure 4–9)**.

The clutch release or throw-out bearing is a ball-thrust bearing contained in the clutch release bearing collar, mounted on the front bearing retainer of the transmission case **(Figure 4–10)**. The release

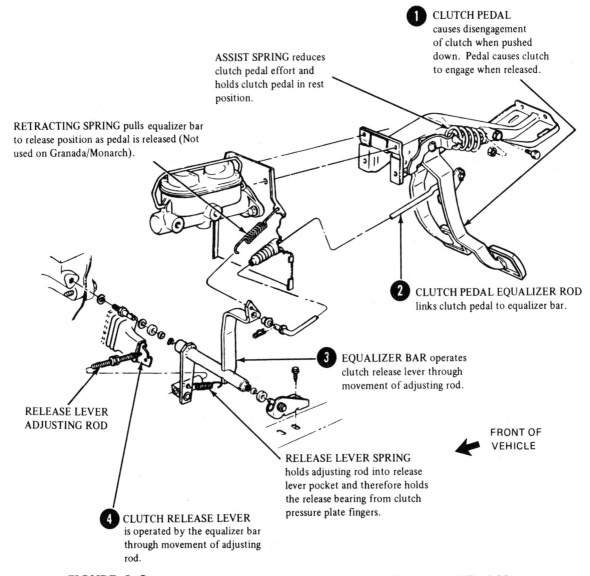

① CLUTCH PEDAL causes disengagement of clutch when pushed down. Pedal causes clutch to engage when released.

ASSIST SPRING reduces clutch pedal effort and holds clutch pedal in rest position.

RETRACTING SPRING pulls equalizer bar to release position as pedal is released (Not used on Granada/Monarch).

② CLUTCH PEDAL EQUALIZER ROD links clutch pedal to equalizer bar.

③ EQUALIZER BAR operates clutch release lever through movement of adjusting rod.

RELEASE LEVER ADJUSTING ROD

FRONT OF VEHICLE

RELEASE LEVER SPRING holds adjusting rod into release lever pocket and therefore holds the release bearing from clutch pressure plate fingers.

④ CLUTCH RELEASE LEVER is operated by the equalizer bar through movement of adjusting rod.

FIGURE 4–9 Rod and lever clutch linkage operation. (Courtesy of Ford Motor Company.)

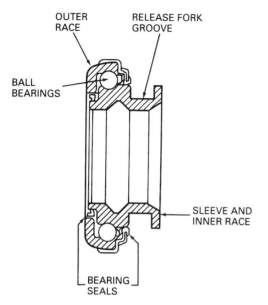

FIGURE 4–10 Cross section of typical clutch release bearing. (Courtesy of F T Enterprises.)

bearing is connected through linkage to the clutch and is moved by the release yoke or hydraulic pressure to engage the release levers and move the pressure plate to the rear, thus separating the clutch driving members from the driven member when the clutch pedal is depressed (**Figures 4–11** and **4–12**). An overcenter spring helps depress the clutch pedal

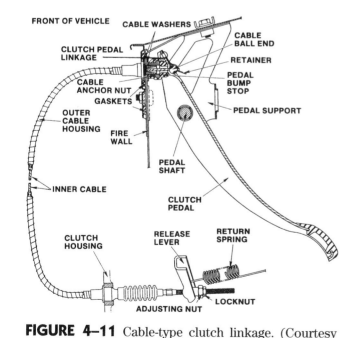

FIGURE 4–11 Cable-type clutch linkage. (Courtesy of Ford Motor Company.)

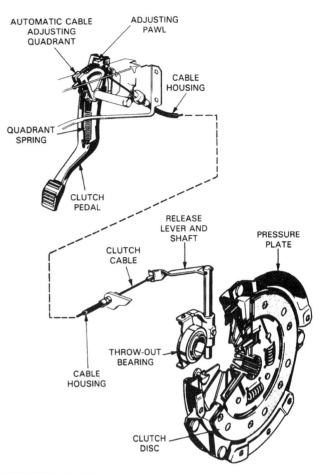

FIGURE 4–12 Cable type of clutch control with self-adjusting mechanism. (Courtesy of Ford Motor Company.)

after initial pedal movement. A pedal return spring keeps the pedal against its stop when the pedal is released. The clutch free pedal travel will increase with linkage wear and decrease with driven disc wear.

Hydraulic Clutch Control

The hydraulic control consists of a hydraulic master cylinder operated by a pushrod connected to the brake pedal, and a servo cylinder, which operates the clutch release fork (**Figures 4–13** to **4–17**). The master cylinder and servo cylinder are connected hydraulically by a steel tube. Brake fluid is used in the system. The advantage of the hydraulic control is that force multiplication is easily achieved hydraulically, and the need for complicated linkage is eliminated.

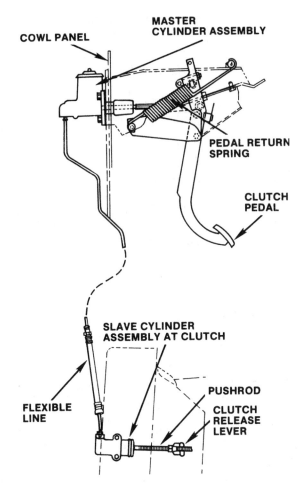

FIGURE 4–13 Hydraulic clutch control components. (Courtesy of General Motors Corporation.)

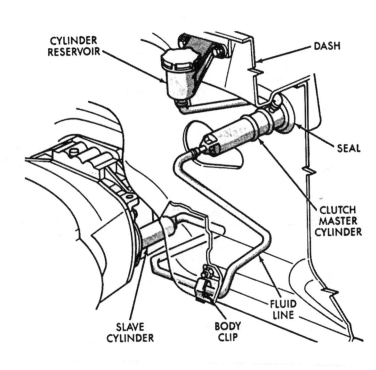

FIGURE 4–14 Hydraulic clutch control with remote mounted fluid reservoir. (Courtesy of Chrysler Corporation.)

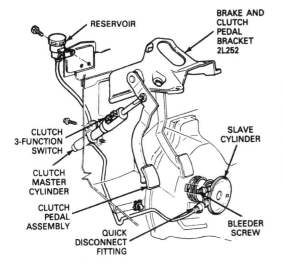

FIGURE 4–15 Hydraulic clutch control with integrated slave cylinder and release bearing. The three functions of the clutch switch are; 1: to prevent starting the engine unless the pedal is depressed to the floor; 2: to cut off the speed control when the pedal is depressed; 3: to provide a fuel control signal to the engine control computer. (Courtesy of Ford Motor Company.)

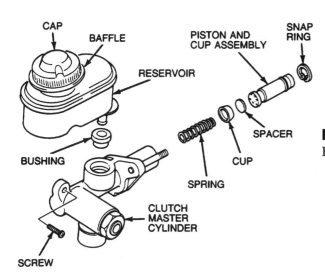

FIGURE 4–16 Clutch master cylinder parts. (Courtesy of Ford Motor Company.)

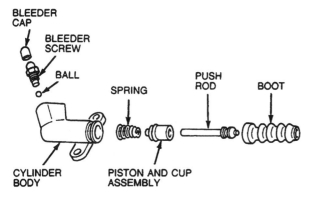

FIGURE 4–17 Clutch slave cylinder parts. (Courtesy of Ford Motor Company.)

Clutch Pedal Free Play

Clutch linkage is usually designed to provide clearance between the release bearing and release fingers when the clutch is fully applied (pedal in return position; **Figure 4–18**). This results in some clutch pedal free play being provided. Other units are designed to provide continuous running of the release bearing (see **Figure 4–2**).

Clutch linkage adjustment is extremely important in either case. Without proper linkage adjustment, full clutch engagement may not be achieved or full clutch release may not be possible.

Automatic Clutch Linkage Adjustment

Automatic clutch linkage adjustment is provided on some cars by a spring-loaded pawl connected to the clutch pedal and a toothed quadrant connected to the clutch control cable. When sufficient pedal free play has developed (due to wear on clutch parts), the pawl engages the next tooth on the quadrant to reduce pedal free play when the pedal is depressed. This eliminates the need for periodic adjustment **(Figure 4–19)**. Clutch life and transmission shifting

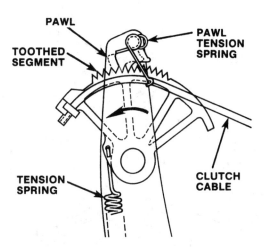

FIGURE 4–19 Ratchet-type automatic clutch linkage adjuster. (Courtesy of Ford Motor Company.)

are adversely affected if the linkage is not properly adjusted.

Clutch Vacuum Booster

Some vehicles are equipped with a vacuum booster designed to reduce the effort required to depress the clutch pedal. The booster consists primarily of a diaphragm, an input pushrod connected to one side of the diaphragm and an output pushrod connected to the other side. Engine intake manifold vacuum acts on one side of the diaphragm while atmospheric pressure acts on the other when the clutch pedal is depressed. When the clutch pedal is released, pressure is equalized on both sides of the diaphragm. A valve inside the booster controls the vacuum and atmospheric pressure ports. When the clutch pedal is depressed, atmospheric pressure acting on the input side of the diaphragm helps to release the clutch with reduced pedal effort. It is the pressure difference on the two sides of the diaphragm that causes it to move.

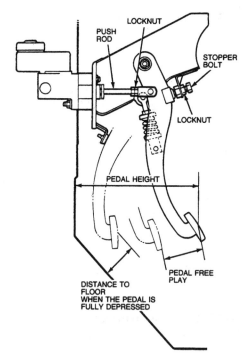

FIGURE 4–18 Clutch pedal free play is needed to ensure that clutch is fully applied and release bearing clears clutch levers. (Courtesy of Ford Motor Company.)

Electronic Clutching and Shifting

Electronic clutching and gear shifting use signals from sensors indicating engine speed, engine load, and vehicle speed to inform a computer when to clutch and shift. Electric solenoids perform the actual operations in response to computer signals. Although available on some vehicles, this system is not a common option.

Clutch Start Switch

The clutch start switch is connected into the starting circuit. The switch is normally open when the clutch pedal is released. When the clutch pedal is depressed, the switch closes, allowing the starting circuit to be completed between the ignition switch and starter relay or solenoid. A transmission neutral switch bypasses the clutch start switch to allow the engine to be started when the transmission is in Neutral without depressing the clutch pedal (see **Figure 4–15**).

CLUTCH PROBLEMS

The following clutch problems and their causes are typical.

Clutch Fails to Release (Clutch Drag)

When the clutch pedal is depressed, the clutch does not release. The transmission input shaft keeps on turning and gears clash and grind when shifting is attempted. Possible causes include:

1. Linkage adjustment incorrect
2. Clutch disc stuck to flywheel
3. Warped clutch disc
4. Clutch disc hub stuck on clutch shaft splines
5. Clutch shaft pilot seized in pilot bearing
6. Clutch linkage disconnected
7. Low fluid in clutch master cylinder
8. Fluid bypass leak inside master cylinder or slave cylinder

Clutch Slips

Clutch slippage is most noticeable during acceleration. When the accelerator pedal is pressed down, the engine speeds up, but the car doesn't. Possible causes are:

1. No clutch pedal free play (incorrect linkage adjustment)
2. Oil-soaked clutch disc
3. Worn clutch facings
4. Weak clutch pressure plate springs
5. Warped pressure plate or flywheel friction surface

Clutch Chatter (Grabbing)

Clutch grab or chatter produces severe vibration resulting from repeated and rapid gripping and slipping of the clutch even when the clutch pedal is being released slowly. Possible causes are:

1. Oily patches on clutch facing
2. Burned or glazed clutch facing
3. Warped pressure plate or flywheel
4. Loose motor mounts

Hard Clutch Pedal Effort

A clutch pedal that is hard to depress is caused by excessive friction anywhere in the clutch release linkage, by a faulty overcenter spring, or by the release fork slipping off its pivot.

No Pedal Return

The clutch pedal stays down on the floor after having been depressed. This is caused by:

1. Bind in release linkage
2. Weak pressure plate springs

Abnormal Clutch Noise

Abnormal clutch noise includes rattles, squeaks and squealing, or grinding. Noise may originate from the clutch linkage, release bearing, pilot bearing, or transmission/transaxle.

1. *Clutch linkage noise:* squeaks or scraping noises may be caused by dry or rusted linkage or cable mechanism, clutch fork pivot, or clutch pedal pivot. With the engine shut off, operate the clutch pedal and listen with a stethoscope to isolate the source. The parts causing the problem may only require lubrication; if worn, they may have to be replaced.

2. *Release bearing noise:* normally occurs only while the clutch pedal is depressed or held down. A dry or worn release bearing that is causing noise must be replaced.

3. *Pilot bearing noise:* occurs only when the crankshaft and clutch shaft turn at different speeds

during clutch disengagement. A dry or worn pilot bearing or bushing must be replaced.

4. *Transmission noise:* occurs only in neutral and stops when the clutch pedal is depressed. With the clutch disengaged, the transmission input shaft stops turning and the noise stops. The problem is usually the input shaft bearing at the front of the transmission/transaxle.

Pulsating Clutch Pedal

Slight up-and-down pedal movement is felt with light foot pressure on the pedal. Causes include a warped flywheel, pressure plate release levers bent or worn, or the clutch housing misaligned.

CLUTCH SERVICE PRECAUTIONS

SAFETY CAUTION: ASBESTOS DANGER: Some clutch facings are made with asbestos. Asbestos dust inhaled or ingested can cause cancer. Wear a respirator or use a vacuum or proper wash to remove dust. Avoid inhaling asbestos dust. Do not use an air hose to blow dust off clutch parts. Wash hands thoroughly after handling asbestos.

1. Avoid getting burned by hot clutch or exhaust parts.

2. Disconnect the battery to avoid accidental cranking of the engine during clutch or transmission work.

3. Support the vehicle safely before doing any work under the vehicle. Use hoist or safety stands (do not work under a vehicle supported by hydraulic jacks or bumper jacks).

4. Support the engine properly before transaxle, transmission, or cross-member removal.

5. Use proper transmission or transaxle jack for removal procedure.

6. Make sure that heavy clutch parts and flywheel do not drop during removal (injury and damage could result).

7. Support the transmission or transaxle properly to prevent clutch plate damage during removal and installation. The transmission must move straight back from the flywheel during removal to disengage the clutch shaft from the clutch. Allowing the weight of the transmission to hang on the input shaft and clutch disc will damage the clutch disc.

8. Do not use compressed air to blow out the clutch housing. Asbestos dust (from clutch facing) can cause cancer if inhaled. Use a proper vacuum cleaner. Use a filter for breathing protection.

9. Do not allow any grease, oil, or other contamination to come in contact with clutch friction surfaces. Even dirty hands can damage the coefficient of friction and cause clutch problems.

CLUTCH PROBLEM DIAGNOSIS

Clutch Booster Operating Check

To check the operation of the clutch booster, proceed as follows[1]:

1. Run the engine for one or two minutes, and then stop it.

2. Step on the clutch pedal several times with normal pressure. If the pedal depressed fully the first time but gradually becomes higher when depressed succeeding times, the booster is operating properly. If the pedal height remains unchanged, the booster is faulty.

3. With the engine stopped, step on the clutch pedal several times with the same foot pressure to make sure that the pedal height will not change. Then step on the clutch pedal and start the engine. If the pedal moves downward slightly, the booster is in good condition. If there is no change, the booster is faulty.

4. With the engine running, step on the clutch pedal and then stop the engine. Hold the pedal depressed for 30 seconds. If the pedal height does not change, the booster is in good condition. If the pedal rises, the booster is faulty.

If these three tests are okay, the booster performance can be determined as good. If one of these three tests is not okay at last, the check valve, vacuum hose, or booster will be faulty.

For detailed clutch problem diagnosis, refer to the following diagnostic charts:

Figure 4–20, Clutch Problem Diagnosis

Figure 4–21, Self-Adjusting Clutch Linkage Diagnosis

[1]Courtesy of Chrysler Corporation.

PROBLEM	POSSIBLE CAUSE	CORRECTION
Will Not Disengage (Pedal to the floor and hard to shift into reverse)	1. Air in the hydraulic system. 2. Master or secondary hydraulic cylinder seals worn. 3. Not enough pedal travel. 4. Release bearing worn or damaged. 5. Driven plate worn or damaged. 6. Clutch fork off the ball stud. 7. Driven plate binding. 8. Driven plate warped. Run-out more than 5.08 mm (0.20 in.).	1. Bleed and check for damage. 2. Repair. 3. Adjust the linkage or trim the pedal bumper. 4. Replace. 5. Replace. 6. Install correctly and lubricate. 7. Repair or replace the plate or clutch gear. 8. Replace.
Slipping	1. Driven plate friction pads worn or oil soaked. 2. Pressure plate or flywheel warped. 3. Diaphragm spring weak. 4. Driven plate overheated or not seated.	1. Replace. Check for leaks as needed. 2. Replace as needed. 3. Replace. 4. Allow to cool and make 30-40 normal starts - DO NOT OVERHEAT.
Grabbing (Chattering)	1. Engine mounts loose or damaged. 2. Driven plate friction pads oil soaked. 3. Pressure plate or flywheel warped. 4. Driven plate friction pad material burned or smeared onto the pressure plate or flywheel. 5. Clutch gear worn.	1. Tighten or replace. 2. Replace and check for leaks. 3. Replace as necessary. 4. Clean off or replace as needed. 5. Repair the transmission.
Rattling (Transmission Click)	1. Diaphragm spring weak. 2. Clutch fork loose or off the ball stud. 3. Driven plate springs weak or oil in the damper.	1. Replace the pressure plate. 2. Replace the retaining spring or install the fork correctly. 3. Replace and check for leaks as needed.
Release Bearing Noisy With The Clutch Engaged	1. Release bearing binding. 2. Clutch fork off the ball stud or loose spring tension. 3. Linkage return springs weak.	1. Clean, or replace if damaged, and lubricate. 2. Install, and lubricate. 3. Replace.
Noisy	1. Release bearing worn or damaged. 2. Clutch fork off the ball stud. 3. Pilot bearing loose.	1. Replace. 2. Install correctly and lubricate. 3. Replace. Refer to ENGINE (SEC. 6A).
Pedal Stays On The Floor When Disengaged	1. Release bearing binding. 2. Diaphragm spring weak.	1. Free up, or replace, and lubricate. 2. Replace the pressure plate.
Pedal Is Hard To Push	1. Hydraulic line blocked or crimped. 2. Master or secondary cylinders binding. 3. Driven plate worn.	1. Clean out or replace. 2. Repair or replace as needed. 3. Replace.
Squeaking	1. Ball stud not lubricated or incorrectly lubricated.	1. Lubricate with high temperature (wheel-bearing) grease.

FIGURE 4–20 Clutch problem diagnosis. (Courtesy of Chrysler Corporation.)

Figure 4–22, Continuous Running Release Bearing Diagnosis

Figure 4–23, Clutch Noise Diagnosis

Figure 4–24, Clutch Slip Diagnosis

Figure 4–25, Clutch Grab/Chatter Diagnosis

Figure 4–26, Improper Clutch Release Diagnosis

CONDITION	POSSIBLE SOURCE	ACTION
• Clutch Does Not Disengage Properly or Gears Clash While Shifting	• Improper clutch pedal travel. • Pawl does not fully engage due to missing, damaged, or weak pawl spring. • Improper clutch cable installed. • Damaged rubber insulators. • Loose pedal support attachments. • Carpet, sound deadener out of position. • Floor mats interfering with pedal travel. • Pawl binding due to entrapped sound absorber. • Broken components inside of clutch housing. • External linkage worn or damaged.	• Install new spring. • Install correct cable. • Correct insulators. • Loosen and retighten to specification. • Position correctly. • Reposition floor mats. • Remove contamination and free up pawl. • Replace or service. Refer to Section 16-02. • Service or replace linkage parts as required.
• Pedal Makes Racheting Noise While Traveling To or From Floor	• Teeth stripped on pawl or quadrant.	• Replace quadrant, pawl and pawl spring.
• Pedal Travels To Floor With No Effort or Noise	• Pawl does not engage quadrant due to missing spring. • Broken clutch cable. • Damaged or loose components inside of clutch housing.	• Install spring. • Replace clutch cable. • Replace or service. Refer to Section 16-02.
• Clutch Squeaks or Scrubs When the Pedal is in Motion—Noise Originating in Engine Compartment	• Clutch release linkage and/or cable—lack of lubrication binding, interference, worn or kinked. • Lack of lubrication on the clutch release lever to release bearing contact. • Lack of lubricant in the clutch release bearing bore and the release bearing guide. • Flywheel housing out of alignment. • Damaged release bearing.	• Lubricate with Long-Life Lubricant C1AZ-19590-BA or equivalent. Service as required. • Remove transaxle and release bearing. Lubricate with Long-Life Lubricant C1AZ-19590-BA or equivalent, accordingly. • Lubricate with Long-Life Lubricant C1AZ-19590-BA or equivalent, accordingly. • Replace or service. Refer to Section 16-02.

FIGURE 4–21 Self-adjusting clutch linkage diagnosis. (Courtesy of Ford Motor Company.)

DIAGNOSIS OF SUSPECTED RELEASE BEARING NOISE — CONTINUOUS RUNNING TYPE

Chirp, squeak, and clatter, with clutch pedal up, can be caused by insufficient bearing pre-load, out-of-plane pressure plate fingers or transmission, or a worn or damaged release bearing. The following procedures will isolate the cause:

ACTION	RESULT	CONCLUSION	NEXT STEP
With engine idling and transaxle in neutral, depress clutch pedal to the floor.	Still noisy	Release bearing is damaged or worn	Replace bearing
	Noise gone	Release bearing is OK	Proceed to next action
Disconnect clutch cable from release lever and move lever away from cable to disengage bearing from pressure plate fingers.	Still noisy	Noise is from transaxle	Refer to section on transaxle diagnosis
	Noise gone	Transmission is OK	Proceed to next action
Apply 5 lb. load to release lever at cable junction in direction of cable—pull to pre-load bearing.	Still noisy	Binding release lever pivot	Lube/free pivot/bushing
		Pressure plate fingers out of plane	Note I
	Noise gone	Clutch control system damaged	Note II

I. Binding pivots will reduce bearing pre-load, resulting in possible scrubbing between pressure plate fingers and bearing face. Out-of-plane fingers will cause oscillation of the release lever, resulting in noise if pivot is dry. Lever plane is affected by pressure plate mounting bolt torque. Assure bolts are properly tightened.
II. Service/replace as necessary any sticky or binding clutch control components.

FIGURE 4–22 Continuous-running clutch release bearing diagnosis. (Courtesy of Ford Motor Company.)

CLUTCH NOISE

	Condition Found	Cause	Correction
1.	Clutch components damaged or worn out prematurely.	Incorrect or sub-standard clutch parts.	Replace with parts of correct type and quality.
2.	Pilot bearing seized or bearing rollers are brinneled.	a) Bearing cocked or scored during installation. b) Bearing not lubricated prior to installation. c) Bearing defect. d) Clutch misalignment.	a), b), c) Replace bearing. Be sure it is properly seated and lubricated before installing clutch. d) Check and correct misalignment caused by excessive runout of flywheel, disc, or cover. Replace input shaft if bearing hub is damaged.
3.	Loose components.	Attaching bolts loose at flywheel, cover, or clutch housing.	Tighten bolts to specified torque. Replace any clutch bolts that are damaged.
4.	Components appear overheated. Hub of disc cracked or torsion damper springs are distorted or broken.	Frequent high load, full throttle operation.	Replace parts as needed. Alert driver to condition causes.
5.	Contact surface of concentric bearing damaged.	a) Clutch cover incorrect, or release fingers are bent or distorted causing damage. b) Concentric bearing defect. c) Concentric bearing misaligned.	a) Replace clutch cover and concentric bearing. b) Replace concentric bearing. c) Check and correct runout of clutch components. Also check input shaft and bearing condition. Replace shaft and bearing if worn or damaged.
6.	Concentric bearing is noisy.	Concentric bearing defect.	Replace concentric bearing.
7.	Clutch pedal squeak.	a) Pivot pin loose. b) Pedal bushings worn out or cracked.	Tighten pivot pin. Replace bushings if worn or damaged. Lubricate pin and bushings with silicone base lubricator chassis grease.

FIGURE 4–23 (Courtesy of Chrysler Corporation.)

CLUTCH SLIPS

Condition Found	Cause	Correction
1. Disc facing worn out.	a) Normal wear. b) Driver frequently "rides" (slips) clutch. Results in rapid wear overheating. c) Insufficient clutch cover diaphragm spring tension.	Replace clutch disc. Also replace cover if spring is weak or pressure plate surface is damaged.
2. Clutch disc facing contaminated with oil, grease, or clutch fluid.	a) Leak at rear main seal or at transmission input shaft seal. b) Excessive amount of grease applied to input shaft splines. c) Road splash, water entering housing. d) Slave cylinder leaking.	a), b), c), d) Replace leaking seals. Apply less grease to input shaft splines. Replace clutch disc (do not clean and reuse). Clean clutch cover and reuse only if cover is in good condition. Replace slave cylinder if leaking.
3. Clutch is running partially disengaged.	Release bearing sticking–binding. Does not return to normal running position.	Verify that bearing is actually binding, then replace bearing and transmission front bearing retainer if sleeve surface is damaged.
4. Flywheel height incorrect.	Flywheel surface improperly machined. Too much stock removed or surface is tapered.	Replace flywheel.
5. Wrong disc or pressure plate installed.	Incorrect parts order or model number.	Replace with correct parts. Compare old and new parts before installation.
6. Clutch disc, cover and/or diaphragm spring, warped, distorted.	a) Rough handling (impact) bent cover, spring, or disc. b) Incorrect bolt tightening sequence and method caused warped cover.	Install new disc or cover as needed. Follow installation/tightening instructions.
7. Facing on flywheel side of disc torn, gouged, worn.	Flywheel surface scored and nicked.	Reduce scores and nicks by sanding or surface grinding. Replace flywheel if scores–nicks are deeper than .002-.004 inch.
8. Clutch disc facing burnt (charred). Flywheel and cover pressure plate surfaces heavily glazed.	a) Frequent operation under high loads or hard acceleration conditions. b) Driver frequently "rides" (slips) clutch. Results in rapid wear and overheating of disc and cover.	Scuff sand flywheel. Replace clutch cover and disc. Alert driver to problem cause.

FIGURE 4–24 (Courtesy of Chrysler Corporation.)

CLUTCH GRAB/CHATTER

Condition Found	Cause	Correction
1. Clutch disc facing covered with oil, grease, or clutch fluid.	a) Oil leak at rear main or input shaft seal. b) Too much grease applied to splines or disc and input shaft.	a) Correct leak and replace disc (do not clean and reuse the disc). b) Apply lighter grease coating to splines and replace disc (do not clean and reuse the disc).
2. Clutch disc and/or cover warped, or disc facings exhibit unusual wear or appear to be wrong type.	Incorrect or substandard parts.	Replace disc and/or cover with correct parts.
3. Clutch master or slave cylinder plunger dragging–binding.	a) Master or slave cylinder components worn or corroded.	a) Replace both cylinders as assembly (and reservoir).
4. No fault found with clutch components.	a) Problem actually related to suspension or driveline component. b) Engine related problem.	a) Further diagnosis required. Check engine/transmission mounts, propeller shafts and U-joints, tires, suspension attaching parts and other driveline components as needed. b) Check EFI and igniton systems.
5. Partial engagement of clutch disc (one side worn–opposite side glazed and lightly worn).	a) Clutch pressure plate position setting incorrect or modified. b) Clutch cover, spring, or release fingers bent, distorted (rough handling, improper assembly). c) Clutch disc damaged or distorted. d) Clutch misalignment.	a) Replace clutch cover and disc. b) Replace clutch cover and disc. c) Replace disc. d) Check alignment and runout of flywheel, disc, or cover and/or clutch housing. Correct as necessary.

FIGURE 4–25 (Courtesy of Chrysler Corporation.)

IMPROPER CLUTCH RELEASE

Condition Found	Cause	Correction
1. Clutch disc warped.	New disc not checked for axial runout before installation.	Replace disc. Be sure runout of new disc is less than .5 mm (.020 in.).
2. Clutch disc binds on input shaft splines.	a) Clutch disc hub splines damaged during installation. b) Input shaft splines rough, damaged. c) Corrosion, rust formations on splines of disc and input shaft.	Clean, smooth and lubricate disc and shaft spines. Replace disc and/or input shaft if splines are severely damaged.
3. Clutch disc rusted to flywheel and/or pressure plate.	Occurs in vehicles stored, or not driven for extended periods of time.	Remove clutch cover and disc. Sand rusted surfaces clean with 180 grit paper.
4. Clutch disc facing sticks to flywheel.	Vacuum may form in pockets over rivet heads in clutch disc. Occurs as clutch cools down after use.	Drill 1/16 inch diameter hole through rivets and scuff sand disc facing with 180 grit paper.
5. Clutch disc too thick.	Wrong disc installed.	Replace disc.
6. Pilot bearing seized.	a) Bearing cocked during installation. b) Bearing defective. c) Bearing not lubricated. d) Clutch misalignment.	Lubricate and install new bearing. Check and correct any misalignment.
7. Clutch will not disengage properly.	a) Low fluid level in cutch master cylinder. b) Air in clutch hydraulic system. c) Clutch cover loose. d) Wrong clutch disc. e) Disc bent, distorted during installation. f) Clutch cover diaphragm spring bent or warped during transmission installation. g) Clutch disc installed backwards.	a) Top off cylinder and check for leaks. b) Bleed and refill system. c) Tighten bolts. d) Install correct disc. e) Replace disc. f) Replace cover. g) Remove and reinstall disc correctly. Be sure disc side marked "to flywheel" is actually toward flywheel.

FIGURE 4–26 (Courtesy of Chrysler Corporation.)

CLUTCH REMOVAL

To remove the clutch disc, pressure plate, clutch fork, and release bearing, the transmission/transaxle must first be removed. Refer to Chapter 6 and the service manual for this procedure. After transmission/transaxle removal, the typical procedure for clutch removal is as follows:

1. Remove the release bearing assembly.

2. Mark both the flywheel and pressure plate cover with a center punch to ensure correct reassembly if the pressure plate is to be used again.

3. Loosen the pressure plate attaching bolts progressively a little at a time until all spring pressure has been relieved.

4. Remove the bolts (be sure to have a firm grip on the heavy assembly); then remove the pressure plate and clutch disc **(Figure 4–27)**.

INSPECTING CLUTCH PARTS

Carefully inspect all the parts as follows (see **Figures 4–28 to 4–39**).

1. Check to see if the clutch disc was installed with the "flywheel side" toward the flywheel.

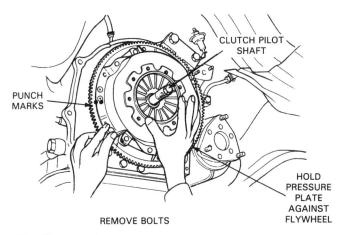

PUNCH MARKS

CLUTCH PILOT SHAFT

HOLD PRESSURE PLATE AGAINST FLYWHEEL

REMOVE BOLTS

FIGURE 4–27 With the transmission/transaxle removed, center-punch mark the pressure plate cover and flywheel for assembly reference. Insert a clutch pilot shaft or arbor to prevent the disc from falling out while loosening and removing the pressure plate bolts. (Courtesy of Ford Motor Company.)

2. Check the flywheel bolt torque. If the bolts are loose, replace them. Use thread lock sealer to secure the new bolts and tighten to specifications.

3. Check the pilot bearing. Replace the bearing if brinnelled, seized, or noisy. Lube the bearing before installation.

4. Check the transmission input shaft. The clutch disc must slide freely on the shaft splines. Lightly grease the splines before installation. Replace the shaft if the splines or pilot bearing hub are damaged.

5. Check the crankshaft flange (if the flywheel is removed). Be sure that the flange is clean and that the flywheel bolt threads are in good condition.

6. Check the rear main seal if the clutch disc and cover were oil covered. Replace the seal if necessary.

7. Check the clutch disc facing. Replace the disc if the facing is charred, scored, flaking off, or worn. Also check runout of the new disc. The runout should not exceed 0.02 in. (0.5 mm) maximum.

8. Check the flywheel condition. Scuff sand the flywheel face to remove glaze. Afterward, clean the surface with a wax and grease remover. Replace the flywheel if severely scored, worn, or cracked. Secure the flywheel with new bolts (if removed). Do not reuse old bolts. Use Lock and Seal on bolts.

9. Check the clutch housing bolts. Tighten if loose. Be sure that housing is fully seated on engine block. Also be sure that locating dowels are in place.

10. Check the flywheel face runout if chatter or grab was encountered. Runout should not exceed 0.003 in. (0.08 mm).

11. Tighten the clutch cover bolts two or three threads at a time, alternately and evenly (in a diagonal pattern), to the specified torque. Failure to do so could warp the cover.

12. Check the clutch cover. Replace if warped, cracked, or bent. Be sure that the cover is the correct size and properly aligned on the disc and flywheel.

13. Check the clutch cover diaphragm spring and release fingers. Replace the cover if the spring or fingers are bent, warped, broken, or cracked.

14. Inspect the concentric bearing hydraulic lines (hydraulic release bearing). Be sure that the connections are tight and not cross threaded. Replace the bearing assembly if the lines are loose or leaking.

15. The transmission input shaft bearing will cause noise, chatter, or improper release if damaged. Check its condition before installing the transmission.

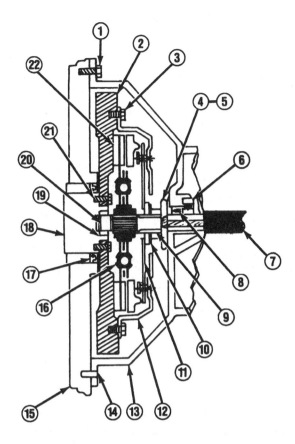

9   Inspect release bearing slide surface of trans. front bearing retainer. Surface should be smooth, free of nicks, scores. Replace retainer if necessary. Lubricate slide surface before installing release bearing.

10   Do not replace release bearing unless actually faulty. Replace bearing only if seized, noisy, or damaged.

11   Check clutch cover diaphragm spring and release fingers. Replace cover if spring or fingers are bent, warped, broken, cracked. Do not tamper with factory spring setting as clutch problems will result.

12   Check condition of clutch cover. Replace clutch cover if plate surface is deeply scored, warped, worn, or cracked. Be sure cover is correct size and properly aligned on disc and flywheel.

13   Inspect clutch housing. Be sure bolts are tight. Replace housing if damaged.

14   Verify that housing alignment dowels are in position before installing housing.

15   Clean engine block surface before installing clutch housing. Dirt, grime can produce misalignment.

16   Make sure side of clutch disc marked "flywheel side" is toward flywheel.

17   Check rear main seal if clutch disc and cover were oil covered. Replace seal if necessary.

18   Check crankshaft flange (if flywheel is removed). Be sure flange is clean and flywheel bolt threads are in good condition.

19   Check pilot bearing. Replace bearing if damaged. Lube with Mopar high temp. bearing grease before installation.

20   Check transmission input shaft. Disc must slide freely on shaft splines. Lightly grease splines before installation. Replace shaft if splines or pilot bearing hub are damaged.

21   Check flywheel bolt torque. If bolts are loose, replace them. Use Mopar Lock N'Seal to secure new bolts.

22   Check clutch disc facing. Replace disc if facing is charred, scored, flaking off, or worn. Also check runout of new disc. Runout should not exceed 0.5 mm (0.02 in.).

1   Check clutch housing bolts. Tighten if loose. Be sure housing is fully seated on engine block.

2   Check flywheel. Scuff sand face to remove glaze. Clean surface with wax and grease remover. Replace flywheel if severely scored, worn or cracked. Secure flywheel with new bolts (if removed). Do not reuse old bolts. Use Mopar Lock N'Seal on bolts.

3   Tighten clutch cover bolts 2-3 threads at a time, alternately and evenly (in a diagonal pattern) to specified torque. Failure to do so could warp the cover.

4   Check release fork. Replace fork if bent or worn. Make sure pivot and bearing contact surfaces are lubricated.

5   Check release fork pivot (in housing). Be sure pivot is secure and ball end is lubricated.

6   Transmission input shaft bearing will cause noise, chatter, or improper release if damaged. Check condition before installing transmission.

7   Check slave cylinder. Replace it if leaking. Be sure cylinder is properly secured in housing and cylinder piston is seated in release fork.

8   Check input shaft seal if clutch cover and disc were oil covered. Replace seal if worn, or cut.

FIGURE 4–28 Clutch inspection points. (Courtesy of Chrysler Corporation.)

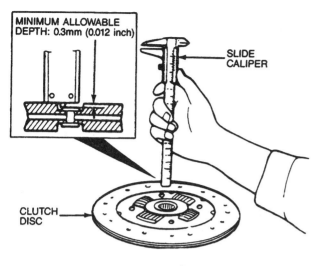

MINIMUM ALLOWABLE
DEPTH: 0.3mm (0.012 inch)

SLIDE
CALIPER

CLUTCH
DISC

FIGURE 4–29 Measuring clutch facing thickness (top) and disc runout (bottom). (Courtesy of Ford Motor Company.)

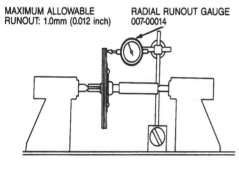

MAXIMUM ALLOWABLE
RUNOUT: 1.0mm (0.012 inch)

RADIAL RUNOUT GAUGE
007-00014

EXCESSIVE WEAR

NORMAL FINGER WEAR

EXCESSIVE FINGER WEAR

EXCESSIVE WEAR

EXCESSIVE FINGER WEAR

BROKEN OR BENT FINGERS

EXCESSIVE SCORING

CLUTCH CHATTER

FIGURE 4–30 Clutch pressure plate inspection points. (Courtesy of Ford Motor Company.)

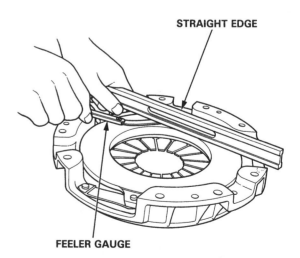

STRAIGHT EDGE

FEELER GAUGE

FIGURE 4–31 Measure pressure plate warpage at three positions. (Courtesy of Ford Motor Company.)

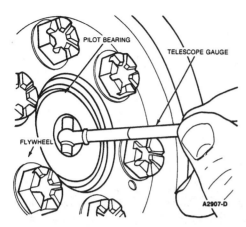

FIGURE 4–32 Measuring pilot bushing ID. Replace bushing if wear is excessive. (Courtesy of Ford Motor Company.)

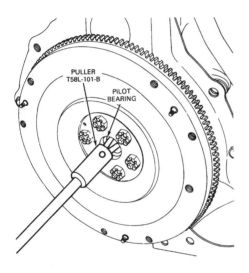

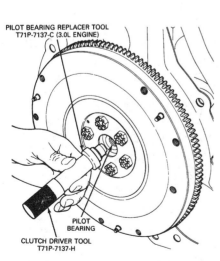

FIGURE 4–33 Use puller to remove pilot bushing (top). Drive new bushing in to specified depth with bushing driver. (Courtesy of Ford Motor Company.)

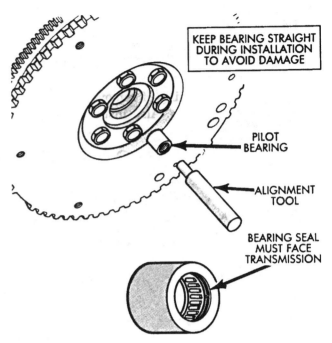

FIGURE 4–34 Clutch pilot bearing installation. (Courtesy of Chrysler Corporation.)

16. Check the input shaft seal if the clutch cover and disc were oil covered. Replace the seal if worn or cut.

17. Check the concentric bearing mounting pin and retaining nut (hydraulic release bearing). Never reuse an old retaining nut; use a new part only. Be sure that the pin is secure and in good condition.

18. Do not replace the hydraulic concentric bearing unless actually faulty. Replace the bearing only if it leaks, is seized, or is damaged.

19. Inspect the clutch housing. Be sure that the locating dowels are in position and the bolts are tight. Replace the housing if cracked or damaged. If clutch problems occurred, check the runout to be sure that the housing is square with the flywheel and transmission input shaft.

20. Check the condition of the pressure plate surface. Replace the clutch cover if the plate surface is deeply scored, warped, worn, or cracked.

CLUTCH INSTALLATION

1. Use a clutch aligning arbor or suitable dummy shaft to assemble the clutch disc and pressure plate to the flywheel **(Figure 4–40).** (Make sure that the

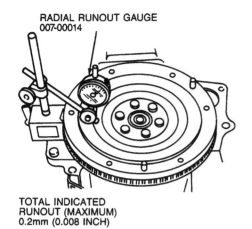

RADIAL RUNOUT GAUGE
007-00014

TOTAL INDICATED
RUNOUT (MAXIMUM)
0.2mm (0.008 INCH)

FIGURE 4–35 Measuring flywheel runout. (Courtesy of Ford Motor Company.)

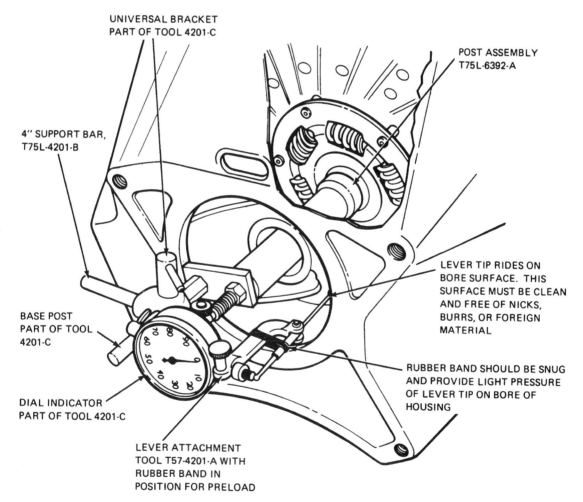

UNIVERSAL BRACKET
PART OF TOOL 4201-C

POST ASSEMBLY
T75L-6392-A

4" SUPPORT BAR,
T75L-4201-B

LEVER TIP RIDES ON
BORE SURFACE. THIS
SURFACE MUST BE CLEAN
AND FREE OF NICKS,
BURRS, OR FOREIGN
MATERIAL

BASE POST
PART OF TOOL
4201-C

RUBBER BAND SHOULD BE SNUG
AND PROVIDE LIGHT PRESSURE
OF LEVER TIP ON BORE OF
HOUSING

DIAL INDICATOR
PART OF TOOL 4201-C

LEVER ATTACHMENT
TOOL T57-4201-A WITH
RUBBER BAND IN
POSITION FOR PRELOAD

FIGURE 4–36 Measuring clutch housing bore run-out with dial indicator. Housing, clutch shaft, pilot bearing, and transmission must be in concentric alignment for proper clutch operation. (Courtesy of Ford Motor Company.)

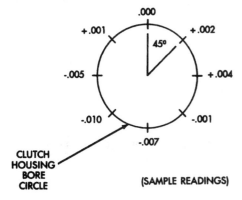

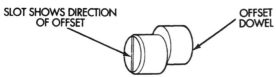

DOWEL SELECTION	
TIR VALUE	**OFFSET DOWEL REQUIRED**
0.011 – 0.021 inch	0.007 inch
0.022 – 0.035 inch	0.014 inch
0.036 – 0.052 inch	0.021 inch

FIGURE 4–37 Clutch housing bore measurement points and sample readings (top). Offset dowel selection chart (bottom). (Courtesy of Chrysler Corporation.)

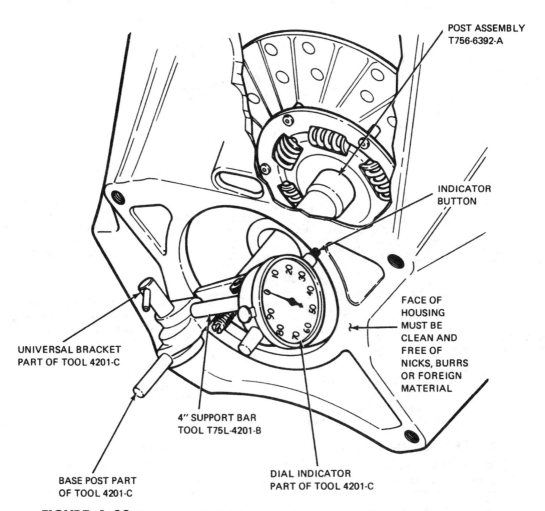

FIGURE 4–38 Measuring clutch housing face run-out. Transmission mounting surface must be at 90 degrees to clutch shaft centerline for proper shaft and clutch alignment. (Courtesy of Ford Motor Company.)

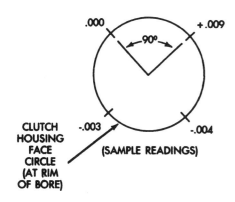

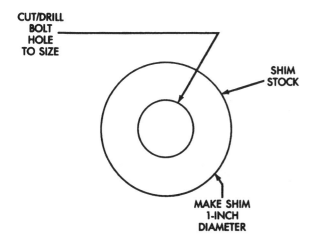

FIGURE 4–39 (Courtesy of Chrysler Corporation.)

proper side of the disc faces the flywheel.) Tighten the bolts progressively to the specified torque.

2. Install the release bearing (lubricate interior of sleeve if recommended; **Figure 4–41**).

3. Install the transaxle or transmission, cross member, and drive line or half-shafts as applicable.

4. Adjust the pedal height, clutch linkage, and transmission linkage as specified in the manufacturer's manual **(Figure 4–42).**

5. Check the transmission lubricant level and correct if required.

6. Road test the performance of the clutch, making sure that there is sufficient pedal travel and free play for proper clutch apply and release and good transmission shifting.

HYDRAULIC CLUTCH CONTROL SERVICE

The hydraulic clutch master cylinder, sleeve cylinder, and hydraulic line are serviced in much the same way

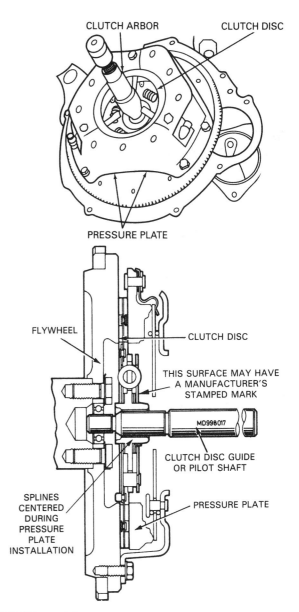

FIGURE 4–40 Use clutch aligning arbor to center the clutch disc while tightening the pressure plate cover bolts. [Courtesy of Ford Motor Company (top) and Chrysler Corporation (bottom).]

as brake hydraulic system parts. The units are disassembled and cleaned. The master cylinder and slave cylinder may have to be honed to remove minor imperfections. Repair kits are installed with new cups and seals. After installing the master cylinder, slave cylinder, and hydraulic line, the master cylinder is filled with fluid and air is bled from the slave cylinder bleeder **(Figure 4–43).** Finally, the linkage between the slave cylinder and clutch fork is adjusted to provide the required clutch pedal free play (see **Figure 4–44**).

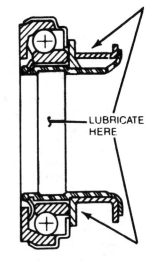

FIGURE 4–41 Lubricate release bearing hub ID and fork groove before installation. (Courtesy of General Motors Corporation.)

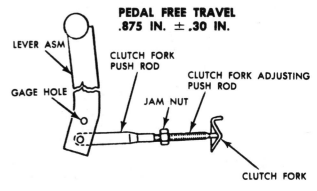

FIGURE 4–42 Typical mechanical linkage adjustment. (Courtesy of General Motors Corporation.)

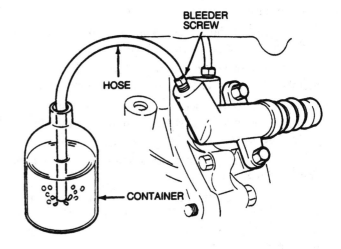

FIGURE 4–43 Bleed any air out of the hydraulic clutch control system. (Courtesy of Ford Motor Company.)

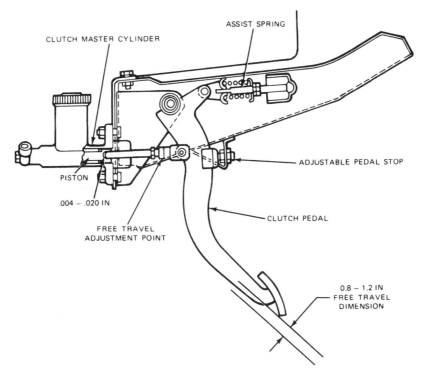

FIGURE 4–44 Hydraulic clutch master cylinder pushrod adjustment. (Courtesy of Ford Motor Company.)

REVIEW QUESTIONS

1. Name the seven major components of an automotive clutch.

2. The _____ and _____ _____ drive the clutch disc.

3. The clutch disc is designed with _____ springs to aid in gradual clutch engagement and _____ springs to absorb _____ vibrations from the crankshaft.

4. The pilot bearing or bushing supports the front of the _____ _____ shaft.

5. The clutch facings are _____ to steel segments of the clutch disc.

6. Clutch facings may contain _____, which is heat resistant.

7. Clutch pedal free play _____ as a result of linkage wear and _____ as a result of clutch lining wear.

8. Clutch control linkage may be the _____ or the _____ type.

9. The clutch start switch allows engine starting only when the clutch pedal is _____.

10. If the clutch fails to release properly, the _____ could be out of adjustment, the clutch disc could be _____ to the flywheel, the clutch disc could be _____, or the clutch shaft pilot could be seized in the _____ _____.

11. List five possible causes of clutch slippage.

12. A pulsating clutch pedal could be caused by a warped _____, bent or worn pressure plate _____ _____, or misaligned _____ _____.

13. Clutch release bearing noise normally occurs only while the clutch pedal is _____ or _____.

14. True or false? What appears to be clutch chatter may be caused by loose motor mounts.

15. True or false? Inhaling asbestos dust can cause cancer.

16. When installing a clutch pressure plate, use an _____ _____ to center the clutch disc.

17. When tightening clutch pressure plate mounting bolts, tighten them only _____ or _____ threads at a time in an _____ pattern to specified _____.

18. After completing clutch installation, the _____ _____ must be adjusted to _____.

TEST QUESTIONS

1. Clutch capacity is determined by
   a. linkage length, clutch diameter, surface area, apply pressure, and coefficient of friction
   b. clutch diameter, pedal leverage, surface area, and apply pressure
   c. apply pressure, clutch diameter, surface area, and coefficient of friction
   d. coefficient of friction, surface area, pedal pressure, and clutch diameter

2. Clutch assembly-driven members are the
   a. disc and clutch shaft
   b. pressure plate and clutch shaft
   c. flywheel and clutch shaft
   d. pressure plate and flywheel

3. The clutch is operated by
   a. a cable
   b. a system of rods
   c. a hydraulic system
   d. any of the above

4. Clutch slippage may be caused by
   a. no pedal free play
   b. weak clutch springs
   c. contaminated clutch disc
   d. any of the above

5. A clutch failing to release may be caused by
   a. incorrect linkage adjustment
   b. weak clutch springs
   c. no pedal free play
   d. a faulty pilot bearing

6. The clutch pressure plate may have
   a. coil or leaf springs
   b. leaf springs or a diaphragm spring
   c. a diaphragm spring or torsion bars
   d. coil springs or a diaphragm spring

7. Clutch pedal free play provides clearance between the
   a. pressure plate and flywheel
   b. release fingers and pressure plate
   c. flywheel and clutch cover
   d. release bearing and release fingers

8. The clutch start switch
   a. ensures positive clutch engagement
   b. prevents clutch lockup
   c. prevents starting the engine when the pedal is released
   d. avoids starting too soon

9. "Clutch drag may be caused by incorrect linkage adjustment." "Clutch slippage may be caused by incorrect linkage adjustment." Which of these statements is correct?
   a. the first
   b. the second
   c. both are correct
   d. both are incorrect

10. Technician A says that a warped pressure plate or flywheel can cause clutch chatter. Technician B says that clutch chatter may be caused by loose motor mounts. Who is right?
    a. technician A
    b. technician B
    c. both are right
    d. both are wrong

11. Flywheel face runout should not exceed
    a. 0.3 in. (7.6 mm)
    b. 0.03 in. (0.76 mm)
    c. 0.003 in. (0.076 mm)
    d. 0.33 in. (8.4 mm)

12. The hydraulic clutch master cylinder uses
    a. power steering fluid
    b. brake fluid
    c. ATF
    d. none of the above

◆ CHAPTER 5 ◆

MANUAL TRANSMISSION AND TRANSAXLE PRINCIPLES

INTRODUCTION

Front-engine, rear-wheel-drive vehicles use a transmission and differential to provide the various gear ratios. Front-wheel-drive vehicles use a transaxle that combines the transmission and differential in a single unit. The operating principles of the gears, shafts, bearings, and shift mechanisms in manual transmissions and manual transaxles are basically the same. The operation of the differential section of the transaxle is the same as that of a rear-wheel-drive axle differential, with the exception of the final drive gears. This chapter discusses these principles and the various transmission and transaxle designs and their operation (see **Figures 5–1** and **5–2**.)

LEARNING OBJECTIVES

After completing this chapter, you should be able to:

- Describe the functions of a transmission and a transaxle.
- List the major components of a manual transmission and a manual transaxle.
- Describe the operating principles of manual transmission/transaxle gears.
- Describe the operation of a manual transmission and a manual transaxle.

- Trace the powerflow through a manual transmission and a manual transaxle.
- Describe the different types of manual transmissions and transaxles.
- Describe the operation of the differential section of a manual transaxle.
- Describe the benefits and operation of a transmission/transaxle overdrive gear ratio.

TERMS YOU SHOULD KNOW

Look for these terms as you study this chapter and learn what they mean.

input shaft	bearings
clutch shaft	case
countershaft	final drive
countergears	differential
output shaft	spur gear
mainshaft	helical gear
output gears	gear reduction
synchronizers	overdrive
shift forks	direct drive
shift linkage	gear ratio
shift lever	constant mesh

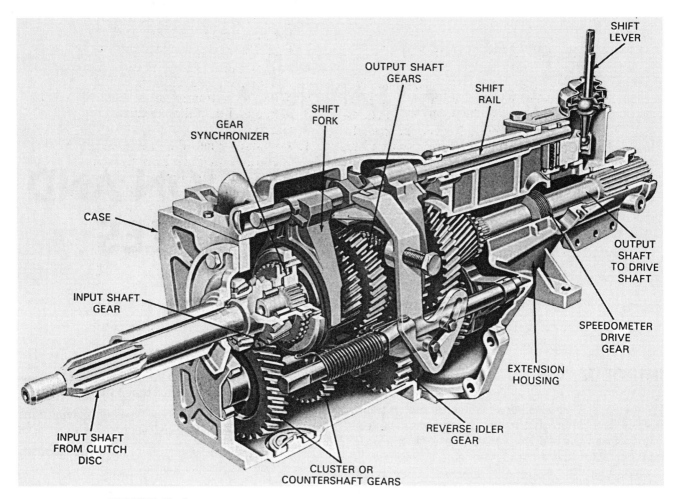

FIGURE 5–1 Typical five-speed transmission used on rear-wheel-drive vehicles. (Courtesy of Ford Motor Company.)

drive

coast

backlash

climbing

synchronizer hub

synchronizer sleeve

synchronizer inserts

blocking rings

electronic gear shifing

speedometer drive gear

backup light switch

MANUAL TRANSMISSION AND TRANSAXLE FUNCTIONS AND COMPONENTS

The automotive engine does not have enough power to put a car into motion without the use of gear reductions provided by the transmission or transaxle and differential. Gear reductions allow the engine to start

moving the car slowly and then shift into higher gears as speed increases and power requirements are less. The functions of the manual transmission and transaxle are:

1. To provide several gear ratios (power and speed combinations) to allow the driver to obtain the acceleration and fuel economy desired.

2. To provide a reverse gear to move the car backward.

3. To provide the means for the driver to select the gear (forward or reverse) and gear ratio desired for all operating conditions.

4. The transaxle provides differential action in addition to the transmission functions and a final gear reduction not found on manual transmissions.

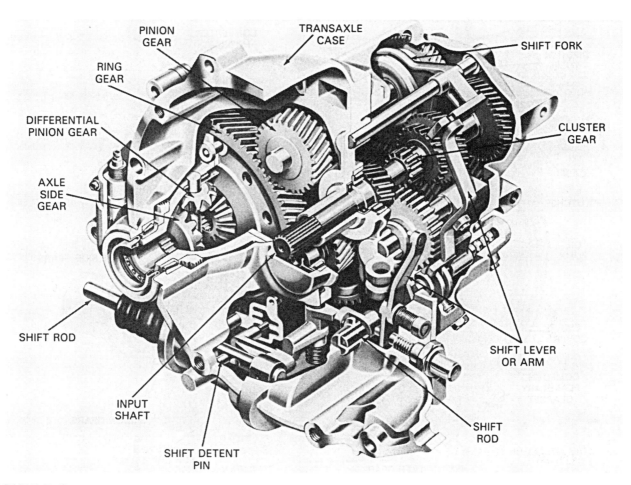

FIGURE 5–2 Five-speed manual transaxle used on front-wheel-drive car. (Courtesy of Ford Motor Company.)

The following parts are used in transmissions and transaxles (**Figures 5–3** and **5–4**):

1. *Input shaft* (also called clutch shaft): driven by the clutch disc, the input shaft and input gear drive all the other gears

2. *Countershaft* (also called clustergear shaft): holds countergears in position; countergears mesh with input gear and output gears

3. *Countergears* (also called clustergear): mounted on the countershaft, they transmit power from the input gear to output gears and provide a gear reduction

4. *Output shaft* (also called mainshaft): holds output gears that are meshed with countergears and reverse idler gear

5. *Output gears* (also called mainshaft gears): mounted on output shaft; can be connected and disconnected from the output shaft; are in mesh with countergears and the reverse idler

6. *Synchronizers:* used to make gear shifting easier, they also lock gears to shafts

7. *Shift forks:* used to shift synchronizers or gears

8. *Shift linkage:* connects shift lever to shift forks

9. *Shift lever:* driver-operated lever used to shift gears

10. *Bearings:* Ball, roller, needle, and bushing-type bearings used to support gears on shafts and shafts in transmission or transaxle case

11. *Case:* one-, two-, or three-piece die cast aluminum housing that contains and supports shafts, gears, synchronizers, and lubricant

12. *Final drive pinion* (transaxle only): final output gear that drives differential ring gear

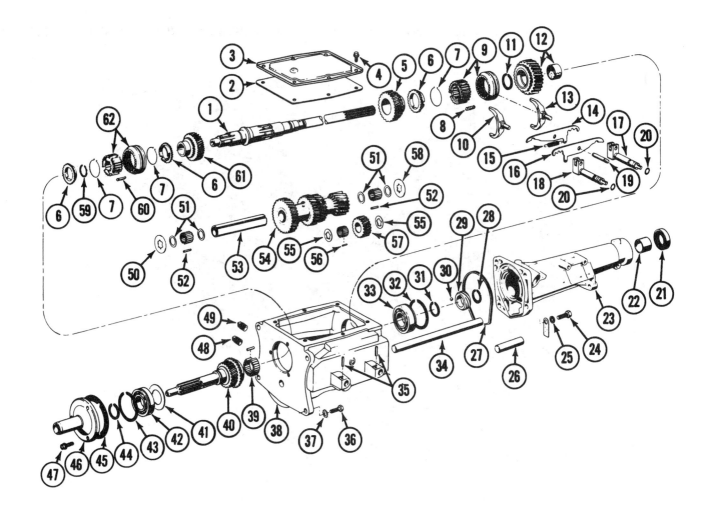

1. MAIN SHAFT
2. GASKET
3. CASE COVER
4. BOLT
5. FIRST GEAR
6. CLUTCH FRICTION RING SET
7. SHAFT PLATE RETAINING SPRING
8. CLUTCH SHAFT FIRST AND REVERSE SHIFT PLATE
9. FIRST AND REVERSE CLUTCH ASSEMBLY
10. SHIFTER SECOND AND HIGH FORK
11. CLUTCH FIRST AND REVERSE GEAR SNAP RING
12. REVERSE GEAR
13. SHIFTER FIRST AND REVERSE R FORK
14. SHIFTER INTERLOCK FIRST AND REVERSE LEVER
15. INTERLOCK POPPET SPRING
16. SHIFTER INTERLOCK SECOND AND THIRD LEVER
17. SHIFTER FORK FIRST AND REVERSE SHAFT
18. SHIFTER FORK SECOND AND THIRD SHAFT
19. SHIFTER FORK INTERLOCK LEVER PIVOT PIN

20. SHIFTER FORK SHAFT SEAL
21. OIL SEAL
22. BUSHING
23. EXTENSION HOUSING
24. BOLT
25. LOCK WASHER
26. IDLER GEAR SHAFT
27. GASKET
28. SPEEDOMETER DRIVE GEAR RING
29. SPEEDOMETER DRIVE GEAR
30. SPEEDOMETER DRIVE GEAR BALL
31. REAR BEARING LOCKRING
32. REAR BEARING LOCKRING
33. REAR BEARING
34. COUNTERSHAFT
35. SHIFTER FORK RETAINING PIN
36. BOLT
37. LOCK WASHER
38. CASE
39. SPLINE SHAFT PILOT BEARING ROLLER
40. CLUTCH SHAFT
41. FRONT BEARING WASHER
42. FRONT BEARING
43. FRONT BEARING LOCKRING
44. FRONT BEARING SNAP RING
45. GASKET

46. FRONT BEARING CAP
47. BOLT
48. DRAIN PLUG
49. FILLER PIPE PLUG
50. FRONT COUNTERSHAFT GEAR THRUST WASHER
51. COUNTERSHAFT GEAR BEARING ROLLER WASHER
52. COUNTERSHAFT GEAR BEARING ROLLER
53. COUNTERSHAFT GEAR ROLLER BEARING SPACER
54. COUNTERSHAFT GEAR
55. REVERSE IDLER GEAR BEARING ROLLER WASHER
56. REVERSE IDLER GEAR BEARING ROLLER
57. REVERSE IDLER GEAR
58. REAR COUNTERSHAFT THRUST
59. CLUTCH SECOND AND THIRD SNAP RING
60. CLUTCH SHAFT SECOND AND THIRD SHIFT PLATE
61. SECOND AND THIRD CLUTCH ASSEMBLY
62. SECOND GEAR

FIGURE 5–3 Three-speed manual transmission components. (Courtesy of Chrysler Corporation.)

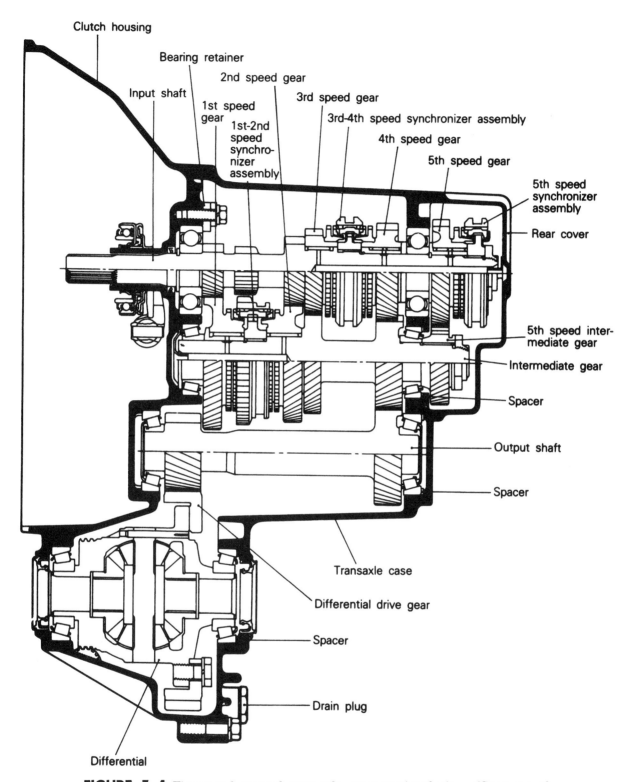

FIGURE 5–4 Five-speed manual transaxle cross-sectional view. (Courtesy of Chrysler Corporation.)

13. *Final drive ring gear* (transaxle only): attached to differential case and driven by final drive pinion

14. *Differential* (transaxle only): provides driving torque to both front-drive axles and provides differential action for turning corners

GEAR PRINCIPLES

Gears are round metal wheels with teeth around the circumference. Gears are used to drive other gears or shafts. Gears are classified as input (drive), output (driven), or idler gears. Gears may have straight-cut teeth (spur gears) or angled teeth (helical gears) **(Figure 5–5).** Gears are mounted on shafts and may be free to turn on the shaft or are connected to the shaft by splines or keys. Gears are used to reduce output speed (gear reduction), increase output speed (overdrive), or provide direct drive (input and output speeds the same). Reducing the output speed provides a torque increase. Increasing the output speed results in reduced torque output. The ratio between the input and output gears determines the output speed and torque output. The number of teeth on each gear in a gear set determines the gear ratio.

Gear Ratios

A gear ratio is the proportional difference in speed and torque between a drive gear and a driven gear **(Figure 5–6).** When a drive gear turns a driven gear at one-half the driven gear speed, the gear ratio is 2:1. For example, if the drive gear has 12 teeth and the driven gear has 24 teeth, the ratio is 2:1. The drive gear must make two turns to make the driven gear make one turn. The ratio is calculated as follows: $24 \div 12 = 2$. To calculate any gear ratio, always use the "driven over drive" for-

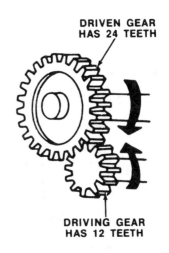

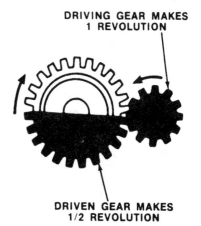

FIGURE 5–6 Example of a 2:1 gear ratio. This gear ratio reduces speed by 50% and increases torque output by 100%. When a similar large gear drives a similar small gear, the gear ratio is 0.5:1 which increases the output speed by 100% and decreases the output torque by 50%. In both cases, output gear rotation is opposite to input gear rotation.

mula (number of teeth on the driven gear divided by the number of teeth on the drive gear).

When power flows through a series of gears, the ratio can be calculated in a similar manner. For example, if a 20-tooth drive gear drives a 24-tooth cluster gear, and the second-speed cluster gear has 16 teeth driving a 20-tooth second-speed-driven gear, the result would be a 1.5:1 ratio. This is calculated as follows:

$$\frac{\text{driven}}{\text{drive}} \times \frac{\text{driven}}{\text{drive}} \text{ or } \frac{24}{20} \times \frac{20}{16} = 1.5\text{:}1$$

which is an acceptable second gear ratio.

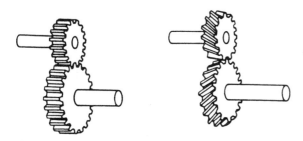

FIGURE 5–5 Spur gears (left) have straight-cut teeth. Helical gears (right) have angled teeth. Helical gears run quieter and are stronger.

Transmission/Transaxle Torque Capacity

Transmissions and transaxles are designed with an adequate torque capacity to meet the requirements of the engines with which they are matched. A transmission or transaxle must be able to handle all the torque a particular engine is able to produce plus a little extra as a safety margin. The gears and shafts in a transmission/transaxle designed for large, high torque engines are larger than those designed for smaller engines. The maximum torque output of any transmission/transaxle occurs in low gear. The torque increase from the input shaft through the low-speed gears to the output shaft rise fourfold with a 4:1 low gear ratio. The output shaft, therefore, must be considerably larger in diameter than the input shaft. For example, an engine able to produce 200 pound feet of torque at 2500 rpm would produce 800 pound feet of torque at the transmission/transaxle output shaft.

Constant Mesh Gears

The term *constant mesh* refers to gears that remain in mesh with each other and are not engaged or disengaged from each other by transmission or driver action when shifting gears. These gears remain in the same position on the shaft, that is, they do not slide along the shaft. Synchronizers are used to engage or disengage constant mesh gears as the synchronizer sleeve is moved by the shift linkage.

Helical Gears

A helical gear has gear teeth that are at an angle to the axis of rotation of the gear. One advantage of helical gears is that more than one tooth is doing the driving at all times, which is not the case with straight spur gears. Helical gears also run quieter since they create a wiping action as they engage and disengage the teeth on another gear. A disadvantage is that helical teeth on a gear cause the gear to move fore or aft on a shaft (depending on the direction of the angle of the gear (teeth). This axial thrust must be absorbed by thrust washers and other transmission gears, shafts, or the transmission case (see **Figure 5–5**).

Drive and Coast

The drive side of gear teeth is the side that is in contact with teeth of another gear while torque is being ap-

plied. This is the side of gear teeth that is subject to the most wear. The coast side of gear teeth is the opposite side from the drive side. This side of the teeth is in contact when the drive wheels are driving the engine (for example, during deceleration).

Gear Backlash

Backlash is the term used to describe the amount one gear is able to move when the gear with which it is in mesh is held stationary. All gears have some backlash to allow for expansion of metal due to heat and for proper lubrication. Excessive backlash is an indication of gear tooth wear.

Gear Climbing

Gear climbing is a problem caused by excessive wear in gears, bearings, and shafts whereby the gears move sufficiently apart to cause the apex (or point) of the teeth on one gear to climb over the apex of the teeth on another gear with which it is meshed. This results in a loss of drive until other teeth are engaged; it also causes rapid destruction of the gears.

SHAFT AND BEARING LOADS

Transmission and transaxle shafts, bearings, gears, and housings are subjected to several kinds of loads during vehicle operation. Torsional loads are imposed on shafts and gears as they turn **(Figure 5–7)**. Axial loads are imposed on shafts, gears, and bearings. As torsional

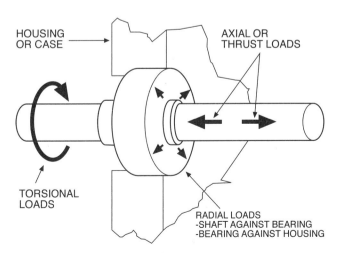

FIGURE 5–7 Different kinds of loads imposed on transmission/transaxle parts.

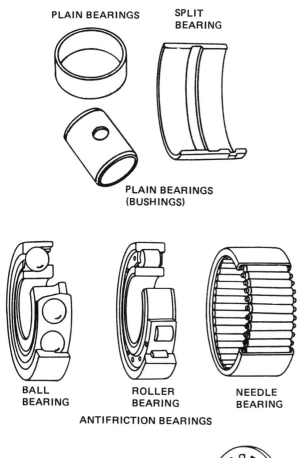

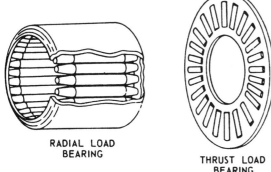

FIGURE 5–8 Different bearing designs used in transmissions and transaxles. (Courtesy of Deere & Co.)

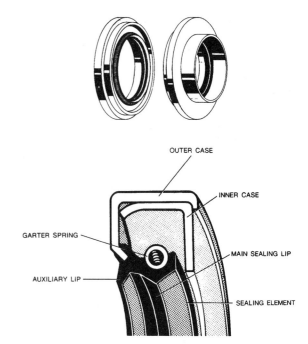

FIGURE 5–10 Typical seal design and common seal terminology.

loads are imposed on the gears, the angle of the gear teeth causes thrust loads against gears, bearings, thrust washers, and the transmission/transaxle case. Bearings and thrust washers are used to reduce friction and wear on transmission/transaxle parts. The size and design of bearings and thrust washers varies depending on the loads they are expected to carry (**Figures 5–8 and 5–9**).

TRANSMISSION/TRANSAXLE SEALS AND GASKETS

Transmission and transaxle seals and gaskets are designed to keep lubricants in and prevent the entry of dirt and moisture, A typical seal consists of a metal case, rubber sealing lip, and a garter spring (**Figure 5–10**). The garter spring increases the contact pressure of the sealing lip against the sealing surface. Seals

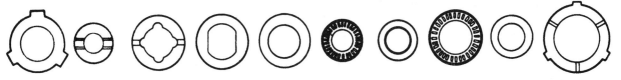

FIGURE 5–9 Several types of thrust bearings. Thrust bearings are designed to absorb axial loads. (Courtesy of Ford Motor Company.)

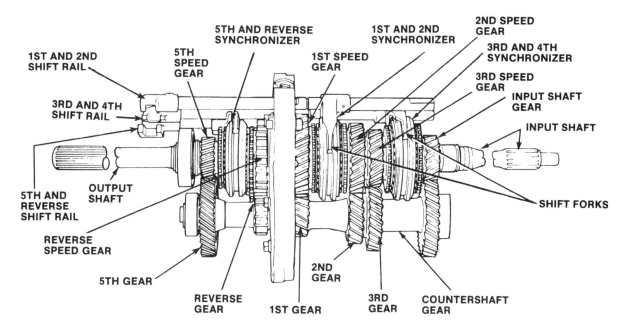

FIGURE 5–11 Synchronizers, shift forks, and shift rails for a five-speed transmission. Can you determine in which direction to shift the synchronizer sleeves for various gear positions? (Courtesy of Ford Motor Company.)

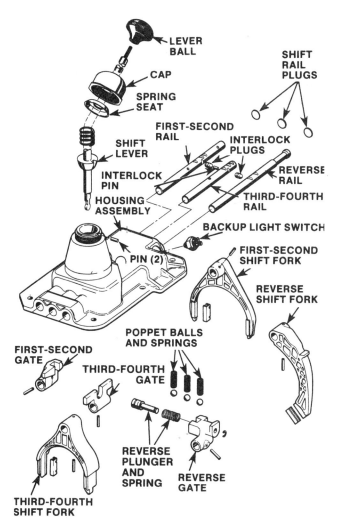

FIGURE 5–12 Direct transmission shift mechanism has no external linkage. (Courtesy of Chrysler Corporation.)

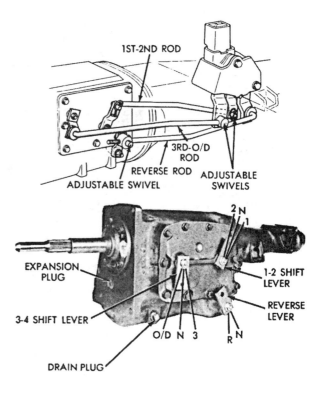

FIGURE 5–13 External view of typical manual transmission (four-speed) and shift linkage arrangement (console shift). (Courtesy of Chrysler Corporation.)

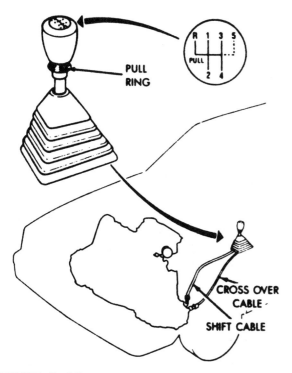

FIGURE 5–14 Shift linkage for five-speed overdrive transaxle. (Courtesy of Chrysler Corporation.)

are used between the transmission/transaxle case and the input and output shafts, and between the shift shafts and case. O-ring seals are often used at shift shafts and at the speedometer drive gear adapter or speed sensor. Fiber or cork compound gaskets are used at the cover plate, shift cover, extension housing, and front-bearing retainer.

SHIFT MECHANISM

Gear shifting is done by means of forks that are positioned in grooves in synchronizer sleeves **(Figures 5–11 to 5–20).** The forks are connected to sliding shift rails or shaft-operated cams. The shafts or cams are operated by cable- or rod-type linkage connected to the gear shift lever; the gear shift lever may, in some instances, actuate the shift rails directly, without any linkage. In the latter case, the shift lever is mounted directly to the transmission case.

The gear shift lever is mounted so that it is able to select the desired shift rail or shift cam; then the shift is completed by moving the lever forward or pulling back. Shift rails or shafts are equipped with spring-loaded balls that snap into notches in the shift rail—one for each gear position and Neutral position. This device, known as a detent, helps keep the synchronizer or gear in the position selected. An interlock device is also pro-

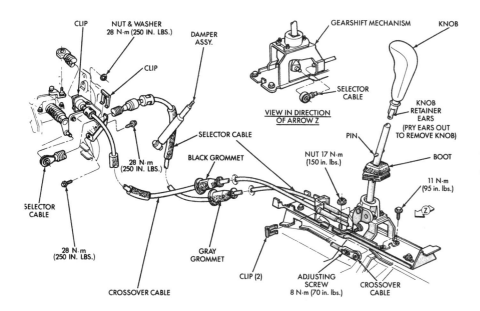

FIGURE 5–15 Cable-type transaxle shift linkage. (Courtesy of Chrysler Corporation.)

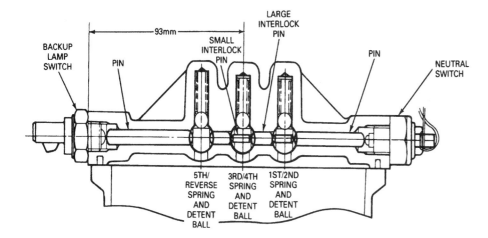

FIGURE 5–16 Detents help transmission stay in selected gear position. Interlock prevents shifting into two gears at once. (Courtesy of Ford Motor Company.)

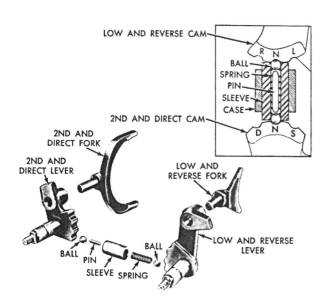

FIGURE 5–17 Cam-and-lever-type shift system showing interlock pin and detent balls and spring. (Courtesy of Chrysler Corporation.)

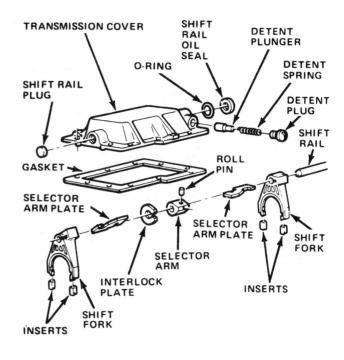

FIGURE 5–18 Single-rail-type shift cover showing forks, selector plates, interlock, and detent. (Courtesy of Chrysler Corporation.)

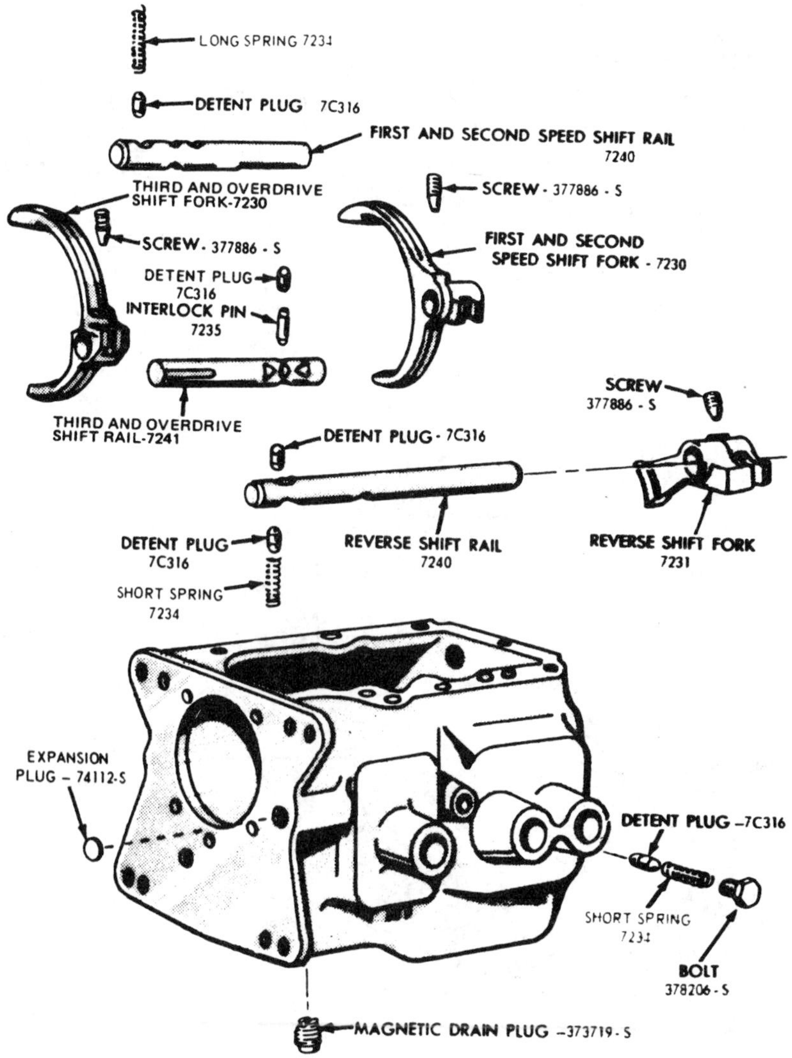

TRANSMISSION COVER

SHIFT RAIL OIL SEAL

O-RING

DETENT PLUNGER

DETENT SPRING

DETENT PLUG

SHIFT RAIL PLUG

SHIFT RAIL

GASKET

ROLL PIN

SELECTOR ARM PLATE

SELECTOR ARM PLATE

SHIFT FORK

SELECTOR ARM

INTERLOCK PLATE

INSERTS

SHIFT FORK

INSERTS

FIGURE 5–19 Exploded view of shift rails, forks, detents, and interlock mounted in transmission case. (Courtesy of Ford Motor Company.)

LONG SPRING 7234

DETENT PLUG 7C316

FIRST AND SECOND SPEED SHIFT RAIL 7240

THIRD AND OVERDRIVE SHIFT FORK-7230

SCREW - 377886 - S

SCREW - 377886 - S

FIRST AND SECOND SPEED SHIFT FORK - 7230

DETENT PLUG 7C316

INTERLOCK PIN 7235

THIRD AND OVERDRIVE SHIFT RAIL-7241

SCREW 377886 - S

DETENT PLUG - 7C316

REVERSE SHIFT FORK 7231

DETENT PLUG 7C316

REVERSE SHIFT RAIL 7240

SHORT SPRING 7234

EXPANSION PLUG – 74112-S

DETENT PLUG –7C316

SHORT SPRING 7234

BOLT 378206 - S

MAGNETIC DRAIN PLUG –373719-S

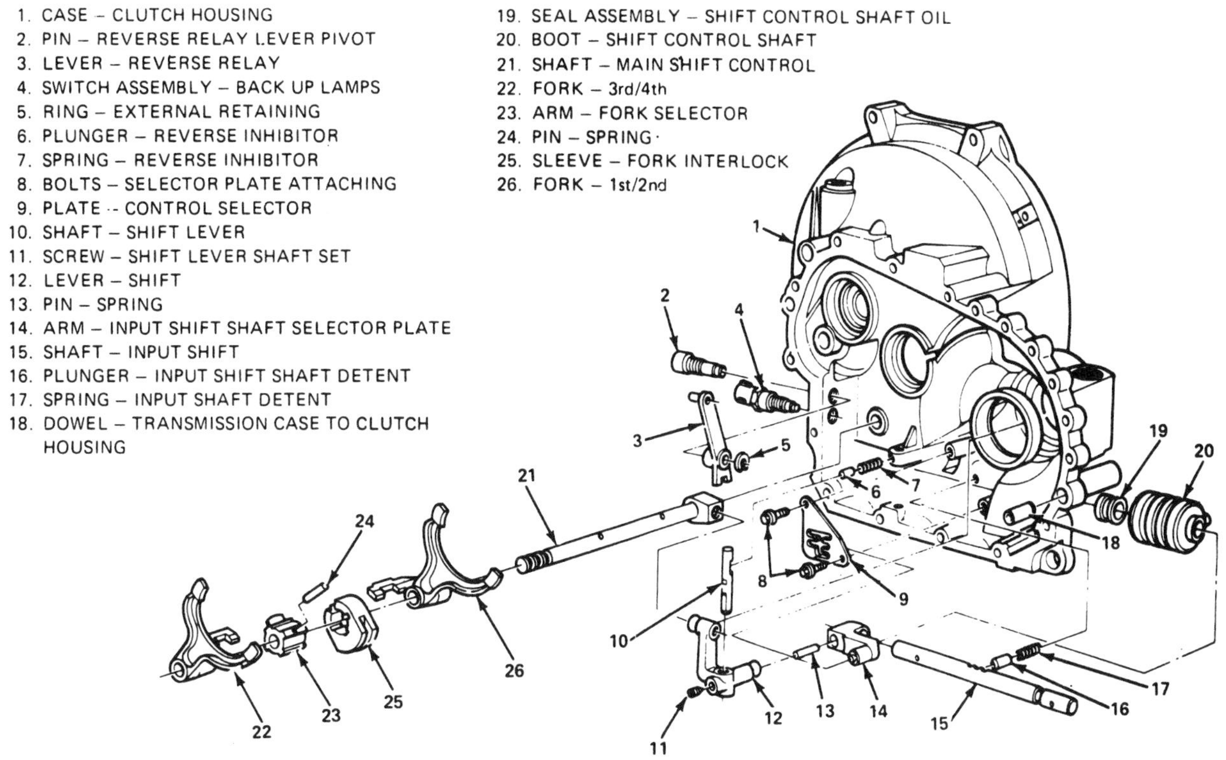

1. CASE – CLUTCH HOUSING
2. PIN – REVERSE RELAY LEVER PIVOT
3. LEVER – REVERSE RELAY
4. SWITCH ASSEMBLY – BACK UP LAMPS
5. RING – EXTERNAL RETAINING
6. PLUNGER – REVERSE INHIBITOR
7. SPRING – REVERSE INHIBITOR
8. BOLTS – SELECTOR PLATE ATTACHING
9. PLATE – CONTROL SELECTOR
10. SHAFT – SHIFT LEVER
11. SCREW – SHIFT LEVER SHAFT SET
12. LEVER – SHIFT
13. PIN – SPRING
14. ARM – INPUT SHIFT SHAFT SELECTOR PLATE
15. SHAFT – INPUT SHIFT
16. PLUNGER – INPUT SHIFT SHAFT DETENT
17. SPRING – INPUT SHAFT DETENT
18. DOWEL – TRANSMISSION CASE TO CLUTCH
    HOUSING

19. SEAL ASSEMBLY – SHIFT CONTROL SHAFT OIL
20. BOOT – SHIFT CONTROL SHAFT
21. SHAFT – MAIN SHIFT CONTROL
22. FORK – 3rd/4th
23. ARM – FORK SELECTOR
24. PIN – SPRING·
25. SLEEVE – FORK INTERLOCK
26. FORK – 1st/2nd

FIGURE 5–20 Internal shift mechanism for four-speed manual transaxle. (Courtesy of General Motors Corporation.)

vided, which makes it impossible to shift the transmission into two gears at once. The interlock in the shift rail system is usually a plate or pin located in the case between two shift rails or plates. The pin or plate is able to slide toward either rail. Notches in the rail are arranged so that the pin is pushed into a notch in the stationary rail or selector plate as the other rail is shifted. This prevents shifting of more than one shift rail at any time.

A similar interlock pin is provided between two cams on the cam and shaft arrangement. A spring-loaded detent is used to hold the shift cam in the selected position.

SYNCHRONIZERS

Synchronizers are used in transmissions and transaxles to:

1. Bring the drive and driven members to the same rotating speed to prevent gears from grinding when shifting.
2. Lock the driven gear to the output shaft or mainshaft when shifting into that gear.

A common type of synchronizer consists of a hub, sleeve, inserts, insert springs, and blocking rings (**Figures 5–21** and **5–22**). The synchronizer hub is splined to the mainshaft and usually retained by a snap ring. The sleeve is splined to the hub but can slide on the hub. The shift fork engages a groove in the sleeve and controls sleeve position. When a particular gear is selected, the sleeve slides on the splined hub toward the driven gear required. Movement of the sleeve annular groove pushes the inserts against the brass blocking ring, forcing it into contact with a cone on the driven gear. Friction between the two parts brings them to the same rotating speed. At this point the sleeve is able to move into full engagement with the synchronizer teeth on the driven gear. This prevents clashing of gears during shifting. Finely cut grooves in the inner surface of the blocking ring cut through the lubricant to aid in the braking action. They also hold lubricant to prevent severe wedging and locking of the ring onto the gear cone. A more recent design uses a paper-based compound on the inner surface of the brass ring. Since equalization of speed of rotating parts is required for engagement, sufficient time is required during shifting for this to occur. Force shifting can damage synchronizers and gears.

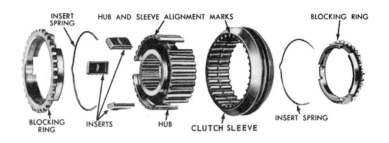

FIGURE 5–21 Typical synchronizer parts. (Courtesy of Ford Motor Company.)

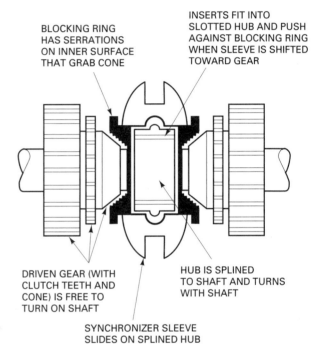

FIGURE 5–22 When the synchronizer sleeve is shifted, the blocking ring brings the gear and shaft to the same speed, allowing the sleeve to lock the synchronizer teeth on the gear to the sleeve, hub, and shaft. In neutral, the driven gears are free to turn on the shaft.

BLOCKING RING HAS SERRATIONS ON INNER SURFACE THAT GRAB CONE

INSERTS FIT INTO SLOTTED HUB AND PUSH AGAINST BLOCKING RING WHEN SLEEVE IS SHIFTED TOWARD GEAR

DRIVEN GEAR (WITH CLUTCH TEETH AND CONE) IS FREE TO TURN ON SHAFT

HUB IS SPLINED TO SHAFT AND TURNS WITH SHAFT

SYNCHRONIZER SLEEVE SLIDES ON SPLINED HUB

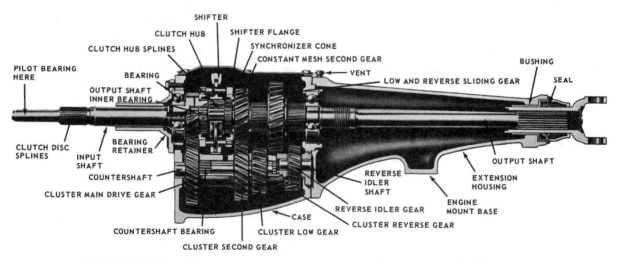

FIGURE 5–23 Cutaway view of three-speed manual transmission. (Courtesy of Chrysler Corporation.)

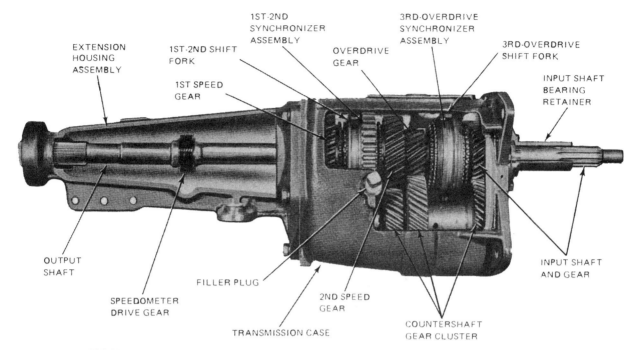

FIGURE 5–24 Four-speed overdrive transmission cutaway showing gear arrangement. In this transmission, third gear is direct (1:1) drive. Overdrive is provided by moving the third and overdrive synchronizer sleeve to the rear to connect the overdrive-driven gear to the output shaft. Power flow is from the input shaft gear, to counter-gear, to overdrive gear, and output shaft. (Courtesy of Ford Motor Company.)

Electronic Clutching and Shifting

Electronic clutching and gear shifting uses signals from sensors indicating engine speed, engine load, and vehicle speed to inform a computer when to clutch and shift. Electric solenoids perform the actual operations in response to computer signals. This system, although available on some vehicles, is not a common option.

TRANSMISSION AND TRANSAXLE TYPES

Transmissions and transaxles may be three-speed, four-speed, five-speed, or six-speed (**Figures 5–23** to **5–28**). In the three-speed versions (used on older cars), third gear is direct drive. In the four-speed version, fourth gear may be direct drive or overdrive, depending on vehicle application. In the five-speed version, fourth gear is usually direct drive, and fifth gear is an overdrive. In the six-speed unit, fifth gear is usually direct drive, and sixth gear is an overdrive.

TRANSMISSION AND TRANSAXLE POWERFLOW

Study the powerflow of transmissions and transaxles shown in **Figures 5–29** to **5–34**.

The following describes the powerflow in a typical four-speed transmission:

Neutral

Powerflow is from the input shaft drive pinion to the countergears. The countergears drive the mainshaft gears. In Neutral, none of the mainshaft gears have been locked to the output shaft by the synchronizers, and there is no powerflow to the output shaft.

First Gear

When the driver selects first gear, the first-gear synchronizer locks the driven first gear to the output shaft. When the driver releases the clutch pedal, power flows

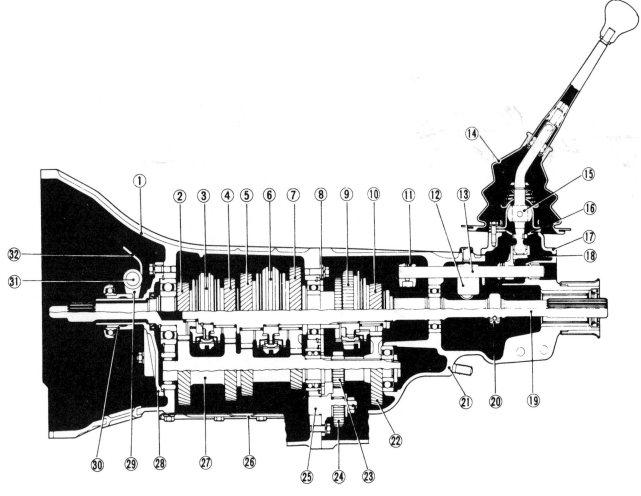

1. Transmission case
2. Main drive pinion
3. Synchronizer assy. (3-4 speed)
4. 3rd speed gear
5. 2nd speed gear
6. Synchronizer assy. (1-2 speed)
7. 1st speed gear
8. Rear bearing retainer
9. Synchronizer assy. (overdrive)
10. Overdrive gear
11. Control finger
12. Neutral return finger
13. Control shaft
14. Control lever cover
15. Control lever assy.
16. Stopper plate
17. Control housing
18. Change shifter
19. Mainshaft
20. Speedometer drive gear
21. Extension housing
22. Counter overdrive gear
23. Counter reverse gear
24. Reverse idler gear
25. Reverse idler gear shaft
26. Case cover
27. Counter gear
28. Front bearing retainer
29. Clutch shift arm
30. Release bearing carrier
31. Clutch control shaft
32. Return spring

FIGURE 5–25 Typical five-speed overdrive transmission for rear-wheel-drive vehicle. (Courtesy of Chrysler Corporation.)

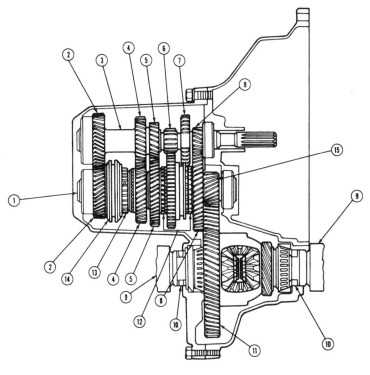

FIGURE 5–26 Four-speed manual transaxle cutaway view. (Courtesy of Ford Motor Co. of Canada Ltd.)

1. MAINSHAFT
2. 4TH SPEED GEARS
3. INPUT CLUSTER
4. 3RD SPEED GEARS
5. 2ND SPEED GEARS
6. REVERSE GEAR
7. REVERSE IDLER GEAR
8. 1ST SPEED GEARS

9. HALF SHAFTS
10. DIFFERENTIAL OIL SEALS
11. FINAL DRIVE RING GEAR
12. 1ST/2ND SPEED SYNCHRONIZER
    BLOCKER RINGS
13. 3RD/4TH SPEED SYNCHRONIZER HUB
14. 3RD/4TH SPEED SYNCHRONIZER SLEEVE
15. PINION GEAR PART OF MAINSHAFT

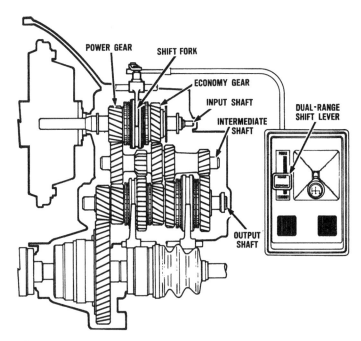

FIGURE 5–27 Dual-range transaxle provides four speeds in each range, for a total of eight forward speeds. Low range is for power, and high range is for economy. Note two shift levers. (Courtesy of Chrysler Corporation.)

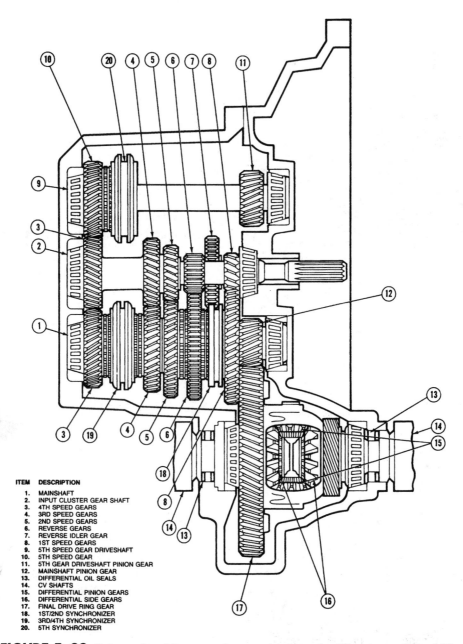

ITEM	DESCRIPTION
1.	MAINSHAFT
2.	INPUT CLUSTER GEAR SHAFT
3.	4TH SPEED GEARS
4.	3RD SPEED GEARS
5.	2ND SPEED GEARS
6.	REVERSE GEARS
7.	REVERSE IDLER GEAR
8.	1ST SPEED GEARS
9.	5TH SPEED GEAR DRIVESHAFT
10.	5TH SPEED GEAR
11.	5TH GEAR DRIVESHAFT PINION GEAR
12.	MAINSHAFT PINION GEAR
13.	DIFFERENTIAL OIL SEALS
14.	CV SHAFTS
15.	DIFFERENTIAL PINION GEARS
16.	DIFFERENTIAL SIDE GEARS
17.	FINAL DRIVE RING GEAR
18.	1ST/2ND SYNCHRONIZER
19.	3RD/4TH SYNCHRONIZER
20.	5TH SYNCHRONIZER

FIGURE 5–28 Schematic of five-speed manual transaxle. (Courtesy of Ford Motor Company.)

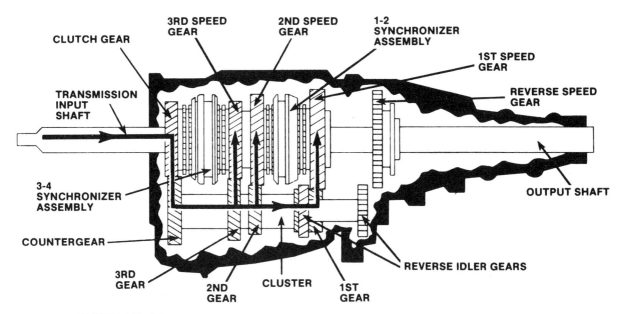

FIGURE 5–29 Three-speed manual transmission power flow in neutral. (Courtesy of General Motors Corporation.)

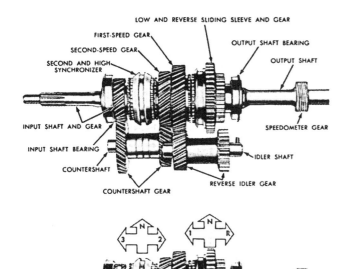

POWER FLOW – THREE-SPEED TRANSMISSION

FIGURE 5–30 Three-speed manual transmission gears and synchronizer arrangement. (Courtesy of General Motors Corporation.)

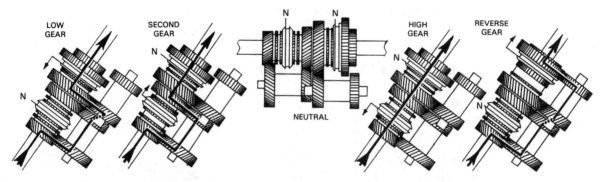

FIGURE 5–31 Power flow in different gear positions of a three-speed manual transmission with synchronized forward gears. Note synchronizer positions in each diagram. N = neutral position of synchronizer. (Courtesy of General Motors Corporation.)

from the input shaft drive pinion to the countergear, and from the first-speed counter to the first-speed driven gear, to the synchronizer sleeve, synchronizer hub, and output shaft.

Second Gear

To shift to second, the clutch pedal is depressed, and the lever is shifted to second. This shifts the synchronizer sleeve away from the first-speed gear on the output shaft to the second-speed gear and locks it to the output shaft. The driver then releases the clutch pedal.

Third, Fourth, and Fifth Gears

The procedure to shift from second to third, then to fourth and to overdrive is similar to the first-to-second shift. The difference is that a different output gear is locked to the output shaft for each gear selection. Overdrive gear ratios of less than 1:1 are used to reduce fuel consumption at highway speeds and to reduce engine wear through reduced engine speed. Overdrive ratios range from approximately 0.7:1 to about 0.85:1. On some four-speed units, fourth gear is direct drive (1:1). On others, fourth gear is an overdrive ratio. On five-speed units, fourth gear is usually direct drive, and fifth gear is overdrive.

Reverse

When reverse gear is selected, the reverse synchronizer locks the reverse-driven gear to the output shaft. Power flows from the drive pinion to the cluster gear, to the reverse idler, and to the reverse-driven gear, synchronizer sleeve, synchronizer hub, and output shaft.

TRANSAXLE FINAL DRIVE AND DIFFERENTIAL

Helical gear and hypoid gear final drives are used. Both types provide a final gear reduction in the drive train. The helical gear type is used with engines mounted in the transverse position, where the drive axles and the engine crankshaft are parallel to each other. The hypoid gear final drive is used with engines mounted in a longitudinal position, where power flow from the crankshaft must make a 90 degree turn to the drive axles.

    1. *Helical gear final drive.* The transaxle output shaft gear drives a large ring gear mounted on the differential case, which turns at reduced speed (**Figures 5–35** and **5–36**).

    2. *Hypoid gear final drive.* The transaxle output shaft and gear drive the ring gear and differential case at reduced speed. The hypoid gears provide for a lower drive pinion and the bevel gears produce the 90 degree turn in powerflow required with engines mounted in a longitudinal position (**Figure 5–37**).

    The transaxle differential operates in the same manner as the drive axle differential described in Chapter 3 (see **Figure 5–38**).

Speedometer Drive Gear

A worm-type speedometer gear mounted on the output shaft drives a speedometer drive pinion, speedometer

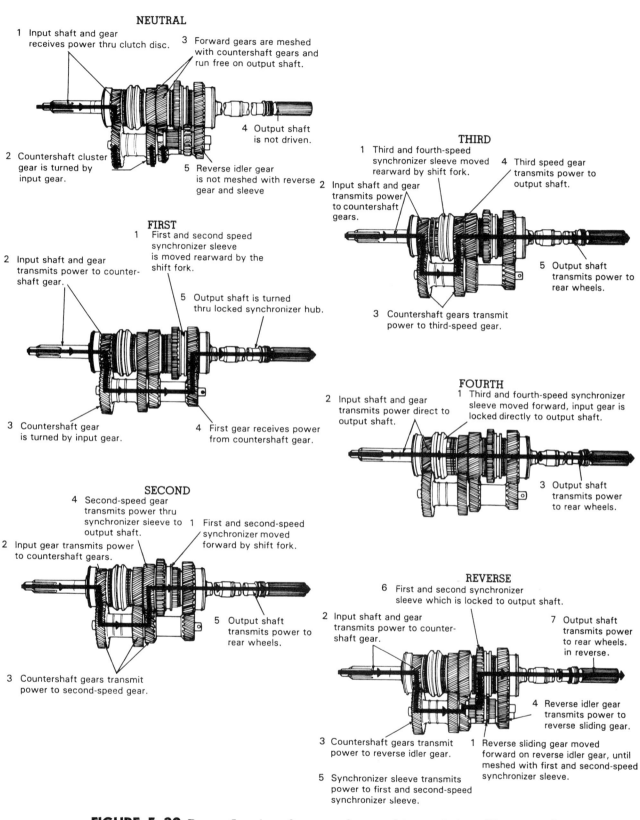

NEUTRAL

1 Input shaft and gear receives power thru clutch disc.

3 Forward gears are meshed with countershaft gears and run free on output shaft.

4 Output shaft is not driven.

2 Countershaft cluster gear is turned by input gear.

5 Reverse idler gear is not meshed with reverse gear and sleeve

FIRST

1 First and second speed synchronizer sleeve is moved rearward by the shift fork.

2 Input shaft and gear transmits power to counter-shaft gear.

5 Output shaft is turned thru locked synchronizer hub.

3 Countershaft gear is turned by input gear.

4 First gear receives power from countershaft gear.

SECOND

4 Second-speed gear transmits power thru synchronizer sleeve to output shaft.

1 First and second-speed synchronizer moved forward by shift fork.

2 Input gear transmits power to countershaft gears.

5 Output shaft transmits power to rear wheels.

3 Countershaft gears transmit power to second-speed gear.

THIRD

1 Third and fourth-speed synchronizer sleeve moved rearward by shift fork.

4 Third speed gear transmits power to output shaft.

2 Input shaft and gear transmits power to countershaft gears.

5 Output shaft transmits power to rear wheels.

3 Countershaft gears transmit power to third-speed gear.

FOURTH

1 Third and fourth-speed synchronizer sleeve moved forward, input gear is locked directly to output shaft.

2 Input shaft and gear transmits power direct to output shaft.

3 Output shaft transmits power to rear wheels.

REVERSE

6 First and second synchronizer sleeve which is locked to output shaft.

2 Input shaft and gear transmits power to counter-shaft gear.

7 Output shaft transmits power to rear wheels. in reverse.

4 Reverse idler gear transmits power to reverse sliding gear.

3 Countershaft gears transmit power to reverse idler gear.

1 Reverse sliding gear moved forward on reverse idler gear, until meshed with first and second-speed synchronizer sleeve.

5 Synchronizer sleeve transmits power to first and second-speed synchronizer sleeve.

FIGURE 5–32 Power flow in a four speed manual transmission. (Courtesy of Ford Motor Company.)

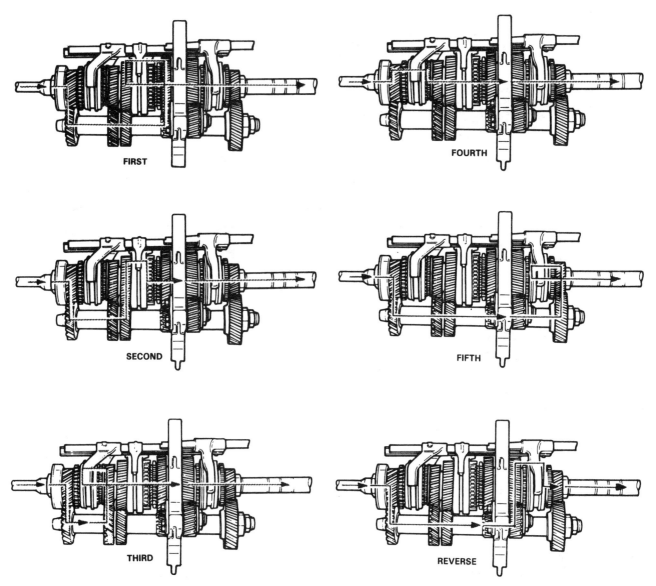

FIGURE 5–33 Five speed manual transmission power flow.

First Gear: From input shaft, to countergear, to first-speed gear, to 1–2 synchronizer sleeve and hub, to output shaft.

Second Gear: From input shaft, to countergear, to second-speed gear, to 1–2 synchronizer sleeve and hub, to output shaft.

Third Gear: From input shaft, to countergear, to third-speed gear, to 3–4 synchronizer sleeve and hub, to output shaft.

Fourth Gear: From input shaft, to 3–4 synchronizer sleeve and hub, to output shaft.

Fifth Gear: From input shaft, to countergear, to fifth-speed gear, to R–5 synchronizer sleeve and hub, to output shaft.

Reverse Gear: From input shaft, to countergear, to reverse gear, to reverse idler gear, to reverse-driven gear, to R–5 synchronizer sleeve and hub, to output shaft. (Courtesy of General Motors Corporation.)

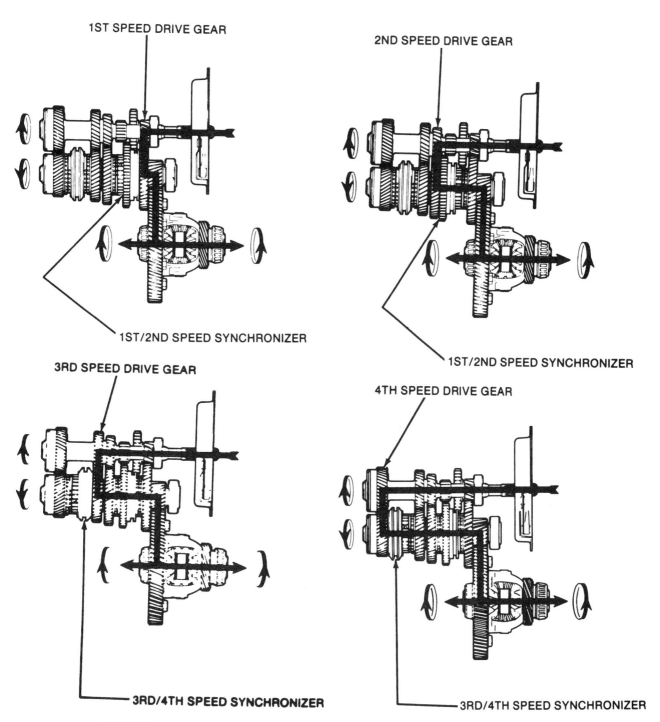

1ST SPEED DRIVE GEAR

2ND SPEED DRIVE GEAR

1ST/2ND SPEED SYNCHRONIZER

1ST/2ND SPEED SYNCHRONIZER

3RD SPEED DRIVE GEAR

4TH SPEED DRIVE GEAR

3RD/4TH SPEED SYNCHRONIZER

3RD/4TH SPEED SYNCHRONIZER

FIGURE 5–34 Power flow in forward speeds for four-speed manual transaxle. (Courtesy of Ford Motor Company.)

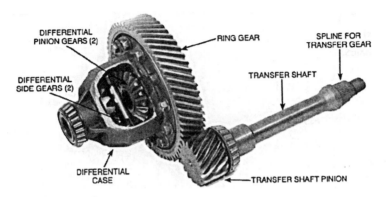

FIGURE 5–35 Helical final drive ring gear and pinion. (Courtesy of Chrysler Corporation.)

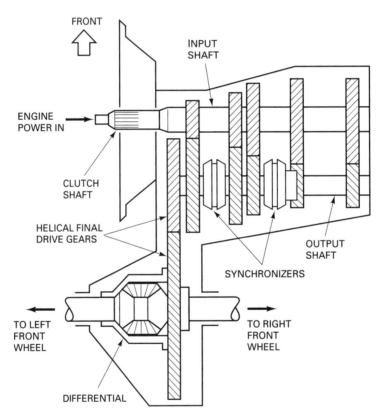

FIGURE 5–36 Transaxle with helical gear final drive is used with transverse engine front-wheel-drive cars. Hypoid gears are not needed since transaxle shafts, drive axles, and engine crankshaft are all parallel.

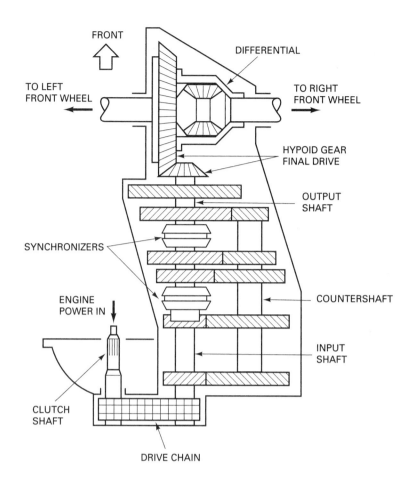

FRONT

DIFFERENTIAL

TO LEFT
FRONT WHEEL

TO RIGHT
FRONT WHEEL

HYPOID GEAR
FINAL DRIVE

OUTPUT
SHAFT

SYNCHRONIZERS

COUNTERSHAFT

ENGINE
POWER IN

INPUT
SHAFT

CLUTCH
SHAFT

DRIVE CHAIN

FIGURE 5–37 Transaxle with hypoid gear final drive is used on front-wheel-drive cars with longitudinally mounted engines. Hypoid gears turn power flow 90 degrees. This is necessary because engine crankshaft is at right angle to the drive axles.

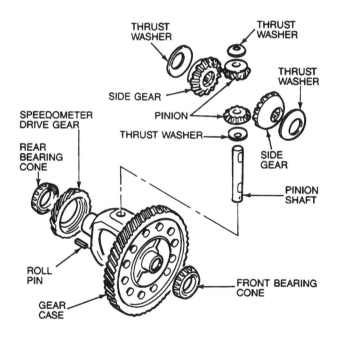

THRUST
WASHER

THRUST
WASHER

THRUST
WASHER

SIDE GEAR

PINION

SPEEDOMETER
DRIVE GEAR

THRUST WASHER

SIDE
GEAR

REAR
BEARING
CONE

PINION
SHAFT

ROLL
PIN

FRONT BEARING
CONE

GEAR
CASE

FIGURE 5–38 Transaxle differential parts. (Courtesy of Ford Motor Company.)

cable, and speedometer head in the dash. The speedometer cable is enclosed in a flexible housing. Cars with electronic speedometers have a magnetic pulse type speed sensor instead of a gear-driven speedometer.

TRANSMISSION/TRANSAXLE LUBRICATION

Manual transmissions and transaxles use either a gear oil, engine oil, or ATF (automatic transmission fluid) as a lubricant depending on the make and model of the unit. The gears and shafts in the lower part of the case are submerged in the lubricant. As the gears rotate during operation, the remaining gears, shafts and bearings are splash lubricated from the oil throw-off caused by gear rotation. The lubricant fill level is usually a little below the mid-point of the case. A threaded fill and level checking plug is located at this point. Grooves on shafts, thrust surfaces, and gear bores help in spreading and channeling lubricant to wear areas. Troughs, tubes, or funnels direct oil to other critical areas.

The gears, shafts, and lubricant expand as they warm up during operation. To prevent any resulting pressure buildup in the transmission/transaxle, a vent is provided. If there were no vent or if the vent were plugged, pressure could force oil past the seals in the case.

REVIEW QUESTIONS

1. What is the major difference in function between a transmission and a transaxle?

2. Why are different gear ratios needed in a transaxle or transmission?

3. List the 11 major parts found in transaxles and transmissions.

4. Gears are round metal wheels with _____ around the circumference.

5. Gears are used to _____ output speed, _____ output speed, or provide _____ drive.

6. The ratio between the _____ and _____ gears determines the output speed and _____ output.

7. A gear ratio is the proportional difference in _____ and _____ between a _____ gear and a _____ gear.

8. A helical gear has teeth that are at an _____.

9. Gear backlash is the amount that one gear is able to _____ when the gear with which it is in mesh is _____ _____.

10. What two jobs do synchronizers perform?

11. The synchronizer is splined to the _____ and is held in place by a _____ _____.

12. When the synchronizer sleeve is shifted toward a gear, the _____ _____ contacts a _____ on the driven gear.

13. A _____ in the shift mechanism helps keep the synchronizer in the gear position selected.

14. A shift _____ makes it possible to shift into two gears at once.

15. What benefits does an overdrive gear provide?

16. In a transaxle, a gear mounted on the _____ drives the _____ _____ mounted on the differential case.

TEST QUESTIONS

1. Technician A says that the differential is part of the transaxle. Technician B says that a transmission-equipped car does not need a differential. Who is right?
   a. technician A
   b. technician B
   c. both are right
   d. both are wrong

2. The transmission/transaxle input shaft may also be called a
   a. countershaft
   b. clustershaft
   c. clutch shaft
   d. mainshaft

3. Transmission/transaxle output gears are
   a. splined to the output shaft
   b. keyed to the output shaft
   c. free to turn on the output shaft
   d. geared to the output shaft

4. In a manual transaxle, the final drive pinion drives the
   a. output shaft
   b. countershaft
   c. clutch gear
   d. ring gear

5. The number of gears on a fully synchronized three-speed transmission mainshaft is
   a. two
   b. three
   c. four
   d. five

6. The second- and third-speed synchronizer hub on a three-speed manual transmission is splined to the
   a. clutch shaft
   b. mainshaft

   c. cluster gear
   d. input shaft

7. The only gear not turning when the three-speed fully synchronized transmission is in Neutral with the engine running and the clutch applied is the
   a. clutch gear
   b. cluster gear
   c. low-driven gear
   d. reverse-driven gear

8. The transmission section of the four-speed transaxle has how many forward driven gears?
   a. three
   b. four
   c. five
   d. none of the above

9. The five-speed transmission for rear-wheel-drive vehicles has how many synchronizers?
   a. three
   b. four
   c. five
   d. six

10. When shifting gears in a manual transmission/transaxle, the
    a. shift fork moves the synchronizer sleeve
    b. inserts push against the blocking ring
    c. the synchronizer sleeve connects the driven gear to the synchronizer hub
    d. all of the above

◆ CHAPTER 6 ◆

MANUAL TRANSMISSION AND TRANSAXLE SERVICE

INTRODUCTION

This chapter discusses common manual transmission and transaxle problems, problem diagnosis, removal, disassembly, inspection, reassembly, and installation of manual transmissions and transaxles. Due to the many differences in transmission and transaxle design, the instructions in the appropriate service manual should be followed.

LEARNING OBJECTIVES

After completing this chapter, you should be able to:

- Describe common manual transmission and transaxle problems.
- Diagnose manual transmission and transaxle problems.
- Remove and replace a manual transmission and manual transaxle.
- Disassemble, clean, repair, and reassemble a manual transmission and manual transaxle.

TERMS YOU SHOULD KNOW

Look for these terms as you study this chapter and learn what they mean.

gear clashing   locked in gear
gear grinding   bearing noise
jumping out of gear   cleaning the parts
hard shifting   inspecting the parts

MANUAL TRANSMISSION AND TRANSAXLE PROBLEM DIAGNOSIS

After extended use, a manual transmission or transaxle may develop problems due to normal wear and possible driver abuse. Typical transmission and transaxle problems include the following. See **Figures 6–1** and **6–2** for problem diagnosis.

Gears Clash or Grind When Shifting

Clashing or grinding gears when shifting can cause further internal damage to the transmission or transaxle. The synchronizer teeth grind while trying to equalize the drive and the driven speeds. Gear clashing and grinding may be caused by the clutch not releasing properly. The clutch linkage may not be adjusted properly, there may be an internal clutch problem, or the lubricant level may be too low in the transmission/transaxle, allowing the gears to continue spinning. Badly worn gearshift linkage, worn or damaged synchronizers, shift forks, shift rails, or bearings can also cause gears to grind.

PROBLEM	CAUSE	CORRECTION
Transmission shifts hard	1. Clutch adjustment incorrect. 2. Clutch linkage binding. 3. Shift rail binding. 4. Internal bind in transmission caused by shift forks, selector plates, or synchronizer assemblies. 5. Clutch housing misalignment. 6. Incorrect lubricant.	1. Adjust clutch. 2. Lubricate or repair as necessary. 3. Check for mispositioned selector arm roll pin, loose cover bolts, worn shift rail bores, worn shift rail, distorted oil seal, or extension housing not aligned with case. Repair as necessary. 4. Remove, disassemble, and inspect transmission. Replace worn or damaged components as necessary. 5. Check runout at rear of clutch housing. Correct runout. 6. Drain and refill transmission.
Gear clash when shifting from one gear to another	1. Clutch adjustment incorrect. 2. Air in hydraulic system. 3. Clutch linkage or cable binding. 4. Clutch housing misalignment. 5. Lubricant level low or incorrect lubricant. 6. Gearshift components or synchronizer assemblies worn or damaged.	1. Adjust clutch. 2. Bleed hydraulic control system. 3. Lubricate or repair as necessary. 4. Check runout at rear face of clutch housing. Correct runout. 5. Drain and refill transmission and check for lubricant leaks if level was low. Repair as necessary. 6. Remove, disassemble, and inspect transmission. Replace worn or damaged components as necessary.
Will not shift into one gear	1. Gearshift selector plates, interlock plate, or selector arm, worn, damaged, or incorrectly assembled. 2. Shift rail detent plunger worn, spring broken, or plug loose. 3. Gearshift lever worn or damaged. 4. Synchronizer sleeves or hubs damaged or worn.	1. Remove, disassemble, and inspect transmission cover assembly. Repair or replace components as necessary. 2. Tighten plug or replace worn or damaged components as necessary. 3. Replace gearshift lever. 4. Remove, disassemble, and inspect transmission. Replace worn or damaged components.
Locked in one gear—cannot be shifted out of that gear	1. Shift rail(s) worn or broken, shifter fork bent, setscrew loose, center detent plug missing or worn. 2. Broken gear teeth on countershaft gear, clutch shaft, or reverse idler gear. 3. Gearshift lever broken or worn, shift mechanism in cover incorrectly assembled or broken, worn or damaged gear train components.	1. Inspect and replace worn or damaged parts. 2. Inspect and replace damaged part. 3. Disassemble transmission. Replace damaged parts or assemble correctly.

FIGURE 6–1 Manual transmission problem diagnosis. (Courtesy of General Motors Corporation.)

Clutch Spin Down Time

Clutch spin down time varies between different vehicle makes and models. Some spin down time is normal and may be as high as 10 seconds on some vehicles. If spin down time is excessive, grinding of gears may occur when shifting from Neutral to Reverse. To check spin down time, proceed as follows:

1. Start the engine and run at normal idle with the transmission/transaxle in Neutral and the clutch engaged (pedal released).

2. Push the clutch pedal down and hold it there for 10 seconds, then shift into Reverse.

3. If gear clashing or grinding is heard, check the clutch linkage adjustment to ensure full clutch release. Adjust the linkage to specifications if necessary. If this does not correct the problem, there may be an internal clutch problem. (See Chapter 4 for detailed clutch problem diagnosis.)

Abnormal Transmission/Transaxle Noise

A humming, whirring, or grinding sound coming from the transmission or transaxle may be the result of low

Jumps out of gear	1. Clutch housing misalignment. 2. Offset lever nylon insert worn or lever at-tached nut loose. 3. Gearshift mechanism, shift forks, selector plates, interlock plate, selector arm, shift rail, detent plugs, springs, or shift cover worn or damaged. 4. Clutch shaft or roller bearings worn or dam-aged. 5. Gear teeth worn or tapered, synchronizer as-semblies worn or damaged, excessive end play caused by worn thrust washers or output shaft gears. 6. Pilot bushing worn.	1. Check runout at rear face of clutch housing. 2. Remove gearshift lever and check for loose off-set lever nut or worn insert. Repair or replace as necessary. 3. Remove, disassemble, and inspect transmis-sion cover assembly. Replace worn or dam-aged components as necessary. 4. Replace clutch shaft or roller bearings as nec-essary. 5. Remove, disassemble, and inspect transmis-sion. Replace worn or damaged components as necessary. 6. Replace pilot bushing.
Transmission noisy	1. Lubricant level low or incorrect lubricant. 2. Clutch housing-to-engine, or transmission-to-clutch housing bolts loose. 3. Dirt, chips, or foreign material in transmission. 4. Gearshift mechanism or transmission gear, or bearing components worn or damaged. 5. Clutch housing misalignment.	1. Drain and refill transmission. If lubricant level is low, check for leaks and repair as neces-sary. 2. Check and correct bolt torque as necessary. 3. Drain, flush, and refill transmission. 4. Remove, disassemble, and inspect transmis-sion. Replace worn or damaged components as necessary. 5. Check runout at rear face of clutch housing. Correct runout.
Leaks lubricant	1. Excessive amount of lubricant in transmission. 2. Loose or broken main drive gear bearing re-tainer. 3. Main drive gear bearing retainer gasket dam-aged. 4. Side cover loose or gasket damaged. 5. Rear bearing retainer oil seal leaks. 6. Countershaft loose in case. 7. Shift lever seals leak.	1. Drain to correct level. 2. Tighten or replace retainer. 3. Replace gasket. 4. Tighten cover or replace gasket. 5. Replace seal. 6. Replace case. 7. Replace seal.

FIGURE 6–1 *(Continued)*

lubricant level, contaminated lubricant, or worn or rough bearings, gears, or thrust washers. If the noise occurs only in one gear, the parts involved in the power flow for that gear are at fault. If the noise occurs in all gear positions, the problem is in those parts common to all gear positions (for example, final drive gears in the transaxle).

Transmission/Transaxle Jumps Out of Gear

When the shift lever jumps into the Neutral position while driving, the problem could be improperly ad-justed or badly worn shift linkage, bent or worn shift forks, worn synchronizer teeth, worn synchronizer in-serts, weak insert springs, worn clutch pilot bearing, worn input shaft bearing, worn countershaft bearings, worn thrust washers, worn output shaft gears, or clutch housing misalignment.

Transmission/Transaxle Hard to Shift

Hard shifting may be caused by binding shift linkage due to lack of lubrication, wear, bent linkage or im-properly adjusted linkage, or a clutch that does not fully disengage. Vacuum may hold a worn disc against the flywheel.

Transmission/Transaxle Locked in Gear

When a transmission or transaxle is locked in one gear, the problem could be bent shift linkage, badly worn shift linkage, a bent shift fork, loose shift rail fork set screw, or a damaged detent or shift interlock.

Lubricant Leaks

Lubricant leaks may be caused by a lubricant level that is too high, damaged gaskets, worn or damaged seals,

CONDITION	PROBABLE CAUSE
Excessive shift effort (all forward gears)	Improper fluid or level. Use synchromesh transaxle fluid GM P/N 12345349 or equivalent. Automatic transmission fluid or engine oil does not work well with synchronizers resulting in increased shift effort. (Check for proper clutch spin-down time)
Shifting effort high into or out of gear (engine running or not)	a. Shift cable binding, kinked, worn, or not routed correctly. NOTE: Water can get past grommets and corrode the cable, causing an increased shift effort and/or increased effort or no movement of cable when water freezes b. Shifter mechanism in vehicle worn, damaged, or not lubricated. c. Shift lever nut loose, allowing shift lever to cock and bind while shifting (NVG – T550) d. Shift rails or bushings damaged, binding, or worn (NVG – T550)
Excessive reverse shift effort	a. Reverse and/or idler gear teeth are damaged or mutilated (mushroomed) b. Reverse lever bent (both ears must be in same plane) (NVG – T550) c. Reverse shift rail or bushing worn, missing or binding (NVG – T550) d. Engine idle speed too high
Hard to shift into shift gates (1-2, 3-4, 5-rev.) and (side to side)	Shift cable binding, kinked, worn, or not routed correctly. NOTE: Water can get past grommets and corrode the cable, causing an increased shift effort and/or increased effort or no movement of cable when water freezes.
Hard shift into 1-2 gate	Shift shaft cover installed too deep or top of cover is damaged and not allowing full travel of the shift shaft. (NVG – T550)
Hard shift into 1st-2nd gear	Output gear shim missing or too thin causing excessive output shaft end play. (NVG – T550)
Hard shift into 5th gear	Bent reverse lever (NVG – T550)
Unable to shift out of 5th gear	Missing reverse shift rail assembly or gear disengage roller (NVG – T550)
Unable to shift into any gear	Missing snap ring and/or detent plug (NVG – T550)
No block out in any forward gear	Replace synchronizer sleeve of affected gear only if there is NO bronze transfer from blocking ring to speed gear cone (NVG – T550)

FIGURE 6–2 Manual transaxle (five-speed) problem diagnosis. (Courtesy of General Motors Corporation.)

CONDITION	PROBABLE CAUSE
Knock at low speeds	a. Worn drive axle joint b. Worn side gear hub counterbore
Noise most pronounced on turns	Differential gear noise
Clunk on acceleration or deceleration	a. Loose engine mounts b. Worn inboard drive axle joint c. Worn differential pinion shaft in case d. Side gear hub counterbore in case worn oversize
Clicking noise on turns	Worn outboard CV joint
Vibration	a. Rough wheel bearing b. Bent drive axle shaft c. Out of round tires d. Tire unbalance e. Worn CV joint in drive axle shaft f. Incorrect drive axle angle (Trim Height)
Noisy in Neutral with Engine Running	a. Worn or damaged input gear bearings b. Broken or rubbing, input shaft bearing sleeve (NVG – T550) c. Worn or damaged clutch release bearing d. Damaged or worn speed gear bearing e. Damaged or worn bearing races f. Damaged or worn thrust surfaces g. Improper running engine h. Slight noise is normal
Noisy in First Only	a. Chipped, scored, or worn first-speed constant-mesh gears b. Worn 1-2 synchronizer
Noisy in Second Only	a. Chipped, scored, or worn second speed constant-mesh gears b. Worn 1-2 synchronizer
Noisy in Third Only	a. Chipped, scored, or worn third-gear constant-mesh gears b. Worn 3-4 synchronizer
Noisy in Fourth Only	a. Worn 3-4 gear synchronizer b. Chipped, scored, or worn fourth-gear or output gear
Noisy in Fifth Gear Only	a. Worn 5th gear synchronizer b. Chipped, scored, or worn fifth-speed gear or output gear
Noisy in Reverse Only	a. Chipped, scored, or worn reverse idler gear, idler gear bushing, input or output gear(s) b. Worn or damaged synchronizer sleeve (Isuzu)

FIGURE 6–2 (Continued)

CONDITION	PROBABLE CAUSE
Noisy in All Gears	a. Insufficient lubricant b. Worn bearings c. Chipped, scored, or worn input gear (shaft) and/or output gear (shaft) d. Differential housing cracked or foreign object between shaft and differential. e. Output gear bearing worn or damaged. f. Shift rail guide bolt loose, rubbing on gear (NVG – T550)
Noisy Differential	a. Output bearing race retainer installed upside down (NVG – T550) b. Detent holder cover not installed flush with bore (NVG – T550) c. Worn or damaged output shaft
Slips out of Gear	a. Worn or improperly adjusted linkage b. Transmission loose on engine housing c. Shift linkage binds d. Bent or worn cables e. Input gear bearing retainer broken or loose f. Worn or bent shift fork g. Dirt between clutch housing and engine h. Stiff shift lever seal
Slips out of gear on acceleration or deceleration	a. 1st Gear: Thrust bearing and/or washer missing or worn (too much end play) (NVG – T550) b. 1st and/or 2nd Gear: Damaged or worn spline lock on 1st/2nd synchronizer sleeve and/or hub (NVG – T550) c. 3rd and/or 4th Gear: Damaged or worn spline lock on 3rd/4th synchronizer sleeve and/or hub (NVG – T550) d. 5th Gear: Damaged or worn spline lock on 5th synchronizer sleeve and/or reverse gear (NVG – T550)
Slips out of gear on coast	Shift rail(s) detent damaged, worn or missing parts.
Leaks Lubricant	a. Fluid level indicator not seated in fill port causing fluid leakage at vent plug b. Worn axle shaft seals c. Excessive amount of lubricant in transaxle because of improper checking of fluid d. Loose or broken input gear (shaft) bearing retainer e. Worn input gear bearing and/or lip seal damaged f. Worn shift lever seal g. Lack of sealant between case and clutch cover or loose clutch cover h. Loose end plate or lack of sealant i. Loose or lack of sealant from back up lamp switch j. Speedometer signal assembly internal leakage

FIGURE 6–2 *(Continued)*

loose cover bolts, loose countershaft plug, or damaged shift lever seals. Lubricant leaks and shift linkage problems are usually checked out in the shop. Inspect each gasket and seal for leakage. Make sure that all cover bolts and housing bolts are tight.

Shift Linkage Check

Inspect the linkage for damage, excessive wear, or binding. Lubricate the linkage and operate it to ensure that it operates freely. Adjust the linkage if necessary to ensure that the linkage is able to select each gear and that shift travel is adequate.

CHECKING THE LUBRICANT

The transmission/transaxle lubricant should be checked to ensure that it is at the level specified in the vehicle service manual. It should not be above or below that level. Fluid should be added or removed as required to correct the level. If fluid is low, inspect the unit for leaks at the front and rear seals, cover and housing gaskets, and where the shift linkage enters the case. Make sure the case vent is not plugged since this can cause fluid to be forced out. Seals, gaskets, and O-rings that leak should be replaced.

The condition of the fluid should also be noted. It should smell and look like new fluid. Dirty lubricant should be changed. Shiny metal particles in the fluid indicate major wear of internal parts. Check the metal particles on the drain plug magnet as well.

To check the fluid level in a manual transmission/transaxle on most vehicles, raise the vehicle and remove the fill/level plug. Have a container handy to contain any fluid spill caused by overfilling. The fluid level should be at the bottom of the opening **(Figure 6–3)**. If necessary, check the fluid level by inserting a short piece of rod bent at 90 degrees partway into the opening to contact the fluid. Add the specified fluid if necessary.

To check the fluid level on some transaxles, park the vehicle on a level surface. With the engine off, remove the transaxle dipstick and wipe it clean. Insert the dipstick until fully seated and remove it again **(Figure 6–4)**. The fluid should be at the level specified on the dipstick. Add or remove fluid if necessary to bring it to the correct level.

On some transaxles, the speed sensor must be removed to check the fluid level. The speed sensor used to check the fluid level is similar to a dipstick **(Figure 6–5)**.

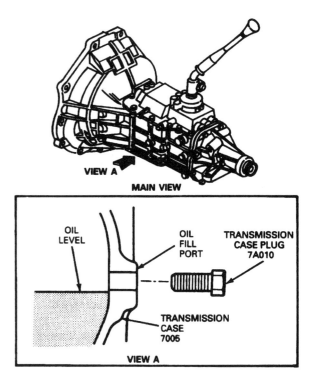

FIGURE 6–3 Transmission must be filled to correct level with specified lubricant. (Courtesy of Ford Motor Company.)

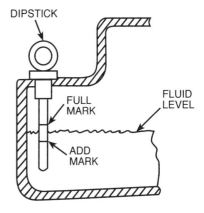

FIGURE 6–4 Many transaxles have a dipstick for checking the fluid level.

SHIFT EFFORT TEST

Two tests can be made to determine if shift effort is normal or excessive: the engine-off test and the engine-running test. The engine-off test is performed with the engine off and measures the effort required to move the shift linkage, shift rail, shift fork, and synchronizer sleeve from Neutral to each gear posi-

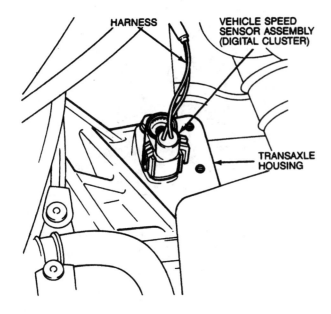

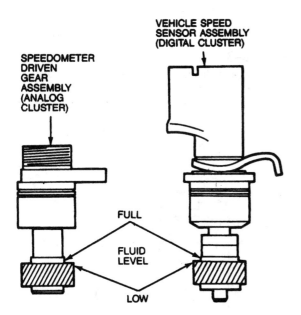

FIGURE 6–5 To check the fluid level on some transaxles, the speed sensor must be removed. The sensor is then used in a manner similar to using a dipstick. (Courtesy of Ford Motor Company.)

tion and back. Depress the clutch pedal during these checks. Compare the shift effort required to that of a similar vehicle in good condition. Excessive shift effort may be caused by the linkage or by internal transmission/transaxle problems. Disconnecting the linkage at the transmission/transaxle allows checking linkage operation and internal shift mechanism separately.

The engine-running test checks the shift effort required in the same way but also checks for clutch spindown time and clutch drag. To perform the engine-running test, apply the parking brake securely, start the engine, and let it run at idle. Depress the clutch pedal, and shift into first gear. Compare the effort required to that during the engine-off test. Shift back to Neutral and release the clutch pedal. Repeat the test for each gear position. If excessive effort is required when shifting into one gear position only, the problem may be internal. If excessive effort is required shifting into all positions, the problem may be clutch drag. (See Chapter 4 for details on clutch problem diagnosis.)

ROAD TEST

Road test the car to check for clutch and transmission operation and noise. Test the transmission in each gear under acceleration, deceleration, and coast or float modes. Check for any abnormal noise or operating condition and note in which gear and during which driving mode the problem occurs. This will help isolate the problem area in the transmission/transaxle. Remember that CV joints, drive axles, differentials, drive shafts, and wheel bearings can also cause noise problems.

TRANSMISSION REMOVAL

Removal procedures for manual transmissions are generally quite similar. Procedures for transaxle removal are quite different. The following procedures are typical. For detailed instructions, refer to the service manual.

See **Figures 6–6** and **6–7.**

1. Disconnect the negative battery cable.
2. Support the vehicle on a hoist or on safety jack stands.
3. Drain the transmission lubricant.
4. Scribe mark the drive line to the flange connection at the rear.
5. Disconnect the rear-wheel-drive drive shaft at the rear and tape the U-joint bearings in place to prevent loss of bearings or entry of dirt.
6. Slide the drive line from the transmission output shaft and cap the opening to prevent lubricant leakage.

FIGURE 6–6 Hydraulic transmission jack supports transmission during removal and installation. (Courtesy of OTC Division, SPX Corporation.)

7. Disconnect all transmission linkages, speedometer cable, and any electrical connections.

8. Support the engine as required. It may have to be lowered at the rear to provide room for the transmission to slide out.

9. Remove the cross member (if required). Note the location of any alignment shims and identify for later assembly.

10. Support the transmission on a transmission jack.

11. Remove the transmission attaching bolts.

12. Move the transmission straight out of the clutch assembly; avoid any binding in the clutch to prevent clutch damage.

TRANSAXLE REMOVAL

Transaxle removal procedures vary depending on the make and model of the vehicle. In some cases the engine and transaxle must be removed together through the top of the engine compartment. In most cases the transaxle is disconnected from the engine and removed from underneath the car (**Figures 6–8** to **6–10**).

1. Disconnect the negative battery cable from the battery.

2. Support the car on a hoist or jack stands.

3. Disconnect the clutch linkage, shift linkage, and speedometer cable.

4. Disconnect any electrical wiring from the transaxle.

5. Drain the lubricant from the transaxle.

6. Install the engine support fixture.

7. Remove the front drive axles.

8. Remove the starting motor.

9. Support the transaxle on a transmission jack.

10. Remove the transaxle-to-engine mounting bolts.

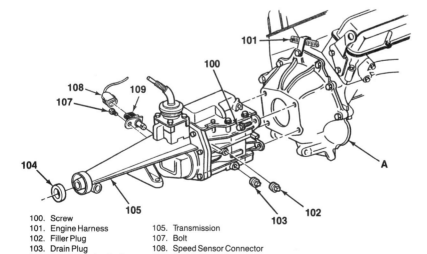

100. Screw
101. Engine Harness
102. Filler Plug
103. Drain Plug
104. Rear Extension Seal
105. Transmission
107. Bolt
108. Speed Sensor Connector
109. Vehicle Speed Sensor

FIGURE 6–7 Manual transmission removal. (Courtesy of General Motors Corporation.)

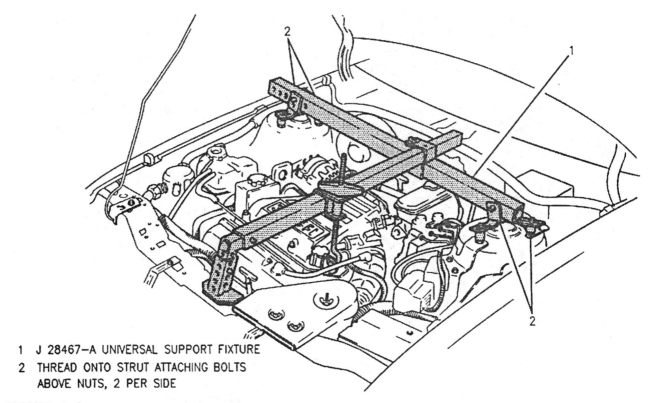

1 J 28467-A UNIVERSAL SUPPORT FIXTURE
2 THREAD ONTO STRUT ATTACHING BOLTS
  ABOVE NUTS, 2 PER SIDE

FIGURE 6–8 Engine support tool used in transaxle removal. (Courtesy of General Motors Corporation.)

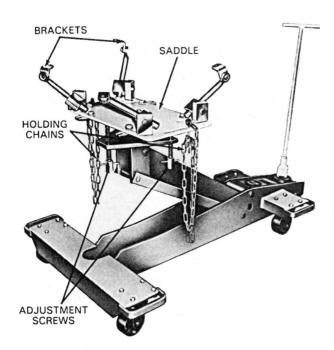

FIGURE 6–9 Jack used for transaxle removal. (Courtesy of OTC Division, SPX Corporation.)

11. Remove the transaxle-to-frame mount.

12. Remove the engine support subframe if necessary.

13. Separate the transaxle from the engine and remove the transaxle.

TRANSMISSION AND TRANSAXLE DISASSEMBLY GUIDELINES

Disassembly procedures differ considerably between different models of manual transmissions and transaxles. Refer to the service manual to ensure that the proper sequence is followed. See **Figures 6–11** to **6–17** for examples of transmission disassembly procedures. Four- and five-speed transmission parts are shown in **Figures 6–18** and **6–19**. **Figures 6–20** to **6–23** are examples of transaxle disassembly procedures. Typical transaxle parts are shown in **Figures 6–24** to **6–29**.

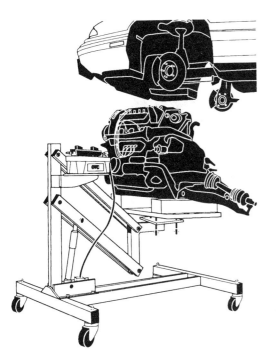

FIGURE 6–10 The engine and transaxle are removed together on some models of transaxle overhaul. On others, the transaxle is disconnected from the engine and removed. In both cases, a suitable jack such as the one shown is used. (Courtesy of OTC Division, SPX Corporation.)

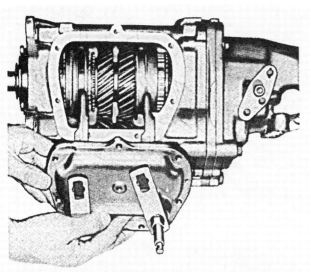

FIGURE 6–11 Removing the shift cover from a manual transmission. (Courtesy of General Motors Corporation.)

CASE

MAINSHAFT

INPUT SHAFT

REVERSE IDLER
GEAR SHAFT

EXTENSION
HOUSING

FIGURE 6–12 Removing/installing the extension housing and mainshaft on a Ford four-speed transmission. (Courtesy of Ford Motor Company.)

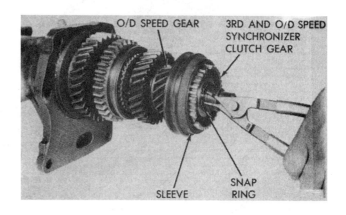

FIGURE 6–13 Transmission parts mounted on output shaft (mainshaft) of four-speed overdrive transmission. Note smaller overdrive driven gear. (Courtesy of Chrysler Corporation.)

O/D SPEED GEAR

3RD AND O/D SPEED SYNCHRONIZER CLUTCH GEAR

SLEEVE

SNAP RING

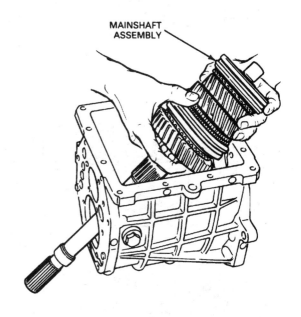

FIGURE 6–14 Removing a mainshaft assembly. (Courtesy of Ford Motor Company.)

MAINSHAFT ASSEMBLY

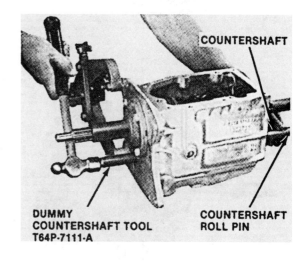

FIGURE 6–15 Using a dummy countershaft tool to drive out the countershaft. (Courtesy of Ford Motor Company.)

COUNTERSHAFT

DUMMY COUNTERSHAFT TOOL T64P-7111-A

COUNTERSHAFT ROLL PIN

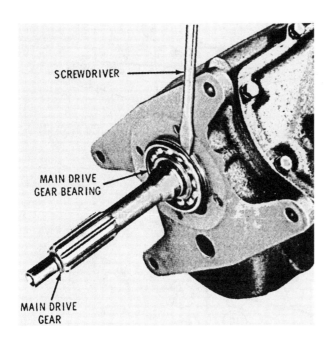

FIGURE 6–16 Removing the front bearing from the main drive gear prior to removing the gear and shaft from the case. (Courtesy of General Motors Corporation.)

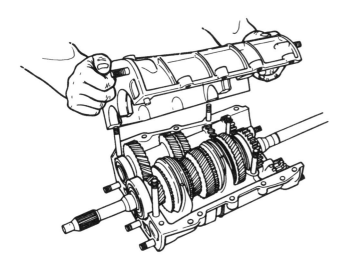

FIGURE 6–17 Split case transmission provides easy access to gear train. (Courtesy of Ford Motor Company.)

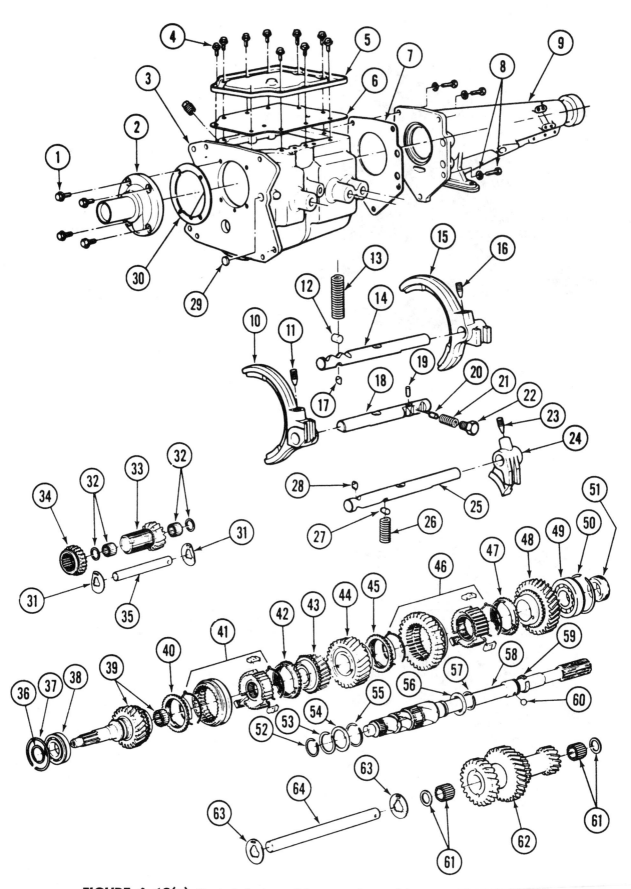

FIGURE 6-18(a) Exploded view of four-speed overdrive transmission. (Courtesy of Ford Motor Company.)

1. INPUT SHAFT BEARING RETAINER ATTACHING BOLT
2. INPUT SHAFT BEARING RETAINER
3. TRANSMISSION CASE
4. COVER ATTACHING BOLT
5. COVER
6. COVER GASKET
7. EXTENTION HOUSING GASKET
8. EXTENTION-TO-CASE BOLT AND LOCKWASHER
9. EXTENTION HOUSING ASS'Y.
10. 3RD-OVERDRIVE SHIFT FORK
11. SET SCREW
12. DETENT PIN
13. LONG SPRING
14. 1ST-2ND SPEED SHIFT RAIL
15. 1ST-2ND SPEED SHIFT FORK
16. SET SCREW
17. INTERLOCK DETENT PIN
18. 3RD-OVERDRIVE SHIFT RAIL
19. INTERLOCK PIN
20. PIN
21. DETENT SPRING
22. SIDE DETENT BOLT
23. SET SCREW
24. REVERSE SHIFT FORK
25. REVERSE SHIFT RAIL
26. DETENT PIN SPRING
27. REVERSE DETENT PIN
28. DETENT PIN
29. EXPANSION PLUG
30. RETAINER GASKET
31. THRUST WASHER
32. BEARINGS AND 3/4" FLAT WASHER

33. REVERSE IDLER GEAR
34. REVERSE SLIDING GEAR
35. REVERSE IDLER GEAR SHAFT
36. SNAP RING
37. SNAP RING
38. INPUT SHAFT BEARING
39. INPUT SHAFT GEAR AND BEARINGS
40. BLOCKING RING
41. 3RD-OVERDRIVE SYNCHRONIZER ASS'Y.
42. BLOCKING RING
43. OVERDRIVE GEAR
44. SECOND SPEED GEAR
45. BLOCKING RING
46. 1ST-2ND SYNCHRONIZER ASS'Y.
47. BLOCKING RING
48. 1ST SPEED GEAR
49. OUTPUT SHAFT BEARING
50. SNAP RING
51. SPEEDOMETER DRIVE GEAR
52. SNAP RING
53. SNAP RING
54. THRUST WASHER
55. SNAP RING
56. THRUST WASHER
57. SNAP RING
58. OUTPUT SHAFT
59. SNAP RING
60. SPEEDOMETER GEAR DRIVE BALL
61. BEARINGS AND 7/8" FLAT WASHER
62. COUNTERSHAFT GEAR CLUSTER
63. THRUST WASHER
64. COUNTERSHAFT

FIGURE 6–18(b) Key for Figure 6–18(a).

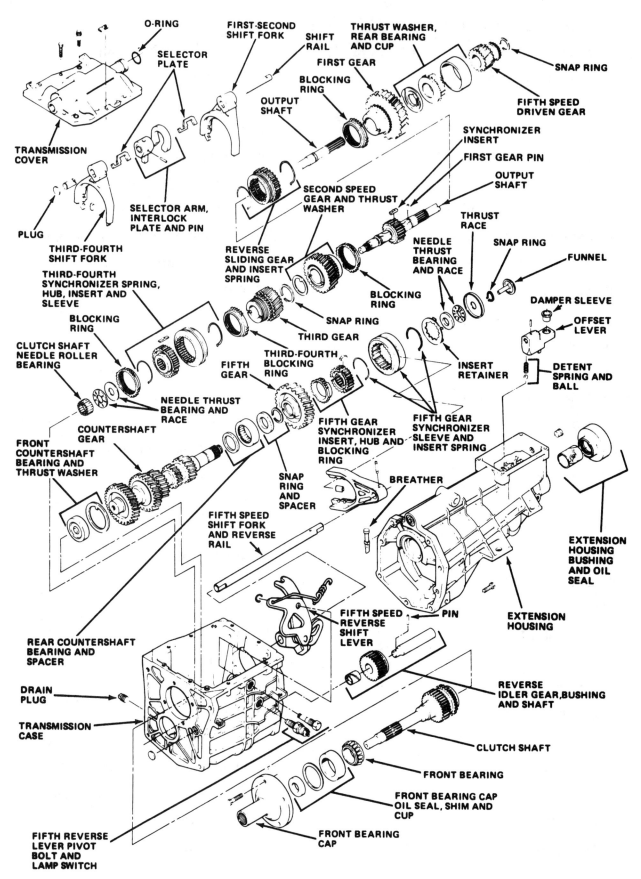

FIGURE 6–19 Five-speed manual transmission parts. (Courtesy of Chrysler Corporation.)

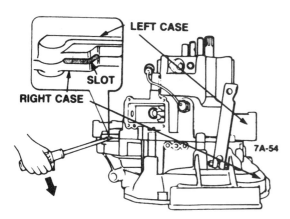

FIGURE 6–20 The transaxle case and cover are often stuck together and must be pried apart with a screwdriver. This transaxle has slots to make the job easier and avoids damage to mating surfaces. (Courtesy of General Motors Corporation.)

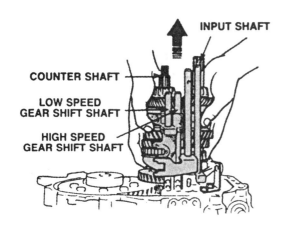

FIGURE 6–21 After removing the gear housing, the gear assemblies and shift mechanism can be removed as an assembly. (Courtesy of General Motors Corporation.)

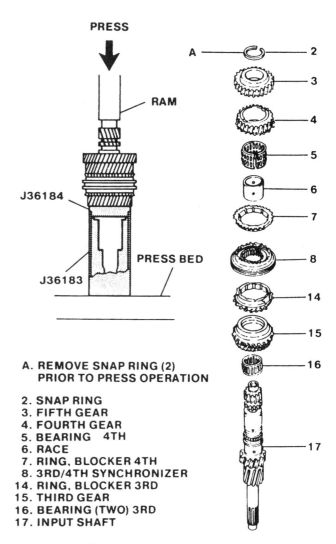

A. REMOVE SNAP RING (2) PRIOR TO PRESS OPERATION

2. SNAP RING
3. FIFTH GEAR
4. FOURTH GEAR
5. BEARING 4TH
6. RACE
7. RING, BLOCKER 4TH
8. 3RD/4TH SYNCHRONIZER
14. RING, BLOCKER 3RD
15. THIRD GEAR
16. BEARING (TWO) 3RD
17. INPUT SHAFT

FIGURE 6–22 Using a press to remove input shaft components of a five-speed transaxle. (Courtesy of General Motors Corporation.)

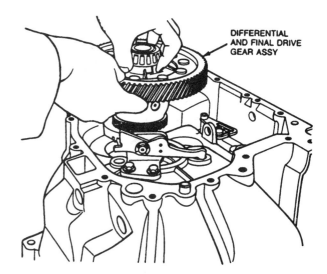

FIGURE 6–23 After removing the gear assemblies, the differential is removed from this transaxle. (Courtesy of Ford Motor Company.)

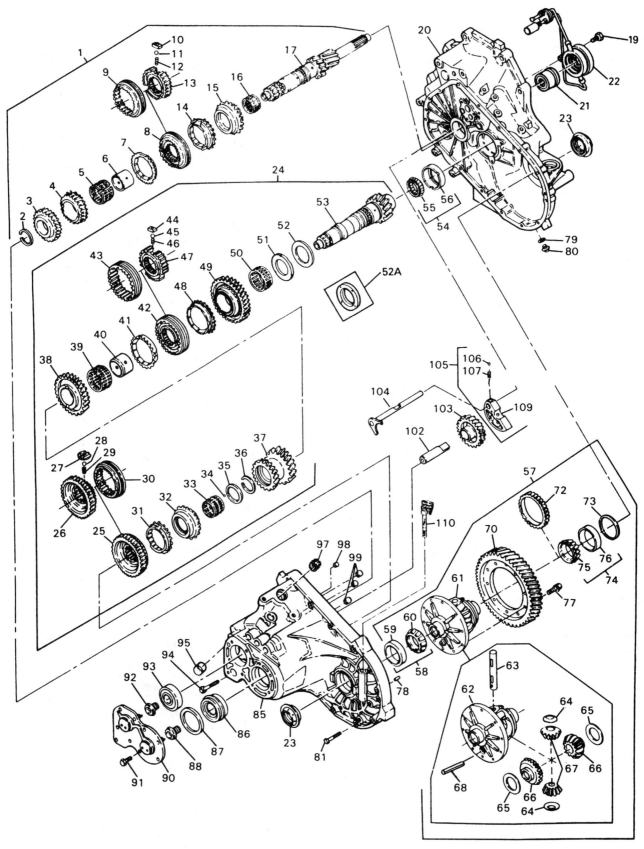

FIGURE 6–24(a) Five-speed manual transaxle parts (typical). See Figure 6–24(b) for key to numbered parts. (Courtesy of General Motors Corporation.)

1 SHAFT & GEAR ASSEMBLY, INPUT CLUSTER	34 BALL, THRUST WASHER POSITIONER	70 GEAR, RING DIFFERENTIAL
2 SNAP RING	35 WASHER, THRUST	72 GEAR, SPEEDO OUTPUT (ELECTRONIC)
3 GEAR, FIFTH INPUT	36 SNAP RING	73 SHIM, DIFFERENTIAL (SELECTIVE)
4 GEAR, FOURTH INPUT	37 GEAR, 3RD/4TH CLUSTER	74 BEARING ASSEMBLY, DIFFERENTIAL
5 BEARING, CAGE	38 GEAR, 2ND OUTPUT	75 BEARING, DIFFERENTIAL
6 RACE, NEEDLE	39 BEARING, 2ND OUTPUT	76 RACE, BEARING DIFFERENTIAL
7 RING, BLOCKER 4TH	40 RACE, BEARING 2ND OUTPUT	77 BOLT/SCREW, DIFFERENTIAL RING (10)
8 SYNCHRONIZER ASSEMBLY, 3RD/4TH	41 RING, BLOCKER 2ND GEAR	78 PIN (TWO)
9 SLEEVE, 3RD/4TH SYNCHRONIZER	42 SYNCHRONIZER ASSEMBLY, 1ST/2ND GEAR	79 PLUG, OIL DRAIN
10 KEY, 3RD/4TH SYNCHRONIZER (THREE)	43 SLEEVE, 1ST/2ND SYNCHRONIZER	80 WASHER
11 BALL, 3RD/4TH SYNCHRONIZER (THREE)	44 KEY, 1ST/2ND SYNCHRONIZER (THREE)	81 BOLT/SCREW, TRANSAXLE CASE, M8 x 1.25 x 50 (15)
12 SPRING, 3RD/4TH SYNCHRONIZER (THREE)	45 BALL, 1ST/2ND SYNCHRONIZER (THREE)	85 CASE, TRANSAXLE
13 HUB, CLUTCH, 3RD/4TH SYNCHRONIZER	46 SPRING, 1ST/2ND SYNCHRONIZER (THREE)	86 BEARING ASSEMBLY, OUTPUT SHAFT
14 RING, BLOCKER 3RD	47 HUB, 1ST/2ND SYNCHRONIZER	87 SHIM, OUTPUT GEAR (SELECTIVE)
15 GEAR, THIRD INPUT	48 RING, BLOCKER 1ST GEAR	88 RETAINER, OUTPUT GEAR BEARING
16 BEARING, CAGE (TWO)	50 BEARING, 1ST OUTPUT	90 END PLATE, TRANSAXLE CASE
17 SHAFT, INPUT	51 BEARING, THRUST	91 BOLT/SCREW, M8 x 1 x 18 (9)
19 PIN	52 WASHER, THRUST	92 RETAINER, INPUT GEAR BEARING
20 HOUSING, CLUTCH AND DIFFERENTIAL	52A WASHER, THRUST (REPLACES 51 AND 52 FOR MV5 ONLY)	93 BEARING ASSEMBLY, INPUT SHAFT
21 BEARING/SEAL ASSEMBLY, INPUT SHAFT	53 SHAFT, OUTPOUT	94 BOLT/SCREW, REVERSE IDLER, M8 x 1.25 x 50
22 BEARING ASSEMBLY, CLUTCH RELEASE	54 BEARING, OUTPUT SHAFT SUPPORT	95 BUSHING, DETENT LEVER
23 SEAL, OIL DRIVE AXLE	55 BEARING, OUTPUT	97 BEARING, NEEDLE SHIFT SHAFT
24 SHAFT & GEAR ASSEMBLY, OUTPUT CLUSTER	56 RACE, BEARING OUTPUT	98 BUSHING, REVERSE RAIL
25 GEAR, REVERSE OUTPUT/5TH SYNCHRONIZER ASSEMBLY	57 GEAR AND DIFFERENTIAL ASSEMBLY	99 BUSHING, SHIFT RAIL (THREE)
26 GEAR, REVERSE	58 BEARING ASSEMBLY, DIFFERENTIAL	102 SHAFT, REVERSE IDLER
27 KEY, 5TH SYNCHRONIZER (THREE)	59 RACE, BEARING DIFFERENTIAL	103 GEAR, REVERSE IDLER
28 BALL, 5TH SYNCHRONIZER (THREE)	60 BEARING, DIFFERENTIAL	104 RAIL, REVERSE SHIFT IDLER GEAR
29 SPRING, 5TH SYNCHRONIZER (THREE)	61 CASE, DIFFERENTIAL ASSEMBLY	105 BRACKET ASSEMBLY, REVERSE IDLER GEAR
30 SLEEVE, 5TH SYNCHRONIZER	62 CASE, DIFFERENTIAL	106 BALL, BRACKET REVERSE IDLER GEAR
31 RING, BLOCKER 5TH GEAR	63 PIN, CROSS DIFFERENTIAL	107 SPRING, BRACKET REVERSE IDLER GEAR
32 GEAR, 5TH SPEED OUTPUT	64 WASHER, THRUST PINION GEAR	109 BRACKET, REVERSE IDLER GEAR
33 BEARING, 5TH SPEED OUTPUT	65 WASHER, THRUST SIDE GEAR	110 INDICATOR ASSEMBLY, TRANSAXLE FLUID LEVEL
	66 GEAR, SIDE DIFFERENTIAL	
	67 GEAR, PINION DIFFERENTIAL	
	68 ROLL PIN, PINION GEAR SHAFT	

FIGURE 6–24(b) Key for Figure 6–24(a).

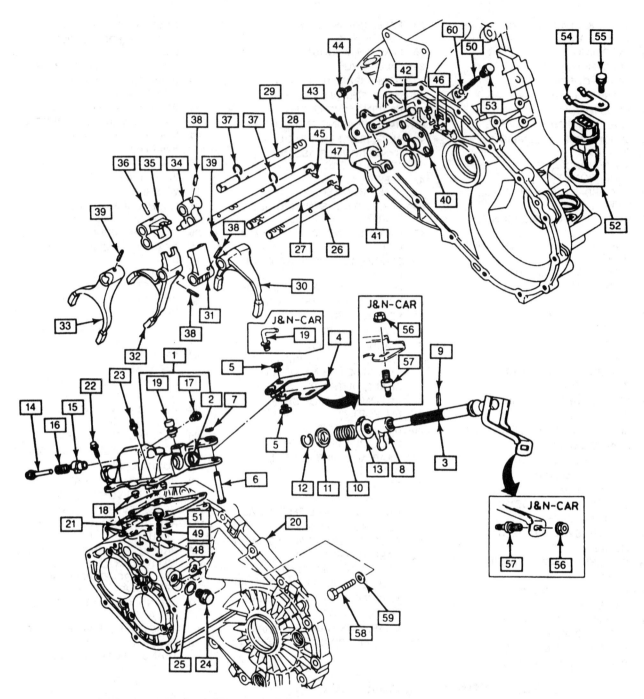

FIGURE 6–25(a) Five-speed transaxle case and shift mechanism components. See Figure 6–25(b) for key to numbered parts. (Courtesy of General Motors Corporation.)

1	QUADRANT BOX ASSEMBLY
2	QUADRANT BOX OIL SEAL
3	SHIFT LEVER
4	SELECT LEVER
5	SELECT LEVER BUSHING
6	SELECT LEVER PIN
7	C-CLIP
8	INTERNAL SHIFT LEVER
9	ROLL PIN
10	SELECT LEVER SPRING
11	LOWER SPRING SEAT
12	C-CLIP
13	UPPER SPRING SEAT
14	QUADRANT BOX REVERSE INHIBITOR BOLT
15	REVERSE INHIBITOR CAM
16	REVERSE INHIBITOR CAM SPRING
17	STOPPER CAM BOLT
18	KNOCK PINS
19	BREATHER
20	TRANSAXLE CASE
21	GASKET

22	QUADRANT BOX RETAINING BOLT
23	STUD
24	PLUG
25	GASKET
26	1ST/2ND SHIFT SHAFT
27	3RD/4TH SHIFT SHAFT
28	5TH SHIFT SHAFT
29	REVERSE SHIFT SHAFT
30	1ST/2ND SHIFT FORK
31	1ST/2ND SHIFT BLOCK
32	3RD/4TH SHIFT FORK
33	5TH SHIFT FORK
34	REVERSE SHIFT LEVER BLOCK
35	REVERSE/5TH SHIFT BLOCK
36	10 mm INTERLOCK PIN
37	C-CLIP
38	ROLL PIN
39	ROLL PIN
40	REVERSE SHIFT LEVER BRACKET
41	REVERSE SHIFT LEVER
42	REVERSE SHIFT LEVER PIN

43	CLEVIS PIN
44	REVERSE SHIFT LEVER BRACKET BOLT
45	12 mm LOCK PIN
46	10 mm LOCK PIN
47	13 mm LOCK PIN
48	REVERSE DETENT BALL
49	1ST/2ND, 3RD/4TH AND 5TH DETENT SPRINGS
50	REVERSE DETENT SPRING
51	1ST,2ND, 3RD/4TH AND 5TH RETAINING BOLTS
52	VEHICLE SPEED SENSOR (VSS)
53	REVERSE DETENT SPRING RETAINING BOLT
54	VSS RETAINER
55	VSS RETAINING BOLT
56	NUT
57	STUD
58	TRANSAXLE CASE BOLT
59	WASHER
60	REVERSE DETENT BALL

FIGURE 6–25(b) Key for Figure 6–25(a).

1	DIFFERENTIAL CASE
2	VEHICLE SPEED SENSOR (VSS) RING (J AND N CARS ONLY)
3	SPEEDOMETER DRIVE GEAR (R CAR ONLY)
4	SIDE GEAR THRUST WASHER
5	SIDE GEAR
6	PINION GEAR THRUST WASHER
7	PINION GEAR
8	DIFFERENTIAL SIDE BEARING
9	PINION SHAFT

10	PINION SHAFT ROLL PIN
11	DIFFERENTIAL RING GEAR
12	DIFFERENTIAL SIDE BEARING SELECTIVE SHIM
13	DIFFERENTIAL RING GEAR BOLT

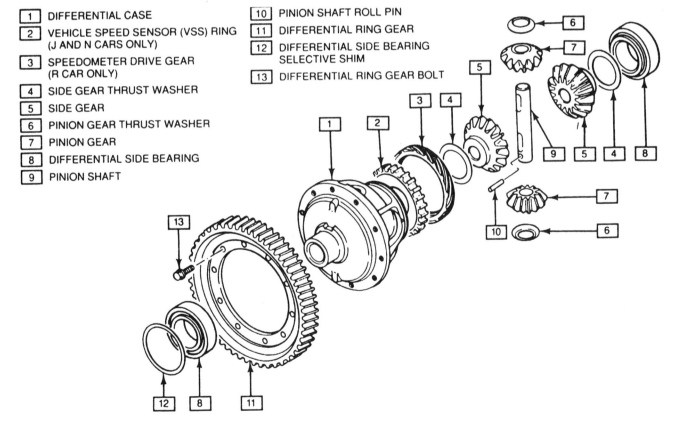

FIGURE 6–26 Typical transaxle differential components. (Courtesy of General Motors Corporation.)

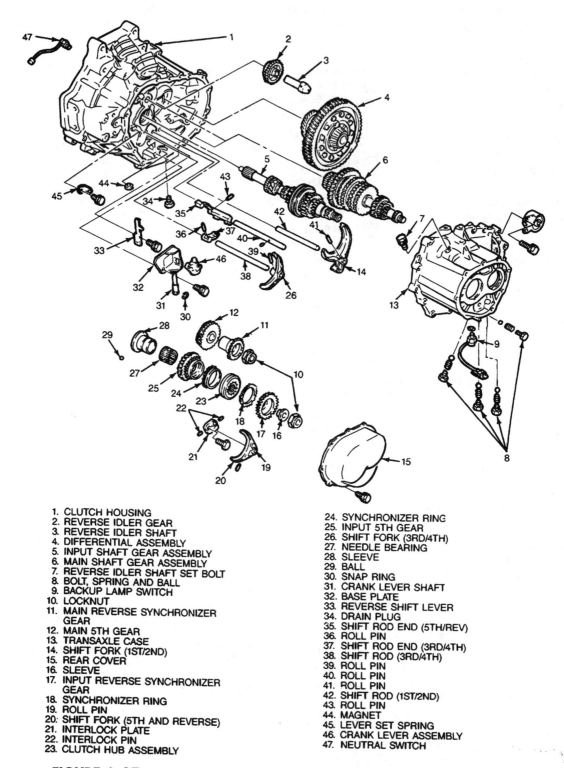

1. CLUTCH HOUSING
2. REVERSE IDLER GEAR
3. REVERSE IDLER SHAFT
4. DIFFERENTIAL ASSEMBLY
5. INPUT SHAFT GEAR ASSEMBLY
6. MAIN SHAFT GEAR ASSEMBLY
7. REVERSE IDLER SHAFT SET BOLT
8. BOLT, SPRING AND BALL
9. BACKUP LAMP SWITCH
10. LOCKNUT
11. MAIN REVERSE SYNCHRONIZER
    GEAR
12. MAIN 5TH GEAR
13. TRANSAXLE CASE
14. SHIFT FORK (1ST/2ND)
15. REAR COVER
16. SLEEVE
17. INPUT REVERSE SYNCHRONIZER
    GEAR
18. SYNCHRONIZER RING
19. ROLL PIN
20. SHIFT FORK (5TH AND REVERSE)
21. INTERLOCK PLATE
22. INTERLOCK PIN
23. CLUTCH HUB ASSEMBLY

24. SYNCHRONIZER RING
25. INPUT 5TH GEAR
26. SHIFT FORK (3RD/4TH)
27. NEEDLE BEARING
28. SLEEVE
29. BALL
30. SNAP RING
31. CRANK LEVER SHAFT
32. BASE PLATE
33. REVERSE SHIFT LEVER
34. DRAIN PLUG
35. SHIFT ROD END (5TH/REV)
36. ROLL PIN
37. SHIFT ROD END (3RD/4TH)
38. SHIFT ROD (3RD/4TH)
39. ROLL PIN
40. ROLL PIN
41. ROLL PIN
42. SHIFT ROD (1ST/2ND)
43. ROLL PIN
44. MAGNET
45. LEVER SET SPRING
46. CRANK LEVER ASSEMBLY
47. NEUTRAL SWITCH

FIGURE 6–27 Five-speed manual transaxle components. (Courtesy of Ford Motor Company.)

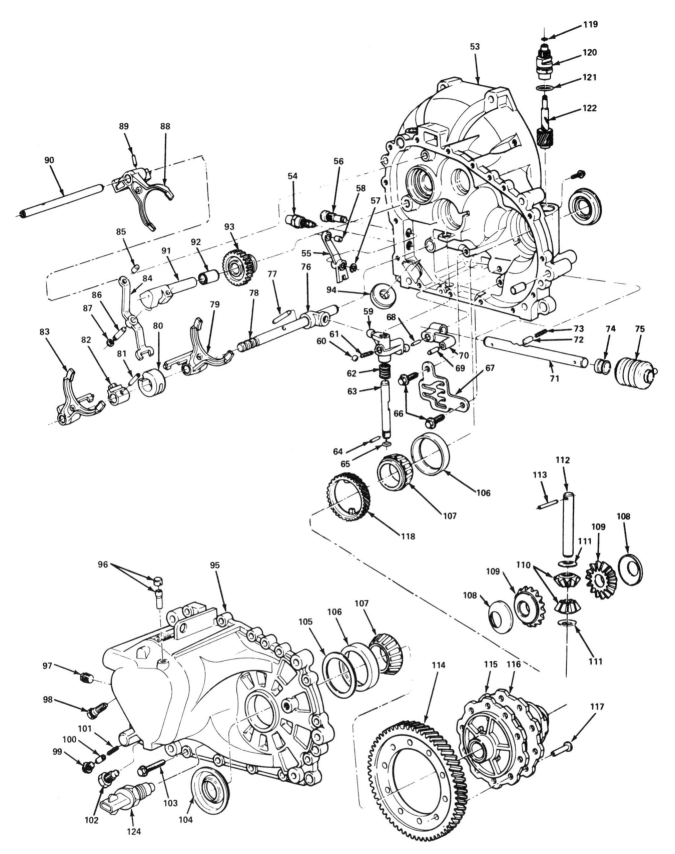

FIGURE 6–28 Five-speed transaxle shift mechanism and final drive components must also be inspected. See Figure 6–29 for key to numbered parts. (Courtesy of Ford Motor Company.)

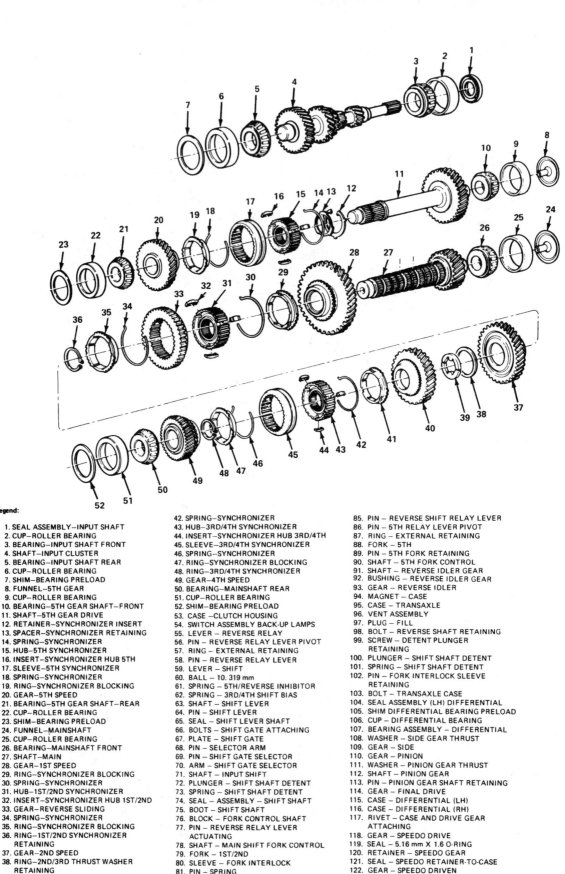

Legend:

1. SEAL ASSEMBLY—INPUT SHAFT
2. CUP—ROLLER BEARING
3. BEARING—INPUT SHAFT FRONT
4. SHAFT—INPUT CLUSTER
5. BEARING—INPUT SHAFT REAR
6. CUP—ROLLER BEARING
7. SHIM—BEARING PRELOAD
8. FUNNEL—5TH GEAR
9. CUP—ROLLER BEARING
10. BEARING—5TH GEAR SHAFT—FRONT
11. SHAFT—5TH GEAR DRIVE
12. RETAINER—SYNCHRONIZER INSERT
13. SPACER—SYNCHRONIZER RETAINING
14. SPRING—SYNCHRONIZER
15. HUB—5TH SYNCHRONIZER
16. INSERT—SYNCHRONIZER HUB 5TH
17. SLEEVE—5TH SYNCHRONIZER
18. SPRING—SYNCHRONIZER
19. RING—SYNCHRONIZER BLOCKING
20. GEAR—5TH SPEED
21. BEARING—5TH GEAR SHAFT—REAR
22. CUP—ROLLER BEARING
23. SHIM—BEARING PRELOAD
24. FUNNEL—MAINSHAFT
25. CUP—ROLLER BEARING
26. BEARING—MAINSHAFT FRONT
27. SHAFT—MAIN
28. GEAR—1ST SPEED
29. RING—SYNCHRONIZER BLOCKING
30. SPRING—SYNCHRONIZER
31. HUB—1ST/2ND SYNCHRONIZER
32. INSERT—SYNCHRONIZER HUB 1ST/2ND
33. GEAR—REVERSE SLIDING
34. SPRING—SYNCHRONIZER
35. RING—SYNCHRONIZER BLOCKING
36. RING—1ST/2ND SYNCHRONIZER RETAINING
37. GEAR—2ND SPEED
38. RING—2ND/3RD THRUST WASHER RETAINING
39. WASHER—2ND/3RD GEAR THRUST
40. GEAR—3RD SPEED
41. RING—SYNCHRONIZER BLOCKING

42. SPRING—SYNCHRONIZER
43. HUB—3RD/4TH SYNCHRONIZER
44. INSERT—SYNCHRONIZER HUB 3RD/4TH
45. SLEEVE—3RD/4TH SYNCHRONIZER
46. SPRING—SYNCHRONIZER
47. RING—SYNCHRONIZER BLOCKING
48. RING—3RD/4TH SYNCHRONIZER
49. GEAR—4TH SPEED
50. BEARING—MAINSHAFT REAR
51. CUP—ROLLER BEARING
52. SHIM—BEARING PRELOAD
53. CASE —CLUTCH HOUSING
54. SWITCH ASSEMBLY BACK-UP LAMPS
55. LEVER – REVERSE RELAY
56. PIN – REVERSE RELAY LEVER PIVOT
57. RING – EXTERNAL RETAINING
58. PIN – REVERSE RELAY LEVER
59. LEVER – SHIFT
60. BALL – 10. 319 mm
61. SPRING – 5TH/REVERSE INHIBITOR
62. SPRING – 3RD/4TH SHIFT BIAS
63. SHAFT – SHIFT LEVER
64. PIN – SHIFT LEVER
65. SEAL – SHIFT LEVER SHAFT
66. BOLTS – SHIFT GATE ATTACHING
67. PLATE – SHIFT GATE
68. PIN – SELECTOR ARM
69. PIN – SHIFT GATE SELECTOR
70. ARM – SHIFT GATE SELECTOR
71. SHAFT – INPUT SHIFT
72. PLUNGER – SHIFT SHAFT DETENT
73. SPRING – SHIFT SHAFT DETENT
74. SEAL – ASSEMBLY – SHIFT SHAFT
75. BOOT – SHIFT SHAFT
76. BLOCK – FORK CONTROL SHAFT
77. PIN – REVERSE RELAY LEVER ACTUATING
78. SHAFT – MAIN SHIFT FORK CONTROL
79. FORK – 1ST/2ND
80. SLEEVE – FORK INTERLOCK
81. PIN – SPRING
82. ARM – FORK SELECTOR
83. FORK – 3RD/4TH
84. LEVER – 5TH SHIFT RELAY

85. PIN – REVERSE SHIFT RELAY LEVER
86. PIN – 5TH RELAY LEVER PIVOT
87. RING – EXTERNAL RETAINING
88. FORK – 5TH
89. PIN – 5TH FORK RETAINING
90. SHAFT – 5TH FORK CONTROL
91. SHAFT – REVERSE IDLER GEAR
92. BUSHING – REVERSE IDLER GEAR
93. GEAR – REVERSE IDLER
94. MAGNET – CASE
95. CASE – TRANSAXLE
96. VENT ASSEMBLY
97. PLUG – FILL
98. BOLT – REVERSE SHAFT RETAINING
99. SCREW – DETENT PLUNGER RETAINING
100. PLUNGER – SHIFT SHAFT DETENT
101. SPRING – SHIFT SHAFT DETENT
102. PIN – FORK INTERLOCK SLEEVE RETAINING
103. BOLT – TRANSAXLE CASE
104. SEAL ASSEMBLY (LH) DIFFERENTIAL
105. SHIM DIFFERENTIAL BEARING PRELOAD
106. CUP – DIFFERENTIAL BEARING
107. BEARING ASSEMBLY – DIFFERENTIAL
108. WASHER – SIDE GEAR THRUST
109. GEAR – SIDE
110. GEAR – PINION
111. WASHER – PINION GEAR THRUST
112. SHAFT – PINION GEAR
113. PIN – PINION GEAR SHAFT RETAINING
114. GEAR – FINAL DRIVE
115. CASE – DIFFERENTIAL (LH)
116. CASE – DIFFERENTIAL (RH)
117. RIVET – CASE AND DRIVE GEAR ATTACHING
118. GEAR – SPEEDO DRIVE
119. SEAL – 5.16 mm X 1.6 O-RING
120. RETAINER – SPEEDO GEAR
121. SEAL – SPEEDO RETAINER-TO-CASE
122. GEAR – SPEEDO DRIVEN
123. DOWEL – CASE-TO-CLUTCH HOUSING
124. **SWITCH – TRANSAXLE NEUTRAL SENSING**

FIGURE 6–29 Five-speed transaxle gear train parts. See Figure 6–28 for listed parts not shown here. (Courtesy of Ford Motor Company.)

Cleaning the Parts

1. Wash all parts (except the sealed bearings and seals) in a suitable cleaning solvent. Brush or scrape all foreign matter from the parts. Be careful not to damage any parts with the scraper. Do not clean, wash, or soak transmission seals in cleaning solvents. Dry all parts with compressed air.

2. Rotate the nonsealed ball bearings in a cleaning solvent until all lubricant is removed. Hold the bearing assembly to prevent it from rotating, and dry it with compressed air.

3. Lubricate the bearings with approved transmission lubricant, and wrap them in a clean, lint-free cloth or paper until ready for use.

4. Clean the magnet in the bottom of the case with kerosene or mineral spirits.

Inspecting the Parts

See **Figures 6–30** to **6–47** for inspection procedures.

1. Inspect the transmission case for cracks, worn or damaged bearing bores, damaged threads, or

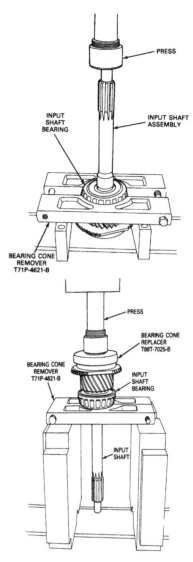

FIGURE 6–31 Removing (top) and installing (bottom) a clutch shaft bearing. (Courtesy of Ford Motor Company.)

any other damage that could affect the operation of the transmission.

2. Inspect the front face of the case for small nicks or burrs that could cause misalignment of the transmission with the flywheel housing. Remove all small nicks or burrs with a fine stone on cast iron cases or with a fine file on aluminum cases.

3. Replace any cover that is bent or distorted. Make sure that the vent hole is open.

4. Check the condition of the shift levers, forks, shift rails, and the lever and shafts.

5. Inspect the ball bearings according to the instructions in the section on ball bearing inspection.

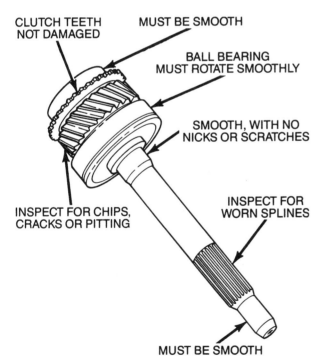

FIGURE 6–30 Inspect the clutch shaft (input shaft) carefully as above. (Courtesy of Chrysler Corporation.)

6. Replace roller bearings that are broken, worn, or rough, and check their respective races for wear or damage.

7. Replace the countershaft (cluster) gear if the teeth are chipped, broken, or worn. Replace the countershaft if it is bent, scored, or worn.

8. Replace the reverse idler gear or sliding gear if the teeth are chipped, worn, or broken. Replace the idler gear shaft if bent, worn, or scored.

9. Replace the input shaft and gear if the splines are damaged or if the teeth are chipped, worn, or broken. If the roller bearing surface in the bore of the gear is worn or rough or if the cone surface is damaged, replace the gear and the gear rollers.

10. Replace all other gears that are chipped, broken, or worn.

11. Check the synchronizer sleeves for free movement on their hubs. Make sure that the alignment marks (if present) are properly indexed.

12. Inspect the synchronizer blocking rings for widened insert slots, rounded clutch teeth, and smooth internal surfaces (must have machined grooves). With the blocker ring on the cone, the distance between the face of the blocker ring and the clutch teeth on the gear must not be less than 0.020 in. (0.5 mm).

13. Replace the speedometer drive gear if the teeth are stripped or damaged. Make certain to install the correct-size replacement gear. Test the speed sensor output signal. Replace if faulty.

INSPECTING THE GEARS AND SHAFTS

Inspect each gear carefully for any abnormal condition. Inspect both sides of the gear teeth, the cone surface, clutch teeth, thrust surfaces, and the gear bore surface. Look for any of the following conditions (**Figures 6–32 to 6–34**):

Cracks: breaks in the metal that show up as a line or as a complete break.

Wear: shows up as loss of metal in areas where friction occurs as compared to surrounding area where there is no friction.

Chips: are seen as small bits of missing metal that have broken off.

Nicks and Burrs: indentations caused by small amounts of metal being raised or displaced from the point of impact of another part or object.

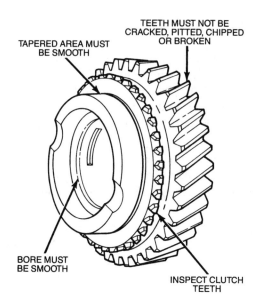

FIGURE 6–32 Check all gears for wear or damage. (Courtesy of Chrysler Corporation.)

Overheating: shows up as discoloration from blue to black due to lack of lubrication, overloading, or both.

Galling: damage to surfaces of parts in frictional contact with each other. Material from one part may tear loose and be deposited on the other by welding due to loss of lubricant, overloading, or overheating.

Inspect each shaft for any of these same conditions. Inspect the friction areas, splines, and snap ring grooves. Place the shaft in V-blocks and check for straightness with a dial indicator (**Figures 6–35 to 6–38**).

Minor nicks and burrs can be removed from both gears and shafts with a fine stone. Be careful not to damage any of the surrounding area. Badly damaged gears or shafts must be replaced.

SYNCHRONIZER INSPECTION

Synchronizers must be disassembled for proper inspection of all its parts. The sleeve and hub are factory-mated parts, and they must be marked to ensure that they are mated during later reassembly. Remove the retaining springs and inserts, and slide the sleeve from the hub. The hub must not be allowed to drop since it is easily bent. After disassembly, check that the sleeve slides freely back and forth on the hub without sticking. Inspect the hub and sleeve for wear or damage to the splines and gear teeth. Check the inserts for wear

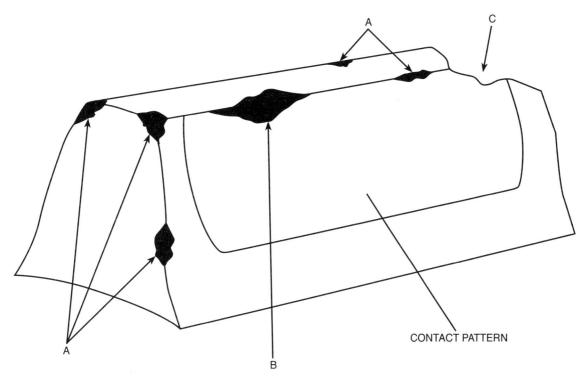

FIGURE 6–33 (A) Small chips in these areas of gear teeth are usually acceptable. (B) Larger chips that extend into tooth contact area are not acceptable. (C) Broken tooth is not acceptable.

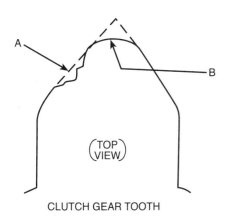

FIGURE 6–34 If clutch gear teeth or blocking ring are chipped (A) or rounded (B), the gear or ring should be replaced.

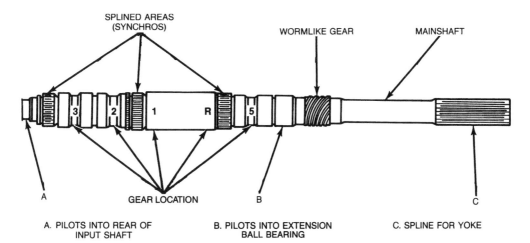

FIGURE 6–35 Carefully examine shaft for wear or damage in the areas shown. (Courtesy of Chrysler Corporation.)

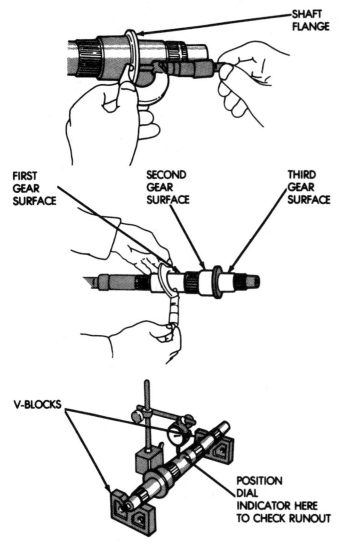

FIRST GEAR SURFACE

SECOND GEAR SURFACE

THIRD GEAR SURFACE

V-BLOCKS

POSITION DIAL INDICATOR HERE TO CHECK RUNOUT

FIGURE 6–36 Measure output shaft wear and runout. If excessive, replace the shaft. (Courtesy of Ford Motor Company.)

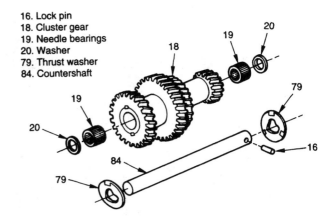

16. Lock pin
18. Cluster gear
19. Needle bearings
20. Washer
79. Thrust washer
84. Countershaft

FIGURE 6–37 Inspect cluster gear teeth, bearing race inside each end of cluster gear, needle bearings, thrust washers, and cluster gear shaft for excessive wear or damage. (Courtesy of Ford Motor Company.)

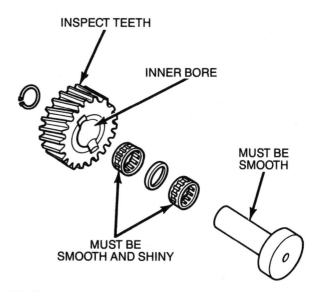

INSPECT TEETH

INNER BORE

MUST BE SMOOTH

MUST BE SMOOTH AND SHINY

FIGURE 6–38 Inspect the reverse idler assembly as illustrated. (Courtesy of Chrysler Corporation.)

or damage. Check the springs to make sure they are not distorted **(Figure 6–39).**

To assemble the synchronizer, position the sleeve on the hub with the index marks aligned and the front of both the hub and sleeve facing the same direction. Place the inserts into the grooves. Install the retaining springs, and index them as specified in the service manual. Usually the tanged end of the spring is placed inside one of the inserts and the spring spiraled into place. The remaining spring is installed on the other side in the same manner but in the opposite direction, with the tanged end inserted in the other end of the same insert. This distributes spring force equally against the inserts **(Figures 6–40 and 6–41).**

Examine the brass blocking rings for wear or damage to the teeth (see Figure 6–34) and the grooved inner surface. Make sure the ring is not cracked **(Figure 6–42).** Check paper-faced blocking rings for glazing and discoloration due to overheating and for pits and cracking. Place the blocking ring on the gear cone, and try to turn it while holding the gear. The ring should have a grabbing effect but should pull off easily without sticking. Place the ring on the gear cone and measure the clearance with a feeler gauge **(Figure 6–43).** A minimum clearance of 0.020 in. (0.51 mm) is specified in some service manuals. If clearance is below specifications, the ring should be replaced.

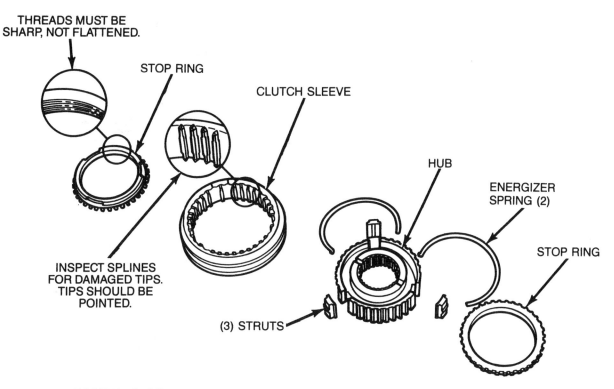

FIGURE 6–39 Inspect each synchronizer part as illustrated. (Courtesy of Chrysler Corporation.)

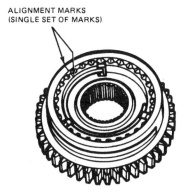

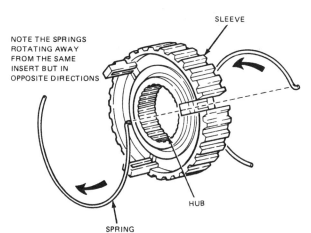

FIGURE 6–40 Be sure the synchronizers are all assembled correctly and the springs are positioned as specified in the service manual. (Courtesy of Ford Motor Company.)

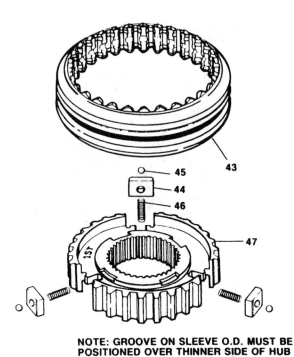

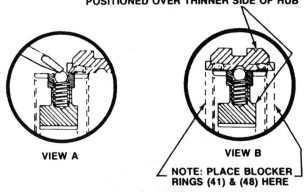

NOTE: GROOVE ON SLEEVE O.D. MUST BE
POSITIONED OVER THINNER SIDE OF HUB

VIEW A

VIEW B

NOTE: PLACE BLOCKER
RINGS (41) & (48) HERE

FIGURE 6–41 Assembling a ball-type synchronizer.
(Courtesy of General Motors Corporation.)

43. SLEEVE, 1ST/2ND SYNCHRONIZER
44. KEY, 1ST/2ND SYNCHRONIZER (THREE)
45. BALL, 1ST/2ND SYNCHRONIZER (THREE)
46. SPRING, 1ST/2ND SYNCHRONIZER (THREE)
47. HUB, 1ST/2ND SYNCHRONIZER

1ST/2ND ASSEMBLY PROCEDURES

→← Install

1. Sleeve (43), small O.D. groove **MUST** be positioned over **THINNER** side of hub (47).
2. Spring (46) into key (44).
3. Spring and key assemblies, bevel cut on keys toward sleeve.
4. Position assembly as in View A.
5. Balls (45):
    • push the ball into the sleeve using a screwdriver
    • push the sleeve (43) down just enough to retain the ball
    • "cock" the sleeve just enough to allow installation of the remaining balls (one at a time).
6. Blocker rings (41) and (48):
    • make sure blocker ring tangs line up with the keys.
7. Center the hub, keys and balls by pushing on both blocker rings, View B. Balls will "click" into position.

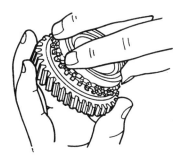

FIGURE 6–42 Checking blocker ring against gear cone. Push the ring against the cone, and try to turn the ring on the cone. It should grab the cone but still release freely when pulled away. (Courtesy of Ford Motor Company.)

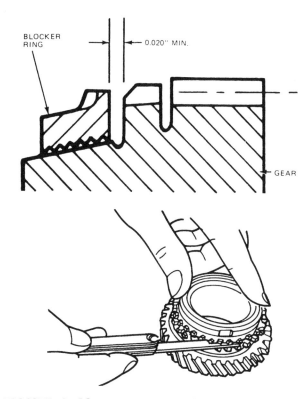

FIGURE 6–43 Measure clearance between blocking ring and gear face with a feeler gauge. If less than specified, replace the blocker ring. (Courtesy of Ford Motor Company.)

BEARING INSPECTION

Transmission bearings must be carefully examined to determine whether they are in good condition and can be used again or whether they must be replaced. The following procedures may be used:

Ball Bearing Inspection

1. *Inner ring raceway.* While holding the outer ring stationary, rotate the inner ring at least three revolutions. Examine the raceway of the inner ring from both sides for pits or spalling. A bearing assembly should be replaced when thus damaged. Light particle indentation is acceptable.

2. *Outer ring raceway.* While holding the inner ring stationary, rotate the outer ring at least three revolutions. Examine the raceway of the outer ring from both sides as with the raceway of the inner ring. If the raceway is spalled or pitted, replace the bearing assembly **(Figure 6–44)**.

Bearing External Surfaces

The bearing must be replaced if damage is found in any of the following areas:

1. Radial cracks on the front and rear faces of the outer or inner rings

2. Cracks on the outside diameter or outer ring (particularly around snap ring groove)

3. Deformation or cracks in the ball cage (particularly around rivets)

Spin Testing the Bearings

1. Lubricate the bearing raceways with a slight amount of clean oil. Turn the bearing back and forth slowly until the raceways and balls are coated with oil.

2. Hold the bearing by the inner ring in a vertical position. Vertical movement between the inner and outer rings is acceptable. Spin the outer ring several times by hand (do not use an air hose). If roughness or vibration is noticeable or the outer ring stops abruptly, the bearing should be replaced.

Roller Bearing Inspection

There are several types of roller bearings used in transmissions and transaxles: tapered, straight, and thrust. The rollers in a tapered bearing and thrust bearings are always caged. The rollers in a straight roller bearing may or may not be caged. In applications where the rollers are not caged, they fit between an inner race such as a shaft and an outer race such as the inside of a gear bore. Their endwise movement is re-

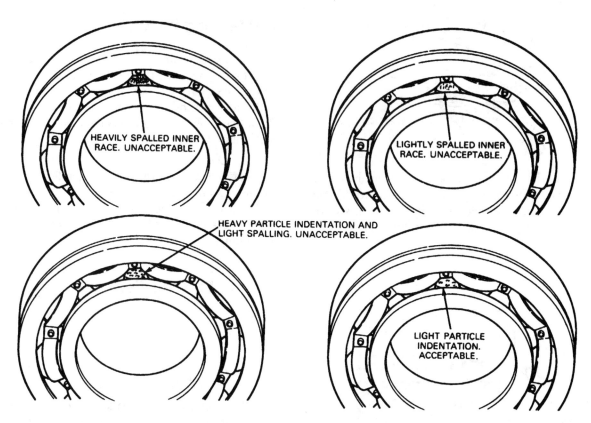

FIGURE 6–44 Ball bearing inspection points. (Courtesy of Ford Motor Company.)

stricted by spacers and washers. Regardless of design, every bearing has an inner and an outer race which are subject to wear or damage. Always inspect these surfaces, the rollers, and the cage as outlined in **Figure 6–45**.

SHIFT MECHANISM INSPECTION

Depending on transmission or transaxle design, the shift mechanism may be located in the case cover (**Figure 6–46**), in the case, or in several parts of the case. Each part of the shift mechanism should be carefully inspected for wear or damage. Smooth shifting is not possible with damaged shift or badly worn shift mechanism parts. The following parts should be inspected:

Shift Forks: Check for distortion wear and cracks at the fork end. Place the fork in the groove of the synchronizer and measure the clearance between the fork and sleeve groove (**Figure 6–47**). Check the shift rail end as well. Check the threaded hole and set screw for damage if so equipped.

Shift Rails: Check for bends, scoring, grooving, or damaged detent grooves and holes.

Detent Springs: Check for distortion, collapse, and breakage.

Detent Balls or Pins: Check for excessive wear or other damage.

Detent Cams: Check for excessive wear, damage, or cracks.

Interlock Plates and Pins: Check for wear, scoring, or bent plates.

Shift Selector Plates: Check for wear scoring or other damage.

These parts should all be checked during transmission/transaxle assembly for proper operation and movement. (See **Figures 6–18, 6–19,** and **6–25 to 6–27** for shift mechanism parts.)

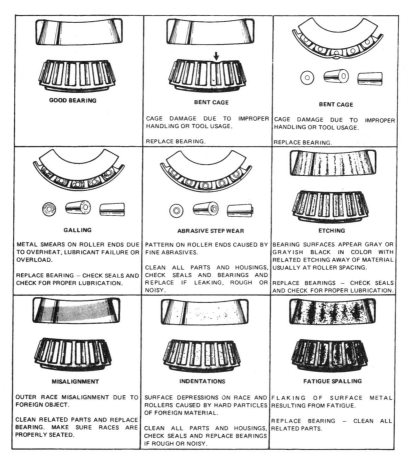

FIGURE 6–45 Inspect bearings carefully for any abnormal conditions or damage. Some typical conditions and damage are shown here. (Courtesy of General Motors Corporation.)

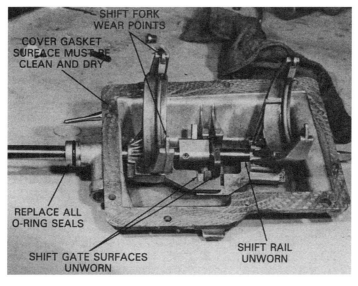

FIGURE 6–46 Inspect the shift mechanism for wear or damage. Make sure that the detents and interlocks work properly. (Courtesy of Chrysler Corporation.)

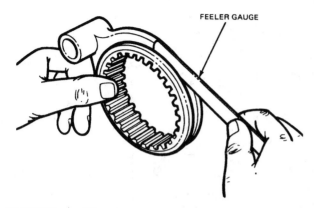

FIGURE 6–47 Measure the clearance between the shift fork and synchronizer sleeve shift fork groove. If excessive, the shift fork and/or the sleeve may need replacing. (Courtesy of Ford Motor Company.)

REPLACING BEARINGS AND SEALS

Transmission seals can be replaced without disassembly since they are located externally. Bearing replacement requires transmission disassembly.

Removing and installing transmission/transaxle bearings requires following some basic procedures carefully to avoid injury and prevent damage to the bearing and related parts. The outer race may be a press fit in the housing bore with the inner race a sliding fit on the shaft, or the inner race may be a press fit on the shaft and the outer race a sliding fit in the housing bore. When removing or installing bearings, the force must always be applied to the tight (press fit) race. However, if access is restricted to the side of the race, force should be applied normally. Since the force is transmitted through the bearing, special precautions are required for this type of bearing removal. Make sure that equipment and vehicle manufacturers' procedures are followed to avoid injury. Special shields should be used to contain the bearing in case it explodes while high pressure is transmitted through the bearing.

To remove or install a bearing, select a press adapter that will apply the force evenly on the tight race. The part from which the bearing is to be removed (or installed) must be well supported in order to avoid slipping or cocking when the force is applied. Slipping or cocking can cause parts breakage and personal injury. With the parts properly positioned, apply the force gradually while observing that no slipping or cocking occurs. Then continue the procedure until the bearing is removed (or installed into its proper location) (**Figures 6–48** and **6–49**).

Transmission and transaxle seals are removed and installed with special pullers and seal drivers. Some seals can be removed simply by prying them out with a screwdriver. When installing a new seal, the outside of the case is usually coated with the specified sealer to avoid leakage. Of course, the housing bore must first be cleaned and any slight roughness removed. The sealing lip must be lubricated with transmission/transaxle lubricant. Select the appropriate seal driver and install the seal to the specified depth. Avoid cocking the seal during installation. A distorted seal will leak (**Figure 6–50**).

CLEANING AND REPAIRING THREADED HOLES

Threaded holes in transmission/transaxle case components should be cleaned and inspected for damage. Threads in good condition can be cleaned with a tap or die to remove any foreign material or minor burrs.

FIGURE 6–48 Incorrect (1) and correct (2) methods of bearing removal. (Courtesy of Deere & Company.)

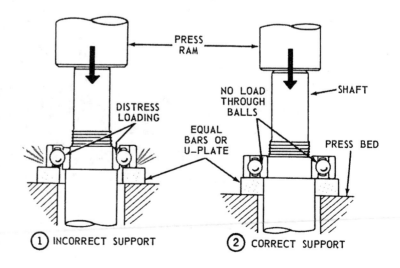

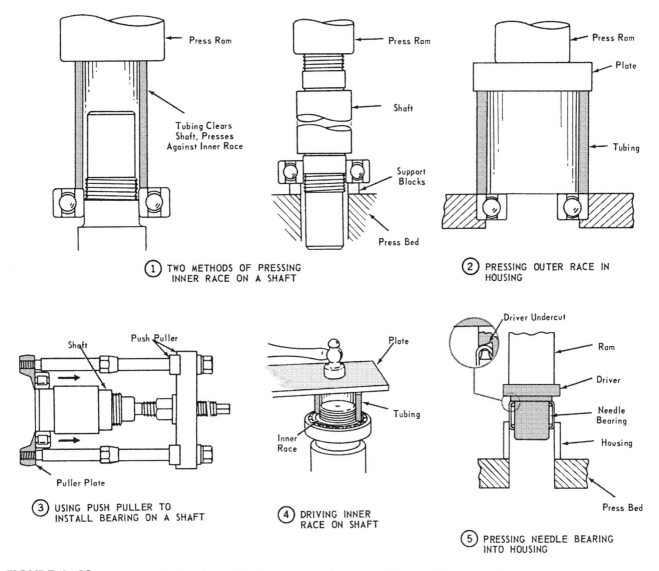

FIGURE 6–49 Proper methods of installing bearings. (Courtesy of Deere & Company.)

Damaged threads must be repaired by drilling out the damaged threads, tapping new threads in the hole thus prepared, and installing a suitable-size thread repair insert (**Figures 6–20** and **6–21**). First, establish the size, pitch, and length of thread required. Refer to the kit manufacturer's instructions for the proper-size drill to use for the thread size to be repaired. Drill out the damaged threads with the specified drill. Clean out all metal chips from the hole. Tap new threads in the hole using the specified tap. Lubricate the tap while threading the hole. Back out the tap every turn or two. When the hole is threaded to the proper depth, remove the tap and all metal chips from the hole. Select the proper-size thread insert and thread it onto the installing mandrel. Lubricate the thread insert with motor oil if in cast iron (do not lubricate if installing in alu-

minum). Install the thread insert into the hole until flush with, or to one turn below, the surface. Remove the installer. If the tang of the insert does not break off during mandrel removal, break the tang off with a drift punch and remove it. This completes the repair and allows normal fastener use and torque (**Figures 6–51** and **6–52**).

TRANSMISSION AND TRANSAXLE ASSEMBLY

Since the procedures and sequence of assembly vary considerably, refer to the appropriate service manual for instructions. Some general guidelines follow (see

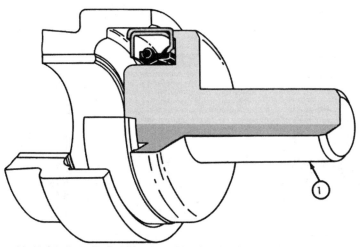

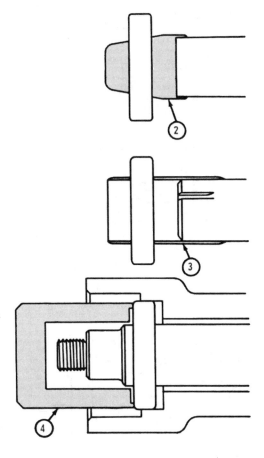

SOME OF THE FIXTURES USED FOR PROPERLY INSTALLING A LIP TYPE OIL SEAL:

① AN INSTALLATION TOOL IS EMPLOYED TO PRESS FIT THE SEAL IN A HOUSING BORE PRIOR TO INSTALLING THE SHAFT. THE O.D. OF THE TOOL IS SLIGHTLY SMALLER THAN THE O.D. OF THE SEAL.

② A CONE IS USED TO PERMIT THE SEAL TO PASS OVER SHARP CORNERED SHAFT ENDS.

③ A SLEEVE WILL PROTECT THE SEALING LIP WHEN PASSING OVER KEYWAYS, SPLINES, SHARP EDGES OR ROUGH SURFACES.

④ A TOOL FOR INSTALLING AN OIL SEAL OVER A SHAFT MUST APPLY PRESSURE EVENLY AND NEAR THE OUTER EDGE OF THE SEAL. SEAT SEAL WELL WITHIN THE HOUSING BORE, ALLOW FOR SHAFT AND BORE CLEARANCE IN AND AROUND THE TOOL.

FIGURE 6–50 Proper method of seal installation. (Courtesy of Deere & Company.)

FIGURE 6–51 Damaged threads can be restored in a threaded part by the use of a thread repair insert. The damaged hole is drilled to a precise oversize, tapped, and a coiled insert installed. This provides new threads of original diameter and type.

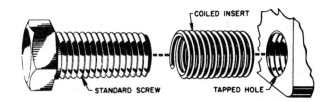

FIGURE 6–52 How to use a thread repair kit to repair damaged internal threads. (Courtesy of General Motors Corporation.)

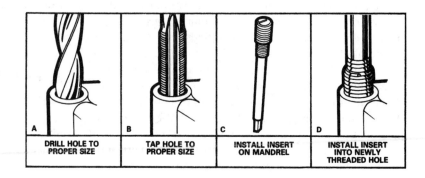

Figures 6–53 to **6–77** for examples of assembly procedures):

1. Make sure that you have on hand all the replacement parts, gaskets, and seals that you will need.

2. Never use undue force during assembly. Use only a soft-faced hammer for striking.

3. When replacing a worn gear, always replace the matching gear with which it is in mesh. If a new gear is meshed with a worn gear, rapid tooth wear and noise may result.

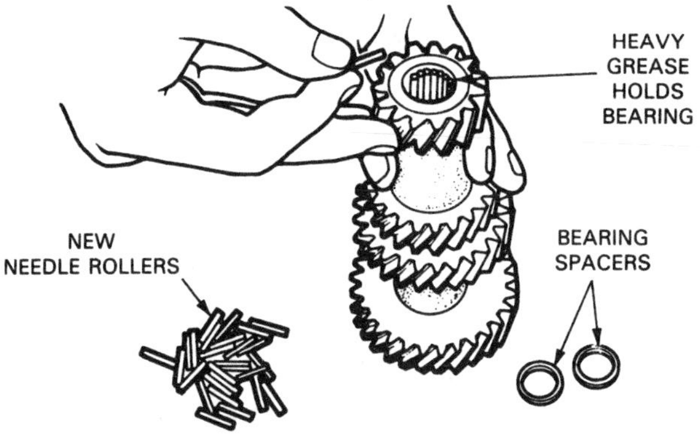

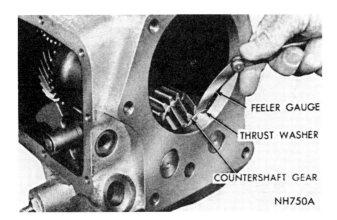

FIGURE 6–53 Use grease to hold non-caged needle bearings in place. (Courtesy of Chrysler Corporation.)

FIGURE 6–54 Measuring cluster gear end play with a feeler gauge. (Courtesy of Chrysler Corporation.)

FIGURE 6–55 Using a dial indicator to measure cluster gear end play as the gear is moved all the way forward and all the way back. (Courtesy of Ford Motor Company.)

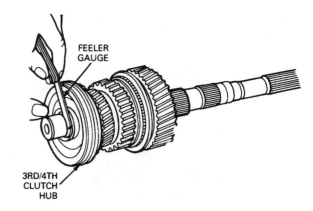

FIGURE 6–56 Measure clearance in output shaft gear train with a feeler gauge. (Courtesy of Ford Motor Company.)

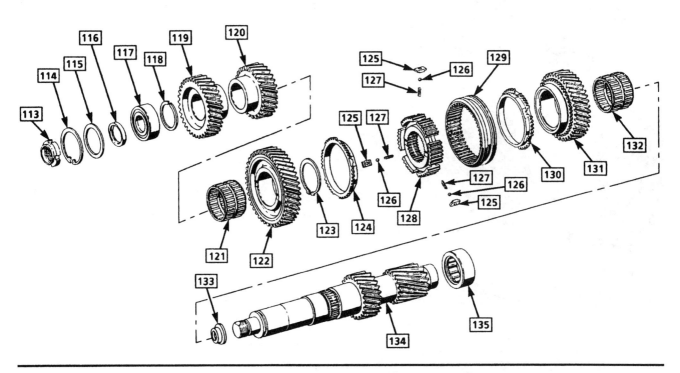

113 COUNTERSHAFT NUT	**121** 6TH GEAR BEARING	**129** SYNCHRONIZER SLEEVE
114 SNAP RING	**122** 6TH GEAR	**130** SYNCHRONIZER RING
115 SELECTIVE SHIM	**123** SNAP RING	**131** 5TH GEAR
116 BEARING WASHER	**124** SYNCHRONIZER RING	**132** 5TH GEAR BEARING
117 INPUT BEARING	**125** PRESSURE PIECE	**133** FRONT BEARING RACE
118 SNAP RING	**126** SYNCHRONIZER BALL	**134** COUNTERSHAFT
119 4TH SPEED COUNTER GEAR	**127** SYNCHRONIZER SPRING	**135** REAR BEARING
120 3RD SPEED COUNTER GEAR	**128** SYNCHRONIZER BODY	

FIGURE 6–57 Countershaft assembly for five-speed manual transmission. (Courtesy of General Motors Corporation.)

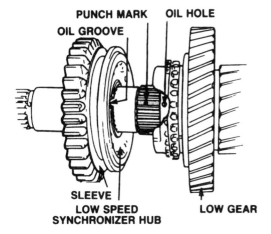

PUNCH MARK   OIL HOLE
OIL GROOVE

SLEEVE
LOW SPEED
SYNCHRONIZER HUB   LOW GEAR

FIGURE 6–58 The low-speed synchronizer hub oil groove and the oil hole in the mainshaft must be aligned during assembly of this unit. (Courtesy of General Motors Corporation.)

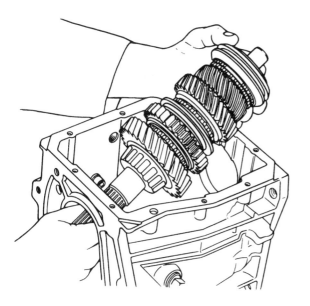

FIGURE 6–59 Removing/installing the mainshaft assembly on a three-speed transmission. (Courtesy of General Motors Corporation.)

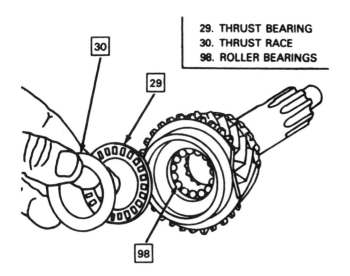

29. THRUST BEARING
30. THRUST RACE
98. ROLLER BEARINGS

FIGURE 6–60 Installing the mainshaft support-bearing rollers and thrust bearing in the main drive gear. (Courtesy of General Motors Corporation.)

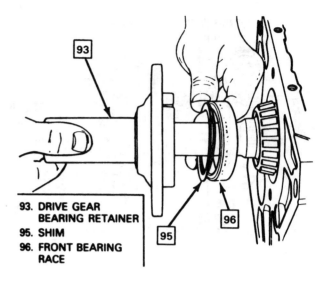

FIGURE 6–61 Front bearing retainer and shim installation. (Courtesy of General Motors Corporation.)

93. DRIVE GEAR
    BEARING RETAINER
95. SHIM
96. FRONT BEARING
    RACE

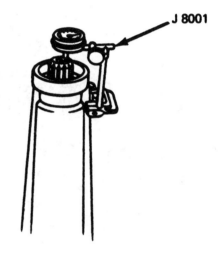

FIGURE 6–62 Measuring mainshaft (output shaft) end play with a dial indicator. (Courtesy of General Motors Corporation.)

J 8001

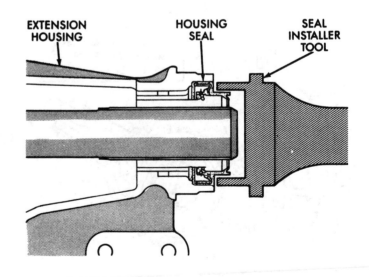

EXTENSION
HOUSING

HOUSING
SEAL

SEAL
INSTALLER
TOOL

FIGURE 6–63 Installing an extension housing seal. (Courtesy of Chrysler Corporation.)

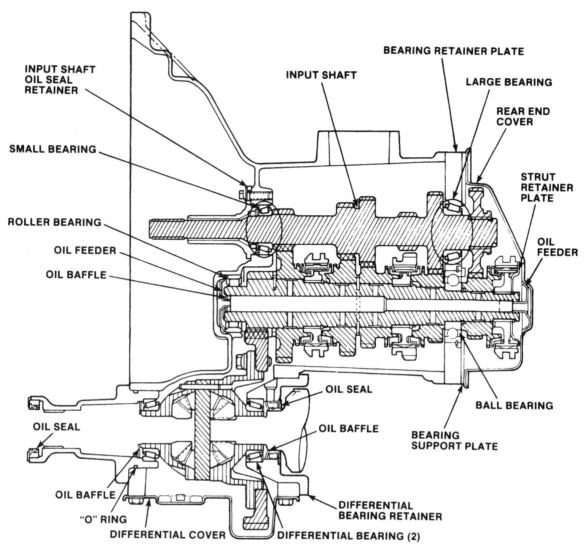

FIGURE 6–64 Seal and bearing locations of a typical five-speed manual transaxle. (Courtesy of General Motors Corporation.)

4. Use grease to hold needle bearings in place during assembly.

5. Lubricate all friction surfaces with transmission/transaxle lubricant or special assembly lubricant or gel during assembly.

6. Measure end play and clearances as required to make sure that they are correct.

7. If bearing preload adjustment is required, measure preload with a dial indicator. If a shim change is required, measure the existing shim thickness and increase or decrease the shim thickness by adding or replacing shims as required. Recheck the preload after assembling the shims and retainer.

8. Always use new snap rings. Old snap rings may be distorted or have lost tension.

9. Use only new gaskets, seals, and O-rings. Use sealer only where specified.

10. Replace any damaged fasteners. Use only fasteners of the correct size and type (metric or U.S.).

11. Tighten all fasteners to specifications.

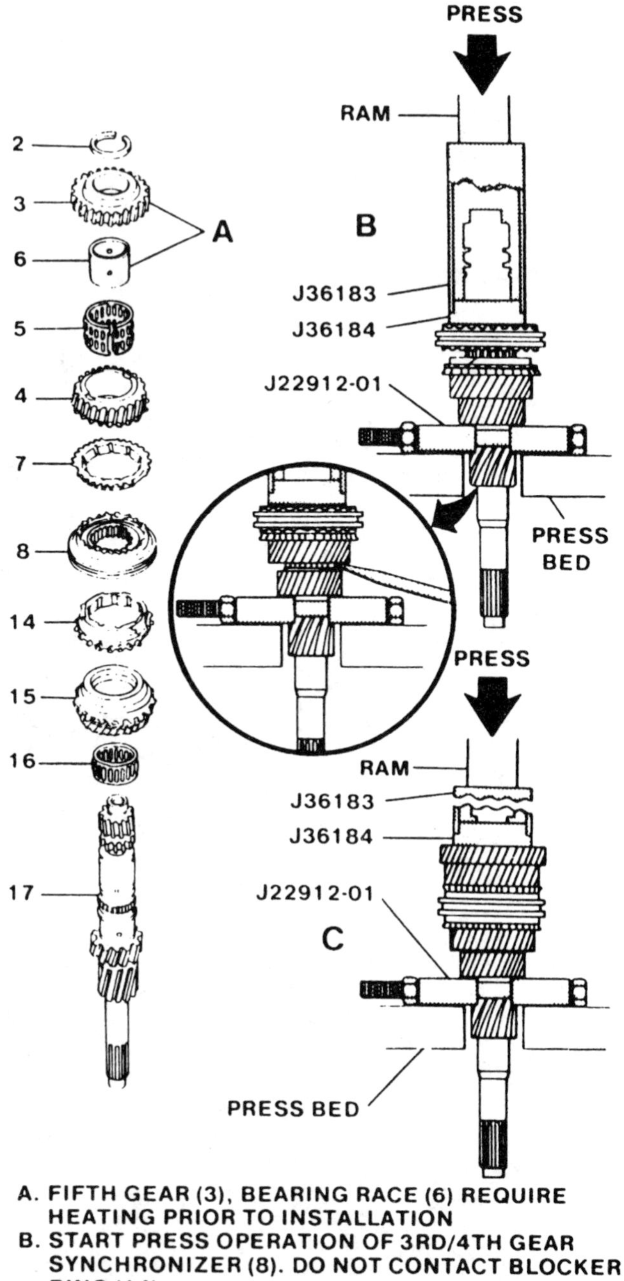

FIGURE 6–65 Installing input shaft components of a five-speed transaxle. (Courtesy of General Motors Corporation.)

A. FIFTH GEAR (3), BEARING RACE (6) REQUIRE HEATING PRIOR TO INSTALLATION
B. START PRESS OPERATION OF 3RD/4TH GEAR SYNCHRONIZER (8). DO NOT CONTACT BLOCKER RING (14)
LIFT GEARS (15) AND (14) WITH PROBE TO ENGAGE BLOCKER RING (14) INTO SYNCHRONIZER (8). CONTINUE PRESS OPERATION
C. PRESS FIFTH GEAR (3)
2. SNAP RING
3. 5TH GEAR
4. 4TH GEAR
5. BEARING, 4TH GEAR
6. RACE, BEARING 4TH GEAR
7. BLOCKER RING, 4TH GEAR
8. SYNCHRONIZER ASSEMBLY, 3RD/4TH GEAR
14. BLOCKER RING, 3RD GEAR
15. 3RD GEAR
16. BEARING, 3RD GEAR
17. SHAFT, INPUT

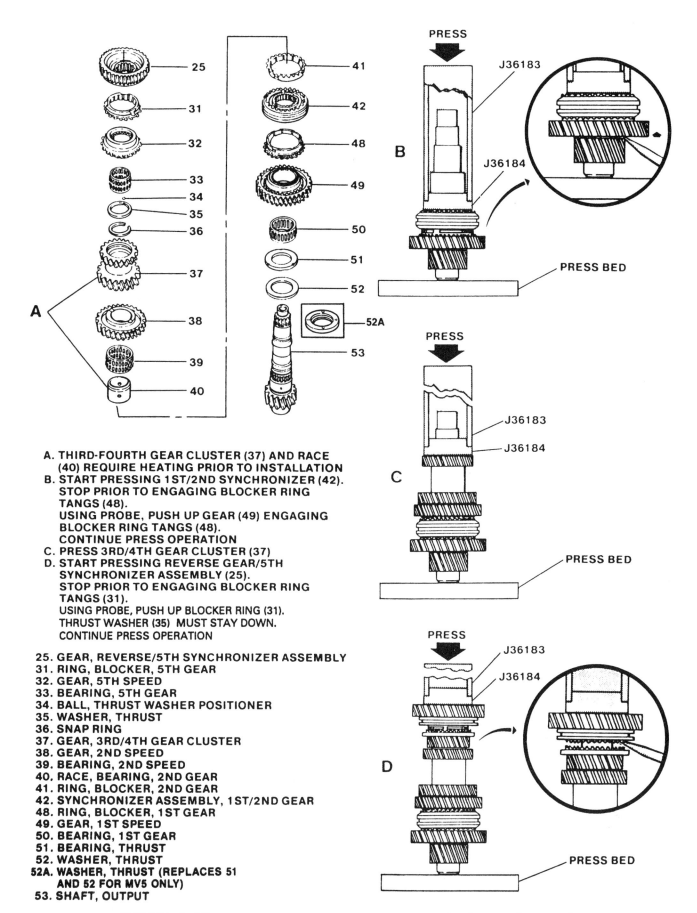

A. THIRD-FOURTH GEAR CLUSTER (37) AND RACE
   (40) REQUIRE HEATING PRIOR TO INSTALLATION
B. START PRESSING 1ST/2ND SYNCHRONIZER (42).
   STOP PRIOR TO ENGAGING BLOCKER RING
   TANGS (48).
   USING PROBE, PUSH UP GEAR (49) ENGAGING
   BLOCKER RING TANGS (48).
   CONTINUE PRESS OPERATION
C. PRESS 3RD/4TH GEAR CLUSTER (37)
D. START PRESSING REVERSE GEAR/5TH
   SYNCHRONIZER ASSEMBLY (25).
   STOP PRIOR TO ENGAGING BLOCKER RING
   TANGS (31).
   USING PROBE, PUSH UP BLOCKER RING (31).
   THRUST WASHER (35) MUST STAY DOWN.
   CONTINUE PRESS OPERATION

25. GEAR, REVERSE/5TH SYNCHRONIZER ASSEMBLY
31. RING, BLOCKER, 5TH GEAR
32. GEAR, 5TH SPEED
33. BEARING, 5TH GEAR
34. BALL, THRUST WASHER POSITIONER
35. WASHER, THRUST
36. SNAP RING
37. GEAR, 3RD/4TH GEAR CLUSTER
38. GEAR, 2ND SPEED
39. BEARING, 2ND SPEED
40. RACE, BEARING, 2ND GEAR
41. RING, BLOCKER, 2ND GEAR
42. SYNCHRONIZER ASSEMBLY, 1ST/2ND GEAR
48. RING, BLOCKER, 1ST GEAR
49. GEAR, 1ST SPEED
50. BEARING, 1ST GEAR
51. BEARING, THRUST
52. WASHER, THRUST
52A. WASHER, THRUST (REPLACES 51
    AND 52 FOR MV5 ONLY)
53. SHAFT, OUTPUT

FIGURE 6–66 Assembling output shaft components of a five-speed transaxle.
(Courtesy of General Motors Corporation.)

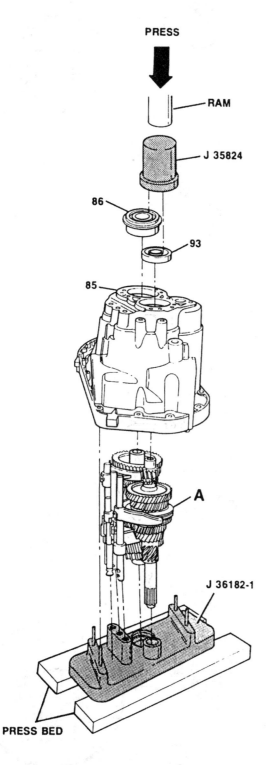

A. GEAR CLUSTER/SHIFT RAIL ASSEMBLY
85. TRANSMISSION CASE
86. BEARING, OUTPUT SHAFT
93. BEARING, INPUT SHAFT

FIGURE 6–67 Installing the gear cluster and shift rail assembly of a five-speed transaxle. (Courtesy of General Motors Corporation.)

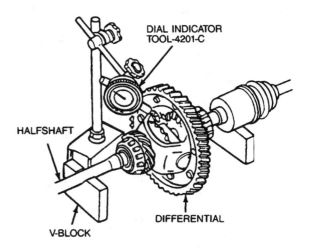

FIGURE 6–68 Differential side gear and pinion backlash being measured with a dial indicator. Excessive backlash indicates worn gears. (Courtesy of Ford Motor Company.)

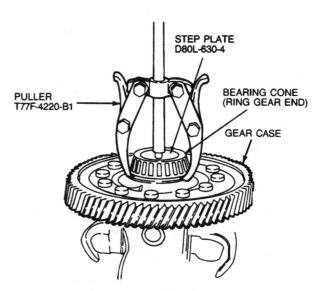

FIGURE 6–69 Removing a differential side bearing. (Courtesy of Ford Motor Company.)

INSTALLING THE TRANSMISSION/TRANSAXLE

Installation procedures vary between different transmissions and transaxles. Refer to the service manual for specific procedures. Some guidelines to remember are:

1. If required, check the clutch parts and perform required service as outlined in Chapter 4 before installing transmission.

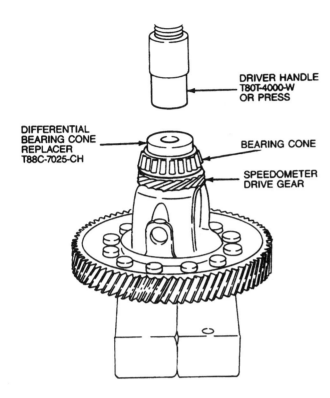

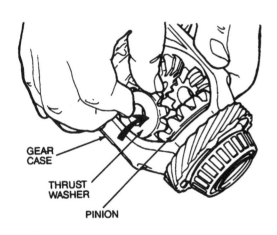

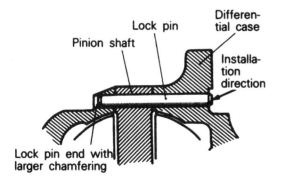

FIGURE 6–70 Installing a differential case side bearing. (Courtesy of Ford Motor Company.)

FIGURE 6–71 Assembling the differential side gears, pinions, and thrust washers. (Courtesy of Ford Motor Company.)

FIGURE 6–72 Installing a press-fit pinion shaft lock-pin. Some transaxles use a lock screw to hold the pinion shaft. (Courtesy of Chrysler Corporation.)

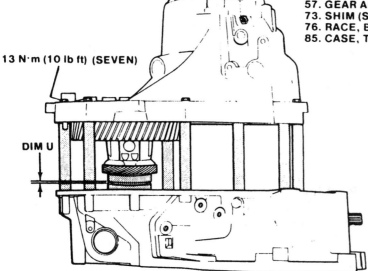

BOLT, M8 X 1.25-6G/
LENGTH - 160 mm (SEVEN)
13 N·m (10 lb ft)

57

NOTE:
BEARING
RACE (76)
MUST BE
REMOVED
FROM CASE

A

J26935-3

J26935-13
(SEVEN)

85

76

73

20

23

13 N·m (10 lb ft) (SEVEN)

DIM U

DIMENSION U
— DETERMINE LARGEST SHIM WITHOUT BINDING
— USE SHIM TWO SIZES LARGER

SHIM PART NO.	DIM U mm (IN.)	COLOR	STRIPES
14082132	0.30 (0.012)	ORANGE	1
14082133	0.35 (0.014)	ORANGE	2
14082134	0.40 (0.016)	ORANGE	3
14082135	0.45 (0.018)	ORANGE	4
14082136	0.50 (0.020)	YELLOW	1
14082137	0.55 (0.022)	YELLOW	2
14082138	0.60 (0.024)	YELLOW	3
14082139	0.65 (0.026)	YELLOW	4
14082140	0.70 (0.028)	WHITE	1
14082141	0.75 (0.030)	WHITE	2
14082142	0.80 (0.031)	WHITE	3
14082143	0.85 (0.033)	WHITE	4
14082144	0.90 (0.035)	GREEN	1
14082145	0.95 (0.037)	GREEN	2
14082146	1.00 (0.039)	GREEN	3
14082147	1.05 (0.041)	GREEN	4
14082148	1.10 (0.043)	BLUE	1
14082149	1.15 (0.045)	BLUE	2
14082150	1.20 (0.047)	BLUE	3
14082151	1.25 (0.049)	BLUE	4
14082152	1.30 (0.051)	RED	1

A. BEARING CUP (76) MUST BE INSTALLED OVER BEARING

20. HOUSING, CLUTCH AND DIFFERENTIAL
23. SEAL, DRIVE AXLE
57. GEAR AND DIFFERENTIAL ASSEMBLY
73. SHIM (SELECTIVE)
76. RACE, BEARING DIFFERENTIAL
85. CASE, TRANSMISSION

FIGURE 6–73 Transaxle differential selective shim bearing preload procedure.
(Courtesy of General Motors Corporation.)

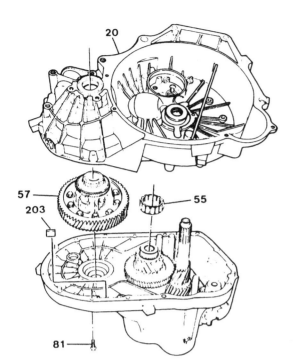

FIGURE 6–74 Transaxle case and differential assembly. (Courtesy of General Motors Corporation.)

20. **CASE, CLUTCH AND DIFFERENTIAL**
55. **BEARING ASSEMBLY, OUTPUT SHAFT**
57. **DIFFERENTIAL ASSEMBLY**
81. **BOLT (15), 21 N·m (15 lb ft)**
203. **MAGNET**

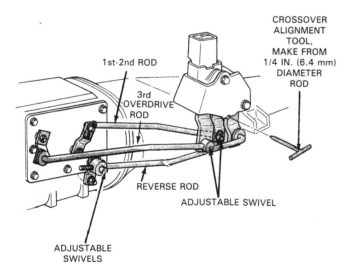

FIGURE 6–75 After transmission or transaxle installation, the shift linkage must be adjusted. Many different rod and cable shift designs are used. Follow service manual instructions for proper adjustment. (Courtesy of Chrysler Corporation.)

2. Apply a coat of high-temperature lubricant to such areas as the pilot bushing, release bearing hub or transmission bearing retainer extension, and clutch release fork, as recommended.

3. Place the transmission or transaxle securely on a transmission jack.

4. Install guide pins in bell housing to align transmission/transaxle during installation.

(Install shims if any were present during removal.)

5. Slide transmission/transaxle into place without using undue force. Make sure that input shaft splines and clutch disc hub splines are aligned.

6. With transmission/transaxle firmly against engine or bell housing, install attaching bolts and tighten to specified torque.

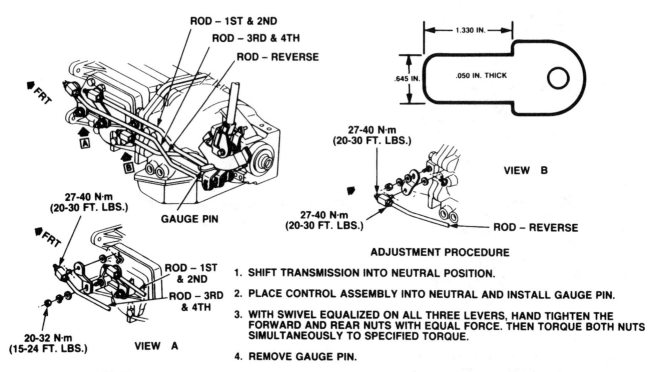

ADJUSTMENT PROCEDURE

1. SHIFT TRANSMISSION INTO NEUTRAL POSITION.

2. PLACE CONTROL ASSEMBLY INTO NEUTRAL AND INSTALL GAUGE PIN.

3. WITH SWIVEL EQUALIZED ON ALL THREE LEVERS, HAND TIGHTEN THE FORWARD AND REAR NUTS WITH EQUAL FORCE. THEN TORQUE BOTH NUTS SIMULTANEOUSLY TO SPECIFIED TORQUE.

4. REMOVE GAUGE PIN.

FIGURE 6–76 A fabricated gauge pin (top right) is used on this four-speed shift linkage to hold all the shift levers in Neutral while making linkage adjustments. (Courtesy of General Motors Corporation.)

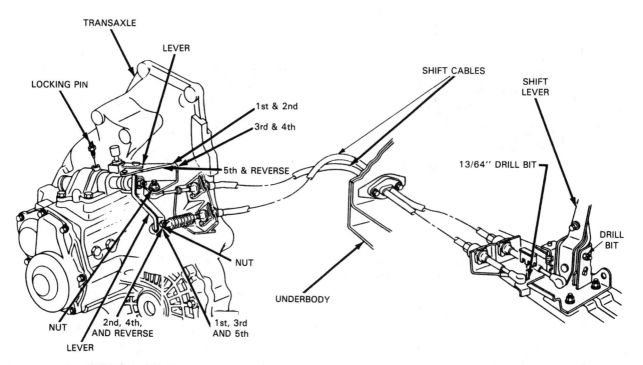

FIGURE 6–77 Transaxle shift linkage adjustment (typical). (Courtesy of General Motors Corporation.)

7. Install the cross member (replace any shims that were removed) and mount.

8. Remove the jack and engine support.

9. Install the drive axle shafts or drive line (lubricate the slip yoke before sliding into the transmission) as per scribe marks.

10. Reconnect and adjust the linkage; connect the speedometer cable and electrical connections.

11. Fill the transmission with the recommended lubricant to the proper level.

12. Lower the vehicle to the floor and check for leaks. Reconnect the negative battery cable.

13. Road test the vehicle for proper performance of transmission/transaxle.

14. Inspect for possible leakage.

REVIEW QUESTIONS

1. List all the possible causes of gear clashing or grinding when shifting.

2. What causes abnormal transmission or transaxle noise?

3. What could cause a transmission or transaxle to jump out of gear?

4. A loose shift rail fork setscrew can cause a transmission or transaxle to be _____ in gear.

5. When diagnosing a transmission or transaxle during a road test, the car should be operated in _____ _____ under _____ , _____ and _____ modes.

6. Most transaxles can be removed by _____ them from the engine and removing them from _____ the engine car.

7. When drying a bearing with compressed air, hold it to _____ it from _____ .

8. Synchronizer blocking rings should be inspected for _____ insert slots, _____ clutch teeth, and _____ internal surfaces.

9. When replacing a worn gear, always replace the _____ _____ as well.

10. Always use new snap rings since used snap rings may be _____ or have lost their _____ .

TEST QUESTIONS

1. Technician A says that gear clashing or grinding when shifting may be caused by the clutch not releasing fully. Technician B says that the cause may be worn synchronizers. Who is right?
   a. technician A
   b. technician B
   c. both are right
   d. both are wrong

2. A noisy transmission/transaxle may be caused by
   a. low lubricant level or worn bearings
   b. worn bearing or synchronizers
   c. worn synchronizers or low lubricant level
   d. low lubricant level or worn shift forks

3. Hard shifting may be caused by
   a. bent shift linkage or lack of lubrication

   b. incorrectly adjusted shift linkage or a clutch not fully releasing
   c. both (a) and (b)
   d. none of the above

4. If a transaxle does not stay in the gear selected, look for
   a. worn synchronizer teeth
   b. faulty detent
   c. worn bearings
   d. any of the above

5. An excessively high lubricant level may cause
   a. foaming
   b. lubricant loss
   c. seal failure
   d. any of the above

6. If a transmission can be shifted into two gears at once, the cause could be
   a. worn countershaft bearings
   b. worn second and third gears
   c. worn synchronizers
   d. faulty interlock

7. Guide pins should be used during transmission installation to
   a. prevent damage to the pressure plate
   b. prevent damage to the release bearing
   c. prevent damage to the clutch disc
   d. all of the above

8. To spin test a bearing
   a. use the air hose to spin the outer race
   b. spin the inner race by hand
   c. hold the outer race by hand
   d. hold the inner race and spin the outer race by hand

◆ CHAPTER 7 ◆

AUTOMATIC TRANSMISSION AND TRANSAXLE PRINCIPLES

INTRODUCTION

Automatic transmissions and transaxles use a torque converter, planetary gears, clutches and bands, and a hydraulic system to transmit engine power to the drive wheels. A manually operated shift lever allows the driver to select the drive range desired. Upshifts and downshifts occur automatically. Automatic shifting may be computer controlled or hydraulically controlled. The automatic transaxle contains a final drive gear and differential unit not included in automatic transmissions. Automatic transaxles are used in front-wheel-drive cars. Automatic transmissions are used in rear-wheel-drive cars. This chapter explains the function, design, and operation of automatic transmissions and transaxles.

LEARNING OBJECTIVES

After completing this chapter, you should be able to:

- Describe the function of automatic transmissions and transaxles.
- List the major components of an automatic transaxle.
- List the major components of an automatic transmission.
- Describe the difference between an automatic transaxle and an automatic transmission.

- Describe the function and operation of conventional and lockup torque converters.
- Describe the function and operation of three-speed and four-speed planetary gear systems.
- Describe the function and operation of multiple disc clutches, bands, and servos.
- Trace the powerflow through automatic transmissions and transaxles.
- Describe how automatic shifting occurs in electronic and nonelectronic automatic transmissions and transaxles.

TERMS YOU SHOULD KNOW

Look for these terms as you study this chapter and learn what they mean.

automatic transmission	hydraulic pump
automatic transaxle	clutch piston
torque converter	clutch cylinder
impeller	driving clutch
turbine	holding clutch
stator	band
lockup torque converter	servo
input shaft	valve body
drive link	planetary gears

output shaft

transfer shaft

final drive

output pinion

differential

automatic transmission fluid

case

vortex flow

rotary flow

stator shaft

torque multiplication stage

coupling stage

lockup stage

sun gear

planet pinions

carrier

ring gear

clutch retainer

clutch plates

clutch hub

pressure plate

cushion spring

return spring

torque capacity

one-way clutch

sprag clutch

roller clutch

park pawl

pressure regulator valve

manual valve

throttle valve

vacuum modulator

governor valve

shift valves

shift solenoids

upshifts

downshifts

shift timing

shift quality

static seals

dynamic seals

flow control rings

transmission cooler

AUTOMATIC TRANSMISSION AND TRANSAXLE FUNCTIONS

The functions of an automatic transmission or transaxle are:

1. To provide several gear ratios (power and speed combinations) to allow the driver to obtain the acceleration and fuel economy desired.

2. To provide a reverse gear to move the car backward.

3. To provide the means for the driver to select the gear operating range desired for all operating conditions.

4. To provide automatic upshifts and downshifts as required by operating conditions.

5. The transaxle also provides a final gear reduction and differential action not found on automatic transmissions.

Automatic transmissions are used in rear-wheel-drive and four-wheel-drive vehicles with the engine mounted longitudinally in front. Automatic transaxles are used in front-wheel-drive and all-wheel-drive vehicles with the engine in front and in some midengine and rear engine rear-wheel-drive cars.

AUTOMATIC TRANSMISSION AND TRANSAXLE COMPONENTS

The major components of an automatic transaxle and automatic transmission are very similar and operate on the same principles. The major difference is that the automatic transaxle incorporates a final drive gear reduction and differential unit into the assembly. The following components are typical (**Figures 7–1** and **7–2**):

1. *Torque converter:* hydraulic fluid coupling that transmits and multiplies torque from the engine to the transmission or transaxle input shaft. The converter cover drives the hydraulic pump.

2. *Drive link:* chain and sprocket that transmit torque converter power output to the transaxle input shaft on transaxles where the converter and gear train are offset.

3. *Input shaft:* transmits torque from torque converter to clutch and planetary gears. May also be called turbine shaft.

4. *Hydraulic pump:* circulates and pressurizes automatic transmission fluid to operate clutches, bands, and valves in transaxle or transmission.

5. *Clutch pistons and cylinders:* hydraulic actuators that operate clutches.

6. *Clutches (driving type):* hydraulically operated to connect or disconnect planetary gear components to input shaft.

7. *Clutches (holding type):* hydraulically operated to hold (prevent from turning) or release planetary gear components by connecting or disconnecting them from the transmission or the transaxle case.

8. *Bands:* operated by hydraulic servos, they can hold (prevent from turning) or release (allow to turn) planetary gear components.

9. *Servo:* hydraulic cylinder and piston applies (tightens) and releases bands.

10. *Valve body:* contains hydraulic control valves that are operated by the shift lever, hydraulic pressure, and electronically controlled solenoids. Valves control fluid flow to clutches and servos.

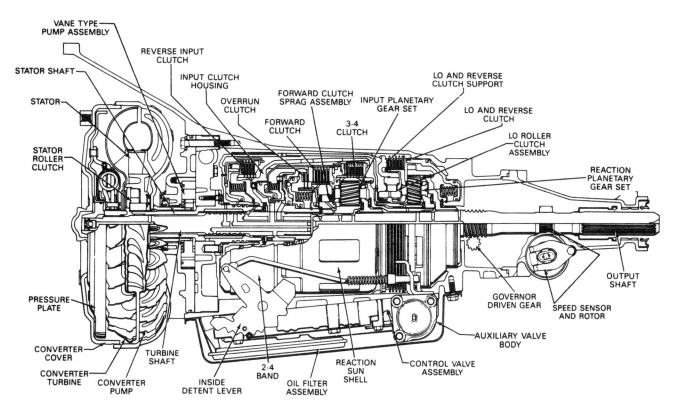

FIGURE 7–1 Four-speed electronic automatic transmission used on rear-wheel-drive cars has two simple planetary gears. (Courtesy of General Motors Corporation.)

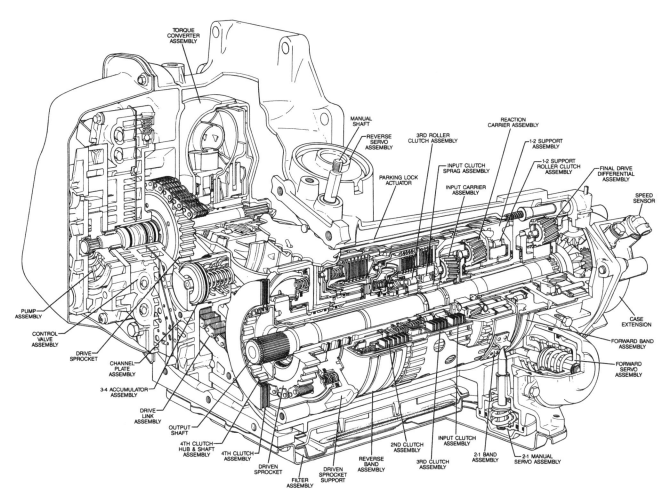

FIGURE 7–2 Four-speed electronic automatic transaxle with planetary gear final drive. (Courtesy of General Motors Corporation.)

11. *Planetary gears:* transmit torque to output shaft. Provide several gear ratios and reverse.

12. *Output shaft:* transmits torque from planetary gears to drive shaft on transmissions only.

13. *Transfer shaft and gears:* transmit power from output shaft to the final drive gears on some transaxles.

14. *Output pinion:* transmits torque from planetary gears (or transfer shaft) to final drive ring gear on transaxles only. Final drive provides final gear reduction.

15. *Differential:* provides differential action to allow wheels to turn at different speeds when cornering.

16. *Automatic transmission fluid:* transmits torque from torque converter impeller to torque converter turbine. Operates clutches, servos, and valves. Provides lubrication and cooling to transaxle and transmission components.

17. *Case:* holds shafts, gears, and pump in place. Contains transmission fluid. Bell-housing section of case surrounds the torque converter and provides the means for bolting the transmission or transaxle to the engine. Case is made of aluminum. Bottom of case is covered by the oil pan.

18. *Electronic control module (ECM):* receives information from input sensors. Uses information from input sensors and programmed information in ECM memory to control the action of the shift valve solenoids and the torque converter clutch.

19. *Input sensors:* provide information to the electronic control module about throttle position, engine speed, engine load (intake manifold vacuum), vehicle speed, engine coolant temperature, transmission/transaxle fluid temperature, and shift lever position.

20. *Output devices* (actuators): electric solenoids that actuate the converter clutch control valve and the shift valves for upshifts and downshifts.

TORQUE CONVERTER CONSTRUCTION AND OPERATION

The three-member torque converter consists of the impeller, the turbine, and the stator. The entire assembly is enclosed in a steel shell and is full of transmission fluid at all times. The steel shell or housing of the converter is bolted to a flex plate that is attached to the engine crankshaft. Inside the shell or housing the rear

portion contains a series of vanes known as the impeller. Whenever the crankshaft turns, this part of the converter turns with it (**Figures 7–3 to 7–5**).

The turbine is located in this same shell and is splined to the transmission or transaxle input shaft. The turbine is free to rotate independently from the impeller. The turbine is similar in appearance to the impeller but has curved vanes.

When the engine is running, the rotating impeller causes fluid to be thrown toward the turbine vanes. When this occurs with sufficient force to overcome the resistance to rotation, the turbine begins to turn, turn-

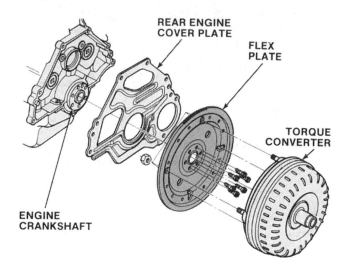

FIGURE 7–3 The torque converter attaches to a flex plate that bolts to the engine crankshaft. (Courtesy of Ford Motor Company.)

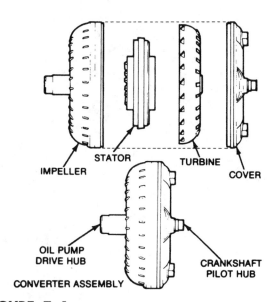

FIGURE 7–4 Torque converter components. (Courtesy of Ford Motor Company.)

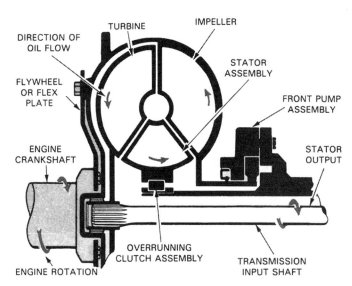

FIGURE 7–5 The engine drives the impeller. The impeller throws fluid at the turbine, causing it and the turbine shaft (transmission/transaxle input shaft) to turn. The converter hub drives the hydraulic pump. (Courtesy of Chrysler Corporation.)

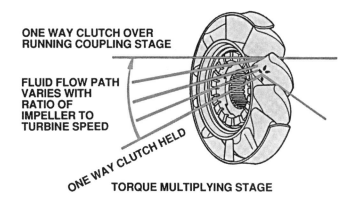

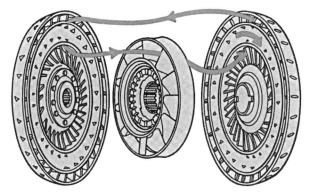

FIGURE 7–6 Stator redirects fluid flow to aid impeller rotation. (Courtesy of Ford Motor Company.)

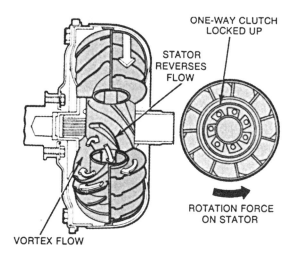

FIGURE 7–7 Fluid flow from turbine is redirected by stator vanes (during torque multiplication) to same direction as impeller. This aids impeller rotation. This flow is called vortex flow. (Courtesy of Ford Motor Company.)

ing the transmission input shaft. Without a stator between the impeller and the turbine, the fluid flow leaving the turbine would be in a direction opposite to impeller rotation and would resist impeller rotation.

The stator vanes redirect the fluid flow back to the same direction as impeller rotation, thereby assisting impeller rotation. This fluid flow, from the impeller to the turbine, to the stator, and back to the impeller is called vortex flow. The circular fluid flow is called rotary flow.

The vortex flow of the fluid in the torque converter results in torque multiplication. In other words, the impeller is turning faster than the turbine, and fluid striking the stationary vanes is redirected to aid in impeller rotation **(Figures 7–6** and **7–7)**.

The stator consists of a series of vanes surrounding a one-way clutch **(Figure 7–8)**. The one-way clutch hub is splined to an extension of the hydraulic pump, which is bolted to the transmission case. This extension is referred to as a stator shaft (although it is tubular) or reaction shaft, and it cannot rotate. The one-way clutch prevents the stator vane assembly from rotating counterclockwise (opposite to impeller rotation) but allows clockwise rotation.

When turbine speed increases to the point where it approaches impeller speed (approximately nine-tenths), fluid leaving the turbine vanes begins to strike the reverse side of the stator vanes, causing the stator to rotate in the same direction as the impeller and the turbine. This is called the coupling stage, which provides almost a 1:1 ratio through the torque converter **(Figure 7–9)**.

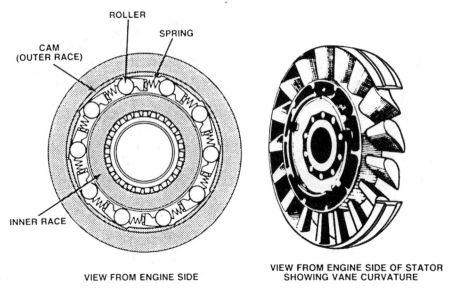

VIEW FROM ENGINE SIDE

VIEW FROM ENGINE SIDE OF STATOR SHOWING VANE CURVATURE

FIGURE 7–8 Stator assembly. (Courtesy of Chrysler Corporation.)

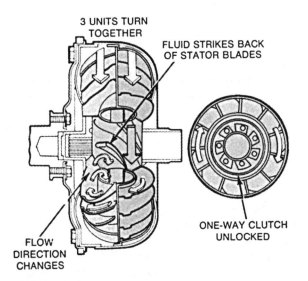

FIGURE 7–9 As the turbine approaches impeller speed, fluid from the turbine strikes the back side of the stator vanes, causing the entire assembly to rotate as a unit. (Courtesy of Ford Motor Company.)

As long as the engine is transmitting torque, the impeller is the drive member and the turbine is the driven member. An infinite series of ratios is possible between the two because of the hydrodynamic connection (transfer of torque through hydraulic fluid). The range of drive ratios through the converter is from approximately 2.2:1 to almost 1:1.

During deceleration, the vehicle's momentum (kinetic inertia) causes the turbine to drive the impeller

hydraulically. This tends to drive the engine. Since the engine is trying to return to idle speed, engine braking helps slow down vehicle speed.

Converter Stall Speed and Torque Capacity

The stall speed of a torque converter refers to the speed (rpm) of the engine when the transmission/transaxle is in gear, the vehicle is held stationary, and the engine is operated at wide-open throttle for a few seconds. At this point, the maximum torque capacity of the converter is reached. Engine speed is stabilized, and the torque converter slips. The torque capacity and stall speed of the torque converter are carefully matched to the torque output of the engine by the vehicle manufacturer. If too large a converter is used, the power output of the engine cannot be utilized efficiently. Too much engine power would be required to drive the large diameter impeller. If too small a converter is used, engine speed would be excessive before the converter could transmit maximum torque. Fuel consumption would also be too high.

Factors that affect the performance and torque capacity of the torque converter are converter diameter and the angle of the converter blades or vanes. A large diameter converter is harder to turn than a small diameter converter. The angle of the converter vanes affects the velocity and direction of the fluid leaving the vanes, both of which have a bearing on converter performance.

To maintain the correct converter-to-engine match, a replacement converter must be of the same size and torque capacity as the original. Anything else will adversely affect performance and fuel economy.

Variable-Pitch Converter

One of the design factors affecting converter capacity and performance is stator vane angle. The fixed stator vane design is a compromise between performance and economy.

Some torque converters are designed with a variable-pitch (angle) stator. The stator vanes are mounted to allow them to pivot. A hydraulic piston connected to the vanes by small connecting rods causes the vanes to open or close, depending on operating conditions.

Moving the piston to close the stator vanes results in changing the exit angle of the fluid to aid impeller rotation better. This position also reduces the exit openings of the stator. Since the impeller is still trying to move the same volume of fluid through the stator, the velocity of the fluid increases, resulting in greater torque multiplication, higher engine speed, and more rapid acceleration. As the stator angle changes to the more open position, torque multiplication and acceleration are reduced.

This design was used with some early two-speed transmissions. The increased number of gear ratios available in more modern transmissions eliminated the need for the variable-pitch stator design.

Dual Stator Torque Converter

Some automatic transmissions with greater torque capacity use a dual stator torque converter to increase torque multiplication. Increased torque multiplication improves acceleration and pulling power during acceleration. This design is used on some full-sized pickups and four-wheel-drive vehicles. Torque multiplication may be as high as 3.5 to 1.

In this converter, the primary stator is located next to the turbine. The secondary stator is located between the primary stator and the impeller. During low-speed, maximum torque multiplication, fluid from the turbine strikes the front of the primary stator vanes. This locks up the primary stator one-way clutch. The primary stator vanes redirect the fluid to strike the front of the secondary stator vanes causing the secondary stator one-way clutch to lock up. The secondary stator vanes redirect the fluid to the impeller in the same direction as impeller rotation, thereby aiding impeller rotation.

As vehicle speed increases and less torque multiplication is needed, centrifugal force changes the direction of fluid leaving the turbine so that it strikes the back side of the primary stator vanes. This causes the primary stator one-way clutch to unlock and overrun and torque multiplication to decrease. Secondary stator operation remains relatively unchanged until vehicle speed is further increased. As vehicle speed increases and torque multiplication is no longer needed, centrifugal force further changes the direction of fluid flow causing it to strike the back side of both the primary and secondary stator vanes. Both stator one-way clutches are unlocked and overrun, and torque multiplication has ceased.

Hydraulic Lockup Torque Converters

This type of torque converter is similar in design and operation to the conventional three-member torque converter. The difference is in the addition of a hydraulically operated single-plate direct-drive clutch. A clutch apply piston or pressure plate assembly is splined to the turbine. It is equipped with a series of torsional springs through which torque is transmitted from the clutch to the turbine shaft. The purpose of the torsional springs is to dampen the effects of engine power impulses and the shock of clutch lockup (**Figures 7–10** to **7–12**).

The clutch piston or pressure plate is applied and released by hydraulic pressure from the transmission hydraulic system. Clutch friction material is attached to the inside of the converter cover. When applied, mechanical powerflow is from the converter cover through the clutch to the torsional springs, the pressure plate hub, and the turbine shaft. When operating in lower gears, the lockup clutch is released. In direct drive or overdrive, the clutch is applied. Electronic control of converter lockup is handled by a computer based on signals received from various sensors and switches. The following sensors are typical:

1. *Brake switch:* when brakes are applied, the converter clutch is released to prevent stalling the engine

2. *Coolant temperature sensor:* prevents lockup until engine warms up

3. *Manifold vacuum sensor (or throttle position sensor):* releases lockup clutch during acceleration

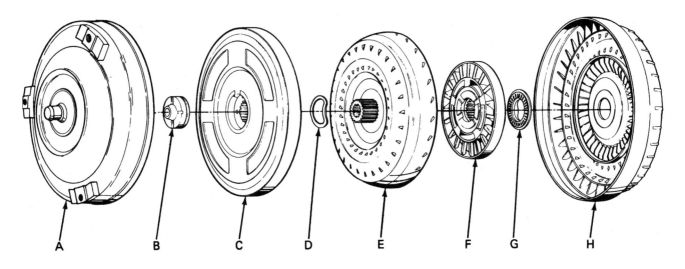

A HOUSING COVER ASSEMBLY, CONVERTER
B SPACER, TURBINE THRUST
C PRESSURE PLATE ASSEMBLY
D SPRING, PRESSURE PLATE

E TURBINE ASSEMBLY
F STATOR ASSEMBLY
G THRUST BEARING ASSEMBLY
H CONVERTER PUMP ASSEMBLY

FIGURE 7–10 Components of lockup clutch torque converter. (Courtesy of General Motors Corporation.)

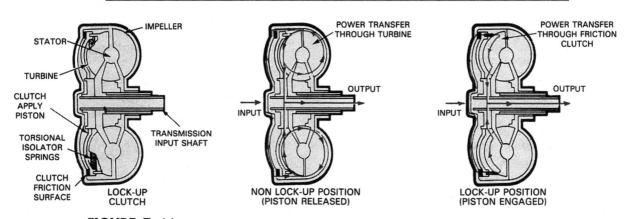

FIGURE 7–11 Hydraulic lockup converter operation and powerflow. (Courtesy of Chrysler Corporation.)

FIGURE 7–12 Electronic control circuit for converter hydraulic clutch lockup. (Courtesy of General Motors Corporation.)

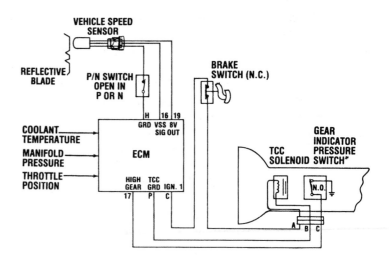

4. *Gearshift lever position sensor:* prevents converter lockup in lower gears

5. *Vehicle speed sensor:* prevents converter lockup until proper road speed is reached

Centrifugal Clutch Lockup Converter

This unit is similar to the conventional three-member torque converter. It has the impeller, turbine, and stator assembly, which operate in the usual manner described earlier. The added features are the centrifugal clutch and damper assembly, which includes a coasting one-way clutch **(Figures 7–13** and **7–14)**.

The converter clutch consists of a series of sliding friction shoes arranged around the circumference of the damper assembly. As the speed of the turbine increases, the friction shoes slide outward due to increased centrifugal force. When the friction shoes are fully applied against the converter cover, power flows from the converter cover to the one-way clutch through the torsional springs to the turbine hub and turbine shaft, thereby providing mechanical drive through the converter. Torsional shocks are dampened by the torsional springs.

The centrifugal clutch is designed to provide some slippage as torque demand from the engine increases. Consequently, when the vehicle is under load, there may be a split between mechanical drive and hydraulic drive through the converter.

The factors determining whether the centrifugal clutch will be applied, and the degree of application, are rotating speed and vehicle load. During mechanical drive, the clutch and damper assembly drive the turbine and turbine shaft through the one-way clutch assembly. During coasting conditions, the one-way clutch freewheels or overruns.

Viscous Converter Clutch

The viscous converter clutch serves the same purpose as the torque converter clutch described earlier. The clutch apply and release functions operate in a similar manner. The difference is that the viscous clutch converter has silicone fluid sealed between the converter cover and the clutch assembly. This fluid provides a limited amount of slippage between the rotor and body to reduce torsional shock and vibration when the clutch is applied. The ECM (Electronic Control Module) controls the clutch solenoid in relation to vehicle speed, throttle position, gear range, transmission fluid temperature, engine coolant temperatures, and barometric pressure. The slight amount of slippage cushions torsional shock and vibration and still provides very close to 1:1 drive.

Planetary Splitter Gear Torque Converter

Some automatic transaxles use a torque converter equipped with a single planetary gearset to provide me-

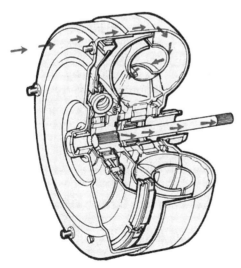

FIGURE 7–13 Centrifugal clutch lockup torque converter cutaway. (Courtesy of Ford Motor Company.)

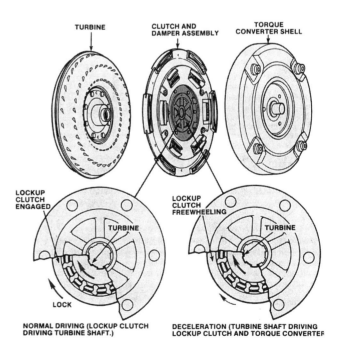

FIGURE 7–14 Centrifugal clutch lockup torque converter parts. (Courtesy of Ford Motor Company.)

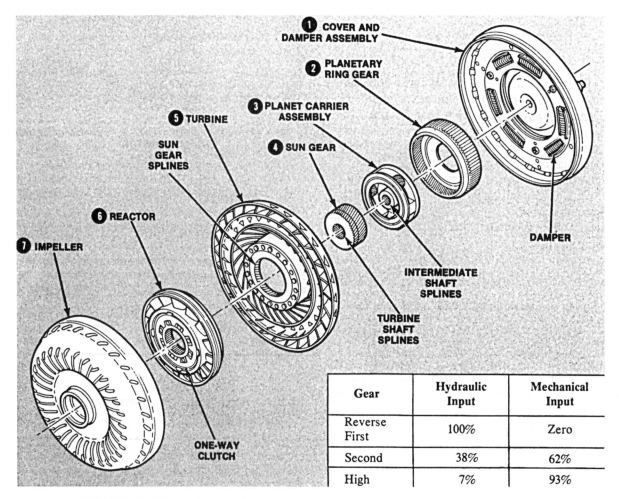

Gear	Hydraulic Input	Mechanical Input
Reverse First	100%	Zero
Second	38%	62%
High	7%	93%

FIGURE 7–15 Exploded view of splitter gear type of torque converter used in some transaxles. (Courtesy of Ford Motor Co. of Canada Ltd.)

chanical drive through the converter. This unit is sometimes referred to as a splitter gear since it splits or divides engine torque transmission between mechanical and hydraulic means in second and third gears (**Figure 7–15**).

In second gear, the turbine supplies 38% of the torque hydraulically; 62% is transmitted mechanically. In third gear, the planetary gear mechanical torque output is increased to 93% with only 7% torque transmitted hydraulically.

Operation of the unit is dependent on the interaction between the torque converter and the planetary gear train in the transmission. Understanding the operation of this unit may require studying planetary gear operation and powerflow.

Construction of this converter includes a torsional spring damper assembly riveted to the inside of the converter cover. The planetary ring gear (internal gear) is splined into the damper assembly so that these parts always turn at engine speed. The planet pinion carrier is splined to the transmission intermediate shaft and the pinions are, of course, in mesh with the ring gear. The sun gear, which is in mesh with the planet pinions, is splined to the turbine hub and to the turbine shaft.

Mechanical transmission of torque through the torque converter is dampened by the torsional springs located between the converter cover and planetary ring gear. The degree of mechanical transmission of torque is dependent on gear position and the interaction between the transmission planetary gear train and the torque converter.

Torque Converter Drive Link

In some transaxle designs, torque converter and gear train are offset. The torque converter transmits driving torque to the gear train input shaft through a chain and sprockets called a drive link. This arrangement reduces the overall length of the transaxle (**Figure 7–16**).

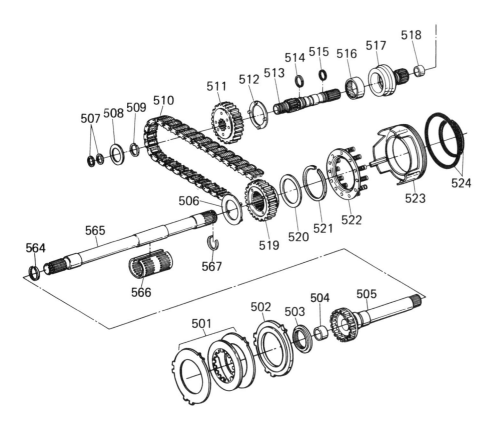

FIGURE 7–16 Chain link is used on some transaxles to transmit power from torque converter to transaxle. (Courtesy of General Motors Company.)

PLANETARY GEAR PRINCIPLES

A simple planetary gearset consists of three components: a sun gear, a carrier (with pinion gears mounted in it), and an internally toothed ring gear (**Figure 7–17**). Power transmission through a planetary gearset

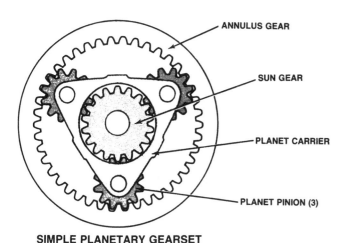

SIMPLE PLANETARY GEARSET

FIGURE 7–17 Planetary gear components. Annulus gear is also called an internal gear or ring gear. Planet carrier is also called a cage. Planetary gears transmit torque when one of the three members is the drive member, one is the held member, and the other is the driven member. (Courtesy of Chrysler Corporation.)

is possible only if one of the three members is held (prevented from rotating) or if two members are locked together. A number of ratios—Forward, Reverse, and Neutral—are possible, depending on which member is the drive, driven, or held unit (**Figures 7–18** to **7–23**).

Planetary gears are compact and are in constant mesh (no shifting of gears required). Clutches are used to connect or disconnect planetary gear members to the input shaft. Clutches or bands are used to hold planetary gear members. Several drive ranges are possible with a simple planetary gearset. Study the illustrations to learn how they work.

Simple Planetary Gear Ratios

In a simple planetary gearset with a sun gear that has 30 teeth and a ring gear that has 90 teeth, the effective number for the carrier is 120 teeth. This is calculated by adding the number of teeth on the sun gear to the number of teeth on the ring gear: $30 + 90 = 120$. In other words, $S + R = C$.

To calculate the gear ratio through this gearset, simply divide the number of teeth of the drive member into the number of teeth on the driven member: driven/drive. For example, if the sun gear is the drive member, the ring gear is the driven member, and the carrier is being held, the ratio would be

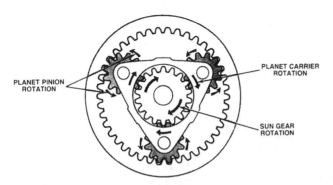

FIGURE 7–18 With the sun gear as the input and the carrier as the output, the gearset is in maximum forward reduction. The pinions walk around the inside of the stationary ring gear. (Courtesy of Chrysler Corporation.)

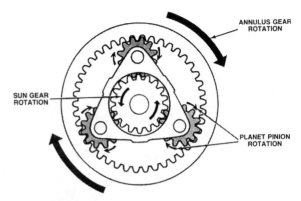

FIGURE 7–20 With the ring gear as the input and the sun gear as the output, the gearset is in maximum reverse overdrive. The carrier is stationary, and the pinions act as idler gears. (Courtesy of Chrysler Corporation.)

$$\tfrac{90}{30} \quad \text{or} \quad 3{:}1$$

If the carrier is the drive member and the ring gear is the driven member with the sun gear being held, the ratio would be

$$\tfrac{90}{120}{:}1 \quad \text{or} \quad 0.75{:}1$$

There are eight possible conditions that can be used with a simple planetary gearset. Six of these are shown in **Figures 7–18** to **7–23.** The other two conditions are (1) direct drive when two members are locked to each other, and (2) Neutral when there is no drive

member or no held member. When two planetary gear members are locked together, the entire planetary gearset rotates as an assembly for direct drive.

Calculating gear ratios through two or three sets of planetary gears becomes a little more complicated and is not really essential. Two or three sets of planetary gears may be used to provide Reverse, Neutral, and three or four forward speeds, including overdrive. When two simple planetary gearsets are used back to back, the assembly is called a Simpson planetary gearset. Another planetary gear design with two sun gears, two sets of pinions in a single carrier, and a single ring gear is used in some transmissions and transaxles. This design is called a Ravigneaux planetary gearset.

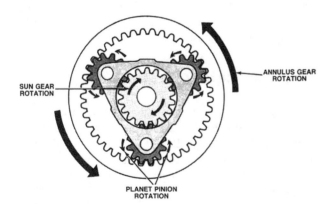

FIGURE 7–19 With the sun gear as the input and the ring gear as the output, the gearset is in reverse reduction. The carrier is stationary, and the pinions act as idler gears. (Courtesy of Chrysler Corporation.)

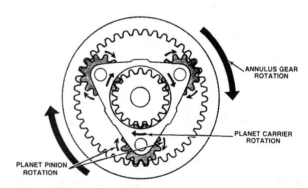

FIGURE 7–21 With the ring gear as the input and the carrier as the output, the gearset is in forward reduction. The pinions walk around the stationary sun gear. (Courtesy of Chrysler Corporation.)

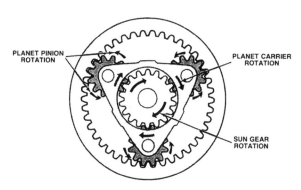

FIGURE 7–22 With the carrier as the input and the sun gear as the output, the maximum forward overdrive is achieved. The pinions walk around the inside of the stationary ring gear. (Courtesy of Chrysler Corporation.)

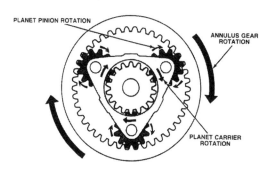

FIGURE 7–23 With the carrier as the input and the ring gear as the output, the gearset is in forward overdrive. The pinions walk around the stationary sun gear. (Courtesy of Chrysler Corporation.)

COMPOUND PLANETARY GEAR OPERATION AND POWERFLOW

Three-Speed Planetary Gear Powerflow

To provide three forward speeds and reverse, it is necessary to use a compound planetary gearset. A common compound planetary gearset consists of two simple planetary gearsets with a common sun gear, which connects the two gearsets. This is known as the Simpson compound planetary gearset. In this unit, the forward gearset ring gear and the sun gear can be connected to the input shaft by means of two separate multiple-disc clutches. The sun gear and the rear gearset carrier can be held. The sun gear can be held by a band (intermediate or kickdown band). Other transaxles or transmissions use a multiple-disc clutch to lock the sun gear to the transmission case **(Figure 7–24)**.

In manually selected low gear, the rear carrier is held by a band or a multiple-disc clutch. In both cases, there is also a one-way clutch that prevents backward rotation of the carrier but allows forward rotation. When the drive position has been selected, the one-way clutch only does the holding while in low gear. The forward carrier and the rear ring gear are splined to the transmission or transaxle output shaft. This is accomplished by the output shaft extending through the hollow sun gear to reach the forward gearset carrier.

Four-Speed Planetary Gear Powerflow

A typical planetary gear arrangement that provides four forward speeds and reverse consists of two simple planetary gearsets with different-size sun gears and five clutches. The input clutch retainer contains the underdrive, overdrive, and reverse drive clutches. The 2/4 and low/reverse holding clutches are contained in the case. The input members of the gearset are:

- Underdrive clutch when applied drives the rear (larger) sun gear.
- Overdrive clutch when applied drives the front planetary carrier.
- Reverse clutch when applied drives the front (smaller) sun gear. The front ring gear and rear carrier assembly is splined to the output shaft.

The planetary gear members that can be held stationary (locked to the case) are:

- The front sun gear is held when the 2/4 clutch is applied.
- The front carrier is held stationary when the low/reverse clutch is applied.

Powerflow through this gearset is as follows:

1. *Neutral.* No clutches are applied. Only the input shaft and input clutch retainer turn.

2. *First gear.* Only the rear gearset is used in first gear. Power flows from the underdrive clutch, to the rear (larger) sun gear, to the pinions, which walk around the stationary ring gear (held by the low/re-

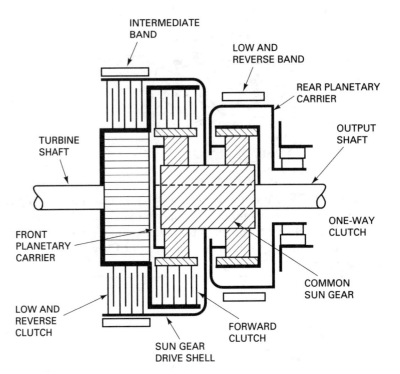

FIGURE 7–24 Three-speed Simpson planetary gear arrangement.

verse clutch) driving the rear carrier and output shaft in a forward direction. The gear ratio is 2.84:1.

3. *Second gear.* Both gearsets are used in second gear. Power flows from the underdrive clutch to the rear sun gear, to the rear pinions, to the gear ring gear and front carrier assembly, to the output shaft. The front pinions walk around the stationary front sun gear, which is held by the 2/4 clutch. The gear ratio is 1.57:1.

4. *Third gear.* In third gear, both gearsets are locked together to the input shaft, causing them and the output shaft to rotate as a unit. Powerflow is from the underdrive clutch, which drives the rear sun gear, and from the overdrive clutch, which drives the front carrier. This locks both gearsets to the output shaft for direct drive, 1:1.

5. *Fourth gear (overdrive).* The front gearset provides the overdrive ratio. Powerflow is from the overdrive clutch to the front carrier, to the front pinions, to the front ring gear and rear carrier assembly, to the output shaft. The 2/4 clutch holds the front sun gear stationary, causing the front pinions to walk around the held sun gear. The overdrive ratio is 0.69:1.

6. *Reverse.* In Reverse, the gear reduction and reverse are obtained through the front gearset. Powerflow is from the reverse clutch to the front sun gear, to the pinions, to the front ring gear and rear carrier assembly, to the output shaft. The front pinions walk around the stationary sun gear (held by the low/reverse

clutch), causing the front ring gear to turn in reverse. The gear ratio is 2.21:1.

Examples of this gear train arrangement are shown in **Figures 7–25** and **7–26.** Other four-speed overdrive gear trains are shown in **Figures 7–27** to **7–31.**

PLANETARY GEAR OVERDRIVE

Some four-speed overdrive automatic transmissions utilize a Simpson planetary gearset combined with a planetary gear overdrive unit. The Simpson gearset is used to provide three forward speeds and Reverse. The overdrive planetary unit is attached to the back of the Simpson gear train **(Figure 7–32).**

The overdrive unit consists of the following major components **(Figure 7–33):**

1. *Overrunning clutch:* a roller clutch that locks the intermediate shaft to the output shaft.

2. *Overdrive clutch:* a multiple-disc clutch that holds the overdrive sun gear during fourth gear (overdrive).

3. *Direct clutch:* a multiple-disc clutch that locks the overdrive sun gear and ring gear together to prevent the roller clutch from overrunning

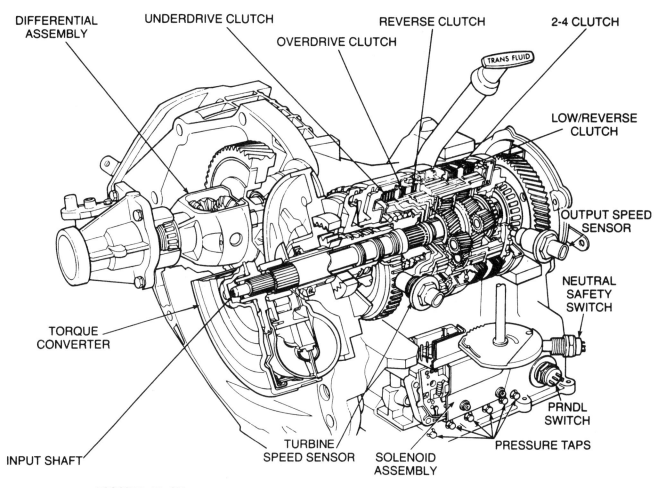

FIGURE 7–25 Four-speed automatic overdrive transaxle (A604). (Courtesy of Chrysler Corporation.)

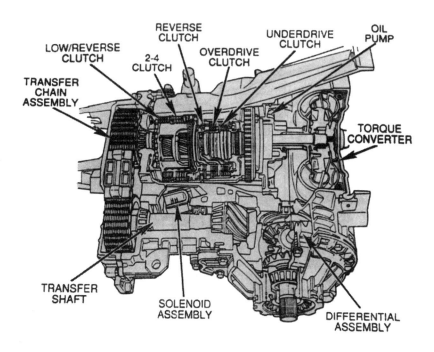

FIGURE 7–26 Four-speed electronic automatic transaxle (42LE) with hypoid gear final drive. (Courtesy of Chrysler Corporation.)

HYDRA-MATIC 4L60 - GEAR RATIOS
FIRST 3.06 FOURTH .70
SECOND 1.62 REVERSE 2.29
THIRD 1.00

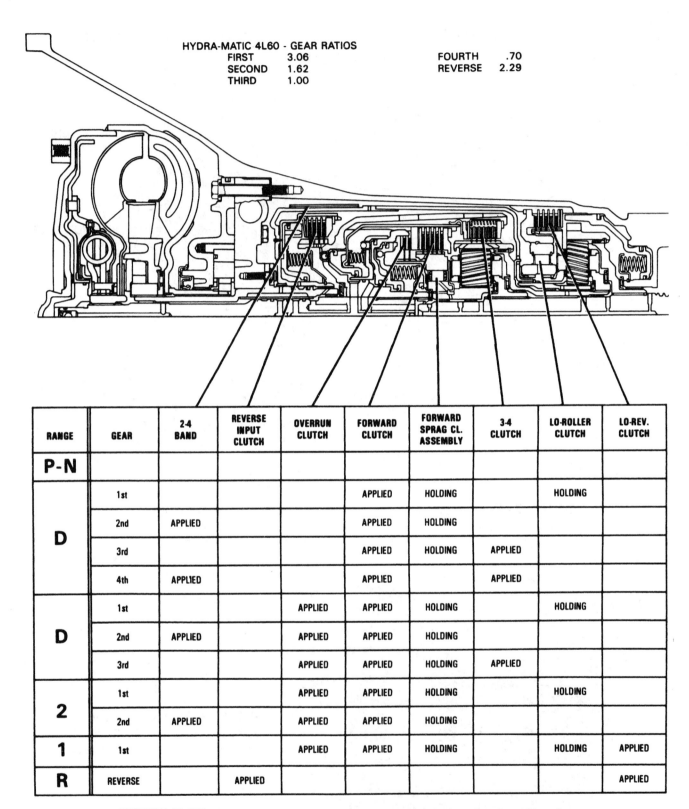

RANGE	GEAR	2-4 BAND	REVERSE INPUT CLUTCH	OVERRUN CLUTCH	FORWARD CLUTCH	FORWARD SPRAG CL. ASSEMBLY	3-4 CLUTCH	LO-ROLLER CLUTCH	LO-REV. CLUTCH
P-N									
D	1st				APPLIED	HOLDING		HOLDING	
	2nd	APPLIED			APPLIED	HOLDING			
	3rd				APPLIED	HOLDING	APPLIED		
	4th	APPLIED			APPLIED		APPLIED		
D	1st			APPLIED	APPLIED	HOLDING		HOLDING	
	2nd	APPLIED		APPLIED	APPLIED	HOLDING			
	3rd			APPLIED	APPLIED	HOLDING	APPLIED		
2	1st			APPLIED	APPLIED	HOLDING		HOLDING	
	2nd	APPLIED		APPLIED	APPLIED	HOLDING			
1	1st			APPLIED	APPLIED	HOLDING		HOLDING	APPLIED
R	REVERSE		APPLIED						APPLIED

FIGURE 7–27 Four-speed overdrive automatic transmission clutch and band application chart (GM4L60). (Courtesy of General Motors Corporation.)

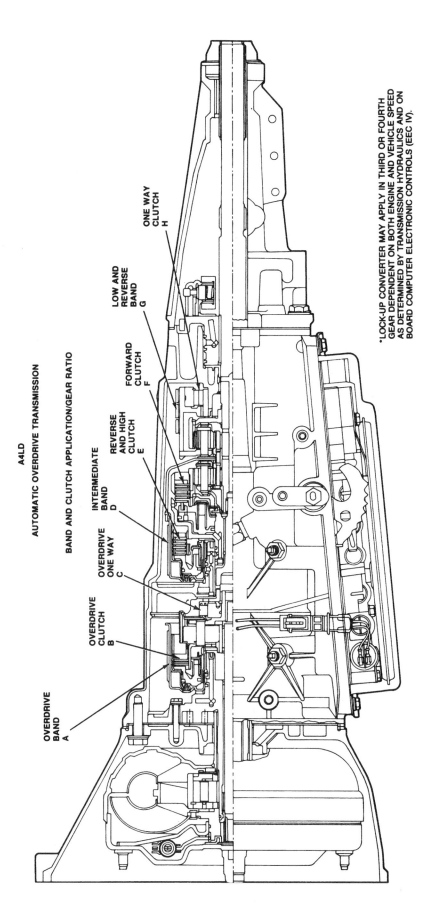

A4LD

AUTOMATIC OVERDRIVE TRANSMISSION

BAND AND CLUTCH APPLICATION/GEAR RATIO

OVERDRIVE BAND A · OVERDRIVE CLUTCH B · OVERDRIVE ONE WAY C · INTERMEDIATE BAND D · REVERSE AND HIGH CLUTCH E · FORWARD CLUTCH F · LOW AND REVERSE BAND G · ONE WAY CLUTCH H

*LOCK-UP CONVERTER MAY APPLY IN THIRD OR FOURTH GEAR DEPENDENT ON BOTH ENGINE AND VEHICLE SPEED AS DETERMINED BY TRANSMISSION HYDRAULICS AND ON BOARD COMPUTER ELECTRONIC CONTROLS (EEC IV).

GEAR	OVERDRIVE BAND A	OVERDRIVE CLUTCH B	OVERDRIVE ONE WAY CLUTCH C	INTERMEDIATE BAND D	REVERSE AND HIGH CLUTCH E	FORWARD CLUTCH F	LOW AND REVERSE BAND G	ONE WAY CLUTCH H	GEAR RATIO
1 — MANUAL FIRST GEAR (LOW)		APPLIED	HOLDING			APPLIED	APPLIED	HOLDING	2.47:1
2 — MANUAL SECOND GEAR		APPLIED	HOLDING	APPLIED		APPLIED			1.47:1
D — DRIVE AUTO — 1ST GEAR		APPLIED	HOLDING			APPLIED		HOLDING	2.47:1
D — O/D AUTO — 1ST GEAR			HOLDING			APPLIED		HOLDING	2.47:1
D — DRIVE AUTO — 2ND GEAR		APPLIED	HOLDING	APPLIED		APPLIED			1.47:1
D — O/D AUTO — 2ND GEAR			HOLDING	APPLIED		APPLIED			1.47:1
D — DRIVE AUTO — 3RD GEAR		APPLIED	HOLDING		APPLIED	APPLIED			1.0:1
D — O/D AUTO — 3RD GEAR			HOLDING		APPLIED	APPLIED			1.0:1
D — OVERDRIVE AUTOMATIC FOURTH GEAR	APPLIED				APPLIED	APPLIED			0.75:1
REVERSE		APPLIED	HOLDING		APPLIED		APPLIED		2:1

FIGURE 7–28 Four-speed automatic overdrive transmission clutch and band application and gear ratio chart (GMA4LD). (Courtesy of Ford Motor Company.)

213

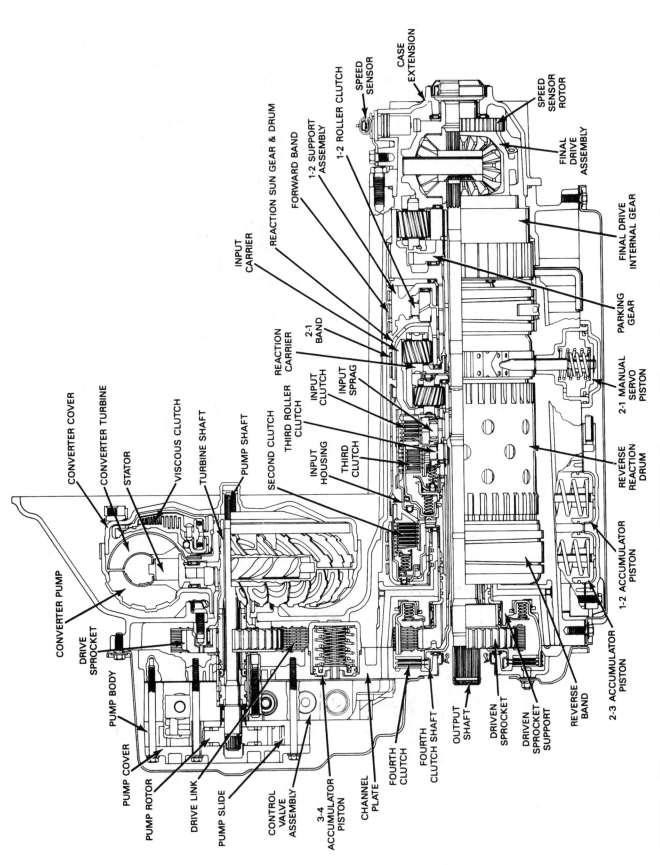

FIGURE 7-29 Four-speed overdrive automatic axle. (GM4T60-E) (Courtesy of General Motors Corporation.)

CONVERTER COVER

CONVERTER TURBINE

STATOR

VISCOUS CLUTCH

TURBINE SHAFT

PUMP SHAFT

CONVERTER PUMP

DRIVE SPROCKET

PUMP BODY

PUMP COVER

PUMP ROTOR

DRIVE LINK

PUMP SLIDE

CONTROL VALVE ASSEMBLY

3-4 ACCUMULATOR PISTON

CHANNEL PLATE

FOURTH CLUTCH

FOURTH CLUTCH SHAFT

OUTPUT SHAFT

DRIVEN SPROCKET

DRIVEN SPROCKET SUPPORT

REVERSE BAND

2-3 ACCUMULATOR PISTON

1-2 ACCUMULATOR PISTON

REVERSE REACTION DRUM

2-1 MANUAL SERVO PISTON

PARKING GEAR

FINAL DRIVE INTERNAL GEAR

SPEED SENSOR ROTOR

FINAL DRIVE ASSEMBLY

CASE EXTENSION

SPEED SENSOR

1-2 ROLLER CLUTCH

1-2 SUPPORT ASSEMBLY

FORWARD BAND

REACTION SUN GEAR & DRUM

INPUT CARRIER

REACTION CARRIER

2-1 BAND

INPUT CLUTCH

INPUT SPRAG

THIRD ROLLER CLUTCH

INPUT HOUSING

THIRD CLUTCH

SECOND CLUTCH

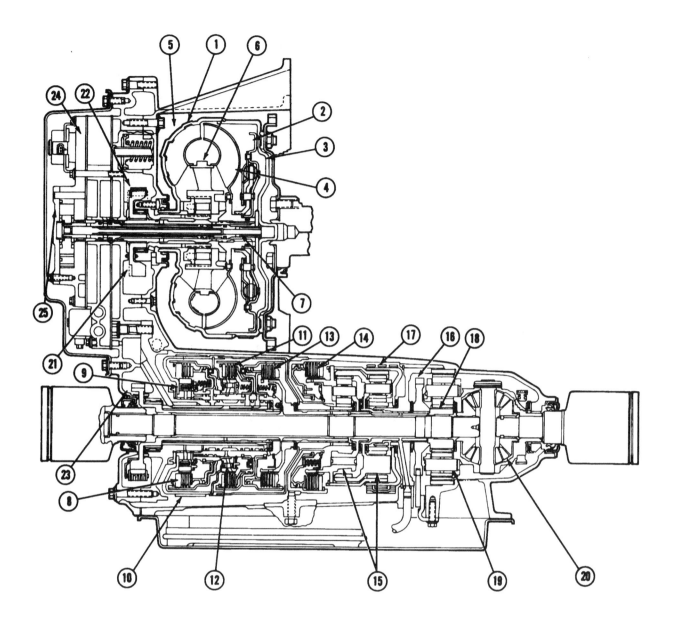

ITEM	DESCRIPTION
1.	TORQUE CONVERTER
2.	CONVERTER CLUTCH (PISTON PLATE CLUTCH AND DAMPER ASSEMBLY)
3.	CONVERTER COVER
4.	TURBINE
5.	IMPELLER
6.	REACTOR
7.	OIL PUMP DRIVESHAFT
8.	FORWARD CLUTCH
9.	LOW ONE-WAY CLUTCH
10.	OVERDRIVE BAND
11.	DIRECT CLUTCH
12.	DIRECT ONE-WAY CLUTCH

ITEM	DESCRIPTION
13.	INTERMEDIATE CLUTCH
14.	REVERSE CLUTCH
15.	PLANETARY GEARS
16.	PARKING GEAR
17.	LOW/INTERMEDIATE BAND
18.	FINAL DRIVE SUN GEAR
19.	FINAL DRIVE PLANET
20.	DIFFERENTIAL ASSEMBLY
21.	DRIVE SPROCKET
22.	DRIVE LINK ASSEMBLY (CHAIN)
23.	DRIVEN SPROCKET
24.	VALVE BODY (MAIN CONTROL ASSEMBLY)
25.	OIL PUMP

FIGURE 7–30 Four-speed overdrive automatic transaxle (Ford AXOD-E) (Courtesy of Ford Motor Company.)

GEAR	OVER DRIVE BAND	FOR- WARD CLUTCH	LOW ONE-WAY CLUTCH	DIRECT CLUTCH	DIRECT ONE-WAY CLUTCH	INTER- MEDIATE CLUTCH	REV CLUTCH	LOW INTER BAND	RATIO
MANUAL LOW		APPLIED	HOLD	APPLIED				APPLIED	2.77:1
• COASTING		APPLIED		APPLIED	HOLD			APPLIED	2.77:1
DRIVE 1st GEAR		APPLIED	HOLD					APPLIED	2.77:1
• COASTING		APPLIED	O/R					APPLIED	Freewheel
DRIVE 2nd GEAR		APPLIED	O/R			APPLIED		APPLIED	1.543:1
DRIVE 3rd GEAR				APPLIED	HOLD	APPLIED			1.000:1
• COASTING		APPLIED	HOLD	APPLIED	HOLD	APPLIED			1.000:1
OVERDRIVE 3rd GEAR • COASTING			O/R	APPLIED	HOLD	APPLIED			Freewheel
OVERDRIVE 4th GEAR	APPLIED			APPLIED	O/R	APPLIED			.694:1
REVERSE		APPLIED	HOLD				APPLIED		2.263:1

FIGURE 7–31 Clutch and band application chart for Ford AXOD-E transaxle. (Courtesy of Ford Motor Company.)

during deceleration in Drive, second, first, and Reverse, thereby providing engine braking.

4. *Direct clutch spring:* a powerful, large-diameter coil spring that provides 800 lbs (3558 N) of force to apply the direct clutch.

5. *Overdrive piston:* used to control the application and release of the direct clutch and the overdrive clutch.

Direct-Drive Operation

Direct drive occurs in first, second, third, and Reverse gears. The powerflow in direct drive is as follows **(Figure 7–34)**:

The intermediate shaft drives the carrier and overrunning clutch. During acceleration, the overrunning clutch locks up and drives the output shaft. At the same time, with the direct clutch applied, the planetary gears are locked up with the output shaft to provide direct drive at 1:1. During deceleration, the overrunning clutch is released while engine braking is provided through the locked-up planetary gearset.

Overdrive Operation

The transmission shifts into overdrive when the overdrive piston is applied. This action first compresses the direct clutch spring to release the direct clutch. The overrunning clutch momentarily provides the only powerflow to the output shaft.

The overdrive piston continues to move until the overdrive clutch is fully applied. This locks the overdrive sun gear to the extension housing of the transmission. With the sun gear held and the planet carrier as the input member, the planet pinions walk around the stationary sun gear to drive the ring gear and output shaft at a ratio of 0.69 to 1 overdrive. Since the output shaft is now turning faster than the intermediate shaft, the overrunning clutch freewheels **(Figure 7–35)**.

Ravigneaux Planetary Gears (Three-Speed)

The Ravigneaux compound planetary gear train consists of two sun gears, one planet pinion carrier containing two sets of pinions, and one ring gear. In the three-speed arrangement of this planetary gearset, there are two sun gears, one behind the other and each free to turn separately. The front sun gear is slightly larger than the rear sun gear.

The rear sun gear is in mesh with one set of short pinions. These short pinions are in mesh with a set of long pinions mounted in a single carrier. The long pinions are in mesh with the front or larger sun gear and also with the ring gear or internal gear. This completes the physical arrangement of these gears.

The ring gear also has external teeth on it, which are used to provide the Park position for this gearset. All gears have helical teeth for quiet operation and are highly finished high-grade steel for toughness and durability. The gearset is controlled by two multiple-disc

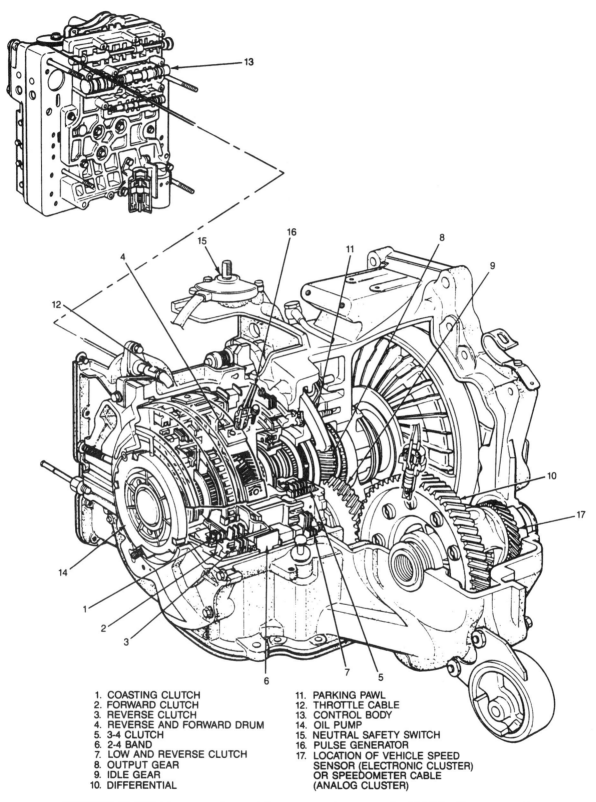

1. COASTING CLUTCH
2. FORWARD CLUTCH
3. REVERSE CLUTCH
4. REVERSE AND FORWARD DRUM
5. 3-4 CLUTCH
6. 2-4 BAND
7. LOW AND REVERSE CLUTCH
8. OUTPUT GEAR
9. IDLE GEAR
10. DIFFERENTIAL

11. PARKING PAWL
12. THROTTLE CABLE
13. CONTROL BODY
14. OIL PUMP
15. NEUTRAL SAFETY SWITCH
16. PULSE GENERATOR
17. LOCATION OF VEHICLE SPEED
    SENSOR (ELECTRONIC CLUSTER)
    OR SPEEDOMETER CABLE
    (ANALOG CLUSTER)

FIGURE 7–32 Four-speed overdrive automatic transaxle (4EAT). (Courtesy of Ford Motor Company.)

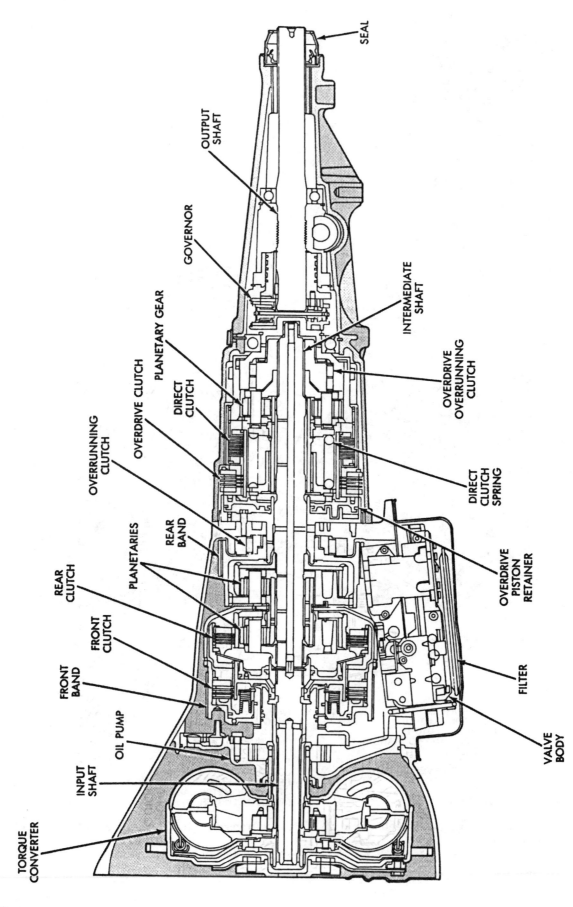

FIGURE 7-33 Four-speed automatic overdrive automatic transmission with Simpson planetary gears and planetary gear overdrive. (Courtesy of Chrysler Corporation.)

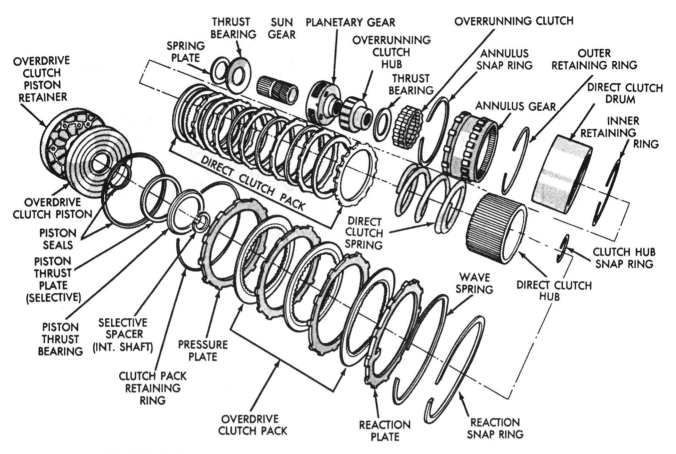

FIGURE 7–34 Planetary gear overdrive components for four-speed overdrive automatic transmission. (Courtesy of Chrysler Corporation.)

clutches, two bands, and a one-way clutch **(Figures 7–36** to **7–38)**.

The selector lever has six positions: Park, Reverse, Neutral, Drive, 2, and 1. In Park, the ring gear and output shaft are held stationary by a park pawl, which engages the external teeth on the ring gear. The park pawl is anchored to the transmission case.

In Reverse, the rear (reverse and high) clutch is applied to drive the front or secondary sun gear in a clockwise direction. The secondary sun gear drives the secondary (long) pinions counterclockwise. The counterclockwise-turning secondary pinions drive the ring gear and output shaft in a counterclockwise direction for Reverse. The low and reverse holding clutch is

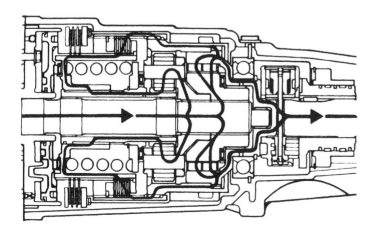

FIGURE 7–35 Powerflow in direct drive. (Courtesy of Chrysler Corporation.)

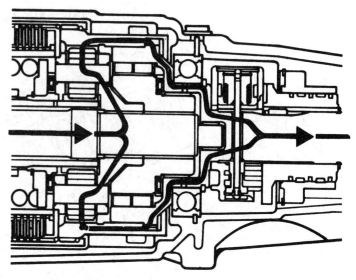

FIGURE 7–36 Powerflow in overdrive. (Courtesy of Chrysler Corporation.)

applied to prevent the carrier from turning in a forward direction. It tries to do this since there is a resistance to motion of the ring gear and output shaft due to vehicle load. In Neutral, no clutches or bands are applied. In the Drive position, the transmission starts in Low and shifts automatically to second and to third.

Four-Speed Overdrive Ravigneaux Planetary Gear Powerflow

The four-speed overdrive Ravigneaux planetary gear arrangement consists of the following components:

- Forward clutch, when applied, drives the forward (smaller) sun gear.
- Direct clutch, when applied, drives the carrier.
- Reverse clutch, when applied, drives the reverse (larger) sun gear.
- Intermediate clutch, when applied, holds the reverse sun gear stationary.
- Intermediate roller clutch prevents the carrier from turning backward in second gear.
- Low and reverse band, when applied, holds the carrier stationary.
- Overdrive band, when applied, holds the reverse sun gear stationary.

The automatic overdrive four-speed transmission uses four multiple-disc clutches, two one-way clutches, two bands, and two input shafts to control a

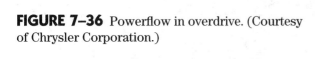
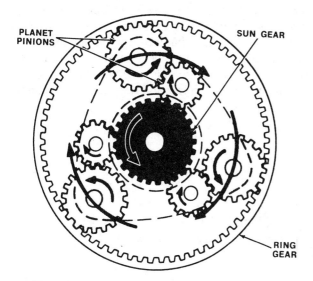

FIGURE 7–37 Ravigneaux planetary gears have a single pinion carrier with two sets of pinions, one ring gear, and two sun gears. (Courtesy of Ford Motor Company.)

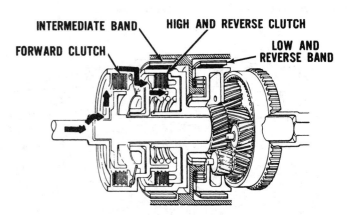

FIGURE 7–38 Three-speed Ravigneaux planetary gear train. (Courtesy of Ford Motor Company.)

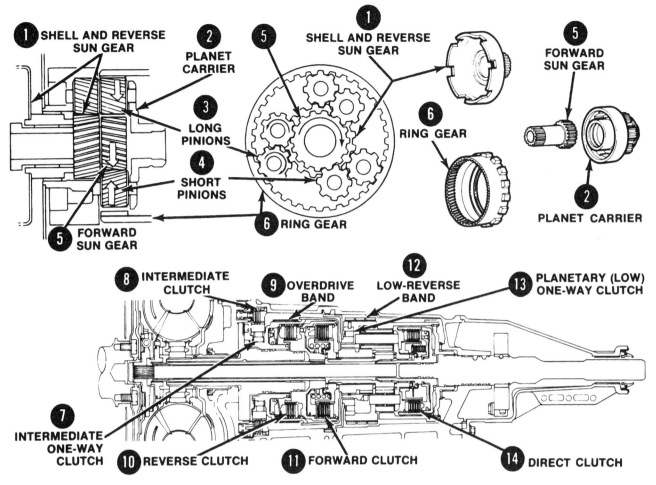

FIGURE 7–39 Four-speed automatic overdrive transmission with Ravigneaux planetary gears (AOD). (Courtesy of Ford Motor Company.)

Ravigneaux-type planetary gear system. A tubular turbine shaft is used, allowing a direct-drive shaft to be located inside the turbine shaft. The direct-drive shaft is spring dampened in the torque converter. Selector lever positions are Park, Reverse, Neutral, Drive, 3, and 1. The Drive position is the overdrive position, and the 3 position locks out the overdrive. Study **Figures 7–39 and 7–40.**

In the Park position, the park pawl locks the ring gear and output shaft to the transmission case. The low and reverse band is applied in Park, but no drive condition is possible since no clutches are applied. In Reverse, the reverse clutch is applied to drive the reverse (front, larger) sun gear clockwise. The low and reverse band holds the carrier to prevent it from turning forward. This allows the reverse sun gear to drive the long pinions counterclockwise. The long pinions drive the ring gear and output shaft in reverse. In Neutral, no clutches or bands are applied.

Low Gear. In Low gear, the forward clutch is applied to drive the forward (rear or smaller) sun gear. This drives the short pinions in a counterclockwise direction. The short pinions drive the long pinions in a clockwise direction, which drives the ring gear and output shaft forward for low gear. Resistance to motion of the ring gear creates a reaction on the carrier, which attempts to turn backward. This is prevented by a one-way clutch.

On deceleration, the one-way clutch overruns, providing no engine braking. In manual Low, the low and reverse band is applied to prevent carrier rotation and provide engine braking on deceleration.

Second Gear. In second gear, the intermediate holding clutch is applied to lock the outer race of the intermediate one-way clutch to the transmission case. This prevents the reverse (larger) sun gear from turning counterclockwise. This is the case during en-

GEAR		OVERDRIVE (BAND)	LOW & REV (BAND)	LOW	INTERMEDIATE (ONE-WAY CLUTCH)	INTERMEDIATE (FRICTION)	FORWARD	DIRECT	REVERSE
1	D			H			A		
1	COAST			OR			A		
1	M		A	H			A		
1	COAST		A	/			A		
2	D			OR	H	A	A		
2	COAST			OR	OR	/	A		
2	M	A		OR	H	/	A		
3				OR	OR	/	A	A	
4		A		OR		/		A	
R			A						A

D = DRIVE/OVERDRIVE RANGE   H = HOLDING
M = MANUAL RANGE   OR = OVERRUNNING
A = APPLIED   / = APPLIED, BUT INEFFECTIVE

FIGURE 7–40 Clutch and band application chart for Ford AODE transmission. (Courtesy of Ford Motor Company.

gine torque application. During deceleration the intermediate one-way clutch overruns, resulting in a freewheeling–no engine braking condition.

In second gear, the reverse sun gear is held by the intermediate holding clutch and one-way clutch. Since the forward clutch is still applied, drive is from the turbine shaft to the forward clutch to the forward (small) sun gear. The forward sun gear drives the short pinions counterclockwise. The short pinions drive the long pinions clockwise. The long pinions are forced to walk around the stationary reverse sun gear, causing the carrier to rotate and driving the ring gear and out-put shaft at an increased speed compared to Low gear.

The intermediate holding clutch remains applied in third and fourth gear but has no effect since the entire gear train is turning in a clockwise direction in third and fourth. The fact that the intermediate clutch remains applied in third and fourth results in smoother 3–2 downshifts.

Third Gear.   To upshift from second gear to third gear, the direct clutch must be applied. The direct clutch

is driven by the direct-drive shaft (not the turbine shaft) and when applied drives the carrier at engine speed.

Since the forward clutch is still applied (driving the forward sun gear), and the carrier is driven through the direct clutch, the entire gear train is forced to turn at engine speed, or 1:1. The direct clutch transmits about 60% of the drive while the forward clutch transmits the other 40%.

However, although the gear train is locked up and rotates as a unit for all practical purposes, there is some converter slip in direct drive, causing the planet pinions to turn on their shafts to a very small degree. The intermediate holding clutch remains applied but has no effect on third-gear operation since the entire gear train is turning clockwise and the intermediate one-way clutch therefore overruns.

Fourth Gear (Overdrive).   As the transmission automatically shifts from third gear direct to fourth gear overdrive, the overdrive band is applied to hold the reverse sun gear stationary. At the same time, the forward clutch is released while the direct-drive clutch is still left applied. The transmission is now driven through the direct-drive shaft only, bypassing the turbine and turbine shaft and thereby eliminating converter slip.

Powerflow is from the direct-drive shaft, through the direct clutch, driving the carrier clockwise. Since the overdrive band is holding the reverse sun gear stationary, carrier rotation causes the long pinions to walk around the reverse sun gear. This causes the pinions to turn on their shafts, forcing the ring gear and output shaft to turn faster than the carrier in overdrive. The result is an overdrive ratio of 0.667:1. The intermediate clutch, though still applied, has no effect on overdrive operation since all gear components are turning clockwise and the intermediate one-way clutch therefore overruns.

MULTIPLE-DISC CLUTCH DESIGN AND OPERATION

Multiple-disc clutches are used in automatic transmissions and transaxles to:

1. Connect planetary gear members to the input shaft.
2. Lock planetary gear members to the case to prevent them from turning.

A multiple-disc clutch consists of the following components (see **Figures 7–41** to **7–43**):

1. *Clutch retainer* (also called clutch cylinder or clutch drum): the clutch retainer encloses the clutch piston, piston seals, clutch plates, clutch discs, pressure plate, cushion spring, and release springs. The clutch retainer has internal grooves that engage external tabs on the clutch plates.

2. *Clutch hub:* positioned inside the clutch retainer, it has external teeth that engage internal teeth on the clutch discs.

3. *Clutch plates:* steel plates with external tabs that engage grooves in the clutch retainer.

4. *Clutch discs:* discs with internal teeth that engage teeth on the clutch hub. Discs have friction material bonded to both sides.

5. *Clutch piston:* slides back and forth in clutch retainer to apply and release clutch pack. Hydraulic pressure applies the piston, and spring pressure moves the piston to the release position. Rubber seals on the piston prevent fluid leakage between the piston and the clutch cylinder and hub.

6. *Pressure plate:* acts as a stop for clutch discs when the clutch is applied. It is held in place by a snap ring that fits into a groove in the clutch retainer.

7. *Clutch springs or spring:* pushes the piston back to the released position when hydraulic pressure is removed from the other side. May be a single large coil spring, a series of small coil springs, or a single wave plate spring called a Belleville spring.

8. *Cushion spring:* a wavy steel plate or a waved snap ring may be used to cushion clutch application.

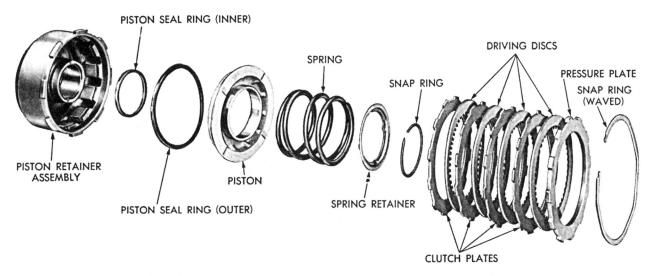

FIGURE 7–41 Multiple-disc clutch components (typical) with steel driving discs and composition driven plates. (Courtesy of Chrysler Corporation.)

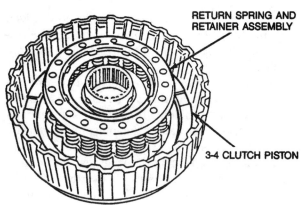

FIGURE 7–42 Clutch with multiple coil springs. (Courtesy of Ford Motor Company.)

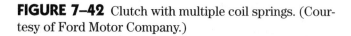

Hydraulic pressure is fed to the clutch retainer to force the piston against the clutch discs and apply the clutch. The drive and driven discs are squeezed tightly between the piston and pressure plate, causing the clutch retainer, clutch discs, and clutch hub to rotate as a unit. Friction between the discs transmits driving torque.

When hydraulic pressure is removed, the return spring forces the piston back to the released position, allowing the clutch discs to separate from each other and turn independently. Precise clutch pack clearance is critical to clutch operation since discs may turn in opposite directions at times. Steel and friction discs are stacked alternately in the clutch pack **(Figures 7–44 to 7–45)**.

A ball type of check valve is located in the clutch piston. The check ball controls a fluid exhaust passage. Fast clutch release is required to provide smooth rapid shifts and prevent unwanted friction in the clutch. The rapidly spinning clutch assembly deposits residual fluid between the piston and cylinder base circumference, which attempts to continue clutch apply. Centrifugal force unseats the fluid exhaust check ball and allows fluid to exhaust, preventing this condition. When the clutch is applied once again, hydraulic pressure seats the check ball and seals off the exhaust orifice.

Clutch Plates and Discs

Steel clutch discs are stamped from steel stock and are finished with a dull surface to facilitate proper break-in with new friction discs. After proper break-in, steel discs become polished. Friction discs are steel plates with friction material bonded to both sides. Friction material may be organic or metallic, depending on friction characteristics required.

Metallic material is usually a sintered or powdered copper and graphite mix with bonding agents. Semimetallic materials include asbestos powders. Nonmetallic organic friction materials are normally a paper

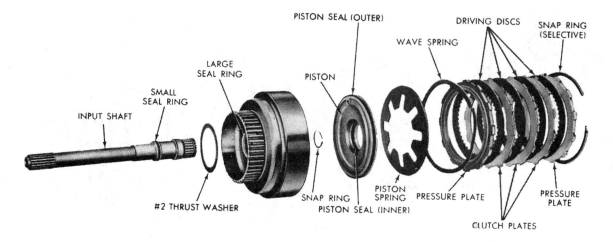

FIGURE 7–43 Multiple-disc input clutch with Belleville spring. (Courtesy of Chrysler Corporation.)

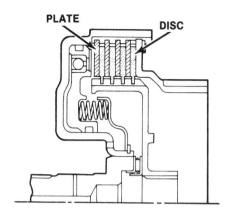

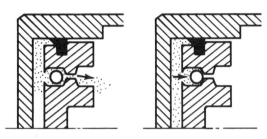

FIGURE 7–44 Cross section of one-half of multiple-disc clutch (top). Clutch position check ball unseats to allow fluid to escape when clutch is released. (Courtesy of Chrysler Corporation.)

type sometimes combined with asbestos and the proper bonding agents.

The friction characteristics of these materials are modified by the type of fluid used and by grooving of the friction discs **(Figure 7–46)**. The slip-lockup characteristics of multiple-disc clutches are critical to shift quality. Due to the nature of the frictional characteris-

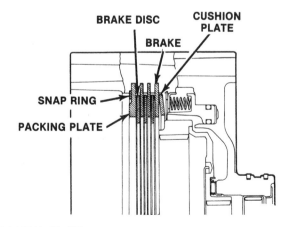

FIGURE 7–45 Clutch pack arrangement with pressure plate on one side and dished cushion plate on the other. (Courtesy of Chrysler Corporation.)

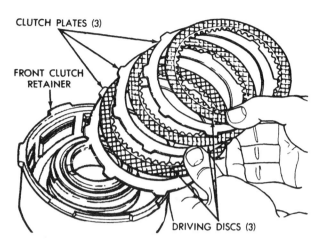

FIGURE 7–46 Example of grooving on clutch discs. (Courtesy of Chrysler Corporation.)

tics of the clutch plates, new and old plates should never be mixed, since glazing could occur.

Clutch Torque Capacity

The maximum torque capacity of the multiple-disc clutch is determined by the following factors:

1. Clutch diameter
2. Frictional surface area (number of plates)
3. Hydraulic pressure
4. Surface area acted on by hydraulic pressure
5. In the case of a Belleville-spring-type clutch, the mechanical advantage gained by the lever action of the spring

The diameter of the clutch is limited by the room available in the transmission case. The frictional surface area can be increased or decreased by the number of plates used in the clutch pack. Increasing hydraulic apply pressure will, of course, increase the torque capacity of a clutch and also will result in harsher shifts. The surface area against which the hydraulic pressure acts (piston size) is also limited by the available room in the clutch cylinder. Engine size and vehicle design are factors that influence the design and balance of torque capacity factors utilized by the vehicle manufacturer.

Multiple-Disc Holding Clutches

Many transmission designs utilize multiple-disc holding clutches in place of bands and servos. A hydraulically applied and spring-released piston is used. Steel and friction plates stacked alternately comprise the clutch pack. The externally tanged steel plates engage corresponding grooves in the transmission case. The internally toothed friction plates engage grooves on a drum attached to the planetary gear member to be held. A heavy pressure plate and snap ring absorb clutch apply reaction pressure. A wave spring may be used to help cushion clutch application.

BANDS AND SERVOS

Many automatic transmission designs use the hydraulic-servo-operated wraparound band as a holding device to control planetary gear operation. The band does not increase the diameter of the gear train as much as a multiple-disc clutch does but requires room for a servo to operate the band.

Hydraulic Servo

A hydraulic servo converts hydraulic force to mechanical force. The servo consists of a piston operating in a bore in the transmission case or in a separate servo cylinder bolted to the transmission case. A piston rod is used to act directly on the band or through a lever and link assembly. The lever usually is used to increase apply force. Reaction force is applied to an anchor at the other end of the band. The anchor is attached to or is part of the transmission case **(Figure 7–47)**.

The piston in a low and reverse band servo is usually single acting. Hydraulic apply force is available on one side of the piston with a spring on the other side of the piston to return the piston to the release position when apply pressure is removed. A piston plug in the servo piston may be used to cushion servo apply. The two piston return springs are located between the piston and a land on the piston plug and between the piston and spring retainer. Band adjustment may be provided at the lever or the anchor to maintain proper operating clearance between the band and the drum.

The intermediate servo usually has a two-land piston and is double acting. The servo bore and piston are stepped—the small end of the piston operating in the smaller-diameter bore and the larger-diameter piston in the larger bore. A piston rod and return spring are located inside the piston. A piston return spring is used between the piston and piston rod guide, which is held in the bore by means of a snap ring.

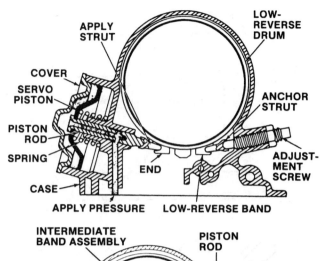

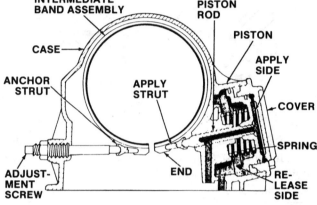

FIGURE 7–47 Single-acting (top) and double-acting (bottom) hydraulic servos. (Courtesy of Ford Motor Company.)

Hydraulic pressure applied between the piston and piston bore applies the intermediate band on a 1–2 upshift or a 3–2 downshift. Spring pressure returns the piston to the release position on a 2–1 downshift. On a 2–3 upshift, hydraulic pressure introduced to the release side of the piston plug spring pressure forces the piston back against apply pressure to release the band for third gear. During a 3–2 downshift, intermediate servo release pressure is dumped. Since apply pressure is still present, the intermediate band applies for second-gear operation.

During a part-throttle or full-throttle 3–2 downshift, it is essential that the intermediate band be applied immediately as the direct clutch is released in order to prevent excessive engine speed increase. The intermediate servo piston rod may be direct acting on the band, or it may act on the band through a lever and link or strut. Reaction force is absorbed by the other end of the band through an anchor in the transmission case.

Proper operating clearance may be adjusted on some transmissions by means of an anchor screw adjustment. Other transmissions may use selective length band actuating rods or may have no adjustment. Proper band-to-drum clearance is required to prevent drag on the drum when the band is in the released position and to assure full band application before the servo piston bottoms in its bore to prevent slippage.

Bands

Transmission bands may be rigid or flexible. The rigid type is also flexible to the extent that it will contract during band application and expand on band release. The flexible type when removed from the transmission does not retain its circular shape to fit the drum. Bands are either single wrap or double wrap **(Figure 7–48)**. The double-wrap design increases the effects of self-energization when the band is applied. Self-energizing is the tendency of a band to tighten around a drum during drum rotation.

The double-wrap band design is used for low and reverse where greater holding force is required due to the high torque of low and reverse gear operation. Bands have either a relatively hard metallic friction lining or a softer organic friction material.

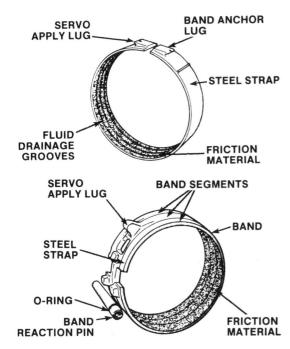

FIGURE 7–48 Single (top) and double wrap (bottom) bands. (Courtesy of Chrysler Corporation.)

The metallic materials are generally more abrasive than the organic materials. For this reason, they are usually used only on the low and reverse band since this band is usually applied to a static or slow-turning drum. The softer organic materials, usually a paper-based compound, are used on bands required to operate on fast-turning drums. Metallic-lined bands used on these drums would result in much more rapid drum wear.

Drum material is also a factor in the slip-lockup characteristics of band operation. The proper combination of drum material, drum surface finish, and band frictional material is designed to provide the required slip-lockup characteristics for smooth positive shifts without causing premature band and drum wear or glazing. Band frictional linings are usually grooved to control the escape of transmission fluid. This helps in providing the desired band application characteristics.

To ensure proper operation of the bands, the fluid specified by the vehicle manufacturer must be used. Using incorrect fluid results in a change of the coefficient of friction of all friction devices (clutches and bands) and consequent changes in shift characteristics. Harsher, more severe shifts or "mushy" delayed shifts can be the result of using improper fluid in the transmission or transaxle.

Torque Capacity of Bands. The torque capacity of a band must be great enough to hold the desired reaction member under all appropriate operating conditions. Torque capacity is determined by the friction characteristics of the band and drum (band friction lining and drum material); surface finish of the drum; drum and band diameter; servo piston diameter; hydraulic pressure to the servo piston; ratio of lever used to apply the band; and whether the servo is positioned to take advantage of the self-energizing effect of drum rotational direction when the band is applied. In the case of a low and reverse band, of course, the held member attempts to rotate counterclockwise in Low and clockwise in Reverse. It is therefore impossible to have self-energizing benefits in both directions. Higher hydraulic pressures are sometimes used in Reverse to offset the difference there would otherwise be in torque capacity.

Higher hydraulic apply pressures are used in Reverse with a multiple-disc low and reverse holding clutch. This is required since the reaction force on the held member is greater in reverse than in Low. In Reverse, only the rear half of the planetary gearset provides the gear reduction while in low gear, reduction is achieved through both the front and rear section of the gear train. In the band and servo design, the self-energizing effect will work against hydraulic servo apply pressure, requiring even greater hydraulic pressure in reverse.

ONE-WAY CLUTCHES

Automatic transmissions and transaxles may use one or more one-way clutches to help control planetary gear operation. One-way clutches allow rotation in one direction and prevent rotation in the opposite direction. There are two kinds of one-way clutches: the sprag clutch and the roller clutch. One-way clutches require no mechanical linkage or hydraulic pressure for operation. They act and react instantly when torque

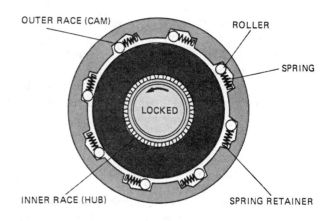

FIGURE 7–50 Roller-type one-way clutch operation. (Courtesy of Chrysler Corporation.)

changes direction. A one-way clutch consists of an inner race and an outer race with rollers or sprags between the races. The sprags tilt to wedge between the races when the clutch locks up. The sprags tilt in the opposite direction when the clutch overruns **(Figure 7–49)**. In a roller clutch, a spring retainer and springs keep the rollers close to the narrowest point between the races. When the clutch locks up, the rollers wedge between the inner and outer races. When the clutch overruns, the rollers slide away from the high point on the ramps against spring pressure **(Figure 7–50)**. A one-way clutch is used in the torque converter stator. It is also used as a reaction device in planetary gear systems and as an input drive clutch in some cases.

TRANSAXLE FINAL DRIVE AND DIFFERENTIAL

Helical gear, planetary gear, and hypoid gear final drives are used. All three types provide a final gear reduction in the drive train. The helical gear and planetary gear types are used with engines mounted in the transverse position, where the drive axles and the engine crankshaft are parallel. The hypoid gear final drive is used with engines mounted in a longitudinal position,

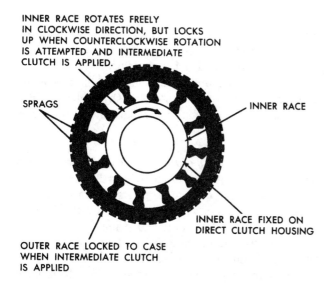

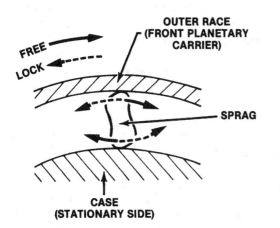

FIGURE 7–49 One-way sprag clutch operation. (Courtesy of General Motors Corporation and Chrysler Corporation.)

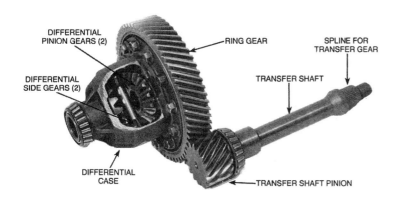

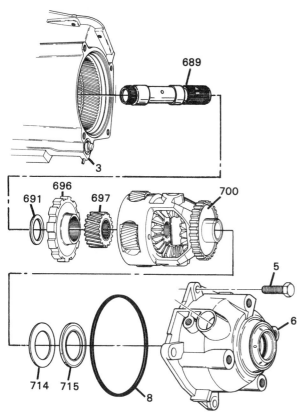

FIGURE 7–51 Helical gear transaxle final drive and differential. (Courtesy of Chrysler Corporation.)

where powerflow from the crankshaft must make a 90 degree turn to the drive axles.

1. *Helical gear final drive.* The transaxle output shaft gear drives a large ring gear mounted on the differential case, which turns at reduced speed **(Figure 7–51)**.

2. *Planetary gear final drive.* The transaxle output shaft and sun gear drive the planet pinions, which are forced to walk around the stationary ring gear, which is locked to the transaxle case. This forces the pinion carrier and differential case assembly to turn at reduced speed **(Figure 7–52)**.

3. *Hypoid gear final drive.* The transaxle output shaft and gear drive the ring gear and differential case at reduced speed. The hypoid gears provide the 90 degree turn in powerflow required with engines mounted in a longitudinal position **(Figure 7–53)**.

Transaxle Differential

The transaxle differential operates in the same manner as the drive axle differential described in Chapter 3.

Park Pawl

The park pawl is mounted in the transmission or transaxle case and is actuated by the transmission shift linkage. When the shift lever is placed in the Park position, the pawl engages a toothed parking gear which is splined to the transmission output shaft or other planetary gear output member. This locks the output shaft to the case and prevents it and the drive wheels from turning. When the shift lever is moved out of the Park position, the park pawl is disengaged **(Figure 7–54)**.

```
  5  BOLT, CASE EXTENSION
  6  EXTENSION, CASE
  8  SEAL, EXTENSION TO CASE
689  SHAFT, FINAL DRIVE SUN GEAR
691  BEARING ASSEMBLY, THRUST (1/2 SUPPORT/
     INTERNAL GEAR)
696  GEAR, PARKING
697  GEAR, FINAL DRIVE SUN
700  CARRIER ASSEMBLY, DIFFERENTIAL/
     FINAL DRIVE COMP
714  WASHER, DIFFERENTIAL CARRIER/CASE (THRUST)
715  BEARING ASSEMBLY, THRUST
     (DIFFERENTIAL CARRIER/CASE)
```

FIGURE 7–52 Planetary gear transaxle final drive and differential. (Courtesy of General Motors Corporation.)

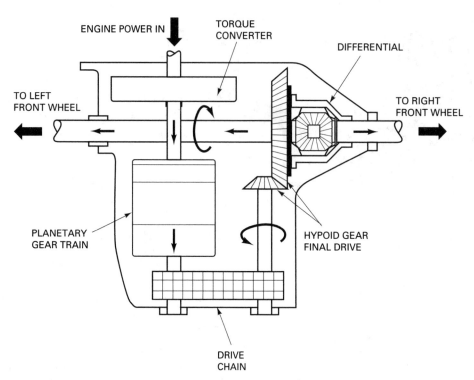

FIGURE 7–53 Hypoid final drive gears turn power 90 degrees from engine crankshaft to front-wheel-drive axles.

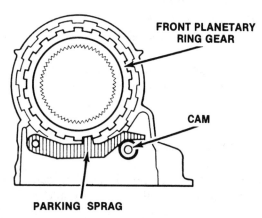

FIGURE 7–54 Park pawl (sprag) locks output shaft to the transmission/transaxle case. (Courtesy of Chrysler Corporation.)

HYDRAULIC AND ELECTRONIC CONTROL SYSTEM COMPONENTS AND OPERATION

All automatic transmissions and transaxles have a hydraulic system to operate the various clutches and bands. For many years there was no electronic control of the hydraulic system. Shift valve operation, shift timing, and shift quality were all a function of the hydraulic system. Selector lever position, throttle position (or intake manifold vacuum), and vehicle speed determined which clutches or bands were applied or released.

With the application of electronics to automatic transmissions and transaxles, shift timing and shift quality have been improved. Electronic control began with electronic control of the torque converter clutch. Electronic control of hydraulic pressure and the shift valves was added later. Full electronic control of the hydraulic system is common on today's transmissions and transaxles.

HYDRAULIC PUMPS

The hydraulic pump is the source of fluid flow and operating pressure. Fluid flow (circulation) is needed to lubricate and cool internal parts. Hydraulic pressure is needed to operate transmission/transaxle components. All automatic transmission/transaxle pumps operate on the same basic principle. Rotation of the pump drive member creates expanding intake chambers and contracting outlet chambers. The pump intake is connected to the fluid reservoir (oil pan) through a filter or screen. The pump outlet is connected to the transmis-

FIGURE 7–55 Gear-type hydraulic pump. (Courtesy of Chrysler Corporation.)

sion/transaxle hydraulic system. The intake and outlet chambers are isolated from each other to prevent backflow from the outlet chambers to the inlet chambers. Filtered oil is drawn into the pump intake and forced out of the pump outlet.

On rear-wheel-drive vehicles with the engine in front, the pump is driven by flats or notches on the torque converter hub. These flats or notches fit into the pump drive member. On front-wheel-drive transaxles, a pump drive shaft is used. One end of the shaft is splined to the center of the torque converter cover. The other end fits into the pump drive member.

Internal/External (IX) Pumps

IX pumps have an inner drive member and an outer driven member. There are two IX pump designs: the gear type and the lobe or rotor type. In both designs, the inner drive member gear teeth or lobes mesh with the teeth or lobes on only one side of the driven member. The drive and driven members turn on different centers causing them to mesh on one side and separate on the other as the pump is driven **(Figures 7–55 to 7–57)**.

As the drive member of the rotary lobe pump turns, the outer driven member turns with it. The lobes that are in mesh separate, creating expanding inlet chambers as the rotors turn. When the lobes of the two members are directly opposite each other (180 degrees) from the meshed position, they pass each other with very little clearance between them. This is the point where the low pressure intake area is separated from the high pressure outlet area. As the lobes pass this point, they come closer together and begin to mesh again. This squeezes the fluid out from between the lobes into the hydraulic system under pressure.

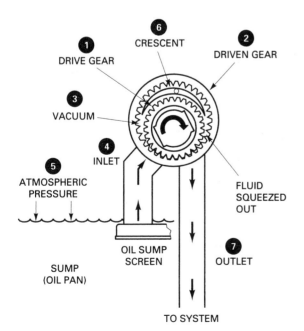

FIGURE 7–56 Gear-type hydraulic pump operation. (Courtesy of Ford Motor Company.)

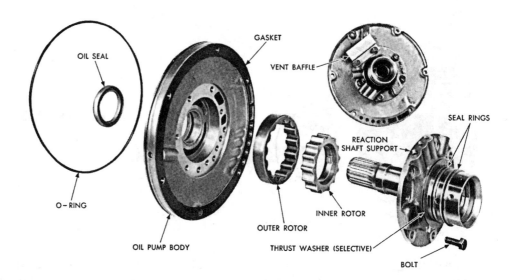

FIGURE 7–57 Rotor-type hydraulic pump. (Courtesy of Chrysler Corporation.)

The IX gear pump operates similarly. The teeth of the inner drive member and the outer driven member are in mesh on one side only. As they turn, they separate, creating a low pressure area at the intake side of the pump. Fluid is carried between the gear teeth of both gears and is trapped between the teeth and a crescent-shaped divider. As the teeth pass the divider, they come closer together and begin to mesh again. This forces the fluid out from between the gear teeth into the pump outlet and into the hydraulic system under pressure. The minimal clearance between the gear teeth and the crescent prevent fluid from bleeding back to the inlet side of the pump.

Pump capacity normally exceeds requirements, usually remaining adequate for the life of the transmission/transaxle. Abnormal wear due to fluid contamination, low fluid levels, or aeration can result in wear that reduces pump capacity below the level required for satisfactory operation.

IX gear and rotor pumps are classified as positive displacement pumps. This means that the pumps deliver a constant volume of fluid for each revolution of the gears or rotors. Pump output increases or decreases only as its rotating speed increases or decreases.

Variable Displacement Vane Pump

A variable displacement vane pump varies its output to meet the changing requirements of the transmission/transaxle. It provides a large volume of fluid when required (as in low-speed operation) and reduces output when demands are low (as when operating at highway speeds). This reduces the load on the engine at higher speeds and reduces fuel consumption **(Figure 7–58)**.

The pump consists of a drive rotor with vanes positioned radially around the outer circumference. The vanes are positioned in slots and are able to slide in and out. This assembly fits inside a circular oil pump slide. The slide is able to move in relation to the rotor and can change the size of the intake and outlet areas of the pump. The slide is held in the maximum off center position by a priming spring at startup. As the rotor turns, the area between the vanes is increased at the pump in-

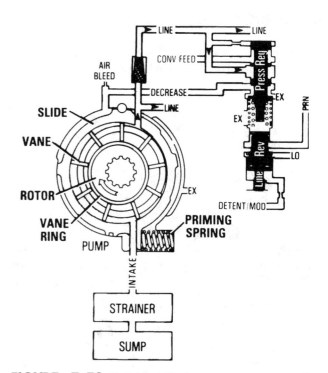

FIGURE 7–58 Variable displacement vane-type hydraulic pump. (Courtesy of General Motors Corporation.)

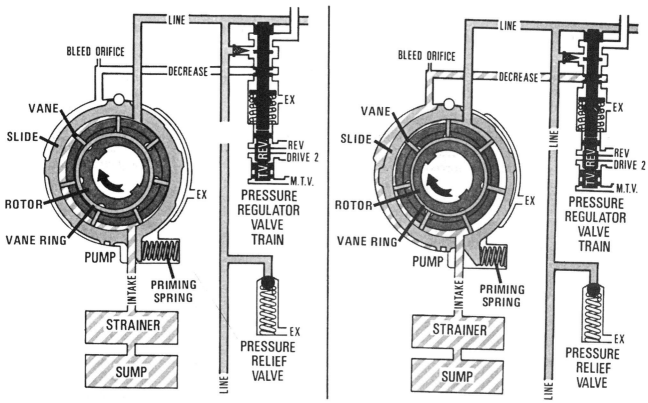

FIGURE 7–59 Operation of variable capacity vane pump. Maximum output on left and minimum output on right. (Courtesy of General Motors Corporation.)

take, creating a low pressure area. Atmospheric pressure forces fluid from the reservoir into the area between the vanes. The fluid is carried around to the pump outlet area where the vanes are pushed back into their slots due to the reduced clearance between the slide and the rotor. During maximum pump output, this forces the fluid out of the pump outlet and into the hydraulic system.

Fluid pressure from the pressure regulator valve is directed to the back of the oil pump slide. This moves the slide to a more centered position over the pump rotor. Slide position is balanced between spring pressure on one side and hydraulic pressure on the other. The more centralized position of the slide reduces the difference in space between the vanes in the inlet and outlet areas of the pump, thereby reducing pump output **(Figure 7–59)**.

Some hydraulic pumps are designed with several pressure regulator and flow control valves incorporated into the pump body. This may include the main pressure regulator valve, converter regulator valve, converter clutch control valve, and the reverse boost valve. Oil passages in the pump body connect these valves to passages in the transmission/transaxle case or to the main control valve body.

Pressure Regulation

A pressure regulator valve controls maximum system pressure (line pressure) and usually also torque converter, lubrication, and cooling circuit pressures. As pressure builds up in the system, the spool type of pressure regulator valve is forced back against spring pressure. When pressure reaches a predetermined maximum (determined by spring pressure), the valve moves far enough to allow some fluid to bypass and return to the sump **(Figures 7–60 and 7–61)**. The torque converter control valve controls pressure to the torque converter **(Figures 7–62 and 7–63)**.

Electronic Pressure Control

Electronic pressure control replaces the throttle-linkage-operated throttle valve and the vacuum modulator valve. The result is more precise control of hydraulic pressure for smoother shifts.

In this system, the control module varies electrical current to an electronic pressure control solenoid.

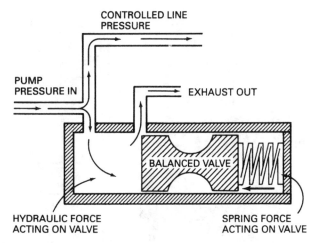

FIGURE 7–60 Basic principle of pressure regulation and balanced valve operation. Line pressure is controlled by spring pressure.

The solenoid controls the position of a flow control spool valve. With no current, the spool valve is held all the way in and allows maximum pressure to flow. As more current is allowed to the solenoid, the valve is pushed back by the solenoid through spring pressure. This restricts fluid flow and reduces hydraulic pressure.

The control module regulates current to the pressure control solenoid based on signals from the throttle position sensor and programmed information stored in the control module memory. As the throttle opening is increased, hydraulic pressure rises. When the throttle opening is reduced, the pressure decreases.

Adaptive Learning

The electronic control module (ECM) or powertrain control module (PCM) may be programmed to provide line pressure adjustments to maintain shift quality and shift timing patterns that could otherwise change due to clutch and band component wear. Pressure changes are achieved by monitoring changes in input signals to the computer. The computer processes this information and compares it to programmed information stored in computer memory.

Manual Shift Valve

The shift lever is on the steering column or console and is connected by linkage to the manual shift valve in the valve body. The driver can select Park, Reverse, Neutral, or any of the various positions. The manual valve directs hydraulic pressure to the appropriate clutches, servos, and valves to provide drive through the planetary gears. Fluid flow is directed to the torque converter, fluid cooler, and lubrication circuit in the transmission/transaxle anytime the engine is running, regardless of shift lever position **(Figure 7–64;** see also **Figure 7–61).**

Throttle Valve (or Modulator Valve)

The throttle valve is operated mechanically through the accelerator linkage or vacuum operated by a vacuum diaphragm modulator connected to intake manifold vacuum. In either case, the throttle valve modifies line

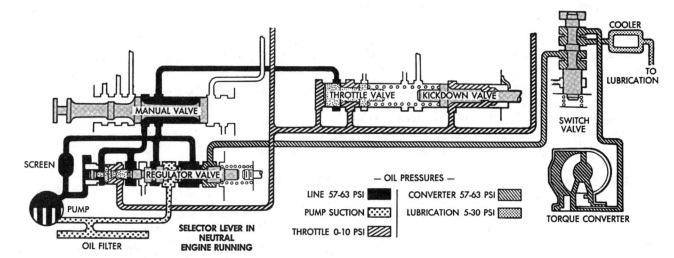

FIGURE 7–61 Pressure regulator valve controls line pressure in hydraulic control system. (Courtesy of Chrysler Corporation.)

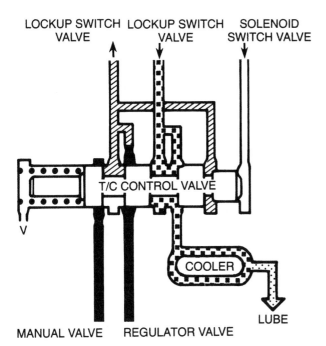

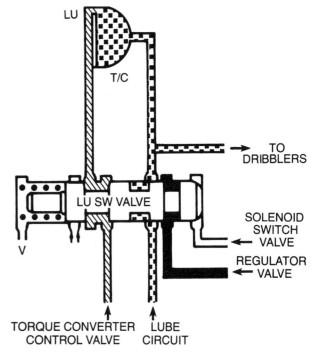

FIGURE 7–62 The torque converter control valve controls hydraulic pressure to the torque converter lockup clutch. (Courtesy of Chrysler Corporation.)

FIGURE 7–63 The lockup switch valve is actuated by a computer-controlled solenoid to operate the torque converter lockup switch. (Courtesy of Chrysler Corporation.)

pressure to produce throttle pressure. The valve of throttle pressure is directly proportional to the carburetor throttle opening in the linkage-operated model and directly proportional to the level of intake manifold vacuum in the case of the vacuum-modulator-operated throttle valve. As throttle opening increases, throttle pressure increases. Throttle pressure is directed at one end of the first-to-second and second-to-third shift valves and is a force that tries to keep these valves in the downshift position. Throttle pressure is aided by spring pressure in both shift valves (**Figures 7–65** to **7–68**).

Governor Valve

The governor valve provides a modified line pressure known as governor pressure in direct proportion to vehicle road speed (**Figures 7–69** and **7–70**). As vehicle speed increases, governor pressure also increases. Governor pressure is directed to the shift valves in opposition to the throttle pressure acting on the shift valves. When vehicle speed has reached a

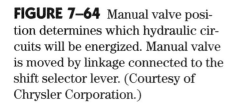

FIGURE 7–64 Manual valve position determines which hydraulic circuits will be energized. Manual valve is moved by linkage connected to the shift selector lever. (Courtesy of Chrysler Corporation.)

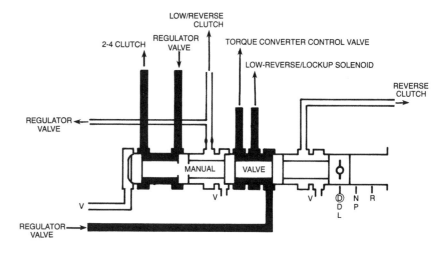

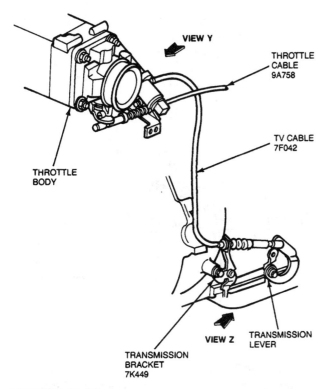

FIGURE 7-65 Many transmissions have a mechanically actuated throttle valve in the transmission/transaxle valve body. A cable from the fuel system throttle body connects it to the throttle valve. (Courtesy of Ford Motor Company.)

point where governor pressure acting on the shift valve is greater than throttle pressure, the spring pressure acting on the shift valve, an upshift takes place. On electronically controlled transmissions/transaxles, the vehicle speed sensor provides a speed signal to the computer. A hydraulic governor is not needed.

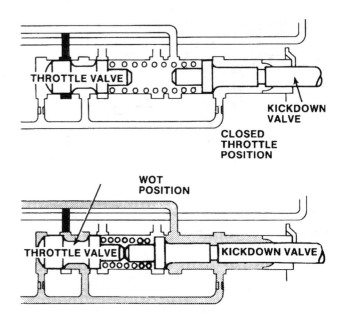

FIGURE 7-66 Throttle valve and kickdown (downshift) valve are mechanically controlled by accelerator linkage in this arrangement. (Courtesy of Chrysler Corporation.)

FIGURE 7-67 Examples of transmission vacuum modulators. Lower modulator is altitude compensated to maintain shift characteristics at all altitudes. Pressure-sensitive evacuated bellows provide compensation for various atmospheric pressures. The modulator controls the throttle valve (and therefore throttle pressure) in direct proportion to engine intake manifold vacuum. Throttle pressure is directed to one end of the first-to-second and second-to-third shift valves, and governor pressure is directed to the other end of the shift valves. (Courtesy of Ford Motor Company.)

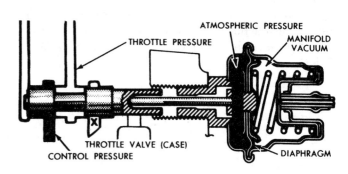

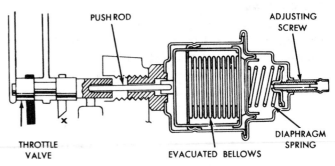

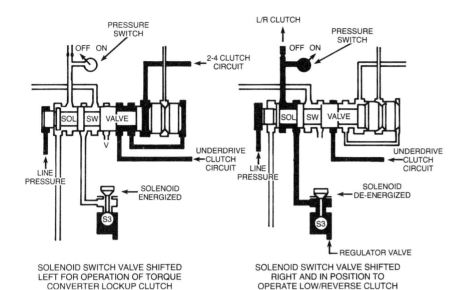

FIGURE 7-68 Solenoid switch valve operates torque converter clutch when shifted to the left. When shifted to the right, it is in position to operate the Low/Reverse clutch. (Courtesy of Chrysler Corporation.)

Shift Valves

Automatic shift valves are controlled electronically by computer-controlled electric solenoids in response to signals from sensors such as the throttle position sensor, engine speed sensor, vehicle speed sensor, coolant temperature sensor, ambient temperature sensor or fluid temperature sensor, manifold absolute pressure sensor, turbine speed sensor, and brake switch on computer-controlled transmissions and transaxles. Governor pressure and throttle pressure valves are not required.

On nonelectronic transmissions and transaxles, the shift valves respond to governor pressure and throttle pressure to provide the automatic upshifts and downshifts at the desired speeds. These valves are simply on/off valves controlling the flow of line pressure to the first-to-second, second-to-third, and third-to-fourth shift circuits **(Figures 7-71** and **7-72(a)** and **(b))**.

Nonelectronic Downshifts

There are three kinds of downshifts possible: a coasting downshift, a forced downshift or kickdown, and a manual-lever-selected downshift. In a coasting downshift, throttle pressure is reduced, allowing the transmission to remain in the higher range until road speed

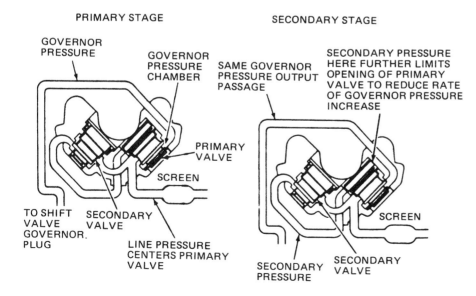

FIGURE 7-69 Output-shaft-mounted governor operation. (Courtesy of Chrysler Corporation.)

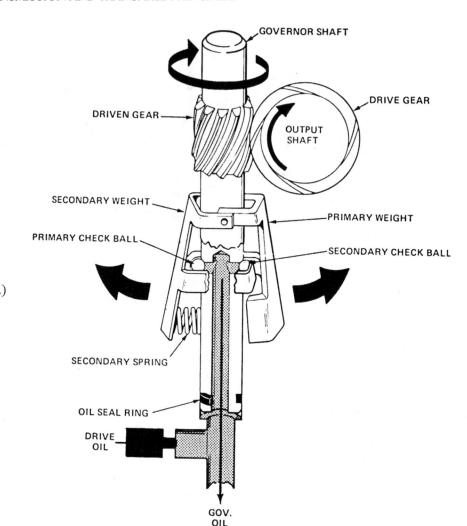

FIGURE 7–70 Output-shaft-gear-driven governor operation. (Courtesy of General Motors Corporation.)

has dropped sufficiently to cause enough drop in governor pressure to occur and allow the springs to cause the shift valves to downshift. This occurs at low road speeds, about 6 to 10 mph (10 to 16 km/h).

In a forced downshift, the accelerator pedal is suddenly depressed. This causes a sudden rise in throttle pressure, and if road speed is not too high, a forced downshift will occur. Forced downshifts or kickdown can occur from fourth to third, third to second, second to first, or from fourth or third to first, depending on transmission design, selector lever position, road speed, and degree of throttle depression. If the road speed is high enough, forced downshift is not possible. Most transmissions provide for two types of forced downshifts: part-throttle (to detent) or full-throttle (through detent) downshift. A throttle-linkage operated detent valve or kickdown valve provides the force downshift function (see **Figures 7–71** and **7–72**(a) and (b). A manual selector lever downshift is also possible. This occurs when the driver moves the selector lever to the

next-lower shift lever position. This results in the manual valve being moved and directing hydraulic pressure to the appropriate clutches and bands. A manual-lever-selected downshift should not be attempted unless recommended by the vehicle manufacturer.

Electronic Shift Control Solenoids. The shift control solenoids are simple on/off types that control fluid flow to the 1–2, 2–3, and 3–4 shift valves. They do not regulate or modify fluid pressures. They simply allow fluid to flow to the shift valves or shut off fluid flow.

The shift control solenoids work together in different on/off combinations to control upshifts and downshifts. The normally closed solenoids de-energize exhaust fluid to reduce hydraulic pressure to the shift valves to a level that does not cause shift valve movement. When the solenoid is energized, the exhaust passage is closed to allow full pressure to the shift valve and cause an upshift. De-energizing the solenoid results in a downshift. When energized, the solenoid ar-

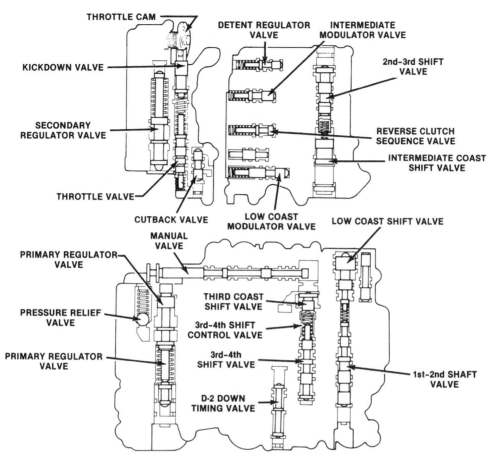

FIGURE 7–71 Typical hydraulic control valves. (Courtesy of Chrysler Corporation.)

mature pushes a check ball against its seat to shut off fluid exhaust. When the solenoid is de-energized, fluid pressure unseats the check ball and opens the fluid exhaust passage.

The electronic control module regulates current to the shift solenoids based on information it receives from a variety of input sensors and switches as well as on information stored in the control module memory.

Electronic Downshifts

The same kinds of downshifts can occur in a computer-controlled transmission or transaxle as those described for a nonelectronic system. Signals received from the throttle position sensor, manifold absolute pressure sensor, turbine speed sensor, fluid temperature sensor, vehicle speed sensor, and engine speed sensor combined with the computer control program information determine when and under what conditions downshifts will occur. Downshifts occur when the shift valves

move to the downshift position as a result of control solenoid action.

Shift Timing and Quality

Several different devices are used in automatic transmissions to control shift timing and quality. Application of clutches and bands is cushioned by such devices as an orifice or an accumulator piston or valve. An orifice restricts apply pressure for a short period until pressure is built up "downstream" from the orifice. An accumulator in the apply circuit is used with a spring-loaded valve or piston. The piston or valve is forced to move against spring pressure during clutch or band engagement, thereby absorbing some of the apply pressure and cushioning the shift. Similar devices are used to control the timed sequence of band and clutch apply and release. For example, during a second-to-third upshift, the reverse and high clutch must not be fully applied before the intermediate band (or intermediate holding clutch) is released. If the apply and release of

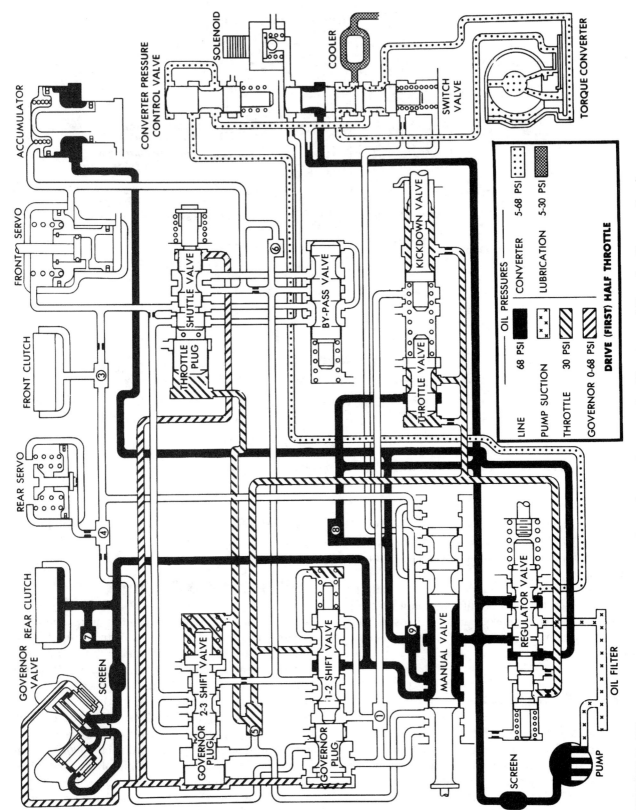

FIGURE 7-72 (a) Hydraulic control system of nonelectronic transaxle. (Courtesy of Chrysler Corporation.)

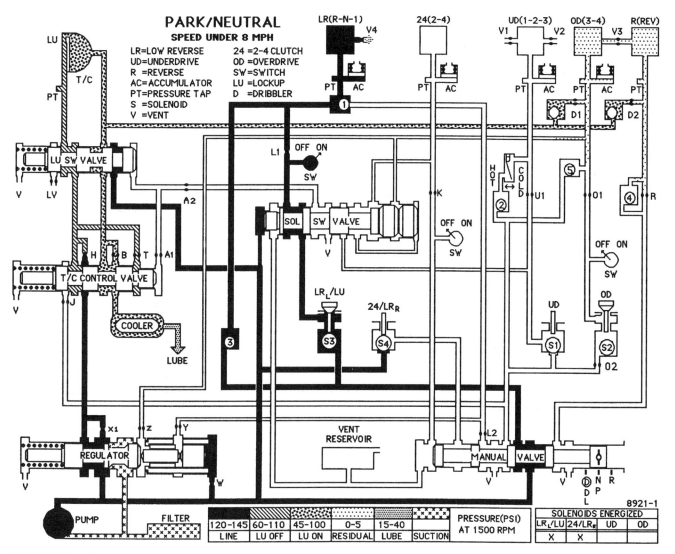

FIGURE 7–72 (b) Electronic four-speed transaxle hydraulic schematic. (Courtesy of Chrysler Corporation.)

these units were not properly timed, a braking effect would result. (See **Figure 7–72** to locate various accumulators and restrictions in hydraulic lines).

Orifice Flow Control. An orifice is a fixed metered restriction in a hydraulic circuit used to delay pressure buildup or to reduce pressure on the downstream side of the orifice. If the downstream side has no fluid exhaust, pressure will build up gradually on the downstream side until it is equal on both sides of the orifice. This provides the delay function used in some apply circuits. If the downstream side of the circuit is not closed, pressure will be lower than it is on the upstream side and will remain lower. Orifices are used to control and cushion the application of clutches and bands by a slight delaying action.

Thermal Valve. A bimetal thermal valve may be used in parallel with an orifice to provide a larger opening and improved fluid flow when the transmission fluid is cold. Cold fluid has a reduced flow rate compared to fluid at operating temperature. Without the thermal valve, clutch and band application is delayed. When the fluid is cold, the thermal valve is open, allowing additional fluid flow in the apply passage. As the fluid warms up, the thermal valve gradually closes, and fluid flow is through the orifice only. Shift quality and shift timing are therefore more equal at varying fluid temperatures.

Check Valves. Ball-type check valves are used in automatic transmissions and transaxles to control fluid flow. A check valve is a one-way flow control valve. It opens or closes a fluid passage depending on the direc-

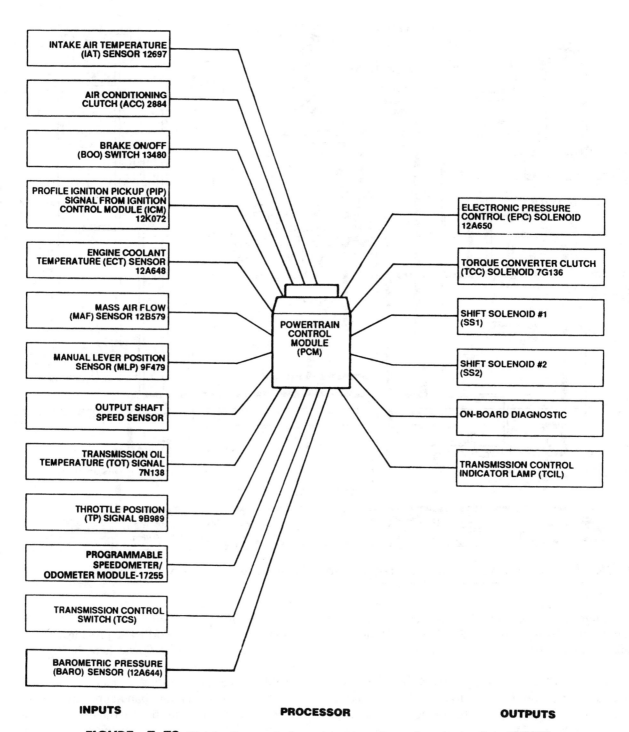

INPUTS   PROCESSOR   OUTPUTS

FIGURE 7–73 Electronic control system inputs and outputs for 4R7OW (AODEW) Ford transmission. (Courtesy of Ford Motor Company.)

tion of fluid flow. When fluid pressure is applied to the seat side, the ball is unseated, and fluid flows through the opening. When pressure is applied to the other side of the ball, the ball is held against the seat, closing off the opening and blocking fluid flow in that direction. Check balls may be made from steel, viton, nylon, or rubber. In some applications, a single check ball is used to control two interconnecting fluid flow paths.

Accumulators. Accumulators are used to cushion full application of clutches and bands. They are de-

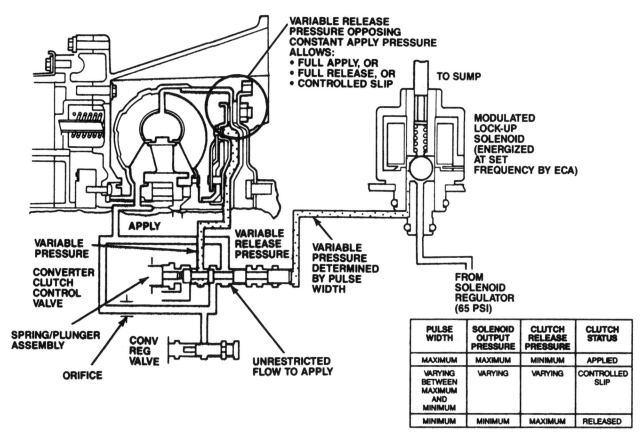

FIGURE 7–74 Ford's modulated converter clutch control (MCCC) system. (Courtesy of Ford Motor Company.)

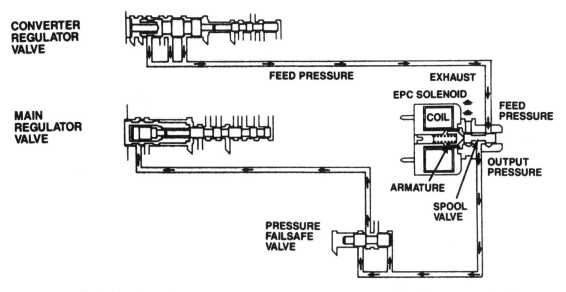

FIGURE 7–75 Ford's electronic pressure control system (EPC). (Courtesy of Ford Motor Company.)

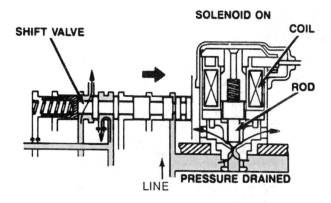

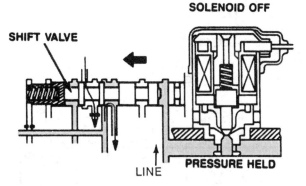

FIGURE 7–76 Electronically controlled solenoid and shift valve operation. (Courtesy of Ford Motor Company.)

signed to improve the quality of both manually selected and automatic shifts.

An accumulator is a spring-loaded piston that operates in a piston bore or cylinder. It is in parallel hydraulically with the clutch or band apply circuit.

It absorbs some of the hydraulic pressure in the circuit to cushion clutch or band application. During the initial apply stage, the clearance between the clutch plates (or band and drum) is taken up, and the accumulator is inactive. After the clearance is taken up, pressure buildup is rapid, pushing the accumulator into its bore against spring pressure. This makes final clutch or band lockup more gradual and the shift much smoother.

When shifts are made under high engine torque (heavy throttle), a throttle-sensitive hydraulic pressure is introduced to the spring side of the accumulator. A much higher apply pressure is therefore required to cause accumulator action. Pressure buildup time in the apply circuit is reduced, and a more firm and aggressive shift is produced. Without this feature, clutch and band slippage would occur under heavy throttle shifts.

Electronic Control Systems

Modern automatic transmissions and transaxles are electronically controlled. A powertrain control module (PCM) or transmission/transaxle controller receives input signals from a variety of vehicle sensors as shown in **Figure 7–73.** The information from these sensors is processed by the control module and compared to programmed information stored in the control module memory. This processing produces output signals to control the operation of the output devices shown in **Figure 7–73.** The result is much more precise control over shift timing and shift quality than was possible without electronic controls. Upshifts and downshifts

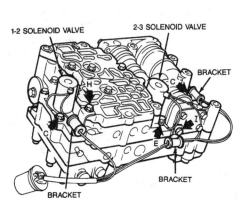

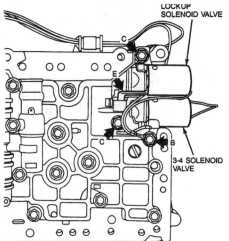

FIGURE 7–77 1–2, 2–3, and 3–4 shift solenoids on valve body. (Courtesy of Ford Motor Company.)

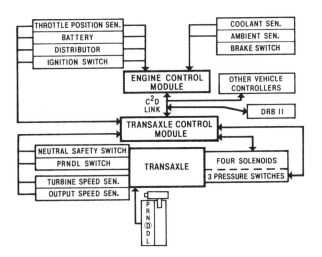

FIGURE 7–78 Chrysler's electronic control system inputs and outputs. Note scan tool (DRB11) connection for system diagnosis. (Courtesy of Chrysler Corporation.)

are smoother and more closely matched to operating conditions. Study **Figures 7–73** to **7–82** to learn how these systems work. The systems shown are examples of current transmissions and transaxles. Systems vary with the make and model of vehicle.

Valve Body

The valve body is usually made of die-cast aluminum and contains the pressure regulator valve, manual valve, shift valves, shift solenoids, and other shift timing and shift quality devices. The valve body is usually bolted to the case in automatic transmissions and is covered by the oil pan. On many transmissions and transaxles, it is part of the pump and valve body assembly. In automatic transaxles, the valve body may be bolted to the bottom, side, or top of the transaxle case. Fluid passages in the case connect the pressure source

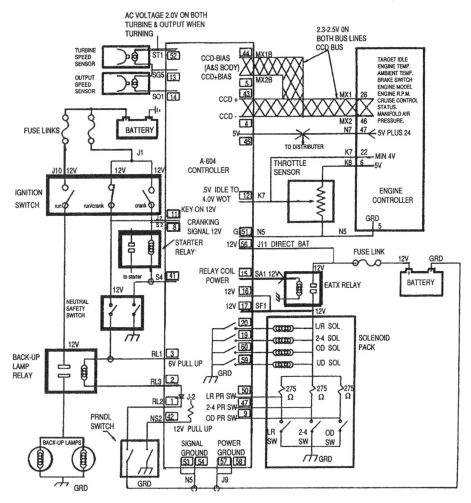

FIGURE 7–79 Chrysler's electronic control system electronic schematic. (Courtesy of Chrysler Corporation.)

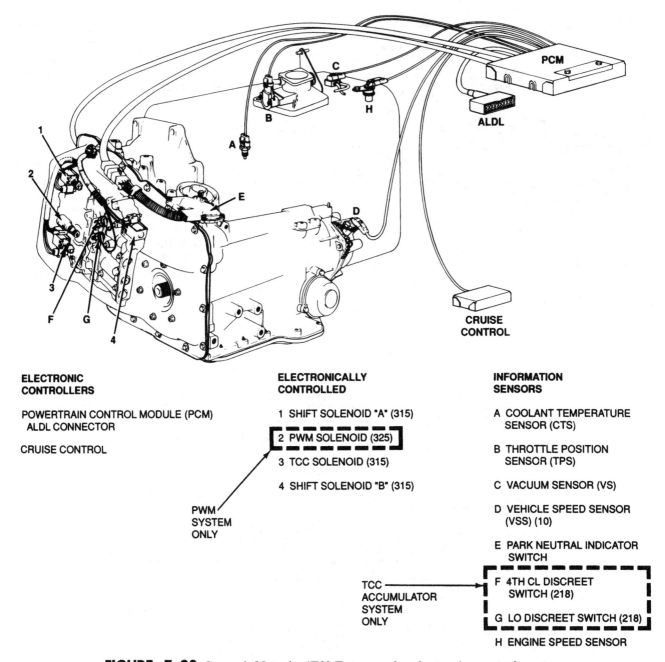

**ELECTRONIC
CONTROLLERS**

POWERTRAIN CONTROL MODULE (PCM)
  ALDL CONNECTOR

CRUISE CONTROL

**ELECTRONICALLY
CONTROLLED**

1 SHIFT SOLENOID "A" (315)

2 PWM SOLENOID (325)

3 TCC SOLENOID (315)

4 SHIFT SOLENOID "B" (315)

PWM
SYSTEM
ONLY

TCC
ACCUMULATOR
SYSTEM
ONLY

**INFORMATION
SENSORS**

A COOLANT TEMPERATURE
   SENSOR (CTS)

B THROTTLE POSITION
   SENSOR (TPS)

C VACUUM SENSOR (VS)

D VEHICLE SPEED SENSOR
   (VSS) (10)

E PARK NEUTRAL INDICATOR
   SWITCH

F 4TH CL DISCREET
   SWITCH (218)

G LO DISCREET SWITCH (218)

H ENGINE SPEED SENSOR

FIGURE 7–80 General Motor's 4T60-E transaxle electronic control system. (Courtesy of General Motors Corporation.)

to the different valves in the valve body and to passages in the transmission/transaxle case that lead to the transmission/transaxle hydraulic units. Valve bodies may be one-, two-, or three-piece construction. A steel transfer plate and gasket are sometimes used between valve body sections to control fluid flow and prevent leakage between sections (**Figures 7–83** and **7–84**).

SEALS AND GASKETS

Static Seals and Gaskets

Gaskets are perhaps the most common type of static seal. The automatic transmission and transaxles use gaskets in such places as between the hydraulic pump

HYDRA-MATIC 4T60-E RANGE REFERENCE CHART

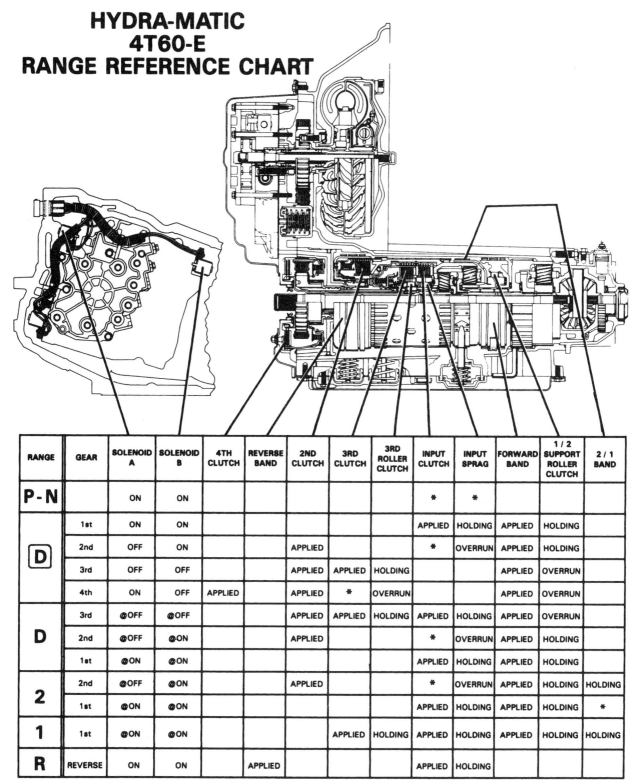

RANGE	GEAR	SOLENOID A	SOLENOID B	4TH CLUTCH	REVERSE BAND	2ND CLUTCH	3RD CLUTCH	3RD ROLLER CLUTCH	INPUT CLUTCH	INPUT SPRAG	FORWARD BAND	1/2 SUPPORT ROLLER CLUTCH	2/1 BAND
P-N		ON	ON						*	*			
D	1st	ON	ON						APPLIED	HOLDING	APPLIED	HOLDING	
	2nd	OFF	ON			APPLIED			*	OVERRUN	APPLIED	HOLDING	
	3rd	OFF	OFF			APPLIED	APPLIED	HOLDING			APPLIED	OVERRUN	
	4th	ON	OFF	APPLIED		APPLIED	*	OVERRUN			APPLIED	OVERRUN	
D	3rd	@OFF	@OFF			APPLIED	APPLIED	HOLDING	APPLIED	HOLDING	APPLIED	OVERRUN	
	2nd	@OFF	@ON			APPLIED			*	OVERRUN	APPLIED	HOLDING	
	1st	@ON	@ON						APPLIED	HOLDING	APPLIED	HOLDING	
2	2nd	@OFF	@ON			APPLIED			*	OVERRUN	APPLIED	HOLDING	HOLDING
	1st	@ON	@ON						APPLIED	HOLDING	APPLIED	HOLDING	*
1	1st	@ON	@ON				APPLIED	HOLDING	APPLIED	HOLDING	APPLIED	HOLDING	HOLDING
R	REVERSE	ON	ON		APPLIED				APPLIED	HOLDING			

*APPLIED BUT NOT EFFECTIVE

@ THE SOLENOID'S STATE FOLLOWS A SHIFT PATTERN WHICH DEPENDS UPON VEHICLE SPEED AND THROTTLE POSITION. IT DOES NOT DEPEND UPON THE SELECTED GEAR.

ON = SOLENOID ENERGIZED

OFF = SOLENOID DE-ENERGIZED

FIGURE 7–81 Clutch band and solenoid application chart for General Motors 4T60-E transaxle. (Courtesy of General Motors Corporation.)

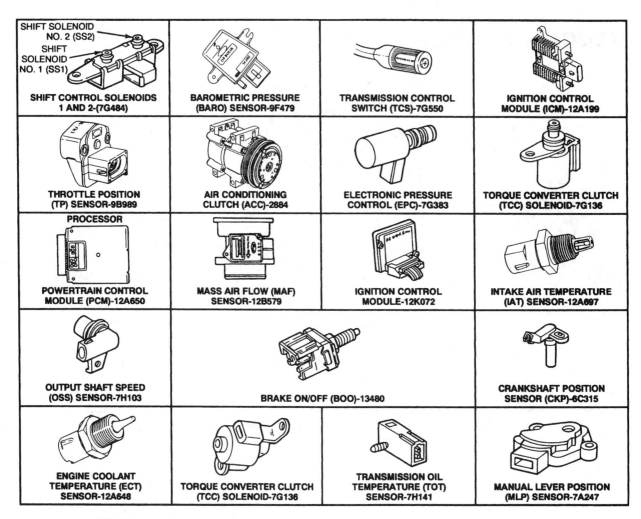

FIGURE 7–82 Information from input sensors like these are fed to the power-train control module to control transmission/transaxle operation. (Courtesy of Ford Motor Company.)

and the case, between the oil pan and the case, between the extension housing and the case, and between some parts of the valve body. Gasket materials include cork and paper compounds. A gasket can do its job properly only if the right gasket is used, if it is installed as recommended, and if proper tightening (tightening sequence and correct torque) of fasteners is done.

Other static seals include O-rings and lathe-cut rectangular or square cross-sectional seal rings **(Figures 7–85 to 7–88)**. These are usually made from synthetic rubber materials. Typical O-ring use is between the selector shaft and transmission case. Lathe-cut seals are often used between the hydraulic pump and the transmission case.

Dynamic Seals

Dynamic seals are used between a moving and a stationary part or between two moving parts. Dynamic seal designs include the O-ring type, the lathe-cut type, and the lip type of synthetic rubber construction. Other types include Teflon, nylon, and cast-iron, square or rectangular cross-section circular seal rings. The latter rings may be of the butt-end design, the tapered-end, or the locking type **(Figures 7–85 to 7–88)**. Lip-type and lathe-cut seals are used between clutch pistons and clutch cylinders as well as servo pistons and piston bores. Lip-type seals are always installed with the edge of the lip facing the fluid or pressure to be confined. Hy-

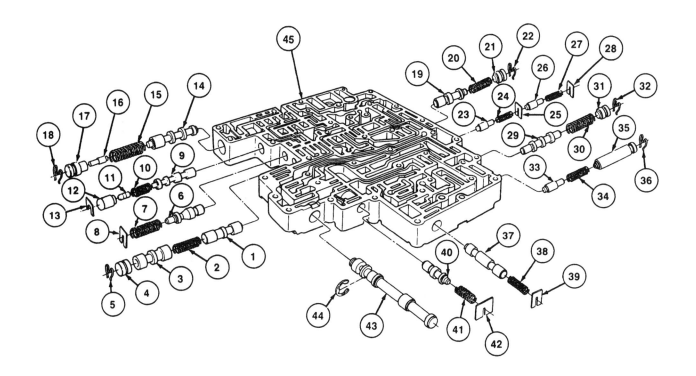

Item	Part Number	Description
1	—	1-2 Shift Valve (Part of 7A100)
2	—	2-3 Shift Valve Spring (Part of 7A100)
3	—	2-3 Shift Valve (Part of 7A100)
4	—	Valve Retaining Plug (Part of 7A100)
5	—	Valve Plug Retainer (Part of 7A100)
6	—	Pressure Regulator Valve (Part of 7A100)
7	—	Pressure Regulator Valve Spring (Part of 7A100)
8	—	Spring Retaining Plate (Part of 7A100)
9	—	Bypass Clutch Control Valve (Part of 7A100)
10	—	Bypass Clutch Control Valve Spring (Part of 7A100)
11	—	Bypass Clutch Control Valve Plunger (Part of 7A100)
12	—	Bypass Clutch Control Plunger Sleeve (Part of 7A100)
13	—	Control Valve Plate (Part of 7A100)
14	—	Main Regulator Valve (Part of 7A100)

Item	Part Number	Description
15	—	Main Oil Pressure Regulator Valve Spring (Part of 7A100)
16	—	Main Oil Pressure Booster Valve (Part of 7A100)
17	—	Main Oil Pressure Booster Valve Sleeve (Part of 7A100)
18	—	Valve Plug Retainer (Part of 7A100)
19	—	Pressure Regulator Valve (Part of 7A100)
20	—	Pressure Regulator Valve Spring (Part of 7A100)
21	—	Valve Retainer Plug (Part of 7A100)
22	—	Valve Plug Retainer (Part of 7A100)
23	—	Capacity Modulator Valve (Part of 7A100)
24	—	Capacity Modulator Valve Spring (Part of 7A100)
25	—	Spring Retaining Plate (Part of 7A100)
26	—	Capacity Modulator Valve (Part of 7A100)
27	—	Capacity Modulator Valve Spring (Part of 7A100)
28	—	Spring Retaining Plate (Part of 7A100)
29	—	3-4 Shift Valve (Part of 7A100)

FIGURE 7–83 Main control valve body for Ford 4R70W (AODE-W) transmission. (Courtesy of Ford Motor Company.)

Item	Part Number	Description
30	—	3-4 Shift Valve Spring (Part of 7A100)
31	—	Valve Retainer Plug (Part of 7A100)
32	—	Valve Plug Retainer (Part of 7A100)
33	—	Capacity Modulator Valve (Part of 7A100)
34	—	Capacity Modulator Valve Spring (Part of 7A100)
35	—	Valve Retainer Plug (Part of 7A100)
36	—	Valve Plug Retainer (Part of 7A100)
37	—	2-3 Backout Valve (Part of 7A100)

Item	Part Number	Description
38	—	2-3 Backout Valve Spring (Part of 7A100)
39	—	Spring Retaining Plate (Part of 7A100)
40	—	Pressure Regulator Valve (Part of 7A100)
41	—	Pressure Regulator Valve Spring (Part of 7A100)
42	—	Spring Retaining Plate (Part of 7A100)
43	—	Control Manual Valve (Part of 7A100)
44	—	Retaining Ring (Part of 7A100)
45	7A100	Main Control Valve Body Assembly

FIGURE 7–83 *(Continued)*

draulic pressure pushes the lip against the bore surface to increase the sealing ability of the seal. Cast-iron seal rings may be used on accumulator pistons and on transmission shafts. Seal rings of synthetic materials such as Teflon are used in these areas in some transmissions and transaxles.

These seal rings are positioned in grooves on the parts to be sealed and must be of the exact cross-sectional size as well as the proper diameter to function effectively. The use of an incorrect seal ring or its improper installation may result in early transmission failure or an inoperative transmission or transaxle after overhaul.

Flow Control Rings (Oil Transfer Rings)

Flow control rings are dynamic seal rings. However, they are part of a hydraulic passage. These rings allow hydraulic flow and pressure to be transferred uninterrupted from a stationary part to a moving or rotating part and from a rotating part such as a shaft to a stationary part. They fit into grooves in either the stationary part or the moving part. One example of the use of flow control rings is in directing hydraulic pressure from the pump housing to the forward clutch. Seal rings in the grooves of the stationary pump housing are inserted against the inner circumference of the rotating clutch drum. Fluid from a passage in the pump housing is directed between the two seal rings to a passage in the clutch drum leading to the area between the clutch piston and clutch drum (**Figures 7–89** and **7–90**).

AUTOMATIC TRANSMISSION AND TRANSAXLE FLUIDS

Automatic transmission clutches and bands are designed to provide the correct coefficient of friction for good shifting and long service life only if the correct transmission fluid is used. The slip-lockup characteristics of different transmission fluids are not the same. If the incorrect fluid is used, the transmission will not shift properly, and its service life will be reduced. Transmission fluids can become extremely hot if the transmission is abused (excessive rocking when stuck). Overheating of transmission fluid causes rapid oxidation of the fluid and shortens life expectancy drastically. Towing heavy trailers with cars not properly equipped with a trailer towing package (which includes a proper auxiliary transmission cooler) can cause serious damage and early failure of the transmission. Many automatic transmissions and transaxles have a fluid cooling system. Fluid is pumped from the transmission/transaxle to a cooling tank inside the radiator (**Figures 7–91** to **7–93**). The engine coolant absorbs heat from the hot transmission fluid, keeping it at proper operating temperature. Cars equipped to pull trailers usually have an auxiliary fluid cooler. It is a small radiator mounted in front of the engine radiator. Fluid pumped through the auxiliary cooler is cooled by airflow over the fins and tubes of the cooler (**Figure 7–94**). Although some original factory-fill transmission fluids may not be dyed red, most replacement fluids are red. The red dye aids in distinguishing oil leaks from the transmission from engine oil leaks.

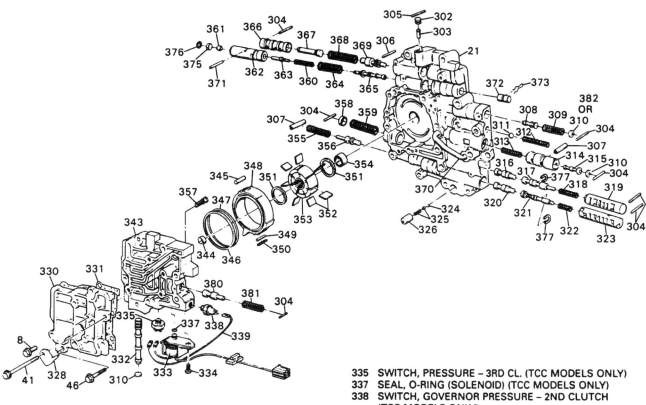

8	SCREW, AUXILIARY VALVE BODY COVER/AUXILIARY VALVE BODY - M6 X 1 X 25
41	SCREW, AUXILIARY VALVE BODY TO CASE COVER - M6 X 1 X 90
46	SCREW, AUX. VALVE BODY COVER/VALVE BODY - M6 X 1 X 45
21	CONTROL VALVE AND FLUID PUMP ASSEMBLY
302	PLUG, BORE LINE BOOST VALVE
303	VALVE, LINE BOOST
304	PIN, VALVE AND SPRING RETAINING
305	PIN, COILED SPRING LINE BOOST PLUG
306	PIN, THROTTLE VALVE BUSHING
307	SLEEVE, SPRING RETAINING
308	VALVE, SHIFT TV
309	SPRING, SHIFT TV
310	PLUG, VALVE BORE
311	BALL, PRESSURE RELIEF (.375mm DIA.)
312	SPRING, PRESSURE RELIEF
313	SPRING, 1-2 ACCUMULATOR
314	BUSHING, 1-2 ACCUMULATOR
315	VALVE, 1-2 ACCUMULATOR
316	VALVE, 2-3 SHIFT
317	VALVE, 2-3 THROTTLE
318	SPRING, 2-3 THROTTLE VALVE
319	BUSHING, 2-3 THROTTLE VALVE
320	VALVE, 1-2 SHIFT
321	VALVE, 1-2 THROTTLE
322	SPRING, 1-2 THROTTLE VALVE
323	BUSHING, 1-2 THROTTLE VALVE
324	BALL, LO BLOW OFF (.3125mm DIA.)
325	SPRING AND PLUG ASSEMBLY, LO BLOW OFF
326	PLUG, LO BLOW OFF VALVE
328	RETAINER, VALVE BODY PIPE
330	COVER, AUXILIARY VALVE BODY
331	GASKET, AUXILIARY VALVE BODY COVER
332	VALVE, CONV. CL. CONTROL (TCC MODELS ONLY)
333	SOLENOID ASSEMBLY (TCC MODELS ONLY)
334	SCREW, SOLENOID (TCC MODELS ONLY)

335	SWITCH, PRESSURE – 3RD CL. (TCC MODELS ONLY)
337	SEAL, O-RING (SOLENOID) (TCC MODELS ONLY)
338	SWITCH, GOVERNOR PRESSURE – 2ND CLUTCH (TCC MODELS ONLY)
339	HARNESS, SOLENOID WIRE
343	BODY, AUXILIARY VALVE
344	SLEEVE, AUXILIARY VALVE BODY
345	PIN, SLIDE PIVOT
346	RING, FLUID SEAL (SLIDE TO COVER)
347	SEAL, O-RING (PUMP SLIDE)
348	SLIDE, PUMP
349	SUPPORT, PUMP SLIDE SEAL
350	SEAL, PUMP SLIDE
351	RING, PUMP VANE
352	VANE, PUMP
353	ROTOR, FLUID PUMP
354	BEARING ASSEMBLY, PUMP SHAFT AND SEAL
355	SPRING, 3-2
356	VALVE, 3-2 REGULATING CONTROL
357	FILTER, AUXILIARY VALVE BODY
358	PLUG, PUMP SPRING RETAINING
359	SPRING, PUMP PRIMING
360	SPRING, TV AND REVERSE BOOST VALVE
361	VALVE, TV BOOST
362	BUSHING, TV AND REVERSE BOOST VALVE
363	VALVE, REVERSE BOOST
364	SPRING, PRESSURE REGULATOR
365	VALVE, PRESSURE REGULATOR
366	BUSHING, TV PLUNGER
367	PLUNGER, THROTTLE VALVE
368	SPRING, THROTTLE VALVE
369	VALVE, THROTTLE
370	PIPE, VALVE BODY
371	PIN, TV AND REVERSE BOOST BUSHING
372	PLUG, BORE (PRESSURE REGULATOR)
373	RETAINER, BORE PLUG PRESSURE REGULATOR
375	PLUG, VALVE BORE ISOLATOR
376	RING, VALVE RETAINING
377	RETAINER, THROTTLE VALVE
380	VALVE, ORIFICE CONTROL (TCC MODELS ONLY)
381	SPRING, ORIFICE CONTROL VALVE (TCC MODELS ONLY)
382	PLUG, VALVE BORE

FIGURE 7–84 Control valve body and oil pump components for 3T40 transaxle. (Courtesy of General Motors Corporation.)

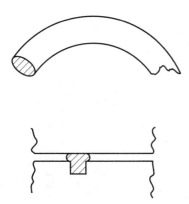

FIGURE 7–85 O-ring seal is squeezed out of shape under pressure of assembly to form positive seal.

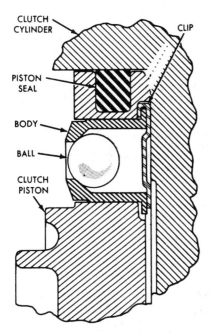

FIGURE 7–86 Example of lathe cut seal use. (Courtesy of General Motors Corporation.)

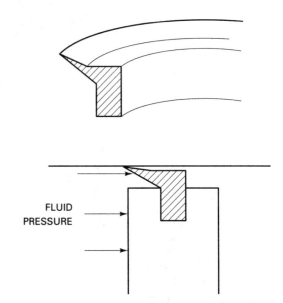

FIGURE 7–87 Lip-type seal fits into groove. Lip must always face fluid pressure when seal is installed.

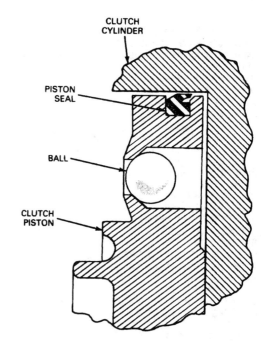

FIGURE 7–88 Example of lip-type seal use. (Courtesy of Ford Motor Company.)

Fluid Types

The development of automatic transmission/transaxle fluids (ATF) has paralleled the development of automatic transmissions and transaxles. The first true ATF was developed by General Motors in 1949 and was designated Type A. An improved version came on the market in 1957 and was called Type A–Suffix A. In 1965 the Ford Motor Company released their Type F fluid for use in their vehicles. General Motors replaced their Type A–Suffix A with Dexron in 1968. Since then, a variety of fluids have been developed, such as Dexron IID and Dexron IIE. Ford introduced their Type H, Type CJ, and Mercon fluids. The Mercon fluid is superior to the earlier Ford fluids and may be used in any of the units except where Type F is recommended. Chrysler-produced vehicles have long used the Type A, Type A–Suffix A, and Dexron fluids. However, in 1968, Chrysler recommended their own Type 7176 for their vehicles and recommends it for use in their older vehicles with lockup torque converters as well.

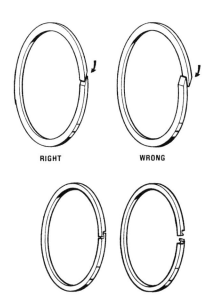

FIGURE 7–89 Teflon (top) and cast-iron (bottom) flow control seal rings. (Courtesy of General Motors Corporation.)

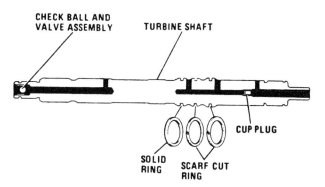

FIGURE 7–90 Typical application of oil transfer rings on turbine shaft. (Courtesy of General Motors Corporation.)

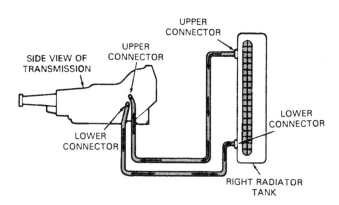

FIGURE 7–91 Transmission fluid cooler in horizontal flow radiator tank. (Courtesy of General Motors Corporation.)

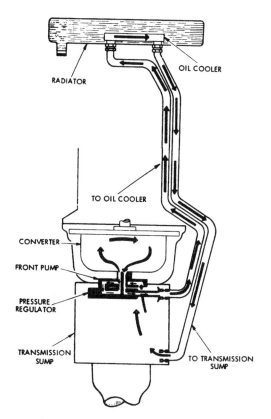

FIGURE 7–92 Fluid cooler mounted in bottom tank of vertical flow radiator. (Courtesy of Ford Motor Company.)

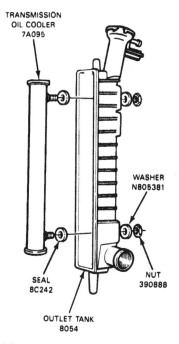

FIGURE 7–93 Transmission/transaxle oil cooler is located in radiator outlet tank. (Courtesy of Ford Motor Company.)

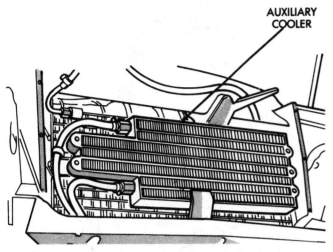

FIGURE 7–94 Auxiliary transmission/transaxle fluid cooler is usually mounted in front, behind the grille. (Courtesy of Chrysler Corporation.)

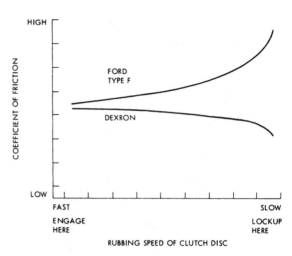

FIGURE 7–95 Difference in coefficient of friction between Type F fluid and Dexron fluid.

Transmission/transaxle fluids have very specific slip-lockup characteristics that differ among fluid types. The frictional characteristics of the fluid and the frictional surfaces of clutches and bands are specifically designed to provide smooth slip-lockup action during application and no-slip holding of applied units **(Figure 7–95)**. If the wrong fluid is used, increased slippage, or grabbing and shudder may occur. Always use the fluid specified by the vehicle manufacturer.

CONTINUOUSLY VARIABLE TRANSMISSION

The continuously variable transmission (CVT) has a nearly unlimited range of drive ratios between the engine and the final drive. It is used in some subcompact import cars. With a CVT, the engine operates at its most efficient, nearly constant speed, with very smooth ratio changes. The CVT has an engine-driven input pulley, a flexible steel drive belt, and an output pulley. The pulley sheaves are widened or narrowed to effect ratio changes. When the input pulley narrows and the output pulley widens, output speed is increased. To reduce speed and increase torque, the input pulley widens, and the output pulley narrows. Widening the pulley reduces its effective diameter, while narrowing the pulley increases its effective diameter. The pulleys are controlled by hydraulic actuators in response to an electronic control system and selector lever position.

REVIEW QUESTIONS

1. What functions are provided by an automatic transaxle that are not provided in an automatic transmission?

2. Vortex flow in a torque converter is fluid flow from the _____ to the _____ to the _____.

3. True or false? There is no vortex flow when the torque converter is in the torque multiplication stage.

4. What is the advantage of a lockup torque converter?

5. Power transmission through planetary gears is possible only when one member is _____ or two members are _____ _____.

6. In a simple planetary gearset when the drive input is through the sun gear and the carrier is stationary, the ring gear turns in _____ direction.

7. Overdrive through a simple planetary gearset occurs when the drive input is through the _____ and the _____ _____ is held.

8. Multiple-disc clutches are used to connect _____ _____ members to the _____ _____ and to _____ planetary gear members to the _____ to prevent them from _____.

9. Clutch pack _____ is critical since alternate clutch discs may turn in _____ _____ at times.

10. Steel and friction clutch discs are stacked in an _____ arrangement in the clutch pack.

11. How can the hydraulic pressure be changed to increase clutch torque capacity?

12. A hydraulic servo is used to tighten a _____ around a steel _____ .

13. Name the two types of one-way clutches used in some automatic transmissions and transaxles.

14. A _____ _____ is mounted in the transmission or transaxle case to prevent the _____ wheels from turning.

15. What three kinds of hydraulic pump are used in automatic transmissions and transaxles?

16. Hydraulic pressure is maintained at the proper level by the _____ _____ valve.

17. When the driver moves the shift lever, it causes the _____ _____ valve in the valve body to move.

18. The transmission or transaxle throttle valve may be operated by the _____ _____ or by a _____ _____ .

19. In a hydraulically controlled automatic transmission, governor pressure is directed to the _____ _____ in opposition to _____ _____ .

20. In electronically controlled automatic transmissions and transaxles, _____ pressure and _____ pressure are not required.

21. In an electronically controlled automatic transaxle, downshifts occur when the _____ _____ move to the _____ position as a result of _____ _____ action.

TEST QUESTIONS

1. Technician A says that automatic transmissions and transaxles are similar in many ways. Technician B says that a major difference is that the transaxle includes a final drive and differential. Who is right?
   a. technician A
   b. technician B
   c. both are right
   d. both are wrong

2. The torque converter turbine drives the
   a. impeller
   b. stator
   c. turbine shaft
   d. one-way clutch

3. A simple planetary gearset consists of
   a. ring gear, annulus gear, and sun gear
   b. sun gear, pinions, and carrier
   c. carrier, ring gear, and annulus gear
   d. ring gear, sun gear, and carrier

4. The transmission/transaxle band is tightened around a drum by a
   a. hydraulic servo
   b. accumulator
   c. shift valve
   d. governor

5. Hydraulic line pressure cannot exceed a specified maximum due to the action of the
   a. shift control valve
   b. governor valve
   c. accumulator
   d. regulator valve

6. Which of the following are holding devices?
   a. multiple-disc clutch
   b. one-way clutch
   c. band
   d. park pawl
   e. any of the above

7. Governor pressure acts on the
   a. accumulator
   b. servo
   c. shift valves
   d. one-way clutch

8. In the hydraulic lockup torque converter, the clutch locks the
   a. turbine to the impeller
   b. impeller to the converter cover
   c. turbine to the stator
   d. turbine to the converter cover

9. In a simple planetary gearset, when the sun gear is the input, and the carrier is held, the result will be
   a. a speed increase and reverse output
   b. a speed decrease and forward output
   c. forward output and direct drive
   d. reverse output and a speed decrease

10. In the Ravigneaux compound planetary gearset, there are
    a. two sets of pinions and two carriers
    b. two sun gears and two sets of pinions
    c. two ring gears and one carrier
    d. two carriers and two sun gears

11. A multiple-disc clutch is used to
    a. drive a planetary gear member
    b. hold a planetary gear member
    c. either (a) or (b)
    d. none of the above

12. When a multiple-disc clutch is applied, hydraulic pressure is forced between the
    a. clutch discs and clutch plates
    b. clutch retainer and clutch piston
    c. pressure plate and clutch discs
    d. clutch retainer and clutch discs

13. In an electronically controlled transmission/transaxle
    a. a hydraulic system is not required
    b. solenoids control the governor and throttle valves
    c. shift valves are controlled by solenoids
    d. all of the above

◆ CHAPTER 8 ◆

AUTOMATIC TRANSMISSION AND TRANSAXLE SERVICE

INTRODUCTION

A thorough understanding of automatic transmission and transaxle construction and operation is needed to be able to diagnose problems, perform tests, and repair faulty components in automatic transmissions and transaxles. The technician must be able to distinguish between engine performance problems that affect the operation of automatic transmissions and transaxles and problems caused by faulty operation of the transmission or transaxle. This chapter discusses the problem diagnosis, testing, and service of automatic transmissions and transaxles.

LEARNING OBJECTIVES

After completing this chapter, you should be able to:

- Describe typical automatic transmission and transaxle problems.
- Perform the preliminary inspection and adjustment procedures.
- Perform required diagnostic test procedures and interpret the test results to identify automatic transmission and transaxle problems.
- Remove, repair, and replace an automatic transmission or transaxle.

TERMS YOU SHOULD KNOW

Look for these terms as you study this chapter and learn what they mean.

harsh engagement	modulator adjustment
delayed engagement	kickdown
harsh shifts	to detent
slippage	through detent
shift points	stall test
no upshift	hydraulic pressure test
fluid level	band adjustment
fluid condition	air pressure test
fluid and filter change	end-play measurements
oil pan deposits	clutch pack clearance
fluid leaks	transaxle drive chain wear
shift linkage adjustment	
throttle linkage adjustment	torque converter service
	cooler flushing

AUTOMATIC TRANSMISSION AND TRANSAXLE PROBLEMS

Automatic transmissions and transaxles may develop problems over an extended period of time and operation. To be able to identify and correct operating problems requires a thorough knowledge of automatic transmission and transaxle construction and operation. Typical problems are described here:

1. *Harsh engagement.* Car jerks when shifted into gear. May be caused by the engine idle speed too high, hydraulic pressures too high, faulty accumulator, valve body leakage.

2. *Delayed engagement.* Car does not respond immediately when shifted into gear. May be caused by incorrect linkage adjustment, low fluid level, low hydraulic pressures, faulty oil pump, valve body leakage, leaking clutch piston seals, faulty accumulator.

3. *Harsh shifts.* Car jerks when it upshifts. May be caused by hydraulic pressure too high, hydraulic pressure too low, worn or faulty clutches, incorrect throttle linkage adjustment.

4. *Slips in forward or reverse drive.* May be caused by low fluid level, low hydraulic pressures, worn hydraulic pump, worn clutch discs, leaking clutch piston seals, valve body leakage.

5. *Incorrect shift points or no upshifts.* May be caused by low fluid level, a faulty vacuum modulator, low hydraulic pressure, faulty governor, problems in the valve body.

6. *Transmission or transaxle noise.* Buzzing, whining, or grinding sounds. May be caused by incorrect fluid level, faulty torque converter, worn bearings, worn planetary gears, worn final drive gears, worn differential gears, worn hydraulic pump.

7. *No converter lockup.* May be caused by incorrect fluid level, aerated fluid, faulty hydraulic pump, incorrect hydraulic pressures, faulty coolant temperature sensor, valve body leakage, faulty electronic control.

PROBLEM DIAGNOSIS STEPS

Transmission/transaxle problems may be caused by malfunctions in the electronic control system, the hydraulic system, or the mechanical components of the unit. What appear to be transmission/transaxle problems may, in fact, be the consequences of poor engine performance. The technician must be able to distinguish among these and identify the problem area and correct the malfunction.

The usual steps in the diagnostic procedure are:

1. Check the fluid level and condition.

2. Check the vacuum line and vacuum modulator for leaks if so equipped.

3. Check the shift linkage adjustment.

4. Check the throttle and downshift linkage adjustment.

5. Check the engine idle speed.

6. Perform self-diagnostic procedures and pinpoint electrical tests.

7. Perform a road test.

8. Perform a stall test (only if recommended by the vehicle manufacturer).

9. Perform hydraulic pressure tests.

The correct interpretation of each of these tests is critical in deciding what is normal about the transmission or transaxle and what is not. Proper test interpretation determines what to do next, whether to proceed to the next step, or whether to make some adjustments or corrections first. The following procedures are typical of transmission/transaxle diagnosis. The diagnostic charts shown in **Figures 8–1** to **8–8** are only a few examples of diagnostic steps as they appear in service manuals. For procedures that apply to any specific transmission or transaxle, refer to the appropriate service manual.

PRELIMINARY INSPECTION AND ADJUSTMENTS

Before taking the car on a road test and before performing a stall test or pressure tests, make sure that the engine is operating properly. Check the transmission/transaxle fluid level and condition, check for fluid leaks, and check the shift linkage adjustment, throttle linkage adjustment, vacuum modulator system, exhaust gas recirculation (EGR) valve operation, and engine idle speed.

Fluid Level

The following conditions should apply when checking the fluid level:

1. Fluid is at operating temperature, at least 185°F (85°C).

2. Vehicle is in a level position.

3. Parking brake is fully applied.

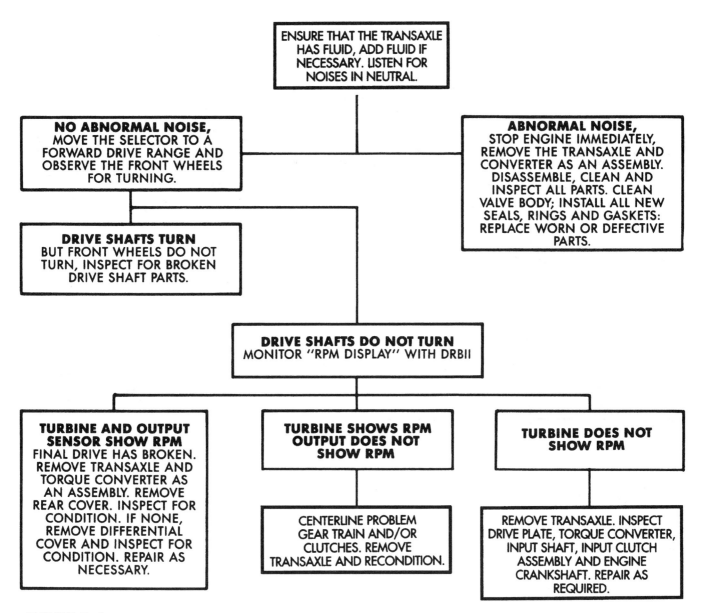

FIGURE 8–1 Transaxle diagnosis when vehicle will not move. (Courtesy of Chrysler Corporation.)

4. With the engine running at idle, move the selector lever through all gear positions.

5. Leave the engine running at idle (most vehicles) and place the selector lever in the position specified by the vehicle manufacturer (usually, Park or Neutral). Many vehicles show a different fluid level in Park from that in Neutral; therefore, it is important to place the selector lever in the specified position. On some vehicles the fluid level is checked with the engine off.

6. Use a clean, lint-free, preferably white cloth. Pull the dipstick and wipe the blade clean. Insert the dipstick, making sure that it is fully seated. Remove the dipstick and check the fluid level and condition (color, smell, contamination; Figure 8–9). The car should not be road tested while the fluid level is too low or too high since further damage is possible. Fluid level must be corrected first.

A fluid level that is too low can result in air in hydraulic system, which in turn can cause insufficient apply pressure to friction elements. Clutch and band slippage can cause overheating and serious transmission damage. Varnish forms on internal transmission parts; it can cause valve malfunctions. Delayed engagement and mushy shifts can also be caused by low fluid levels.

The cause of the low fluid level should be determined and the problem corrected. A fluid level that is too high can cause similar damage. The fluid is churned up by the rotating gear train, causing fluid aeration and

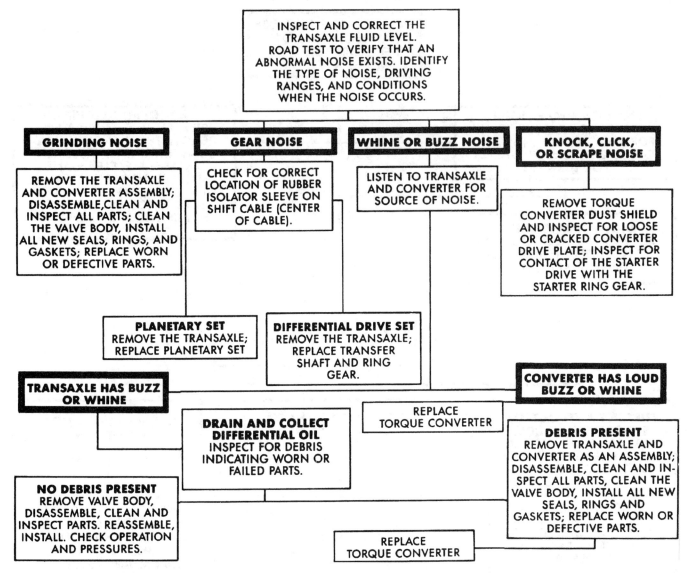

FIGURE 8–2 Abnormal noise diagnosis for 42LE Chrysler transaxle. (Courtesy of Chrysler Corporation.)

foam. Foaming allows air to get into the hydraulic system. This causes clutch and band slippage, wear, overheating, and varnish deposits. Foaming can also result in fluid being forced out of the transmission vent or filler tube, which may be mistaken for a fluid leak.

Fluid Condition

Fluid colors range from an almost clear fluid to a deep red. Some fluids tend to discolor and darken somewhat with age and use. This should be taken into account when checking fluid condition. The oil pan should be removed for further diagnosis of fluid and

deposits if the following conditions are present in the fluid:

- Very dark colored fluid, which has a pungent, burned smell. Fluid temperatures can reach 350°F (177°C) under extreme conditions.

- Presence of metallic particles and particles of friction material from bands or clutches.

- Milky colored fluid, which indicates a coolant leak into the transmission fluid via the fluid cooler in the radiator. The system must be flushed in this case.

- Varnish deposits on the dipstick and fluid that is dark brown in color as a result of overheating.

Possible Cause

NOTE:
Code 36 is not stored alone. It is stored if a speed error (codes 50 through 58) is detected immediately after a shift. Look at the possible causes associated with the speed error code.

Fault Code Number	Condition	Planetary gear sets broken or seized	Faulty cooling system	Torque converter clutch failure	Internal solenoid leak	Pressures too high	Valve body leakage	Regulator valve	Torque converter control valve	Torque converter clutch switch valve	Solenoid switch valve	Stuck/sticky valves	Plugged filter	Worn or damaged accumulator seal rings	Damaged clutch seals	L/R clutch	2/4 clutch	Reverse clutch	OD clutch	UD clutch	Damaged or failed clutches:	Worn pump	Worn or damaged input shaft seal rings	Worn or damaged reaction shaft support seal rings	Aeroled fluid (high fluid level)	Low fluid level
21	OD clutch—pressure too low		×	×	×	×	×	×				×	×	×	×				×			×		×	×	×
22	2/4 clutch—pressure too low		×	×	×	×	×	×				×	×	×	×		×					×			×	×
23	2/4 clutch and OD clutch—pressures too low		×	×	×	×	×	×				×	×	×	×							×			×	×
24	L/R clutch—pressure too low		×	×	×	×	×	×				×	×	×	×	×						×			×	×
25	L/R clutch and OD clutches—pressures too low		×	×	×	×	×	×				×	×	×	×							×			×	×
26	L/R clutch and 2/4 clutches—pressures too low		×	×	×	×	×	×				×	×	×	×							×			×	×
27	OD, 2/4, and L/R clutches—pressures too low		×	×	×	×	×	×				×	×	×	×							×			×	×
31	OD clutch pressure switch response failure			×	×		×												×			×			×	×
32	2/4 pressure switch response failure				×		×										×					×			×	×
33	2/4 and O/D clutch pressure response failures				×		×					×										×			×	×
37	Solenoid switch valve stuck in the LO position				×		×			×	×															
38	Partial torque converter clutch out of range			×	×	×	×		×	×		×										×	×			
47	Solenoid switch valve stuck in the LR position				×		×			×	×															
50	Speed ratio default in reverse	×	×		×	×	×	×				×	×	×	×	×		×				×	×	×		×
51	Speed ratio default in 1st	×	×		×	×	×	×				×	×	×	×	×				×		×	×	×		×
52	Speed ratio default in 2nd	×	×		×	×	×	×				×		×	×		×			×		×	×	×		×
53	Speed ratio default in 3rd	×	×		×	×	×	×				×			×		×		×	×		×	×	×		×
54	Speed ratio default in 4th	×	×		×	×	×	×				×			×		×		×			×	×	×		×
60	Inadequate LR element volume	×					×					×		×	×											
61	Inadequate 2/4 element volume	×					×					×		×			×									
62	Inadequate OD element volume	×					×					×		×					×							

FIGURE 8–3 Diagnostic trouble code chart for 42LE Chrysler transaxle. (Courtesy of Chrysler Corporation.)

POSSIBLE CAUSE

POSSIBLE CAUSE \ CONDITION	HARSH ENGAGEMENT FROM NEUTRAL TO D	HARSH ENGAGEMENT FROM NEUTRAL TO R	DELAYED ENGAGEMENT FROM NEUTRAL TO D	DELAYED ENGAGEMENT FROM NEUTRAL TO R	POOR SHIFT QUALITY	SHIFTS ERRATIC	DRIVES IN NEUTRAL	DRAGS OR LOCKS	GRATING, SCRAPING, GROWLING NOISE	ENGINE MISFIRE	BUZZING NOISE	BUZZING NOISE DURING SHIFTS ONLY	HARD TO FILL OIL BLOWS OUT FILLER TUBE	TRANSAXLE OVERHEATS	HARSH UPSHIFT	NO UPSHIFT INTO OVERDRIVE	NO TORQUE CONVERTER CLUTCH	HARSH DOWNSHIFTS	HIGH SHIFT EFFORTS	HARSH CONVERTER CLUTCH
Engine Performance	X	X			X										X			X		
Worn or faulty clutch(es)	X	X	X	X	X	X	X								X	X		X		
— Underdrive clutch	X		X		X	X	X											X		
— Overdrive clutch					X	X	X								X	X				
— Reverse clutch		X		X	X	X														
— 2/4 clutch					X		X								X			X		
— Low/reverse clutch	X	X			X		X											X		
Clutch(es) dragging							X													
Insufficient clutch plate clearance							X							X						
Damaged clutch seals			X	X														X		
Worn or damaged accumulator seal ring(s)	X	X	X	X														X		
Faulty cooling system														X						
Engine coolant temp. too low																X	X			
Incorrect gearshift control linkage adjustment			X	X		X	X							X						
Shift linkage damaged																			X	
Chipped or damaged gear teeth								X	X											
Planetary gear sets broken or seized								X	X											
Bearings worn or damaged								X	X											
Driveshaft(s) bushing(s) worn or damaged									X											
Worn or broken reaction shaft support seal rings			X	X	X	X												X		
Worn or damaged input shaft seal rings			X	X												X				
Valve body malfunction or leakage	X	X	X	X	X	X	X				X							X	X	X
Hydraulic pressures too low			X	X	X	X								X	X	X				
Hydraulic pressures too high	X	X													X			X		
Faulty oil pump			X	X		X								X		X				
Oil filter clogged			X	X	X	X						X								
Low fluid level			X	X	X	X					X			X		X	X			
High fluid level													X	X						
Aerated fluid			X	X	X	X					X		X	X		X	X			
Engine idle speed too low			X	X																
Engine idle speed too high	X	X												X				X		
Normal solenoid operation												X								
Solenoid sound cover loose												X								
Sticking torque converter clutch position																				X
Torque Converter Failure	X													X		X				X
Drive Plate cracked or bent									X	X										

FIGURE 8–4 Four-speed OD transmission diagnosis. (Courtesy of Chrysler Corporation.)

POSSIBLE CAUSE

	CONVERTER CLUTCH WILL NOT ENGAGE	CLUTCH WILL NOT DISENGAGE	STAYS ENGAGED AT TOO LOW A SPEED IN 4th GEAR	LOCKS UP OR DRAGS IN LOW OR SECOND	STALLS OR IS SLUGGISH IN REVERSE	CHATTER DURING CLUTCH ENGAGEMENT–(COLD)	VIBRATION OR SHUDDER DURING CLUTCH ENGAGEMENT	VIBRATION AFTER CLUTCH ENGAGEMENT	VIBRATION WHEN "REVVED" IN NEUTRAL	OVERHEATING: OIL COMING OUT OF FILL TUBE OR PUMP SEAL	SHUDDER AFTER CLUTCH ENGAGEMENT
FAULTY OIL PUMP	X			X	X		X				X
STICKING GOVERNOR VALVE	X	X	X								
PLUGGED COOLER, LINES OR FITTINGS					X					X	X
VALVE BODY MALFUNCTION	X	X	X	X	X		X				X
STUCK SWITCH VALVE	X	X	X	X	X					X	
STUCK CONVERTER CLUTCH VALVE	X	X	X								
STUCK CONVERTER CLUTCH SOLENOID	X	X									
SOLENOID WIRING DISCONNECTED	X										
FAILED CONVERTER CLUTCH SOLENOID	X										
FAILED CONVERTER CLUTCH RELAY	X	X									
FAULTY TORQUE CONVERTER:	X					X	X	X			X
OUT OF BALANCE									X		
FAILED CONVERTER CLUTCH	X					X					X
LEAKING TURBINE HUB SEAL	X					X					
ALIGN EXHAUST SYSTEM								X			X
TUNE ENGINE							X	X			X
FAULTY INPUT SHAFT OR SEAL RING	X				X						
THROTTLE CABLE MISADJUSTED								X			X

FIGURE 8–5 Torque converter clutch diagnosis (typical). (Courtesy of Chrysler Corporation.)

Depositing several drops of fluid from the dipstick onto a clean white cloth helps determine fluid condition and the presence of metal or friction particles. The fluid should feel smooth and slippery when rubbed between the finger and thumb. If there is a gritty feel to the fluid, further diagnosis is required. Make sure that hands are clean for this test. If further verification of fluid and transmission/transaxle condition is required, the oil pan should be removed and the fluid and deposits examined. Air pressure checks can be used to check clutch and band operation.

Oil Pan Deposits

Remember that the oil pan and the fluid in it may be hot enough to cause severe burns. To remove the pan, use a large drain pan to catch the fluid during pan removal. First, loosen all the oil pan bolts a turn or two. Remove all the bolts from the three sides of the pan, which will allow the pan to drop slightly to drain the fluid. Loosen the remaining bolts an additional few turns to allow the other side of the pan to drop some more. When all the fluid has drained, remove the remaining bolts and the pan.

Before Pinpoint Tests

NOTE: Prior to entering Pinpoint Tests, check the powertrain control module wiring harness for proper connections, bent or broken pins, corrosion, loose wires, proper routing, proper seals and their condition. Check the powertrain control module, sensors and actuators for damage. Refer to the Powertrain Control/Emissions Diagnosis Manual.[6]

On-Board Diagnostic Trouble Code Description Chart

If DTCs appear while performing the On-Board Diagnostics refer to the On-Board Diagnostic Trouble Code Description Chart for the appropriate service procedure. Prior to entering Pinpoint Tests, refer to any TSBs and Oasis messages for E4OD transmission concerns.

NOTE: After Electrical Diagnosis has been performed and a concern still exists, refer to the Diagnosis by Symptom charts in this section.

Diagnostic Trouble Code		Component	Description	Condition	Symptoms/Actions
Two Digit	Three Digit				
11	111	System	Pass	No concern detected.	Concern not detected by powertrain control module[ab]
14	211	RPM sensor/crankshaft position sensor	RPM sensor/crankshaft position sensor concern.	Engine RPM sensor circuit failure. With RPM sensor failure may not run On-Board Diagnostics KOER.	Harsh engagements and shifts, late wide open throttle upshifts, abnormal torque converter clutch operation or does not engage. Crankshaft position sensor failure/engine will stall or not run.) May flash transmission control indicator lamp.[b]
22	126	Manifold absolute pressure sensor or barometric pressure sensor	Manifold absolute pressure sensor or barometric pressure sensor out of On-Board Diagnostics range.	Manifold absolute pressure sensor or barometric pressure sensor signal higher or lower than expected or no response during Dynamic Response (Goose) Test.	Rerun On-Board Diagnostics.
—	128	Manifold absolute pressure sensor	Manifold absolute pressure sensor vacuum circuit failure.	Manifold absolute pressure sensor or barometric pressure sensor signal higher or lower than expected or no response during Dynamic Response (Goose) Test.	Firm shift fell, late shifts at altitude.[b]
23	121	Throttle Position Sensor	Throttle position sensor out of On-Board Diagnostics range.	Throttle position sensor (gasoline engines) not at idle position during KOEO. Throttle position sensor (diesel engines) not at wide open throttle position during KOEO.	Rerun at appropriate throttle position sensor position per the engine application. May flash transmission control indicator lamp.
26	636	Transmission Oil Temperature Sensor	Transmission oil temperature sensor out of On-Board Diagnostics range.	Transmission not at operating temperature during On-Board Diagnostics.	Warm vehicle to normal operating temperature and rerun On-Board Diagnostics.
29	452	Vehicle Speed Sensor	Insufficient vehicle speed input.	Powertrain control module detected a loss of vehicle speed signal during operation.	Harsh engagements, firm shift feel, abnormal shift schedule, unexpected downshifts may occur at closed throttle, abnormal torque converter clutch operation or engages only at Wide Open Throttle. May flash transmission control indicator lamp.[a]

(a)

FIGURE 8–6 Diagnostic trouble code chart for Ford E40D transmission. (Courtesy of Ford Motor Company.)

Diagnostic Trouble Code		Component	Description	Condition	Symptoms/Actions
Two Digit	Three Digit				
33	—	Throttle Position Sensor	Sensor signal input noisy.	Noisy signal indicated at powertrain control module.	Harsh engagements, firm shift feel, abnormal shift schedule, abnormal torque converter clutch operation or does not engage. May flash transmission control indicator lamp.
43	—	Throttle Position Sensor	Sensor signal indicates below idle voltage.	Indicated voltage signal below idle specifications.	Harsh engagements, firm shift feel, abnormal shift schedule, abnormal torque converter clutch operation or does not engage. May flash transmission control indicator lamp. [a]
47	633	4x4 Low Switch	4x4 Low switch closed.	4x4 Low switch closed/or 4x4 Low indicator lamp circuit open.	Failed on — Early shift schedules in 4x2 and 4x4 HI range. Failed off — Shifts delayed in 4x4 Low. NOTE: If the 4x4 low indicator light fuse is blown, the transmission will shift according to the 4x4 Low shift schedule regardless of the transfer case position. [a][b]
49 [d]	617 [d]	Shift Solenoid 1, Shift Solenoid 2 or Internal Transmission Components	1-2 shift error.	Engine RPM drop not detected when 1-2 shift was commanded by powertrain control module.	Improper gear selection depending on failure mode and transmission range selector lever position. Refer to Shift Application Chart. Shift errors may also be due to other internal transmission concerns such as stuck valves or damaged friction material. May flash transmission control indicator lamp. **Refer to Pinpoint Test A**
53	123	Throttle Position Sensor	Throttle position sensor circuit above maximum voltage, (short to vehicle power).	Voltage above or below specification for On-Board Diagnostics or during normal vehicle operation.	Harsh engagements, firm shift feel, abnormal shift schedule, abnormal torque converter clutch operation or does not engage. May flash transmission control indicator lamp. [b]
56	637	Transmission Oil Temperature Sensor	-40°C (-40°F) indicated, transmission oil temperature sensor circuit open.	Voltage drop across transmission oil temperature sensor exceeds scale set for temperature -40°C (-40°F).	Torque converter clutch and stabilized shift schedule may be enabled sooner after cold start. **Refer to Pinpoint Test B**
59 [d]	618 [d]	Shift Solenoid 1, Shift Solenoid 2 or Internal Transmission Components	2-3 shift error.	Engine RPM drop not detected when 2-3 shift was commanded by powertrain control module.	Improper gear selection depending on failure mode and transmission range selector lever position. Refer to Shift Application Chart. Shift errors may also be due to other internal transmission concerns such as stuck valves or damaged friction material. May flash transmission control indicator lamp. **Refer to Pinpoint Test A**
62 [d]	628 [d]	Transmission	Transmission slippage detection.	Excessive amount of clutch slippage was detected.	Transmission slippage, erratic or no torque converter clutch operation. May flash transmission control indicator lamp. **Refer to Diagnosis by Symptom**
63	122	Throttle Position Sensor	Throttle position sensor circuit below minimum voltage, (open/shorted to ground).	Voltage above or below specification for On-Board Diagnostics or during normal vehicle operation.	Harsh engagements, firm shift feel, abnormal shift schedule, abnormal torque converter clutch operation or does not engage. May flash transmission control indicator lamp. [b]

(b)

FIGURE 8–6 *(Continued)*

Diagnostic Trouble Code		Component	Description	Condition	Symptoms/Actions
Two Digit	Three Digit				
—	124	Throttle Position Sensor	TP sensor voltage higher than expected.	Voltage above specification.	Harsh engagements, firm shift feel, abnormal shift schedule, abnormal torque converter clutch operation or does not engage. May flash transmission control indicator lamp.[a]
—	125	Throttle Position Sensor	TP sensor voltage lower than expected.	Voltage below specification.	Harsh engagements, firm shift feel, abnormal shift schedule, abnormal torque converter clutch operation or does not engage. May flash transmission control indicator lamp.[a]
65	632	Transmission Control Switch	Transmission control switch not changing state.	Transmission control switch not cycled during On-Board Diagnostics/circuit open or shorted.	Rerun diagnostics and cycle switch. No overdrive cancel when switch is cycled.[a]
66	638	Transmission Oil Temperature Sensor	157°C (315°F) indicated, transmission oil temperature sensor circuit grounded.	Voltage drop across transmission oil temperature sensor exceeds scale set for temperature of 157°C (315°F).	Torque converter clutch and stabilized shift schedule may be enabled sooner after cold start. **Refer to Pinpoint Test B**
67	539	Air Conditioning Clutch	A/C switch error.	Diagnostic Trouble Code may result from A/C clutch being "ON" during On-Board Diagnostics.	Failed on — electronic pressure control pressure slightly low with A/C off. Failed off — electronic pressure control pressure slightly low with A/C on.[a]
67	654	Manual Lever Position Sensor	Manual lever position sensor not in park.	On-Board Diagnostics not run in park.	Rerun On-Board Diagnostics in park.
67	634	Manual Lever Position Sensor	Manual lever position sensor out of range.	Indicated voltage drop across manual lever position sensor exceeds limits established for each position.	Harsh engagements, firm shift feel. **Refer to Pinpoint Test D**
68	657	Transmission Oil Temperature Sensor	Transmission Overtemp Condition.	Transmission oil temperature exceeded 270°F.	Slight increase in electronic pressure control pressure. May flash transmission control indicator lamp. **Refer to Pinpoint Test B**
—	659	Manual Lever Position Sensor	Manual lever position sensor indicating park during operation.	Manual lever position sensor indicating park during operation.	Electronic pressure control pressure high, all shifts firm **Refer to Pinpoint Test D.**
—	667	Manual Lever Position Sensor	Manual lever position sensor circuit below minimum voltage.	Manual lever position sensor circuit or powertrain control module shorted or grounded.	Increase in electronic pressure control pressure **Refer to Pinpoint Test D.**
—	668	Manual Lever Position Sensor	Manual lever position sensor circuit above maximum voltage.	Manual lever position sensor, circuit or powertrain control module indicates open.	Increase in electronic pressure control pressure **Refer to Pinpoint Test D.**
—	691	4x4L	4x4 low switch failure.	4x4 low switch failure during normal vehicle operation.	Early shifts, harsh shifts, increase in electronic pressure control pressure. **Refer to Powertrain Control/Emissions Diagnosis Manual**

(c)

FIGURE 8–6 *(Continued)*

Diagnostic Trouble Code		Component	Description	Condition	Symptoms/Actions
Two Digit	Three Digit				
—	157, 158, 159, 184, 185	Mass Air Flow Sensor	Mass air flow sensor diagnostic trouble codes	Mass air flow sensor system has a malfunction which may cause a transmission concern.	High[a] electronic pressure control pressure. Firm shifts and engagements. May flash transmission control indicator lamp. **Refer to Powertrain Control/Emissions Diagnosis manual.**[a]
69[d]	619[d]	Shift Solenoid 1, Shift Solenoid 2 or Internal Transmission Components	3-4 shift error.	Engine RPM drop not detected when 3-4 shift was commanded by powertrain control module.	Improper gear selection depending on failure mode and transmission range selector lever position. Refer to Shift Application Chart. Shift errors may also be due to other internal transmission concerns such as stuck valves or damaged friction material. May flash transmission control indicator lamp. **Refer to Pinpoint Test A**
72	129	Manifold absolute pressure sensor	Insufficient manifold absolute pressure sensor change dynamic response test (gasoline engines only).	Manifold absolute pressure sensor or barometric pressure sensor signal higher or lower than expected or no response during Dynamic Response (Goose) Test.	Rerun On-Board Diagnostics and perform Dynamic Response Test.
73	167	Throttle Position Sensor	Insufficient throttle position sensor change dynamic response test.	Throttle not depressed during KOER.	Rerun On-Board Diagnostics and depress (goose) throttle when indicated.
74	536	Brake On/Off Switch	Brake not actuated during On-Board Diagnostics. Brake on/off switch circuit failed.	Brake not cycled during KOER. Brake on/off circuit failure.	Failed on or not connected — Torque converter clutch will not engage at less than 1/3 throttle. Failed off — Torque converter clutch will not disengage when brake is applied. [a]
91[c]	621[c]	Shift Solenoid 1	Shift solenoid circuit failure.	Solenoid 1 circuit failed to provide voltage drop across solenoid. Circuit open or shorted or powertrain control module driver failure during KOEO.	Improper gear selection depending on failure mode and transmission range selector lever position. Refer to Shift Solenoid Application Chart. **Refer to Pinpoint Test A**
92[c]	622[c]	Shift Solenoid 2	Shift Solenoid 2 solenoid circuit failure.	Solenoid 2 circuit fails to provide voltage drop across solenoid. Circuit open or shorted or powertrain control module driver failure during KOEO.	Improper gear selection depending on failure mode and lever position. Refer to the Shift Solenoid Application Chart. **Refer to Pinpoint Test A**
93[c]	626[c]	Coast Clutch Solenoid	Coast clutch solenoid circuit failure.	Coast clutch solenoid failed to provide voltage drop across solenoid. Circuit open or shorted or powertrain control module driver failure during KOEO.	Failed off — No third gear engine braking in overdrive cancel. Failed on — Third gear engine braking in overdrive range. Coast Clutch may be damaged/eventual failure. **Refer to Pinpoint Test G**
94[c]	627[c] 629[c]	Torque Converter Clutch Solenoid	Torque converter clutch solenoid circuit failure.	Torque converter clutch solenoid circuit fails to provide voltage drop across solenoid. Circuit open or shorted or powertrain control module driver failure during KOEO.	Short circuit — Engine stalls in Drive or manual 2 at idle with brake applied. Open circuit — Torque converter clutch never engaged. **Refer to Pinpoint Test C**

(d)

FIGURE 8–6 *(Continued)*

Diagnostic Trouble Code		Component	Description	Condition	Symptoms/Actions
Two Digit	**Three Digit**				
97	631	Transmission Control Indicator Lamp	Transmission control indicator lamp circuit failure.	Transmission control indicator lamp circuit open or shorted.	Failed on — Overdrive cancel mode always indicated, no flashing for electronic pressure control failure. Failed off — Overdrive cancel mode never indicated, no flashing for electronic pressure control failure. °
98ᶜ	998ᶜ		Failure Mode Effects Management failure.	Failure detected in one or more critical inputs.	Powertrain control module enables alternate functions. Check for other error codes.°
99ᶜ	624ᶜ	Electronic Pressure Control	Electronic pressure control circuit failure, shorted circuit or powertrain control module.	Voltage through electronic pressure control circuit is checked and compared after a time delay. An error will be noted if tolerance is exceeded during KOEO and continuous On-Board Diagnostics.	Short circuit — (Gasoline engines): Causes minimum electronic pressure control pressure (minimum capacity). Limits engine torque (partial fuel shut-off, heavy misfire). Flashing transmission control indicator lamp. Diesel engines — Cuts power on powertrain control module pin 35 (powertrain control module power) to attain maximum electronic pressure control (maximum capacity). Harsh engagements and shifts, flashing transmission control indicator lamp. Open circuit — (Gasoline and diesel engines): Causes maximum electronic pressure control, harsh engagements and shifts. May flash transmission control indicator lamp. **Refer to Pinpoint Test E.**
	625	Electronic Pressure Control	Powertrain control module failure — electronic pressure control driver	Voltage through electronic pressure control circuit is checked and compared after a time delay. An error will be noted if tolerance is exceeded during KOEO and continuous On-Board Diagnostics.	Short circuit — (Gasoline engines): Causes minimum electronic pressure control pressure (minimum capacity). Limits engine torque (partial fuel shut-off, heavy misfire). Flashing transmission control indicator lamp. Diesel engines — Cuts power on powertrain control module pin 35 (powertrain control module power) to attain maximum electronic pressure control (maximum capacity). Harsh engagements and shifts, flashing transmission control indicator lamp. Open circuit — (Gasoline and diesel engines): Causes maximum electronic pressure control, harsh engagements and shifts. May flash transmission control indicator lamp. **Refer to Pinpoint Test E**

(e)

FIGURE 8–6 *(Concluded)*

Carefully pour the remaining fluid out of the oil pan. Before disturbing the deposits in the pan, examine them for type and quantity. Metallic particles are shiny. Friction metal deposits are very dark or black. A small amount of deposits is normal. Larger amounts indicate that overhaul is required. Examine the metal particles on the drain plug magnet as well.

Fluid contaminated by engine coolant (water or antifreeze) appears milky and requires repair of the leak, reverse flushing of the cooler and lines, a complete draining of the transmission and torque converter, replacement of the filter, and filling with new fluid.

DETERMINING PROPER SOLENOID
ELECTRONIC OPERATION IN THE TRANSAXLE

The following tests will isolate electronic operation in the transaxle from the vehicle and determine if there is an electrical problem in the transaxle.

VERIFYING POWER SUPPLY TO TRANSAXLE:

1. Unplug wiring harness at transaxle.

2. Turn key to run position.

3. Using a circuit tester or unpowered test light, ensure a good negative ground and place the probe in the vehicle harness power connector first at A then at connector E. Each must light.

4. With a DVM using steps 2 and 3 check for voltage supply, DVM should read about 11.5 - 12 volts of battery voltage.

BRAKE SWITCH TEST:

With probe in A which is the power supply for the TCC Solenoid (the P.C.M. will issue a ground to command TCC on) apply brake pedal unpowered test light must go out. If it does not then the brake switch is not adjusted correctly or not functioning properly.

TESTING SHIFT SOLENOIDS A, B AND TCC SOLENOID OPERATION:

5. Turn key to off position.

6. Using jumper wire (about 6 inches long) connect wires to connector pins A and E at transaxle and then to A and E lead connectors at vehicle harness. Connect 4 more wires to pins B, D, F and G at transaxle harness.

   If this is not done properly P.C.M. fuses can be blown during test.

7. Isolate other wires so they do not contact each other or vehicle. Label each wire with tape and write pin letter on tape.

8. Using the DVM turn to DCA range of the meter to the 2 amp position and ensure a good negative ground.

9. Turn key to run position.

10. Using the positive probe ground wire F, SOLENOID A should apply and a single click sound (light) will be heard inside transaxle. Amp draw will be about .5 - .8 amps.

11. Repeat procedure in step 9 but this time ground wire G, SOLENOID B should apply and a single click sound (light) will be heard inside transaxle. Amp draw will be about .5 - .8 amps.

12. Repeat procedure in step 9 but this time ground wire D, the TCC SOLENOID should apply and a single click sound (light) will be heard inside transaxle. Amp draw will be about .5 - .8 amps.

* If any of the solenoids do not apply, check jumper wire connections and repeat steps 9-11. If no solenoid apply still exists, check for these possible causes:

— loose pins in transaxle connector
— pinched or bare wire
— foreign material in solenoid
— loose or defective connectors at solenoids
— inoperative solenoids, broken coil in solenoids
— open wire

FIGURE 8–7 Solenoid operation check chart for 4T60E transaxle. (Courtesy of General Motors Corporation.)

3800 TPI (L27) ENGINE & 4T60-E POWERTRAIN ELECTRICAL DIAGNOSIS CHART

CONDITION	INSPECT	FOR CAUSE
1ST AND 4TH GEAR ONLY EXTENDED 1ST GEAR BY PASSING 2ND & 3RD THEN SHIFT TO 4TH **3RD AND 2ND GEAR DOWNSHIFTS ATTAINABLE IN MANUAL GEAR RANGES** POSSIBLE CODE: — 26 QUAD DRIVER MODULE CIRCUIT	• Solenoid A For "On" Failure	— Foreign material in solenoid. — P.C.M. signal grounded. — Pinched solenoid return wire to ground.
2ND AND 3RD GEAR ONLY POSSIBLE CODE: — 26 QUAD DRIVER MODULE CIRCUIT	• Solenoid A For "Off" Failure	— Insufficient force of solenoid. — Foreign material. — P.C.M. not grounding. — O-ring failure. — No supply voltage to Solenoid A. — Wires not connected to solenoid.
3RD AND 4TH GEAR OPERATION (4-3-3-4); 2ND GEAR DOWN-SHIFTS ATTAINABLE THROUGH MANUAL GEAR RANGES POSSIBLE CODES: — 26 QUAD DRIVER MODULE CIRCUIT — 36 TRANSAXLE SHIFT CONTROL PROBLEM	• Solenoid B For "Off" Failure	— Foreign material in solenoid. — Insufficient force of solenoid. — O-ring failure. — Open wire from Solenoid B to P.C.M. — P.C.M. not grounding. — No supply voltage to Solenoid B. — Wires not connected to Solenoid B.
1ST & 2ND GEAR ONLY (1-2-2-1) POSSIBLE CODES: — 26 QUAD DRIVER MODULE CIRCUIT — 36 TRANSAXLE SHIFT CONTROL PROBLEM	• Solenoid B For "On" Failure	— Foreign material in solenoid. — P.C.M. signal grounded. — Pinched solenoid return wire to ground.
3RD GEAR ONLY (2ND GEAR POSSIBLE THROUGH MANUAL GEAR RANGE) POSSIBLE CODES: — 36 TRANSAXLE SHIFT CONTROL PROBLEM POSSIBLE CODES: — 36 TRANSAXLE SHIFT CONTROL PROBLEM — 16 BATTERY VOLTAGE HIGH OR LOW — 24 SPEED SENSOR — 26 QUAD DRIVER MODULE CIRCUIT	• P.C.M. And Transaxle Wiring • P.C.M. And Transaxle Wiring • Generator And Wiring • Speed Sensor & Wiring • P.C.M. And Wiring Solenoids A And B	— Loose connector. — Corroded connector. — Defective P.C.M. — Loose connector. — Corroded connector. — Defective P.C.M. — Loose connector. — Corroded connector. — Defective generator. — Loose connector. — Corroded connector. — Defective speed sensor. — Loose connector. — Corroded connector. — Defective quad driver.

(a)

FIGURE 8–8 (Courtesy of General Motors Corporation.)

CONDITION	INSPECT	FOR CAUSE
INACCURATE SHIFT POINTS POSSIBLE CODES: — 21 THROTTLE POSITION SENSOR HIGH — 22 THROTTLE POSITION SENSOR LOW — 31 PRNDL CIRCUIT PROBLEM	• Output Speed Sensor (Speedometer Will Not Work Or Be Inaccurate) • Throttle Position Sensor • PRNDL Circuit Problem	— No connection. — Pinched wire. — Wire breakage (coil). — Inadequate signal. — Rotor/sensor interference. — No connection. — Pinched wire. — Incorrect resistance. — Connector loosens. — Corroded connector. — Switch contact corrosion. — Mis-adjustment. — Mis-wired (switched wires).
STUCK IN 1ST GEAR POSSIBLE CODES: — 24 SPEED SENSOR — 26 QDM CIRCUIT — 31 PRNDL MALFUNCTION	• Output Speed Sensor (Speedometer Will Not Work) • Solenoid A & B For "On" Failure • PRNDL Failure	— No connection. — Pinched wire. — Wire breakage (coil). — Inadequate signal. — Rotor/sensor interference. — Solenoids return wires ground. — PRNDL indicates only Manual Lo — no D4, D3 or D2.
STUCK IN 1ST GEAR 2ND WITH HIGH RPM POSSIBLE CODES: — 31 PRNDL SWITCH PROBLEM — 21 THROTTLE POSITION SENSOR HIGH	• PRNDL Switch Stuck In Low • Throttle Position Sensor	— Connector loosens. — Defective switch contact. — Corroded connector. — Switch contact corrosion. — Pinched wire. — No connection. — Pinched wire. — Incorrect resistance. — Mechanical linkage.

(b)

FIGURE 8–8 *(Continued)*

CONDITION	INSPECT	FOR CAUSE
T.C.C. STUCK ON IN 3RD AND 4TH GEAR POSSIBLE CODE: — 26 QUAD DRIVER MODULE CIRCUIT	• T.C.C. Solenoid For "On" Failure	— Foreign material. — Pinched solenoid wire to ground. — P.C.M. signal grounded.
T.C.C. APPLIES WITH MAX PRESSURE POSSIBLE CODE: — 26 QUAD DRIVER MODULE CIRCUIT	• T.C.C. P.W.M. For "Off" Failure	— Foreign material in P.W.M. solenoid. — No P.C.M. signal. — Insufficient force of P.W.M. — O-rings failure. — Open wire. — No supply voltage to P.W.M. solenoid.
INCORRECT APPLY AND RELEASE OF T.C.C. (WRONG GEAR RANGE) POSSIBLE CODES: — 31 PRNDL SWITCH CIRCUIT — 38 BRAKE SWITCH CIRCUIT — 14 COOLANT TEMP HIGH — 15 COOLANT TEMP LOW	• PRNDL Circuit Problem • Brake Switch (No T.C.C. Apply) • Coolant Temp Sensor	— Connector loosens. — Connector corroded. — Switch contact corrosion. — Pinched wire. — Wires switched or misadjusted. — Connector corroded. — Switch contact corrosion. — No supply voltage. — Defective device. — Connector loosens. — Incorrect resistance. — Pinched wire. — Connector corroded.

(c)

FIGURE 8–8 *(Continued)*

CONDITION	INSPECT	FOR CAUSE

NO T.C.C.
 	
POSSIBLE CODES:
— 26 QUAD DRIVER
  MODULE CIRCUIT
	• T.C.C. Solenoid For "Off"
	  Failure
		— Foreign material.
		— Insufficient force.
		— O-ring failure.
		— No P.C.M. signal.
		— Open wire.
		— No supply voltage to T.C.C. solenoid.

	• T.C.C. P.W.M. For "On" Failure	— Foreign material. — Pinched wire. — P.C.M. signal grounded.
— 38 BRAKE SWITCH CIRCUIT	• Brake Switch (No T.C.C. Apply)	— No supply voltage. — Connector corroded. — Switch contact corrosion. — Connector loosens. — Pinched wire.
— 31 PRNDL SWITCH PROBLEM	• PRNDL Circuit Problem	— Connector loosens. — Connector corroded. — Switch contact corrosion. — Pinched wire. — PRNDL connector wires A and B switched around if PRNDL indicates anything but D3 or D4.

— 15 COOLANT TEMP LOW
  (T.C.C. WILL COME ON
  WITH A CODE 15 AFTER
  ENGINE HAS BEEN DRIVEN
  AWHILE
  — ENGINE RUN TIMER
    ELAPSED)
	• Coolant Temp Sensor	— Connector corroded.
		— Incorrect resistance.
		— Connector loosens.
		— Pinched wire.

(d)

FIGURE 8–8 *(Continued)*

CONDITION	INSPECT COMPONENT	FOR CAUSE
LEAKS AT:	• Side Cover (53) • Flanged Nuts (50) • Bolt & Washer Assy. (52)	— Cracks or not flat. — Low torque. — Low torque.
	• Side Cover Gasket (54) • Flanged Nuts (50) • Bolt & Washer Assy. (52)	— Split. — High torque. — High torque.
	• Inner Gasket (55) • Flanged Nuts (50) • Bolt & Washer Assy. (52)	— Split. — High torque. — High torque.
	• Fluid Fill Tube	— Cut seal, case porosity or bad bracket weld.
	• Electrical Connector (35) • "O" Ring Seal (36)	— Case porosity. — Cut or nicked.
	• Reverse Servo Cover (40) • "O" Ring Seal (41)	— Cracks or porosity. — Cut or nicked.
	• Forward Servo Cover (13) • "O" Ring Seal (14) • Case	— Cracks or porosity. — Cut or nicked. — Porosity.
	• Cooler Ball Check Assy. (28) And Cooler Pipe Fitting (29)	— Stripped threads, low torque or porosity in case. — Bad flare.
	• Modulator Assembly (32) • "O" Ring Seal (33)	— Split or cracked seams. — Cut or nicked.
	• Case Extension (6) • Extension Seal (8)	— Cracks or porosity. — Cut or nicked.
	• Right Hand Axle Seal Assy. (4) And Left Hand Axle Seal Assy. (409)	— Cut, nicked or worn. — Missing garter spring. — Bushing (7) worn allowing right axle seal leak.
	• Manual Shaft Seal (806)	— Cut or nicked.
	• Converter Seal Assy. (525)	— Cut, nicked or worn. — Missing garter spring.
	• Speed Sensor Assy. (10) • "O" Ring Seal (11)	— Damaged housing. — Cut or nicked.
	• Parking Plunger Guide (809)	— Porosity in case.
	• "O" Ring Seal (810)	— Cut or nicked.
OIL OUT THE VENT OR FOAMING	• Oil Level	— Transaxle overfilled.
	• Transaxle Oil (Foaming)	— Contaminated with antifreeze or engine overheating. — Lube pipes (126-130) leaking.
	• Oil Filter (Foaming) (100) And/Or Seal (101)	— Damaged seal assembly.
	• Thermo Element (Case) (120-123)	— Does not close when hot. — Not installed correctly. — Incorrect pin heights.
	• Channel Plate (Upper) Gasket (430)	— Not installed correctly or damaged.
	• Drive Sprocket Support (522)	— Plugged drain back holes.

(e)

FIGURE 8–8 *(Continued)*

CONDITION	INSPECT COMPONENT	FOR CAUSE
HIGH OR LOW OIL PRESSURE (VERIFY WITH GAGE, ENGINE MUST BE PROPERLY TUNED) ENGINE MUST DEVELOP 13-18 HG. IN. OF VACUUM	• Oil Level • Vacuum Line • Modulator (32) • Modulator Valve (34) • Oil Pump Assembly • Pressure Regulator Valve (313) Or Springs (311 & 312) • Pressure Relief Valve (321)	— High or low; correct as required. — Leaking, pinched, disconnected or cut. — Leaks or damaged diaphragm. (A bent modulator will not function correctly.) — Nicked, scored or stuck. — Slide stuck, seals damaged, vanes damaged. — Pump drive shaft damaged. — Nicked or scored, springs damaged. — Damaged spring, ball missing.
DELAYED ENGAGEMENT	• Fluid Level • Cooler Check Ball (28) • Reverse Servo Assembly • Forward Servo Assembly	— Low. — Not seating, allowing converter drain back. — Seal (43) cut or damaged. — Seal (105) damaged or mislocated. — Seal (18) damaged or cut.
SLIPS IN DRIVE 2ND GEAR START SOLENOID A FOR "OFF" FAILURE 3RD GEAR START SEE 3RD GEAR ONLY 4TH GEAR START SOLENOID B FOR "OFF" FAILURE OR TCC WIRES AND SOLENOID B WIRES SWITCHED	• Fluid Level • Vacuum Line • Modulator (32) • Oil Pressure • Modulator Valve (34) • Forward Servo Assembly • Forward Servo Piston (16) • Oil Filter (100) • Filter Seal (101) • Forward Servo Seal (105) • Torque Converter (1) • Bolt (380) • Input Clutch Assembly • Pump Assembly	— Low - correct. — Pinched, slowing vacuum response. — Damaged. — See Causes of Low Pressure. — Stuck or binding. — Damaged or missing cushion spring (19) or retainer (20). — Seal (18) damaged. — Plugged. — Cut or damaged. — Leaking, damaged or missing seal or low torque of bolts (103). — Stator roller clutch not holding. — Low torque allowing leakage for driven sprocket support. — Leaks at ball capsule (633) or seals. — Seals damaged (634 & 635). — Slide sticking. — Leak at slide seals.
NO DRIVE IN DRIVE RANGE (INSTALL PRESSURE GAGE)	• Oil Level • Oil Pressure • Manual Linkage	— Low (correct). — Low (See Causes of Low Pressure). — Misadjusted or disconnected.

(f)

FIGURE 8–8 *(Continued)*

CONDITION	INSPECT COMPONENT	FOR CAUSE
NO DRIVE IN DRIVE RANGE (INSTALL PRESSURE GAGE) (Cont.)	• Forward Servo Assembly	— Piston or seal damaged.
	• 1/2 Roller Clutch	— Damaged.
	• Drive Axles	— Disengaged.
	• Oil Pump Assembly	— Damaged. (See Causes of Low Oil Pressure.)
		— Pump drive shaft (227) damaged.
	• #3 Checkball	— Missing.
	• Torque Converter (1)	— Stator roller clutch (vehicle moves, but is very sluggish).
		— Converter not bolted to flex plate.
	• Drive Link Assembly	— Damaged or broken drive link chain.
		— Sprockets damaged.
	• Input Clutch Assembly	— Burned, clutch plates or missing.
		— Damaged piston seals or piston.
		— Housing checkball assembly leaking.
		— Input shaft seals damaged.
		— Input shaft feed passages blocked.
	• Input Sprag And Input Sun Gear Assembly	— Improper assembly.
		— Sprag damaged - roll over.
	• Input Carrier And Reaction Carrier Assembly	— Pinions damaged.
		— Internal gear damaged.
		— Sun gear damaged.
	• Output Shaft (510)	— Damaged, misassembled with axles.
	• Forward Band Assembly (688)	— Burned.
		— Band apply pin (21) mislocated with band. (Will still move in Manual Lo and Manual 2nd.)
	• Parking Pawl (694)	— Spring broken, pawl remains engaged.
	• Final Drive Assembly Or Final Drive Sun Gear Shaft (689)	— Damaged side gear, gears, pinion, internal gear.
FIRST SPEED ONLY NO 1-2 SHIFT	• Control Valve Assembly (300)	— 1-2 Shift valve (318) stuck or binding.
		— Spacer plate (370) or gaskets (364 & 371) mispositioned or damaged.
	• Driven Sprocket Support (609)	— Oil seal rings (612 & 613) damaged.
	• 2nd Clutch Assy. (617)	— Clutch plates damaged.
		— Piston or seals damaged.
		— Parts misassembled.
	• Reverse Reaction Drum (669)	— Splines damaged.
1-2 SHIFT FEEL — HARSH OR SOFT	• Oil Pressure	— (See Causes of High or Low Oil Pressure.)
	• 1-2 Accumulator Piston (136 & 137) And Cover (132)	— Cover bolts (131) improperly torqued.
		— Piston or seal damaged.
		— Spring damaged.
		— Gaskets (133) mispositioned, damaged or low torque of bolts (131).

(g)

FIGURE 8–8 *(Continued)*

CONDITION	INSPECT COMPONENT	FOR CAUSE
1-2 SHIFT FEEL — HARSH OR SOFT (Cont.)	• Control Valve Assy. (300) • #2 Checkball	— 1-2 Accumulator valve (341) stuck. — Mislocated.
SOFT/SLIPPING	• Driven Sprocket Support (609)	— Rolled or twisted seal (612) for Vespel ring. — Worn sleeve in 2nd clutch housing (616 or 619).
SLIPS ON TURNS	• Fluid Level • Filter (100)	— Low. — Cracked or damaged.
SHUDDER 1-2 SHIFT	• 2nd Clutch (616-627)	— Worn (fiber) plates (624). — Leaking check valve ball (618). — Cut seal (620) — Damaged (steel) plates (625). — Mispositioned snap ring (627 or 622).
	• Driven Sprocket Support (609)	— Damaged seal rings (612 & 613). — (See Causes of Low Oil Pressure.)
1-2 SHIFT SPEED — HIGH OR LOW	• Refer To Shift Speed Chart And Section 6E • Check Service Bulletins If An Update To PROM • Wrong PROM	
1ST & 2ND GEAR ONLY (1-2-2-1) POSSIBLE CODES: — 26 QUAD DRIVER MODULE CIRCUIT — 36 TRANSAXLE SHIFT CONTROL PROBLEM	• Solenoid B For "On" Failure	— Foreign material in solenoid. — P.C.M. signal grounded. — Pinched solenoid return wire to ground.
1ST AND 4TH GEAR ONLY EXTENDED 1ST GEAR BY PASSING 2ND & 3RD THEN SHIFT TO 4TH POSSIBLE CODE: — 26 QUAD DRIVER MODULE CIRCUIT	• Solenoid A For "On" Failure	— Foreign material in solenoid. — P.C.M. signal grounded. — Pinched solenoid return wire to ground.
2ND AND 3RD GEAR ONLY POSSIBLE CODE: — 26 QUAD DRIVER MODULE CIRCUIT	• Solenoid A For "Off" Failure	— Insufficient force of solenoid. — Foreign material, plugging filter [374(A)]. — P.C.M. not grounding. — "O" ring failure. — No supply voltage to Solenoid A. — Wires not connected to solenoid.
NO 2-3 SHIFT (1st, 2nd & 4th SPEEDS ONLY)	• Control Valve Assy. (300)	— 2-3 Shift valve (357) stuck. — 3-2 Manual downshift valve (356) stuck.

(h)

FIGURE 8–8 *(Continued)*

CONDITION	INSPECT COMPONENT	FOR CAUSE
3RD GEAR ONLY (Cont.) — 26 QUAD DRIVER MODULE CIRCUIT	• P.C.M. And Wiring Solenoids A And B	— Loose connector. — Corroded connector. — Defective quad driver.
3RD AND 4TH GEAR OPERATION (4-3-3-4) 2ND GEAR DOWNSHIFTS ATTAINABLE THROUGH MANUAL GEAR RANGES POSSIBLE CODES: — 26 QUAD DRIVER MODULE CIRCUIT — 36 TRANSAXLE SHIFT CONTROL PROBLEM	• Solenoid B For ''Off'' Failure	— Foreign material, plugging filter [374(B)]. — Insufficient force of solenoid. — ''O'' ring failure. — Open wire from Solenoid B to P.C.M. — P.C.M. not grounding. — No supply voltage to Solenoid B. — Wires not connected to Solenoid B.
NO 3-4 SHIFT	• Control Valve Assembly (300) • 4th Clutch Shaft (504) • 4th Clutch Assembly (500-502) • Shift Cable Adjustment	— 3-4 Shift valve (362) stuck. — 4-3 Manual downshift valve (360) stuck. — Spline damage. — Clutch plates burned. — Piston or seals damaged. — Clutch plates or piston mislocated.
3-4 SHIFT FEEL — HARSH OR SOFT	• See Causes Of High Or Low Oil Pressure • Accumulator Cover (421) And Piston (428 & 427) • #10 Checkball • Control Valve Assy. (300)	— Damaged seals (427 or 422). — Missing springs (423, 424 or 425). — Missing. — 3-4 Accumulator valve (350) stuck.
3-4 SHIFT SPEED — HIGH OR LOW	• Refer To Shift Speed Chart And Section 6E • Check Service Bulletins If An Update To PROM • Wrong PROM	
NO REVERSE	• Oil Pressure (See Causes Of High Or Low Pressure) • Reverse Servo (17, 39-49) • Oil Pump Assembly (See No Drive) • Drive Link Assembly (See No Drive) • Reverse Band (615) • Input Clutch (See No Drive)	— Misassembled. — Piston or seal damaged. — Missing cushion spring (45) or retainers (46). — Burned, damaged, or mislocated.

(i)

FIGURE 8–8 *(Continued)*

CONDITION	INSPECT COMPONENT	FOR CAUSE
NO 2-3 SHIFT (1st, 2nd & 4th SPEEDS ONLY (Cont.)	• Channel Plate Gasket (429)	— Mispositioned or damaged.
	• Driven Sprocket Support (609)	— Blocked 3rd clutch passage.
	• Input Housing And Shaft Assembly	— Seals (628) damaged. — Blocked oil passages.
	• 3rd Clutch Assembly	— Clutch plates burned. — Damaged piston or seals. — Damaged checkball assembly (piston).
	• 3rd Roller Clutch Assembly	— Damaged cage. — Rollers out of cage. — Damaged springs. — Misassembled on input sun gear shaft. — No third gear and no engine braking in Manual Lo.
2-3 SHIFT FEEL — HARSH OR SOFT	• See Causes Of High Or Low Oil Pressure	
	• #4 Checkball	— Mislocated for a soft shift.
	• #9 Checkball	— Missing for a harsh shift.
	• 2-3 Accumulator Piston, Gaskets And Seals	— Missing springs (138A & 138B), cut seal (137), damaged gaskets (133) and low torque of bolts (131).
2-3 SHIFT SPEED — HIGH OR LOW	• Refer To Shift Speed Chart And Section 6E	
	• Wrong PROM	
	• Check Service Bulletins If An Update To PROM	
3RD GEAR ONLY (2ND GEAR POSSIBLE THROUGH MANUAL GEAR RANGE) POSSIBLE CODES: — 36 TRANSAXLE SHIFT CONTROL PROBLEM	• P.C.M. And Transaxle Wiring	— Loose connector. — Corroded connector. — Defective P.C.M.
(1ST AND 2ND GEAR POSSIBLE THROUGH MANUAL GEAR RANGES) POSSIBLE CODES: — 36 TRANSAXLE SHIFT CONTROL PROBLEM — 16 BATTERY VOLTAGE HIGH OR LOW — 24 SPEED SENSOR	• P.C.M. And Transaxle Wiring	— Loose connector. — Corroded connector. — Defective P.C.M.
	• Generator And Wiring	— Loose connector. — Corroded connector. — Defective generator.
	• Speed Sensor And Wiring	— Loose connector. — Corroded connector. — Defective speed sensor.

(j)

FIGURE 8–8 *(Continued)*

CONDITION	INSPECT COMPONENT	FOR CAUSE
NO REVERSE (Cont.)	• Reverse Reaction Drum (669) • Input Sprag (See No Drive) • Input And Reaction Carriers (See No Drive)	— Splines damaged. — (See No Drive.)
LOCKED UP IN REVERSE OR DRIVE	• Final Drive Internal Gear (693)	— Deformed/dented parking pawl (694).
SLIPS IN REVERSE (ALSO SEE SLIPS IN DRIVE)	• Oil Pressure • Reverse Servo Assembly • Reverse Reaction Drum (669)	— See Causes of Low Pressure. — Damaged seal (43). — Damaged splines.
NO PARK RANGE	• Final Drive Internal Gear (693 & 694) • Actuator Assembly (800) • Shift Cable Adjustment	— Park pawl spring. — Park pawl. — Parking gear. — Spring damaged.
HARSH NEUTRAL TO REVERSE OR HARSH NEUTRAL TO DRIVE	• Modulator (32), And/Or Lines • Reverse Servo Cushion Spring (45) • Control Valve Assy. (300) • Forward Servo Cushion Spring (19) • Spacer Plate (370)	— Loss of vacuum due to damaged lines or modulator. — Broken or wrong spring. — #5 Checkball missing - results in harsh reverse. — #6 Checkball missing - results in harsh drive. — Broken or wrong spring. — Thermal element does not close when warm, causing harsh Neutral to Drive.
2nd GEAR STARTS	• Control Valve Assembly (300)	— Stuck 1-2 shift valve (318).
HARSH ENGAGEMENT OR ENGAGEMENT SHUDDER IN REVERSE	• 2nd Clutch Housing And Drum Assembly (617) • Reverse Band Assembly (615) • #5 Checkball • Servo Cushion Spring (45)	— Drum surface scored or hot spots caused by band slippage. — Burned fiber material. — Missing or mislocated. — Wrong spring or damaged.
NO ENGINE BRAKING IN MANUAL 2ND OR LO	• 2-1 Manual Band (680) • Apply Pin (111)	— Burned or glazed fiber material. — Not engaging 2-1 manual band.

(k)

FIGURE 8–8 (Continued)

CONDITION	INSPECT COMPONENT	FOR CAUSE
NO ENGINE BRAKING IN MANUAL 2ND OR LO	• Seals (113 & 107)	— Cut or damaged. — Missing filter (115) allowing foreign material to damage seal and bore.
	• Gaskets (133)	— Damaged.
	• Bolts (131)	— Low torque.
CONVERTER CLUTCH DOES **NOT** RELEASE	• TCC Solenoid	— TCC solenoid (315) does not exhaust.
	• Control Valve Assy. (300)	— Converter clutch valve (335) stuck in apply position.
	• TCC Screen [374(C)]	— Missing, allowing foreign material to stick TCC solenoid on.
TCC STUCK ON IN 3RD AND 4TH GEAR POSSIBLE CODE: — 26 QUAD DRIVER MODULE CIRCUIT	• TCC Solenoid For "On" Failure	— Foreign material. — Pinched solenoid wire to ground. — P.C.M. signal grounded.
TCC APPLIES WITH MAX PRESSURE—HARSH APPLY POSSIBLE CODE: — 26 QUAD DRIVER MODULE CIRCUIT	• TCC P.W.M. For "Off" Failure	— Foreign material in P.W.M. solenoid. — No P.C.M. signal. — Insufficient force of P.W.M. — "O" rings failure. — Open wire. — No supply voltage to P.W.M. solenoid.
CONVERTER CLUTCH APPLY, ROUGH, SLIPS, OR SHUDDERS	• Control Valve Assy. (300)	— Converter clutch regulator valve (332 or 334) stuck.
	• Turbine Shaft (518)	— Seals damaged or missing. — Converter clutch blow off checkball (420) not seated or damaged.
	• Channel Plate (401)	
	• Drive Sprocket Support (522)	— Worn bushing (523).
	• Torque Converter	— Worn or glazed fiber material. (Replace converter.)
4-3 DOWNSHIFT — HARSH	• Control Valve Assy. (300) • 3-4 Accumulator Seal • 3-4 Accumulator Valve	— #10 Checkball missing. — Cut seal (427). — Valve stuck (350).
3-2 DOWNSHIFT — HARSH	• Control Valve Assy. (300) • 2-3 Accumulator Seal • 2-3 Accumulator Valve	— #9 Checkball missing. — Cut seal (137). — Valve stuck (343).
2-1 DOWNSHIFT — HARSH	• Spacer Plate (370) • 1-2 Accumulator Seal • 1-2 Accumulator Valve	— Wrong spacer plate. — Cut seal (137). — Valve stuck (341).

(I)

FIGURE 8–8 *(Continued)*

CONDITION	INSPECT COMPONENT	FOR CAUSE
NO CONVERTER CLUTCH APPLY	• Verify Proper P.C.M. Operation And Vehicle Wiring	— Improper operation or wiring.
	• Wiring Harness (224)	— Connector damaged or loose. — Pinched wires. — TCC Solenoid (315) inoperative.
	• Control Valve Assy. (300)	— Converter clutch valve (335) stuck. — Converter clutch regulator valve (332 or 334) stuck.
	• TCC Solenoid (315)	— Solenoid "O" ring (316) leaking.
	• Solenoid Screen [374(C)]	— Blocked.
	• Torque Converter (1)	— Inspect - Refer to Transaxle Unit Repair Section and Section 6E.
	• Turbine Shaft (518)	— Seals (519 or 520) damaged.
	• Oil Pump Drive Shaft (227)	— Damaged seal (228).
	• Channel Plate (401)	— Converter clutch blow off checkball not seated or damaged. — #1 Checkball [372(A)] missing.
NO TCC POSSIBLE CODES: — 26 QUAD DRIVER MODULE CIRCUIT	• TCC Solenoid For "Off" Failure	— Foreign material, plugging filter [374(D)]. — Insufficient force. — "O" ring failure. — No P.C.M. signal. — Open wire. — No supply voltage to TCC solenoid.
	• TCC P.W.M. For "On" Failure	— Foreign material. — Pinched wire. — P.C.M. signal grounded.
— 38 BRAKE SWITCH CIRCUIT	• Brake Switch (No TCC Apply)	— No supply voltage. — Connector corroded. — Switch contact corrosion. — Connector loosens. — Pinched wire.
— 31 PRNDL SWITCH PROBLEM	• PRNDL Circuit Problem	— Connector loosens. — Connector corroded. — Switch contact corrosion. — Pinched wire. — PRNDL connector wires A and B switched around if PRNDL indicates anything but D3 or D4.
— 15 COOLANT TEMP LOW (TCC WILL COME ON WITH A CODE 15 AFTER ENGINE HAS BEEN DRIVEN AWHILE — ENGINE RUN TIMER ELAPSED)	• Coolant Temp Sensor Engine Up To Operating Temperature Of 54°C (130°F)?	— Connector corroded. — Incorrect resistance. — Connector loosens. — Pinched wire.

(m)

FIGURE 8-8 *(Concluded)*

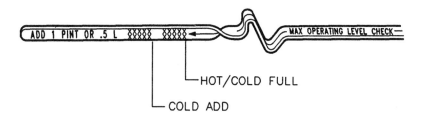

HOT/COLD FULL

COLD ADD

NOTE: Fluid level to be in cross-harched area on fluid level indicator blade. Check at operating temperature..

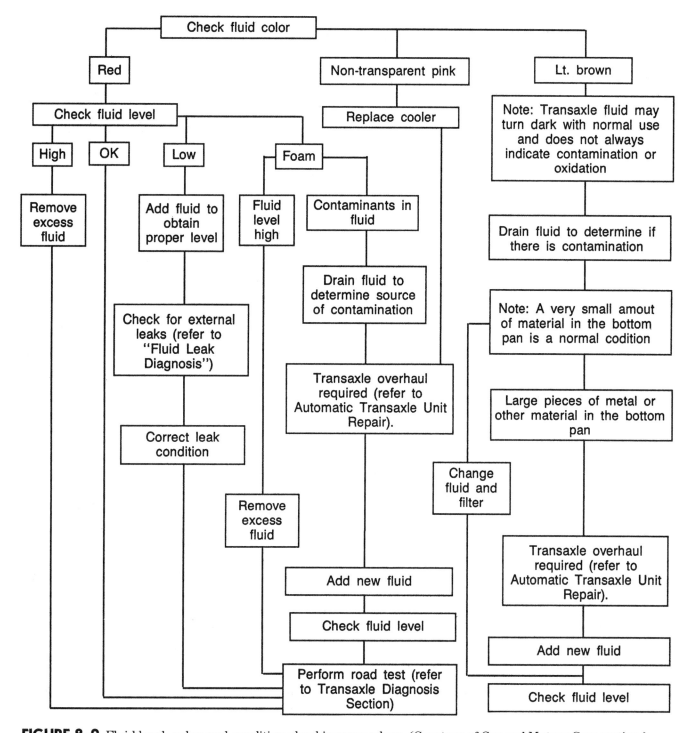

FIGURE 8–9 Fluid level, color, and condition-checking procedure. (Courtesy of General Motors Corporation.)

Fluid and Filter Change

The fluid and filter should be changed at the interval specified in the service manual. In most cases, fluid or filter change is not recommended unless a problem develops. Vehicles operating under severe service conditions may require the fluid and filter to be changed at regular intervals. Severe service includes trailer towing or operating under heavy loads or extreme temperatures.

To change the fluid and filter, obtain the required amount and correct type of fluid, a filter, and a pan gasket, and proceed as follows:

> **SAFETY CAUTION:** Fluid may be hot enough to cause severe burns.

1. Raise the vehicle on a hoist.

2. With a drain pan in position, remove the drain plug from the oil pan to drain the fluid. If there is no drain plug, loosen the oil pan bolts and remove enough of them to allow the pan to tilt and drain. Remove the remaining bolts and the oil pan.

3. Remove and clean or replace the filter or screen.

4. Clean the oil pan and remove all old gasket material.

5. Clean the gasket surface on the transmission/transaxle case.

6. Position the new gasket in place using the recommended sealer.

7. Place the pan in position and start all the bolts by hand. Tighten them alternately to specified torque. Do not overtighten. Overtightening will cause the gasket to crack and leak.

8. Drain the torque converter (if it has a drain plug) with the selector lever in the proper position (some models). Many torque converters cannot be drained.

9. Pour the specified initial amount and type of fluid into the transmission using a long-neck funnel. Pour the fluid in through the dipstick tube.

10. Start the engine and shift through all gear positions.

11. Check the fluid level and top it up to the correct level. Shut off the engine.

12. Check underneath for leaks.

Fluid Leakage

When checking for fluid leaks, it is important to be able to distinguish between transmission/transaxle fluid, engine oil, power steering fluid, and antifreeze. Once it has been determined that it is in fact transmission fluid that is leaking, the suspected area should be cleaned and wiped dry. The transmission/transaxle should then be operated and the point of leakage determined by close examination of new leakage. Areas of leakage are as follows (**Figures 8–10 and 8–11**):

- Torque converter
- Front pump seal or gasket
- Case, oil pan gaskets, servo cover gaskets, and extension housing gasket and seal
- Speedometer cable adapter
- Filler tube O-ring
- Shift linkage shafts and O-rings
- Vacuum modulator (engine vacuum can draw fluid into engine through ruptured modulator diaphragm. To check, remove vacuum line from modulator; there should be no evidence of fluid in modulator or vacuum line)
- Vent or filler tube leakage can result from overfilling

If transmission/transaxle has been operated with a low fluid level sufficiently to cause internal damage, both the internal damage and the leak must be corrected.

Shift Linkage Adjustment and Neutral Switch Check

It is essential to proper transmission/transaxle operation that the selector lever position and the manual valve position be synchronized. In other words, when the driver selects Reverse, for example, it is essential that the manual valve in the valve body also be in the reverse position.

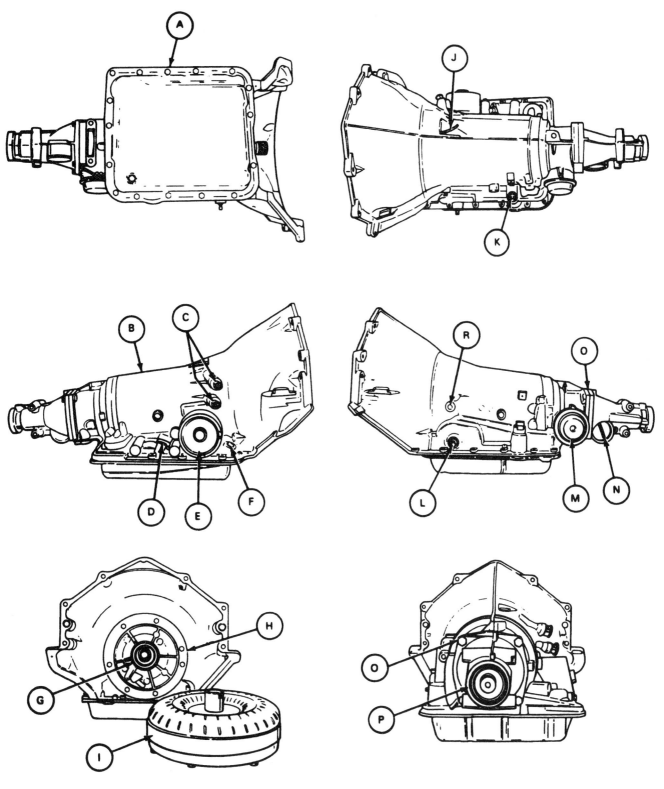

A BOTTOM PAN GASKET	**G** OIL PUMP SEAL ASSEMBLY	**M** GOVERNOR COVER SEAL
B CASE	**H** OIL PUMP TO CASE SEAL	**N** SPEEDO SEAL
C COOLER CONNECTORS & PIPE PLUGS	**I** CONVERTER	**O** EXTENSION TO CASE SEAL
D T.V. CABLE SEAL	**J** VENT	**P** EXTENSION OIL SEAL ASSY.
E SERVO COVER SEAL	**K** ELECTRICAL CONNECTOR SEAL	**R** LINE PRESSURE TAP
F OIL FILL TUBE SEAL	**L** MANUAL SHAFT SEAL	

FIGURE 8–10 Possible transmission fluid leak points. (Courtesy of General Motors Corporation.)

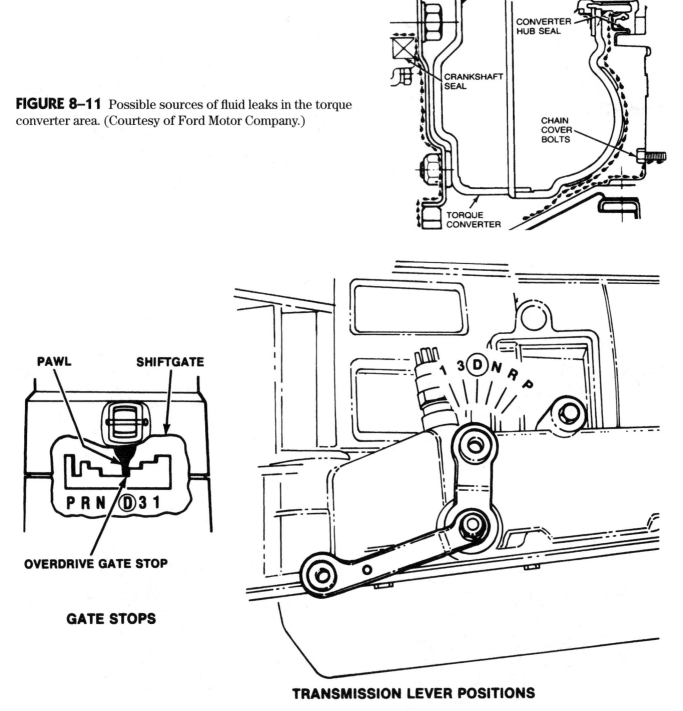

FIGURE 8–11 Possible sources of fluid leaks in the torque converter area. (Courtesy of Ford Motor Company.)

GATE STOPS

TRANSMISSION LEVER POSITIONS

FIGURE 8–12 Shift lever pawl positions in shift gate must be synchronized with transmission/transaxle shift lever and detent positions. (Courtesy of Ford Motor Company.)

The position of the selector lever in each range is determined by gates in the shift mechanism. The position of the manual shift valve in each range is held in place by detents. Synchronization of selector lever position and manual valve position is determined by adjustment of the linkage between the two (**Figures 8–12 and 8–13**).

A typical linkage adjustment involves loosening or disconnecting the linkage at the shift lever bracket. The selector lever is then placed in Park

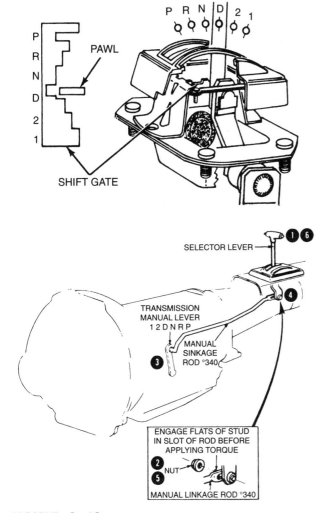

FIGURE 8–13 Manual linkage adjustment requires synchronization of shift lever, pawl, gate, and detent. (Courtesy of Ford Motor Company.)

against the gate, and the shift valve lever is placed in the Park detent position. With these in position, the clamp on the sliding adjustment is tightened to maintain this relationship. On the threaded type of linkage adjustment, the connection is lengthened or shortened as required to make the adjustment.

A further check is required by selecting all gear positions and making sure that the engine will start in the Park and Neutral positions but not in any other positions. Some vehicles may require a neutral start switch adjustment to be made after the linkage adjustment has been corrected. Incorrect manual shift linkage adjustment can cause delayed engagement, slippage, overheating, and shift problems. Manual shift linkage types include those using rods and those with a cable.

Throttle Linkage Adjustment

There are two types of throttle linkage: the type that controls only the downshift valve (equipped with a vacuum modulator to control the throttle valve) and the type that controls both the downshift valve and the throttle valve (these do not have a vacuum modulator). Linkage design includes the rod and lever type and the cable type. Some of these linkage systems are not adjustable.

The importance of throttle valve linkage adjustment stems from the fact that throttle pressure rises proportionately with increased throttle opening. If TV (throttle valve) linkage adjustment is incorrect, it can result in:

1. Throttle pressure that is too high in relation to throttle opening. This results in harsh upshifts. Part-throttle (to detent) and WOT (through detent) downshifts will occur earlier than normal. Part-throttle downshifts can occur at a relatively small increase in throttle opening. This can be annoying in city traffic and on the highway.

2. Throttle pressure that is too low in relation to throttle opening. This results in upshifts occurring too early and "mushy" upshifts and may result in slippage of bands and clutches. Greater than normal throttle opening will be required to effect forced downshifts.

Procedures for adjusting throttle valve and downshift linkage vary considerably. Since transmission/transaxle operating characteristics and life are affected by TV and downshift linkage, it is important that procedures and specifications given in the appropriate service repair manual are followed. Differences in specifications may exist, for example, for the same model and year of transmission on a car equipped with different-size engines.

Modulator System Checks

The vacuum modulator system has the same effect on the hydraulic control system as the throttle valve linkage system. Engine intake manifold vacuum varies with engine speed and load and is related to throttle opening. Any leakage in the vacuum system will have the effect of reducing vacuum. This results in higher than normal throttle (or modulator) pressure, with the same effect on transmission operation as described earlier. The general procedure for checking the vacuum modulator system requires checking the vacuum at the line removed from the modulator. If vacuum readings taken at this point are normal, there are no vacuum leaks in the line, and the engine condition is assumed to be satisfactory. If any transmission fluid is noticeable when the vacuum line is disconnected at the modulator, the vacuum diaphragm in the modulator is leaking, and the engine is consuming some transmission fluid through the vacuum line to the intake manifold. The vacuum modulator must be replaced. If the vacuum source, vacuum lines, and vacuum modulator are in good condition but shift characteristics indicated a vacuum modulator system problem, the vacuum modulator may have to be adjusted. This requires removing the modulator from the transmission. Special modulator wrenches are required to remove some screw-in-type units since there is very little room between the transmission case and the modulator body in some cases. The push-in-type modulator has a clamp and cap screw holding it in place. The cap screw and clamp must be removed, and the modulator can then be pulled out. In some cases, it may have to be pried out. Whenever a vacuum modulator is removed from a transmission, have a pan ready to catch any fluid that may drain from the transmission (about 1 quart or 1 liter). The modulator should be removed carefully to avoid losing the actuating pin, which may drop during modulator removal. After removal, the modulator can be bench tested with the use of a vacuum pump and gauge and with the use of special gauge pins in some cases (**Figures 8–14** and **8–15**). If adjustment is required, this should only be done as specified in the appropriate service manual.

EGR (Exhaust Gas Recirculation) System Checks

EGR system operation affects engine intake manifold vacuum, and manifold vacuum affects modulator operation. This system should be checked. If not operating properly, the necessary corrections should be made. A quick check can be made as follows:

1. Check the engine at operating temperature and at idle speed.
2. Locate and observe movement of the EGR valve stem as engine speed is increased to at least 1700 rpm.

If no movement is evident, check the EGR vacuum source. If OK, the EGR valve is stuck and requires service.

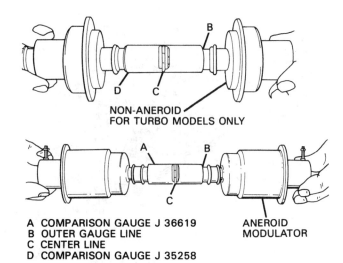

A   COMPARISON GAUGE J 36619
B   OUTER GAUGE LINE
C   CENTER LINE
D   COMPARISON GAUGE J 35258

FIGURE 8–14 Vacuum modulator check. (Courtesy of General Motors Corporation.)

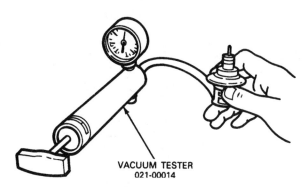

FIGURE 8–15 Testing a vacuum modulator with a hand vacuum pump. If vacuum does not hold, the diaphragm has a leak. (Courtesy of Ford Motor Company.)

Engine Idle Speed

The engine idle speed should be adjusted to specifications. An engine idle speed that is too high results in harsh engagement of clutches in both forward and reverse. This is perceived by the customer as a clunk during engagement. A harsh closed throttle (coasting) downshift may also be caused by too high an engine idle speed. Use a tachometer and adjust the idle speed where possible to the manufacturer's specifications. These are usually stated on the underhood emission sticker. Most of today's fuel-injected cars do not have an idle speed adjustment. Idle speed is controlled by the idle air control motor or solenoid and computer.

COMPUTER CONTROL SELF-DIAGNOSIS

Computers are designed to monitor their own performance as well as input sensors, switches, output devices, and related wiring harness. When a problem occurs often enough, a fault code is stored in computer memory. A malfunction indicator lamp (check engine light) on the dash goes on to alert the driver that the vehicle needs repair. The technician can activate the computer memory to generate fault codes. These will appear as a flashing light, a number code, or a message on the dash.

A diagnostic connector (self-test connector or assembly line diagnostic link, ALDL) in the wiring harness provides the means for activating fault codes. The diagnostic connector may be located in the engine compartment, under the dash, behind the side panel below the dash, behind the glove compartment, or in some other location. To activate the self-diagnostic mode and generate the fault codes, different methods are used on different vehicle makes and models. Some typical methods are described here.

1. Turn the ignition key on and off in the specified sequence and time to activate the dash light. Light flashes are converted to a fault code number.

2. Connect a test light to specified terminals in the diagnostic connector. Light flashes are converted to a fault code number.

3. Press two specified climate control buttons at the same time. Light flashes, fault code numbers, or word messages are generated depending on the vehicle make and model.

4. Connect a scanner into the diagnostic connector and note the display on the scanner. The display may be a fault code number, a flashing light, or a bar graph depending on the type of scanner being used.

Follow the procedures given in the appropriate service manual to generate fault codes and how to use them.

Fault Code Charts

Fault code charts are provided in service manuals. They list all the possible fault code numbers and what each fault code number means. Fault codes direct the technician to the malfunctioning circuit. However, the circuit itself may not be causing the trouble. Trouble in

a related component can cause the fault code to be triggered. It is therefore important to understand which vehicle systems are interrelated and may have common sensors. See **Figures 8–3** and **8–6** to **8–8** for examples of fault codes.

A scanner (scan tool) is used by plugging it into the wiring harness diagnostic connector. The vehicle's computer communicates a variety of information to the scanner, which is displayed in digital form as fault codes or in word form. Some of this information is difficult or impossible to obtain without a scanner. Using a scanner saves diagnosis time and can avoid the unnecessary replacement of good parts when other testing methods are used. The scanner is not able to pinpoint the exact location of a problem in a circuit but is able to identify the problem circuit. Pinpoint tests with a digital voltmeter or ohmmeter are performed to isolate the problem within the circuit. Substituting suspected components with known good components is another method of pinpointing faulty components.

A scanner can be used to detect intermittent problems related to the wiring harness and wiring connectors. The scanner is plugged into the diagnostic connector with the engine not running. The wiring harness, connectors, and terminals can then be manipulated and wiggled while observing the scanner display. Faulty wires and connectors can be detected in this way.

The scanner can also be used to check operation while the vehicle is being driven under conditions that caused the check engine light to turn on, indicating a problem. The scanner should be observed in each test position while driving the vehicle. Modern scan tools allow the technician to perform a number of pinpoint checks and tests under actual operating conditions. Refer to the wiring diagrams in the service manual to locate wiring connectors and circuits and the test procedures in each case. Each test is independent of the others. Test sequences within each test can identify a condition or a problem without requiring the completion of the entire test procedure. The test strategy usually involves the following steps.

1. Check the voltage or resistance value.
2. Change the input signal.
3. Perform a click test.
4. Perform a wiggle test.
5. Perform a coil resistance test.
6. Perform an output signal test.
7. Check for harness shorts.
8. Check for harness opens.

ROAD TESTING—SHIFT ANALYSIS

A road test is performed to obtain the following information about transmission/transaxle operation: what is normal and what is abnormal about transmission/transaxle operation.

PRO TIPS

Fluid level, engine oil level, and coolant level should be corrected before road testing. The engine and transmission must be at operating temperature for a road test to be valid.

Traffic conditions and consideration for others on the road are prime safety considerations during road-testing procedures. Unexpected maneuvers can cause accidents. Select a section of road where speed limits and traffic conditions will allow safe road testing.

Look for the following points during a road test:

1. *Proper engagement as the selector lever is moved to each gear position including Park.* Things to look for are delayed or harsh engagement.

2. *Proper transmission operation in all forward ranges.* This includes:

    a. The 1–2, 2–3, 3–4 upshifts and converter lockup during light throttle operation. Shifts should be smooth, yet noticeable, with no engine flare-up or run-up during shifts. Upshifts should occur at proper speeds.

    b. The same shifts during medium and heavy throttle operation. Shifts should be firmer and have a more positive feel with no engine flare-up or run-up during upshifts. Compare to specifications.

3. *To detent (part-throttle or torque demand) downshift operation.* Downshifts and downshift pattern should correspond to those given for the particular vehicle make, model, engine, and differential ratio combination. Tire size will also have a bearing on shift speed patterns.

4. *Through detent (WOT downshift or kickdown) operation.* Compare to specifications.

5. *Coasting downshift (closed-throttle downshift) operation.* Brakes can be used to retard the vehicle for this check. Note downshift speed and quality and compare with specifications.

6. *Noisy operation.* Note any abnormal noise (this may require a window to be open), and note the gear position in which noise occurs. If disassembly is required later, this will help pinpoint the problem if you know the powerflow patterns.

7. *Manually selected downshifts.* While driving in third or fourth gear at approximately 35 mph (56 km/h), manual selection of second- or first-gear position can help determine band (or clutch) operation, both apply and release.

Some typical conclusions that can be drawn from abnormal operation during a road test include the following:

1. Clutch slippage, causing delayed engagement in all forward gears, poor acceleration

2. Slippage, causing delayed engagement in Reverse, delayed 2–3 and 3–4 upshift, engine speedup (Neutral feel) during 2–3 upshift, and poor acceleration in third, direct, or overdrive

3. Intermediate band or clutch slippage, causing delayed 1–2 upshift, engine speedup (Neutral feel) during 1–2 upshift, and poor acceleration in second gear

4. Leaking vacuum modulator or vacuum supply line, causing delayed or no upshift

5. Governor sticking, possibly causing delayed or no upshift or early upshift regardless of throttle opening

6. Worn hydraulic pump, causing delayed engagement and slippage in all gear positions if severe wear present.

7. Stator one-way clutch not holding, causing very poor low-speed acceleration.

For more detailed and more specific problems, refer to the diagnostic charts and procedures in the appropriate service manual.

STALL TESTING

PRO TIP

Perform a stall test only on vehicles when the manufacturer recommends a stall test. Follow all safety precautions required during a stall test.

Since a stall test is performed at wide-open throttle, the following procedure and safety precautions should be rigidly observed during a stall test **(Figures 8–16** and **8–17).**

1. Connect the tachometer to the engine. You must know your powerflow for this test to be meaningful. This will tell you which clutch, band, or servo is being tested in each case.

2. The engine cooling system should be in good condition and all fluid levels correct.

3. The engine and transmission/transaxle should be at normal operating temperature. This requires approximately 15 minutes of operation.

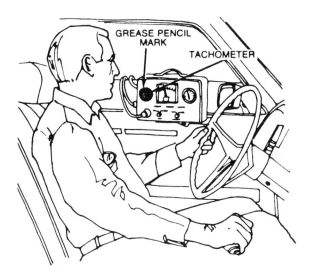

FIGURE 8–16 Stall testing transmission. (Courtesy of Ford Motor Company of Canada Ltd.)

4. Block vehicle wheels for safety front and back.

5. Parking brake and service brakes must be fully applied during the stall test.

6. No one should be in front of the vehicle or behind the vehicle during stall tests.

7. Never hold the throttle at the wide-open position for more than 5 seconds at a time.

8. After each 5-second test, place the selector lever in Neutral and run the engine at 1000 to 1500 rpm for at least 15 seconds to cool the converter before making the next test.

9. If specified engine speed is exceeded during any specific test, release the accelerator pedal immediately since clutch or band slippage is indicated. Continued testing in this position would result in further internal damage.

10. Place the selector lever in each specified position in turn and make the test. Record engine rpm in each case.

All stall test results should be compared with those given in the appropriate service repair manual. Some variation in readings should be allowed for possible reduced engine power output and for higher altitudes.

1. *Stall speed above normal:* clutch or band slippage

2. *Stall speed slightly below normal:* engine power output below normal; engine requires tuneup or mechanical repair

Stall speeds in "D" and "R" range are equal to each other but lower than the nominal value.	1. Engine output is low 2. Stator one-way clutch is faulty (Faulty torque converter is suspected if it is lower than nominal by more than 600 rpm)
Stall speed in "D" range is higher than nominal.	1. OD clutch slipping 2. OD one-way clutch faulty 3. Forward clutch slipping 4. One-way clutch No. 2 faulty 5. Low line pressure
Stall speed in "R" range is higher than nominal.	1. OD clutch slipping 2. OD one-way clutch faulty 3. Direct clutch slipping 4. Brake No. 3 slipping 5. Low line pressure

FIGURE 8–17 Typical stall test interpretation. (Courtesy of Chrysler Corporation.)

3. *Stall speed well below (about two-thirds) normal:* stator one-way clutch in converter not holding

HYDRAULIC PRESSURE TESTS

Although road testing provides the means to identify which area in the transmission is causing a problem, hydraulic pressure testing may be required to verify the diagnosis and isolate the problem further **(Figures 8–18 to 8–22).**

The number of hydraulic circuits that can be tested varies among different makes and models of transmissions and transaxles. Generally, all can be

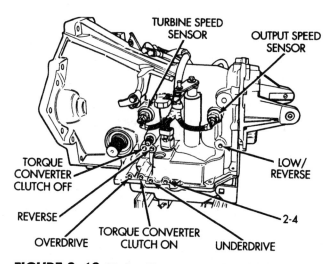

FIGURE 8–18 Hydraulic pressure test port locations on Chrysler 42LE transaxle. (Courtesy of Chrysler Corporation.)

tested for proper line (or control) pressures, including proper line pressure increase and decrease in the various modes of operation. From this it can easily be seen that pressure testing may be required to solve a shift timing or shift quality problem since pressure changes affect both.

Pressure testing will indicate whether the following systems are operating properly:

1. *Pressure supply system:* pump and pressure regulator valve

2. *Throttle pressure system:* throttle valve and vacuum modulator system (if so equipped)

3. *Governor pressure system:* governor valve, weights, and springs

The following equipment is required to perform a hydraulic pressure test:

1. A tachometer (capable of being read from the driver's position).

2. One or two hydraulic pressure gauges (depending on the transmission being tested) with fittings and hoses long enough to hang gauges inside the vehicle for the driver to observe. Gauges should be capable of at least 400 psi (2800 kPa).

3. A vacuum gauge (for those transmissions/ transaxles equipped with a vacuum modulator) with a long hose capable of reaching the driver's position for easy reading.

4. A vacuum supply pump, possibly needed to provide adequate vacuum in some cases to verify accurately and distinguish between transmission-caused problems and engine-caused transmission/transaxle problems.

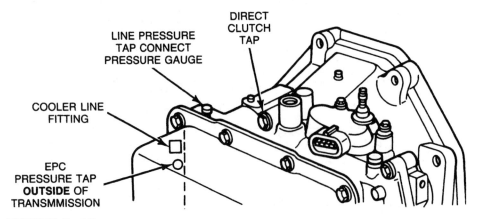

FIGURE 8–19 Pressure tap locations on AXOD-E transaxle. (Courtesy of Ford Motor Company.)

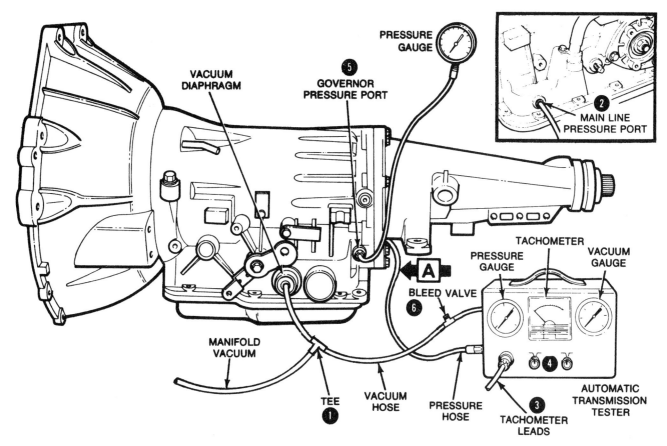

FIGURE 8–20 Typical pressure testing hookup. (Courtesy of Ford Motor Company.)

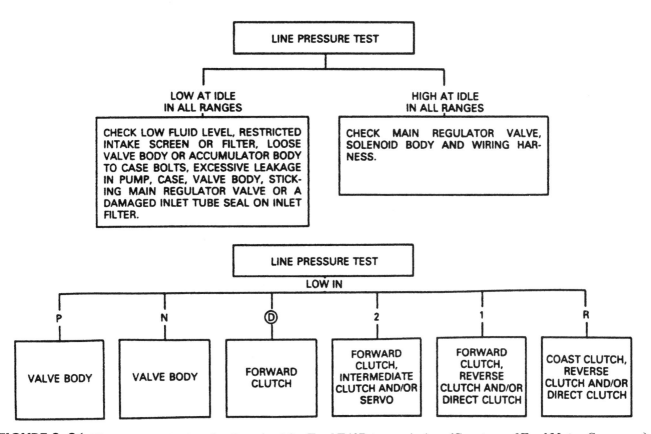

FIGURE 8–21 Line pressure test evaluation chart for Ford E40D transmission. (Courtesy of Ford Motor Company.)

ALL PRESSURE SPECIFICATIONS ARE PSI

(on hoist, with front wheels free to turn)

Gear Selector Position	Actual Gear	PRESSURE TAPS					
		Under-Drive Clutch	Over-Drive Clutch	Reverse Clutch	Torque Converter Clutch Off	2/4 Clutch	Low/Reverse Clutch
PARK * 0 mph	PARK	0-2	0-5	0-2	60-110	0-2	115-145
REVERSE * 0 mph	REVERSE	0-2	0-7	165-235	50-100	0-2	165-235
NEUTRAL * 0 mph	NEUTRAL	0-2	0-5	0-2	60-110	0-2	115-145
L # 20 mph	FIRST	110-145	0-5	0-2	60-110	0-2	115-145
3 # 30 mph	SECOND	110-145	0-5	0-2	60-110	115-145	0-2
3 # 45 mph	DIRECT	75-95	75-95	0-2	60-90	0-2	0-2
OD # 30 mph	OVERDRIVE	0-2	75-95	0-2	60-90	75-95	0-2
OD # 50 mph	OVERDRIVE WITH TCC	0-2	75-95	0-2	0-5	75-95	0-2

*Engine speed at 1500 rpm
#CAUTION: Both front wheels must be turning at same speed.

FIGURE 8–22 Pressure test specifications for Chrysler 42LE transaxle. (Courtesy of Chrysler Corporation.)

The tap plug is removed and the pressure gauge fitting screwed into the threaded opening. Make sure that you have the correct fitting with the correct size and type of thread. The fitting should screw easily into the hole by hand at least several turns; then tighten it with a wrench.

The vacuum gauge is connected to the vacuum line at the modulator with a T-fitting. The vacuum gauge is necessary to determine whether specified hydraulic pressures are achieved at specified vacuum values.

All pressure test results, both vacuum and hydraulic, should be recorded in order to be valid and for accurate comparison and analysis with the manufacturer's specifications. Use the appropriate chart from the service manual for comparison analysis.

BAND ADJUSTMENT

Band adjustment may be required on transmissions or transaxles with bands. The clearance between the band and drum must be precise. Too little clearance causes drag, friction, and overheating. Too much clearance may cause band slippage or harsh engagement. The adjustment procedure usually involves loosening the adjuster locknut, turning the adjusting screw to

specified torque, and then backing off the adjustment the specified number of turns and tightening the locknut **(Figure 8–23)**. Most late-model transmissions and transaxles are not provided with any band adjustment.

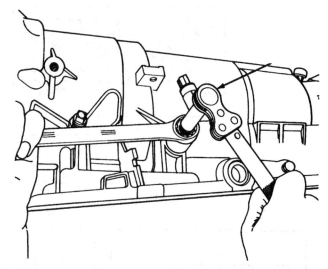

FIGURE 8–23 Band adjustment requires holding the locknut with a wrench while tightening the adjusting screw to specified torque. (Courtesy of Ford Motor Company.)

When a band problem develops, internal repairs are needed.

AIR PRESSURE TESTS

Air pressure tests may be used to aid in problem diagnosis. On many transmissions and transaxles, air pressure tests are used to check the operation of clutches, servos, bands, and other components while on the bench after overhaul. After the oil pan and valve body have been removed, air is applied to specified passages in the transmission or transaxle to check the apply and release of clutches and bands, to check for leaks or blockage, and to check the operation of accumulators and valves in some cases **(Figure 8–24)**.

To perform a pressure test requires a rubber-tipped air nozzle and air pressure regulated at about 35 psi (240 kPa). The service manual specifies the passages to which air pressure should be applied. A dull thud should be heard when a clutch or servo is applied by air pressure. When air pressure is removed, the unit should release. No sound when the passage is pressurized indicates a blocked passage. A hissing sound in the clutch or servo indicates leakage.

ELECTRICAL AND ELECTRONIC CONTROL SYSTEM TESTING

Electronic transmission and transaxle control systems are described in Chapter 7. Review this information as needed to become more familiar with the various inputs and outputs of these systems. A block diagram of one such system is shown in **Figure 8–25.**

After the usual preliminary checks and the self-diagnostics test are performed, a transmission tester or scan tool is used to allow the technician to operate the transmission/transaxle portion of the electrical control system separately from the other vehicle electronics. This determines whether there is a problem in the transmission/transaxle electrical/electronic components. One such tester is shown in **Figures 8–26** and **8–27.** Several different harness adapters are used to connect the tester to the various models. Tester face overlays are changed to adapt the tester to different models of transmissions/transaxles. Abbreviations used in these illustrations and in the tester instructions that follow are shown in **Figure 8–28.** The following description of test procedures and tester use are provided through the courtesy of the Ford Motor Company.

Using the Transmission Tester

The transmission tester allows a technician to operate the electrical portion of the transmission independent of the vehicle electronics. The transmission tester usage is divided into five steps:

1. Preliminary testing and diagnosis
2. Installing the transmission tester
3. Static testing—Vehicle OFF
4. Dynamic testing—Vehicle running (ON)
5. Removing the transmission tester and clearing fault codes

Preliminary Testing and Diagnosis. Before any diagnostic testing is done on a vehicle, some preliminary checks must be performed, as follows. Be sure to write down your findings, especially any fault codes found, for future reference.

1. Check transmission fluid level and condition.
2. Check for add-on items (phones, computers, CB radio, etc.)
3. Visually inspect wiring harness and connectors.
4. Check for vehicle modifications.
5. Verify that the shift linkage is properly adjusted.
6. Verify customer concern.
   a. Upshift
   b. Downshift

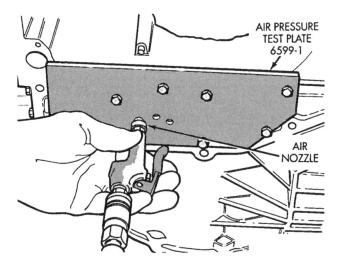

FIGURE 8–24 Using air pressure to check underdrive clutch operation in a Chrysler 42LE transaxle. (Courtesy of Chrysler Corporation.)

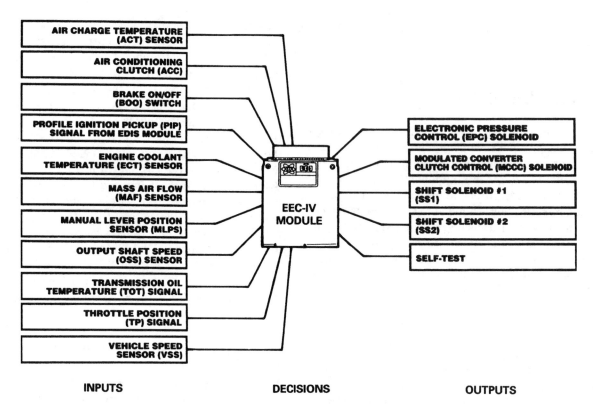

INPUTS   DECISIONS   OUTPUTS

FIGURE 8–25 Inputs and outputs of AOD-E transmission electronic control system. (Courtesy of Ford Motor Company.)

c. Coasting

d. Engagement

e. Noise/vibration

7. Vehicle must be at a normal operating temperature.

8. Perform vehicle EEC-IV self-test.

9. Record all fault codes.

10. Repair all nontransmission codes.

Installing the Transmission Tester (Setup Procedures). Installing the transmission tester *at the transmission connector* allows the separation of the vehicle electronics from the transmission electronics. Disconnecting the normal vehicle electronics will in itself set additional codes and cause firm shifts. Disconnecting the transmission connector defaults the transmission to its maximum line pressure.

NOTE: During tester usage, additional fault codes may be set. Therefore, it is important that all codes are erased after repairs have been made. To verify elimination of all codes, rerun self-test.

1. Disconnect the vehicle harness at the transmission connector.

CAUTION: Do not attempt to pry off connectors with a screwdriver. This will damage the connector and could result in a transmission concern. If you have transmission heat shields, remove them first. Always replace heat shields after service.

2. Turn the tester solenoid select switch to the "OHMS/DIODE CHECK" position.

3. Install the appropriate overlay onto the tester. Connect the appropriate interface cable to the transmission tester and then to the appropriate transmission connectors.

CAUTION: Route all cables away from HEAT SOURCES.

4. Install the line pressure gauge into the line pressure tap on transmission. Refer to the ap-

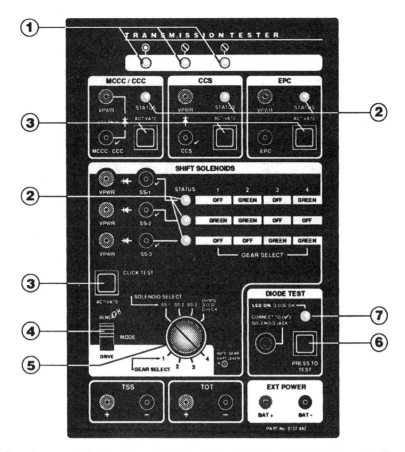

1. **Overlay and Cable Correctly Installed LEDs:** Only LEDs with ◎ symbol and cable correctly match.

2. **Status LEDs:** LED **"OFF"** when not activated by tester (solenoid not activated, open circuit or signal line short to ground).
   LED **"GREEN"** when activated by tester and current draw is correct.
   LED **"RED"** when activated by tester and current draw is excessive (short to VPWR).
   All LEDs light orange during self-test.

3. **Solenoid Activate Buttons:** Energize respective solenoids during click testing and activate selected circuits during DRIVE MODE testing.

4. **Tester Mode Switch:** Selects operating mode, either BENCH or DRIVE.

5. **Solenoid Select/Gear Select Knob:** Has three functions.
   In BENCH MODE: acts as shift solenoid selector for click testing.
   In DRIVE MODE: acts as forward gear selector in place of vehicle's processor-controlled shifting. Hydraulic safety mechanisms and overrides are built into the transmission.
   In OHMS/DIODE check: allows you to measure ohms and check for presence of a diode on specific solenoids.

6. **Diode Test Button:** Activates DIODE TEST circuit.

7. **Diode OK LED:** With DIODE TEST BUTTON depressed, indicates condition of diode. (LED on: diode OK.)

FIGURE 8–26 Transmission tester controls. (Courtesy of Ford Motor Company.)

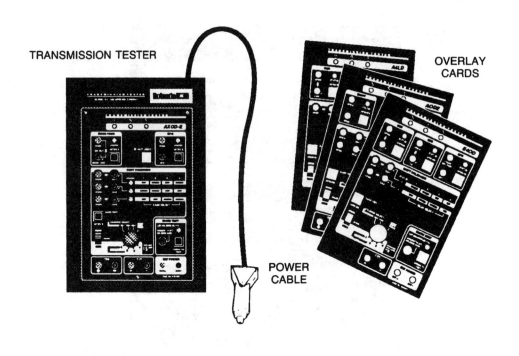

TRANSMISSION TESTER

OVERLAY CARDS

POWER CABLE

A4LD ADAPTER CABLE

AODE ADAPTER CABLE

AXODE ADAPTER CABLE

E4OD ADAPTER CABLE

EXTENDER CABLE

FIGURE 8–27 Tester overlays and adapter cables. (Courtesy of Ford Motor Company.)

ACC	Air Conditioning Clutch		**OWC**	One-Way Clutch
ACT	Air Charge Temperature		**PIP**	Profile Ignition Pickup
BAT	Battery		**PSPS**	Power Steering Pressure Switch
BOO	Brake On/Off		**ROM**	Read Only Memory
CCC	Converter Clutch Control		**SS1**	Shift Solenoid 1
CONT	Continuous Codes		**SS2**	Shift Solenoid 2
DVOM	Digital Volt-Ohm Multimeter		**SS3**	Shift Solenoid 3
ECA	Electronic Control Assembly		**ST**	Self-Test
ECT	Engine Coolant Temperature		**STI**	Self-Test Input
EEC	Electronic Engine Control		**STO**	Self-Test Output
EPC	Electronic Pressure Control		**TOT**	Transmission Oil Temperature
FMEM	Failure Mode Effects Management		**TPS**	Throttle Position Sensor
KAM	Keep Alive Memory		**TSS**	Turbine Speed Sensor
KOEO	Key On Engine Off		**VFS**	Variable Force Solenoid
KOER	Key On Engine Running		**VPWR**	Vehicle Power
MAF	Mass Air Flow Sensor		**VSS**	Vehicle Speed Sensor
MCCC	Modulated Converter Clutch Control		**WOT**	Wide-Open Throttle
MLPS	Manual Lever Position Sensor			

FIGURE 8–28 Transmission/transaxle abbreviations for Ford EEC-IV system. (Courtesy of Ford Motor Company.)

propriate year service manual for tap locations.

> **CAUTION:** Route all gauge lines away from heat sources.

5. Plug the transmission tester power supply plug into the cigarette lighter receptacle. At this time, all LEDs should illuminate for a short period and then turn off. This is the tester internal circuit check.

6. Set the Bench/Drive switch to "BENCH" mode.

Static Testing—Vehicle "Off". Static testing procedures allow for shop testing of the transmission in the vehicle or on the bench. Completion of these tests prove out the transmission electronically.

> **CAUTION:** For resistance checks, be sure that the tester solenoid select switch is set to the "OHMS/DIODE CHECK" position or damage to the ohmmeter may result.

Resistance/Continuity Tests

1. Refer to the appropriate year service manual or transmission reference manual for the proper pinpoint test to be performed based on the self-test fault codes displayed.

2. Using a digital volt-ohmmeter and the transmission tester, perform the pinpoint tests as indicated in the service manual or transmission reference manual based on the self-test fault codes which were displayed.

3. Perform repairs as indicated by the pinpoint tests. Always retest and road test the vehicle after a repair.

Transmission Solenoids and Sensors Resistance Tests

EPC SOLENOID

1. Set the ohmmeter to the 100–200 ohm range.

2. Connect the positive lead of the ohmmeter to the VPWR jack.

3. Connect the negative lead of the ohmmeter to the EPC jack.

4. Record resistance.

5. Refer to the service manual for values and transmission applications. If out of range, refer to pinpoint test E in the service manual or transmission reference manual.

TRANSMISSION OIL TEMPERATURE (TOT) SENSOR

1. Set the ohmmeter to 1000 ohms (K).

2. Connect the ohmmeter positive (+) lead to +TOT jack.

3. Connect the ohmmeter negative (−) lead to −TOT jack.

4. Record resistance. Resistance will vary with temperature.

5. If out of range, refer to pinpoint test B in the appropriate service manual or transmission reference manual.

TURBINE SHAFT SPEED SENSOR (TSS)—AXODE

1. Set the ohmmeter to 1000 ohm (K) range.

2. Connect the positive lead of the ohmmeter to the +TSS jack.

3. Connect the negative lead of the ohmmeter to the −TSS jack.

4. TSS should be 100–200 ohms.

Temperature °F	Resistance Ohms (K)
32–68	100–37
69–104	37–16
105–158	16–5
159–194	5–2.7
195–230	2.7–1.5
231–266	1.5–0.8

Solenoid	Transmission Application AXODE Solenoid Resistance (ohms)
S1	15–25
S2	15–25
S3	15–25
CCC	21–36
MCCC	.98–1.6
EPC	3.23–5.5

5. Record the resistance.

6. If out of range, refer to pinpoint test F in the service manual or transmission reference manual.

SOLENOIDS (SS1, SS2, SS3, MCCC/CCC)

1. Set the ohmmeter to the 100–200 ohm range.

2. Connect the positive lead of the ohmmeter to the appropriate VPWR jack for the solenoid being tested.

3. Connect the negative lead of the ohmmeter to the appropriate solenoid (SS1, SS2, SS3, MCCC/CCC) jack.

4. Record resistance.

5. Refer to the service manual for values and transmission applications. If out of range, refer to the following pinpoint tests in the service manual or transmission reference manual: pinpoint test A (SS1, SS2, SS3); pinpoint test C (MCCC/CCC)

Dynamic Testing—Vehicle "On". Dynamic testing is the final step in the transmission tester usage. It allows the transmission to be proven out electronically and hydraulically.

Following are the transmission solenoid cycling and drive test procedures:

PRELIMINARY SETUP

1. Bench/Drive switch set to Drive mode.

2. Rotate gear select switch to 1st gear position.

3. Vehicle in Park.

4. Start vehicle.

EPC SOLENOID

> **CAUTION:** Do not attempt to hold the EPC switch depressed (minimum line pressure) and stall the transmission (holding the vehicle with the brake while depressing the throttle with the transmission in gear); transmission damage will result.

5. Observe line pressure. Record the value. Line pressure should go to maximum. If not, refer to the Condition/Cause chart in the service manual for diagnostic tips or the reference manual for pinpoint test E concerning EPC solenoid.

6. Depress the EPC switch. Line pressure should drop to a minimum value. Record the value. If not, refer to the Condition/Cause chart in the service manual for diagnostic tips or the reference manual for pinpoint test E concerning EPC solenoids.

ENGAGEMENTS

7. Verify that the Bench/Drive switch is in the Drive mode and gear select switch to 1st gear position.

8. Depress the EPC switch. Line pressure should drop to idle pressure. While holding the EPC switch down, shift vehicle from Park to Reverse.

Does vehicle shift into Reverse?

Shift vehicle from Reverse to Drive.

Does vehicle shift into Drive?

Release the EPC switch; pressure should return to maximum. Repeat engagements. With the EPC switch release, engagements should be firm.

UPSHIFT/DOWNSHIFT

> **NOTE:** Upshifts and downshifts will be FIRM during this procedure.

> **NOTE:** Pressure gauges may be removed from the vehicle during these tests.

> **NOTE:** These tests should be performed on the road. If performed on the hoist, the technician may not feel all of the shifts when they are engaged.

LEDs will turn GREEN when solenoids are activated and turn OFF when deactivated. Refer to the appropriate overlay for the proper status/shift sequence of the shift solenoids during upshifts and downshifts.

9. Move the shift lever into Overdrive and accelerate to 15 mph; select 2nd gear by rotating the gear selector to 2nd.

Did the vehicle shift into 2nd gear?

Did the appropriate shift solenoids activate/deactivate?

10. Accelerate to 25 mph and select 3rd gear.

Did the vehicle shift into 3rd gear?

Did the appropriate shift solenoids activate/deactivate?

11. Accelerate to 35/45 mph and select 4th gear.

Did the vehicle upshift to 4th gear?

Did the appropriate shift solenoids activate/deactivate?

12. Reverse the order to downshift.

Does the vehicle downshift from 4 to 3, 3 to 2, and 2 to 1?

Did the appropriate shift solenoids activate/deactivate?

Another type of tester is shown in **Figure 8–29.** Tester manufacturer and vehicle manufacturer instructions must be followed for tests to be valid.

TESTING SHIFT SOLENOIDS AND SPEED SENSORS

The shift solenoids can be tested with an ohmmeter. Disconnect the solenoid wiring, then connect the ohmmeter leads to the solenoid terminals **(Figures 8–30 to 8–33).** If resistance is above or below specifications, replace the solenoid. To test the speed sensor, discon-

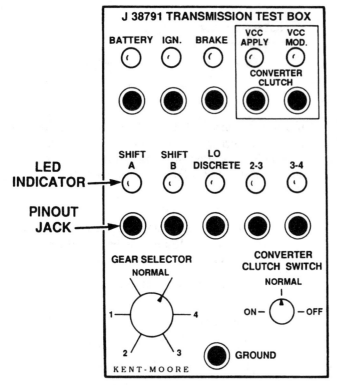
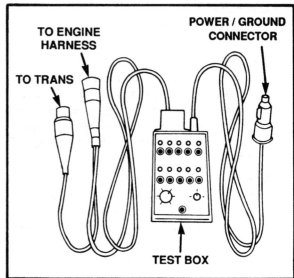

FIGURE 8–29 Transmission test box is used to isolate the cause of a problem in the ECM/PCM, wiring, or transaxle. (Courtesy of General Motors Corporation.)

nect the wiring from the sensor. Connect the voltmeter leads to the sensor terminals. Rotate the transmission output shaft and observe the readings. The voltmeter should display a reading each time a signal is generated by the sensor **(Figure 8–34).** If there is no reading, replace the sensor.

TRANSMISSION AND TRANSAXLE REMOVAL AND DISASSEMBLY

If testing procedures indicate internal problems, the transmission or transaxle may have to be removed for repairs. Some repairs are possible without removing the unit from the car. Valve bodies, governors, accumulators, and servos are accessible in some cases without removing the entire unit. Consult the service manual for specific procedures.

Removal procedures for automatic transmissions and transaxles vary considerably. A transmission jack must be used, and the engine may have to be supported with a special holding fixture. The torque converter is usually disconnected from the engine and removed with the transmission or trans-

axle. Steering linkage and exhaust pipes may have to be disconnected to provide clearance for removal. For detailed removal procedures, follow the instructions in the appropriate service manual. **Figures 8–35** to **8–39** show removal steps that are typical.

Disassembly and Assembly Guidelines

After the transmission/transaxle has been removed and the exterior cleaned and mounted on a holding fixture **(Figure 8–40),** the overhaul should proceed in an organized and systematic manner. The sequence of operations includes the following. First, all subassemblies are removed from the transmission/transaxle. This includes:

- Torque converter
- Oil pan and filter
- Valve body
- Hydraulic pump
- Clutch units, gear train, bands, and servos

Determine proper solenoid and electrical operation in the transaxle.

Before removing side cover or removing transaxle from vehicle, perform on-vehicle functional test for solenoid A, solenoid B and T.C.C. solenoid.

Solenoid A can be checked at connector terminals E and F.
Solenoid B can be checked at connector terminals E and G.
T.C.C. solenoid can be checked at connector terminals A and D.

NOT USED

TRANSAXLE CONNECTOR

USING DVM, MEASURE RESISTANCE OF TRANSAXLE SOLENOIDS A,B ANDT.C.C. BY PROBING TRANSAXLE CONNECTOR TERMINALS. "E-F", "E-G" AND "A-D" SHOULD BE 20-30 OHMS. ARE THEY?

YES

NO

4T60-E
3800 TPI (L27)
ELECTRICAL
CIRCUIT

T.C.C./V.C.C. SOLENOID

DIODE

P.W.M. SOLENOID

"B" SOLENOID

BRAKE SWITCH

12V

A RED

B WHITE

D BLACK

EZ RED

EY RED

EX RED

F BLUE

G GREEN

ECM

"A" SOLENOID

CHECK CONNECTIONS OF TRANSAXLE CONNECTOR. IF OK THEN REPAIR TRANSAXLE. (POSSIBLE STUCK SHIFT VALVE).

REPAIR TRANSAXLE INTERNAL WIRING OR REPLACE SOLENOID.

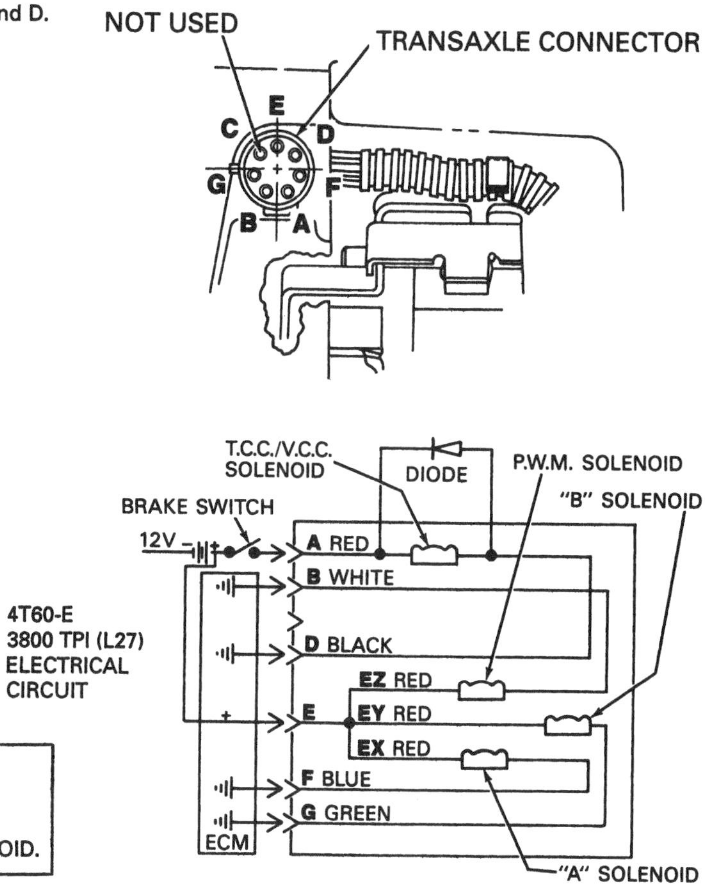

FIGURE 8–30 How to check shift solenoids and torque converter clutch solenoid on a 4T60-E transaxle. (Courtesy of General Motors Corporation.)

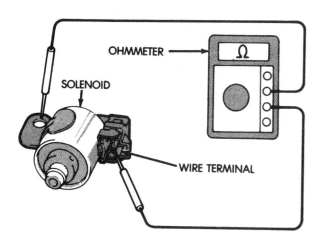

OHMMETER

Ω

SOLENOID

WIRE TERMINAL

FIGURE 8–31 Shift solenoid coil resistance can be tested with an ohmmeter. Compare the result to specifications. (Courtesy of Chrysler Corporation.)

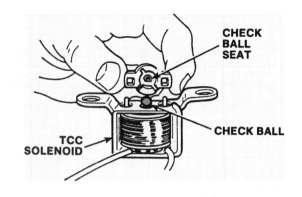

FIGURE 8–32 Converter clutch solenoid check ball and seat may require cleaning if leakage is present. (Courtesy of General Motors Corporation.)

FIGURE 8–33 AXOD-E transaxle oil temperature (TOT) sensor resistance value at different temperatures. (Courtesy of Ford Motor Company.)

TRANSAXLE FLUID TEMPERATURE

Degrees °C	Degrees °F	Resistance Ohms
0-20	32-58	107K-33.5K
21-40	59-104	33.5K-14.5K
41-70	105-158	14.5K-5.0K
71-90	159-194	5.0K-2.5K
91-110	195-230	2.5K-1.5K
111-130	231-266	1.5K-0.8K

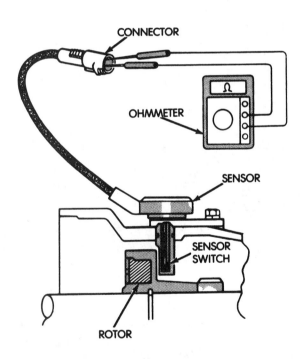

FIGURE 8–34 To test this speed sensor, connect a voltmeter to the sensor leads and turn the transmission output shaft. The needle should deflect each time the rotor passes the sensor. (Courtesy of Chrysler Corporation.)

- Extension housing
- Governor
- Output shaft

Measuring End Play

End-play measurements are taken and recorded before and during disassembly. These measurements are used to determine selection of proper thrust washer thick-ness during assembly. Thrust washer thickness determines end-play requirements. Excessive end play indicates excessive wear internally and allows clutch drums to move back and forth excessively in the case. Assembled end-play measurements should be between minimum and maximum specifications with preference being at the low end of specifications since end play will increase as the transmission is put in service. Refer to the appropriate shop manual for specifications and for information on the proper procedure for end-play measurements (**Figures 8–41** and **8–42**).

FIGURE 8–35 Transmissions and transaxles are heavy. Use the appropriate jack and secure the unit to the lift bracket on the jack. (Courtesy of OTC Division, SPX Corporation.)

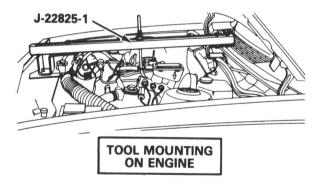

FIGURE 8–36 Engine support fixture used for transaxle removal. (Courtesy of General Motors Corporation.)

Correcting End Play

The following procedure is typical for correcting shaft or gear train end play. For example, if end play is 0.140 in. (3.55 mm), required end play is 0.062 to 0.125 in. (1.57 to 3.17 mm), and present thrust washer measures

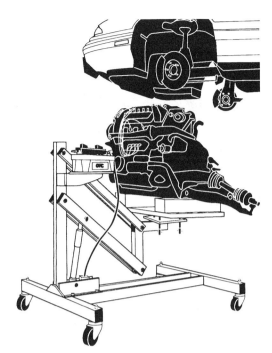

FIGURE 8–37 The engine and transaxle are removed together on some models for transaxle overhaul. On others, the transaxle is disconnected from the engine and removed. In both cases, a suitable jack such as the one shown is used. (Courtesy of OTC Division, SPX Corporation.)

0.125 in. (3.17 mm). To reduce end play to within specifications obviously requires a thicker thrust washer. This can be calculated as follows:

$$0.140 - 0.125 = 0.015$$
$$0.140 - 0.062 = 0.078$$

Therefore, a thrust washer that is 0.015 to 0.078 in. thicker must be used. Since the old thrust washer measures 0.125 in., simply add to that figure as follows:

$$0.125 + 0.015 = 0.140 \text{ in.}$$
$$0.125 + 0.078 = 0.203 \text{ in.}$$

To bring end play within specifications therefore requires a thrust washer between 0.140 and 0.203 in. thick.

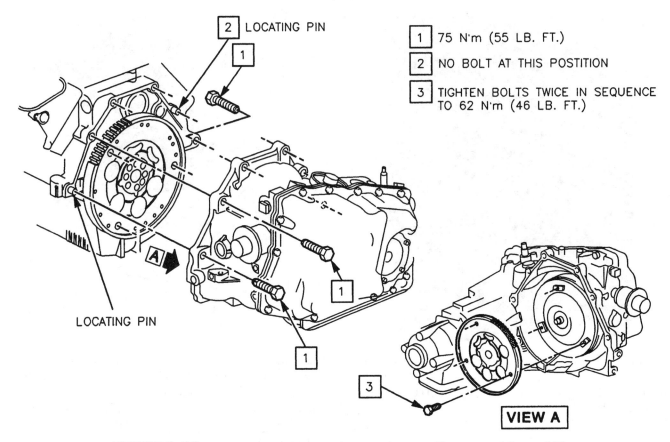

1	75 N·m (55 LB. FT.)
2	NO BOLT AT THIS POSTITION
3	TIGHTEN BOLTS TWICE IN SEQUENCE TO 62 N·m (46 LB. FT.)

FIGURE 8–38 Typical transaxle to engine attachment. (Courtesy of General Motors Corporation.)

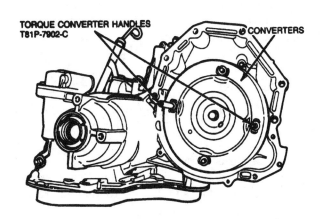

FIGURE 8–39 Using torque converter handles makes removal of a heavy converter easier and safer. (Courtesy of Ford Motor Company.)

Checking Transaxle Drive Chain Wear

On transaxles with a drive chain linking the converter to the transaxle, check the drive chain wear. The usual procedure is to deflect the chain inward on one side until tight, and scribe mark the housing at the point of maximum deflection in line with the outside edge of the chain as follows:

1. Deflect the drive chain inward on one side until stretched tight **(Figure 8–43).**

2. Holding the chain in this position, scribe mark the housing in line with the outside edge of the chain at the point of maximum deflection.

3. Deflect the chain outward on the same side until stretched tight.

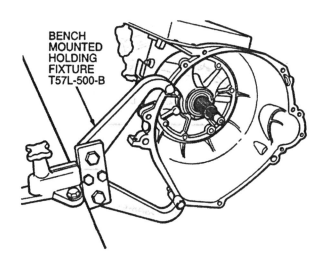

FIGURE 8–40 Transmission (top) and transaxle (bottom) bench-mounted holding fixtures allow unit to be rotated to aid in disassembly/assembly. (Top— Courtesy of Ford Motor Company. Bottom—Courtesy of General Motors Corporation.)

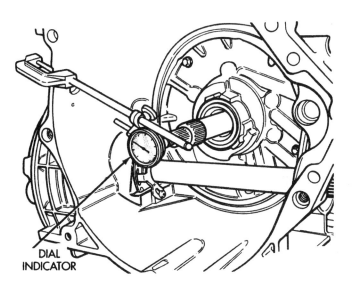

FIGURE 8–41 Measuring input shaft end play. Other end-play measurements may be required during disassembly. (Courtesy of Chrysler Corporation.)

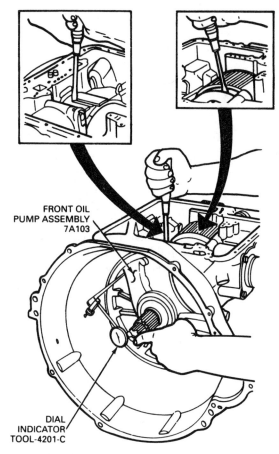

FIGURE 8–42 Measuring gear train end play on a C6 transmission. (Courtesy of Ford Motor Company.)

4. Holding the chain in this position, scribe mark the housing in line with the outside edge of the chain at the point of maximum deflection.

5. Measure the distance between the two scribe marks. If this dimension exceeds specifications, replace the drive chain.

See **Figures 8–44** to **8–53** for examples of disassembly procedures.

CLEANING, INSPECTION, AND ASSEMBLY GUIDELINES

1. Follow the disassembly sequence and procedure given in the appropriate service repair manual.

2. Remove all old gasket material from metal surfaces with a suitable scraper. Avoid scoring or gouging the metal since this can cause fluid leakage. A spray-on gasket remover helps loosen gasket material.

3. Replace all old gaskets and seals with those supplied in the gasket and seal kit.

4. Replace oil transfer rings and metal seal rings if worn. Overhaul kits usually contain all gaskets, seals, oil transfer rings, check balls, and in some cases servo pistons.

5. Use only filtered, moisture-free compressed air regulated at 35 psi (242 kPa) maximum for cleaning passages, and so on.

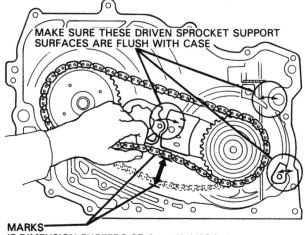

FIGURE 8–43 Torque converter link inspection. (Courtesy of General Motors Corporation.)

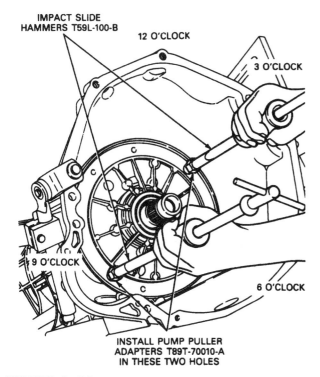

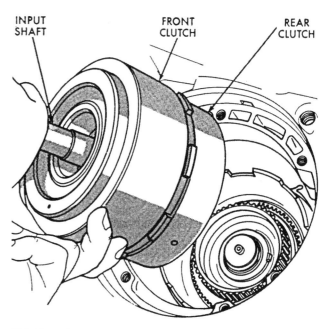

FIGURE 8–45 (b) Removing front and rear clutch assemblies from 32RH transmission. (Courtesy of Chrysler Corporation.)

FIGURE 8–44 Using slide hammer pullers to remove the transmission oil pump. (Courtesy of Ford Motor Company.)

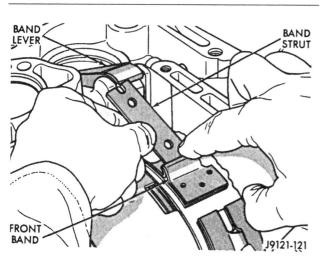

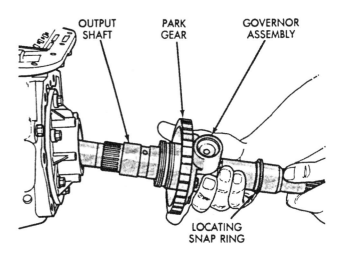

FIGURE 8–45 (c) Removing/installing the output shaft assembly in a 36RH or 37RH transmission. (Courtesy of Chrysler Corporation.)

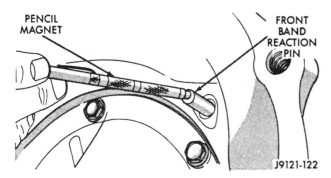

FIGURE 8–45 (a) Removing the front band strut and reaction pin on a 32RH Chrysler transmission. (Courtesy of Chrysler Corporation.)

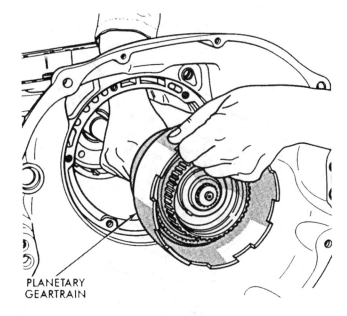

FIGURE 8–46 Removing/installing the planetary gear train on a 32RH transmission. (Courtesy of Chrysler Corporation.)

PLANETARY
GEARTRAIN

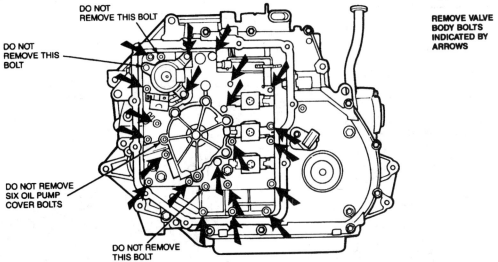

DO NOT
REMOVE THIS BOLT

DO NOT
REMOVE THIS
BOLT

REMOVE VALVE
BODY BOLTS
INDICATED BY
ARROWS

DO NOT REMOVE
SIX OIL PUMP
COVER BOLTS

DO NOT REMOVE
THIS BOLT

FIGURE 8–47 AXOD-E transaxle valve body removal. (Courtesy of Ford Motor Company.)

FIGURE 8–48 It is a good practice to tag accumulator springs for proper location during later assembly. (Courtesy of Ford Motor Company.)

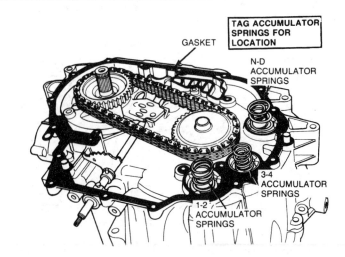

TAG ACCUMULATOR
SPRINGS FOR
LOCATION

GASKET

N-D
ACCUMULATOR
SPRINGS

3-4
ACCUMULATOR
SPRINGS

1-2
ACCUMULATOR
SPRINGS

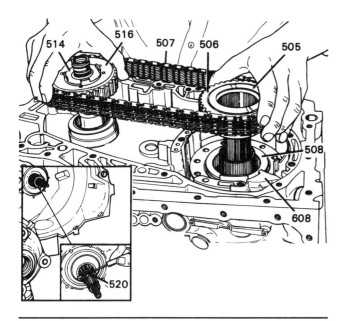

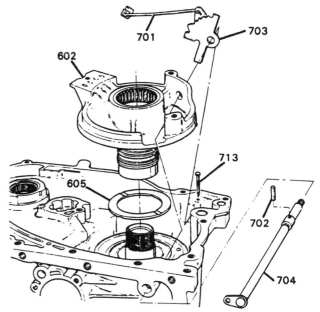

602 SUPPORT, DRIVEN SPROCKET
605 WASHER, THRUST — DRIVEN SPROCKET
     SUPPORT TO DIRECT CLUTCH HOUSING
701 ROD & RETAINER ASSEMBLY
702 PIN/DETENT LEVER TO SHAFT
703 LEVER & HUB ASSEMBLY, MANUAL DETENT
704 SHAFT, MANUAL
713 PIN, MANUAL SHAFT/CASE RETAINING

FIGURE 8–50 Driven sprocket support and manual linkage removal/installation, 3T40 transaxle. (Courtesy of General Motors Corporation.)

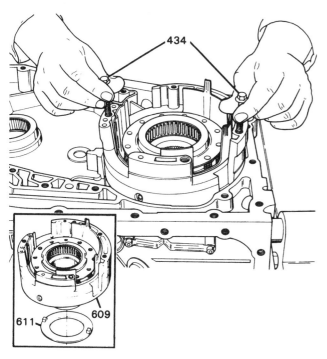

434 BOLT, M8 X 1.25 X 45.0 LG (CHANNEL PLATE/CASE)
505 WASHER, THRUST (4TH CLUTCH HUB/
     DRIVEN SPROCKET)
506 SPROCKET, DRIVEN
507 LINK ASSEMBLY, DRIVE
508 WASHER, THRUST (DRIVEN & 2ND CLUTCH DRUM)
514 WASHER, THRUST (DRIVE SPROCKET/CHANNEL PLATE)
516 SPROCKET, DRIVE
520 SEAL, O-RING (TURBINE SHAFT/HUB) GREEN
608 SCOOP, CHAIN SCAVENGING
609 SUPPORT, DRIVEN SPROCKET
611 WASHER, THRUST (DRIVEN SPROCKET SUPPORT/
     2ND CLUTCH DRUM)

FIGURE 8–49 Removing sprockets, drive link assembly, and driven sprocket support from a 4T60-E transaxle. (Courtesy of General Motors Corporation.)

6. Do not use solvents, detergents, or vapor degreasers on composition clutch plates, bands, synthetic seals, and check balls.

7. Use only lint-free cloth for any wiping of parts. Lint can cause valves to stick and oil to leak.

8. Do not overexpand snap rings. Damaged snap rings must be replaced.

9. Do not overstretch seals and seal rings. Fluid leaks and malfunction are caused by stretched and distorted seals and seal rings.

10. Ends of angle-cut seal rings must be installed with angled cuts facing each other **(Figure 8–54).**

Following are the guidelines for cleaning, inspecting, and assembling transaxles and transmissions:

11. Hooked cast-iron seal rings must be properly hooked and flush with no step in hooked ends when installed **(Figure 8–54).**

12. Use only the recommended type of fluid for lubrication during assembly. In some cases a lu-

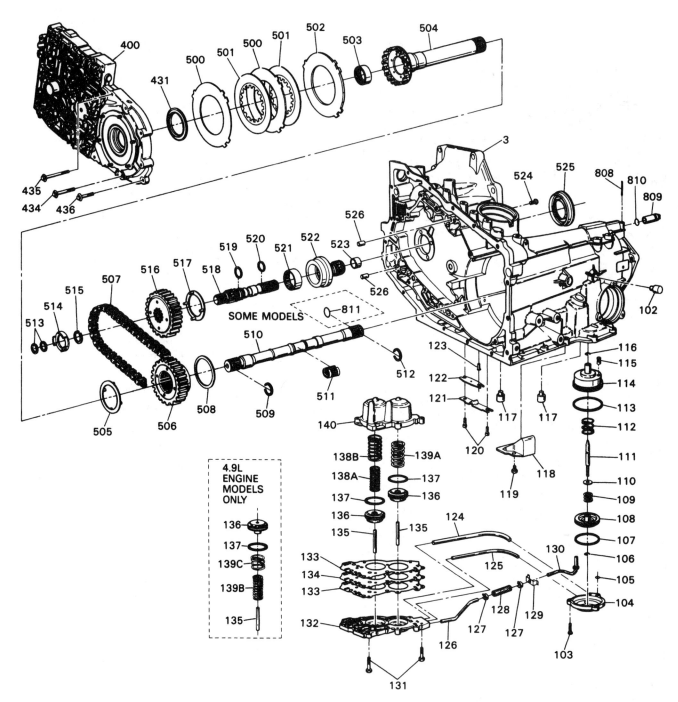

FIGURE 8–51 Drive link, 4th clutch, accumulators and case seals, 4T60-E transaxle. (Courtesy of General Motors Corporation.)

3	CASE, TRANSMISSION
102	PIN, BAND ANCHOR (2-1 MANUAL)
103	BOLT, 2-1 MANUAL SERVO COVER
104	COVER, 2-1 MANUAL SERVO BODY
105	SEAL, SQUARE CUT (2-1 SERVO)
106	CLIP, RETAINING (BOTTOM)
107	SEAL, LIP
108	PISTON, 2-1 MANUAL SERVO
109	SPRING, 2-1 MANUAL SERVO CUSHION
110	RETAINER, INT. SERVO SPRING MANUAL CUSHION
111	PIN, 2-1 MANUAL APPLY
112	SPRING, 2-1 MANUAL SERVO RETURN
113	SEAL, O-RING
114	BODY, 2-1 MANUAL SERVO
115	FILTER, 2-1 SERVO
116	CLIP, RETAINING (TOP)
117	PIN, BAND ANCHOR FORWARD AND REVERSE
118	SCAVENGER, OIL SCOOP (BOTTOM PAN)
119	BOLT, M8 $\times$ 1.25 $\times$ 20.0 LG.
120	PIN WASHER ASSEMBLY, THERMO ELEMENT
121	THERMOSTATIC ELEMENT
122	PLATE, THERMOSTATIC ELEMENT
123	PIN, THERMAL ELEMENT
124	PIPE, FORWARD SERVO APPLY
125	PIPE, MANUAL SERVO APPLY
126	PIPE, LUBE OIL
127	CLAMP, HOSE
128	HOSE, LUBE OIL
129	RETAINER, LUBE PIPE CLIP
130	PIPE & WASHER ASSEMBLY
131	BOLT, M8 $\times$ 1.0 $\times$ 30 (2)
132	COVER, ACCUMULATOR
133	GASKET, ACCUMULATOR COVER
134	PLATE, ACCUMULATOR SPACER
135	PIN, 2-3 ACCUMULATOR
136	PISTON, 1-2 & 2-3 ACCUMULATOR
137	RING, OIL SEAL ACCUMULATOR PISTON
138A	SPRING, 2-3 ACCUMULATOR (INNER)
138B	SPRING, 2-3 ACCUMULATOR (OUTER)
139A	SPRING, 1-2 ACCUMULATOR
139B	SPRING, 1-2 ACCUMULATOR (INNER)
139C	SPRING, 1-2 ACCUMULATOR (OUTER)
140	HOUSING, ACCUMULATOR (MACHINED)
400	CHANNEL PLATE ASSEMBLY, COMPLETE
431	BEARING ASM., 4TH CHANNEL HUB/CHANNEL PLATE
434	BOLT, M8 $\times$ 1.25 $\times$ 45.0 LG (CHANNEL PLATE/CASE)
435	BOLT, M8 $\times$ 1.25 $\times$ 50.0 LG (CHANNEL PLATE/CASE)
436	BOLT, M8 $\times$ 1.25 $\times$ 30.0
500	PLATE, 4TH CLUTCH REACTION
501	PLATE ASSEMBLY, 4TH CLUTCH
502	PLATE, 4TH CLUTCH APPLY
503	BEARING ASSEMBLY, 4TH CLUTCH
504	HUB & SHAFT ASSEMBLY, 4TH CLUTCH
505	WASHER, THRUST (4TH CLUTCH HUB/DRIVEN SPROCKET)
506	SPROCKET, DRIVEN
507	LINK ASSEMBLY, DRIVE
508	WASHER, THRUST (DRIVEN & 2ND CLUTCH DRUM)
509	RING, OUTPUT SHAFT/DRIVE AXLE (SNAP)
510	SHAFT, OUTPUT
511	BEARING, INPUT SUN GEAR
512	RING, OUTPUT SHAFT/DIFFERENTIAL INBOARD (SNAP)
513	RING, TURBINE SHAFT TO SUPPORT OIL SEAL
514	WASHER, THRUST (DRIVE SPROCKET/CHANNEL PLATE)
515	RING, TURBINE SHAFT TO DRIVE SPROCKET (SNAP)
516	SPROCKET, DRIVE
517	WASHER, THRUST (DRIVE SPROCKET/SUPPORT)
518	SHAFT, TURBINE
519	RING, TURBINE SHAFT TO SUPPORT OIL SEAL
520	SEAL, O-RING (TURBINE SHAFT/HUB) GREEN
521	BEARING ASSEMBLY, DRIVE SUPPORT/SPROCKET (DRAW CUP)
522	SUPPORT, DRIVE SPROCKET
523	BUSHING, DRIVE SPROCKET SUPPORT
524	SCREW, DRIVE SPROCKET SUPPORT (MS $\times$ 1.25 $\times$ 23.5)
525	HELIX SEAL ASSEMBLY, CONVERTER OIL
528	PIN, DOWEL
808	PIN, GUIDE RETAINING
809	GUIDE, ACTUATOR
810	SEAL, O-RING
811	SEAL, O-RING

FIGURE 8–51 *(Continued)*

bricant such as Door Ease may be useful in keeping a clutch seal in place for assembly. Never use high-temperature lubricant such as white grease. It will clog oil passages since it is not compatible with transmission fluids. Use petroleum jelly or other transmission gel.

13. Every passage in every component must be free and clear of all obstructions.

14. Where fasteners of unequal length are used, be sure that each fastener is installed in the correct location. Installing a shorter fastener in place of the normal length will destroy the threads when it is tightened.

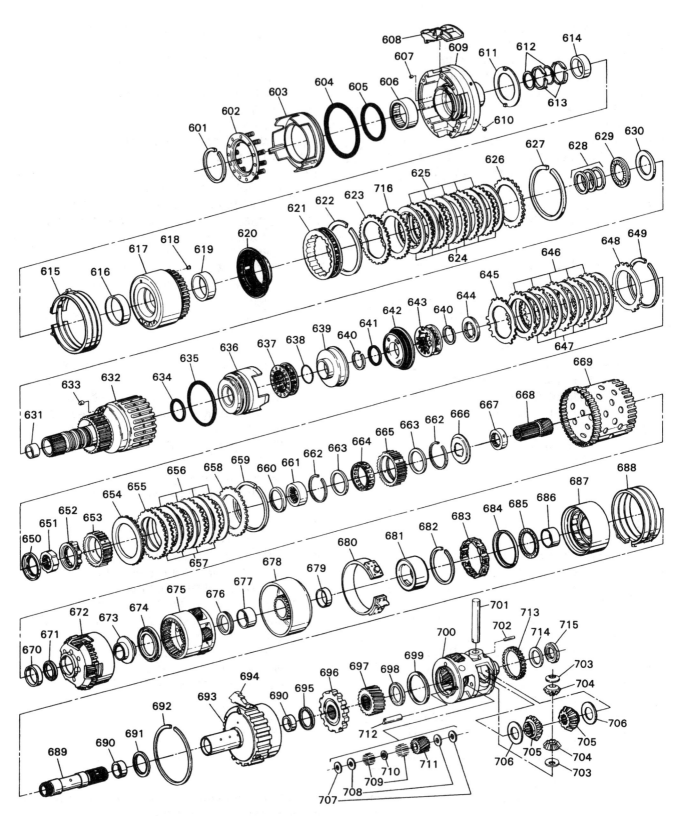

FIGURE 8–52 4T60-E transaxle gear train components. (Courtesy of General Motors Corporation.)

601 RING, SNAP (4TH CLUTCH RETURN SPRING)
602 SPRING ASSEMBLY, 4TH CLUTCH PISTON RETURN
603 PISTON, 4TH CLUTCH
604 SEAL, 4TH CLUTCH PISTON (OUTER)
605 SEAL, 4TH CLUTCH PISTON (INNER)
606 BEARING ASSEMBLY, DRAWN CUP
607 PLUG, CUP ORIFICE
608 SCOOP, CHAIN SCAVENGING
609 SUPPORT, DRIVEN SPROCKET
610 PLUG, CUP
611 WASHER, THRUST (DRIVEN SPROCKET SUPPORT/
2ND CLUTCH DRUM)
612 SEAL, RING FOUR LOBBED
613 RING, OIL SEAL
614 BUSHING, DRIVEN SPROCKET SUPPORT
615 BAND ASSEMBLY, REVERSE
616 BUSHING, 75.5 O.D. X 8.0
617 HOUSING, 2ND CLUTCH
618 RETAINER & BALL ASSEMBLY, CHECK VALVE
(FORWARD CLUTCH)
619 BUSHING, 70.0 O.D. X 11.0
620 PISTON, 2ND CLUTCH W/MOLDED SEAL
621 APPLY RING & RELEASE SPRING ASSEMBLY,
2ND CLUTCH
622 RING, SNAP
623 PLATE, 2ND CLUTCH (WAVED)
624 PLATE ASSEMBLY, 2ND CLUTCH (FIBER)
625 PLATE, 2ND CLUTCH REACTION (STEEL)
626 PLATE, BACKING SUPPORT RING (STEEL)
627 RING, SNAP 2ND CLUTCH (OUTER)
628 RING, OIL SEAL (INPUT SHAFT)
629 BEARING, THRUST (SUPPORT SPROCKET/
THRUST WASHER)
630 WASHER, THRUST (BEARING/INPUT CLUTCH HUB)
' (SELECTIVE)
631 BUSHING, INPUT SHAFT
632 HUB HOUSING SLEEVE & SHAFT ASSEMBLY, INPUT
633 RETAINER & BALL ASSEMBLY, CHECK VALVE
634 SEAL, INPUT CLUTCH PISTON (INNER)
635 SEAL, INPUT CLUTCH PISTON (OUTER)
636 PISTON, INPUT CLUTCH
637 SPRING & RETAINER ASSEMBLY, INPUT
638 SEAL, O-RING
639 HOUSING, 3RD CLUTCH PISTON
640 RING, SNAP (3RD, PISTON HSG./INPUT SHAFT)
641 SEAL, 3RD CLUTCH PISTON (INNER)
642 PISTON, SEAL & BALL CAPSULE ASM., 3RD CLUTCH
643 SPRING RETAINER & GUIDE ASSEMBLY, 3RD CLUTCH
644 BEARING ASSEMBLY, THRUST
645 PLATE, 3RD CLUTCH (WAVED)
646 PLATE ASSEMBLY, 3RD CLUTCH
(SPROCKET SUPPORT/SPLINE O.D.)
647 PLATE ASSEMBLY, 3RD CLUTCH
(SPROCKET SUPPORT/SPLINE I.D.)
648 PLATE, BACKING
649 RING, SNAP
650 DAM, 3RD ROLLER CLUTCH OIL
651 CAM, 3RD ROLLER CLUTCH
652 ROLLER ASSEMBLY, 3RD CLUTCH
653 RACE, 3RD ROLLER CLUTCH
654 PLATE, INPUT CLUTCH APPLY
655 PLATE, INPUT CLUTCH (WAVED)
656 PLATE ASSEMBLY, INPUT CLUTCH (FIBER)
657 PLATE, INPUT CLUTCH (1.9 FLAT)
658 PLATE, CLUTCH BACKING (STEEL)
659 RING, SNAP
660 DAM, INPUT SPRAG RACE LUBE

661 RACE, INPUT SPRAG CLUTCH (INNER)
662 RING, SNAP
663 BEARING, END
664 SPRAG ASSEMBLY, INPUT CLUTCH
665 RACE, INPUT SPRAG CLUTCH (OUTER)
666 RETAINER, INPUT SPRAG CLUTCH
667 SPACER, INPUT SUN GEAR
668 GEAR, INPUT SUN
669 DRUM, REVERSE REACTION
670 BUSHING, REACTION INTERNAL GEAR
671 BEARING ASSEMBLY, THRUST
672 CARRIER ASSEMBLY, INPUT COMPLETE
673 DAM, INPUT CARRIER TO REACTION CARRIER
674 BEARING ASSEMBLY, THRUST (INPUT/
REACTION CARRIER)
675 CARRIER ASSEMBLY, REACTION COMPLETE
676 BEARING ASSEMBLY, THRUST (REACTION CARRIER/
SUN GEAR)
677 BUSHING, REACTION SUN GEAR (LEFT HAND)
678 GEAR, DRUM BUSHING ASSEMBLY, REACTION SUN
679 BUSHING, REACTION SUN GEAR (RIGHT HAND)
680 BAND ASSEMBLY, 2/1
681 RACE, 1/2 SUPPORT (INNER)
682 RING, SNAP (1/2 ROLLER ASSEMBLY)
683 ROLLER ASSEMBLY, 1/2 SUPPORT
684 SPACER, 1/2 SUPPORT
685 BEARING ASSEMBLY, THRUST ASSEMBLY/
LO RACE
686 BUSHING, 1/2 SUPPORT
687 RACE, 1/2 SUPPORT (OUTER)
688 BAND ASSEMBLY, FORWARD
689 SHAFT, FINAL DRIVE SUN GEAR
690 BUSHING, FINAL DRIVE INTERNAL GEAR
691 BEARING ASSEMBLY, THRUST (1/2 SUPPORT/
INTERNAL GEAR)
692 RING, SNAP (FINAL DRIVE INTERNAL GEAR SPROCKET)
693 GEAR, FINAL DRIVE INTERNAL
694 PAWL & PIN ASSEMBLY, PAWL LOCKOUT
695 BEARING ASSEMBLY, THRUST (INTERNAL GEAR/
PARKING GEAR)
696 GEAR, PARKING
697 GEAR, FINAL DRIVE SUN
698 BEARING ASSEMBLY, THRUST CARRIER/SUN GEAR
699 RING, SPIRAL PIN RETAINING
700 CARRIER ASSEMBLY, DIFFERENTIAL/
FINAL DRIVE COMP
701 SHAFT, DIFFERENTIAL PINION
702 PIN, DIFFERENTIAL PINION SHAFT RETAINING
703 WASHER, THRUST (DIFFERENTIAL PINION)
704 GEAR, DIFFERENTIAL PINION
705 GEAR, DIFFERENTIAL SIDE
706 WASHER, THRUST (DIFFERENTIAL SIDE GEAR)
(BRONZE)
707 WASHER, PINION THRUST (BRONZE)
708 WASHER, PINION THRUST (STEEL)
709 BEARING, ROLLER NEEDLE
710 SPACER, PINION NEEDLE BEARING
711 PINION, FINAL DRIVE PLANET
712 PIN, PLANET PINION
713 ROTOR, SPEED SENSOR (29 OR 30 T)
714 WASHER, DIFFERENTIAL CARRIER/CASE (THRUST)
715 BEARING ASSEMBLY, THRUST
(DIFFERENTIAL CARRIER/CASE)
716 PLATE, 2ND CLUTCH APPLY REACTION (TAPERED)

FIGURE 8–52 (*Continued*)

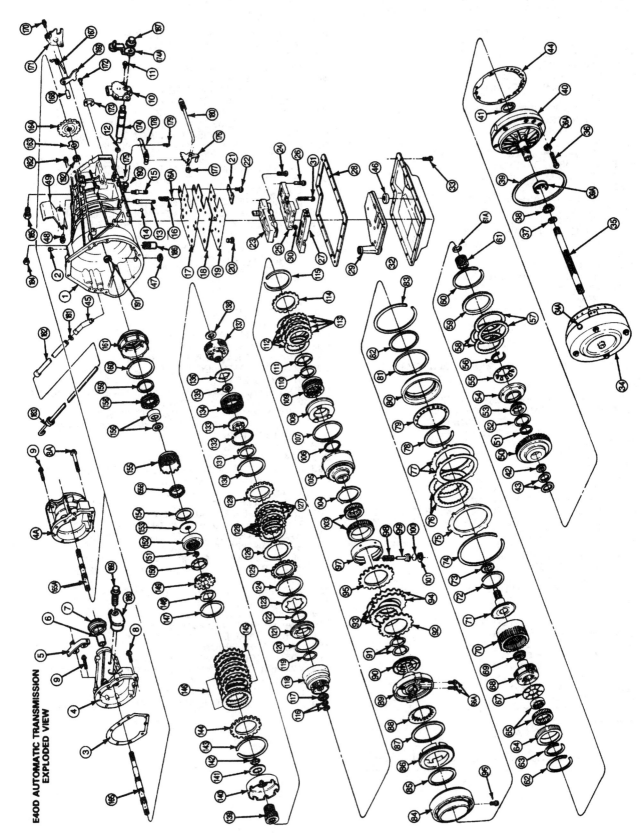

FIGURE 8–53 Ford E40D transmission components. (Courtesy of Ford Motor Company.)

Item	Description
73	Overdrive Center Shaft Thrust Bearing Assembly
74	Clutch Pressure Plate Retainer Snap Ring
75	Clutch Pressure Plate
76	Overdrive Clutch Plate Internal Spline—Friction
77	Overdrive Clutch Plate External Spline—Steel
78	Overdrive Clutch Disc Spring Retaining Ring
79	Overdrive Clutch Piston Disc Spring
80	Overdrive Clutch Piston
81	Clutch Piston Seal—Outer
82	Clutch Piston Seal—Inner
83	Intermediate Cylinder Retaining Ring
84	Intermediate/Overdrive Clutch Cylinder
85	Intermediate Clutch Piston Inner Seal
86	Intermediate Clutch Piston
87	Intermediate Clutch Piston Outer Seal
88	Intermediate Clutch Piston Disc Spring
89	Center Support Assembly
90	Center Support Thrust Washer
91	Direct Clutch Cast Iron Seal
92	Clutch Pressure Plate
93	Intermediate Clutch Internal Spline Plate—Friction
94	Intermediate Clutch External Spline Plate—Steel
95	Clutch Pressure Plate—Rear
96	Bolt—Cylinder Hydraulic Feed (1 Required) M10-1.5 × 24mm
96A	Bolt—Center Support Hydraulic Feed (2 Required) M12-1.75 × 31mm
97	Intermediate Band Assembly
98	Servo Piston Spring
99	Intermediate Band Servo Piston
100	Rear Band Servo Retainer
101	Servo Piston Retaining Ring
103	One-Way Clutch (Serviced in Kits Only)
104	Intermediate One-Way Clutch Thrust Washer
105	Intermediate Brake Drum
106	Direct Clutch Piston Seal—Inner
107	Direct Clutch Piston Seal—Outer
108	Direct Clutch Piston

Item	Description
109	Direct Clutch Retainer and Spring Assembly
110	Direct Clutch Support Spring Retaining Ring
111	Intermediate Brake Drum Thrust Washer
112	Direct Clutch Internal Spline Plate—Friction
113	Direct Clutch External Spline Plate—Steel
114	Direct Clutch Pressure Plate
115	Clutch Plate Retaining Ring (Selective Fit)
116	Forward Clutch Cylinder Seal
117	Forward Clutch Needle Thrust Bearing
118	Forward Clutch Cylinder
119	Forward Clutch Piston Seal —Inner
120	Forward Clutch Piston Seal —Outer
121	Forward Clutch Piston
122	Forward Clutch Piston Spring Ring
123	Forward Clutch Piston Disc Spring
124	Forward Clutch Spring Ring
125	Forward Clutch Pressure Plate
126	Forward Clutch Pressure Spring
127	Forward Clutch External Spline Plate—Steel
128	Forward Clutch Internal Spline Plate—Friction
129	Forward Clutch Pressure Plate—Rear
130	Forward Clutch Pressure Retaining Ring (Selective Fit)
130	Retaining Ring
130	Retaining Ring
130	Forward Clutch Hub Thrust Washer
130	Retaining Ring
131	Forward Clutch Hub Thrust Washer
132	Forward Hub Retaining Ring
133	Forward Hub Ring Gear
134	Forward Ring Gear
135	Forward Clutch Thrust Bearing Assembly
136	Forward Planet Carrier Thrust Washer
137	Forward Planet Assembly
138	Forward Clutch Thrust Bearing Assembly
139	Forward/Reverse Sun Gear Assembly

FIGURE 8–53 *(Continued)*

Item	Description
140	Input Shell
141	Input Shell Thrust Washer
142	Retaining Ring
143	Reverse Clutch Pressure Plate Retaining Ring
144	Reverse Clutch Pressure Plate
145	Reverse Clutch External Spline Plate—Steel
146	Reverse Clutch Internal Spline Plate—Friction
147	Reverse Planet Retaining Ring
148	Planet Carrier Thrust Washer
149	Reverse Planet
150	Planet Carrier Thrust Washer
151	Retaining Ring (for Output Shaft) (1-½ In. Dia.)
152	Output Shaft Ring Gear
153	Output Shaft Hub and Race (Serviced in Kits Only)
154	Retaining Ring
155	Reverse Clutch Hub Assembly
155B	Reverse One-Way Clutch (Serviced in Kits Only)
156	Output Shaft Hub Thrust Bearing
158	Reverse Clutch Retainer and Spring Assembly
159	Reverse Clutch Piston Inner Seal
160	Reverse Clutch Piston Outer Seal
161	Reverse Clutch Piston
162	Bolts (5 Required) ⁵⁄₁₆ In.-24 (One Way Clutch to Case)
163	Output Shaft Thrust Washer—Rear
164	Overdrive Shaft Parking Gear

Item	Description
165	Output Shaft—(4 × 2)
165A	Output Shaft—(4 × 4)
167	Parking Pawl Return Spring
168	Parking Pawl Shaft
169	Parking Pawl
170	Bolt and Washer Assembly (2 Required) M8-1.25 × 23.8mm
171	Parking Rod Guide Plate
172	Bolt M8-1.25 × 25.9mm
173	Parking Pawl Actuating Abutment
174	Manual Control Lever Shaft
174A	Manual Control Lever
175	Manual Lever Shaft Retaining Pin
176	Manual Valve Detent Lever—Inner
177	Inner Detent Lever Nut M14-1.5 Hex
178	Manual Valve Detent Lever Spring
179	Bolt—Hex Flange Head M6-1.0 × 16.5mm
180	Parking Pawl Actuating Rod Assembly
181	Filler Tube O-Ring
182	Oil Filler Tube
183	Oil Level Indicator
184	Oil Tube Inlet Connector
185	Converter Drain Back Check Valve Assembly—Rear
186	Accum. Regulator Filter Assembly
187	Nut, M10-1.5 Hex
188	Extension Housing Plug Assembly
189	Screw and Washer Assembly, ¼-20 × .62
190	Test Port Hex Head Plug (2 Required) ⅛-27
191	Front Case Bushing
192	Rear Case Bushing

FIGURE 8–53 *(Continued)*

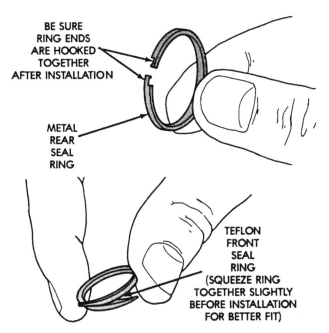

FIGURE 8–54 Seal ring installation instructions. Seal rings should be lubricated with a light coat of petroleum jelly after installation. (Courtesy of Chrysler Corporation.)

Tighten all fasteners to specifications with a torque wrench.

15. Install all paper gaskets dry. The cork pan gasket should also be installed dry with dry mating surfaces. Oily, greasy, or slippery sealant surfaces cause cork gaskets to crack at bolt holes and squish out as fasteners are tightened to specified torque. A little petroleum jelly may be used on paper gaskets to help keep the gasket in place during assembly.

16. Always maintain the original position of parts to be reused.

SUBASSEMBLY SERVICE

It is normal practice to service each subassembly separately and prepare it for installation later. Subassemblies include the pump, clutches, servos and bands, planetary gear units and shafts, the valve body, and the governor. Each unit is disassembled, cleaned, carefully inspected for wear or damage, faulty parts replaced, and the unit assembled as outlined in the service manual. Also refer to any updating information in revised service manual information and manufacturer's service bulletins. The following procedures are typical for subassembly reconditioning:

Pump Service

Careful visual inspection of all pump parts is critical in deciding whether repairs or replacement are needed. In general, if the pump body shows excessive wear, the pump should be replaced. The pumping elements (gears, rotors, or vanes) are replaceable on some units.

Examine each pump part carefully for excessive wear or scoring. The following areas are subject to the highest loading and therefore the most wear:

IX Gear Pump. Inspect both sides of the crescent **(Figure 8–55)**, on the pump inlet side, the outer surface of the internal gear, the internal gear to pump body contact area at the outlet side, the teeth on both

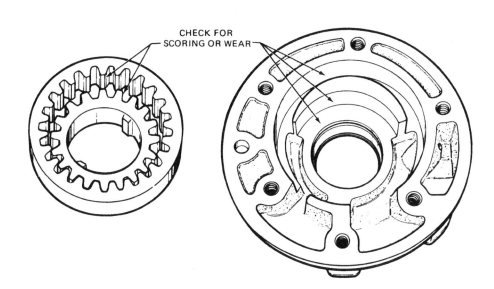

FIGURE 8–55 Checking IX gear pump condition. (Courtesy of General Motors Corporation.)

gears, the surfaces of the pump body and pump cover against which the gears bear, the clearance between the crescent and the gear teeth, the clearance between the internal gear and the pump body, and the clearance between the gears and the pump cover. To check wear on the gear teeth, lay both gears on a flat surface with the teeth engaged. If the external gear can be pulled away from the internal gear at the point where they are in mesh, the gear teeth are excessively worn and must be replaced.

IX Rotor Pump. Inspect the rotors, pump body, pump cover, and rotor-to-pump-cover clearance as for the IX gear pump. To check rotor lobe wear, measure the clearance between the inner and outer rotor lobes when their high points are exactly aligned (**Figures 8–56 to 8–66**).

Vane Pump. Inspect the pump body and pump cover as described before (**Figures 8–67 to 8–75**). The rotor, vanes, and slide must be measured for wear with an outside micrometer. Replacement parts are available in several different dimensions to provide the correct clearances. A selective vane, rotor, and slide

chart is shown in **Figure 8–69.** Slide and rotor-to-pump-cover clearance is measured with a straightedge and feeler gauge.

Clutch Service

There are two general types of transmission/transaxle multiple disc clutches: driving (rotating) and holding (stationary). Each has a number of steel plates and friction discs stacked alternately in a clutch housing or drum. A hydraulically operated piston squeezes these plates and discs together to apply the clutch. When hydraulic pressure is removed, the return springs return the piston to its released position. The number of discs and plates used varies with transmission and transaxle model and application. Always keep clutch parts in their proper order and position when laying them out during disassembly. This provides valuable guidance during assembly later. Clutch parts often look very similar from one clutch to another, but they are usually not the same and must not be interchanged. Keeping all the parts in order during disassembly is therefore critical to proper assembly.

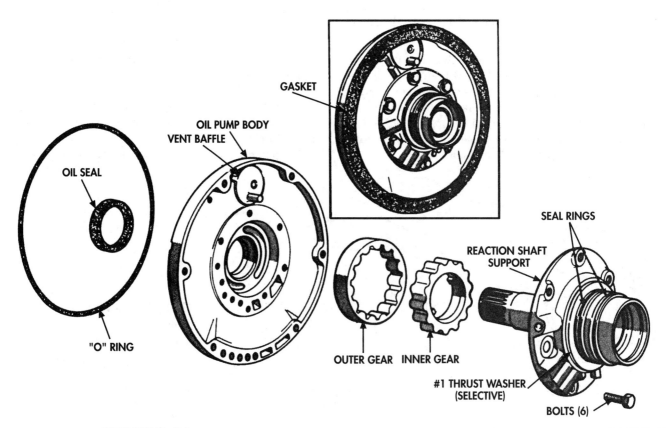

FIGURE 8–56 IX gerotor pump components. (Courtesy of Chrysler Corporation.)

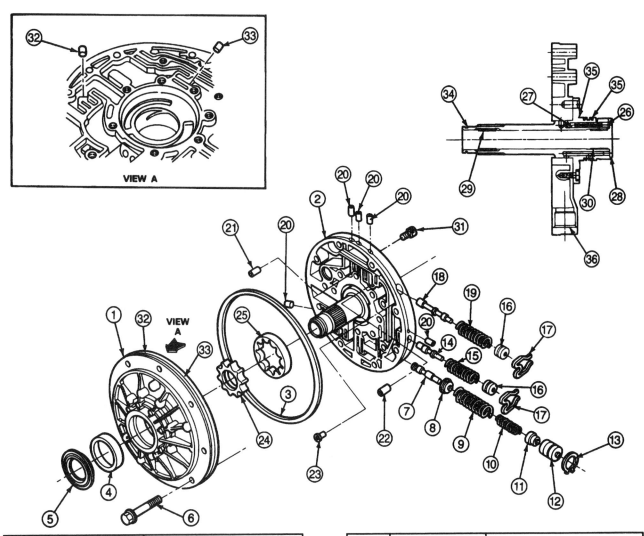

Item	Part Number	Description
1	—	Pump Body (Part of 7A103)
2	—	Body and Support Assembly (Part of 7A103)
3	7A248	Front Oil Pump Seal — O-Ring
4	—	Front Oil Pump Bushing (Part of 7A103)
5	7A248	Front Oil Pump Seal — Small
6	N805260-S	Bolt and Washer Assembly (9 Req'd)
7	—	Main Regulator Valve (Part of 7A103)
8	—	Spring Retainer (Part of 7A103)
9	—	Outer Spring (Part of 7A103)
10	—	Inner Spring (Part of 7A103)
11	—	Main Regulator Booster Valve (Part of 7A103)

Item	Part Number	Description
12	—	Main Regulator Booster Sleeve (Part of 7A103)
13	—	Retainer (Part of 7A103)
14	—	Converter Regulator Valve (Part of 7A103)
15	—	Spring (Part of 7A103)
16	—	Plug (Part of 7A103)
17	—	Clip (Part of 7A103)
18	—	Converter Clutch Control Valve (Part of 7A103)
19	—	Spring (Part of 7A103)
20	—	Solid Cup Plug (Part of 7A103)
21	—	Orificed Cup Plug (Part of 7A103)
22	—	Orificed Cup Plug (Part of 7A103)
23	—	Air Bleed Check Valve Assembly (Part of 7A103)

FIGURE 8–57 This pump assembly contains several valves in the pump body (E40D transmission). (Courtesy of Ford Motor Company.)

MEASURING TOOTH CLEARANCE

FIGURE 8–58 On this pump, tooth clearance (top) and side clearance should be between 0.0035 and 0.0075 in. (0.08 and 0.19 mm). (Courtesy of Chrysler Corporation.)

MEASURING SIDE CLEARANCE

FIGURE 8–59 Measuring pump gear end clearance with straightedge and feeler gauge. On this unit, clearance should be from 0.004 to 0.0025 in. (0.010 to 0.06 mm). (Courtesy of Chrysler Corporation.)

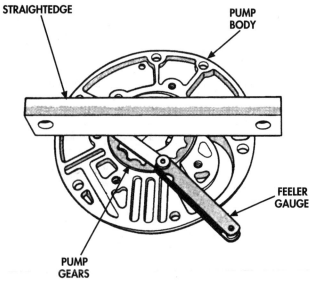

STRAIGHTEDGE

PUMP BODY

FEELER GAUGE

PUMP GEARS

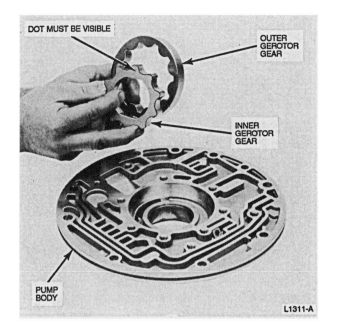

FIGURE 8–60 Location of identification marks is an important part of pump assembly. (Courtesy of Ford Motor Company.)

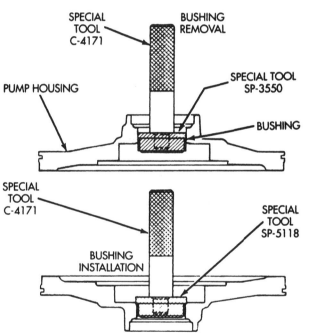

FIGURE 8–61 Replacing the oil pump bushing. (Courtesy of Chrysler Corporation.)

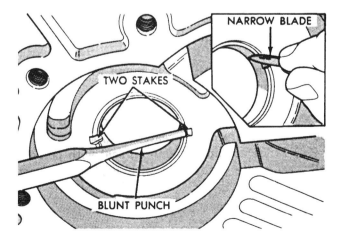

FIGURE 8–62 Staking the oil pump bushing. Use a narrow blade knife to remove burrs after staking. (Courtesy of Chrysler Corporation.)

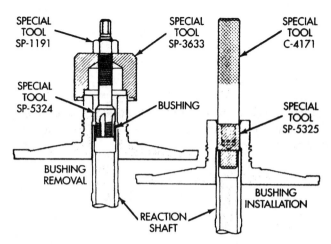

FIGURE 8–63 Replacing the reaction shaft support bushing in a 32RH transmission. (Courtesy of Chrysler Corporation.)

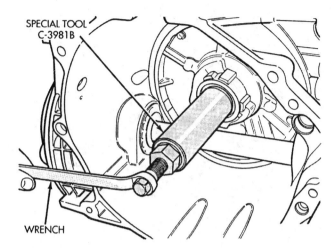

FIGURE 8–65 Removing the pump seal. (Courtesy of Chrysler Corporation.)

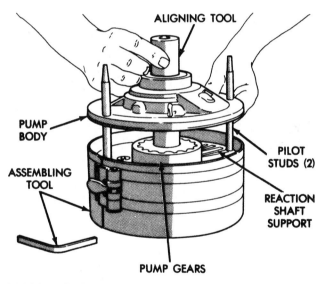

FIGURE 8–64 Some pumps must be assembled with an aligning tool. Even slight misalignment can prevent the pump from fitting into the case bore. (Courtesy of Chrysler Corporation.)

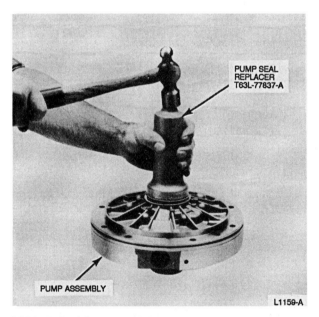

FIGURE 8–66 Installing the pump seal. (Courtesy of Ford Motor Company.)

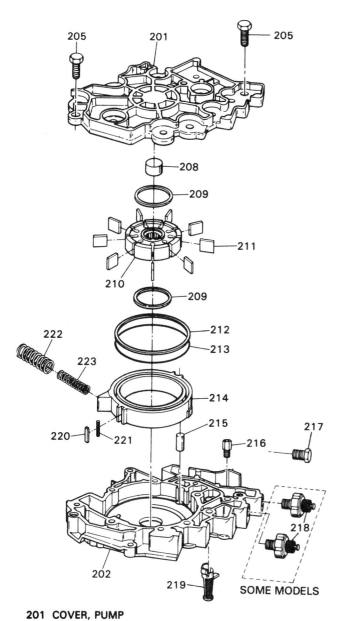

FIGURE 8–67 Pump components for a 4T60-E transaxle. (Courtesy of General Motors Corporation.)

201 COVER, PUMP
202 BODY, OIL PUMP
205 BOLT, METRIC HEAVY HEX FLANGE HEAD
208 BUSHING, AUXILIARY VALVE BODY (PUMP SHAFT)
209 RING, PUMP VANE
210 ROTOR, OIL PUMP SELECTIVE
211 VANE, PUMP SELECTIVE
212 RING, OIL SEAL (SLIDE TO COVER—SELECTIVE)
213 SEAL, O-RING
214 SLIDE, OIL PUMP SELECTIVE
215 PIN, PIVOT (PUMP SLIDE)
216 PLUG, AIR BLEED (HEX HEAD ORIFICED)
217 PLUG, SWITCH HOLE
218 SWITCH ASSEMBLY, PRESSURE
219 SCREEN ASSEMBLY, OIL PUMP PRESSURE
220 SEAL, PUMP SLIDE
221 SUPPORT, OIL PUMP SLIDE SEAL
222 SPRING, PUMP PRIMING (OUTER)
223 SPRING, PUMP PRIMING (INNER)

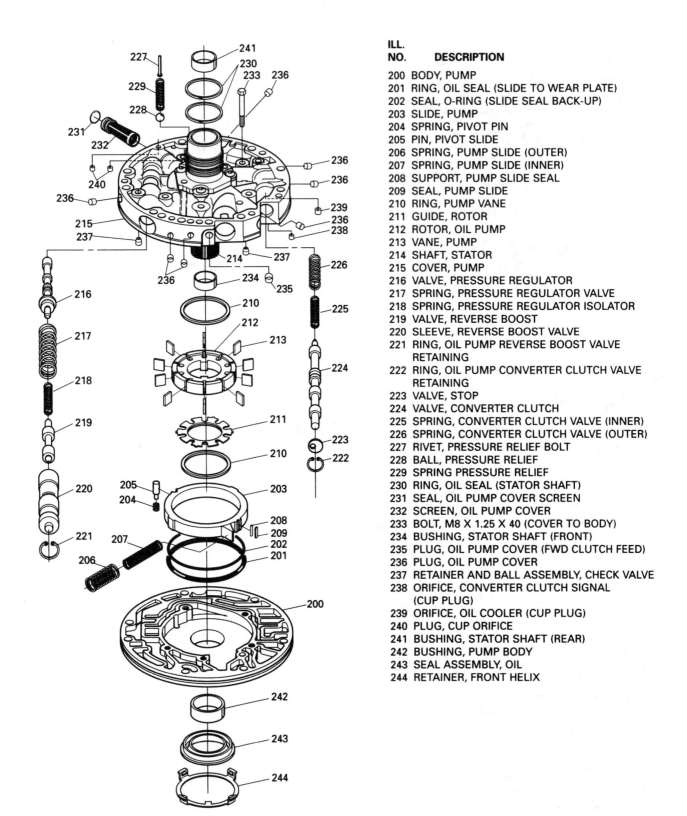

ILL. NO.	DESCRIPTION
200	BODY, PUMP
201	RING, OIL SEAL (SLIDE TO WEAR PLATE)
202	SEAL, O-RING (SLIDE SEAL BACK-UP)
203	SLIDE, PUMP
204	SPRING, PIVOT PIN
205	PIN, PIVOT SLIDE
206	SPRING, PUMP SLIDE (OUTER)
207	SPRING, PUMP SLIDE (INNER)
208	SUPPORT, PUMP SLIDE SEAL
209	SEAL, PUMP SLIDE
210	RING, PUMP VANE
211	GUIDE, ROTOR
212	ROTOR, OIL PUMP
213	VANE, PUMP
214	SHAFT, STATOR
215	COVER, PUMP
216	VALVE, PRESSURE REGULATOR
217	SPRING, PRESSURE REGULATOR VALVE
218	SPRING, PRESSURE REGULATOR ISOLATOR
219	VALVE, REVERSE BOOST
220	SLEEVE, REVERSE BOOST VALVE
221	RING, OIL PUMP REVERSE BOOST VALVE RETAINING
222	RING, OIL PUMP CONVERTER CLUTCH VALVE RETAINING
223	VALVE, STOP
224	VALVE, CONVERTER CLUTCH
225	SPRING, CONVERTER CLUTCH VALVE (INNER)
226	SPRING, CONVERTER CLUTCH VALVE (OUTER)
227	RIVET, PRESSURE RELIEF BOLT
228	BALL, PRESSURE RELIEF
229	SPRING PRESSURE RELIEF
230	RING, OIL SEAL (STATOR SHAFT)
231	SEAL, OIL PUMP COVER SCREEN
232	SCREEN, OIL PUMP COVER
233	BOLT, M8 X 1.25 X 40 (COVER TO BODY)
234	BUSHING, STATOR SHAFT (FRONT)
235	PLUG, OIL PUMP COVER (FWD CLUTCH FEED)
236	PLUG, OIL PUMP COVER
237	RETAINER AND BALL ASSEMBLY, CHECK VALVE
238	ORIFICE, CONVERTER CLUTCH SIGNAL (CUP PLUG)
239	ORIFICE, OIL COOLER (CUP PLUG)
240	PLUG, CUP ORIFICE
241	BUSHING, STATOR SHAFT (REAR)
242	BUSHING, PUMP BODY
243	SEAL ASSEMBLY, OIL
244	RETAINER, FRONT HELIX

FIGURE 8–68 Pump components for a 4L60-E transmission. (Courtesy of General Motors Corporation.)

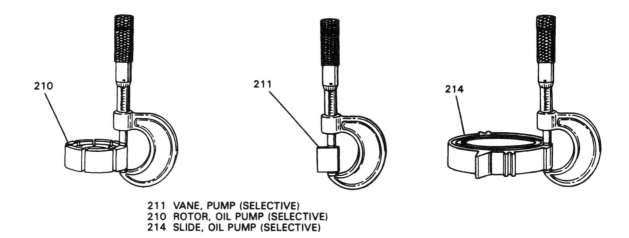

211 VANE, PUMP (SELECTIVE)
210 ROTOR, OIL PUMP (SELECTIVE)
214 SLIDE, OIL PUMP (SELECTIVE)

ROTOR SELECTION		VANE SELECTION		SLIDE SELECTION	
THICKNESS (mm)	THICKNESS (in.)	THICKNESS (mm)	THICKNESS (in.)	THICKNESS (mm)	THICKNESS (in.)
17.953 - 17.963	.7068 - .7072	17.943 - 17.961	.7064 - .7071	17.983 - 17.993	.7080 - .7084
17.963 - 17.973	.7072 - .7076	17.961 - 17.979	.7071 - .7078	17.993 - 18.003	.7084 - .7088
17.973 - 17.983	.7076 - .7080	17.979 - 17.997	.7078 - .7085	18.003 - 18.013	.7088 - .7092

FIGURE 8–69 Rotor, vane, and slide selection chart for a 4T60-E transaxle. (Courtesy of General Motors Corporation.)

To disassemble a clutch, the snap ring and clutch plates are removed first. A spring compressor is used on coil spring clutches to compress the return springs to allow the spring retainer snap ring to be removed. Compress the springs just enough to clear the snap ring, remove the snap ring, then remove the spring compressor. Shop air may be used to remove the clutch piston. Apply the air to the passage specified in the service manual **(Figures 8–76 to 8–82)**. After piston removal, remove the clutch piston seals. Use a seal pick to lift the seal out of its groove. Next, clean all the metal parts in mineral spirits and allow them to air dry. Never wash friction plates. Washing them removes ATF and changes their coefficient of friction.

Inspect the bushing in the clutch drum. Replace it if wear is excessive. Inspect the piston bore for scoring. Minor scoring can be dressed down with crocus cloth. Do not use emery cloth or sandpaper since they produce scratches. Inspect the oil ring grooves for side wear or damage. Inspect the bore against which the oil rings seal for grooved wear. Excessive wear here reduces the sealing capacity of the oil rings. Inspect the clutch piston and check ball. The check ball must be able to move freely in order to seal properly. If the ball is stuck, it must be cleaned and checked for leakage. Pour some

clean solvent into the piston cavity or clutch bore to test for leakage. There should not be any leakage **(Figure 8–83)**. Inspect the piston return coil springs for collapse, distortion, or discoloration from overheating. Replace damaged springs. Inspect the spring fingers for wear on a Belleville spring clutch. Inspect the condition of any splines, snap rings, and snap ring grooves.

Friction plates may be used again if:

- they are flat and not dished or warped
- the friction material is not pitted, glazed, flaked, loose, or excessively worn
- ATF is visible when the plate is squeezed between the thumb and forefinger

If any friction plate fails the test, replace all the friction plates. Never mix old and new friction plates. Their coefficient of friction will not be the same, and slippage may result.

Steel plates may be used again if:

- they are flat and not dished or warped
- surfaces on both sides show no evidence of wear, scuffing, scoring, or overheating

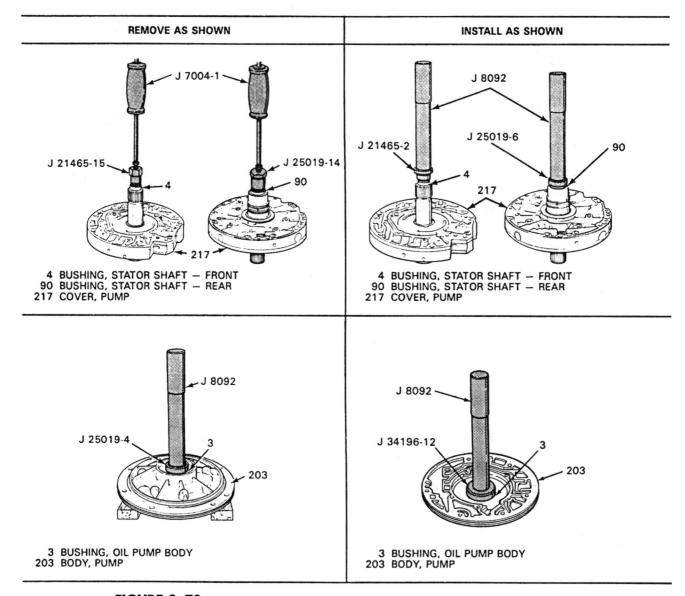

REMOVE AS SHOWN	INSTALL AS SHOWN
J 7004-1 · J 25019-14 · J 21465-15 · 4 · 90 · 217	J 8092 · J 21465-2 · J 25019-6 · 90 · 4 · 217
4 BUSHING, STATOR SHAFT — FRONT 90 BUSHING, STATOR SHAFT — REAR 217 COVER, PUMP	4 BUSHING, STATOR SHAFT — FRONT 90 BUSHING, STATOR SHAFT — REAR 217 COVER, PUMP
J 8092 · J 25019-4 · 3 · 203	J 8092 · J 34196-12 · 3 · 203
3 BUSHING, OIL PUMP BODY 203 BODY, PUMP	3 BUSHING, OIL PUMP BODY 203 BODY, PUMP

FIGURE 8–70 Oil pump bushing replacement on a 4L60 transmission. (Courtesy of General Motors Corporation.)

> **CAUTION:** Do not confuse a wavy or dished cushion plate for a steel plate. A cushion plate is often used next to the clutch piston to cushion clutch application.

Clutch Assembly

Critical points of clutch assembly include checking clutch piston height, lip seal installation procedure, po-

sitioning and number of return springs, clutch plate thickness, number of plates and discs required, order of plate and disc assembly, clutch pack clearance, and snap ring thickness. Specifications for these points must be obtained from the service manual.

Lip seals are always installed with the sealing lip facing the oil pressure side. On a two-seal piston, both seals are installed with the lips facing into the piston cylinder. A piston with two pressure chambers has a third seal located on the sleeve hub of the clutch drum. This seal is installed with the lip facing away from the clutch cylinder. Always use new seals to avoid pressure

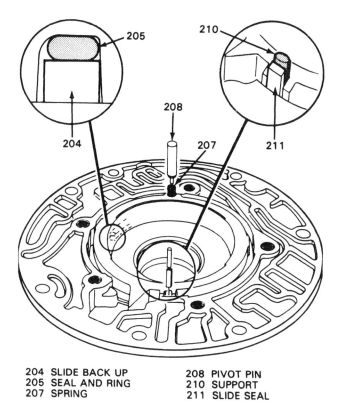

204 SLIDE BACK UP
205 SEAL AND RING
207 SPRING

208 PIVOT PIN
210 SUPPORT
211 SLIDE SEAL

FIGURE 8–71 Installing the slide backup and slide seal in a 4L60 transmission. (Courtesy of General Motors Corporation.)

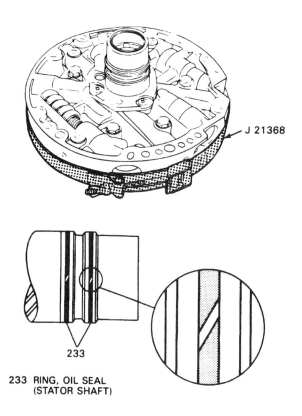

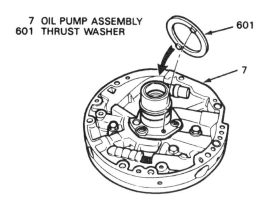

233 RING, OIL SEAL
     (STATOR SHAFT)

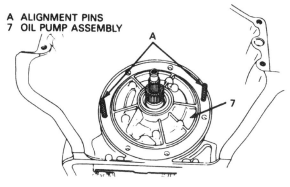

FIGURE 8–72 Oil pump assembly and installation on a 4L60 transmission. (Courtesy of General Motors Corporation.)

loss and clutch slippage. Lubricate the seals with ATF or other approved assembly lubricant. Damage to the seals must be avoided. Assembly can be aided with the use of a smooth feeler gauge with no sharp edges, a fabricated piano wire tool, and a seal protector sleeve. Carefully press the piston into the cylinder bore while observing that the sealing lips are not damaged or folded back. Press the piston into the cylinder by hand until it bottoms **(Figures 8–84 to 8–88).** Place the correct number of return springs into the specified position and place the spring retainer plate in position **(Figures 8–89 and 8–90).** Use a spring compressor to compress the springs just enough to allow snap ring installation. Make sure the snap ring is fully seated, then remove the compressor.

New friction discs must be soaked in ATF for at least 30 minutes before installation. Friction plates installed dry or poorly lubricated result in harsh shifts and early clutch failure. Be sure to install the specified number of plates and discs in proper order in each clutch **(Figures 8–91 to 8–94).** Refer to the service manual for specific assembly procedures. Install the snap ring and make sure it is fully seated. All clutch packs must have some clearance to ensure full clutch

FIGURE 8–73 Installing pump vanes in an AXOD-E transaxle. (Courtesy of Ford Motor Company.)

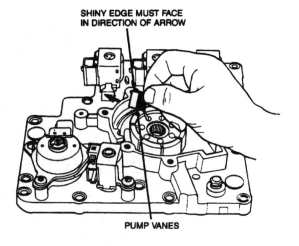

FIGURE 8–74 Installing pump vane support in an AXOD-E transaxle. (Courtesy of Ford Motor Company.)

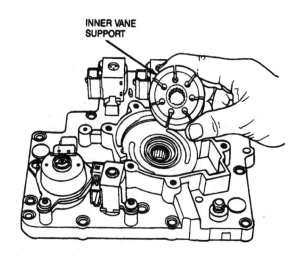

FIGURE 8–75 Installing an AXOD-E transaxle pump vane outer ring. (Courtesy of Ford Motor Company.)

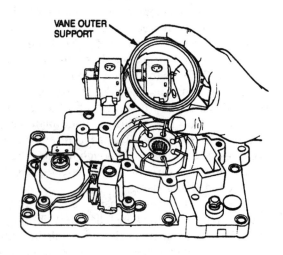

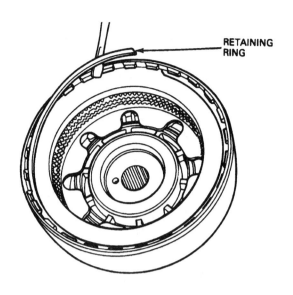

RETAINING
RING

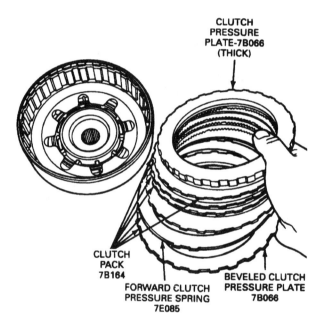

CLUTCH
PRESSURE
PLATE-7B066
(THICK)

CLUTCH
PACK
7B164

FORWARD CLUTCH
PRESSURE SPRING
7E085

BEVELED CLUTCH
PRESSURE PLATE
7B066

FIGURE 8–76 Removing the snap ring and clutch pack from the clutch drum. (Courtesy of Ford Motor Company.)

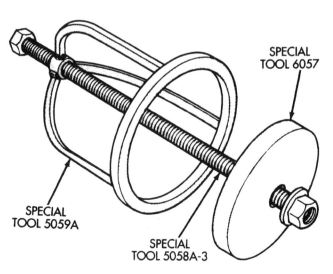

SPECIAL
TOOL 6057

SPECIAL
TOOL 5059A

SPECIAL
TOOL 5058A-3

FIGURE 8–77 Clutch spring compressor tool. (Courtesy of Chrysler Corporation.)

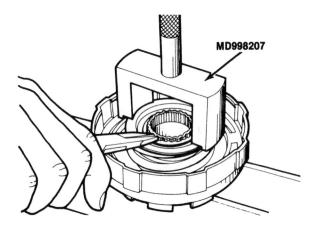

FIGURE 8–78 Using a clutch spring compressor allows snap ring removal. (Courtesy of Chrysler Corporation.)

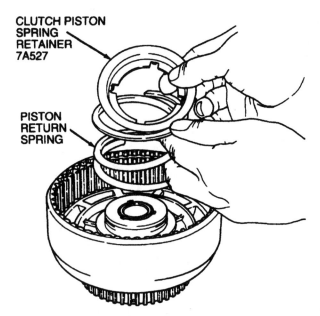

FIGURE 8–79 Clutch with single coil piston return spring. (Courtesy of Ford Motor Company.)

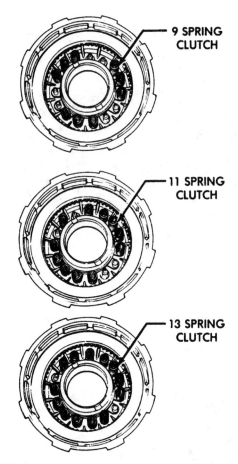

FIGURE 8–80 Multiple return spring clutches vary in the number of springs required. (Courtesy of Chrysler Corporation.)

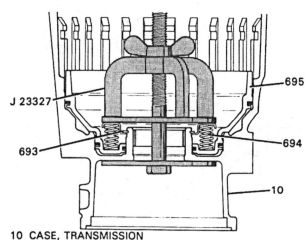

10 CASE, TRANSMISSION
693 RING, LO & REVERSE CLUTCH RETAINER
694 SPRING ASSEMBLY, LO & REVERSE CLUTCH.
695 PISTON, LO & REVERSE CLUTCH

FIGURE 8–81 Removing/installing the Low and Reverse clutch snap ring in a GM 4L60 transmission case. (Courtesy of General Motors Corporation.)

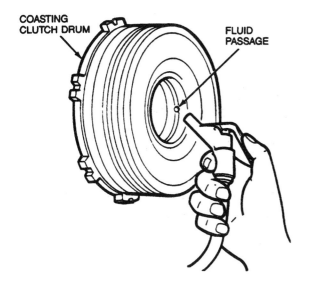

FIGURE 8–82 Using shop air to remove a clutch piston. (Courtesy of Ford Motor Company.)

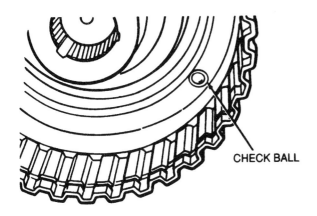

FIGURE 8–83 Clutch piston check ball must be able to move freely and be leak free. (Courtesy of Ford Motor Company.)

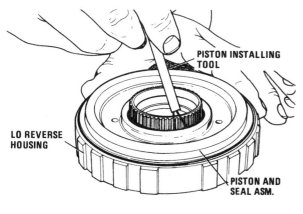

FIGURE 8–84 Fabricated tool for installing clutch piston and seal assembly. (Courtesy of General Motors Corporation.)

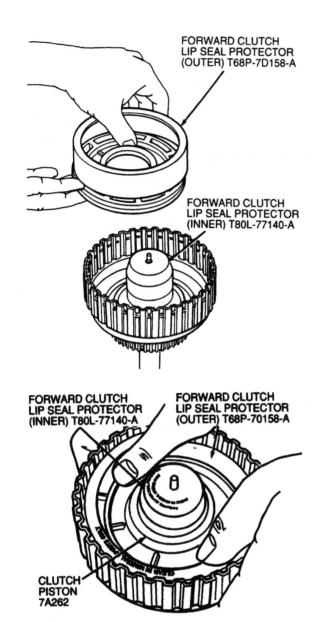

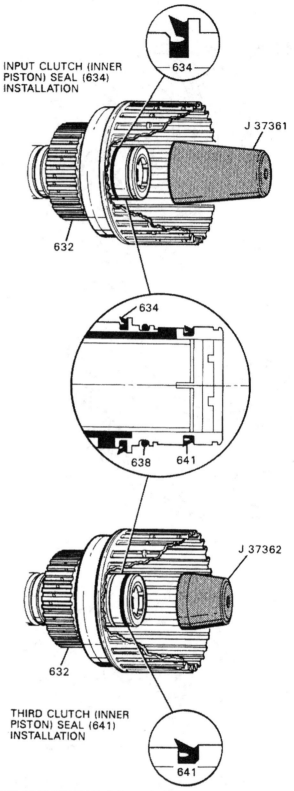

FIGURE 8–85 Using a lip seal protector to install a clutch piston on an AODE transmission. (Courtesy of Ford Motor Company.)

632 HUB HOUSING SLEEVE & SHAFT ASSEMBLY, INPUT
634 SEAL, INPUT CLUTCH PISTON (INNER)
638 SEAL, O-RING
641 SEAL, 3RD CLUTCH PISTON (INNER)

FIGURE 8–86 Input clutch inner piston seal installation, 4T60-E transaxle. (Courtesy of General Motors Corporation.)

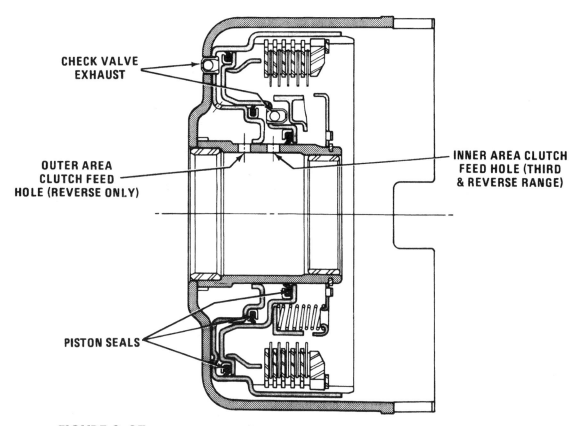

FIGURE 8–87 Cross section of clutch with three seals and two check balls. Note that sealing lips do not all face the same direction. (Courtesy of General Motors Corporation.)

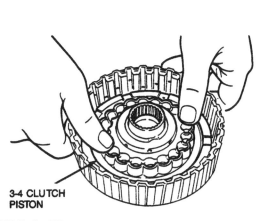

FIGURE 8–88 Pushing a clutch piston into its bore. (Courtesy of Ford Motor Company.)

FIGURE 8–89 Spring placement in a C6 direct clutch. (Courtesy of Ford Motor Company.)

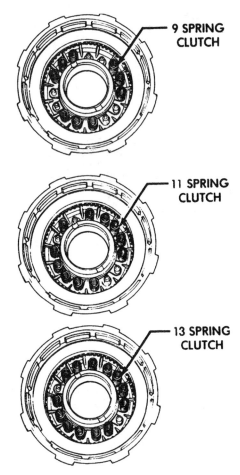

9 SPRING CLUTCH

11 SPRING CLUTCH

13 SPRING CLUTCH

FIGURE 8–90 The correct number of springs must be used in a clutch, and they must be located as specified since torque capacity and shift quality are affected. (Courtesy of Chrysler Corporation.)

release. Insufficient clearance results in clutch drag and overheating. A selective thickness snap ring, apply ring, or pressure plate may be used to increase or decrease clearance to meet specifications depending on clutch design. A rule of thumb allows 0.010 in. (0.25 mm) per friction plate minimum. Consult the service manual for accurate specifications. Clearance is measured with a feeler gauge or a dial indicator, **(Figures 8–95** and **8–96).** To check clutch operation, apply shop air at 35 psi (242 kPa) to the opening specified in the service manual. On some clutches, other holes may have to be blocked by placing a finger over them for this test. If the clutch does not apply properly, check for a missing snap ring, reversed snap ring, reversed clutch apply plate, or damaged piston seals due to improper assembly procedures **(Figure 8–97).**

Servos and Accumulators

Check the pistons, bore surfaces, seal ring grooves, and snap ring grooves for wear, scoring, pitting, or other damage. Minor scoring can be smoothed with crocus cloth. Inspect the return springs for distortion or damage. Clean all parts with mineral spirits and air dry. Make sure all oil passages are clean and unobstructed. Lubricate seal rings, pistons, and bores with ATF during assembly. Use a spring compressor where required for assembly. Compress the spring just far enough to allow snap ring installation. Make sure the snap rings are fully seated. Measure and select the correct servo rod to provide proper band to drum clearance **(Figures 8–98** to **8–103).**

Bands

Inspect the friction surfaces of the bands for pitting, flaking, glazing, looseness, or excessive wear. If the friction surface is in good condition and the band is not distorted, it may be used again. New bands should be soaked in ATF for at least 30 minutes prior to installation to ensure good lubrication and to prevent overheating and glazing.

One-Way Clutches

Inspect the rollers or sprags, inner and outer races, sprag or roller cage, and springs for wear or damage. Damaged or excessively worn parts must be replaced. The clutch must be free to turn in one direction and must lock up in the other. If a one-way clutch is installed in the reverse position, it will overrun when it should lock up and lock up when it should overrun. Obviously, this would not allow proper transmission/transaxle operation. Follow service manual instructions when installing a one-way clutch **(Figures 8–104** to **8–107).**

Planetary Gear Train

Carefully inspect each unit for excessive wear or damage to gear teeth, thrust surfaces, and thrust washers or thrust bearings **(Figures 8–108** to **8–113).** Check pinion gear end play with a feeler gauge and compare to specifications. If end play is excessive, the unit must be repaired or replaced. One example of end-play specifications allows from 0.005 to 0.035 in. (0.13 to 0.89 mm). Follow service manual specifications

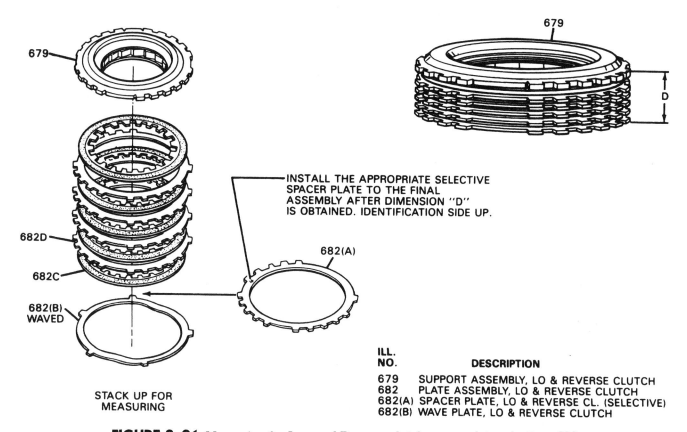

INSTALL THE APPROPRIATE SELECTIVE
SPACER PLATE TO THE FINAL
ASSEMBLY AFTER DIMENSION "D"
IS OBTAINED. IDENTIFICATION SIDE UP.

682(A)

STACK UP FOR
MEASURING

ILL. NO.	DESCRIPTION
679	SUPPORT ASSEMBLY, LO & REVERSE CLUTCH
682	PLATE ASSEMBLY, LO & REVERSE CLUTCH
682(A)	SPACER PLATE, LO & REVERSE CL. (SELECTIVE)
682(B)	WAVE PLATE, LO & REVERSE CLUTCH

FIGURE 8–91 Measuring for Low and Reverse clutch spacer plate selection, GM 4L60 transmission. (Courtesy of General Motors Corporation.)

LO & REVERSE CLUTCH SPACER PLATE SELECTION CHART

IF GAGE DIMENSIONS 'D' IS		USE THIS SELECTIVE PLATE		
FROM	TO	IDENTIFICATION	PLATE THICKNESS	
29.559mm (1.164")	28.844mm (1.136")	NONE	1.671mm (.066")	1.842mm (.073")
28.844mm (1.136")	28.129mm (1.107")	4	2.386mm (.094")	2.557mm (.101")
28.129mm (1.107")	27.414mm (1.079")	5	3.101mm (.122")	3.272mm (.129")

FIGURE 8–92 Low and Reverse clutch spacer plate selection chart for a GM 4L60 transmission. (Courtesy of General Motors Corporation.)

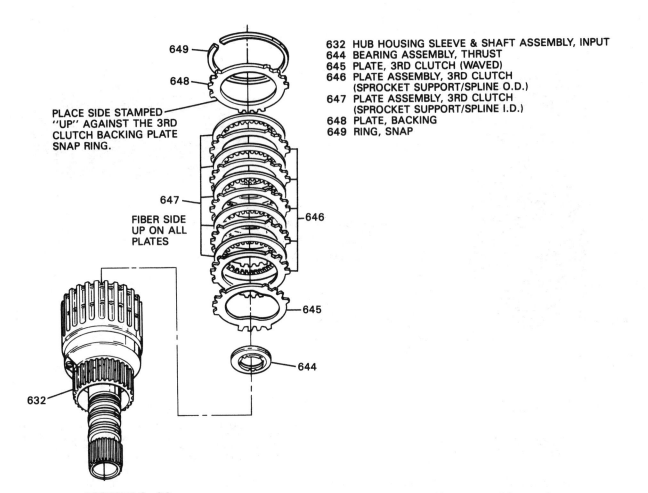

649

648

PLACE SIDE STAMPED
"UP" AGAINST THE 3RD
CLUTCH BACKING PLATE
SNAP RING.

647

FIBER SIDE
UP ON ALL
PLATES

646

645

644

632

632 HUB HOUSING SLEEVE & SHAFT ASSEMBLY, INPUT
644 BEARING ASSEMBLY, THRUST
645 PLATE, 3RD CLUTCH (WAVED)
646 PLATE ASSEMBLY, 3RD CLUTCH
    (SPROCKET SUPPORT/SPLINE O.D.)
647 PLATE ASSEMBLY, 3RD CLUTCH
    (SPROCKET SUPPORT/SPLINE I.D.)
648 PLATE, BACKING
649 RING, SNAP

FIGURE 8–93 Transaxle third clutch assembly instructions. (Courtesy of General Motors Corporation.)

FIGURE 8–94 Alignment of forward and 3–4 clutch plates in a 4L60 transmission. (Courtesy of General Motors Corporation.)

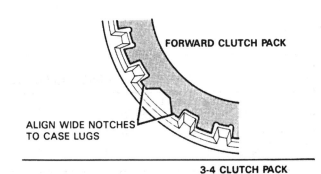

FORWARD CLUTCH PACK

ALIGN WIDE NOTCHES
TO CASE LUGS

3-4 CLUTCH PACK

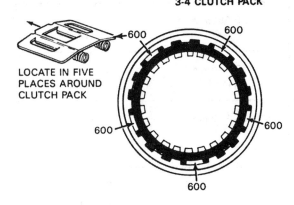

600

LOCATE IN FIVE
PLACES AROUND
CLUTCH PACK

600 SPRING ASM., BOOST 3-4 CLUTCH

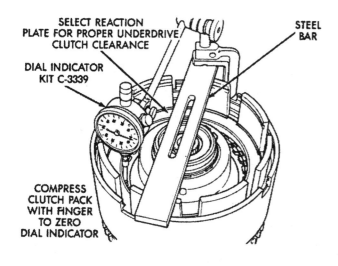

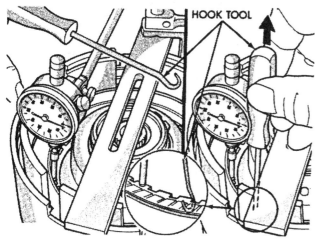

FIGURE 8-95 Using a dial indicator and hook tool to measure clutch pack clearance. (Courtesy of Chrysler Corporation.)

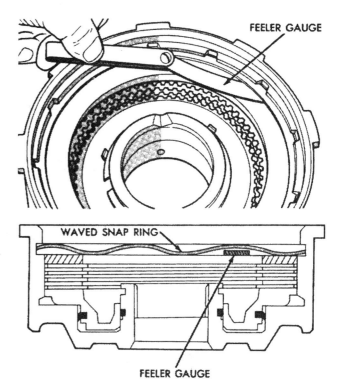

FIGURE 8-96 Measuring clutch pack clearance with a feeler gauge. (Courtesy of Chrysler Corporation.)

and procedures for correction of end play. Some planetary units can be repaired, while parts are not available for others. If this is the case, the unit must be replaced.

Transmission and transaxle shafts include the turbine shaft, intermediate shaft, output shaft, direct drive shaft, and final drive shaft. Not all shafts are found on all transmissions/transaxles, depending on design. Shafts should be checked for straightness, bearing journal wear, thrust surface wear, and wear or damage to splines and snap ring grooves. The inspection and measurement of shafts and the inspection of bearings is described in Chapter 6. Refer to it and the service manual for procedures.

Valve Body Service

To properly service the valve body, it must be completely disassembled, and the parts cleaned in mineral spirits and air dried. Rubber check balls must not be soaked in cleaning fluids since this will cause them to swell and lose their sealing ability. Disassembly must be done in the order and manner described in the applicable service manual. Failure to do so can result in parts damage requiring the replacement of the entire valve body assembly.

Disassembly should be done over a large tray containing mineral spirits **(Figures 8-114** to **8-116).** Stuck valves may have to be sprayed with valve body cleaner or carburetor cleaner to loosen varnish or dirt. Metal particles sometimes cause valves to be stuck. Cleaning fluids do not help in this case. Tapping the open end of the valve bore may dislodge the valve. Another method is to place several layers of a shop towel on the bench top. Tapping the flat open end of the valve bore sharply and squarely on the shop towel several times may loosen the valve. Repeat if necessary. If the valve body casting openings allow, force may be applied to the grooved portion of the valve using a screwdriver and tapping it lightly. Care must be taken not to damage the valve or the valve body in any way during this procedure.

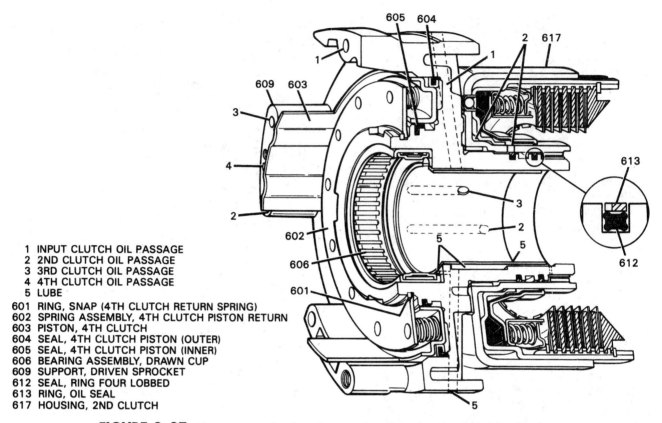

1   INPUT CLUTCH OIL PASSAGE
2   2ND CLUTCH OIL PASSAGE
3   3RD CLUTCH OIL PASSAGE
4   4TH CLUTCH OIL PASSAGE
5   LUBE
601   RING, SNAP (4TH CLUTCH RETURN SPRING)
602   SPRING ASSEMBLY, 4TH CLUTCH PISTON RETURN
603   PISTON, 4TH CLUTCH
604   SEAL, 4TH CLUTCH PISTON (OUTER)
605   SEAL, 4TH CLUTCH PISTON (INNER)
606   BEARING ASSEMBLY, DRAWN CUP
609   SUPPORT, DRIVEN SPROCKET
612   SEAL, RING FOUR LOBBED
613   RING, OIL SEAL
617   HOUSING, 2ND CLUTCH

FIGURE 8–97 Air pressure check points on fourth and second clutch of a four-speed transaxle. (Courtesy of General Motors Corporation.)

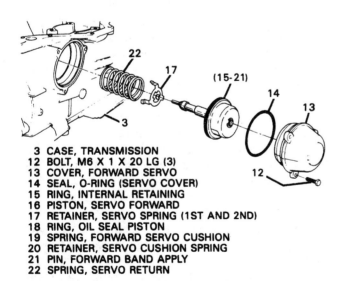

3   CASE, TRANSMISSION
12   BOLT, M6 X 1 X 20 LG (3)
13   COVER, FORWARD SERVO
14   SEAL, O-RING (SERVO COVER)
15   RING, INTERNAL RETAINING
16   PISTON, SERVO FORWARD
17   RETAINER, SERVO SPRING (1ST AND 2ND)
18   RING, OIL SEAL PISTON
19   SPRING, FORWARD SERVO CUSHION
20   RETAINER, SERVO CUSHION SPRING
21   PIN, FORWARD BAND APPLY
22   SPRING, SERVO RETURN

FIGURE 8–98 4T60-E transaxle forward servo assembly. (Courtesy of General Motors Corporation.)

Keep all the parts in order as they are removed from each valve bore, and place them on a clean, lint-free shop towel. Although some springs and valves may look alike, they are not interchangeable or reversible.

Spray all valve body parts with valve body cleaner or carburetor cleaner, wash them in mineral spirits, and air dry. Maintain parts in their proper order at all times. While some manufacturers do not allow any service procedures to be performed on valves or valve bores, others allow the use of crocus cloth to remove minor scoring. Emery cloth or sandpaper should never be used since they leave scratches. To remove minor scoring from a valve bore, roll up a piece of crocus cloth and rotate it in the bore. An accurately dimensioned wooden dowel may be used inside the roll of crocus cloth to aid in the procedure. Wash the bore to remove any grit before trying to insert the valve. Minor imperfections on valves can be removed with crocus cloth. Place a sheet of crocus cloth on a true flat-machined surface or on a piece of plate glass (or use an Arkansas stone), and rotate the valve on the crocus cloth without allowing the valve to roll. This results in a scrubbing action on the valve lands and avoids dulling the lands

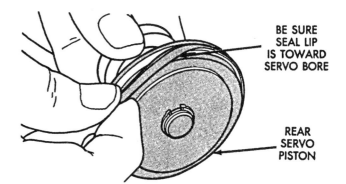

FIGURE 8–100 Servo piston seal installation. (Courtesy of Chrysler Corporation.)

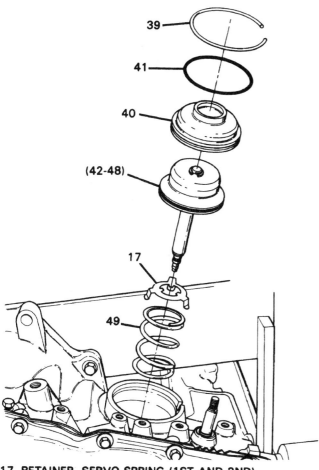

17 RETAINER, SERVO SPRING (1ST AND 2ND)
39 RING, SERVO COVER RETAINING
40 COVER, SERVO
41 SEAL, O-RING (SERVO COVER)
42 RING, INTERNAL RETAINING
43 RING, OIL SEAL PISTON
44 PISTON, SERVO REVERSE
45 SPRING, REVERSE SERVO CUSHION
46 RETAINER, SERVO CUSHION SPRING
47 SPRING, REVERSE SERVO CURVED
48 PIN, REVERSE APPLY (SELECTIVE)
49 SPRING. SERVO RETURN

FIGURE 8–99 4T60-E transaxle reverse servo components. (Courtesy of General Motors Corporation.)

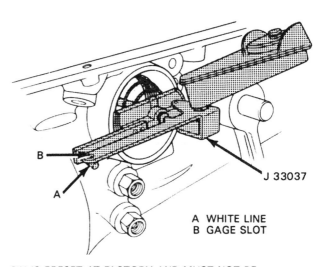

A WHITE LINE
B GAGE SLOT

PIN IS PRESET AT FACTORY AND MUST NOT BE READJUSTED

2-4 SERVO PIN SELECTION		
PIN LENGTH		PIN I.D.
mm	INCH	
66.37 - 66.67	2.61 - 2.62	2 RINGS
67.74 - 68.04	2.67 - 2.68	3 RINGS
69.11 - 69.41	2.72 - 2.73	WIDE BAND

FIGURE 8–101 Servo pin length selection, 4L60 transmission. (Courtesy of General Motors Corporation.)

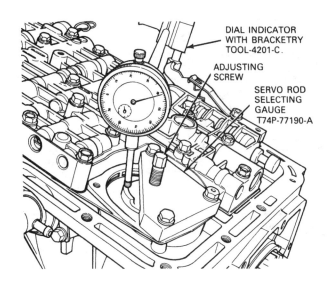

DIAL INDICATOR
WITH BRACKETRY
TOOL-4201-C.

ADJUSTING
SCREW

SERVO ROD
SELECTING
GAUGE
T74P-77190-A

Length — mm	Length — Inches	I.D.
54/53 mm	2.112/2.085	1 Groove
51/50 mm	2.014/1.986	No Groove
49/48 mm	1.915/1.888	2 Grooves

FIGURE 8–102 Servo rod selecting gauge and dial indicator are used to select rod length required on an A4LD reverse servo. (Courtesy of Ford Motor Company.)

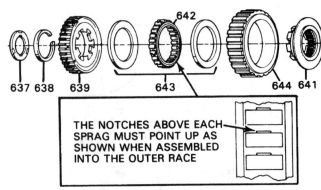

642

637 638 639 643 644 641

THE NOTCHES ABOVE EACH
SPRAG MUST POINT UP AS
SHOWN WHEN ASSEMBLED
INTO THE OUTER RACE

637 BEARING ASSEMBLY, INPUT SUN GEAR
638 SNAP RING, OVERRUN CLUTCH HUB RET.
639 HUB, OVERRUN CLUTCH
641 RETAINER & RACE ASSEMBLY, SPRAG
642 FORWARD SPRAG ASSEMBLY
643 RETAINER RINGS, SPRAG ASSEMBLY
644 RACE, FORWARD CLUTCH OUTER

FIGURE 8–104 Forward clutch sprag (one-way clutch) assembly in a GM 4L60 transmission. (Courtesy of General Motors Corporation.)

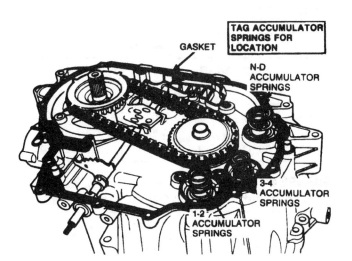

TAG ACCUMULATOR
SPRINGS FOR
LOCATION

GASKET

N-D
ACCUMULATOR
SPRINGS

3-4
ACCUMULATOR
SPRINGS

1-2
ACCUMULATOR
SPRINGS

FIGURE 8–103 Install accumulator springs in accordance with position tagged during disassembly. (Courtesy of Ford Motor Company.)

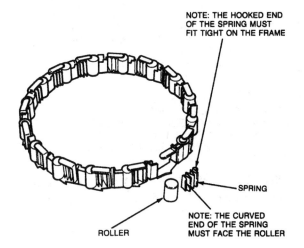

NOTE: THE HOOKED END
OF THE SPRING MUST
FIT TIGHT ON THE FRAME

SPRING

ROLLER

NOTE: THE CURVED
END OF THE SPRING
MUST FACE THE ROLLER

FIGURE 8–105 Typical one-way roller clutch assembly instructions. (Courtesy of Ford Motor Company.)

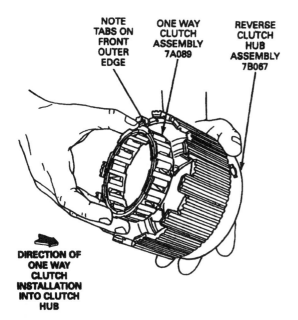

FIGURE 8–106 Installing a one-way clutch, E40D transmission. (Courtesy of Ford Motor Company.)

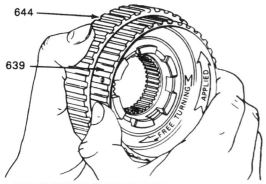

THE OVERRUN CLUTCH HUB MUST TURN
CLOCKWISE, BUT NOT COUNTERCLOCKWISE

639 HUB, OVERRUN CLUTCH
644 RACE, FORWARD CLUTCH (OUTER)

FIGURE 8–107 Checking sprag clutch operation in a GM 4L60 transmission. (Courtesy of General Motors Corporation.)

sharp edges (**Figure 8–117**). These sharp edges must not be dulled since this would allow foreign particles to wedge between the valve and valve bore and cause the valve to stick. After washing away all abrasives and with the parts air dried, check each valve in its bore. Valves should move freely back and forth in their bores by their own weight as the valve body is tilted back and forth. Make sure springs are not distorted, and assemble the valve body in the order prescribed in the service

manual. Make sure all check balls are in their proper location (**Figure 8–118**). Procedures and torque specifications vary. All screws and bolts must be installed in the order specified and tightened in the proper sequence to the torque specified in the service manual (**Figures 8–119** to **8–124**).

Governor Valve Service

The governor should be serviced during transmission/transaxle overhaul to avoid governor-related shift problems (**Figures 8–125** and **8–126**). On output shaft-mounted governors, inspect the valves and valve bores as described earlier in the section on Valve Body Service. Remove any minor imperfections with crocus cloth as described there as well. Make sure the filter screen is clean and is not collapsed or distorted. Inspect the oil seal ring grooves for scoring and wear. Inspect the bore where the seal rings ride for grooved wear. Follow service manual directions for assembly and air-testing the governor.

Case-mounted governors are gear driven with either a weight-actuated valve or ball (**Figures 8–127** and **8–128**). Inspect and service the valve and valve bore as outlined in Valve Body Service. Remove minor imperfections with crocus cloth as described earlier. Inspect the governor weight springs for distortion. Check for free movement of the governor weights and valve by moving the governor weights through their travel limits. Correct any binding action. Inspect the driven gear for any damage or excessive wear. Check the valve inlet and outlet ports to make sure they provide the required opening and do not restrict fluid flow. The inlet can be measured with a feeler gauge with the weights fully extended. The outlet can be measured with the weights in the fully retracted position. Check the service manual for port opening specifications. A minimum of 0.020 in. (0.50 mm) is typical. Check the governor-to-case clearance by installing the governor in the case and performing a leak test with solvent as outlined in the service manual. If leakdown is excessive, it may be possible to restore proper clearance by machining the case bore and installing a repair sleeve. Consult the service manual for detailed procedures.

On the check-ball type of governor, check the weights and springs as described earlier. To check the condition of the ball and seat, perform a leak test as described in the service manual (**Figure 8–129**). Check for proper clearance at the points indicated in **Figures 8–130** and **8–131**. Install the governor cover (**Figure 8–132**).

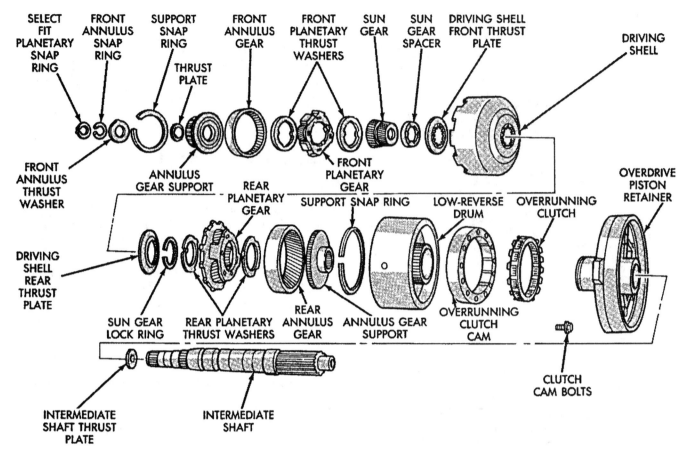

FIGURE 8–108 Gear train parts for a 42RH four-speed transmission. (Courtesy of Chrysler Corporation.)

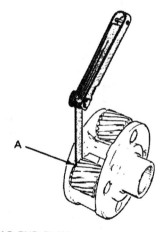

A PINION GEAR END PLAY —
.20mm/.60mm (.008"/.024")

FIGURE 8–109 Checking pinion gear end play. (Courtesy of General Motors Corporation.)

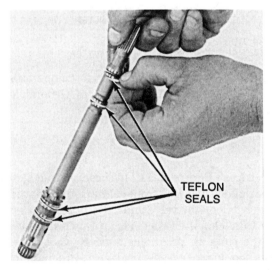

FIGURE 8–110 Teflon seal rings on a transaxle pump drive shaft. (Courtesy of Ford Motor Company.)

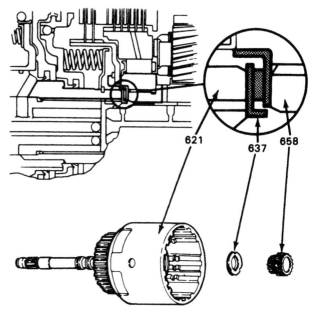

621 HOUSING & SHAFT ASSEMBLY, INPUT
637 BEARING ASSEMBLY, INPUT SUN GEAR
658 GEAR, INPUT SUN

FIGURE 8–112 Proper assembly of input sun gear thrust bearing in a GM 4L60 transmission. (Courtesy of General Motors Corporation.)

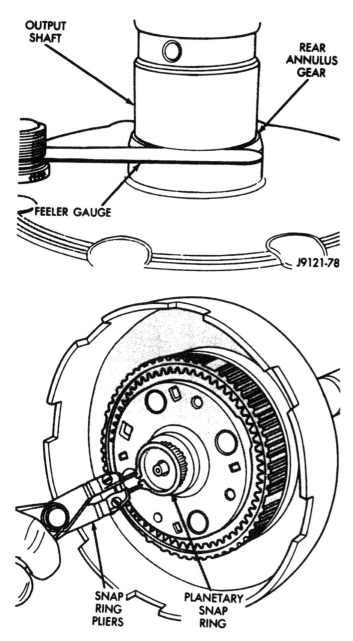

FIGURE 8–111 Measuring gear train end play (top). Thinner or thicker snap ring is used to correct end play. (Courtesy of Chrysler Corporation.)

Transaxle Final Drive and Differential

There are three general types of transaxle final drive: the helical gear, hypoid gear, and planetary gear. All three use conventional differential gears. Critical inspection points include checking for excessive wear or damage to:

1. Gear teeth on all gears, final drive, and differential (**Figures 8–133** to **8–136**)

2. Differential side gear thrust washers

3. Pinion gear thrust surfaces and thrust washers

4. Differential case thrust surfaces (at side gear and pinion gear contact areas)

5. Holes in case where the pinion gear shaft is mounted

6. Pinion gear shaft

7. Differential side bearings (if equipped) cone and roller assemblies and bearing cups

8. Differential side bearing preload or end play (where applicable).

Consult the service manual for detailed procedures and specifications for any specific model of transaxle. Procedures vary considerably among helical gear, planetary gear, and hypoid gear designs.

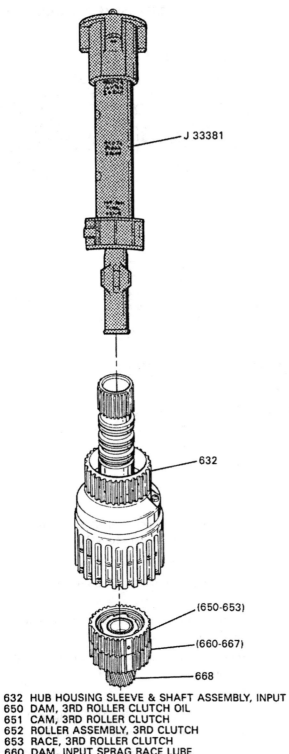

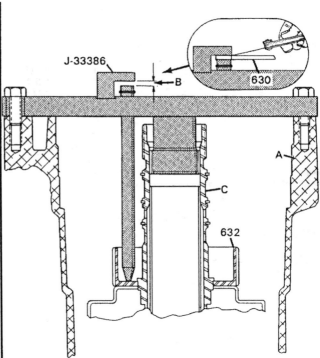

J 33381

632

(650-653)

(660-667)

668

632 HUB HOUSING SLEEVE & SHAFT ASSEMBLY, INPUT
650 DAM, 3RD ROLLER CLUTCH OIL
651 CAM, 3RD ROLLER CLUTCH
652 ROLLER ASSEMBLY, 3RD CLUTCH
653 RACE, 3RD ROLLER CLUTCH
660 DAM, INPUT SPRAG RACE LUBE
661 RACE, INPUT SPRAG CLUTCH (INNER)
662 RING, SNAP
663 BEARING, END
664 SPRAG ASSEMBLY, INPUT CLUTCH
665 RACE, INPUT SPRAG CLUTCH (OUTER)
666 RETAINER, INPUT SPRAG CLUTCH
667 SPACER, INPUT SUN GEAR
668 GEAR, INPUT SUN

J-33386

J-33386

630

B

A

C

632

A CASE
B INSERT SELECTIVE THRUST WASHER TO
   DETERMINE PROPER SIZE
C INPUT SHAFT
630 WASHER, THRUST (SELECTIVE)
632 HOUSING & SHAFT ASSEMBLY, INPUT

If a .152 mm (.006") feeler gauge or larger can be inserted
between thrust washer and tool, use next size larger thrust
washer.

GUIDE FOR SELECTIVE THRUST WASHER

I.D. NO.	DIMENSION		COLOR
	MM	INCHES	
1	2.90-3.00	(0.114-0.118)	ORANGE/GREEN
2	3.05-3.15	(0.120-0.124)	ORANGE/BLACK
3	3.20-3.30	(0.126-0.130)	ORANGE
4	3.35-3.45	(0.132-0.136)	WHITE
5	3.50-3.60	(0.138-0.142)	BLUE
6	3.65-3.75	(0.144-0.148)	PINK
7	3.80-3.90	(0.150-0.154)	BROWN
8	3.95-4.05	(0.156-0.159)	GREEN
9	4.10-4.20	(0.161-0.165)	BLACK
10	4.25-4.35	(0.167-0.171)	PURPLE
11	4.40-4.50	(0.173-0.177)	PURPLE/WHITE
12	4.55-4.65	(0.179-0.183)	PURPLE/BLUE
13	4.70-4.80	(0.185-0.189)	PURPLE/PINK
14	4.85-4.95	(0.191-0.195)	PURPLE/BROWN
15	5.00-5.10	(0.197-0.200)	PURPLE/GREEN

FIGURE 8–113 Installing the input housing and selecting the proper thrust washer, 4T60-E transaxle. (Courtesy of General Motors Corporation.)

EQUIPMENT FOR CLEANING

- Valve body is a precision "hydraulic computer."
- Clinical cleanliness is necessary for proper operation.
- All items shown are essential.

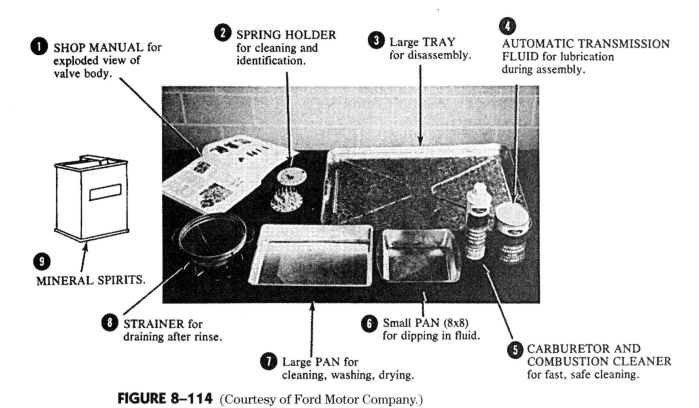

❶ SHOP MANUAL for exploded view of valve body.

❷ SPRING HOLDER for cleaning and identification.

❸ Large TRAY for disassembly.

❹ AUTOMATIC TRANSMISSION FLUID for lubrication during assembly.

❾ MINERAL SPIRITS.

❽ STRAINER for draining after rinse.

❼ Large PAN for cleaning, washing, drying.

❻ Small PAN (8x8) for dipping in fluid.

❺ CARBURETOR AND COMBUSTION CLEANER for fast, safe cleaning.

FIGURE 8–114 (Courtesy of Ford Motor Company.)

Transmission/Transaxle Case

The transmission or transaxle case consists of two or more sections or units. This includes the main housing that contains the gear train and usually, though not always, the torque converter, an extension housing that contains the output shaft, a bushing and seal **(Figure 8–137),** and/or the transaxle differential and a transaxle case cover. All other transmission/transaxle components are attached to these parts in some way. It is these attachment points that must be carefully inspected for excessive wear or damage. All sealing surfaces must be smooth and flat **(Figures 8–138 to 8–141).** Threaded holes must be cleaned and damaged threads repaired with a thread repair insert (see Chapter 6 for thread repair procedures). Check all oil passages to ensure that they are clean and unobstructed.

TORQUE CONVERTER INSPECTION

The converter must be replaced if one of the following conditions exists **(Figures 8–142 to 8–148):**

1. Stator one-way clutch failure; stator locked or free wheels in both directions
2. Badly scored or damaged converter hub, worn drive lugs, or badly scored hub surface
3. Fluid leakage from seams or welds on the converter
4. Loose drive studs, worn drive stud shoulders, or stripped drive stud threads
5. Metal grindings in converter evidenced by cast iron or aluminum in fluid
6. Excessive turbine end play

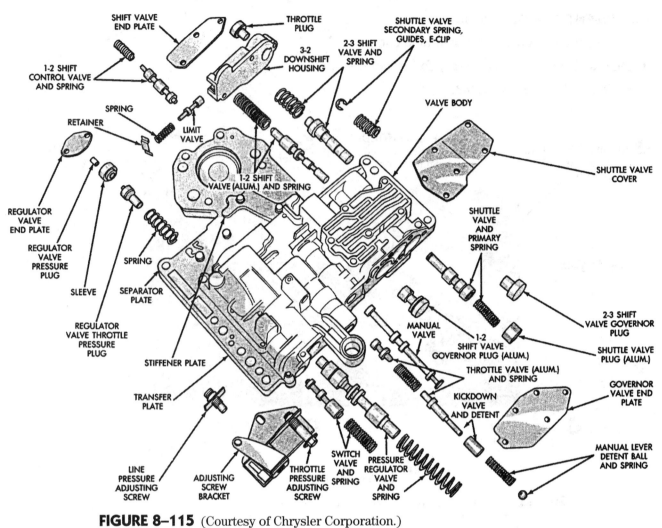

FIGURE 8–115 (Courtesy of Chrysler Corporation.)

A converter that passes inspection on all the first five points should be checked for turbine end play. Excessive wear of the thrust bearings and surfaces requires converter replacement. Measure turbine end play. If turbine end play is within specifications and the converter is not equipped with a lockup clutch, it can be cleaned by flushing using torque converter flushing equipment. Do not flush the torque converter unless recommended by the vehicle manufacturer. Follow the equipment manufacturer's instructions during the flushing procedure. Light scratches or scoring of the hub surface can be polished with crocus cloth. Check flex plate condition and runout. Replace if damage or runout are excessive.

COOLER AND COOLER LINE SERVICE

In a major transmission/transaxle failure, where particles of metal have been carried with the oil through-out the system, it will be necessary to flush out the oil cooler and connecting lines. To flush the oil cooler and lines, use the following procedures (**Figure 8–149**):

1. Disconnect both cooler lines at the transmission/transaxle.

2. Place a hose over the end of the cooler inlet line (from the bottom of the cooler) and insert the hose into an empty container.

3. Flush clean solvent through the return line (from the top of the cooler) using an oil suction gun until clean solvent comes out of the hose. This will back-flush the cooler.

4. Remove the hose from the inlet cooler line and place it on the return line.

5. Flush clean solvent through the inlet line until clean solvent comes out the return line. Remove the remaining solvent from the cooler with compressed air

WASHING AND DRYING

CLEANING PAN

LARGE
TRAY

SEPARATOR
PLATE

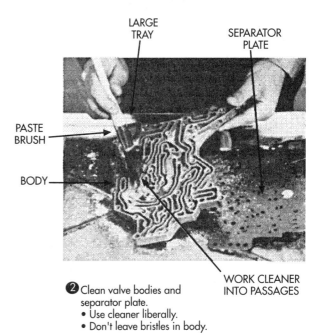

PASTE
BRUSH

BODY

WORK CLEANER
INTO PASSAGES

❶ Spray all small parts with
cleaner.
  • Cover all parts with foam.
  • Spray spring holder also.

❷ Clean valve bodies and
separator plate.
  • Use cleaner liberally.
  • Don't leave bristles in body.

❸ Rinse thoroughly.
  • Use **hot** tap water.
  • Cleaner will rinse away readily.

SPRINGS

BASKET

MINERAL
SPIRITS

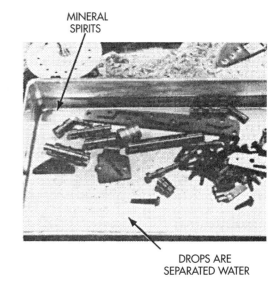

DROPS ARE
SEPARATED WATER

❹ Drip dry small parts.

❺ Dip **all** parts in mineral spirits
for final water separation.

FIGURE 8–116 (Courtesy of Ford Motor Company.)

CORRECTING STICKING, BURRS, SCORING

- Inspect valves and bores during disassembly.

- Remove burrs, nicks, scores before cleaning.

1 Remove burr or nick.
  - Do **not** round edges of lands

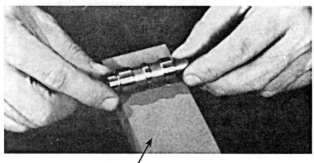

FLAT ARKANSAS
STONE

2 Clean slight scoring in bores.

  - **No** hard pressure on crocus cloth.

TURN IN   CROCUS CLOTH #600
"UNROLL"
DIRECTION

FIGURE 8–117 (Courtesy of Ford Motor Company.)

applied to the return line and flush with transmission fluid.

PRO TIP

Maximum air pressure should not exceed 50 psi (345 kPa).

---

6. Reconnect oil cooler lines and torque nuts to specified torque.

This procedure can also be done with converter flushing equipment. Follow the equipment manufacturer's instructions for procedures and pressures to use.

Oil Cooler Lines

If replacement of steel cooler lines is required, use only double-wrapped and brazed steel tubing. Never use copper or aluminum tubing to replace steel tubing. Those materials do not have satisfactory fatigue durability to withstand normal car vibrations. Steel tubing

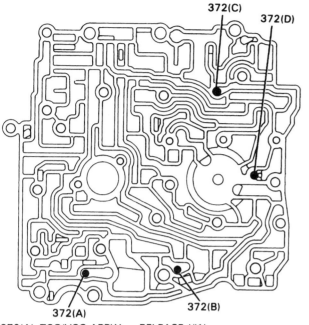

372(C)   372(D)

SHIFT CONDITIONS IF A CHECKBALL IS MISSING OR
MISLOCATED FOR EACH CHECKBALL:

372(A) #1 NO CONVERTER CLUTCH APPLY

372(B) #2 1-2 SHIFT HARSH

372(C) #3 NO DRIVE IN DRIVE RANGES

372(D) #4 SOFT 2-3 SHIFT AND SLIPS IN 3RD GEAR
UNDER LOAD.

ALSO, MANUAL LO PRESSURE BOOST BELOW
SPECIFICATION.

372(A)   372(B)

372(A) TCC/VCC APPLY — RELEASE (#1)
372(B) 2ND — 2ND CL. (#2)
372(C) INPUT CLUTCH — PRN (#3)
372(D) 3RD CLUTCH — LO/1ST (#4)

CHANNEL PLATE SIDE

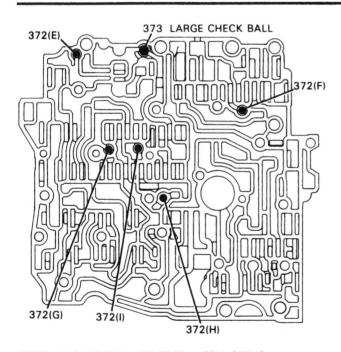

372(E)   373 LARGE CHECK BALL

372(F)

372(E) #5 HARSH NEUTRAL TO REVERSE

372(F) #7 HARSH APPLY OF 3RD CLUTCH FOR MANUAL
LO AND MANUAL LO LOCK-OUT SPEED ABOVE 35
MPH.

372(G) #8 HARSH APPLY OF 2-1 MANUAL BAND IN
MANUAL 2ND AND LO

372(H) #9 2-3 SHIFT HARSH AND 3-2 SHIFT HARSH

372(I) #10 3-4 AND 4-3 SHIFT FEEL — HARSH

373   #6 HARSH NEUTRAL TO DRIVE

372(G)   372(I)

372(H)

372(E) #5 CHECKBALL, REVERSE — REV. SERVO
372(F) #7 CHECKBALL, LO — LO/1ST
372(G) #8 CHECKBALL, D2 — MANUAL 2-1 SERVO FEED
372(H) #9 CHECKBALL, 3RD CL — 3RD CL EX
372(I) #10 CHECKBALL, 4TH — 4TH CL
373   #6 CHECKBALL, D4 — SERVO APPLY

VALVE BODY SIDE

FIGURE 8–118 4T60-E transaxle shift conditions resulting from missing or mislocated check balls. (Courtesy of General Motors Corporation.)

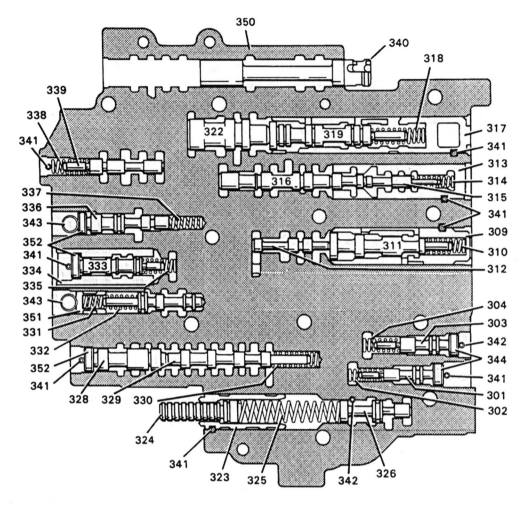

ILL. NO.	DESCRIPTION
301	VALVE, T.V. MODULATOR DOWNSHIFT
302	SPRING, T.V. MODULATOR DOWNSHIFT VALVE
303	VALVE, T.V. MODULATOR UPSHIFT
304	SPRING, T.V. MODULATOR UPSHIFT VALVE
309	SLEEVE, 3-4 THROTTLE VALVE
310	SPRING, 3-4 THROTTLE VALVE
311	VALVE, 3-4 THROTTLE
312	VALVE, 3-4 SHIFT
313	SLEEVE, 2-3 THROTTLE VALVE
314	SPRING, 2-3 THROTTLE VALVE
315	VALVE, 2-3 THROTTLE
316	VALVE, 2-3 SHIFT
317	SLEEVE, 1-2 THROTTLE VALVE
318	SPRING, 1-2 THROTTLE VALVE
319	VALVE, 1-2 THROTTLE
322	VALVE, 1-2 SHIFT
323	SLEEVE, THROTTLE VALVE PLUNGER
324	PLUNGER, THROTTLE VALVE
325	SPRING, THROTTLE VALVE
326	VALVE, THROTTLE
328	VALVE, 3-4 RELAY
329	VALVE, 4-3 SEQUENCE

ILL. NO.	DESCRIPTION
330	SPRING, 4-3 SEQUENCE VALVE
331	SPRING, T.V. LIMIT VALVE
332	VALVE, T.V. LIMIT
333	VALVE, 1-2 ACCUMULATOR
334	SLEEVE, 1-2 ACCUMULATOR VALVE
335	SPRING, 1-2 ACCUMULATOR VALVE
336	VALVE, LINE BIAS
337	SPRING, LINE BIAS VALVE
338	SPRING, 3-2 CONTROL
339	VALVE, 3-2 CONTROL
340	VALVE, MANUAL
341	PIN, COILED SPRING
342	PIN, COILED SPRING
343	RETAINER, SPRING (SLEEVE)
344	PLUG, VALVE BORE
350	BODY, CONTROL VALVE
351	PLUG, T.V. LIMIT
352	PLUG, VALVE BORE (12.5 - O.D.)

FIGURE 8–119 Valve body cross section, GM 4L60 transmission. (Courtesy of General Motors Corporation.)

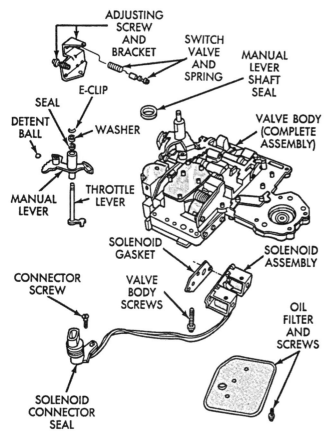

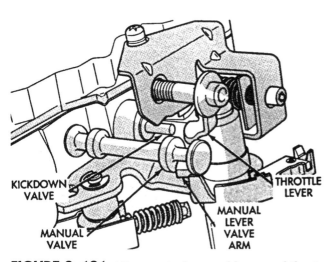

FIGURE 8–120 Serviceable valve body parts for a typical Chrysler transmission. (Courtesy of Chrysler Corporation.)

FIGURE 8–121 Alignment of manual lever and throttle lever on a Chrysler 32RH transmission. (Courtesy of Chrysler Corporation.)

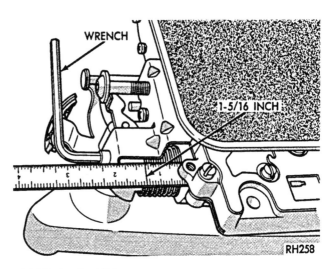

FIGURE 8–122 Line pressure adjustment on a Chrysler 32RH transmission. (Courtesy of Chrysler Corporation.)

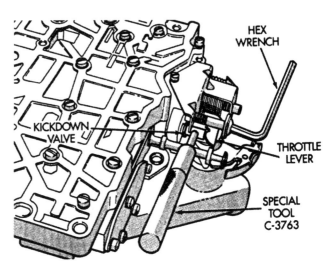

FIGURE 8–123 Throttle pressure adjustment on a Chrysler 32RH transmission. (Courtesy of Chrysler Corporation.)

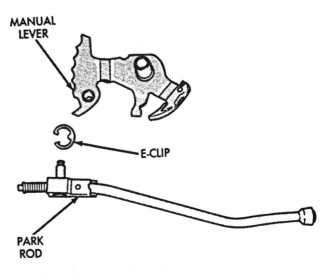

FIGURE 8–124 Park rod components for a typical Chrysler transmission. (Courtesy of Chrysler Corporation.)

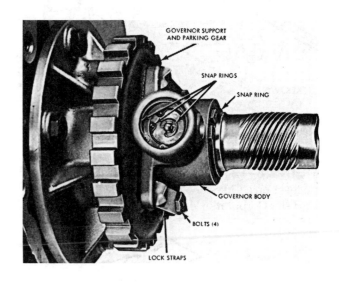

FIGURE 8–125 Transmission output shaft-mounted governor. (Courtesy of Chrysler Corporation.)

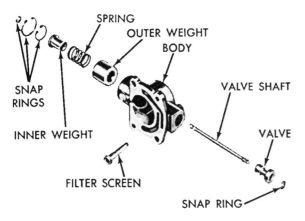

FIGURE 8–126 Output shaft-mounted governor components. (Courtesy of Chrysler Corporation.)

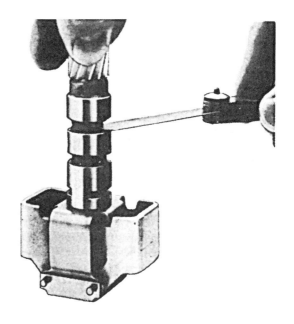

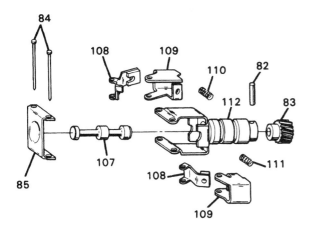

GOVERNOR ASSEMBLY

82 PIN, GOVERNOR GEAR RETAINER
83 GEAR, GOVERNOR DRIVEN
84 PIN, GOVERNOR WEIGHT
85 CAP, GOVERNOR THRUST
107 VALVE, GOVERNOR
108 WEIGHT, GOVERNOR SECONDARY
109 WEIGHT, GOVERNOR PRIMARY
110 SPRING, GOVERNOR WEIGHT PRIMARY
111 SPRING, GOVERNOR WEIGHT SECONDARY
112 SLEEVE & CARRIER ASSEMBLY

FIGURE 8–127 Components of case-mounted valve type governor. (Courtesy of General Motors Corporation.)

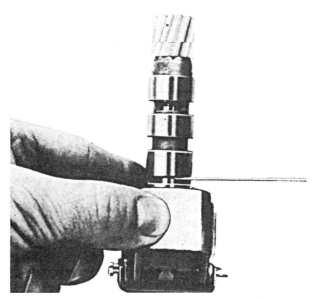

FIGURE 8–128 Measuring inlet (top) and outlet (bottom) openings on a spool valve governor. (Courtesy of General Motors Corporation.)

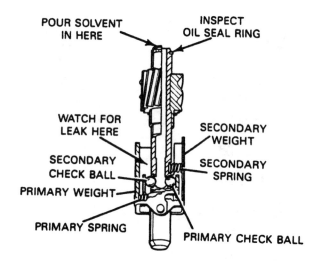

FIGURE 8–129 Leak testing a check-ball governor. (Courtesy of General Motors Corporation.)

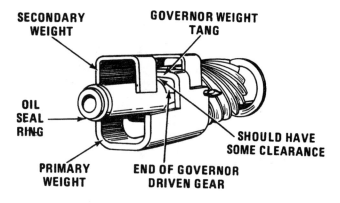

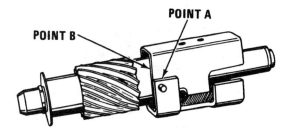

FIGURE 8–130 Check-ball governor clearance points. (Courtesy of General Motors Corporation.)

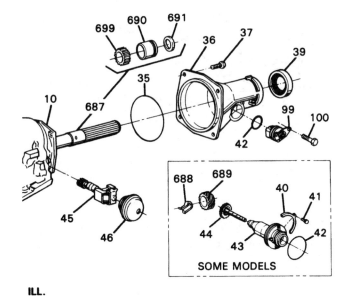

ILL. NO.	DESCRIPTION
10	CASE, TRANSMISSION
35	SEAL, CASE EXTENSION TO CASE
36	EXTENSION, CASE
37	BOLT, CASE EXTENSION TO CASE
39	SEAL ASSEMBLY, CASE EXTENSION OIL
40	RETAINER, SPEEDO DRIVEN GEAR FITTING
41	BOLT & WASHER ASSEMBLY
42	SEAL, O-RING (SPEEDO FITTING TO CASE EXTENSION)
43	FITTING ASSEMBLY, SPEEDO DRIVEN GEAR
44	GEAR, SPEEDO DRIVEN
45	GOVERNOR ASSEMBLY
46	COVER, GOVERNOR
99	SPEED SENSOR, INTERNAL TRANSMISSION
100	BOLT, SPEEDO SENSOR RETAINING
687	SHAFT, OUTPUT
688	CLIP, SPEEDO DRIVE GEAR
689	GEAR, SPEEDO DRIVE
690	SLEEVE, OUTPUT SHAFT NOT USED ON
691	SEAL, OUTPUT SHAFT ALL MODELS
699	ROTOR, INTERNAL TRANSMISSION SPEED SENSOR

FIGURE 8–131 GM 4L60 transmission case extension and associated parts. (Courtesy of General Motors Corporation.)

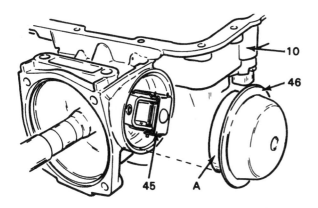

A APPLY SEALANT ON THIS FLANGE BEFORE
  INSTALLATION
10 CASE, TRANSMISSION
45 GOVERNOR, ASSEMBLY
46 COVER, GOVERNOR

FIGURE 8–132 Governor cover installation on a GM 4L60 transmission. (Courtesy of General Motors Corporation.)

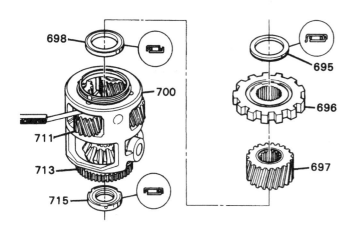

695 BEARING ASSEMBLY, THRUST (INTERNAL GEAR/
    PARKING GEAR)
696 GEAR, PARKING
697 GEAR, FINAL DRIVE SUN
698 BEARING ASSEMBLY, THRUST CARRIER/SUN GEAR
700 CARRIER ASSEMBLY, DIFFERENTIAL/
    FINAL DRIVE COMP
711 PINION, FINAL DRIVE PLANET
713 ROTOR, SPEED SENSOR (29 OR 30 T)
715 BEARING ASSEMBLY, THRUST
    (DIFFERENTIAL CARRIER/CASE)

FIGURE 8–133 Planetary final drive and parking gear components. Checking pinion end play. (Courtesy of General Motors Corporation.)

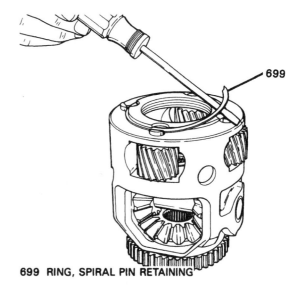

699 RING, SPIRAL PIN RETAINING

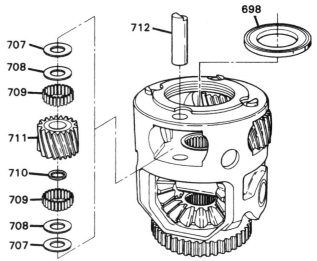

698 BEARING ASSEMBLY, THRUST CARRIER/SUN GEAR
707 WASHER, PINION THRUST (BRONZE)
708 WASHER, PINION THRUST (STEEL)
709 BEARING, ROLLER NEEDLE
710 SPACER, PINION NEEDLE BEARING
711 PINION, FINAL DRIVE PLANET
712 PIN, PLANET PINION

FIGURE 8–134 Planetary final drive disassembly, 4T60-E transaxle. (Courtesy of General Motors Corporation.)

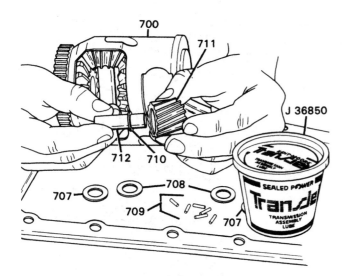

700 CARRIER ASSEMBLY, DIFFERENTIAL/
    FINAL DRIVE COMP
707 WASHER, PINION THRUST (BRONZE)
708 WASHER, PINION THRUST (STEEL)
709 BEARING, ROLLER NEEDLE
710 SPACER, PINION NEEDLE BEARING
711 PINION, FINAL DRIVE PLANET
712 PIN, PLANET PINION

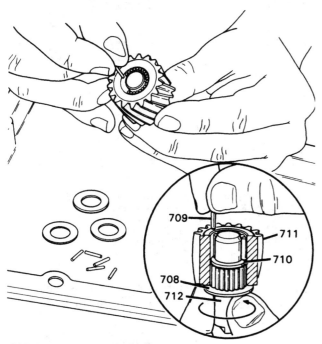

708 WASHER, PINION THRUST (STEEL)
709 BEARING, ROLLER NEEDLE
710 SPACER, PINION NEEDLE BEARING
711 PINION, FINAL DRIVE PLANET
712 PIN, PLANET PINION

FIGURE 8–135 Planetary final drive pinion bearing assembly, 4T60-E transaxle. (Courtesy of General Motors Corporation.)

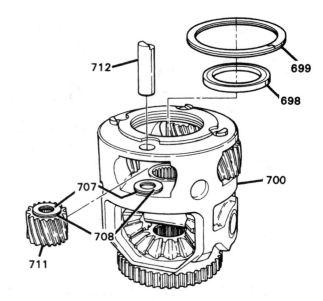

698 BEARING ASSEMBLY, THRUST CARRIER/SUN GEAR
699 RING, SPIRAL PIN RETAINING
700 CARRIER ASSEMBLY, DIFFERENTIAL/
    FINAL DRIVE COMP
707 WASHER, PINION THRUST (BRONZE)
708 WASHER, PINION THRUST (STEEL)
711 PINION, FINAL DRIVE PLANET
712 PIN, PLANET PINION

FIGURE 8–136 Planetary final drive pinion and pin installation, 4T60-E transaxle. (Courtesy of General Motors Corporation.)

should be flared using the double-flare method and the proper fittings.

> **CAUTION:** Do not reverse cooler lines. Air may enter the system if lines are reversed.

TRANSMISSION/TRANSAXLE ASSEMBLY

Some general rules apply to the assembly of any transmission or transaxle. Many of these are provided earlier in this chapter in the section on Disassembly and Assembly Guidelines. Review this information as it applies to assembling the unit.

The procedures used in transmission and transaxle assembly vary too much to allow a single set of instructions to cover them all. The only reliable source for this information is the manufacturer's service manual. Always refer to any updates of service manuals and to any manufacturer's service bulletins on the unit

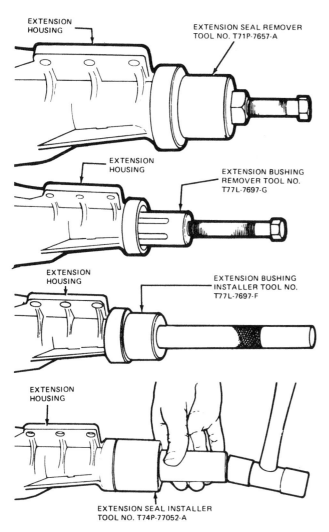

FIGURE 8–137 Removing the extension housing seal bushing (top). Installing the bushing and seal (bottom). (Courtesy of Ford Motor Company.)

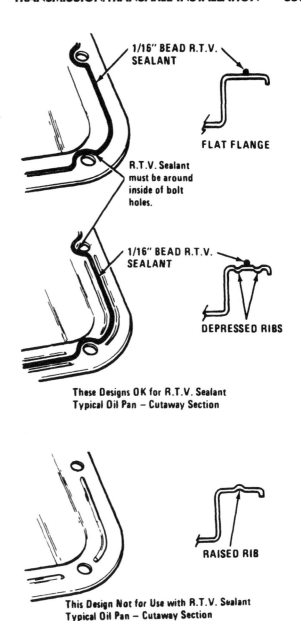

FIGURE 8–138 Oil pan flange designs. (Courtesy of General Motors.)

being serviced. Failure to do so can result in the use of incorrect parts, procedures, and specifications. Follow their instructions carefully to avoid duplication of work and to avoid failure of the unit to perform satisfactorily.

TRANSMISSION/TRANSAXLE INSTALLATION

After completing transmission/transaxle assembly, install the torque converter over the stator support. Make sure the converter has fully engaged the pump drive lugs. Measure the distance from the converter housing mounting face to the converter drive lug to determine whether the converter is fully engaged.

Install a clamp on the converter housing to keep the converter in place during transmission/transaxle installation.

Place the transmission/transaxle on a transmission jack and use the tie down to keep it in place. Raise the unit and align it with the dowel pins on the engine block. Push the unit into place so that the mating surface of the converter housing contacts the engine block mating surface. Install the mounting bolts and tighten them to specifications. After tightening the mounting bolts, the torque converter should be about 0.25 in. (6 mm) from the flex plate. Remove the clamp installed

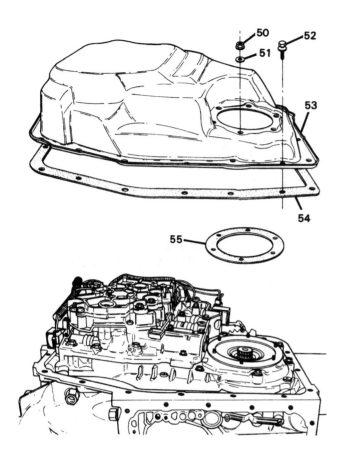

50 NUT, FLANGED HEX (M6 X 1.0)
51 WASHER, CONICAL
52 SCREW & CONICAL WASHER ASSEMBLY
53 PAN, CASE SIDE COVER
54 GASKET, CASE SIDE COVER
55 GASKET, INNER CASE SIDE COVER

FIGURE 8–139 Side cover installation, 4T60-E transaxle. (Courtesy of General Motors.)

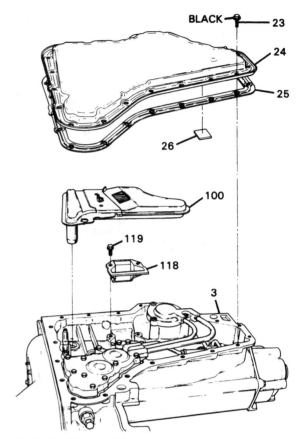

3 CASE, TRANSMISSION
23 BOLT, M6 X 1.0 X 18
24 PAN, TRANSMISSION OIL
25 GASKET, TRANSMISSION OIL PAN
26 MAGNET, CHIP COLLECTOR
100 FILTER ASSEMBLY, TRANSMISSION OIL
118 SCAVENGER, OIL SCOOP (BOTTOM PAN)
119 BOLT, M8 X 1.25 X 20.0 LG.

FIGURE 8–141 4T60-E transaxle oil pan installation. (Courtesy of General Motors Corporation.)

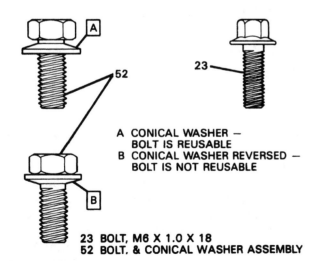

A CONICAL WASHER —
  BOLT IS REUSABLE
B CONICAL WASHER REVERSED —
  BOLT IS NOT REUSABLE

23 BOLT, M6 X 1.0 X 18
52 BOLT, & CONICAL WASHER ASSEMBLY

FIGURE 8–140 4T60-E transaxle side cover bolt usage. (Courtesy of General Motors Corporation.)

INSPECT DRIVE HUB AND PILOT HUB
- Scoring may not be as deep as it appears to the eye.

CHECK FOR DAMAGE
- **Burrs or nicks** — clean up.

CHECK WITH TIP OF FINGERNAIL.
- **Light scoring** — remove as shown below.
- **Deeply scored** — replace converter.
- Cover impeller hub to prevent dirt from entering.

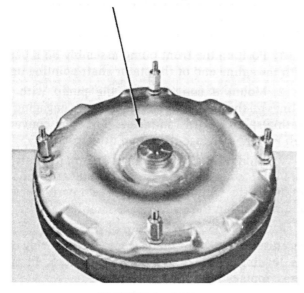

FIGURE 8–142 (Courtesy of Ford Motor Company.)

REMOVE LIGHT SCORING
- Check and replace pump seal and bushing as required.

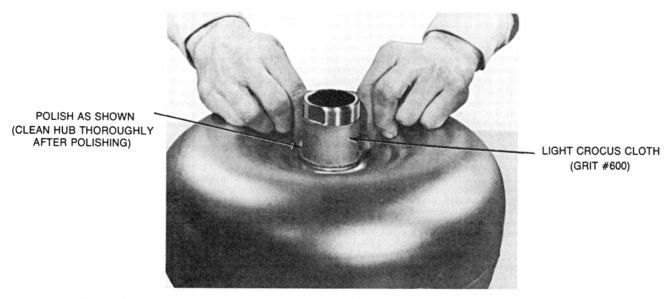

POLISH AS SHOWN
(CLEAN HUB THOROUGHLY
AFTER POLISHING)

LIGHT CROCUS CLOTH
(GRIT #600)

If scoring cannot be removed by light polishing, the converter must be replaced.

FIGURE 8–143 (Courtesy of Ford Motor Company.)

INSPECT DRIVE STUDS

- Studs pilot converter to run true with flywheel.

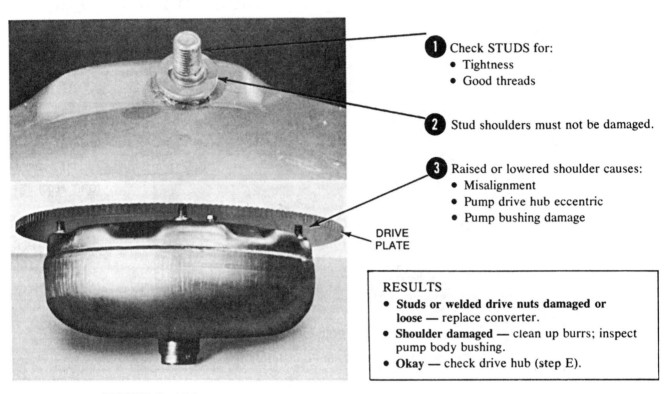

1. Check STUDS for:
   - Tightness
   - Good threads

2. Stud shoulders must not be damaged.

3. Raised or lowered shoulder causes:
   - Misalignment
   - Pump drive hub eccentric
   - Pump bushing damage

DRIVE PLATE

RESULTS
- **Studs or welded drive nuts damaged or loose** — replace converter.
- **Shoulder damaged** — clean up burrs; inspect pump body bushing.
- **Okay** — check drive hub (step E).

FIGURE 8–144 (Courtesy of Ford Motor Company.)

---

earlier. Align the converter with the flex plate. Install the converter drive bolts and tighten to specifications. Install all the parts removed earlier during transmission/transaxle removal. Adjust the shift linkage and throttle linkage to specifications.

Install the correct amount and type of transmission fluid as specified in the service manual. The following steps are typical of this procedure:

1. Apply the parking brake.
2. Remove the transmission/transaxle dipstick.
3. Use a funnel with a long flexible spout and insert the spout into the dipstick tube.
4. Pour in the specified amount of the recommended fluid.
5. Start the engine and run at idle for one minute.
6. With the engine running at idle and the parking and service brakes applied, move the selector lever momentarily into each gear position.
7. Place the selector lever in the Park or Neutral position as specified.

8. Add enough fluid to bring it to the specified level on the dipstick.

Recheck the fluid level after it has reached operating temperature (180 degrees F) to ensure that it is within the hot range on the dipstick. Correct the fluid level as required.

CAUTION: Do not overfill. Overfilling causes fluid to foam resulting in clutch slippage and transmission/transaxle damage.

---

9. Raise the vehicle on a hoist and check for fluid leaks. Correct if necessary.

Road test the vehicle as outlined earlier in this chapter to determine whether shift patterns and quality are correct.

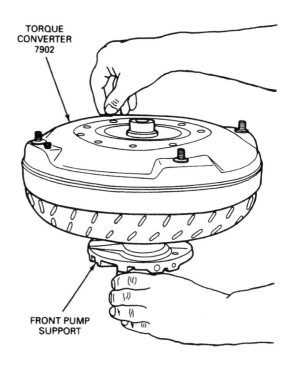

CONVERTER
CLUTCH
HOLDING TOOL
T77L-7902-R

TORQUE
CONVERTER
7902

FRONT PUMP
SUPPORT

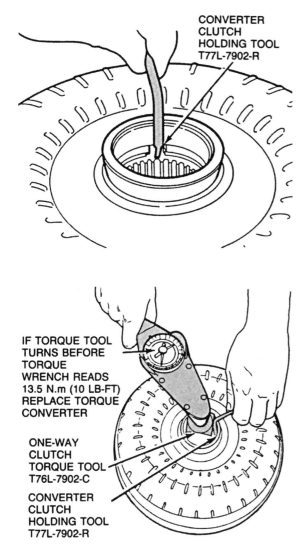

IF TORQUE TOOL
TURNS BEFORE
TORQUE
WRENCH READS
13.5 N.m (10 LB-FT)
REPLACE TORQUE
CONVERTER

ONE-WAY
CLUTCH
TORQUE TOOL
T76L-7902-C

CONVERTER
CLUTCH
HOLDING TOOL
T77L-7902-R

FIGURE 8–145 Checking the stator one-way clutch.
(Courtesy of Ford Motor Company.)

Stator to Turbine Interference Check

1. Position the torque converter on the bench front side down.
2. Install a front pump support to engage the mating splines of the front pump support, and pump drive gear lugs.
3. Install the input shaft, engaging the splines with the turbine hub.
4. Hold the front oil pump support stationary and attempt to rotate the turbine with the input shaft. The turbine should rotate freely in both directions without any signs of interference or scraping noise.

FIGURE 8–146 (Courtesy of Ford Motor Company.)

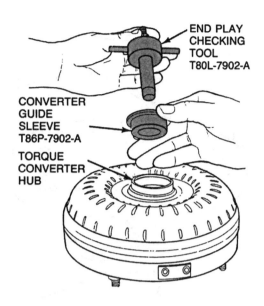

END PLAY
CHECKING
TOOL
T80L-7902-A

CONVERTER
GUIDE
SLEEVE
T86P-7902-A

TORQUE
CONVERTER
HUB

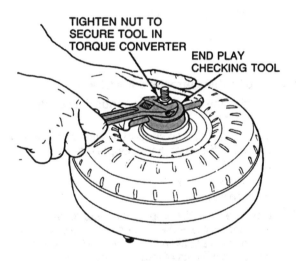

TIGHTEN NUT TO
SECURE TOOL IN
TORQUE CONVERTER

END PLAY
CHECKING TOOL

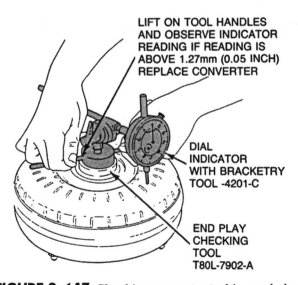

LIFT ON TOOL HANDLES
AND OBSERVE INDICATOR
READING IF READING IS
ABOVE 1.27mm (0.05 INCH)
REPLACE CONVERTER

DIAL
INDICATOR
WITH BRACKETRY
TOOL -4201-C

END PLAY
CHECKING
TOOL
T80L-7902-A

FIGURE 8–147 Checking converter turbine end play. (Courtesy of Ford Motor Company.)

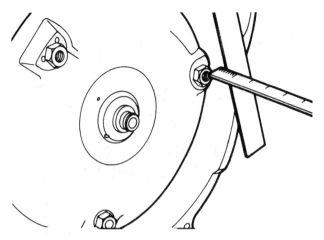

FIGURE 8–148 Measuring converter for full engagement in transmission. (Courtesy of Chrysler Corporation.)

FIGURE 8–149 Flushing the oil cooler and cooler lines. Flushing equipment has a pump and fluid reservoir. (Courtesy of OTC Division, SPX Corporation.)

REVIEW QUESTIONS

1. Harsh engagement of a transmission or transaxle may be caused by _____ _____ _____ too high, _____ _____ too high, a faulty _____, or valve body _____.

2. Slipping in forward or reverse may be caused by a low _____ _____ , low _____ _____, worn _____ _____ , worn _____ _____, leaking clutch piston _____ , or valve body _____.

3. To check the fluid level, the car should be in a _____ position and the fluid should be at _____ _____.

4. Fluid temperatures may reach _____ °F or _____ °C.

5. Milky-colored fluid indicates the presence of _____ _____ in the fluid.

6. Any large amount of deposits in the oil pan indicate that the transmission or transaxle should be _____.

7. The _____ lever position and the _____ _____ position must be _____.

8. Incorrect shift linkage adjustment can cause delayed _____ , _____ , _____ , and _____ problems.

9. When throttle pressure is too high in relation to throttle opening, the result is _____ upshifts and _____ upshifts.

10. When throttle pressure is too low in relation to throttle opening, the result is _____ upshifts and _____ upshifts.

11. A leak in the vacuum modulator system results in higher than normal _____ pressure.

12. During a road test check for proper _____ when the selector lever is moved into each position, check for proper _____ , converter _____ , and torque demand _____.

13. If engine speed is above normal during a stall test, there is _____ or _____ _____.

14. If engine speed is well below normal during a stall test, the stator one-way _____ is not _____.

15. Hydraulic pressure testing indicates whether the _____ _____ system, the _____ pressure system, and the _____ pressure system are working.

16. Air pressure tests can be used to check the operation of the _____ and _____.

17. Excessive transmission/transaxle gear train end play indicates excessive _____ _____ .

18. Transaxle drive chain wear is determined by measuring chain _____.

19. A torque converter that passes visual inspection should be checked for internal wear by measuring _____ _____ _____.

20. In a major transmission or transaxle failure, the _____ and _____ _____ should be _____.

TEST QUESTIONS

1. Technician A says that harsh engagement may be caused by an engine idle speed that is too low. Technician B says that harsh engagement may be caused by hydraulic pressures being too low. Who is right?
   a. technician A
   b. technician B
   c. both are right
   d. both are wrong

2. "A torque converter that does not lock up may be caused by a faulty hydraulic pump." "Incorrect shift point or no upshifts may be caused by a

low fluid level." Which of these statements is correct?
a. the first
b. the second
c. both are correct
d. both are incorrect

3. When checking the fluid in an automatic transmission/transaxle, check the
a. level
b. color
c. smell
d. all of the above

4. The manual shift linkage in an automatic transmission/transaxle is connected to the
a. regulator valve
b. manual shift valve
c. both (a) and (b)
d. none of the above

5. When an automatic transmission/transaxle is overhauled, the hydraulic pump should be measured for
a. pump cover warpage
b. tooth or rotor tip clearance
c. gear or rotor to cover clearance
d. all of the above

6. Overfilling an automatic transmission can cause
a. excessive lubrication
b. excessive converter pressure
c. insufficient clutch apply pressure
d. insufficient cooling

7. A harsh upshift may be caused by
a. incorrect throttle linkage adjustment
b. excessive hydraulic pressure
c. neither (a) nor (b)
d. both (a) and (b)

8. Slipping in all gear positions may be caused by
a. hydraulic pressure too low
b. low fluid level

c. neither (a) nor (b)
d. both (a) and (b)

9. Harsh engagement into Drive or Reverse may be caused by
a. idle speed too low
b. hydraulic pressure too low
c. neither (a) nor (b)
d. both (a) and (b)

10. A condition that allows the engine to be started in any gear position may be caused by incorrect
a. gearshift linkage adjustment
b. throttle linkage adjustment
c. backup switch adjustment
d. neutral switch adjustment

11. Excessive clutch pack clearance can cause
a. too much clutch apply pressure
b. poor clutch release
c. too little shift lag time
d. insufficient clutch application

12. Precise band adjustment is required to ensure
a. full band application when needed
b. full band release when needed
c. both (a) and (b)
d. neither (a) nor (b)

13. A governor valve stuck in the closed or at rest position can cause
a. no downshifts
b. no upshifts
c. both (a) and (b)
d. neither (a) nor (b)

14. Gear train end play can be corrected with the use of
a. selective gear sizes
b. oversize shafts
c. selective carrier sizes
d. selective thrust washers

◆ CHAPTER 9 ◆

FOUR-WHEEL-DRIVE SYSTEM PRINCIPLES AND SERVICE

INTRODUCTION

Four-wheel-drive systems continue to increase in popularity on a variety of vehicle types. The dual-mode two-wheel-drive (2WD)/four-wheel-drive (4WD) system is used on cars, vans, pickup trucks, sport utility vehicles, and commercial trucks. Another popular design is the the full-time 4WD system which shifts from two-wheel drive to four-wheel drive and back automatically. With the part-time 4WD system, the driver decides when to shift from 2WD to 4WD or from 4WD to 2WD (**Figures 9–1** to **9–4**). This chapter describes the various systems, their operation, and service.

LEARNING OBJECTIVES

After completing this chapter, you should be able to:

- Explain basic four-wheel-drive system operation.
- Explain the difference between the various 4WD systems.
- Describe the operation of a viscous coupling.
- Describe the function of a center differential.
- Describe the operation of a transfer case.
- Diagnose four-wheel-drive system problems.

TERMS YOU SHOULD KNOW

Look for these terms as you study this chapter and learn what they mean.

4WD	center differential
2WD	electromagnetic clutch
AWD	transfer case
part-time 4WD	shift motor
full-time 4WD	mode selector switch
manual locking hubs	difficult to shift
automatic locking hubs	will not shift
axle disconnect	transfer case noise
drive train windup	lubricant leaks
viscous coupling	abnormal tire wear

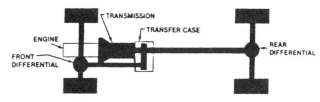

FIGURE 9–1 Part-time 4WD. When engaged, both front and rear axles are mechanically locked together and turn at the same speed. This may cause windup or a binding condition in the drive line when operated excessively on dry pavement or in turns. (Courtesy of Chrysler Corporation.)

PART-TIME FOUR-WHEEL-DRIVE COMPONENTS AND FUNCTION

The following description applies to a basic part-time 4WD system equipped with a two-speed transfer case and no third differential or viscous coupling. The term *part-time* stems from the fact that the vehicle is operated in the 4WD mode only part of the time (during off-road operation). The following are the major components:

1. *Transfer case:* attached to the transmission and driven by the transmission output shaft. It provides Neutral, 2WD, 4WD LO, and 4WD HI positions that can be selected by the driver.

2. *Drive shafts (propeller shafts):* two drive shafts are connected to the transfer case output. The front drive shaft drives the differential pinion in the front drive axle. The rear drive shaft drives the differential pinion in the rear drive axle.

3. *Rear drive axle:* contains the rear-axle drive pinion, ring gear, differential, and drive axles.

4. *Front drive axle:* contains the front-axle drive pinion, ring gear, differential, and drive axles. The outer ends of the front drive axle are equipped with

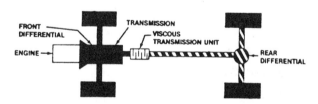

FIGURE 9–2 On-demand 4WD. One axle primarily drives the vehicle. Power is transferred automatically to the other axle when traction is lost on the drive axle. This system may be operated on all road surfaces. (Courtesy of Chrysler Corporation.)

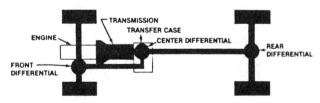

FIGURE 9–3 Full-time 4WD. Both front and rear axles are permitted to turn at different speeds through an interaxle differential system. This eliminates drive line windup and permits vehicle operation in 4WD 100% of the time. (Courtesy of Chrysler Corporation.)

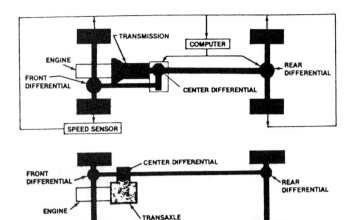

FIGURE 9–4 Integrated 4WD. Wheel speed sensors send information to a computer that locks the center and axle differentials as necessary to maintain traction. The transaxle acts as both transmission and transfer case distributing power to front and rear axles. The transaxle center differential normally functions as an open differential but may incorporate a viscous coupling or lock feature for added traction. The low range is achieved using a gearset internal to the transaxle. (Courtesy of Chrysler Corporation.)

universal joints and pivoting hubs to allow front wheel steering.

5. *Shift control:* driver-operated lever connected through linkage to the shift collar in the transfer case. Allows the driver to select 2WD, 4WD LO, or 4WD HI. An electric switch and electric shift motor are used on some 4WD systems. Others use a vacuum switch, vacuum shift motor, and vacuum storage tank.

6. *Locking hubs:* connect the front wheels to the front drive axles when in the locked position. Manual locking hubs must be turned by hand to the 2WD or 4WD position with the vehicle stopped. Automatic locking hubs can be locked or unlocked without leaving the vehicle, usually by slowly backing up or moving ahead, depending on the transfer case shift position selected.

7. *Axle disconnect:* a vacuum motor or mechanical linkage shifts a splined sleeve to connect or disconnect the front drive axle. No wheel locking hubs are used. Only one side of the axle is disconnected, allowing the differential, ring gear, and pinion to stop turning when in the 2WD mode. However, the other axle keeps turning. When shifted into 4WD, the shift collar connects the two sections of the axle shaft together.

Basic part-time four-wheel drive operates in the following modes (**Figures 9–5** to **9–13**):

1. *2WD mode.* In this mode, power is not transmitted to the front drive wheels, and the vehicle operates as a normal 2WD.

2. *4WD LO.* In this mode, the front and rear axles are driven at reduced speed through the transfer case. Power is transmitted equally to the front and rear drive axles, and they turn at the same speed. This mode is used on rough terrain and severe traction conditions.

3. *4WD HI.* In this mode, the front and rear drive axles are driven at a higher speed than in the 4WD LO mode. Power is transmitted equally to the front and rear drive axles, and they turn at the same speed.

INTERAXLE CONFLICT AND DRIVE TRAIN WINDUP

During normal straight-ahead driving, the front and rear drive shafts turn at the same speed, all four wheels travel the same distance, and there is no interaxle conflict. However, when turning a corner, the front wheels travel farther and turn faster than the rear wheels. Without a center differential in the transfer case, the front and rear drive shafts are forced to turn at the same speed during turns when in four-wheel drive. Since the front and rear wheels do not travel the same distance (because of the difference in turning radius), the tires are forced to slip and scrub. If a part-time four-wheel-drive vehicle is driven on dry pavement in the 4WD mode, interaxle conflict and drive train

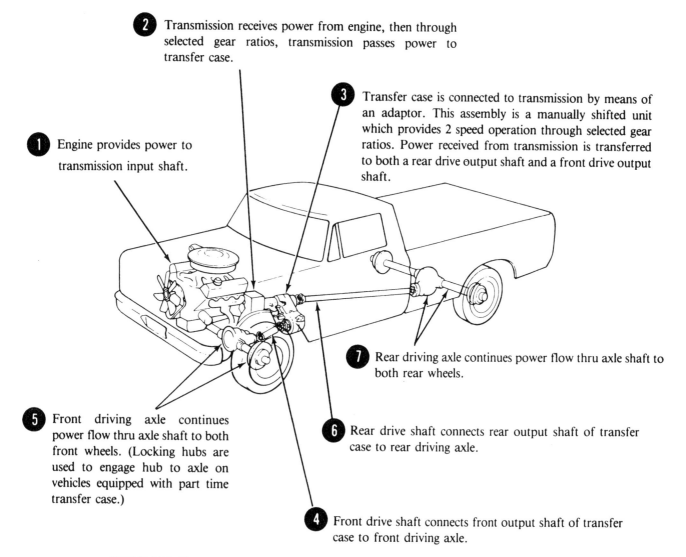

2 Transmission receives power from engine, then through selected gear ratios, transmission passes power to transfer case.

3 Transfer case is connected to transmission by means of an adaptor. This assembly is a manually shifted unit which provides 2 speed operation through selected gear ratios. Power received from transmission is transferred to both a rear drive output shaft and a front drive output shaft.

1 Engine provides power to transmission input shaft.

7 Rear driving axle continues power flow thru axle shaft to both rear wheels.

5 Front driving axle continues power flow thru axle shaft to both front wheels. (Locking hubs are used to engage hub to axle on vehicles equipped with part time transfer case.)

6 Rear drive shaft connects rear output shaft of transfer case to rear driving axle.

4 Front drive shaft connects front output shaft of transfer case to front driving axle.

FIGURE 9–5 (Courtesy of Ford Motor Company.)

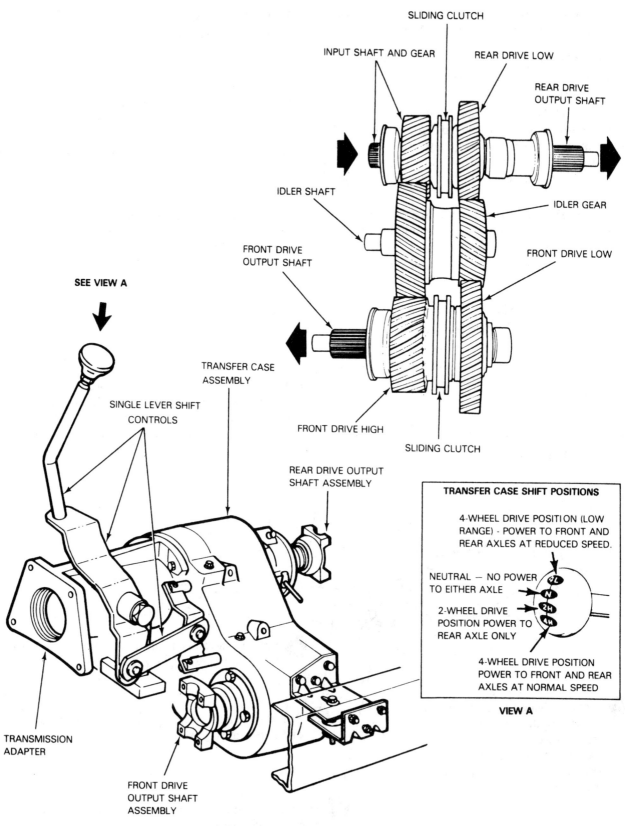

SLIDING CLUTCH

INPUT SHAFT AND GEAR

REAR DRIVE LOW

REAR DRIVE
OUTPUT SHAFT

IDLER SHAFT

IDLER GEAR

FRONT DRIVE
OUTPUT SHAFT

FRONT DRIVE LOW

SEE VIEW A

SINGLE LEVER SHIFT
CONTROLS

TRANSFER CASE
ASSEMBLY

FRONT DRIVE HIGH

SLIDING CLUTCH

REAR DRIVE OUTPUT
SHAFT ASSEMBLY

TRANSFER CASE SHIFT POSITIONS

4-WHEEL DRIVE POSITION (LOW
RANGE) - POWER TO FRONT AND
REAR AXLES AT REDUCED SPEED.

NEUTRAL — NO POWER
TO EITHER AXLE

2-WHEEL DRIVE
POSITION POWER TO
REAR AXLE ONLY

4-WHEEL DRIVE POSITION
POWER TO FRONT AND REAR
AXLES AT NORMAL SPEED

VIEW A

TRANSMISSION
ADAPTER

FRONT DRIVE
OUTPUT SHAFT
ASSEMBLY

FIGURE 9–6 (Courtesy of Ford Motor Company.)

NEW PROCESS 205 PART TIME TRANSFER CASE POWER FLOW

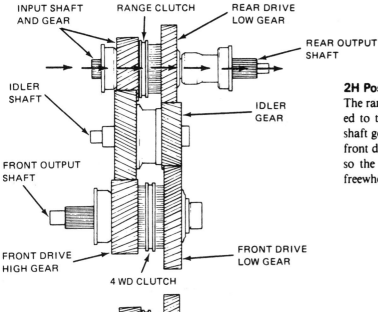

2H Position

The range clutch is shifted forward. The input shaft is locked to the rear output shaft to turn rear driveshaft. Input shaft gear also turns idler gear which turns the freewheeling front drive high gear. The 4 WD clutch is in center position so the front drive low gear, turned by the idler gear, is freewheeling. Rear drive low gear is also freewheeling.

4H Position

Both the range sliding clutch and 4 WD clutch are shifted forward. The input shaft is locked to the rear output shaft to turn rear drive shaft. Input shaft gear also turns idler gear which turns the front drive high gear and front output shaft. Rear drive low gear and front drive low gear are turned by rear idler and are freewheeling.

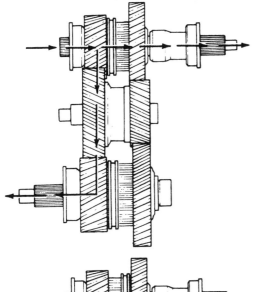

4L Position

Both the range clutch and 4 WD clutch are shifted rearward. The input shaft gear turns the idler gear which turns the rear drive low gear. This gear is locked to rear drive output shaft which then turns rear driveshaft. The idler gear also turns front drive low gear. This gear is locked to the front drive output shaft which then turns front driveshaft.

FIGURE 9–7 (Courtesy of Ford Motor Company.)

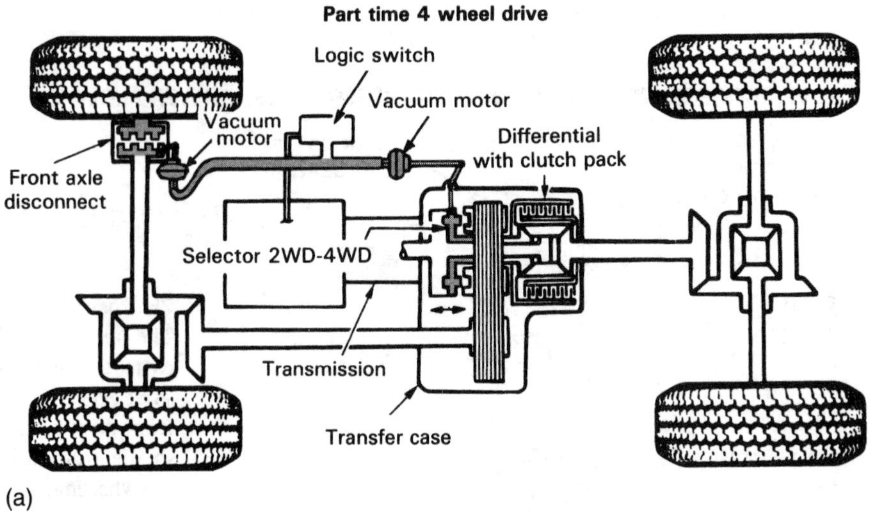

Part time 4 wheel drive

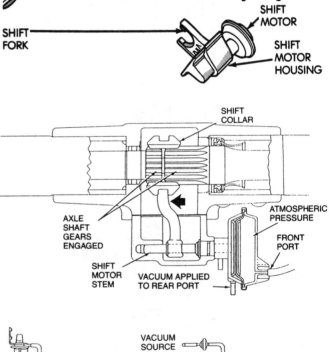

Logic switch

Vacuum motor

Vacuum motor

Differential with clutch pack

Front axle disconnect

Selector 2WD-4WD

Transmission

Transfer case

FIGURE 9-8 Part-time four-wheel drive. (Courtesy of Chrysler Corporation.)

(a)

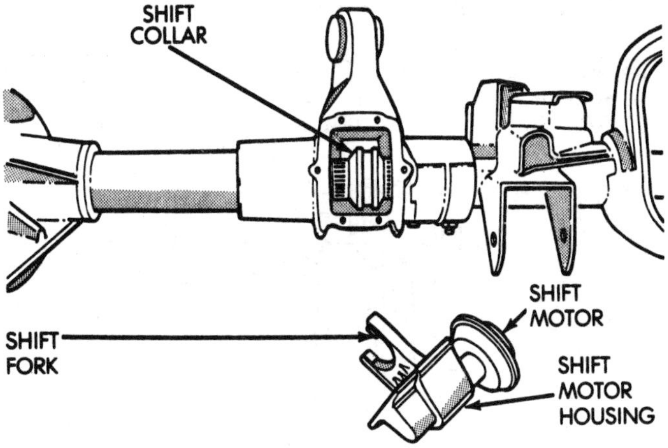

FIGURE 9-9 Front axle disconnect shift motor. (Courtesy of Chrysler Corporation.)

SHIFT COLLAR

SHIFT MOTOR

SHIFT FORK

SHIFT MOTOR HOUSING

SHIFT COLLAR

AXLE SHAFT GEARS ENGAGED

SHIFT MOTOR STEM

VACUUM APPLIED TO REAR PORT

ATMOSPHERIC PRESSURE

FRONT PORT

FIGURE 9-10 When the driver selects 4WD, the transfer case delivers power to the front and rear axles. At the same time, the vacuum control switch on the range selector directs vacuum to the axle shift motor to connect the front axle shaft splines together. (Courtesy of Chrysler Corporation.)

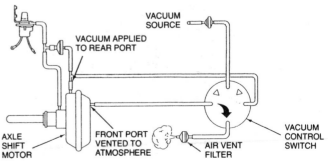

VACUUM SOURCE

VACUUM APPLIED TO REAR PORT

AXLE SHIFT MOTOR

FRONT PORT VENTED TO ATMOSPHERE

AIR VENT FILTER

VACUUM CONTROL SWITCH

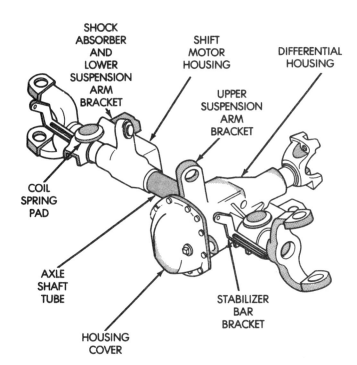

SHOCK
ABSORBER
AND
LOWER
SUSPENSION
ARM
BRACKET

SHIFT
MOTOR
HOUSING

DIFFERENTIAL
HOUSING

UPPER
SUSPENSION
ARM
BRACKET

COIL
SPRING
PAD

AXLE
SHAFT
TUBE

STABILIZER
BAR
BRACKET

HOUSING
COVER

FIGURE 9–11 Four-wheel-drive solid front axle. (Courtesy of Chrysler Corporation.)

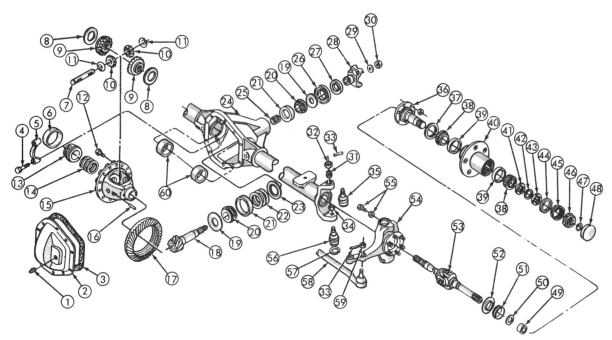

1. FILL PLUG
2. DIFFERENTIAL HOUSING COVER
3. SILICONE RUBBER ADHESIVE SEALANT
4. BEARING CAP BOLT
5. BEARING CAP
6. BEARING CUP (2)
7. PINION MATE SHAFT
8. THRUST WASHER
9. SIDE GEAR
10. PINION GEAR
11. THRUST WASHER
12. RING GEAR MOUNTING BOLTS
13. BEARING (2)
14. BEARING PRELOAD SHIMS
15. DIFFERENTIAL CASE

16. PINION MATE SHAFT PIN
17. RING GEAR
18. PINION DRIVE GEAR
19. SLINGER
20. PINION BEARING
21. DRIVE PINION BEARING CUP
22. DRIVE PINION DEPTH SHIMS
23. BAFFLE
24. DIFFERENTIAL HOUSING
25. DRIVE PINION PRELOAD SHIMS
26. OIL SEAL
27. DUST CAP
28. YOKE
29. WASHER
30. DRIVE PINION NUT

31. UPPER BALL STUD SPLIT RING SEAT
32. UPPER BALL STUD NUT
33. COTTER PIN
34. LOWER BALL STUD JAMNUT
35. UPPER BALL STUD
36. SPINDLE
37. SEAL
38. BEARING
39. BEARING CUP
40. HUB
41. INNER LOCKNUT
42. WASHER
43. OUTER LOCKNUT
44. SPRING CUP
45. PRESSURE SPRING

46. DRIVE GEAR
47. SNAP RING
48. HUB CAP
49. SPINDLE BEARING
50. WASHER
51. SEAL
52. SEAL SEAT
53. AXLE SHAFT
54. STEERING KNUCKLE
55. STEERING STOP BOLT
56. LOWER BALL STUD
57. SNAP RING
58. TIE ROD
59. TIE ROD END NUT
60. INNER OIL SEAL

FIGURE 9–12 Solid front drive axle with axle disconnect system. (Courtesy of Chrysler Corporation.)

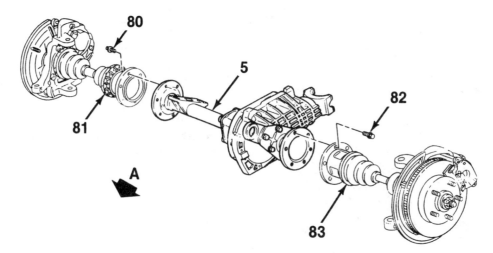

FIGURE 9–13 Independent suspension front drive axle for 4WD has inner and outer CV joints on each axle. (A) front; (5) axle tube; (80) bolt; (81) right side drive axle; (82) bolt; (83) left-side drive axle. (Courtesy of General Motors Corporation.)

windup will occur. The driver experiences this as an intermittent braking sensation that may cause the vehicle to vibrate and shudder. If driven extensively on dry pavement in this mode, rapid tire wear will be the result. During off-road driving where there is less traction and the surface is more uneven, momentary slippage occurs frequently enough at all four wheels to accommodate the difference in speed between the front and rear axles. The difference in traction between the four wheels determines which wheels will do the slipping. With a center differential in the transfer case splitting the powerflow between the front and rear drive shafts, the problem is solved. The transfer case center differential does the same job between the front and rear drive shafts as the conventional drive axle differential does between the left and right drive wheels.

LOCKING FRONT WHEEL HUB OPERATION

See **Figures 9–14** to **9–16.** Locking hubs are used on four-wheel-drive systems to engage or disengage the front drive axles from the front wheels. When in the 2WD mode, the hubs must be unlocked. If the hubs are locked while driving on dry pavement, the tires scrub and wear rapidly. They must be locked to operate in the 4WD mode to drive the front wheels. When the hubs are unlocked, the front wheels are free to turn. This prevents the front drive axles from being driven by the front wheels. This reduces wear on them and on the differential, the front drive shaft, and certain parts in the transfer case.

Some front wheel hubs lock automatically. Others require the driver to stop the vehicle and get out to turn

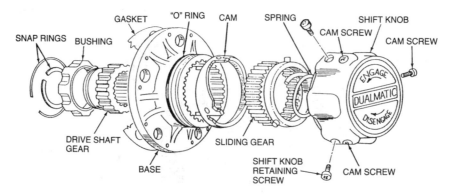

FIGURE 9–14 Locking hub is engaged for 4WD and disengaged for 2WD. In the disengaged position, the front-wheel-drive axles do not turn while driving in the 2WD mode. (Courtesy of Chrysler Corporation.)

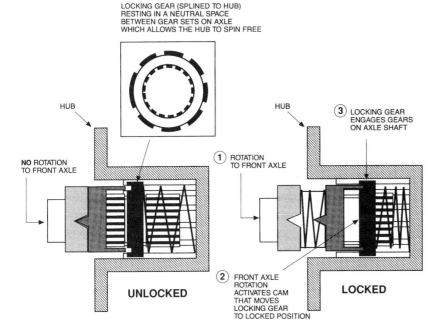

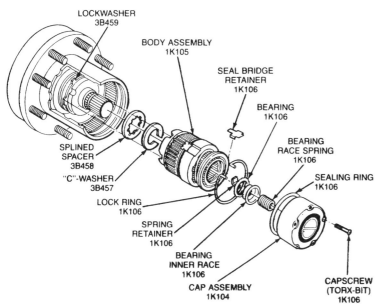

FIGURE 9–15 Manual front wheel hub locking action. (Courtesy of Ford Motor Company.)

FIGURE 9–16 Automatic locking front-wheel-drive hub for four-wheel drive. (Courtesy of Ford Motor Co. of Canada Ltd.)

the locks by hand. To unlock automatic locking hubs, disengage the 4WD and back up about 3 feet. Often, the hubs will unlock without backing up. A disadvantage of automatic locking hubs is that they do not drive the front wheels in reverse.

FULL-TIME 4WD

The full-time four-wheel-drive system provides power to all four wheels all the time. No wheel locking hubs or axle disconnect are used (**Figures 9–17** and **9–18**). The transfer case has a center differential that can be locked to provide equal power to all four wheels when operating on surfaces where one or more wheels could slip. The center differential may be locked by a viscous coupling, the driver using a switch on the dash, or it may be a computer-controlled electromagnetic clutch operating in response to wheel speed sensors (usually, the same sensors used with antilock brakes).

INTEGRATED FULL-TIME 4WD

The transaxle and transfer case are an integrated unit. The center differential may incorporate an electroni-

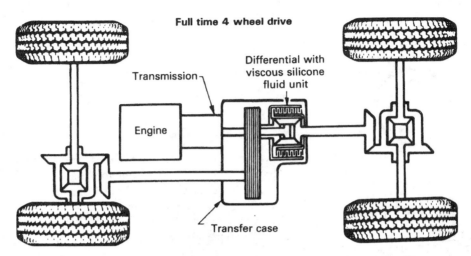

FIGURE 9–17 Full-time four-wheel drive. (Courtesy of Chrysler Corporation.)

cally controlled lockup or a viscous coupling. A low-range mode is provided by a gearset in the transaxle. Wheel speed sensors send wheel spin information to a computer that locks the center and rear differentials as required to maintain traction (see **Figure 9–4**).

PART-TIME/FULL-TIME 4WD

The part-time/full-time 4WD provides the drive modes possible in part-time 4WD and full-time 4WD. It allows the driver to select 2WD, full-time 4WD LO, and full-time 4WD HI.

ALL-WHEEL DRIVE (AWD)

All-wheel drive (AWD) systems do not use a conventional two-speed transfer case. All-wheel-drive systems were developed from front-wheel-drive systems with a transaxle. A single-speed rear-wheel-drive transfer case is added to the transaxle. A viscous coupling is usually used to allow limited slip between the front and rear drive wheels. This provides power to all four wheels but prevents drive line windup **(Figures 9–19** to **9–23).**

VISCOUS COUPLING

A viscous coupling is used on many AWD systems to prevent drive line windup and interaxle conflict. The unit consists of an input shaft connected to a series of splined drive plates, a series of driven plates splined in-

ternally to a housing or drum, and an output shaft splined to the drum. The drive plates and driven plates are arranged alternately and are evenly spaced. The unit contains a measured amount of thick silicon fluid **(Figure 9–23)**.

When the speed difference between the front and rear axles is more than 6%, shearing action begins in the coupling. As the speed difference between the drive shaft and front axles increases, the slippage in the viscous coupling causes the silicon fluid to heat up and expand. Expansion of the fluid results in coupling drive and driven plates to lock up, providing virtual direct drive.

Lockup occurs in about $\frac{1}{10}$ of a second or a quarter turn of the wheels. The unit is self-regulating, since once it is locked up, the temperature of the silicon drops, reducing the pressure and providing limited slippage between the front and rear wheels. A viscous coupling is also used in transfer cases that operate in either part-time or full-time modes.

CENTER DIFFERENTIAL

A center differential is used in the transfer case of full-time 4WD systems to prevent drive line windup and interaxle conflict. It is used in a two-speed transfer case between the front-axle-drive output shaft and the rear-axle-drive output shaft **(Figures 9–24** and **9–25)**. The center differential allows the front and rear drive axles to turn at different speeds when driving on surfaces with uneven traction and during turns. The center differential is often used in conjunction with a viscous coupling to prevent the four-wheel-drive vehicle from being stuck when only one wheel loses trac-

NEW PROCESS 203 FULL TIME TRANSFER CASE POWER FLOW

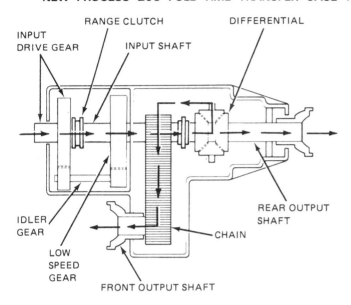

Hi Position

The range clutch is shifted forward. The input drive gear is locked to the input shaft assembly which transfers power through the differential to the chain sprockets and chain. The chain turns the front output shaft which turns front driveshaft. The input shaft assembly also transfers power through the differential to the rear output shaft which turns the rear driveshaft. The input drive gear is also turning the idler gear which then turns the freewheeling low speed gear.

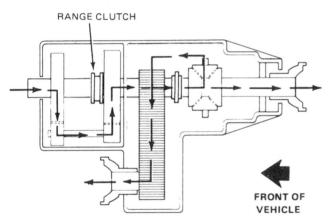

Lo Position

The range clutch is shifted rearward. The input drive gear is turning the idler gear which then turns the low speed gear. The low speed gear is now locked to the input shaft assembly by the sliding clutch in the rearward position. The input shaft assembly transfers power through the differential to both the chain sprocket and rear output shaft, which then power the front driveshaft and rear driveshaft respectively.

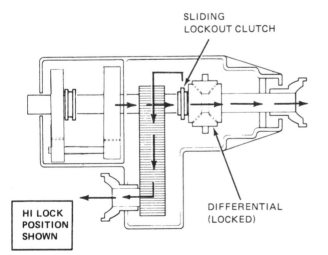

Hi Lock and Lo Lock Positions

The shift to either HI LOCK or LO LOCK position moves the sliding lockout clutch rearward to lock-up the differential. This prevents the front and rear axle from rotating independently of each other. In HI LOCK, the range clutch is shifted forward and power flow is the same as HI except the differential action is not part of the flow. In LO LOCK, the range clutch is shifted rearward and the power flow is the same as LO except the differential action is not part of the flow.

FIGURE 9–18 (Courtesy of Ford Motor Co. of Canada Ltd.)

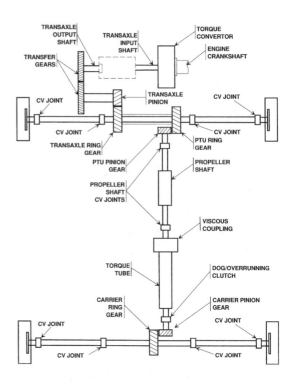

FIGURE 9–19 All-wheel-drive schematic. (Courtesy of Chrysler Corporation.)

tion and spins. In some designs, the center differential is attached to the rear axle differential. One design uses three differentials: front, rear, and center. The center differential is attached to the transaxle. A drive shaft is used to connect it to the rear differential. A transfer case is not used. The center differential takes care of interaxle conflict. The center and rear axle differentials can be locked when slippery road conditions are encountered. Locking the front differential is not practical since this would have negative effects on steering and would cause tire scrubbing.

ELECTROMAGNETIC CLUTCH

An electromagnetic clutch is used in some transfer cases to provide lockup on the center differential when traction conditions require power to be transmitted to all four wheels. The clutch may be activated by a switch on the dash, or it may be controlled electronically by a computer in response to wheel slip speed sensor signals. The clutch operates basically the same as the magnetic clutch on an air conditioning compressor.

In another application, a magnetic clutch is used to spin up the front drive system to rear drive speed in milliseconds. This allows a shift to be made from 2WD HI to 4WD HI at any speed. As soon as the transfer case front and rear output shafts reach the same speed, a

spring-loaded shift collar automatically engages the mainshaft hub to the drive chain sprocket (**Figures 9–23** and **9–24**).

TRANSFER CASE TYPES

A transfer case is used to transmit torque to both front and rear drive axles on a 4WD vehicle. The transfer case is usually attached to the transmission or transaxle and receives its power from the transmission/transaxle output shaft. Two drive shafts extend from the transfer case, one for the rear drive axle and one for the front drive axle.

There are three basic types of transfer case. They may be shifted manually or electronically. The following are typical examples (see **Figures 9–6, 9–7, 9–24, and 9–26 to 9–30**):

1. *Part-time transfer case:* provides Neutral, 2WD HI, 4 WD LO, and 4WD HI. The helical gear part-time transfer case drive train uses an input shaft and gear, a double idler gear and shaft, a front output shaft with a high gear and a low gear, a rear drive low gear and output shaft, and two sliding clutch collars and two shift forks. The chain drive part-time transfer case drive train uses an input gear, two-speed planetary gearset, a drive chain and two sprockets, a front output shaft, a mainshaft, a synchronizer, a range hub and gear, and two shift forks.

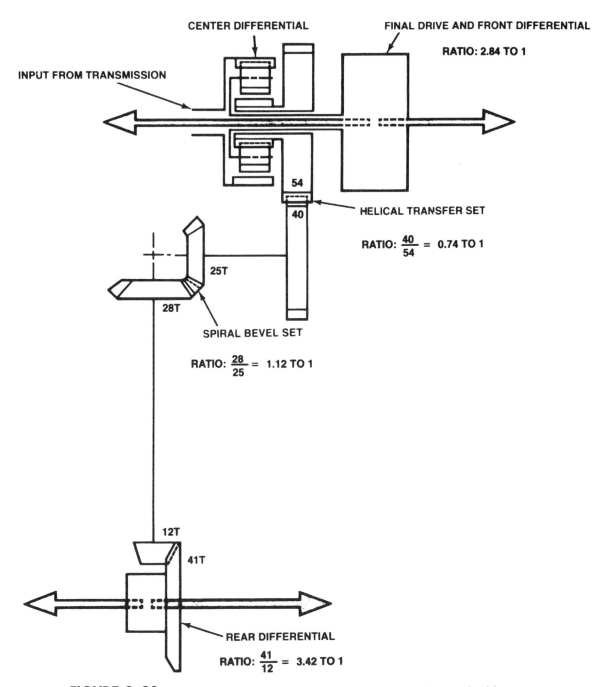

FIGURE 9–20 The rotating speed of the front and rear wheels matched by providing the correct ratio at each set of gears. The rear drive ratio is the result of a combination of ratios: $0.74 \times 1.12 \times 3.42 = 2.84$ to 1. (Courtesy of General Motors Corporation.)

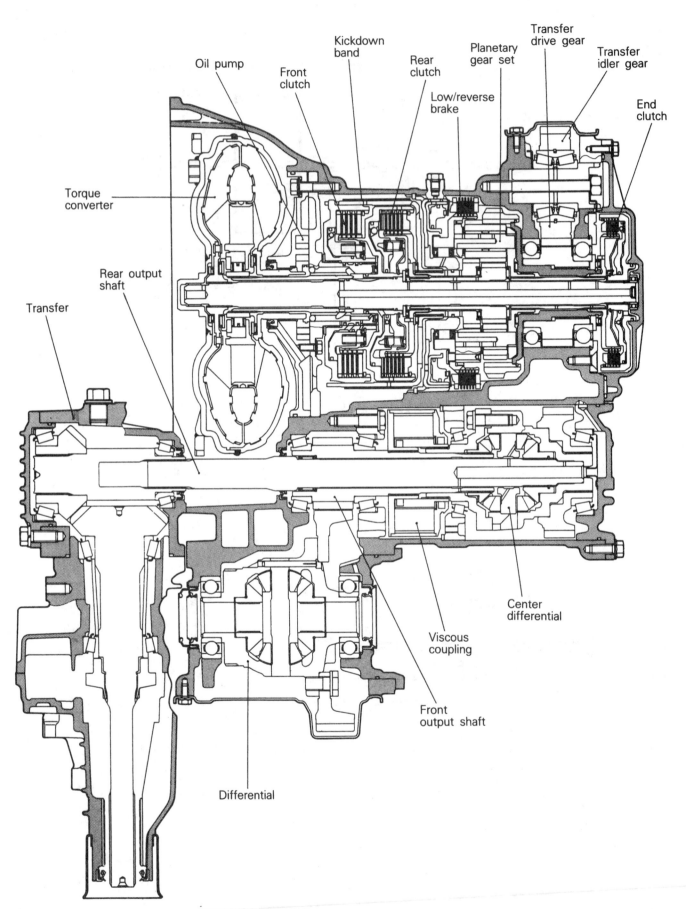

FIGURE 9–21 All-wheel-drive transaxle with gears providing drive to rear wheels. (Courtesy of Chrysler Corporation.)

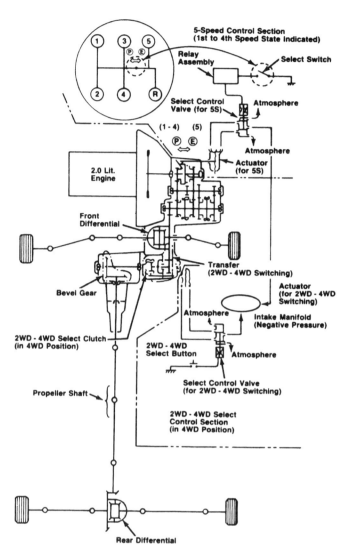

FIGURE 9–22 All-wheel-drive system. (Courtesy of Chrysler Corporation.)

2. *Full-time transfer case:* provides 2WD HI, 4WD HI, and 4WD LO. The full-time transfer case drive train consists of the input gear, two-speed planetary gearset, mainshaft, rear output shaft, front output shaft, a chain and two sprockets, a viscous coupling differential, and three shift forks. The differential can be locked to provide equal power to front and rear drive axles.

3. *Part-time/full-time transfer case:* provides 2WD HI, full-time 4WD HI, and part-time 4WD LO. The part-time/full-time transfer case drive train consists of the input gear, a two-speed planetary gearset, intermediate shaft, mainshaft, front output shaft, planetary differential, drive chain, two sprockets, two shift sleeves, and two shift forks.

Part-Time Four-Wheel-Drive Application

1. *Ford Bronco:* part-time four-wheel drive only.

2. *GEO Tracker:* part-time four-wheel drive only.

3. *Honda Passport:* part-time four-wheel drive only with a 50 mph (80 km/h) speed limit.

4. *Isuzu Rodeo:* part-time four-wheel drive only with a 50 mph (80 km/h) speed limit.

5. *Isuzu Trooper:* part-time four-wheel drive only with a 50 mph (80 km/h) speed limit.

6. *JEEP Cherokee:* although the base system is part-time, it has a center differential and is able to shift on-the-fly.

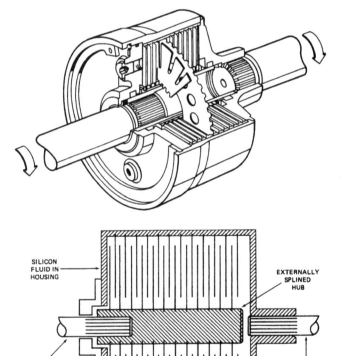

FIGURE 9–23 Viscous coupling. As silicone fluid temperature increases (due to friction caused by difference in speed between drive and driven discs), the fluid expands, locking the discs together.

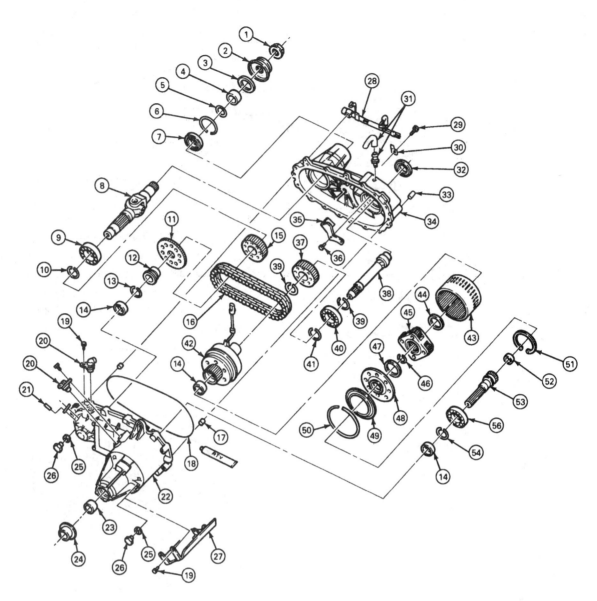

1	Locknut	21	Stud	41	Snap Ring
2	Deflector	22	Rear Case Half	42	Electric Clutch Assembly
3	Oil Seal	23	Steel Bushing	43	Planetary Ring Gear
4	Steel Bushing	24	Oil Seal	44	Thrust Washer
5	O-Ring	25	Washer	45	Planetary Carrier Assembly
6	Snap Ring	26	Hex Head Plug	46	Snap Ring
7	Ball Bearing	27	Shield	47	Thrust Washer
8	Front Output Shaft	28	Wiring Harness	48	Plate
9	Ball Bearing	29	Round-Head Drive Screw	49	Cover
10	Snap Ring	30	Clip	50	Retaining Ring
11	Tone Wheel Ring	31	Vent	51	Snap Ring
12	Speedometer Gear	32	Oil Seal	52	Steel Bushing
13	Snap Ring	33	Dowel Pin	53	Rear Output Shaft
14	Needle Bearing Assembly	34	Front Case Half	54	Snap Ring
15	Drive Sprocket	35	Oil Baffle	55	Ball Bearing
16	Drive Chain	36	Hex Tapping Screw		
17	Dowel Pin	37	Drive Sprocket		
18	RTV Sealant	38	Input Shaft		
19	Hex-Head Self-Tapping Screw	39	Snap Ring		
20	Sensor	40	Ball Bearing		

FIGURE 9–24 Transfer case with magnetic clutch and center differential. (Courtesy of Ford Motor Company.)

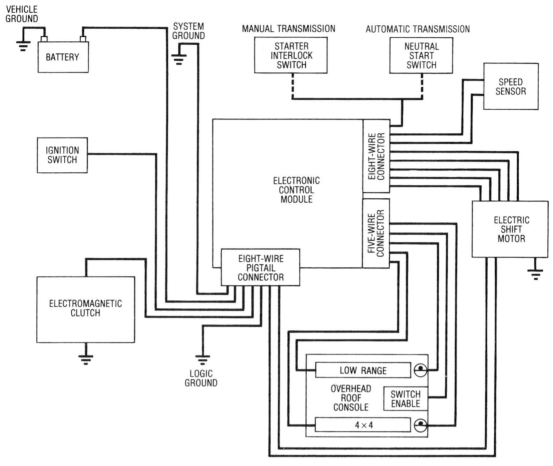

FIGURE 9–25 Computer-controlled transfer case electrical schematic. (Courtesy of Ford Motor Company.)

7. *JEEP Grand Cherokee:* base system is part-time, has a center differential, and is able to shift on-the-fly.

8. *JEEP Wrangler:* part-time four-wheel drive only.

9. *Kia Sportage:* part-time four-wheel drive only.

10. *Nissan Pathfinder:* part-time four-wheel drive only.

11. *Suzuki Samurai:* part-time four-wheel drive only.

12. *Suzuki Sidekick:* part-time four-wheel drive only.

Full-Time Four-Wheel-Drive Application

1. *AM General Hummer:* has a locking center differential.

2. *Chevrolet Blazer:* late model has a locking center differential.

3. *GMC Jimmy:* late model has a locking center differential.

4. *JEEP Grand Cherokee:* has a viscous coupling in the transfer case.

5. *Land Rover Defender 90:* has a locking center differential.

6. *Land Rover Discovery:* has a locking center differential.

7. *Oldsmobile Bravada:* has a locking center differential or viscous coupling.

8. *Range Rover Country Classic:* has a viscous coupling.

9. *Range Rover 4.0 SE:* has a viscous coupling in the transfer case.

10. *Toyota Land Cruiser:* has a locking center differential.

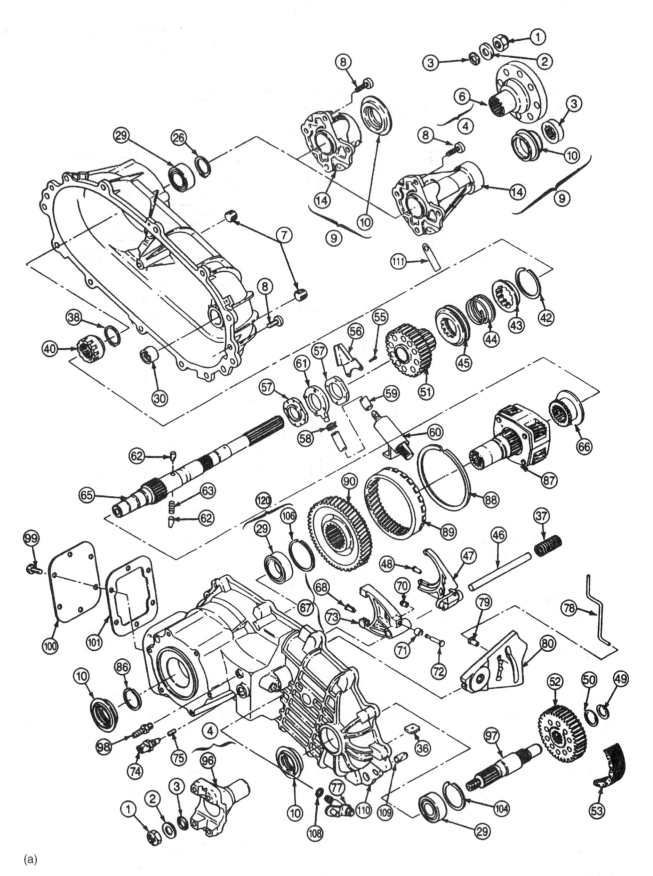

(a)

FIGURE 9–26 Manual shift transfer case components. (Courtesy of Ford Motor Company.)

Item	Part Number	Description
1	7045	Nut (Rear Yoke/Flange)
2	7B368	Output Shaft Yoke Washer
3	7052	Seal, Oil (Rear Spline) Seal, Oil (Rear Flange)
4	7B214	Case Yoke
6	—	Flange (Rear Flange) (Serviced As Part of 7B214 Assembly)
7	7A010	Plug, Pipe
8	7A443	Bolt and Washer Assembly (1989 and Later)
9	7085	Extension Assembly (Rear Spline) Cap Assembly, Bearing (Rear Yoke/Flange)
10	7B215	Yoke to Flange Seal Seal, Oil (Rear Yoke/Flange)
14	—	Extension (Rear Spline) Cap, Bearing (Rear Yoke/Flange) (Serviced As Part of 7085 Assembly)
26	7917	Ring, Snap
28	7005	Case
29	7025	Bearing
30	7127	Caged Needle Bearing
36	7L027	Oil Pan Magnet
37	7219	Shift Fork Spring
38	7917	Ring, Snap
40	7100	Shift Collar Hub
42	7917	Ring, Retaining
43	7D164	Lockup Hub
44	7D126	Spring, Lockup
45	7106	Lockup Collar
46	7240	Shift Rail
47	7289	Fork Assembly, Shift, 2W-4W
48	7C430	Facing, Shift Fork
49	7917	Ring, Retaining
50	7119	Thrust Washer
51	7177	Sprocket, Drive
52	7177	Sprocket, Driven
53	7A029	Chain, Drive
55	7A291	Transfer Housing to Case Bolt
56	7E215	Retainer, Pump
57	7A152	Cover, Pump, Rear

Item	Part Number	Description
58	382486-S	Clamp, Hose
59	7A210	Coupling, Hose
60	7A098	Filter, Oil
61	7A149	Housing, Pump
62	7A250	Pin, Pump
63	7A205	Spring, Pump Pin
65	7061	Output Shaft
66	7100	Shift Collar Hub
67	7289	Ford Assembly Reduction
68	—	Facing, Shift Fork (Serviced As Part of 7289 Assembly)
70	—	Retainer (Serviced As Part of 7289 Assembly)
71	7235	Roller, Cam (Service As Part of 7289 Assembly)
72	—	Pin
73	—	Fork, Reduction (Serviced As Part of 7289 Assembly)
74	7E440	4WD Indicator Switch
75	—	Setscrew (Part of 7E440)
77	7B106	Lever, Shaft and Pin Assembly
78	7C349	Spring, Assist
79	7C191	Bushing, Assist
80	7F063	Cam, Shift
86	—	Ring, Retaining (Part of 7B215)
87	7A398	Front Planet (with PTO) Front Planet (Without PTO)
88	7C122	Ring, Retaining
89	7A153	Ring Gear
90	—	Gear, PTO (with PTO)
96	—	Yoke (Serviced As Part of 7B214 Assembly)
97	7061	Output Shaft
98	7034	Vent
99	381673-S	Bolt (with PTO)
100	7165	Transfer Case Cover
101	7166	Transmission Case Deflector Gasket
104	7917	Ring, Retaining
106	7917	Ring, Retaining
108	7288	Shifter Shaft Seal
109	—	Pin Dowel (Part of 7005)
110	7005	Case

(b)

FIGURE 9–26 (*Continued*)

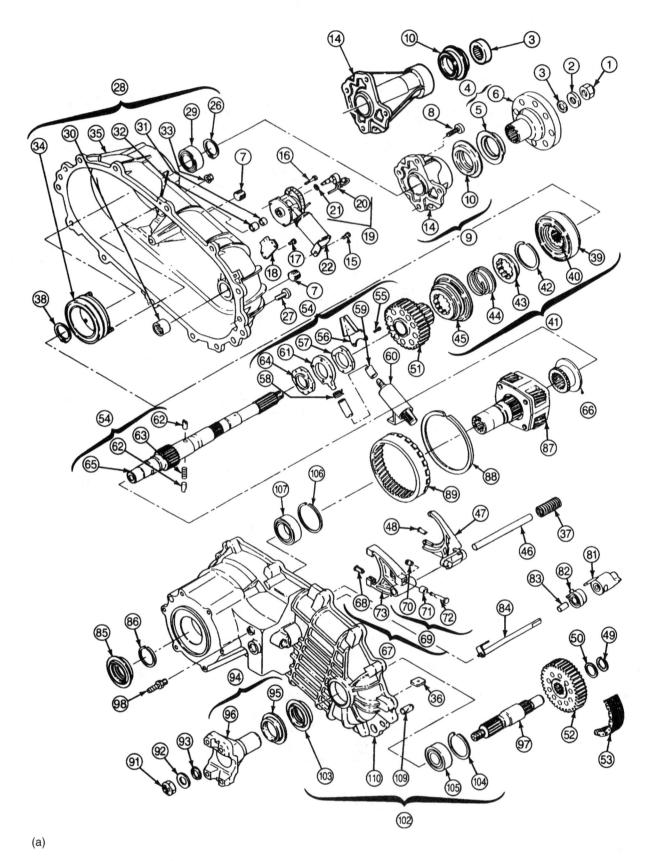

(a)

FIGURE 9–27 Electronic shift transfer case components. (Courtesy of Ford Motor Company.)

Item	Part Number	Description
1	7045	Nut
2	7B368	Output Shaft Yoke Washer
3	7052	Seal, Oil
4	7B214	Case Yoke
5	—	Deflector (Serviced As Part of 7B214 Assembly)
6	—	Yoke (Rear Yoke) (Serviced As Part of 7B214 Assembly) Flange (Rear Flange) (Serviced As Part of 7B214 Assembly)
7	7A010	Plug, Pipe
8	7A443	Bolt and Washer Assembly (1989 and Later) Bolt
9	7085	Bearing Retainer
10	7B215	Yoke to Flange Seal
14	—	Cap, Bearing/Extension (Serviced As Part of 7085 Assembly)
15	—	Bolt (Part of 7G360)
16	—	Bolt (Part of 7A195)
17	—	Bolt (Part of 7A195)
18	14A206	Wire Connector Bracket
19	7A247/7288	Sensor and O-Ring Assembly
20	7A247	Sensor, Speed
21	7288	O-Ring
22	7G360	Motor
26	7917	Ring, Snap
27	7A443	Bolt
28	7005	Case
29	7025	Bearing
30	7127	Caged Needle Bearing
31	7288	Shifter Shaft Seal
32	7W073	Bearing, Sleeve
33	620481-S	Nut
34	7G361	Coil Assembly, Clutch
35	7005	Case
36	7L027	Oil Pan Magnet
37	7219	2W-4W Shift Fork Spring
38	7917	Ring, Snap
39	7G362	Housing, Clutch
40	Part of 7G362	Hub, Shift Collar
41	7106	Lockup Assemby, 2W-4W
42	7917	Ring, Retaining
43	7D164	Lockup Hub
44	7D126	Spring, Lockup
45	7106	Lockup Collar
46	7240	Shift Rail
47	7289	Fork Assemby, Shift, 2W-4W
48	Part of 7289	Facing, Shift Fork
49	7917	Ring, Retaining
50	7119	Thrust Washer
51	7177	Sprocket, Drive

Item	Part Number	Description
52	7177	Sprocket, Driven
53	7A029	Chain, Drive
54	7A149/7061	Shaft and Pump Assemby
55	7A291	Bolt, Hex Head
56	7E215	Retainer, Pump
57	7A152	Cover, Pump, Rear
58	382486-S	Clamp, Hose
59	7A210	Coupling, Hose
60	7A098	Filter, Oil
61	7A149	Housing, Pump
62	7A250	Pin, Pump
63	7A205	Spring, Pump Pin
64	7A152	Cover, Pump, Front
65	7061	Output Shaft
66	7100	Shift Collar Hub
67	7289	Fork Assemby, Reduction
68	—	Facing, Shift Fork (Serviced As Part of 7289 Assembly)
69	—	Pin, Roller and Retainer Assemby (Serviced As Part of 7289 Assembly)
70	—	Retainer (Serviced As Part of 7289 Assembly)
71	—	Roller, Cam (Serviced As Part of 7289 Assembly)
72	—	Pin (Serviced As Part of 7289 Assembly)
73	—	Fork, Reduction (Serviced As Part of 7289 Assembly)
81	7F063	Cam, Electric Shift
82	7W074	Spring, Torsion
83	7Z112	Spacer
84	7N095	Shaft, Shift
85	7B215	Yoke to Flange Seal
86	7917	Ring, Retaining
87	7A398	Front Planet
88	7C122	RIng, Retaining
89	7A153	Ring Gear
91	7045	Nut
92	7B368	Output Shaft Yoke Washer
93	7052	Seal, Oil
94	7B214	Case Yoke
95	—	Deflector (Serviced As Part of 7B214 Assembly)
96	—	Yoke (Serviced As Part of 7B214 Assembly)
97	7061	Output Shaft
98	7034	Vent
102	7005	Case
103	7B215	Yoke to Flange Seal
104	7917	Ring, Retaining
105	7025	Bearing
106	7917	Ring, Retaining
107	7025	Bearing
109	—	Pin Dowel (Part of 7A195)
110	7005	Case

(b)

FIGURE 9–27 *(Continued)*

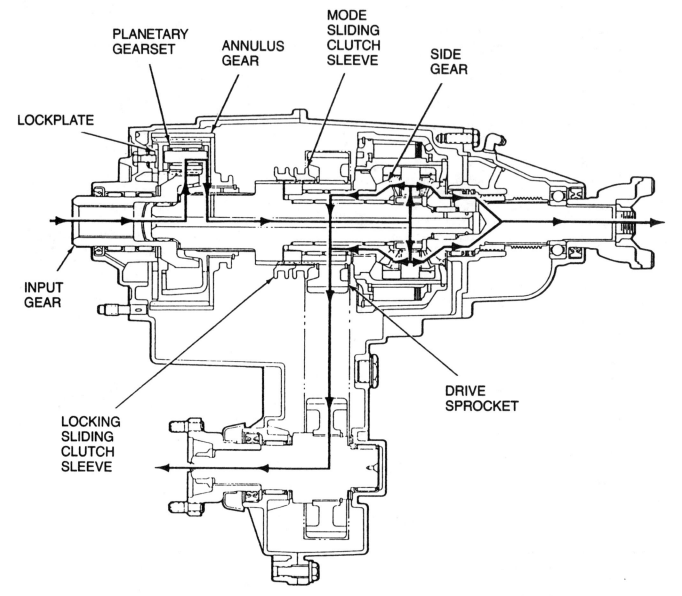

FIGURE 9–28 Full-time transfer case powerflow in Low. (Courtesy of Chrysler Corporation.)

Part-Time/Full-Time Four-Wheel-Drive Application

1. *Chevrolet Blazer:* has a center differential and is able to shift on-the-fly.

2. *Chevrolet/GMC Suburban:* has a center differential and is able to shift on-the-fly.

3. *Chevrolet Tahoe:* has a center differential and is able to shift on-the-fly.

4. *Ford Explorer:* has an automatic progressive locking electronic clutch.

5. *GMC Jimmy:* has a center differential and is able to shift on-the-fly.

6. *GMC Yukon:* has a center differential and is able to shift on-the-fly.

7. *JEEP Cherokee:* has a center differential and is able to shift on-the-fly.

8. *JEEP Grand Cherokee:* has a center differential and is able to shift on-the-fly.

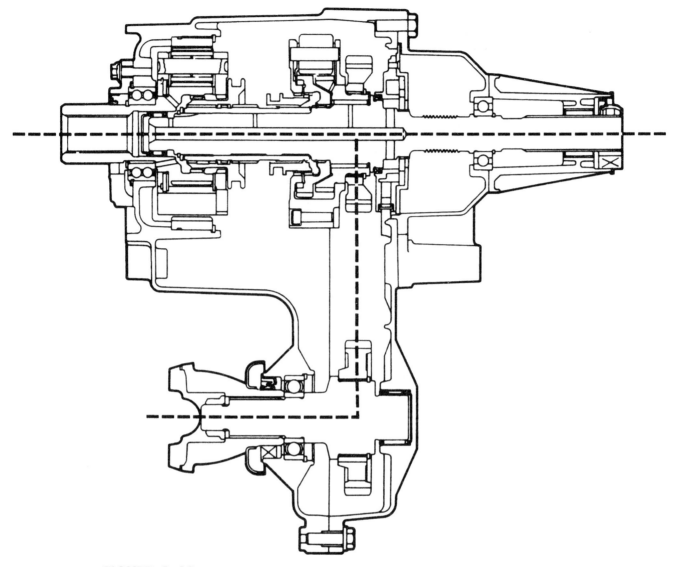

FIGURE 9–29 Part-time/full-time transfer case powerflow in part-time mode. (Courtesy of Chrysler Corporation.)

9. *Mitsubishi Montero:* has a center differential and is able to shift on-the-fly.

10. *Toyota 4-Runner:* has a center differential and is able to shift on-the-fly.

All-Wheel-Drive Application

A number of vehicle manufacturers (North American, European, and Asian) each produce several models of cars and minivans equipped with full-time, four-wheel drive. These vehicles usually have a transaxle with an integrated single-speed transfer case containing a viscous coupling.

FOUR-WHEEL-DRIVE SYSTEM SERVICE

Servicing four-wheel-drive systems includes servicing the drive axles, differentials, drive shafts, transfer case, and control system. Drive axle, differential, and drive shaft service is similar to the drive axle and differential service described in Chapter 3. Servicing transfer case components is similar to servicing transmissions and transaxles. Many four-wheel-drive systems require following a specific sequence when shifting. If shifts are not made in the specified sequence or at the wrong speed, serious damage may be caused on some systems. Four-wheel-drive systems are often subjected to severe operating conditions that result in greater wear

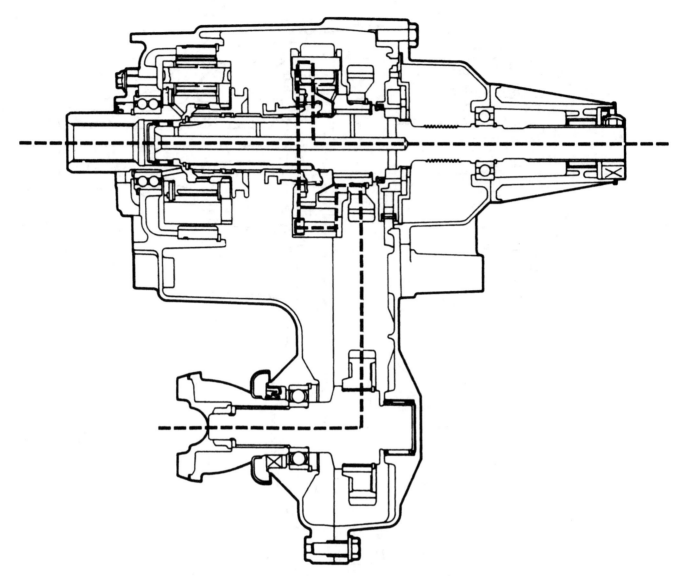

FIGURE 9–30 Part-time/full-time transfer case powerflow in full-time mode. (Courtesy of Chrysler Corporation.)

than in a two-wheel-drive system. Consequently, more frequent maintenance service is often required. Consult the service manual for the type and frequency of lubrication and maintenance service required.

FOUR-WHEEL-DRIVE SYSTEM PROBLEMS

Four-wheel-drive systems are subject to the same kind of problems with tires, wheels, wheel bearings, drive axles, differentials, and drive shafts as two-wheel-drive vehicles, covered in other chapters in this book. Some typical four-wheel-drive system problems that may be encountered include the following (see **Figures 9–31** to **9–34** for problem diagnosis):

Difficult to Shift or Will Not Shift into Desired Range

1. Shift linkage binding or misadjusted
2. Incorrect or low lubricant in transfer case
3. Vehicle speed too great to allow shifting
4. Excessive drive line torque windup
5. Internal shift mechanism binding

PROBLEM	POSSIBLE CAUSE	CORRECTION
Four Wheel Drive Does Not Engage	1. Vacuum hoses kinked, disconnected, or broken 2. Engine vacuum insufficient to activate vacuum actuator. At least – 40 kPa (12 in. hg.) of vacuum is required at the actuator for proper operation. 3. Actuator cable kinked, misrouted, or disconnected. 4. Faulty vacuum actuator. Check for holes in diaphragm or other damage. 5. Faulty transfer case vacuum switch. 6. Faulty 4WD indicator light, switch, or wiring (4WD engaging but indicator light not coming on). 7. Transfer case linkage improperly adjusted or disconnected. 8. Faulty transfer case: Drive chain broken, range selector ring broken, etc. 9. Faulty front axle.	1. Check routing of hoses. Repair or replace as needed. 2. Repair or tune engine as required. 3. Repair or replace as needed. 4. Replace if necessary. 5. Replace. 6. Repair as needed. 7. Adjust or repair. 8. Repair. Refer to the proper Unit Repair Manual. 9. Refer to FRONT AXLE (SEC. 4C).
Four Wheel Drive Will Not Disengage	1. Faulty wiring or front axle switch (4WD disengaging but indicator light staying on). 2. Transfer case vacuum switch vent hose or vacuum actuator hose kinked or plugged. 3. Transfer case vent filter plugged. 4. Actuator cable kinked or damaged. 5. Faulty transfer case vacuum switch. 6. Transfer case linkage binding or improperly adjusted. 7. Faulty front axle shift mechanism.	1. Replace or repair wiring. 2. Repair or replace. 3. Repair or replace. 4. Replace. 5. Replace. 6. Transfer case linkage binding or improperly adjusted. 7. Repair.
Drive Four Wheel Disengages Under Load	1. Insufficient vacuum at vacuum actuator due to vacuum leak, poorly tuned engine, or kinked vacuum hose. – 40 kPa (12 in. hg.) of vacuum is required at the actuator for proper operation. 2. Vacuum system not venting properly due to kinked hose, plugged vent, or faulty transfer case vacuum switch. 3. Faulty transfer case or front axle shift mechanism. Refer to the proper Unit Repair Manual.	1. Tune engine or repair vacuum hoses. 2. Repair. 3. Repair.

(a)

FIGURE 9–31 Transfer case problem diagnosis. (Courtesy of General Motors Corporation.)

PROBLEM	POSSIBLE CAUSE	CORRECTION
Transfer Case Shift Lever Difficult to Shift or Will Not Shift Into 4 LOW or NEUTRAL (Vehicle Moving)	1. Vehicle in motion when attempting to shift. Stop the vehicle when shifting into or out of 4L or N.	1. None required.
Transfer Case Difficult to Shift	1. In extremely cold weather, it may be necessary to reduce vehicle speed or stop before shifting from 2 Wheel to 4 High. 2. If the vehicle has been operated for an extended period in 4 HIGH mode on dry pavement, difficult shifting may result due to driveline torque load. Stop the vehicle, shift transmission to neutral and shift transfer case into desired mode. 3. Transfer case linkage binding. 4. Low transfer case lube level, or improper lubricant used. 5. Internal transfer case problem.	1. None required. 2. Operate the vehicle in 2 WHEEL mode on dry pavement. 3. Adjust or repair. 4. Fill with proper lubricant. 5. Repair.
Transfer Case Noisy In All Modes	1. Low transfer case lube level, or improper lubricant used. 2. Internal transfer case problem.	1. Fill with proper lubricant. 2. Repair.
Noisy In or Jumps out of 4 LOW Range	1. Transfer case not completely engaged in 4 LOW range. Stop vehicle, shift into NEUTRAL, then back to 4 LOW. 2. Shift linkage loose or binding. 3. Transfer case internal shift mechanism faulty.	1. None required. 2. Repair. 3. Repair.
Lubricant Leaking From Transfer Case Vent	1. Transfer case overfilled.	1. Drain lubricant to proper level.
Lubricant Leak At Output Shaft Seals	1. Transfer case overfilled. 2. Vent hose plugged or kinked. 3. Output shaft seals damaged or incorrectly installed.	1. Drain lubricant to proper level. 2. Repair. 3. Replace.
Abnormal Front Tire Wear	1. Front end needs alignment. 2. Extended operation on hard, dry surfaces in 4 HIGH mode.	1. Align to specifications. 2. Operate vehicle in 2 WHEEL mode on hard, dry surfaces.

(b)

FIGURE 9–31 *(Continued)*

CONDITION	POSSIBLE SOURCE	ACTION
Transfer case makes noise.	• Incorrect tire inflation pressures or incorrect size tires and wheels. • Excessive tire tread wear. • Internal components.	• Make sure that all tires and wheels are the same size, and that inflation pressures are correct. • Check tire tread wear to see if there is more than .06 inch difference in tread wear between front and rear. Interchange one front and one rear wheel. Re-inflate tires to specifications. • Operate vehicle in all transmission gears with transfer case in 2HIGH, or HIGH range. • If there is noise in transmission in neutral gear, or in some gears and not in others, remove and repair transmission. • If there is noise in all gears, operate vehicle in all transfer case ranges. If noisy in all ranges or HIGH range only, disassemble transfer case. Check input gear, intermediate and front output shaft gear for damage. Replace as required. If noisy in LOW range only, inspect intermediate gear and sliding gears for damage. Replace as required.
4-wheel drive transfer case jumps out of gear.	• Incomplete shift linkage travel. • Loose mounting bolts. • Front and rear driveshaft slip yokes dry or loose. • Internal components.	• Adjust linkage to provide complete gear engagement. Adjust gearshift lever boot. • Tighten mounting bolts. • Lubricate and repair slip yokes as required. Tighten flange yoke attaching nut to specifications. • Disassemble transfer case. Inspect sliding clutch hub and gear clutch teeth for damage. Replace as required.
Locking hubs will not release.	• Driveline/vehicle torsional lockup. • Extremely cold ambient temperatures.	• Stop vehicle. Drive vehicle in reverse for 10 feet. • Drive vehicle 10 miles to warm axle, then try to disengage hub locks.
Driveline/torsional windup. Vehicle hop, wheel/tire bounce, vehicle skip.	• Incorrect tire inflation pressures or incorrect size tires and wheels. • Excessive tire tread wear. • Driving vehicle on hard surface/dry surface roads or areas. Driving vehicle in tight turns.	• Make sure that all tires and wheels are the same size, and that inflation pressures are correct. • Refer to vehicle owner's guide for correct usage of vehicle. Advise owner.
Delayed shifts to 2WD.	• Driveline/torsional windup. • Extremely cold ambient temperatures.	• Shift transmission into neutral. • Jack the vehicle or lift on hoist with wheels free to rotate. Windup will be released and transfer case will complete its shift. • Drive vehicle 10 miles to warm axle, then try to disengage hub locks.

FIGURE 9–32 Electronic shift transfer case diagnosis. (Courtesy of Ford Motor Company.)

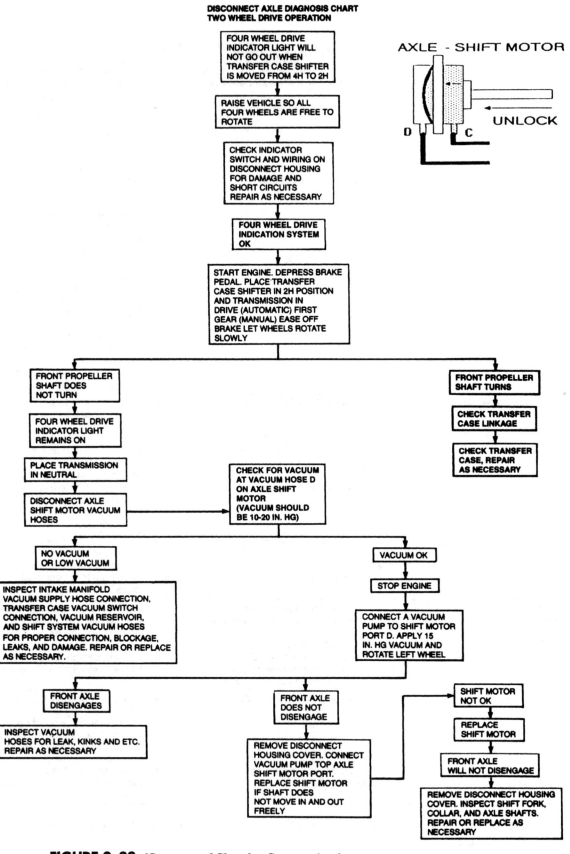

FIGURE 9–33 (Courtesy of Chrysler Corporation.)

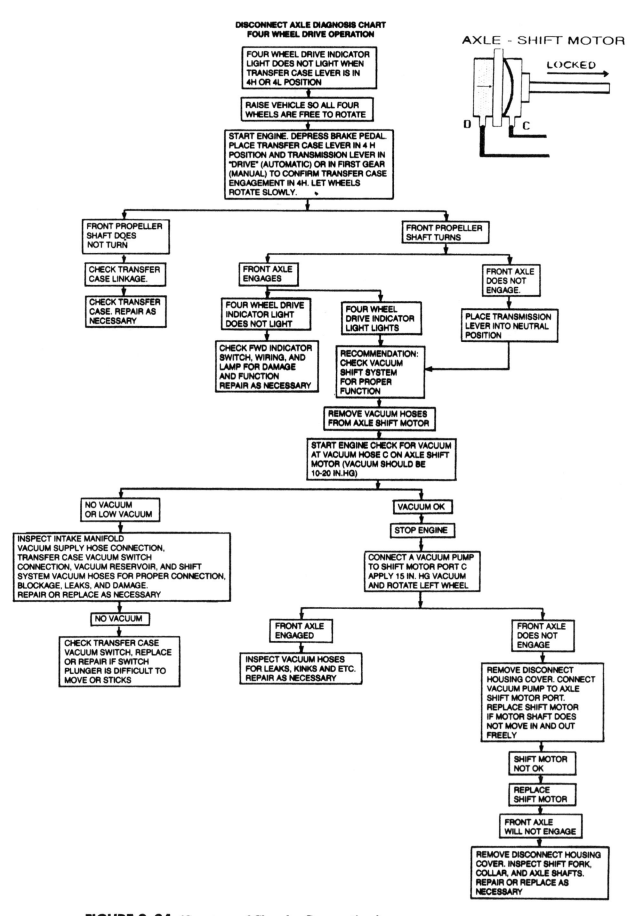

FIGURE 9–34 (Courtesy of Chrysler Corporation.)

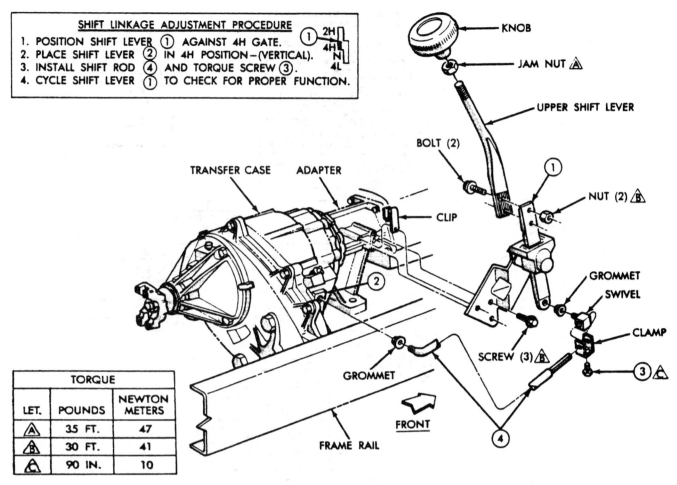

SHIFT LINKAGE ADJUSTMENT PROCEDURE

1. POSITION SHIFT LEVER ① AGAINST 4H GATE.
2. PLACE SHIFT LEVER ② IN 4H POSITION – (VERTICAL).
3. INSTALL SHIFT ROD ④ AND TORQUE SCREW ③.
4. CYCLE SHIFT LEVER ① TO CHECK FOR PROPER FUNCTION.

TORQUE		
LET.	POUNDS	NEWTON METERS
Ⓐ	35 FT.	47
Ⓑ	30 FT.	41
Ⓒ	90 IN.	10

FIGURE 9–35 Typical transfer case shift linkage adjustment. (Courtesy of Chrysler Corporation.)

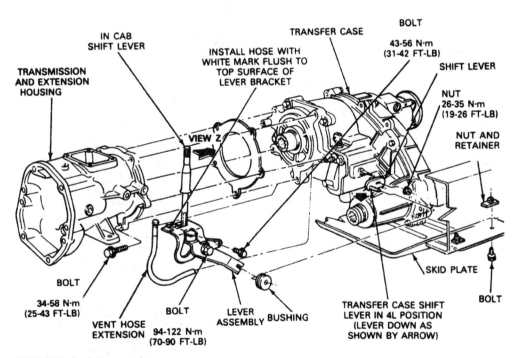

FIGURE 9–36 Transfer case removal requires the use of a transmission jack. All linkage, drive line, and electrical attachments must be disconnected. (Courtesy of Ford Motor Company.)

6. Vacuum leak or low at harness, connecting lines, or vacuum tank

7. Shift motor faulty

8. Mode switch faulty

9. Check valve stuck or leaking

10. Excessive drive train torque load while shifting

11. Incorrect tire pressure or excessively worn tires

Transfer Case Noisy

1. Incorrect or low lubricant level

2. Worn or damaged internal parts

Lubricant Leaks from Transfer Case

1. Lubricant level too high

2. Vent clogged or restricted

3. Output shaft seals damaged, worn, or incorrectly installed

Abnormal Tire Wear

1. Extended operation on hard, dry surface (pavement) in the 4WD HI range

TRANSFER CASE REMOVAL AND OVERHAUL

Transfer case removal and overhaul procedures vary considerably among different models. Select the appropriate service manual and follow the procedures given there.

The transfer case is very heavy and requires the use of a transmission jack for safe removal. The transfer case lubricant should be drained first. Then disconnect the front and rear drive shafts. (Drive shaft and universal joint service is covered in Chapter 2. Drive axle and differential service is described in Chapter 3.) If equipped with a skid plate, it should be removed. Disconnect any electrical or vacuum connections and the shift linkage. Place the transmission jack under the transfer case and tie it to the jack plate with the retainers provided. Remove all the attaching bolts and lower the unit before moving it to the repair bench. Follow service manual disassembly instructions carefully. Examine all gears, synchronizers, shafts, bearings, shift forks and rails, and the chain and sprockets carefully for wear or damage. The procedure is similar to that described in Chapter 6 for transmissions and transaxles. Replace any parts that fail the inspection. Assemble the unit and install it as outlined in the service manual. Fill the transfer case to the specified level with the recommended lubricant. Reconnect the front and rear drive shafts, vacuum and electrical connections, and the shift linkage. Adjust the shift linkage as needed (**Figures 9–35** and **9–36**).

REVIEW QUESTIONS

1. What is meant by the term *part-time four-wheel drive?*

2. The transfer case is attached to the _____ and is driven by the _____ _____ _____ .

3. List three kinds of transfer case shift control systems.

4. True or false? Manual locking hubs are used with a 4WD front axle disconnect system.

5. Automatic locking hubs can be locked or unlocked without _____ the vehicle.

6. The front axle disconnect system allows the _____ , ring gear, and pinion to stop turning when in the _____ mode.

7. In the 4WD LO mode, power is transmitted _____ to the front and rear axles.

8. If a vehicle with part-time 4WD is driven excessively on pavement in the 4WD HI mode, _____ _____ _____ will occur.

9. Full-time 4WD systems do not use wheel _____ _____ or an _____ _____ .

10. The center differential in a full-time 4WD transfer case can be _____ by the driver, or it may be done by a _____ -controlled _____ clutch.

11. All-wheel-drive systems do not use a conventional _____ _____ .

12. A viscous coupling uses a set of _____ plates and _____ plates operating in a heavy _____ fluid.

13. A faulty vacuum _____ _____ could prevent the transfer case from shifting into the desired range.

14. A noisy transfer case may be caused by low _____ _____ or _____ or _____ internal parts.

TEST QUESTIONS

1. In a four-wheel-drive system, the transfer case transmits power
   a. from the engine to the transmission
   b. only when in the 4WD mode
   c. from the engine to the drive shafts
   d. to both drive shaft when in 4WD

2. The least number of differentials required in a 4WD system is
   a. one
   b. two
   c. three
   d. four

3. A 4WD system with a front axle disconnect mechanism
   a. does not require front wheel locking hubs
   b. does not require a transfer case
   c. must have a double reduction differential
   d. none of the above

4. Technician A says that some front wheel locking hubs can be locked or unlocked without leaving the vehicle. Technician B says that manual locking hubs must be operated by hand. Who is right?
   a. technician A
   b. technician B
   c. both are right
   d. both are wrong

5. "In the integrated 4WD system, the transfer case and transaxle are an integrated unit." "The full-time 4WD system provides power to all four wheels all the time." Which of these statements is correct?
   a. the first
   b. the second
   c. both are correct
   d. both are incorrect

6. "All-wheel-drive systems have a three-speed transfer case integrated with the transaxle." "Part-time 4WD allows the driver to select 2WD or 4WD." Which of these statements is correct?
   a. the first
   b. the second
   c. both are correct
   d. both are incorrect

7. Technician A says that a center differential on a 4WD system prevents drive line windup and inter-axle conflict. Technician B says that a viscous coupling may be used for this purpose. Who is right?
   a. technician A
   b. technician B
   c. both are right
   d. both are wrong

8. When it is difficult to shift into 4WD, the problem could be
   a. binding linkage or improperly adjusted linkage
   b. low lubricant level in transfer case
   c. a faulty shift motor
   d. all of the above

9. "A noisy transfer case may be caused by a low lubricant level." "A noisy transfer case may be caused by worn gears or bearings." Which of these statements is correct?
   a. the first
   b. the second
   c. both are correct
   d. both are incorrect

10. Extended operation in the 4WD HI range can cause
    a. abnormal tire wear
    b. added strain on the drive train
    c. both (a) and (b)
    d. none of the above

APPENDIX

English-Metric Equivalents

Fractions	Decimal Inch	Metric mm	Fractions	Decimal Inch	Metric mm
1/64	0.015625	0.397	33/64	0.515625	13.097
1/32	0.03125	0.794	17/32	0.53125	13.494
3/64	0.046875	1.191	35/64	0.546875	13.891
1/16	0.0625	1.588	9/16	0.5625	14.288
5/64	0.078125	1.984	37/64	0.578125	14.684
3/32	0.09375	2.381	19/32	0.59375	15.081
7/64	0.109375	2.778	39/64	0.609375	15.478
1/8	0.125	3.175	5/8	0.625	15.875
9/64	0.140625	3.572	41/64	0.640625	16.272
5/32	0.15625	3.969	21/32	0.65625	16.669
11/64	0.171875	4.366	43/64	0.671875	17.066
3/16	0.1875	4.763	11/16	0.6875	17.463
13/64	0.203125	5.159	45/64	0.703125	17.859
7/32	0.21875	5.556	23/32	0.71875	18.256
15/64	0.234375	5.953	47/64	0.734375	18.653
1/4	0.250	6.35	3/4	0.750	19.05
17/64	0.265625	6.747	49/64	0.765625	19.447
9/32	0.28125	7.144	25/32	0.78125	19.844
19/64	0.296875	7.54	51/64	0.796875	20.241
5/16	0.3125	7.938	13/16	0.8125	20.638
21/64	0.328125	8.334	53/64	0.828125	21.034
11/32	0.34375	8.731	27/32	0.84375	21.431
23/64	0.359375	9.128	55/64	0.859375	21.828
3/8	0.375	9.525	7/8	0.875	22.225
25/64	0.390625	9.922	57/64	0.890625	22.622
13/32	0.40625	10.319	29/32	0.90625	23.019
27/64	0.421875	10.716	59/64	0.921875	23.416
7/16	0.4375	11.113	15/16	0.9375	23.813
29/64	0.453125	11.509	61/64	0.953125	24.209
15/32	0.46875	11.906	31/32	0.96875	24.606
31/64	0.484375	12.303	63/64	0.984375	25.003
1/2	0.500	12.7	1	1.00	25.4

Source: Ford Motor Co. of Canada Ltd.

Torque Conversion

Newton metres (N-m)	Pound-feet (lb-ft)	Pound-feet (lb-ft)	Newton metres (N-m)
1	0.7376	1	1.356
2	1.5	2	2.7
3	2.2	3	4.0
4	3.0	4	5.4
5	3.7	5	6.8
6	4.4	6	8.1
7	5.2	7	9.5
8	5.9	8	10.8
9	6.6	9	12.2
10	7.4	10	13.6
15	11.1	15	20.3
20	14.8	20	27.1
25	18.4	25	33.9
30	22.1	30	40.7
35	25.8	35	47.5
40	29.5	40	54.2
50	36.9	45	61.0
60	44.3	50	67.8
70	51.6	55	74.6
80	59.0	60	81.4
90	66.4	65	88.1
100	73.8	70	94.9
110	81.1	75	101.7
120	88.5	80	108.5
130	95.9	90	122.0
140	103.3	100	135.6
150	110.6	110	149.1
160	118.0	120	162.7
170	125.4	130	176.3
180	132.8	140	189.8
190	140.1	150	203.4
200	147.5	160	216.9
225	166.0	170	230.5
250	184.4	180	244.0

Source: Ford Motor Co. of Canada Ltd.

Decimal Equivalents and Tap Drill Sizes

Drill Size	Decimal	Tap Size	Drill Size	Decimal	Tap Size	Drill Size	Decimal	Tap Size
1/64	0.0156		20	0.1610		T	0.3580	
1/32	0.0312		19	0.1660		23/64	0.3594	
60	0.0400		18	0.1695		U	0.3680	7/16–14
59	0.0410		11/64	0.1719		3/8	0.3750	
58	0.0420		17	0.1730		V	0.3770	
57	0.0430		16	0.1770	12–24	W	0.3860	
56	0.0465		15	0.1800		25/64	0.3906	7/16–20
3/64	0.0469	0–80	14	0.1820	12–28	X	0.3970	
55	0.0520		13	0.1850	12–32	Y	0.4040	
54	0.0550	1–56	3/16	0.1875		12/32	0.4062	
53	0.0595	1–64, 72	12	0.1890		Z	0.4130	
1/16	0.0625		11	0.1910		27/64	0.4219	1/2–13
52	0.0635		10	0.1935		7/16	0.4375	
51	0.0670		9	0.1960		29/64	0.4531	1/2–20
50	0.0700	2–56, 64	8	0.1990		15/32	0.4687	
49	0.0730		7	0.2010	1/4–20	31/64	0.4844	9/16–12
48	0.0760		13/64	0.2031		1/2	0.5000	
5/64	0.0781		6	0.2040		33/64	0.5156	9/16–18
47	0.0785	3–48	5	0.2055		17/32	0.5312	5/8–11
46	0.0810		4	0.2090		35/64	0.5469	
45	0.0820	3–56, 4–32	3	0.2130	1/4–28	9/16	0.5625	
44	0.0860		7/32	0.2187		37/64	0.5781	5/8–18
43	0.0890	4–36	2	0.2210		19/32	0.5937	11/16–11
42	0.0935	4–40	1	0.2280		39/64	0.6094	
3/32	0.0937	4–48	A	0.2340		5/8	0.6250	11/16–16
41	0.0960		15/64	0.2344		41/64	0.6406	
40	0.0980		B	0.2380		21/32	0.6562	3/4–10
39	0.0995		C	0.2420		43/64	0.6719	
38	0.1015	5–40	D	0.2460		11/16	0.6875	3/4–16
37	0.1040	5–44	E, 1/4	0.2500		45/64	0.7031	
36	0.1065	6–32	F	0.2570	5/16–18	23/32	0.7187	
7/64	0.1093		G	0.2610		47/64	0.7344	
35	0.1100		17/64	0.2656		3/4	0.7500	
34	0.1110	6–36	H	0.2660		49/64	0.7656	7/8–9
33	0.1130	6–40	I	0.2720	5/16–24	25/32	0.7812	
32	0.1160		J	0.2770		51/64	0.7969	
31	0.1200		K	0.2810		13/16	0.8125	7/8–14
1/8	0.1250		9/32	0.2812		53/64	0.8281	

Decimal Equivalents and Tap Drill Sizes—*Continued*

Drill Size	Decimal	Tap Size	Drill Size	Decimal	Tap Size	Drill Size	Decimal	Tap Size
30	0.1285		L	0.2900		$^{27}/_{32}$	0.8437	
29	0.1360	8–32, 36	M	0.2950		$^{55}/_{64}$	0.8594	
28	0.1405	8–40	$^{19}/_{64}$	0.2968		$^{7}/_{8}$	0.8750	1–8
$^{9}/_{64}$	0.1406		N	0.3020		$^{57}/_{64}$	0.8906	
27	0.1440		$^{5}/_{16}$	0.3125	$^{3}/_{8}$–16	$^{29}/_{32}$	0.9062	
26	0.1470		O	0.3160		$^{59}/_{64}$	0.9219	
25	0.1495	10–24	P	0.3230		$^{15}/_{16}$	0.9375	1–12, 14
24	0.1520		$^{21}/_{64}$	0.3281		$^{61}/_{64}$	0.9531	
23	0.1540		Q	0.3320	$^{3}/_{8}$–24	$^{31}/_{32}$	0.9687	
$^{5}/_{32}$	0.1562		R	0.3390		$^{63}/_{64}$	0.9844	
22	0.1570	10–30	11/32	0.3437		1	1.000	
21	0.1590	10–32	S	0.3480				

Pipe Thread Sizes

Thread	Drill	Thread	Drill
$^{1}/_{8}$–27	R	$1^{1}/_{2}$–$11^{1}/_{2}$	$1^{47}/_{64}$
$^{1}/_{4}$–18	$^{7}/_{16}$	2–$11^{1}/_{2}$	$2^{7}/_{32}$
$^{3}/_{8}$–18	$^{37}/_{64}$	$2^{1}/_{2}$–8	$2^{5}/_{8}$
$^{1}/_{2}$–14	$^{23}/_{32}$	3–8	$3^{1}/_{4}$
$^{3}/_{4}$–14	$^{59}/_{64}$	$3^{1}/_{2}$–8	$3^{3}/_{4}$
1–$11^{1}/_{2}$	$1^{5}/_{32}$	4–8	$4^{1}/_{4}$
$1^{1}/_{4}$–$11^{1}/_{2}$	$1^{1}/_{2}$		

Source: Frank J. Thiessen and Davis Dales, *Diesel Fundamentals*, 2nd Ed. (Englewood Cliffs, NJ: Prentice Hall, 1986), p. 680.

English-Metric Conversion

Description	Multiply	By	For Metric Equivalent
ACCELERATION	foot/sec^2	0.304 8	metre/sec^2(m/s^2)
	inch/sec^2	0.025 4	metre/sec^2
TORQUE	pound-inch	0.112 98	newton-meters (N-m)
	pound-foot	1.355 8	newton-meters
POWER	horsepower	0.746	kilowatts (kw)
PRESSURE or STRESS	inches of water	0.2488	kilopascals (kPa)
	pounds/sq. in.	6.895	kilopascals (kPa)
ENERGY or WORK	BTU	1.055.	joules (J)
	foot-pound	1.355 8	joules (J)
	kilowatt-hour	3 600 000. or 3.6 × 10^6	joules (J = one W's)
LIGHT	foot candle	10.76	lumens/meter^2 (lm/m^2)
FUEL PERFORMANCE	miles/gal	0.425 1	kilometers/liter (km/l)
	gal/mile	2.352 7	liters/kilometer (l/km)
VELOCITY	miles/hour	1.609 3	kilometers/hr. (km/h)
LENGTH	inch	25.4	millimeters (mm)
	foot	0.304 8	meters (m)
	yard	0.914 4	meters (m)
	mile	1.609	kilometers (km)
AREA	inch^2	645.2	millimeters^2 (mm^2)
		6.45	centimeters^2 (cm^2)
	foot^2	0.092 9	meters^2 (m^2)
	yard^2	0.8361	meters^2
VOLUME	inch^3	16 387.	mm^3
	inch^3	16.387	cm^3
	quart	0.016 4	liters (l)
	quart	0.946 4	liters
	gallon	3.785 4	liters
	yard^3	0.764 6	meters^3 (m^3)
MASS	pound	0.453 6	kilograms (kg)
	ton	907.18	kilograms (kg)
	ton	0.90718	tonne
FORCE	kilogram	9.807	newtons (N)
	ounce	0.278 0	newtons
	pound	4.448	newtons
TEMPERATURE	degree Farenheit	0.556 (°F–32)	degree Celsius (°C)

Source: Ford Motor Co. of Canada Ltd.

INDEX